"To suggest that the merciful, longsuffering, gracious and loving God of the Bible would invent a dreadful doctrine like Calvinism, which would have us believe it is an act of 'grace' to select only certain people for heaven and, by exclusion, others for hell, comes perilously close to blasphemy. And that is why I congratulate Dave Hunt for writing this excellent clarification of the doctrine that has its roots more in Greek humanism, from where it originated, than it does in Scripture. This book could well be the most important book written in the twenty-first century for all evangelical Christians to read. It will help you know and love the real God of the Bible who clearly says of Himself, 'It is not My will that *any* should perish but that *all* should come to repentance.' Calvinism is a far cry from the God of the Bible who loves mankind so much that He sent His only Son to save *whosoever* calls on Him for mercy in the name of His resurrected Son, Jesus Christ. Every evangelical minister should read this book. If they did, we would see a mighty revival of soul-winning passion that would turn this world upside down as multitudes saw the real God of the Bible, not the false God of Augustinianism and Calvinism."

◆ TIM LAHAYE
**Author of more than 50 books including
co-author of the *Left Behind* Series**

"Dave Hunt has done it again. Even as his books, 'The Seduction of Christianity' and 'A Woman Rides the Beast' have stirred the Christian community into taking a serious look at the aberrant teachings of some Pentecostals and the Roman Catholic church, so now in his latest book on Calvinism, he brings to the light the teachings of John Calvin which are bound to cause ripples through the entire church, and send many back to a serious study of TULIP in light of God's Word. He has researched the origins of the teachings of Calvinism and thoroughly documents his findings. It is a must-read for those who are serious in their desire to understand the influence that Calvin has had and continues to have on the Evangelical church."

◆ CHUCK SMITH
Pastor, Calvary Chapel of Costa Mesa

"Dave Hunt has given exact details to show the agonizing faults of Calvinistic abuses that most people have not considered. I would like for all of my students at Liberty University to read this in-depth analysis. It seems that each year Calvinism, like dandelions, comes in the spring. Students get wrapped up in arguing the issues of Calvinism. Those students who don't like aggressive soul-winning use their view of Calvinism to defend their position. Those who are aggressive soul winners attack the weaknesses of Calvinism. Very little of their discussions are grounded in the truth of the Word of God. In the final analysis, their arguments are like weeds, i.e., dandelions that bear no fruit. May many read this volume to 'be no more children, tossed to and fro, and carried about with every wind of doctrine, by the sleight of men, and cunning craftiness,' but may they be grounded in the Word of God."

◆ ELMER L. TOWNS
**Dean, School of Religion
Liberty University**

"This book exposes traditional Calvinism for portraying God in a totally unscriptural manner. Professed Calvinists will want to rethink their position when they realize the Biblical truths that are at stake. This book will stand as a definitive work on the subject."

◆ **WILLIAM MACDONALD**
Author of more than 80 books in 100 languages including the *Believer's Bible Commentary* and *True Discipleship*.

"The character of God has been totally misrepresented by our common denominational traditions. Dave Hunt continues his intrepid commitment to revealing the truth however unfashionable or politically incorrect it may be deemed. Blindfold your prejudices and be ready for a stunning and desperately needed perspective on this highly controversial area. Here is another essential for the serious student of God's Word."

◆ **DR. CHUCK MISSLER**
Founder, Koinonia House

"Rarely has anyone undertaken the exhaustive task of detailing and documenting the misconception of God's sovereign grace as has Dave Hunt. Reading this work should convince even the most staunch Calvinist to recognize the flawed philosophical theology of preselection as an attempt to eliminate man's capacity to exercise his free will, which reduces God's sovereign love to an act of a mere dictator. This book needs to be read by every communicator of the Gospel in defense of the fundamental principles of God's grace."

◆ **ARNO FROESE**
Executive Director, Midnight Call Ministry
Editor, *Midnight Call*

"This incredible book by Dave Hunt is imperative in our generation of 'class warfare.' It is hard to believe that the Christian world has its own system of 'apartheid.' That's exactly what hyper-Calvinism represents, and this book exposes the horror of spiritual apartheid for what it really is. Calvinism makes our Heavenly Father look like the worst of despots and I join Dave in declaring Him: Not Guilty! The biblical revelation of redemption leaves no one uninvited."

◆ **JOSEPH R. CHAMBERS, DD, DSL**
Pastor, author, and radio host

"I am glad to see Dave deal with a tough subject, supply materials that many of us have not accessed until now, and challenge the Biblical basis for TULIP."

◆ JIM CUSTER
Right Start Ministries

"Dave Hunt has given us a fascinating expose of modern five-point Calvinism that is both highly readable and practical. I especially enjoyed the section on perseverance and assurance of salvation."

◆ BOB WILKIN, PH.D.
Founder and Executive Director
Grace Evangelical Society

"As a biblicist, I find this to be a refreshing biblical review of things which for many years have brought confusion to believers. We've allowed words and ideas of men to determine our positions. This book reminds us to listen to what the Word of God has to say."

◆ HARRY BOLLBACK
Co-founder with Jack Wyrtzen of
Word of Life International

"Dave Hunt's treatment of the age-old controversy over election and predestination in his book, *What Love is This? Calvinism's Misrepresentation of God*, is not only thought-provoking but also brings the reader to focus on a scriptural viewpoint in this very thorny theological issue. Many times theology is approached philosophically and not biblically, and this approach will bring havoc in the Church. In Dave's book, we are challenged to go back to the Scriptures as we evaluate the workings of God on this all-important subject of salvation. This is definitely a book that causes us to reflect on how we formulate our doctrine."

◆ JOE JORDAN
Executive Director
Word of Life Fellowship, Inc.

WHAT LOVE IS THIS?

Calvinism's Misrepresentation of God

Dave Hunt

LOYAL

www.loyalpublishing.com

CONTENTS

A Brief Word

Discussions with many people around the world reveal that multitudes of sincere, Bible-believing Christians are "Calvinists" only by default. Thinking that the only choice is between Calvinism with its doctrine of eternal security and Arminianisrn with its falling away, and confident that salvation cannot be lost because of Christ's promise to keep eternally those who believe in Him, they therefore consider themselves to be Calvinists.

It takes only a few simple questions to discover the fact that most of those who regard themselves as Calvinists are largely unaware of what John Calvin and his early followers of the sixteenth and seventeenth centuries actually believed and practiced. Nor do they fully understand what most of today's leading Calvinists believe.

While there are disputed variations of this doctrine, among its chief proponents (whom we quote extensively in context) there is general agreement on certain core beliefs. Multitudes who believe they understand Calvinism will be shocked to discover its Roman Catholic roots and Calvin's grossly un-Christian behavior as the "Protestant Pope" of Geneva, Switzerland.

Most shocking of all, however, is Calvinism's misrepresentation of God who "is love." It is our prayer that the following pages will enable readers to examine more carefully the vital issues involved and to follow God's Holy Word and not man.

1
Why This Book?

"Can you answer some questions about Calvinism?" The query was directed to me by a young man who was among a number of us sitting together around a restaurant table one evening recently in a city where I was speaking at a conference. [1]

"Why do you ask *me*?" was my somewhat puzzled response.

"We heard you were writing a book about Calvinism."

"Yes, I am — a book, in fact, that I didn't want to write. There are fine Christians on both sides. The last thing I want to do is create more controversy — but it's a topic that really has to be faced and dealt with thoroughly." Glancing around the table, I was surprised at the interest reflected on each face which this turn in the conversation had suddenly aroused. Everyone was listening intently.

"I had scarcely given Calvinism a thought for years. Then suddenly — or so it seemed to me — in the last two years Calvinism began emerging as an issue everywhere. Perhaps I'm just waking up, but it seems to me that this peculiar doctrine is being promoted far more widely and aggressively now than I was ever aware of in the past."

The knowing expressions and nodding heads confirmed my impression. "They tell me," I added, "that R.C. Sproul is continually pushing it on radio across the country."

"Our church recently added a new associate pastor to the staff," explained the young man who had raised the question. "He introduces Calvinism in almost every session in the Bible class he teaches."

"Let me suggest how he might do it," I responded. "He asks the class what they think comes first, faith or regeneration. Everyone says, 'Faith, of course — believe on the Lord Jesus Christ and thou shalt be saved.' Then he challenges them, 'But mankind is dead in trespasses and in sins. How can a dead man believe?'"

I had the young man's total attention. "That's it exactly! How did you know?"

"Then he explains," I continued, "that God has to give life sovereignly to those who are spiritually dead before they can believe or even understand the gospel — that regeneration must precede faith."

"You're right! But it seems bizarre . . . like having to get saved before you can get saved!"

"The Calvinist wouldn't put it in those precise words," I responded, "but it's even a bit stranger than that. Without understanding or believing anything about God or Christ or the Bible — because no one supposedly can until they're regenerated —the 'elect' are made spiritually alive by a sovereign act of God without any desire or cooperation on their part and without even knowing what is happening to them at the time."

"That's exactly what he's been teaching," added another member of the same church. "It doesn't make sense. I never read anything like that in the Bible."

"Are you the only ones who have expressed any concern?" I asked. "Do those who thought faith came first immediately accept this new concept?"

"Most do. But it *has* caused some confusion . . . and a few people have left the church."

"No one challenges him," I asked, "with the obvious fact that spiritual death can't be equated with physical death . . . that *physically* dead people not only can't believe, but they can't sin or do anything else?"

"I guess none of us have thought of that."

"What does the senior pastor say?"

"He doesn't seem to know how to handle the confusion being caused by his new assistant. We never heard anything like this from the pulpit before, but now hints of Calvinism are even sneaking into *his* sermons."

The conversation went on like this for some time. Every new aspect of Calvinism I explained was greeted with further exclamations of "Yes! That's exactly what we're hearing."

Others at the table from entirely different areas of the country began to relate their experiences. One man had recently left a church which had split over the issue of Calvinism. The deacon board had voted that every member must sign a Calvinistic statement of faith. Someone else was from a church where the pastor and elders had taken a hard line against what they considered to be a divisive issue and had disfellowshiped a Sunday-school teacher for continuing to indoctrinate his junior high class into Calvinism in spite of several warnings not to do so. A couple had visited a highly recommended church in a large city near their home, pastored by a well-known Calvinist author.

"We don't really know much about Calvinism," my dinner companions confessed. "But it was a strange experience. On the one hand, we had the impression that these people felt they were a bit superior because they were the 'elect.' But at the same time there seemed to be an undercurrent of insecurity. Performance seemed to be a major evidence of one's salvation, which added a rather legalistic flavor."

As we got up to leave the table, a young woman who had sat through the entire discussion in silence asked if she could have a private moment of my time. We sat down again and she began a tale of grief. She was a pastor's wife. Their lives and ministry had been happy and fruitful until her husband and two close friends who were also pastors became interested in a new "truth." All three were very intellectual. As a result of reading current Calvinist authors, they had been drawn into the challenge of studying the writings of John Calvin, Jonathan Edwards, John Knox and others. Their study, taking them all the way back to Augustine, eventually became almost an obsession. Then each of them began to preach their new "light" from their pulpits. After being warned several times to desist from indoctrinating their congregations, they were removed from their pastorates by their denomination. Her husband began to worry whether he was really one of the elect. The nagging questions grew into full-blown doubts about his salvation. The Calvinism which had once seemed so satisfying began to haunt him with uncertainty as to whether he was one of the elect.

"You were never drawn into it?" I asked.

She shook her head. "I'm not an intellectual — which may be why it never appealed to me. But isn't God supposed to be a God of love? In my simple mind it didn't make sense that the God of the Bible didn't love everyone enough to want them all in heaven, that Christ hadn't died for everyone even though the Bible seemed to say that He had . . . ." Tears had come to her eyes. At last she continued, "I kept trying to tell my husband that the God he was now believing in, a God who predestined people before they were even born to spend eternity in the lake of fire, was not the God I knew and loved . . . ."

Troubling encounters such as these became more frequent and demanded a deeper insight on my part into a system which was obviously embraced by a larger portion of the church than I had realized and which seemed so alien to all that I had believed about a God whose sovereignty did not diminish His mercy and love. For my own peace of mind I was compelled to pursue the lengthy investigation which has resulted in this book.

An Issue Of Great Importance

Calvinism has never seemed biblical to me for a number of reasons which we will come to in due order. Over the years, my considerable objections have been discussed privately and in detail with several staunchly Calvinist friends. Thankfully, in spite of our serious differences and the fact that we were unable to resolve them, there was never any loss of good will. We remain in close friendship to this day and have simply avoided this subject in our contacts and fellowship with one another.

It is true that "throughout history many of the great evangelists, missionaries, and stalwart theologians held to the . . . doctrines of grace known as Calvinism." [2] R.C. Sproul declares that "the titans of classical Christian scholarship" are Calvinists. [3] The additional claim is often made that, although many have not made it known publicly, most of today's leading evangelicals in America hold to some form of this doctrine. Whether or not that is the case, I soon discovered that there were far more books in print promoting Calvinism than I had ever imagined. Generally they are produced by major Christian publishers, and their number and influence are growing rapidly.

The *New Geneva Study Bible*, with an introduction by R.C. Sproul and published by Thomas Nelson Publishers in 1995, aggressively promotes Calvinism in its marginal explanations of key passages and calls it "Reformation truth." That bold phrase equates the Reformation with Calvinism — a proposition which is almost universally accepted among evangelicals today. The question of whether this is true, which we will deal with in the following pages, is surely one of great importance.

The significance of our concern is given further weight by the fact that its proponents even claim that "Calvinism is pure biblical Christianity in its clearest and purest expression." [4] D. James Kennedy has said, "I am a Presbyterian because I believe Presbyterianism is the purest form of Calvinism." [5] John Piper writes, "The doctrines of grace (Total depravity, Unconditional election, Limited atonement, Irresistible grace, Perseverance of the saints) are the warp and woof of the biblical gospel cherished by so many saints for centuries." [6] It would seem, then, that those who do not preach Calvinism do not preach the gospel, a serious charge indeed. C.H. Spurgeon was very emphatic that no intelligent Christian could possibly entertain any other position:

> I do not ask whether you believe Calvinism. It is possible you may not. But I believe you will before you enter heaven. I am persuaded that as God may have washed your hearts, He will wash your brains before you enter heaven. [7]

Such a strong statement is impressive, coming from Charles Haddon Spurgeon. John H. Gerstner writes, "We believe with the great Baptist preacher, Charles Haddon Spurgeon, that Calvinism is just another name for Christianity." [8] Again, if Calvinism is true Christianity, would that mean that non-Calvinists are not Christians? Of course, we could cite many other Christian leaders of equal stature in the history of the church, such as D.L. Moody, who were of the opposite opinion. Norman F. Douty lists more than seventy Christian leaders who opposed Calvinism, among them such men as Richard Baxter, John Newton, John and Charles Wesley, John Bunyan, H.C.G. Moule and others. [9] A study of early church history reveals that Calvinistic doctrines were unknown during the church's first three centuries. One of the greatest experts on ecclesiastical history, Bishop Davenant, declares:

> . . . it may be truly affirmed that before the dispute between Augustine and Pelagius, there was no question concerning the death of Christ, whether it was to be extended to all mankind, or to be confined only to the elect. For the Fathers . . . not a word (that I know of) occurs among them of the exclusion of any person by the decree of God. They agree that it is actually beneficial to those only who believe, yet they everywhere confess that Christ died in behalf of all mankind . . . .

> Augustine died A.D. 429, and up to his time, at least, there is not the slightest evidence that any Christian ever dreamed of a propitiation for the elect alone. Even after him, the doctrine of a limited propitiation was but slowly propagated, and for long but partially received. [10]

Today there is growing division on this issue, most Calvinists insisting that Christ died only for the elect. On the other hand, IFCA International, a group of about 700 independent evangelical churches and 1,200 pastors (some of them Calvinists) declares in its doctrinal statement, "We believe that the Lord Jesus Christ died on the cross for all mankind . . . to accomplish the redemption of all who trust in him . . . ." [11] Spurgeon himself, so often quoted by Calvinists to support their view, rejected Limited Atonement, though it lies at the very heart of Calvinism and follows inevitably from its other points — and he did so in unequivocal language:

> I know there are some who think it necessary to their system of theology to limit the merit of the blood of Jesus: if my theological system needed such limitation, I would cast it to the winds. I cannot, I dare not, allow the thought to find lodging in my mind, it seems so near akin to blasphemy. In Christ's finished work I see an ocean of merit; my plummet finds no bottom, my eye discerns no shore . . . . Having a divine Person for an offering, it is not consistent to conceive of limited value; bound and measure are terms inapplicable to the divine sacrifice. [12]

Aggressive Promotion

Calvinists are increasingly insisting that their peculiar dogmas represent the faith of "the Reformers who led the Reformation" and should be accepted by all evangelical Christians as true Christianity and as the biblical expression of the gospel. There is much they stand for with which all Christians would agree. There is much that almost all evangelicals *think* they agree with because of misunderstandings, but actually do not, which will be clarified in the following pages. And there is much with regard to the church, Israel and the return of Christ to which those who believe in the imminent rapture of the church would take strong exception. These latter views have nothing to do with the gospel and therefore will not be dealt with herein.

In the year 2000, the Alliance of Reformation Christians met in London and sent this message to evangelicals worldwide: "We therefore call upon those who bear the label 'evangelical' to affirm their faith once again in accordance with the witness of Scripture and in continuity with the historic testimony of the church." [13] By "historic testimony of the church" they mean the peculiar doctrines which come from Augustine as interpreted and expanded by John Calvin and which were at one time forced by a state church upon all in England and Scotland and those parts of Europe where Calvinists were in control. Historic documentation is provided in Chapters 5 and 6.

Today's Calvinists speak ever more earnestly and boldly about the need for a "new Reformation," by which they very clearly mean a revival of Calvinism as the dominant view in Christendom. Consider some of the resolutions which make up "The London Declaration 2000: Alliance of Reformation Christians – A vision for biblical unity in the modern church, 'The Evangelical Problem'":

Under "The Question of Truth,"
We therefore call upon evangelicals to return to the once-held biblical view...that to lay claim to a particular doctrine [Calvinism] as true is not spiritual arrogance but a biblical duty.

Under "A Vision for Reformation,"
We therefore call upon evangelicals to affirm a vision for reformation which is in accordance with the witness of Scripture and in continuity with the historic testimony of the [Calvinist] church. Such a vision is of a church which is both *Catholic* and *Reformed*. By 'Catholic' we do *not* mean 'Roman Catholic' ... " [See Chapter 4, "Calvinism's Surprising Catholic Connection."] By *Reformed*, we mean that we confess those doctrines about the authority of Scripture and salvation by grace alone which our Reformed [Calvinist] forefathers reaffirmed at the time of the Reformation. (Their emphasis)

Under "Four Affirmations," 1. includes the following:
We likewise affirm that we are *Augustinians* in our doctrine of man and in our doctrine of salvation. This is because we believe that Augustine and his successors, including the [Calvinist] Reformers, faithfully reflect the Bible's

teaching regarding the total spiritual inability of fallen man to respond to God, God the Father's gracious unconditional election of a people to be saved, the design of the incarnate Son's atoning work as intended surely and certainly to secure the salvation of that people [the elect only], the monergistic grace of the Holy Spirit in regeneration [without understanding or faith on man's part], and the perseverance of the elect. Accordingly, we also reject all forms of synergism or Semi-Pelagianism in which man is accorded a cooperative role [even to believe] in his regeneration, e.g. Arminianism. We reject equally any softening of Augustinian soteriology, e.g. Amyraldinianism ('four point' Calvinism), and any hardening of it, e.g. *Hyper-Calvinism* . . . . The notion of one Catholic and Reformed [Calvinist] Church — one main, majestic stream of historic Christian orthodoxy [Augustinianism/Calvinism] — is thus integral to our understanding. This notion we affirm as true and foundational to any evangelical outlook worthy of the name.

Under 2,
Reformed Catholics affirm the importance of the church and its history in any authentic vision of God's redemptive work in space and time. Evangelicalism today is infected with a deadly amnesia with regard to the historic [Calvinist] church . . . . We specifically reject the subjective and often disorderly spectacle of charismatic-style worship, with its attendant practices, such as alleged tongues-speaking, prophecies, 'slayings in the Spirit,' etc.

Under 4.
. . . we bemoan the influence among evangelicals of a pietistic dispensationalism in which the world is considered irredeemably wicked (and thus hardly worth the effort of influencing), and in which the only hope is supposed to be the imminent rapture of the saints.

A Challenge To Remain Silent

With the recent upsurge of Calvinism, a number of leading Calvinists have begun to take a far more aggressive stance in its public promotion. Both sides, in fact, are increasingly making this issue a matter of fellowship in the Lord, resulting in division in a number of otherwise sound churches. In some churches, Calvinism is looked upon as a cult and members are forbidden to promote it even privately. In others only Calvinists are accepted as members. Of course this has been true of pastors and mission candidates for centuries in nearly all Presbyterian churches and even in some Baptist churches — but now that position seems to be growing.

Major evangelical seminaries, even those which generally hold to a dispensational theology, are indoctrinating thousands of future pastors and missionaries into Calvinism's amillennialism, the replacement of Israel with the church and other facets of so-called Reformed theology. Some Christian colleges are increasingly doing the same. Lately a heretofore unsuspected range of confusion and division on this topic seems to be emerging.

In his excellent book, *The Other Side of Calvinism*, Laurence M. Vance claims that there has "of late been a resurgence of Calvinism in the Southern

Baptist Convention." [14] Almost daily I found this subject was claiming a wider interest and greater importance than I had ever imagined. It seemed obvious that there was great need for further research and writing to deal with this important issue.

As it became known that I intended to write such a book, a number of pastors cautioned me to refrain from publicly expressing myself on this subject because out of ignorance of its true teachings I had already misrepresented it. A typical response from the Calvinist friends to whom I sent an early manuscript for comment went like this: "The caricatures you present and the straw men you construct demonstrate to me that you have absolutely no understanding of the Reformed position and until you do I would counsel that you refrain from putting anything in print." [15]

Letters began to pour into our ministry, The Berean Call, from around the world, many from pastors, insisting that I was unqualified to address Calvinism and urging me to seal my lips and drop my pen regarding this topic. It was suggested that I would lose many friends and alienate myself from leading evangelicals, most of whom were said to be convinced Calvinists. Furthermore, who would publish such a book since the major publishers had brought out many books on the other side?

What moved me most was the concern earnestly expressed by close friends that a book from me on this issue could cause division — the last thing I wanted. "We can just hear it now," several friends told me: "Here comes Dave Hunt again; this time he's attacking Calvinists!" That concern weighed heavily upon me.

One must be willing to accept wise counsel. But the advice to remain silent, though given by so many out of genuine concern seemed, after much prayer and soul-searching on my part, to be ill advised. Spurgeon called the debate over God's sovereignty and man's free will "a controversy which . . . I believe to have been really healthy and which has done us all a vast amount of good . . . ." [16] My heart's desire is that this book will be only to God's eternal glory and to the blessing of His people.

1   Narration represents a composite of several of the author's recent actual experiences.
2   Duane Edward Spencer, TULIP: The Five Points of Calvinism in the Light of Scripture (Baker Book House, 1979), 6.
3   R.C. Sproul, Chosen by God (Tyndale House, 1986), 15.
4   Leonard J. Coppes, Are Five Points Enough? The Ten Points of Calvinism (Denver CO: self-published, 1980), xi.
5   D. James Kennedy, Why I Am a Presbyterian (Coral Ridge Ministries, n.d.), 1.
6   John Piper, TULIP, The Pursuit of God's Glory in Salvation (Bethlehem Baptist Church, 2000), back cover.
7   Charles Haddon Spurgeon, Autobiography of Charles H. Spurgeon (American Baptist Society, n.d.), I:92.
8   John H. Gerstner, Wrongly Dividing the Word of Truth: A Critique of Dispensationalism (Wolgemuth and Hyatt, Publishers, Inc., 1991), 107.
9   Norman F. Douty, The Death of Christ (William and Watrous Publishing Company, n.d.), 136-63.
10 James Morrison, The Extent of the Atonement (Hamilton, Adams and Co., 1882), 114-17.
11 IFCA International, What We Believe, I: (3) b (www.ifca.org).
12 Spurgeon, op. cit., I:174.
13 "The London Declaration 2000: Alliance of Reformation Christians - a vision for biblical unity in the modern church, 'The Evangelical Problem.' "
14 "A Study Tool for the Doctrine of Election" (SBC Life, April 1995), 8-9; "Arminian/Calvinist Response" (SBC Life, August 1995), 8-9; cited in Laurence M. Vance, The Other Side of Calvinism (Vance Publications, Pensacola FL, 1999), 25.
15 Personal to Dave Hunt, dated October 19, 2000. On file.
16 Charles Haddon Spurgeon, "God's Will and Man's Will," No. 442 (Newington: Metropolitan Tabernacle, sermon delivered Sunday, March 30, 1862).

2
Is Biblical Understanding Reserved To An Elite?

Calvinists emphasize that their theology rests upon solid biblical exegesis, being "firmly based . . . upon the Word of God." [1] Some have gone so far as to assert that "this teaching was held to be the truth by the apostles," [2] and even that "Christ taught the doctrines which have come to be known as the five points of Calvinism." [3] According to the Bible itself, however, no one should accept such claims without verifying them from Scripture.

Any doctrine claiming to be based upon the Bible must be carefully checked against the Bible. Furthermore, anyone who knows the Bible ought to be able to do so. Relying upon one supposed biblical expert for an evaluation of the opinions of another would be going in circles. No matter whose opinion one accepted, the end result would be the same: one would still be held hostage to human opinion. Each individual must personally check all opinions out directly from the Bible. Yet I was being advised to keep silent on the basis that only those with special qualifications were competent to check Calvinism against the Bible, an idea which in itself contradicted Scripture.

The inhabitants of the city of Berea, though not even Christians when Paul first preached the gospel to them, "searched the scriptures daily, [to see] whether those things [Paul preached] were so" (Acts 17:11) — and they were commended as "noble" for doing so. Yet Calvinists insist that it requires special (and apparently lengthy) preparation for anyone to become qualified to examine that peculiar doctrine in light of the Bible. Why?

After all, the Bible itself declares that a "young man" can understand its instructions and thereby "cleanse his way" (Psalms 119:9). Even a child can know the Holy Scriptures through home instruction from a mother and grandmother (2 Timothy 1:5; 3:15). If special expertise were required to test Calvinism against Scripture, surely that would be proof in itself that this peculiar doctrine did not come from valid biblical exegesis. Anything that enigmatic, by very definition, could not have been derived from the Bible, which itself claims to be written for the simple:

> For ye see your calling, brethren, how that not many wise men after the flesh, not many mighty, not many noble, are called: but God hath chosen the foolish things of the world to confound the wise; and God hath chosen the weak things of the world to confound the things which are mighty . . . that no flesh should glory in his presence. (1 Corinthians 1:26-29)

Is Calvinism So Difficult To Understand?

Should Calvinism really be unfathomable for the common Christian? That very fact, if true, would be additional proof that Calvinism was not derived from the scriptures. How could something so complicated possibly come from that upon which every person is capable of meditating day and night (Psalms 1:1-2)? If the essential nourishment God's Word provides is to be every man's daily sustenance for spiritual life (Deuteronomy 8:3), could Calvinism have come from the Bible and yet be indigestible for the ordinary Christian?

Many, whose obvious sincerity was appreciated, were telling me that in spite of my quoting John Calvin directly from his writings, along with quotations from leading Calvinists of today, I was still likely to misrepresent Calvinism because I didn't understand it. Even after a recent three-hour detailed discussion with Calvinist friends they still told me, "You just don't understand Calvinism." If the gospel is that complex, who could be saved?

Why should Calvinism be such a difficult and apparently esoteric subject that it would require years to comprehend it? Such an attitude could very well intimidate many into accepting this belief simply because such a vast array of highly respected theologians and evangelical leaders espouse it. Surely the great majority of Calvinists are ordinary Christians. On what basis, then, without the expertise that I apparently lacked, were they able to accept it?

As for familiarizing oneself with Calvinism, there are surely more than sufficient resources available for anyone genuinely interested in consulting them. Numerous books on that subject are available, both pro and con. *The five points of calvinism* by Edwin H. Palmer, along with books by R.C. Sproul, John Piper, John MacArthur, A.W. Pink, C.H. Spurgeon and others, are highly recommended by leading Calvinists. On the other side, the books by Samuel Fisk are informative. Laurence M. Vance's *The Other Side of Calvinism* is an exhaustive treatment of more than 700 pages with hundreds of footnotes documenting his quotations. Calvin's *Institutes of the Christian Religion* as well as other of his writings and those of Augustine, John Knox and other classics are also readily available.

Making Certain Of Accuracy And Fairness

To make certain that no mistaken interpretations of the doctrines under consideration survived in this book, a preliminary manuscript was submitted to a number of Calvinist friends and acquaintances for their critique. Reading and discussing with them their valuable comments, for which I am deeply grateful, has been an education in itself. In that process it became clearer than ever that Calvinists don't agree even among themselves on everything.

Most Calvinists agree upon five major points. Others insist that there are ten or even more relevant points. Palmer suggests, "Calvinism is not restricted to five points: it has thousands of points." [4] It's not likely that we can cover all those alleged points in these pages! Palmer himself deals only with five.

There are disagreements between "five-point" and "four-point" Calvinists. For example, Lewis Sperry Chafer, founder of Dallas Theological Seminary, called himself a "four-point" Calvinist because he rejected limited atonement. [5] Vance points out that "Many Baptists in the General Association of Regular Baptist Churches are four-point Calvinists." [6] To deny one point while accepting the other four, however, has been called by five-point Calvinists the "blessed inconsistency."

It is widely declared that one "must hold all five points of Calvinism" [7] because "The Five Points of Calvinism all tie together. He who accepts one of the points will accept the other points." [8] Even those who agree on all five, however, have different ways of understanding and defending them. Obviously, we cannot cover every variety of opinion in this book but must stick to what the majority would accept as a fair presentation of their beliefs.

In the further interest of accuracy, we quote extensively not only Calvin himself, but from the writings of numerous Calvinists who are highly regarded by their colleagues. One book from which we quote extensively is *The Potter's Freedom* by apologist James R. White, which is endorsed by a number of today's evangelical leaders, including R.C. Sproul, Jr., Jay Adams, Irwin Lutzer and many others. It is an especially valuable resource because it was written specifically to answer Norman Geisler's objections to certain points of Calvinism which he raised in his recent book, *Chosen But Free*. There should be more than sufficient citations from authoritative sources for the reader to make absolutely certain that Calvinism is being fairly presented.

An Appeal For Open Discussion

God's foreknowledge, predestination/election, human choice, God's sovereignty and man's responsibility are widely alleged to be mysteries beyond our ability to reconcile. Therefore, some insist that these concepts should be accepted without any attempt at understanding or reconciling apparent conflicts. The illustration is used repeatedly that as we approach heaven's gate we see written above it, "Whosoever will may come," but once we have entered we see from the inside the words, "Chosen in Him before the foundation of the world." We respect the many church leaders who continue to offer such an explanation as though that were sufficient. There are, however, several compelling reasons for not acquiescing to that popular position.

First of all, God intends for us to understand His Word rather than to plead "mystery" over large portions of it. He has given it for our learning. Of God's Word, the psalmist said, "it is a lamp unto my feet, and a light unto my path" (Psalms 119:105) and such it is intended to be for each of us today. Peter acknowledged that there are "things hard to be understood" and warned that Scripture is sometimes twisted, resulting in destruction to those who do so (2 Peter 3:16). God never suggests that there is any part of His Word that we should not attempt to understand fully. Inasmuch as many passages in Scripture are devoted to the difficult themes we will address, we can confidently expect that the Bible itself will clarify the issues.

Second, the history of the church from its earliest beginnings has involved sharp differences of opinion on many vital subjects, including the gospel itself. Numerous destructive heresies have developed and have been vigorously opposed. Neither Christ nor His apostles considered divergent views to be normal or acceptable, but commanded the believers to "earnestly contend for the faith which was once delivered to the saints" (Jude 3). That command applies to us today.

Third, it hardly seems that our Lord would have us draw back from seriously considering and understanding foreknowledge and election/predestination as well as man's responsibility and how it all fits together in God's sovereign grace. While we may never see the entire body of Christ in perfect agreement, each of us is responsible to understand these issues as clearly as we are able through diligent study — and to help one another in the process.

Finally, God calls upon us to seek Him in order that we may know Him, though His ways and His thoughts are as far above ours as "the heavens are higher than the earth" (Isaiah 55:8-9). Surely as we come to know God better we will understand His Word and His will more fully. God is our Savior, and to know Him is life eternal (John 17:3). Knowing God must include a deepening understanding of all He has revealed to us in His Word.

We are to live, as Christ said (quoting His own declaration as the I AM to Israel through Moses in Deuteronomy 8:3), not "by bread alone, but by *every* word that proceedeth out of the mouth of God" (Matthew 4:4). Solomon said, "*Every* word of God is pure" (Proverbs 30:5) (emphases added). Then we must carefully consider and seek to understand *every word*.

The Most Compelling Reason

It is a general assumption that whatever other disagreements we may have, when it comes to the gospel of our salvation both Calvinists and non-Calvinists are in full agreement. Many Calvinists, however, disagree, claiming that the biblical gospel *is Calvinism*. For example: "God's plan of salvation revealed in the Scriptures consists of what is popularly known as the Five Points of Calvinism." [9] Loraine Boettner declares, "The great advantage of the Reformed Faith is that in the framework of the Five Points of Calvinism it sets forth clearly what the Bible teaches concerning the way of salvation."[10] Others insist that "if you do not know the Five Points of Calvinism, you do not know the gospel, but some perversion of it . . . "[11] B.B. Warfield claimed, "Calvinism is evangelicalism in its purest and only stable expression." [12]

Such claims that the Five Points of Calvinism make up the gospel raise the concerns about Calvinism to a new level! If much special study is required to understand Calvinism, and if years of Bible study still leave one ignorant on this subject, and if Calvinism *is the gospel of our salvation* – then where does that leave the multitudes who think they are saved but are ignorant of Calvinism? This question may seem divisive, but it cannot be ignored.

Another grave concern is raised concerning the proclamation of the gospel to the whole world as Christ commanded. Calvinists insist that their doctrine does not diminish the zeal with which the gospel is to be preached. To support this assertion they name some of the great preachers and missionaries who were staunch Calvinists, such as George Whitefield, Adoniram Judson, William Carey and others. And it is true that, although they know that many to whom they preach are not among the elect, some Calvinists indeed preach earnestly so that the elect may hear and believe.

Certainly, however, the zeal of such men and women in bringing the gospel to the world could not be *because* of their Calvinism but only *in spite* of it. To believe that those who will be saved have been fixed by God's decree, that none others can be saved, and that the elect must be regenerated by God's sovereign act without the gospel or any persuasion by any preacher or by any faith in God on their part, could hardly provide motivation for earnestly preaching the gospel.

No matter how the Calvinist tries to argue to the contrary, such a belief can only lessen the zeal a reasonable person might otherwise have to reach the lost with the gospel of God's grace in Christ.

Facing A Real Dilemma

The gospel Peter and Paul and the other apostles preached was for everyone in the audiences they faced, wherever they went: it was not a message which only the elect could believe. Peter told Cornelius and his family and friends, "And he [Christ] commanded us to preach unto the people [not to a select group], . . . that . . . whosoever [among the people to whom He preached] believeth in him shall receive remission of sins" (Acts 10:42-43).

In contrast, Calvin's gospel says that Christ died, and His blood atones, only for the elect. Could this be the same gospel Paul preached? Paul proclaimed to audiences, "We declare unto you [all of you] glad tidings . . . " (Acts 13:32). The "glad tidings" of the gospel which Paul preached echoed what the angel of the Lord had said to the shepherds at the time of Christ's birth: "I bring you tidings of great joy, which shall be to all people . . . " (Luke 2:10). These tidings of great joy concerned the fact that "the Savior of the world" (Luke 2:11; John 4:42) had been born. Calvin's gospel, however, says that Christ is not the Savior of the world but only of the elect.

Paul could and did honestly say to everyone he met, "Christ died for you." In complete contrast, a book we have long recommended to readers declares, "As a reformed Christian, the writer [author] believes that counselors must not tell any unsaved counselee that Christ died for him, for *they cannot say that.* No man knows except Christ himself who are his elect for whom he died" (emphasis added). [13] Obviously, Calvin's message of salvation for a select few *does not* bring "great joy" to "all people."

Palmer writes, "But thank God that Christ's death was an absolute guarantee that every single one of the elect would be saved." [14] So great joy comes to the elect alone! As for the rest, Calvin's gospel that God had predestined their damnation could hardly be "tidings of great joy"! This is the way Calvin put it:

> To many this seems a perplexing subject, because they deem it most incongruous that of the great body of mankind some should be predestinated to salvation, and others to destruction . . . .From this we infer, that all who know not that they are the peculiar people of God, must be wretched [not filled with joy!] from perpetual trepidation . . . . [15]

What gospel is this? Because of the eternal importance of that question for the whole world to whom Christ commanded us to take the gospel, we are compelled to examine Calvinism closely in light of Scripture. Could it really be true, as Arthur C. Custance insists, that "Calvinism is the Gospel and to teach Calvinism is in fact to preach the Gospel"? [16]

Is Calvinism founded upon the plain text of Scripture? Or does it require interpreting common words and phrases such as *all, all men, world, everyone that thirsteth, any man,* and *whosoever will* to mean "the elect"? Is a peculiar interpretation of Scripture required to sustain this doctrine?

Our concern is for the defense of the character of the true God, the God of mercy and love whose "tender mercies are over all his works" (Psalms 145:9). The Bible declares that He is "not willing that any should perish, but that all should come to repentance" (2 Peter 3:9); "who will have all men to be saved, and to come unto the knowledge of the truth" (1 Timothy 2:4). Such is the God of the Bible from Genesis to Revelation.

Open examination and discussion of important issues—especially the gospel and the very nature and character of God—can only be healthy for the body of Christ. It is my prayer that our investigation of Calvinism and its comparison with God's Holy Word, as expressed in the following pages, will bring helpful and needed clarification.

---

1   W.J. Seaton, *The Five Points of Calvinism* (The Banner of Truth Trust, 1970), 8.
2   Jimmie B. Davis (*The Berean Baptist Banner*, February 5, 1995), 30.
3   Mark Duncan, *The Five Points of Christian Reconstruction from the Lips of Our Lord* (Still Waters Revival Books, 1990), 10.25
4   Edwin H. Palmer, foreword to *the five points of calvinism* (Baker Books, enlarged ed., 20th prtg. 1999), 1.
5   Lewis Sperry Chafer, *Systematic Theology* (Dallas Seminary Press, 1948), 3:184.
6   Laurence M. Vance, *The Other Side of Calvinism* (Vance Publications, Pensacola FL, rev. ed. 1999), 147.
7   Charles W. Bronson, *The Extent of the Atonement* (Pilgrim Publications, 1992), 19.
8   Palmer, op. cit., 27.
9   Leonard J. Coppes, *Are Five Points Enough? The Ten Points of Calvinism* (Denver CO: self-published, 1980), 55.
10 Loraine Boettner, *The Reformed Faith* (Presbyterian and Reformed Publishing Co., 1983), 24.
11 Fred Phelps, "The Five Points of Calvinism" (*The Berea Baptist Banner*, February 5, 1990), 21.
12 Benjamin B. Warfield, *Calvin and Augustine,* ed. Samuel G. Craig (Presbyterian and Reformed Publishing Co., 1956), 497.
13 Jay E. Adams, *Competent to Counsel* (Baker Book House, 1970), 70.
14 Palmer, op. cit., 92.
15 John Calvin, *Institutes of the Christian Religion,* trans. Henry Beveridge (Wm. Eerdmans Publishing Company, 1998 ed.), III:xxi,1.
16 Arthur C. Custance, *The Sovereignty of Grace* (Presbyterian and Reformed Publishing Co., 1979), 302.

3
John Calvin And His *Institutes*

Calvinism and the controversies surrounding it have confronted Protestants for more than four hundred years. Of course, the whole dispute in the church goes back long before John Calvin to Augustine, Pelagius and others. Aurelius Augustinus was born November 13, 354 at Tagaste, a small town near the eastern border of modern Algeria. His father was a Roman official and a pagan; his mother Monica, a Christian. In 386, after studies in philosophy, law and the classics (he was greatly inspired by Plato), a year of teaching grammar and a career as a rhetorician, Augustine embraced Christianity, entered the Roman Catholic Church, and established a monastery which he moved to Hippo, Africa upon being appointed its bishop. Often called the father of Roman Catholicism's major doctrines, as we shall see, Augustine heavily influenced later philosophers and even exerts a strong influence among evangelicals today through Calvinism.

Born in Britain near the end of the fourth century, Pelagius rose to prominence after the fall of Rome in August 410 forced him to flee to North Africa. There he came into open conflict with Augustine for his views that there had been sinless beings before Christ and that it was possible through human effort, aided by grace, for anyone to live above sin. He claimed that Adam was mortal when created and that his sin did not bring death upon mankind but affected himself only. Consequently, infants are born in the same state Adam was in before he sinned. Moreover, good works were essential to salvation, especially for the rich to give their goods to the poor to help effect the moral transformation of society, which he believed possible. He considered "forgive us our sins" to be a prayer involving false humility and unsuitable for Christians inasmuch as sin is not a necessity but man's own fault.

Semi-Pelagianism was developed a few years later by a French monk, John Cassianus, who modified Pelagianism by denying its extreme views on human merit and accepting the necessity of the power of the Holy Spirit, but retaining the belief that man can do good, that he can resist God's grace, that he must cooperate in election and does have the will to choose between good and evil. Those who reject Calvinism are often accused of promoting semi-Pelagianism, which is generally a false charge. Labels are often misleading – which is why it is difficult to speak of Calvinism, because of its many shades and variations.

While generally recognizing that Augustine was the source of most of what Calvin taught, Calvinists argue among themselves over the exact composition of this doctrine. Nor would Calvin himself agree completely with many of his followers today. An attempt is made in the following pages to quote those who represent the current view among most Calvinists.

Even without the growing controversy, however, John Calvin is worthy of study because of the enormous impact he has had and continues to have in the Christian world. The Scottish Reformer, John Knox, credited with founding the Presbyterian Church, spent several years in Geneva and brought Calvinism to Scotland and to the Presbyterian movement. Daniel Gerdes said, "Calvin's labors were so highly useful to the Church of Christ, that there is hardly any department of the Christian world to be found that is not full of them. [1] It has been said that "No man in the history of the Church has been more admired and ridiculed, loved and hated, blessed and cursed." [2] Vance claims that "the prodigious impact of Calvin upon Christianity has yet to be fathomed." He goes on to refer to

> . . . such institutions and organizations as Calvin College, Calvin Seminary, the *Calvin Theological Journal*, the International Congress on Calvin Research, the Calvin Translation Society, the Calvin Foundation, and the H. Henry Meeter Center for Calvin Studies, which contains over 3,000 books and 12,000 articles concerning John Calvin. The majority of Calvin's writings are still available today, which is quite an exploit considering that he lived over 400 years ago. There are extant over 2,000 of Calvin's sermons, while Calvin's complete works occupy fifty-nine volumes in the *Corpus Reformatorum*. College and seminary students at both Presbyterian and Reformed schools have the option of taking a whole course on John Calvin. Moreover, Calvin has the eminence of being mentioned in every dictionary, encyclopedia, and history book, both sacred and secular. [3]

How Much Calvin In Calvinism?

There is an attempt today to disassociate Calvin from Calvinism in view of its earlier origins in Augustine and the Latin Vulgate Bible. Moreover, it was not until the Great Synod of Dort (Dordrecht) more than fifty years after Calvin's death that the five points of Calvinism were first set forth in order. Ironically, this declaration came about only as an expression of opposition to the five points of Arminianism. Nevertheless, this system of thought continues to be universally known as "Calvinism." Loraine Boettner says, " . . . it was Calvin who wrought out this system of theological thought with such logical clearness and emphasis that it has ever since borne his name." [4] Where it really came from, as we shall see in the next chapter, is admitted by Custance who says that Augustine was "perhaps the first after Paul to realize the Total Depravity of man." [5] Farrar agrees: "To him [Augustine] . . . [is] due the exaggerated doctrine of total human depravity . . . ." [6]

In spite of its long and varied origins and development, the term "Calvinism" remains as the commonly used identification. As Engelsma says, speaking for the overwhelming majority of Calvinists, "it was Calvin who developed these truths, systematically and fully; and therefore, they came to be called by his name." [7] B.B. Warfield makes it even stronger: "It was he who gave the Evangelical movement a theology." [8] Timothy George goes so far as to say that it was Calvin who "presented more clearly and more masterfully than anyone before him the essential elements of Protestant theology." [9] R. Tudor Jones calls Calvin's *Institutes* "one of the seminal works of Christian theology . . . his thinking was to be the motive force behind revolutionary changes in several European countries. [10] Edwin H. Palmer expresses an admiration for Calvin which seems to grow ever stronger among his followers:

> The name Calvinism has often been used, not because Calvin was the first or sole teacher, but because after the long silence of the Middle Ages, he was the most eloquent and systematic expositor of these truths. To the novitiate, however, it seemed as if Calvin originated them. [11]

Of course, Calvinists are convinced that the Bible itself is the true source of this religious system. C.H. Spurgeon declared, "I believe nothing because Calvin taught it, but because I have found his teaching in the Word of God. [12] . . . We hold and assert again and again that the truth which Calvin preached was the very truth which the apostle Paul had long before written in his inspired epistles, and which is most clearly revealed in the discourses of our blessed Lord Himself." [13]

We respectfully disagree with this great preacher. Certainly some of what Calvin taught (such as limited atonement) was repugnant to Spurgeon, so that he had to pick and choose which of Calvin's beliefs to embrace. In fact, as we shall see, especially in his later years, Spurgeon often made statements which were in direct conflict with Calvinism. His favorite sermon, the one through which he said more souls had come to Christ than through any other, was criticized as being Arminian!

How Much Catholicism In Calvinism?

In the following pages we shall document the fact that the wide praise heaped upon Calvin as a great exegete is badly misplaced. He taught much that was clearly wrong and which his evangelical followers of today either don't know or perhaps don't want to know. There is a great deal contained in Calvin's writings which every true believer must admit was, at the least, serious error and in some cases outright heresy.

On that account alone, Calvin's expertise as an outstanding exegete of God's Word is suspect. Much of his teaching is warmed-over Roman Catholicism. Let those evangelicals who praise Calvin as thoroughly biblical justify, for example, the following from his *Institutes*:

> I believe in the Holy Catholic Church . . . whence flow perpetual remission of sins, and full restoration to eternal life. [14]
> But as it is now our purpose to discourse of the visible Church, let us learn, from her single title of Mother, how useful, nay, how necessary the knowledge of her is, since there is no other means of entering into life unless she conceive us in the womb and give us birth, unless she nourish us at her breasts, and, in short, keep us under her charge and government, until, divested of mortal flesh, we become like the angels . . . . Moreover, beyond the pale of the Church no forgiveness of sins, no salvation, can be hoped for, as Isaiah and Joel testify (Isaiah 37:32, Joel 2:32), . . . hence the abandonment of the Church is always fatal. [15]

Of course, by "Catholic Church" he did not mean the *Roman* Catholic, but the true church universal. Nowhere in Scripture, however, is the church called "Mother" or credited with conceiving us in her womb to spiritual life. The only church called "mother" is the "MOTHER OF HARLOTS" (Revelation 17:5), the false church headquartered at the Vatican. Nor is the true church ever referred to as the means of salvation or forgiveness of sins. Calvin is simply reflecting Roman Catholic ideas which he absorbed as a devout Roman Catholic during the first twenty-four years of his life, and especially through the writings of Augustine, the greatest of all Catholics.

As for Isaiah 37:32 and Joel 2:32, not even an overly active imagination could find the slightest hint of any relationship to the church. Isaiah refers to a remnant of Israel escaping out of Mount Zion during a coming judgment; while Joel refers to a remnant being preserved in Zion. Even if one erroneously equated Israel with the church, these passages do not support Calvin's statements.

Of course, in becoming a Protestant, Calvin rejected the papacy as representing the true church. He declared that "in declining fatal participation in such wickedness, we run no risk of being dissevered from the Church of Christ." [16] Nevertheless, while condemning Romanism as false, he carried over into Protestantism much of her structure and false views, such as infant baptism, a clergy with special powers and efficacy of sacraments performed only by such clergy. More of that later.

Early Life And Conversion

The man known today throughout the world as John Calvin, and who is generally credited as the founder of the system of Protestantism named after him, was born July 10, 1509 in Noyon, France, as Jean Chauvin. His was a devoutly religious Roman Catholic family of prominence in an ecclesiastical town dominated by the local bishop and his assisting priests. As secretary and legal advisor to the bishop, Jean's father, Gerald, was an inside participant in a corrupt religiously-based political system.

In a bit of old-fashioned and quite common nepotism, young Jean was put on the Church payroll at the age of twelve, remaining on it for thirteen years — until one year after his conversion to Luther's Protestantism. From his earliest years Jean was the beneficiary of an ungodly partnership between the civil and religious authorities which held the common people in bondage — a partnership dominated by the Church. It was a pattern which he would later implement with even greater efficiency in Geneva, Switzerland, including church dominance in civil affairs, and persecution and even execution of those accused of heresy.

Upon entering the Collège de La Marche at the University of Paris, Jean's love of Latin was reflected in his registration as Johannes Calvinus. There he diligently pursued knowledge, spending excessively long hours in compulsive study that had ill effects upon his health in later years and possibly shortened his life. He was known for his deep Catholic piety and blunt rebukes of his friends' morals.

Quite unexpectedly in 1528, Jean's father Gerald fell into disfavor with the bishop and was excommunicated from the Roman Catholic Church. Shortly thereafter, Calvin's brother, a priest, was also excommunicated on the grounds of heresy. As a result of the sudden change in circumstances, Gerald ordered Johannes, whom he had previously expected to enter the priesthood, to Orléans for the study of law.

Calvin later explained, "My father had intended me for theology from my childhood. But when he reflected that the career of the law proved everywhere very lucrative for its practitioners, the prospect suddenly made him change his mind." [17] This new pursuit became the young man's passion and possibly laid some of the foundation for the legalism which was later to become so pervasive in the system of theology which he would soon thereafter develop.

After earning a Bachelor of Laws in 1531 (he would later be granted a doctorate in law), Jean — now Johannes (John) — returned to Paris, immersed himself in a passionate study of classical literature and published his first piece of writing, a Latin essay on Seneca's *De elementia*. Historian Will Durant says that John, still a devout Roman Catholic, "seemed dedicated to humanism, when some sermons of Luther reached him and stirred him with their audacity." [18] Secret discussions of daring dissension soon swept Calvin into a circle of young humanist intellectuals who were urging reform of the Church along the lines of Luther's bold rebellion against the Pope.

By January 1534, though not yet a full-fledged Protestant, Calvin had become vocal enough in support of Luther's ideas that he was forced to flee Paris during a crackdown on dissenters by the authorities. Finding refuge in the town of Angoulême, he began to write his voluminous classic, *Institutes of the Christian Religion*, and quite remarkably finished the first and smaller edition the following year. Boettner acknowledges:

> The first [Latin] edition contained in brief outline all the essential elements of his system, and, considering the youthfulness of the author, was a marvel of intellectual precocity. It was later enlarged to five times the size of the original and published in French, but never did he make any radical departure from any of the doctrines set forth in the first edition. [19]

Calvin's *Institutes*

In his *Institutes* Calvin masterfully developed his own brand of Christianity. It was without a doubt an expansion upon Augustinianism and heavily influenced by the Latin Vulgate translation of the Bible — the official Bible of the Roman Catholic Church, and the one Calvin had long studied in its original Latin. The *Institutes*, arising from these two primary sources, has influenced succeeding generations to an extent far beyond anything its young author could have imagined at the time.

Most of those today, including evangelical leaders, who hold Calvin in great esteem, are not aware that they have been captivated by the writings of a devout Roman Catholic newly converted to Luther's Protestantism only two years previously (in the early part of 1533). Oddly, in spite of its paramount importance and his voluminous writings, we have no clear testimony in Calvin's own words concerning his salvation. He refers only to "a sudden conversion" which subdued his "over-much hardened" heart, but gives no description of how or what happened. [20]

Moreover, the exact nature of Calvin's conversion, at least up to that point in time, is placed in further question by two known facts. As late as June of 1533 he helped a young woman to gain entrance to a nunnery, [21] a rather odd thing for a convinced convert to Protestantism to do. Even more peculiar, instead of sending an immediate message withdrawing himself, Calvin kept himself on the payroll of the Roman Catholic Church until a year after he claimed to have been miraculously delivered from the "deep slough" of "obstinate addiction to the superstitions of the papacy." [22] It was not until May 4, 1534 that he returned to Noyon to resign from the Bishop's employ, was arrested, imprisoned, managed to escape and fled. [23] Although he was on the run and changing his place of residence, Calvin finished his original *Institutes* in August 1535. The first edition was published in March 1536. [24]

By any standard, this young man, though unusually bright, was far from mature in the Christian faith. Calvin himself said, "I was greatly astonished that, before a year passed [after his conversion], all those who had some desire for pure doctrine betook themselves to me in order to learn, *although I myself had done little more than begin.*" [25] (Emphasis added) Unquestionably, his *Institutes* could not possibly have come from a deep and fully developed evangelical understanding of Scripture. Instead, they came from the energetic enthusiasm of a recent law graduate and fervent student of philosophy and religion, a young genius devoted to Augustine and a newly adopted cause. Durant says:

> [As] a lad of twenty-six, he completed the most eloquent, fervent, lucid, logical, influential, and terrible work in all the literature of the religious revolution . . . . He carried into theology and ethics the logic, precision, and severity of Justinian's *Institutes* and gave his own masterpiece a similar name. [26]

Commendably, like Luther and the other Reformers, Calvin was determined that Scripture would be his sole authority. Early in the *Institutes* he laid down that foundation, affirming that "if we look at it [the Bible] with clear eyes and unbiased judgment, it will forthwith present itself with a divine majesty which will subdue our presumptuous opposition and force us to do it homage." [27] We can only applaud him for the way in which he affirmed the Bible's sole authority and apparently determined to obey it. Calvin revered God's Word as so far surpassing anything man had ever or could ever produce that "compared with its energetic influence, the beauties of rhetoricians and philosophers will almost entirely disappear; so that it is easy to perceive something divine in the sacred Scriptures . . . ." [28] No one can question Calvin's zeal to follow the Bible or his sincere conviction that what he conceived and taught was true to God's Word. Nevertheless, just as the Bereans daily searched the Scriptures to determine whether Paul's teaching was true to God's Word, so we must do with Calvin's teaching.

If there was a weakness in his approach to Scripture, it was that, in addition to his reliance upon Augustine, he brought his humanistic gift for logic to bear upon that which is "spiritually discerned" (1 Corinthians 2:14). Using his natural abilities, Calvin attempted to organize biblical teaching into an orderly system, which he then presented in his *Institutes*.

At the time of writing his *Institutes* Calvin, far from being an apostle like Paul, was a brand-new convert to the faith who had scarcely begun to walk with the Lord. Therefore, it could not have been spiritual maturity under the guidance of the Holy Spirit that brought forth the *Institutes,* but the power of Calvin's brilliant legal mind. This natural brilliance apparently blinded this young zealot to the fact that the partnership he later forged in Geneva between church and state (as Luther also did) was one of Roman Catholicism's major wrongs all over again and the very antithesis of Christ's life and teaching. The remnants of that error carried over into the Reformation still plague Europe today in the form of state churches.

Basic Elements: Sovereignty And Predestination

A basic foundation of this new religious system that would revolutionize much of Protestantism was an extremist view of God's sovereignty which denied the human will, and considered the church to be God's kingdom on earth — both views inspired by Augustine's writings. Verduin writes of Augustine, "Here we have an early representation of the notion that the Church of Christ was intended by its Founder to enter into a situation radically different from the one depicted in the New Testament . . . .This idea set forth by Augustine . . . led to all sorts of theological absurdities." [29]

Augustine taught that foreknowledge was the same as predestination: "Consequently, sometimes the same predestination is signified also under the name of foreknowledge." [30] Thus God's foreknowledge causes future events. Interestingly, R.C. Sproul writes that "virtually nothing in John Calvin's view of predestination . . . was not first in Martin Luther, and before Luther in Augustine." [31] Calvin's view is so extreme that it makes God the author of every event and thus even of all sin:

> Now . . . God . . . arranges all things . . . . If God merely foresaw human events, and did not also arrange and dispose of them at his pleasure, there might be room for agitating the question, how far his foreknowledge amounts to necessity; but since . . . he has decreed that they are so to happen . . . it is clear that all events take place by his sovereign appointment. [32]

Out of this particular view of God's sovereignty came Calvin's understanding of predestination. According to him (following the teaching of Augustine), in eternity past God had decided to save only a fraction of the human race and decreed that the rest would be consigned to eternal torment.

On what basis then did He predestine so many to hell? Simply because to do so was "the good pleasure of his will":

Scripture clearly proves . . . that God by his eternal and immutable counsel determined once for all those whom it was his pleasure one day to admit to salvation, and those whom, on the other hand, it was his pleasure to doom to destruction. [33]

Those, therefore, whom God passes by he reprobates, and that for no other cause but because he is pleased to exclude them from the inheritance which he predestines to his children . . . . [34]

But if all whom the Lord predestines to death are naturally liable to sentence of death, of what injustice, pray, do they complain . . . because by his eternal providence they were before their birth doomed to perpetual destruction . . . what will they be able to mutter against this defense? [35]

The great God . . . whose pleasure it is to inflict punishment on fools and transgressors, though he is not pleased to bestow his Spirit upon them . . . . Of this no other cause can be adduced than reprobation, which is hidden in the secret counsel of God. [36]

Now since the arrangement of all things is in the hand of God . . . he arranges . . . that individuals are born, who are doomed from the womb to certain death, and are to glorify him by their destruction . . . . [37]

God, according to the good pleasure of his will, without any regard to merit, elects those whom he chooses for sons, while he rejects and reprobates others . . . it is right for him to show by punishing that he is a just judge . . . .

Here the words of Augustine most admirably apply . . . . When other vessels are made unto dishonor, it must be imputed not to injustice, but to judgment.[38]

Throughout his entire *Institutes*, Calvin scarcely mentions or considers God's love which, in Calvin's view, is secondary to His sovereignty. Luther, too, was convinced that God, by His own sovereign choice and independent of anything in man, had from eternity past determined whom He would save and who would be damned. Calvin, like Augustine, said God could foresee the future because He had willed it. [39] Here we have it from Calvin's own pen, echoing once again his mentor, Augustine:

We say, then that Scripture clearly proves this much, that God by his eternal and immutable counsel determined once for all those whom it was his pleasure one day to admit to salvation and those whom, on the other hand, it was his pleasure to doom to destruction. We maintain that this counsel as regards the elect is founded on his free mercy, without any respect to human worth, while those whom he dooms to destruction are excluded from access to life by a just and blameless, but at the same time incomprehensible judgment . . . . But as the Lord seals his elect by calling and justification, so by excluding the reprobate either from the knowledge of his name or the sanctification of his Spirit, he by these marks in a manner discloses the judgment which awaits them. [40]

Depravity And "Mystery"

Clearly, God's mercy as Calvin understood it was very limited. He majors upon God's justice; and there is no disputing that God would be just in damning the entire human race. The real question, however, which we will come to in its own time, is whether God who *is love* would neglect to make salvation available to *anyone*. We believe that the Bible clearly declares God's love for all mankind and His desire that all should be saved. It is in defense of God's love and character that we propose to test Calvinism against God's Word.

According to Calvin, salvation had nothing to do with whether or not a person believed the gospel. No one *could* believe unto salvation without God regenerating and then producing the faith to believe in those whom He had chosen. This conclusion followed logically from Calvin's extreme view of human depravity, which he laid out in his first writings:

> The mind of man is so completely alienated from the righteousness of God that it conceives, desires, and undertakes everything that is impious, perverse, base, impure, and flagitious. His heart is so thoroughly infected by the poison of sin that it cannot produce anything but what is corrupt; and if at any time men do anything apparently good, yet the mind always remains involved in hypocrisy and deceit, and the heart enslaved by its inward perversity. [41]

By Total Depravity Calvin means total *inability*: if left to themselves, all men not only do not seek God but are totally *unable* to seek Him, much less to believe in Jesus Christ to the saving of their souls. He then declares that as a consequence of this total inability on man's part (some Calvinists define inability not as incapacity but as unwillingness), God *causes some* men to believe just as He causes *all* to sin. We must then conclude that God, who *is love*, doesn't love all men enough to rescue them from eternal punishment but reserves His love for a select few called the elect. This evident lack of love Calvin attempted to explain away by pleading the mystery of God's good pleasure, eternal purpose or will.

Some Calvinists, embarrassed by this teaching, attempt to deny that Calvin taught that God decreed the damnation of the lost from whom He withheld the Irresistible Grace which He bestowed upon the elect. Instead, they say that He simply "leaves the non-elect in his just judgment to their own wickedness and obduracy." [42] Like Augustine, Calvin says it both ways. Obviously, however, to allow anyone whom God *could* rescue to go to hell (no matter how much they deserved it) is the same as consigning them to that fate, a consignment which Calvin called "reprobation." Nor is there any question that, through what Calvinists call Irresistible Grace, their God *could* save the entire human race if He desired to do so. Surely Infinite Love would not allow those loved to suffer eternal torment — yet God, according to Calvinism, is pleased to damn billions. Such teaching misrepresents the God of the Bible, as the following pages document from Scripture.

In the final analysis, no rationalization can explain away the bluntness of Calvin's language, that it is God's "pleasure to doom to destruction" those whom He "by his eternal providence . . . before their birth doomed to perpetual destruction . . . ." This sovereign consigning of some to bliss and others to torment was a display of God's power that would, according to Calvin's way of thinking, "promote our admiration of His glory." [43]

Here is an astounding doctrine, but there is no question that Calvin taught it. God is glorified in predestinating some to salvation and others to damnation, though there is no difference in merit between the saved and lost. That God would leave *anyone* to eternal torment who could be rescued, however, would demean God, since to do so is repugnant to the conscience and compassion which God himself has placed within all mankind!

At the same time that he dogmatically pronounced this doctrine, Calvin himself admitted that it was repulsive to intelligent reason. As in Roman Catholicism, Calvin sought to escape the obvious contradictions in his system by pleading "mystery":

Paul . . . rising to the sublime mystery of predestination . . . . [44]

. . . how sinful it is to insist on knowing the causes of the divine will, since it is itself, and justly ought to be, the cause of all that exists . . . . Therefore, when it is asked why the Lord did so, we must answer, Because he pleased . . . . Of this no other cause can be adduced than reprobation, which is hidden in the secret counsel of God. [45]

Calvin claims to derive the teaching from the Bible that God, to His glory, predestined vast multitudes to eternal damnation without allowing them any choice. In fact, while he was still a Roman Catholic he had doubtless already come to such a conclusion from his immersion in the writings of Augustine and the official (and badly corrupted) Roman Catholic Bible, the Latin Vulgate.

1 Cited in Philip Schaff, *History of the Christian Church* (Charles Scribner, 1910; Wm. B. Eerdmans Publishing Co., reprint 1959), 8:281.

2 Georgia Harkness, *John Calvin: The Man and His Ethics* (Abingdon Press, 1958), 3.

3 Laurence M. Vance, *The Other Side of Calvinism* (Vance Publications, Pensacola FL, rev. ed. 1999), 69-70.

4 Loraine Boettner, *The Reformed Doctrine of Predestination* (Presbyterian and Reformed Publishing Co., 1932), 3-4.

5 Arthur C. Custance, *The Sovereignty of Grace* (Presbyterian and Reformed Publishing Co., 1979), 18.

6 Frederic W. Farrar, *History of Interpretation* (E.P. Dutton and Co., 1886), 24.

7   David J. Engelsma, *A Defense of Calvinism as the Gospel* (The Evangelism Committee, Protestant Reformed Church, n.d.), 22.

8   Benjamin B. Warfield, *Calvin and Augustine*, ed. Samuel G. Craig (Presbyterian and Reformed Publishing Co., 1956), 22.

9   Timothy George, *Theology of the Reformers* (Broadman Press, 1988), 179.

10 R. Tudor Jones, *The Great Reformation* (Inter-Varsity Press, n.d.), 133.

11 Edwin H. Palmer, foreword to *the five points of calvinism* (Baker Books, enlarged ed., 20th prtg. 1999), 2.

12 Charles Haddon Spurgeon, *Autobiography of Charles H. Spurgeon* (American Baptist Society, n.d.), 44:402.

13 Op. cit.., 47:398.

14 John Calvin, "Method and Arrangement," in *Institutes of the Christian Religion*, trans. Henry Beveridge (Wm. Eerdmans Publishing Company, 1998 ed.), 29.

15 Op. cit.., IV:i,4.

16 Op. cit.., IV:ii,2.

17 William J. Bouwsma, *John Calvin: A Sixteenth Century Portrait* (Oxford University Press, 1988), 10.

18 Will Durant, "The Reformation," Pt. VI of *The Story of Civilization* (Simon and Schuster, 1957), 460.

19 Boettner, op. cit., 403.

20 Williston Walker, *John Calvin: The Organizer of Reformed Protestantism* (Schocken Books, 1969), 72.

21 John T. McNeil, *The History and Character of Calvinism* (Oxford University Press, 1966), 112.

22 Walker, op. cit..

23 J.D. Douglas, *Who's Who In Christian History*, 128-29; cited in Henry R. Pike, *The Other Side of John Calvin* (Head to Heart, n.d.), 9-10. See also Alister E. McGrath, *A Life of John Calvin* (Blackwell Publishers, 1990), 73; and Jones, op. cit., 127.

24 Jones, op. cit.., 127.

25 Walker, op. cit.

26 Durant, op. cit., 459-60.

27 Calvin, *Institutes*, I:vii,4.

28 Op. cit.., I:viii,1.

29 Leonard Verduin, *The Reformers and Their Stepchildren* (Christian Hymnary Publishers, 1991), 66.

30 Augustine, *Gift of Perseverance*, 47.

31 R.C. Sproul, *Grace Unknown* (Baker Books, 1997), 189.

32 Calvin, op. cit., III:xxiii,6.

33 Op. cit., III:xxi,7.

34 Op. cit., III:xxiii,1.

35 Op. cit., III:xxiii,3.

36 Op. cit., III:xxiii,4.

37 Op. cit., III:xxiii,6.

38 Op. cit., III:xxiii,10-11.

39 Op. cit., III:xxi-xxii.

40 Op. cit., III:xxi,7.

41 Op. cit., II:v,19.

42 Canons of Dort (Dordrecht, Holland, 1619), 1,6.

43 Calvin, op. cit., III:xxi,1.

44 Op. cit., II:xii,5.

45 Op. cit., III:xxiii,2,4.

4
Calvinism's Surprising Catholic Connection

A s for Calvin's theology, there is no question that rather than deriving it from a diligent study of the Bible, he imposed upon the Bible certain preconceived ideas from his Roman Catholic background which locked him into an erroneous interpretation. Many leading Calvinists agree that the writings of Augustine were the actual source of most of what is known as Calvinism today. Calvinists David Steele and Curtis Thomas point out that "The basic doctrines of the Calvinistic position had been vigorously defended by Augustine against Pelagius during the fifth century." [1]

In his eye-opening book, *The Other Side of Calvinism*, Laurence M. Vance thoroughly documents that "John Calvin did not originate the doctrines that bear his name. This is stated emphatically by Calvinists . . . ." [2] Vance quotes numerous well-known Calvinists to this effect. For example, Kenneth G. Talbot and W. Gary Crampton write, "The system of doctrine which bears the name of John Calvin was in no way originated by him . . . ." [3] B.B. Warfield declared, "The system of doctrine taught by Calvin is just the Augustinianism common to the whole body of the Reformers." [4] Thus the debt which the creeds coming out of the Reformation owe to Augustine is also acknowledged. This is not surprising in view of the fact that most of the Reformers had been part of the Roman Catholic Church, of which Augustine was the most highly regarded "saint" — and Calvin and Luther continued to revere him and his doctrines.

C.H. Spurgeon admitted that "perhaps Calvin himself derived it [Calvinism] mainly from the writings of Augustine." [5] Alvin L. Baker wrote, "There is hardly a doctrine of Calvin that does not bear the marks of Augustine's influence." [6] For example, the following from Augustine sounds like an echo reverberating through the writings of Calvin:

> ...even as he has appointed them to be regenerated ... whom he predestinated to everlasting life, as the most merciful bestower of grace, whilst to those whom he has predestinated to eternal death, he is also the most righteous awarder of punishment. [7]

C. Gregg Singer said, "The main features of Calvin's theology are found in the writings of St. Augustine to such an extent that many theologians regard Calvinism as a more fully developed form of Augustinianism." [8] Such statements are staggering declarations in view of the undisputed fact that, as Vance points out, the Roman Catholic Church itself has a better claim on Augustine than do the Calvinists. [9] Consider the following from Calvin himself:

> Augustine is so wholly with me, that if I wished to write a confession of my faith, I could do so with all fulness and satisfaction to myself out of his writings." [10]

Augustine And The Use Of Force

In the fourth century, the Donatists led a movement for purification of the church. They believed that the church should be a pure communion of true believers who demonstrated the truth of the gospel in their lives. Donatists abhorred the apostasy that had come into the church when Constantine wedded Christianity to paganism in order to unify the empire. They considered compromising clergy to be "evil priests working hand in glove with the kings of the earth, men who by their conduct show that they have no king but Caesar." To the Donatists, the church was a "small body of saved surrounded by the unregenerate mass." [11]

Augustine, on the other hand, saw the church as a mixture of believers and unbelievers, in which purity and evil should be allowed to exist side by side for the sake of unity. He used the power of the state to compel church attendance (as Calvin did 1,200 years later): "Whoever was not found within the Church was not asked the reason, but was to be corrected and converted . . . ." [12] Calvin followed his mentor Augustine in enforcing church attendance and participation in the sacraments by threats (and worse) against the citizens of Geneva. Augustine "identified the Donatists as heretics . . . who could be subjected to imperial legislation [and force] in exactly the same way as other criminals and misbelievers, including poisoners and pagans." [13] Frend says of Augustine, "The questing, sensitive youth had become the father of the inquisition." [14]

Though he preferred persuasion if possible, Augustine supported the death penalty for those who were rebaptized as believers after conversion to Christ and for other alleged heretics. In his controversy with the Donatists, using a distorted and un-Christian interpretation of Luke 14:23, Augustine made statements for Christianity which sounded like Islam's forceful measures against those who defect from that religion of violence:

> Why therefore should not the Church use force in compelling her lost sons to return? . . . The Lord Himself said, "Go out into the highways and hedges and compel them to come in . . . ." Wherefore is the power which the Church has received . . . through the religious character and faith of kings . . . the instrument by which those who are found in the highways and hedges — that is, in heresies and schisms — are compelled to come in, and let them not find fault with being compelled. [15]

This is the man whom Calvin admired above all others and upon whom he relied for much of his theology. Sadly, as we shall see later, Calvin put into effect in Geneva the very principles of punishment, coercion and death which Augustine advocated. Henry H. Milman puts it well: "Augustinianism was worked up into a still more rigid and uncompromising system by the severe intellect of Calvin." [16] And he justified his actions by the same erroneous interpretation of Luke 14:23 which Augustine had used to justify suppression of the Donatists with military force. Do those who today hail Calvin as a great exegete accept such usage of this passage?

Augustine's Dominant Influence

There is no question as to the important role Augustine played in molding Calvin's thinking, theology and actions. This is particularly true concerning the key foundations of Calvinism. Warfield refers to Calvin and Augustine as "two extraordinarily gifted men [who] tower like pyramids over the scene of history." [17] Calvin's *Institutes of the Christian Religion* make repeated favorable references to Augustine, frequently citing his writings as authoritative and even using the expression, " . . . confirmed by the authority of Augustine." [18] Calvin often credits Augustine with having formulated key concepts which he then expounds in his *Institutes*. The following are but a very small sampling of such references:

> "We have come into the way of faith," says Augustine: "Let us constantly adhere to it . . . ." [19]

> The truth of God is too powerful, both here and everywhere, to dread the slanders of the ungodly, as Augustine powerfully maintains . . . . Augustine disguises not that . . . he was often charged with preaching the doctrine of predestination too freely, but . . . he abundantly refutes the charge . . . . For it

has been shrewdly observed by Augustine (de Genesis ad Literam, Lib. V.), that we can safely follow Scripture . . . . [20]

For Augustine, rightly expounding this passage, says . . . . [21]

I say with Augustine, that the Lord has created those who, as he certainly foreknew, were to go to destruction, and he did so because he so willed. [22] If your mind is troubled, decline not to embrace the counsel of Augustine . . . . [23]

I will not hesitate, therefore, simply to confess with Augustine that . . . those things will certainly happen which he [God] has foreseen [and] that the destruction [of the non-elect] consequent upon predestination is also most just. [24]

Augustine, in two passages in particular, gives a [favorable] portraiture of the form of ancient monasticism. [Calvin then proceeds to quote Augustine's commendation of the early monks.] [25]

Here the words of Augustine most admirably apply . . . . [26]

This is a faithful saying from Augustine; but because his words will perhaps have more authority than mine, let us adduce the following passage from his treatise . . . . [27]

Wherefore, Augustine not undeservedly orders such, as senseless teachers or sinister and ill-omened prophets, to retire from the Church. [28]

We could multiply many times over the above examples of Augustine's influence upon Calvin and add to them the scores of times Calvin quotes extensively from Augustine's writings. The truth (acknowledged even by leading Calvinists) is that Calvin's basic beliefs were already formed while he was still a devout Roman Catholic, through reading and studying the writings of Augustine and the Latin Vulgate Bible. Clearly, that influence remained with him throughout his life.

Augustinian teachings which Calvin presented in his *Institutes* included the sovereignty that made God the cause of all (including sin), the predestination of some to salvation and of others to damnation, election and reprobation, faith as an irresistible gift from God — in fact, the key concepts at the heart of Calvinism. Nor can we find where Calvin disapproved of any of Augustine's heresies. Reformed Calvinist Richard A. Muller admits, "John Calvin was part of a long line of thinkers who based their doctrine of predestination on the Augustinian interpretation of St. Paul." [29] There is simply no way to claim honestly that Calvin's *Institutes* represent insights which he received from the Holy Spirit through the study of God's Word subsequent to his conversion to Luther's Protestantism. In the latest additions to the original he is quoting and relying upon Augustine even more than ever.

Is Calvinism Really A Protestant Belief?

That many prominent evangelicals today are still under the spell of Augustine is evident — and astonishing, considering his numerous heresies. Norm Geisler has said, "St. Augustine was one of the greatest Christian thinkers of all time."[30] Yet Augustine said, "I should not believe the gospel unless I were moved to do so by the authority of the Catholic Church." That statement was quoted with great satisfaction by Pope John Paul II in his 1986 celebration of the 1600th anniversary of Augustine's conversion. The Pope went on to say:

> Augustine's legacy . . . is the theological methods to which he remained absolutely faithful . . . full adherence to the authority of the faith . . . revealed through Scripture, Tradition and the Church . . . . Likewise the profound sense of mystery — "for it is better," he exclaims, "to have a faithful ignorance than a presumptuous knowledge . . . ."
> I express once again my fervent desire . . . that the authoritative teaching of such a great doctor and pastor may flourish ever more happily in the Church . . . . [31]

Vance provides additional astonishing quotations from Calvinists praising Augustine: "One of the greatest theological and philosophical minds that God has ever so seen fit to give to His church." [32] "The greatest Christian since New Testament times . . . greatest man that ever wrote Latin." [33] "[His] labors and writings, more than those of any other man in the age in which he lived, contributed to the promotion of sound doctrine and the revival of true religion." [34] Warfield adds, "Augustine determined for all time the doctrine of grace." [35] Yet he [Augustine] believed that grace came through the Roman Catholic sacraments. That Calvinists shower such praise upon Augustine makes it easier to comprehend the same praise heaped upon Calvin.

Augustine was no ordinary Roman Catholic but unquestionably the most famous and influential one in history. Vance reminds us that Augustine was "one of Catholicism's original four 'Doctors of the Church' [with] a feast day [dedicated to him] in the Catholic Church on August 28, the day of his death." [36] Pope John Paul II has called Augustine "the common father of our Christian civilization." [37] William P. Grady, on the other hand, writes, "The deluded Augustine (354-430) went so far as to announce (through his book, *The City of God*) that Rome had been privileged to usher in the millennial kingdom (otherwise known as the 'Dark Ages')." [38]

Drawing From A Polluted Stream

Sir Robert Anderson reminds us that "the Roman [Catholic] Church was molded by Augustine into the form it has ever since maintained. Of all the errors that later centuries developed in the teachings of the church, scarcely one cannot be found in embryo in his writings." [39] Those errors include infant baptism for regeneration (infants who die unbaptized are damned), the necessity of baptism for the remission of sins (martyrdom does the same), purgatory, salvation in the Church alone through its sacraments and persecution of those who reject Catholic dogmas. Augustine also fathered acceptance of the Apocrypha (which he admitted even the Jews rejected), allegorical interpretation of the Bible (thus the creation account, the six days, etc. in Genesis are not necessarily literal), and rejection of the literal personal reign of Christ on earth for a thousand years (we are now in the millennial reign of Christ with the Church reigning and the devil presently bound).

Augustine insists that Satan is now "bound" on the basis that "even now men are, and doubtless to the end of the world shall be, converted to the faith from the unbelief in which he [Satan] held them." That he views this promised binding of Satan in the "bottomless pit" (Revelation 20:1-3) allegorically is clear. Amazingly, Satan "is bound in each instance in which he is spoiled of one of his goods" [i.e., someone believes in Christ]. And even more amazing, "the abyss in which he is shut up" is somehow construed by Augustine to be "in the depths" of Christ-rejectors' "blind hearts." It is thus that Satan is continually shut up as in an abyss. [40]

Augustine doesn't attempt to explain how he arrived at such an astonishing idea, much less how one abyss could exist in millions of hearts or how, being "bound" there, Satan would not be free to blind those within whose "hearts" he is supposedly bound (2 Corinthians 4:4). Nor does he explain how or why in spite of Satan being bound, Christ commissioned Paul to turn Jew and Gentile "from the power of Satan unto God" (Acts 26:18), Paul could deliver the Corinthian fornicator to Satan (1 Corinthians 5:5), Satan can transform himself "into an angel of light" (2 Corinthians 11:14), Paul would warn the Ephesian believers not to "give place to the devil" (Ephesians 4:27) and urge them and us today to "stand against the wiles of the devil" (6:11), Satan could still be going about "like a roaring lion . . . seeking whom he may devour" (1 Peter 5:8) and able to continually accuse Christians before God and with his angels to wage war in heaven against "Michael and his angels" and at last be cast out of heaven to earth (Revelation 12:7-10), etc..

Augustine was one of the first to place the authority of tradition on a level with the Bible and to incorporate much philosophy, especially Platonism, into his theology. Exposing the folly of those who praise Augustine, Vance writes:

> He believed in apostolic succession from Peter as one of the marks of the true church, taught that Mary was sinless and promoted her worship. He was the first who defined the so-called sacraments as a visible sign of invisible grace . . . .The memorial of the Lord's supper became that of the spiritual presence of Christ's body and blood. To Augustine the only true church was the Catholic

Church. Writing against the Donatists, he asserted: "The Catholic Church alone is the body of Christ . . . . Outside this body the Holy Spirit giveth life to no one . . . [and] he is not a partaker of divine love who is the enemy of unity. Therefore they have not the Holy Ghost who are outside the Church. [41]

And this is the man whom Geisler calls "one of the greatest Christian thinkers of all time." On the contrary, Calvin drew from a badly polluted stream when he embraced the teachings of Augustine! How could one dip into such contaminating heresy without becoming confused and infected? Yet this bewildering muddle of speculation and formative Roman Catholicism is acknowledged to be the source of Calvinism — and is praised by leading evangelicals! One comes away dumbfounded at the acclaim heaped upon both Calvin and Augustine by otherwise sound Christian leaders.

An Amazing Contradiction

Calvin's almost complete agreement with Augustine is nothing short of astounding. Calvin called himself "an Augustinian theologian." [42] Of Augustine he said, "whom we quote frequently, as being the best and most faithful witness of all antiquity." [43] It is Calvinists themselves who insist upon the connection between Calvin and Augustine. McGrath writes, "Above all, Calvin regarded his thought as a faithful exposition of the leading ideas of Augustine of Hippo." [44] Wendell concedes, "Upon points of doctrine he borrows from St. Augustine with both hands." [45] Vance writes:

> Howbeit, to prove conclusively that Calvin was a disciple of Augustine, we need look no further than Calvin himself. One can't read five pages in Calvin's *Institutes* without seeing the name of Augustine. Calvin quotes Augustine over four hundred times in the *Institutes* alone. He called Augustine by such titles as "holy man" and "holy father." [46]

As Vance further points out, "Calvinists admit that Calvin was heavily influenced by Augustine in forming his doctrine of predestination." [47] How could one of the principal leaders of the Reformation embrace so fully the doctrines of one who has been called "the first real Roman Catholic" [48] and the "principal theological creator of the Latin-Catholic system as distinct from . . . evangelical Protestantism . . . "? [49] And what should be said of the fact that so many evangelical leaders continue to hold both Augustine and Calvin in such high regard?

Calvin's admiration of Augustine and his embracing of much of his teaching is only one of several major contradictions in his life which will be fully documented in this book. Sadly, much Roman Catholicism was carried over by Calvin (as well as by Luther) into Reformed churches, where it remains to this day. The situation is contradictory on the Roman Catholic side as well. Their dogmas reject some of the most important doctrines held by the most famous of their saints — the very Augustinian doctrines which Calvin embraced.

Calvinists seem equally inconsistent. How can Warfield sincerely declare that "it is Augustine who gave us the Reformation" [50] and at the same time acknowledge that Augustine was "in a true sense the founder of Roman Catholicism" [51] and "the creator of the Holy Roman Empire"? [52] Such incongruous statements leave one truly perplexed.

Most inconsistent of all, at least on the part of Calvin himself, was his apparent failure to recognize that Augustine never seems to have understood salvation by grace alone through faith alone in Christ alone. Philip F. Congdon writes, "Another curious parallel is evident between Classical Calvinist theology and Roman Catholic theology. The two share an inclusion of works in the gospel message, and an impossibility of assurance of salvation. ...Both hold to the primacy of God's grace; both include the necessity of our works." [53] Augustine's heresies, especially his Romanist view of faith in Christ being supplemented by good works and the sacraments, were not lost on Luther, who wrote:

> In the beginning, I devoured Augustine, but when . . . I knew what justification by faith really was, then it was out with him. [54]

To make it more confusing, leading Calvinists suggest that I side with Roman Catholicism by rejecting Calvinism even though it comes largely from the ultimate Roman Catholic, Augustine. Here is how one writer expressed it to me:

> And given that the position you espouse is, in fact, utterly opposed to the very heart of the message of the Reformers, and is instead in line with Rome's view of man's will and the nature of grace, I find it *tremendously* inconsistent on your part. You speak often of opposing the traditions of men, yet, in this case, you embrace the very traditions that lie at the heart of Rome's "gospel."[55]

On the contrary, it seems that the Reformers and their creeds are infected with ideas that came from the greatest Roman Catholic, Augustine himself. Furthermore, a rejection of Election, Predestination and the Preservation of the Saints as defined by Calvinists is hardly embracing "the heart of Rome's 'gospel.'" The real heart of Rome's gospel is good works and sacraments. Certainly Calvin's retention of sacramentalism, baptismal regeneration for infants and honoring the Roman Catholic priesthood as valid is a more serious embrace of Catholicism's false gospel than is a rejection of Calvinism. Such a rejection requires no agreement with Rome whatsoever on any part of its heretical doctrines of salvation. On the other hand, Calvinism retains much from Calvin's Roman Catholic heritage.

It is staggering that the predominant influence upon Reformed theology and creeds could be so closely related to the very Roman Catholicism against which the Reformers rebelled. Nevertheless, this is a proven fact readily admitted by ardent Calvinists. Yet those who fail to bow to these creeds are allegedly "in error." How the Protestant creeds came to be dominated by Calvinistic doctrine is an interesting story.

The Role Of The Latin Vulgate

Along with the writings of Augustine, the Latin Vulgate was another source that molded Calvin's thoughts into what he expressed in his *Institutes of the Christian Religion*. Fluent in Latin, Calvin had long used that corrupted translation of the Bible, which, since its composition by Jerome at the beginning of the fifth century, was the official Bible of Roman Catholics. It was again so declared by the Council of Trent in 1546 when Calvin was 37 years of age. More than that, its influence reached into the Protestant movement: "For one thousand years the Vulgate was practically the only Bible known and read in Western Europe. All commentaries were based upon the Vulgate text . . . preachers based their sermons on it." [56]

The Vulgate was permeated with Augustinian views on predestination and the rejection of free will. According to Philip Schaff, "The Vulgate can be charged, indeed, with innumerable faults, inaccuracies, inconsistencies, and arbitrary dealing in particulars." [57] Others have expressed the same opinion. Samuel Berger called the Vulgate "the most vulgarized and bastardized text imaginable." [58] Grady says, "Damasus commissioned Jerome to revive the archaic Old Latin Bible in A.D. 382 . . . the completed monstrosity became known as the Latin 'Vulgate' . . . and was used of the devil to usher in the Dark Ages." [59] Fisk reminds us:

> Well-known examples of far-reaching errors include the whole system of Catholic "penance," drawn from the Vulgate's "do penance" . . . when the Latin should have followed the Greek — *repent*. Likewise the word "sacrament" was a mis-reading from the Vulgate of the original word for *mystery*. Even more significant, perhaps, was the rendering of the word *presbyter* (elder) as "priest."[60]

Augustine described the problem that led to the production of the Vulgate: "In the earliest days of the faith, when a Greek manuscript came into anyone's hands, and he thought he possessed a little facility in both languages, he ventured to make a translation [into Latin]." [61] As a consequence of such individual endeavor, Bruce says, "The time came, however, when the multiplicity of [Latin] texts [of Scripture] became too inconvenient to be tolerated any longer, and Pope Damasus . . . commissioned his secretary, Jerome, to undertake the work" of revision to produce one authorized Latin version.

Bruce continues: "He [Jerome] was told to be cautious for the sake of 'weaker brethren' who did not like to see their favorite texts tampered with, even in the interests of greater accuracy. Even so, he went much too far for the taste of many, while he himself knew that he was not going far enough." [62] *Unger's Bible Dictionary* comments:

> For many centuries it [Vulgate] was the only Bible generally used . . . . In the age of the Reformation the Vulgate [influenced] popular versions. That of Luther (N.T. in 1523) was the most important and in this the Vulgate had great weight. From Luther the influence of the Latin passed to our own Authorized Version [KJV] . . . . [63]

The Geneva And King James Bibles And Protestant Creeds

Of no small importance to our study is the fact that this corrupt translation had an influence upon the Protestant churches in Europe, England and America. That influence carried into the Geneva Bible (which has further problems; see below) as well as into other early versions of the English Bible and even into the King James of today.

The Vulgate contributed erroneous renderings to the King James Bible, two of which are used today by Calvinists to support Unconditional Election and Irresistible Grace: Acts 2:47 ("And the Lord added to the church daily such as should be saved.") and Acts 13:48 ("and as many as were ordained to eternal life believed."). From the Greek, the first should read, "those who were being saved," and the second should read, "as many as were disposed toward eternal life." This will be discussed in more detail later.

As the Vulgate was filled with Augustinianisms, the Geneva Bible was filled with Calvinism in the text as well as in voluminous notes. H.S. Miller's *General Biblical Introduction* says, "It was a revision of Tyndale's, with an Introduction by Calvin . . . the work of English reformers, assisted by Beza, Calvin, and possibly others." J. R. Dore, in *Old Bibles: An Account of the Early Versions of the English Bible*, 2nd edition, adds that "almost every chapter [of the Geneva Bible] has voluminous notes full of Calvinistic doctrine." Andrew Edgar, in *The Bibles of England*, declares, "At the time the Geneva Bible was first published, Calvin was the ruling spirit in Geneva. All the features of his theological, ecclesiastical, political, and social system are accordingly reflected in the marginal annotations . . . .The doctrine of predestination is proclaimed to be the head cornerstone of the gospel." [64]

W. Hoare says in *The Evolution of the English Bible*, "Considered as a literary whole it [the Geneva Bible] has about it the character of a Calvinist manifesto . . . a book with a special purpose." F. F. Bruce adds, "The notes of the Geneva Bible . . . are, to be sure, unashamedly Calvinistic in doctrine . . . the people of England and Scotland . . . learned much of their biblical exegesis from these notes . . . . The Geneva Bible immediately won, and retained, widespread popularity. It became the household Bible of English-speaking Protestants . . . . This became the authorized Bible in Scotland and was brought to America where it had a strong influence." [65] Butterworth points out, "In the lineage of the King James Bible this [Geneva Bible] is by all means the most important single volume . . . . The Geneva Bible . . . had a very great influence in the shaping of the King James Bible." [66] Robinson is even more emphatic:

> A large part of its [Geneva Bible] innovations are included in the Authorized Version [KJV] . . . . Sometimes the Geneva text and the Geneva margin are taken over intact, sometimes the text becomes the margin and the margin the text. Sometimes the margin becomes the text and no alternative is offered. Very often the Genevan margin becomes the Authorized Version text with or without verbal change. [67]

Further documentation could be given, but this should be sufficient to trace the influence from that ultimate Roman Catholic, Augustine, through the Latin Vulgate and his writings, upon Calvin, and through Calvin into the Geneva Bible and on into the King James Bible, thus into the pulpits and homes of Protestants throughout Europe, England and America. It is small wonder, then, that those who, like Ariminius, dared to question Calvinism, were overwhelmed with opposition. Of course, various synods and assemblies were held to formulate accepted creeds and to punish the dissenters, but the decks were stacked in favor of Calvinism, and no influence to mitigate this error was allowed. This will be documented in Chapters 5 and 6.

The *New Geneva Study Bible*

Today's *New Geneva Study Bible* (recently reprinted as *The Reformation Study Bible*) is being widely distributed in an effort to indoctrinate the readers into Calvinism. Its New King James translation is appealing. As with the original Geneva Bible, however, the notes are Calvinistic treatises.

In his foreword, R.C. Sproul writes, "The *New Geneva Study Bible* is so called because it stands in the tradition of the original Geneva Bible . . . . The light of the Reformation was the light of the Bible . . . . The Geneva Bible was published in 1560 . . . [and] dominated the English-speaking world for a hundred years . . . . Pilgrims and Puritans carried the Geneva Bible to the shores of the New World. American colonists were reared on the Geneva Bible . . . . The *New Geneva Study Bible* contains a modern restatement of Reformation truth in its comments and theological notes. Its purpose is to present the light of the Reformation afresh." In fact, its purpose is to indoctrinate the reader into Calvinism, which inaccurately is marketed as "Reformation truth" – as though

Calvinism and Protestantism are identical. There was, in fact, much more to the Reformation than Calvinism.

Calvinism is experiencing a resurgence among evangelicals today. How is that possible apart from ignorance of what Calvin really taught and practiced and of what Augustine, from whom he obtained most of his beliefs, taught and practiced as well? How else, other than ignorance of the truth about these men and their teachings, can one explain Boettner's sincere declaration that "Calvin and Augustine easily rank as the two outstanding systematic expounders of the Christian system since Saint Paul"? [68]   Or the following from Spurgeon who was otherwise so sound in doctrine, "Augustine obtained his views, without doubt, through the Spirit of God, from the diligent study of the writings of Paul, and Paul received them of the Holy Ghost, from Jesus Christ"? [69]

One views these and other similar statements by today's evangelical leaders with utter astonishment. How was it possible that Loraine Boettner, one of the foremost apologists opposing the Roman Catholic Church, could so highly praise Augustine whom the entire world recognizes as the premier Roman Catholic who gave that Church so many of its basic doctrines that he is among the most highly honored of its "saints" to this day? As for Spurgeon, would he have considered that Augustine's teaching of salvation by the Roman Catholic Church alone through its sacraments beginning with regeneration by infant baptism, the use of force even to the death against "heretics," acceptance of the Apocrypha, allegorical interpretation of creation and the prophecies concerning Israel, a rejection of the literal reign of Christ on David's throne and so much other false doctrine had also all been received from the Holy Spirit? How could Augustine, and Calvin who embraced and passed on many of his major errors, be so wrong on so much and yet be inspired of the Holy Spirit as regards predestination, election, sovereignty, etc.? Sadly, the history of the church, both ancient and modern, includes many prominent Christians who were very godly and of sound doctrine in some respects while in grave error in others.

These important doctrines will be addressed in the following pages and compared carefully with the teaching of God's Word.

1   David N. Steele and Curtis C. Thomas, *The Five Points of Calvinism* (Presbyterian and Reformed Publishing Co., 1963), 19.
2   Laurence M. Vance, *The Other Side of Calvinism* (Vance Publications, Pensacola FL, rev. ed., 1999), 37.
3   Kenneth G. Talbot and W. Gary Crampton, *Calvinism, Hyper-Calvinism and Arminianism* (Still Water Revival Books, 1990), 78.
4   Benjamin B. Warfield, *Calvin and Augustine*, ed. Samuel G. Craig (Presbyterian and Reformed Publishing Co., 1956), 22.
5   Charles Haddon Spurgeon, ed., *Exposition of the Doctrine of Grace* (Pilgrim Publications, n.d.), 298.
6   Alvin L. Baker, *Berkouwer's Doctrine of Election: Balance or Imbalance?* (Presbyterian and Reformed Publishing Co., 1981), 25.
7   Augustine, *On the Soul and its Origins*, 4.16.
8   C. Gregg Singer, *John Calvin: His Roots and Fruits* (A Press, 1989), vii.
9   Vance, op. cit., 40.
10 John Calvin, "A Treatise on the Eternal Predestination of God," in *John Calvin, Calvin's Calvinism*, trans. Henry Cole (Reformed Free Publishing Association, 1987), 38; cited in Vance, op. cit., 38.
11 Leonard Verduin, *The Reformers and Their Stepchildren* (Christian Hymnary Publishers, 1991), 33.
12 *Petilian* II.85.189; cited in W.H.C. Frend, *The Rise of Christianity* (Fortress Press, 1984), 671.
13 Frend, op. cit., 671.
14 Op. cit., 672.
15 E.H. Broadbent, *The Pilgrim Church* (Gospel Folio Press, reprint 1999), 49.
16 Henry H. Milman, *History of Christianity* (A.C. Armstrong and Son, 1886), 3:176.
17 Warfield, op. cit., v.
18 John Calvin, contents page of *Institutes of the Christian Religion*, trans. Henry Beveridge (Wm. B. Eerdmans Publishing Company, 1998 ed.), III:xxiii, IV:xvii, etc.
19 Op. cit., III:xxi,2.
20 Op. cit., III:xxi,4.
21 Op. cit., III:xxiii,1.
22 Op. cit., III: xxiii,5.
23 Ibid.
24 Op. cit., III:xxiii,8..
25 Op. cit., IV:xiii,9.
26 Op. cit., III:xxiii, 11.
27 Op. cit., III:xxiii, 13
28 Op. cit., III:xxiii, 14
29 Richard A. Muller, *Christ and the Decree* (Baker Book House, 1988), 22.
30 Norman L. Geisler, *What Augustine Says* (Baker Book House, 1982), 9.
31 John Paul II, Sovereign Pontiff, *Augustineum Hyponensem* (Apostolic Letter, August 28, 1986. Available at: www.cin.org/jp2.ency/augustin.html.)
32 Talbot and Crampton, op. cit., 78; cited in Vance, op. cit., 39.
33 Alexander Souter, *The Earliest Latin Commentaries on the Epistles of St. Paul* (n.p., 1927), 139.
34 N.L. Rice, *God Sovereign and Man Free* (Sprinkle Publications, 1985), 13.
35 Benjamin B. Warfield, "The Idea of Systematic Theology," in *The Princeton Theology*, ed. Mark A. Noll (Presbyterian and Reformed Publishing Co., 1983), 258.
36 Vance, op. cit., 41.
37 Richard N. Ostling, "The Second Founder of the Faith" (*Time*, September 29, 1986).

38   William P. Grady, *Final Authority: A Christian's Guide to the King James Bible* (Grady Publications, 1993), 54.
39   Sir Robert Anderson, *The Bible or the Church?* (Pickering and Inglis, 2nd ed., n.d.), 53.
40   Augustine, *The City of God*, trans. Marcus Dods. In *Great Books of the Western World,* ed. Robert Maynard Hutchins and Mortimer J. Adler (Encyclopaedia Brittanica, Inc., 1952), XX:7,8.
41   Vance, op. cit., 55
42   Talbot and Crampton, op. cit., 79.
43   Calvin, op. cit., IV:xiv, 26.
44   Alister E. McGrath, *The Life of John Calvin* (Blackwell Publishers, 1990), 151.
45   Francois Wendel, *Calvin: Origins and Development of His Religious Thought* (Baker Books, 1997), 124.
46   Vance, op. cit; citing Calvin, op. cit., 139, 146, 148-49.
47   Op. cit., 113; citing Wendel, op. cit., 264, and Timothy George, *Theology of the Reformers* (Broadman Press, 1988), 232.
48   Peter S. Ruckman, *The History of the New Testament* (Pensacola Bible Baptist Bookstore, 1982), 1:1,149.
49   Philip Schaff, *History of the Christian Church* (Charles Scribner's Sons, 1910; Wm. B. Eerdmans Publishing Co., reprint 1959), III: 1018.
50   Warfield, op. cit., 322.
51   Op. cit., 313.
52   Op. cit., 318.
53   Philip F. Congdon, "Soteriological Implications of Five-point Calvinism" (*Journal of the Grace Evangelical Society*, Autumn 1995), 8:15, 55-68.
54   Timothy George, op. cit., 68.
55   James R. White to Dave Hunt, August 4, 2000. On file.
56   David Schaff, *Our Father's Faith and Ours*, 172; cited in Samuel Fisk, *Calvinistic Paths Retraced* (Biblical Evangelism Press, 1985), 68.
57   Philip Schaff, op. cit., II:975-76.
58   Fisk, op. cit., 68.
59   Grady, op. cit., 35.
60   Fisk, op. cit., 67.
61   F.F. Bruce, *The Books and the Parchments* (Pickering and Inglis, Ltd., 1950), 191.
62   Op. cit., 194-95.
63   Merrill F. Unger, *Unger's Bible Dictionary* (Moody Press, 1969), 1151-54.
64   Fisk, op. cit., 70-75.
65   Ibid.
66   Charles C. Butterworth, *The Literary Lineage of the King James Bible* (University of Pennsylvania Press, 1941), 163.
67   H. Wheeler Robinson, *The Bible In Its Ancient and English Versions* (Clarendon Press, 1940), 186, 206-207.
68   Loraine Boettner, *The Reformed Doctrine of Predestination* (Presbyterian and Reformed Publishing Co., 1932), 405.
69   Spurgeon, op. cit., 298; cited in Vance, op. cit., 38.

5
Irresistibly Imposed "Christianity"

Arguably, one of Satan's cleverest and most effective strategies was to delude the Emperor Constantine with a false conversion. Accounts differ, but whether this came about through a vision or a dream as recounted by Eusebius and Lactantius,[1] Constantine saw a "cross" in the sky and heard a "voice" proclaiming (by some accounts the words were inscribed on the cross), "In this sign thou shalt conquer." In the prior year the god Apollo had also promised him victory.

Constantine's edicts of toleration gave every man "a right to choose his religion according to the dictates of his own conscience and honest conviction, without compulsion and interference from the government." [2] Schaff views Constantine's conversion as a wonderful advance for Christianity: "The church ascends the throne of the Caesars under the banner of the cross, and gives new vigor and lustre to the hoary empire of Rome." [3] In fact, that "conversion" began the corruption of the church and its marriage to the world. [4]

How could a true follower of the Christ whose kingdom is not of this world and whose servants do not wage war proceed to wage war in His name, and under the banner of His cross to conquer with the sword? Of course, the Crusaders did the same, slaughtering both Muslims and Jews to retake the "holy land" under Pope Urban II's pledge (matching Muhammad's and the Qur'an's promise to Muslims) of full forgiveness of sins for those who died in this holy war (Muslim *jihad*). But it was all very Augustinian. The City of God had to be defended!

From Constantine To Augustine

As Durant and other historians have pointed out, Constantine never renounced his loyalty to the pagan gods. He abolished neither the Altar of Victory in the Senate nor the Vestal Virgins who tended the sacred fire of the goddess Vesta. The Sun-god, not Christ, continued to be honored on the imperial coins. In spite of the "cross" (actually the cross of the god Mithras) on his shields and military banners, Constantine had a medallion created honoring the Sun for the "liberation" of Rome; and when he prescribed a day of rest it was again in the name of the Sun-god ("the day celebrated by the veneration of the Sun" [5]) and not the Son of God. [6] Durant reminds us that throughout his "Christian" life Constantine used pagan as well as Christian rites and continued to rely upon "pagan magic formulas to protect crops and heal disease." [7]

That Constantine murdered those who might have had a claim to his throne, including his son Crispus, a nephew and brother-in-law, is further evidence that his "conversion" was, as many historians agree, a clever political maneuver to unite the empire. Historian Philip Hughes, himself a Catholic priest, reminds us, "in his manners he [Constantine] remained, to the end, very much the Pagan of his early life. His furious tempers, the cruelty which, once aroused, spared not the lives even of his wife and son, are . . . an unpleasing witness to the imperfection of his conversion." [8]

It was not long after the new tolerance that Constantine found himself faced with a problem he had never anticipated: division within the Christian church to which he had given freedom. As we noted in the last chapter, it came to a head in North Africa with the Donatists, who, concerned for purity of the faith, separated from the Catholic churches, rejected their ordinances and insisted upon rebaptizing clergy who had repented after having denied the faith during the persecutions which arose when the Emperor Diocletian demanded that he be worshiped as a god. [9] After years of futile efforts to reestablish unity through discussion, pleadings, councils and decrees, Constantine finally resorted to force. Frend puts it well:

> In the spring of 317 he [Constantine] followed up his decision by publishing a "most severe" edict against the Donatists, confiscating their property and exiling their leaders. Within four years, the universal freedom of conscience proclaimed at Milan had been abrogated, and the state had become a persecutor once more, only this time in favor of Christian orthodoxy . . . .
>
> [The Donatists] neither understood nor cared about Constantine's conversion. For them it was a case of the Devil insisting that "Christ was a lover of unity" . . . . In their view, the fundamental hostility of the state toward the church had not been altered. [10]

In his own day and way, Augustine followed Constantine's lead in his treatment of the Donatists, who were still a thorn in the side of the Roman Church. "While Augustine and the Catholics emphasized the unity of the Church, the Donatists insisted upon the purity of the Church and rebaptized all those who came to them from the Catholics — considering the Catholics corrupt." [11] Constantine had been "relentless [as would Augustine and his disciple Calvin be] in his pursuit of 'heretics' [forbidding] those outside of the Catholic church to assemble . . . and confiscated their property . . . the very things Christians had endured themselves were now being practiced in the name of Christianity." [12]

As a good Catholic enjoying the blessing of the Emperor and believing in the state church Constantine had established, Augustine persecuted and even sanctioned the killing of the Donatists and other schismatics, as we have already seen. Gibbon tells us that the severe measures against the Donatists "obtained the warmest approbation of St. Augustine [and thereby] great numbers of the Donatists were reconciled to [forced back into] the Catholic Church." [13] Of Augustine it has been well said that "the very greatness of his name has been the means of perpetuating the grossest errors which he himself propagated. More than anyone else, Augustine has encouraged the pernicious doctrine of salvation through the sacraments of an organized earthly Church, which brought with it priestcraft with all the evil and miseries that has entailed down through the centuries." [14]

From Augustine To Calvin

There is no question that John Calvin had a great zeal for God and His Word. As we have already seen, however, there was a serious defect in his understanding of true Christianity. In many ways which colored his perspective until his death, he still viewed the church of Christ through Roman Catholic eyes. One of those ways was his acceptance of the church as Constantine had molded it and Augustine had cemented it: a partner of the state, with the state enforcing orthodoxy (as the state church defined it) upon all its citizens. Based upon this misunderstanding, Calvin applied his legal training and natural brilliance to the development of a *system* of Christianity based upon an extreme view of God's sovereignty which by the sheer force of its logic would compel kings and all mankind to conform all affairs to righteousness. Indeed, in partnership with the church, kings and other civil rulers would enforce Calvinistic Christianity.

Calvin has impossibly been called both an amillennialist and postmillenialist. Of those who believed in a thousand-year reign of Christ upon earth, Calvin said their "fiction is too puerile to need or to deserve refutation." [15] As far as Calvin was concerned, Christ's kingdom began with His advent upon earth and had been in process ever since. Rejecting the literal future reign of Christ upon the earth through His Second Coming to establish his earthly kingdom upon David's throne in Jerusalem, Calvin felt obliged to establish the kingdom by his own efforts in Christ's absence.

The Bible makes it clear that one must be "born again" even to "see the kingdom of God" (John 3:3) and that "flesh and blood cannot inherit the kingdom of God" (1 Corinthians 15:50). Ignoring this biblical truth and following Augustine's error, Calvin determined (along with Guillaume Farel) to establish a beachhead for the kingdom of God on earth in Geneva, Switzerland. His first attempt there ended with his expulsion from that city. Boettner acknowledges, "Due to an attempt of Calvin and Farel to enforce a too severe system of discipline in Geneva, it became necessary for them to leave the city temporarily." [16]

Three years later, however, facing Catholic opposition from within and the threat of armed intervention by Roman Catholics from without, Geneva's city council decided that they needed Calvin's strong measures and invited him back. This time he succeeded in imposing his religion upon Geneva's citizens with an iron hand. His first act was to hand the city council his *Ecclesiastical Ordinances*, which were adopted November 20, 1561. Stefan Zweig tells us:

> One of the most momentous experiments of all time began when this lean and harsh man entered the Cornavian Gate [of Geneva]. A State [the walled city-state of Geneva] was to be converted into a rigid mechanism; innumerable souls, people with countless feelings and thoughts, were to be compacted into an all-embracing and unique system. This was the first attempt made in Europe to impose . . . a uniform subordination upon an entire populace.

> With systematic thoroughness, Calvin set to work for the realization of his plan to convert Geneva into the first Kingdom of God on earth. It was to be a community without corruption, disorder, vice or sin; it was to be the New Jerusalem, a centre from which the salvation of the world would radiate . . . the whole of his life was devoted to the service of this one idea. [17]

Tyranny In Geneva

Perhaps Calvin thought he was God's instrument to force Irresistible Grace (a key doctrine in Calvinism) upon the citizens of Geneva, Switzerland, even upon those who proved their unworthiness by resisting to the death. He unquestionably did his best to be irresistible in imposing "righteousness," but what he imposed and the manner in which he imposed it was far from grace and the teachings and example of Christ.

Many of those who profess a "Reformed" faith today, especially those known as Reconstructionists such as the late Rousas J. Rushdoony, Gary North, Jay Grimstead and others (including organizations such as the Coalition on Revival), take Calvin's Geneva as their model and thus hope to Christianize the

United States and then the world. Many Christian activists of looser attachment to Calvin hope in their own way, through protest marches and the organizing of large enough voting blocks, to force an ungodly American citizenry into godly living. No one ever worked so hard at attempting to do this and for so long a time as Calvin. Durant reports:

> To regulate lay conduct a system of domiciliary visits was established . . . and questioned the occupants on all phases of their lives . . . .The allowable color and quantity of clothing, and the number of dishes permissible at a meal, were specified by law. Jewelry and lace were frowned upon. A woman was jailed for arranging her hair to an immoral height . . . .

> Censorship of the press was taken over from Catholic and secular precedents and enlarged: books . . . of immoral tendency were banned . . . .To speak disrespectfully of Calvin or the clergy was a crime. A first violation of these ordinances was punished with a reprimand, further violation with fines, persistent violation with imprisonment or banishment. Fornication was to be punished with exile or drowning; adultery, blasphemy, or idolatry, with death . . . a child was beheaded for striking its parents. In the years 1558-59 there were 414 prosecutions for moral offenses; between 1542 and 1564 there were seventy-six banishments and fifty-eight executions; the total population of Geneva was then about 20,000. [18]

Certainly, much of Calvin's unusual zeal could not have come from the Holy Spirit's guidance but rather from his powerful personality and extreme view of God's sovereignty that denied all power of choice to man. Thus "grace" had to be irresistibly imposed. This was evident in the unbiblical manner in which he attempted to inflict his understanding of godliness upon the citizens of Geneva. In contrast to the humility, mercy, love, compassion and longsuffering of Christ, whom he loved and tried to serve, Calvin exerted authority much like the papacy which he now despised. Ironically, in spite of opposing the tyranny of the papacy, Calvin wielded the same unbiblical authoritarianism in attempting to enforce godliness upon ungodly people. Moreover, he criticized other Protestant leaders for not doing the same:

> Seeing that the defenders of the Papacy are so bitter and bold in behalf of their superstitions, that in their atrocious fury they shed the blood of the innocent, it should shame Christian magistrates that in the protection of certain truth, they are entirely destitute of spirit. [19]

Calvin's defenders turn a blind eye to the facts when they attempt to exonerate him by blaming events in Geneva on the civil authorities. In the face of so much evidence to the contrary, Boettner even insists that "Calvin was the first of the Reformers to demand complete separation between Church and State." [20] In fact, Calvin not only established ecclesiastical law but he codified the civil legislation. [21] He held the civil authorities responsible to "foster and maintain the external worship of God, to defend sound doctrine and the condition of the church" [22] and to see that "no idolatry, no blasphemy against God's name, no calumnies against his truth, nor other offenses to religion break out and be disseminated among the people . . . [but] to prevent the true religion . . . from being with impunity openly violated and polluted by public blasphemy." [23]

Calvin used the civil arm to impose his peculiar doctrines upon the citizens of Geneva and to enforce them. Zweig, who pored over the official records of the City Council for Calvin's day, tells us, "There is hardly a day, in the records of the settings of the Town Council, in which we do not find the remark: 'Better consult Master Calvin about this.' " [24] Pike reminds us that Calvin was given a "consultant's chair" in every meeting of the city authorities and "when he was sick the authorities would come to his house for their sessions." [25] Rather than diminishing with time, Calvin's power only grew. John McNeil, a Calvinist, admits that "in Calvin's latter years, and under his influence, the laws of Geneva became more detailed and more stringent." [26]

Don't Cross Dr. Calvin!

With dictatorial control over the populace ("he ruled as few sovereigns have done" [27]), Calvin imposed his brand of Christianity upon the citizenry with floggings, imprisonments, banishments and burnings at the stake. Calvin has been called "the Protestant Pope" and "the Genevese dictator" who "would tolerate in Geneva the opinions of only one person, his own." [28] Concerning the adoption in Geneva of a confession of faith that was made mandatory for all citizens, the historian Philip Schaff comments:

> It was a glaring inconsistency that those who had just shaken off the yoke of popery as an intolerable burden, should subject their conscience and intellect to a human creed; in other words, substitute for the old Roman popery a modern Protestant popery." [29]

Durant says that "Calvin held power as the head of this consistory; from 1541 till his death in 1564, his voice was the most influential in Geneva." [30] Vance reminds us that

> Calvin was involved in every conceivable aspect of city life: safety regulations to protect children, laws against recruiting mercenaries, new inventions, the introduction of cloth manufacturing, and even dentistry. He was consulted not only on all important state affairs, but on the supervision of the markets and assistance for the poor. [31]

Most of these were laudable efforts, but matters of faith were legislated as well. A confession of faith drawn up by Calvin was made mandatory for all citizens. It was a crime for anyone to disagree with this Protestant pope. Durant comments:

> All the claims of the popes for the supremacy of the church over the state were renewed by Calvin for his church . . . .[Calvin] was as thorough as any pope in rejecting individualism of belief; this greatest legislator of Protestantism completely repudiated that principle of private judgment with which the new religion had begun . . . .In Geneva . . . those . . . who could not accept it would have to seek other habitats. Persistent absence from Protestant [Calvinist] services, or continued refusal to take the Eucharist was a punishable offense.
>
> Heresy again became [under Calvin as under Augustine] . . . treason to the state, and was to be punished with death . . . in one year, on the advice of the Consistory, fourteen alleged witches were sent to the stake on the charge that they had persuaded Satan to afflict Geneva with plague. [32]

Calvin was again following in the footsteps of Augustine, who had enforced "unity . . . through common participation in the Sacraments . . . ." [33] A medical doctor named Jerome Bolsec dared to disagree with Calvin's doctrine of predestination. He was arrested for saying that "those who posit an eternal decree in God by which he has ordained some to life and the rest to death make of Him a tyrant, and in fact an idol, as the pagans made of Jupiter." [34] Bolsec was arrested and banished from Geneva with the warning that if he ever returned he would be flogged. [35] John Trolliet, a city notary, criticized Calvin's view of predestination for "making God the author of sin." [36] In fact, the charge was true, as Calvin's own writings clearly state. The court decreed that "thenceforward no one should dare to speak against this book [*Institutes*] and its doctrine." [37] So much for the freedom of conscience which had been promised would replace the popes' intolerable oppression!

Calvin's power was so great that it was tantamount to treason against the state to oppose him. A citizen named Jacques Gruet was arrested on suspicion of having placed a placard on Calvin's pulpit which read in part, "Gross hypocrite . . . ! After people have suffered long, they avenge themselves . . . .Take care that you are not served like M. Verle [who had been killed] . . . ." [38]

Gruet was tortured twice daily in a manner similar to which Rome, rightly condemned by the Reformers for doing so, tortured the victims of her inquisitions who were accused of daring to disagree with her dogmas. The use of torture for extracting "confessions" was approved by Calvin. [39] After thirty days of severe suffering, Gruet finally confessed—whether truthfully, or in desperation to end the torture, no one knows. On July 16, 1547, "half dead, he was tied to a stake, his feet were nailed to it, and his head was cut off." [40]

Good Intentions Gone Astray

No one has ever been as successful as John Calvin at totalitarian imposition of "godliness" upon a whole society. And therefore no one has proved as clearly as he that coercion cannot succeed because it can never change the *hearts* of men. Calvin's theology as laid out in his *Institutes* denied that unregenerate man could choose to believe and obey God. Apparently he was ignorant of the commonsense fact that genuine choice is essential if man is to love and obey God or show love and real compassion to his fellows. By his determined efforts to make Geneva's citizens obey, Calvin disproved his own theories of Unconditional Election and Irresistible Grace. What he did prove, seemingly, by years of totalitarian and surely ungodly force, was the first of Calvinism's Five Points, Total Depravity. Try as he might, there were many whom he simply could not persuade to live as he decreed, no matter how severe the penalty for failing to do so. He did succeed in creating many hypocrites who outwardly conformed to the law so long as the authorities were looking, but in their hearts longed for and practiced, when possible, the same old sins of the past.

Yes, there were reports from visitors that "cursing and swearing, unchastity, sacrilege, adultery, and impure living" such as were found elsewhere were absent from Geneva. [41]   John Knox, of course, was enthusiastic. He called Geneva "the most perfect school of Christ that ever was in the earth since the days of the Apostles." [42] A visiting Lutheran minister, who thought Calvin's coercion was commendable, wrote in 1610, "When I was in Geneva I observed something great which I shall remember and desire as long as I live." He praised the "weekly investigations into the conduct, and even the smallest transgressions, of the citizens" and concluded, "If it were not for the difference of religion, I would have been chained to Geneva forever." [43] *Difference of religion?* Yes, Calvinism was not Lutheranism, although both persecuted the Anabaptists. Protestantism involved several rival factions to say nothing of millions of true Christians who had never given allegiance to Rome and thus had not come out of her as "Protestants." These believers had been martyred by Roman Catholics at the instigations of various popes for a thousand years before Luther and Calvin were born. Thus today's representation of Calvinism as "Reformation theology" that supposedly revived true Christianity is grossly inaccurate. Calvinists have, in fact, hijacked the Reformation.

Admirers of John Calvin cite favorable stories as proof of the godly influence he and his theories exerted in changing a godless society into one that honored God. His methods, however, far from Christlike, could not be justified by *any* results. Nor could Calvin's means, as we have already noted, be justified by the fact that torture, imprisonment and execution had been employed by Luther and the popes and other Roman Catholic clergy to force their religious views upon those under their power. A true follower of Christ is not to be conformed to this world but in his behavior is to follow Christ's example.

Calvin's followers boast that he was the greatest of exegetes and followed Scripture meticulously both in formulating his theology and in guiding his life. Supposedly, Calvin "was willing to break sharply with tradition where it was contrary to the Word of God." [44] At the same time, he is defended with the excuse that he was only conforming to the traditions long established by Rome which began with Constantine. Scott says, "In the early years of the Reformation, censorship of manners and morals remained a settled, accepted part of existing, ancient police regulations not only in Geneva, but in all Europe." [45] This is true. Such curbs discouraged rebellious attempts to leave one's "class," etc. But that was not Christianity as taught and exemplified by Christ and His apostles.

There is no way to defend Calvin's conduct from Scripture. Yes, he was loving and caring toward those who agreed with him. Yes, he expended himself and shortened his life through visiting the sick, caring for the flock and preaching continually. But in his treatment of those who disagreed with him he was anything but a Christian.

The Hopelessness Of Imposed "Godliness"

Sadly, upon looking a bit more closely we find that in spite of threats and torture, Calvin's Geneva was not as righteous a city as the selected optimistic stories seem to indicate. The surviving records of the Council of Geneva unveil a city more similar to the rest of the world than Calvin's admirers would like to admit. These documents reveal "a high percentage of illegitimate children, abandoned infants, forced marriages, and sentences of death." [46] The stepdaughter and son-in-law of Calvin were among the many condemned for adultery. [47] Calvin had done his best, but at his death he felt that he had failed. Certainly he had not been able to produce among sinners, by the irresistible grace he sought to impose upon them, the ideal society — Augustine's City of God — which he had envisioned when he wrote *Institutes.*

Some critics have falsely accused Calvinists of teaching that totally depraved man is incapable of responding to God. That is not exactly their position. They believe that the unsaved can and do respond to God but *only* in unbelief, rebellion and opposition. White explains: "Unregenerate men who are enemies of God most assuredly respond to God: in a universally negative fashion." [48] That being the case, by his own theory, Calvin's efforts at Geneva were doomed before they began!

Speaking for all Calvinists, R.C. Sproul explains that according to the "Reformed view of predestination . . . before a person can choose Christ . . . he must be born again" [49] by a sovereign act of God. How could Calvin be sure that God had done this work in the hearts of all in Geneva? If God had not predestined every citizen of Geneva to salvation, then Calvin was wrong in trying to force them into a Christian mold. Yet coercion even by force was an integral part of the system as practiced by Calvin himself and his immediate successors.

Do Calvinists today approve of such conduct? It's doubtful. Then is it not probable that the Calvinism which produced such tyranny was also wrong in other respects?

How many of the "elect" were there in Geneva? As Jay Adams points out, no one, not even Calvin, could know. Calvinism has no explanation for how the elect could have been identified with certainty among the hypocrites who acted as though they were among the elect by behaving themselves, but did so only out of fear of the consequences. No matter how hard Calvin tried, if God had not elected every citizen in Geneva to salvation (and He apparently had not), then evil would still persist – though not as blatantly as in other cities of that day.

One wonders why Calvin, while insisting upon the doctrine of Total Depravity, didn't realize the hopelessness of trying to impose godliness upon the totally depraved citizens of Geneva. One wonders also, considering Calvin's abysmal record of failure, why today's Reconstructionists who hold to the same dogma nevertheless believe they will be able to impose righteous living upon entire nations – or why evangelicals continue to praise Calvin, the oppressor of Geneva.

Servetus: The Arch Heretic

Born Miguel Serveto in Villanova in 1511, the man known to the world as Michael Servetus "discovered the pulmonary circulation of the blood – the passage of the blood from the right chamber of the heart along the pulmonary artery to and through the lungs, its purification there by aeration, and its return via the pulmonary vein to the left chamber of the heart." He was in some ways "a bit more insane than the average of his time," announcing the end of the world in which "the Archangel Michael would lead a holy war against both the papal and Genevese Antichrists." [50]

There is no question that he was a rank heretic whose ravings about Christ reflected a combination of Islam and Judaism, both of which intrigued him. He was, however, right about some things: that God does not predestine souls to hell and that God is love. His otherwise outrageous ideas might have passed unnoticed had he not published them and attempted to force them upon Calvin and his fellow ministers in Geneva with aggressive, contemptuous and blasphemous railings. That Servetus titled one of his published works *The Restitution of*

Christianity could only be taken as an intentional personal affront by the author of the *Institutes of the Christian Religion.*

Servetus's persistence is seen in the fact that he wrote at least thirty letters to Calvin, an attention which must have irritated the recipient greatly. On February 13, 1546, Calvin wrote to Farel, "Servetus has just sent me a long volume of his ravings. If I consent he will come here, but I will not give my word, for should he come, if my authority is of any avail, I will not suffer him to get out alive." [51] Servetus made the mistake of passing through Geneva seven years later on his way to Naples and was recognized when he attended church (possibly out of fear of arrest for nonattendance) by someone who saw through his disguise and notified Calvin, who in turn ordered his arrest.

The Torture And Burning Of Servetus

Early in the trial, which lasted two months, Calvin wrote to Farel, "I hope that sentence of death will be passed upon him." [52] To understand Calvin, we need to consider that if the God one believes in predestines billions of the "totally depraved" to a burning hell (all of whom He *could* rescue), then to burn at the stake an obviously totally depraved heretic would seem quite mild and easily justifiable. That logic, however, seems somehow to escape many of today's evangelical Christians who admire the man and call themselves Calvinists.

The indictment, drawn up by Calvin the lawyer, contained thirty-eight charges (including rejection both of the Trinity and infant baptism) supported by quotations from Servetus's writings. Calvin personally appeared in court as the accuser and as "chief witness for the prosecution." [53] Calvin's reports of the trial matched Servetus's railings with such un-Christian epithets as "the dirty dog wiped his snout . . . the perfidious scamp soils each page with impious ravings," etc. [54] The Council consulted the other churches of Protestant Switzerland, and six weeks later their reply was received: Servetus should be condemned but not executed. Nevertheless, under Calvin's leadership, He was sentenced to death on two counts of heresy: Unitarianism and rejection of infant baptism. Durant writes:

> He asked to be beheaded rather than burned; Calvin was inclined to support this plea, but the aged Farel . . . reproved him for such tolerance; and the Council voted that Servetus should be burned alive.
> The sentence was carried out the next morning, October 17, 1553 . . . .On the way [to the burning] Farel importuned Servetus to earn divine mercy by confessing the crime of heresy; according to Farel the condemned man replied, "I am not guilty, I have not merited death"; and he besought God to pardon his accusers. He was fastened to a stake by iron chains, and his last book was bound to his side. When the flames reached his face he shrieked with agony. After half an hour of burning he died. [55]

The Failure Of Attempted Exonerations

Many attempts have been made by his modern followers to exonerate Calvin for the unconscionably cruel death of Michael Servetus. It is said that Calvin visited him in prison and pleaded with him to recant. Calvin's willingness for Servetus to be beheaded rather than burned at the stake was not necessarily motivated by kindness, however, but was an attempt to transfer the responsibility from himself to the civil authority. Beheading was the penalty for civil crimes; burning at the stake was for heresy. The charges, however, were clearly theological rather than civil and brought by Calvin himself.

There is no question that the civil authority only acted at the behest of the church. According to the laws of Geneva, Servetus, as a traveler passing through, not a citizen and not being guilty of any crime within the city, should have been expelled from the city, not executed. It was only his heresy which doomed him — and only because Calvin pressed the charges. Calvin did exactly what his view of God required in keeping with what he had written to Farel seven years before. Here again, over Calvin's shoulder, we see the long shadow of Augustine. To justify his actions, Calvin borrowed the same perverted interpretation of Luke 14:23 which Augustine had used. Frend said, "Seldom have gospel words been given so unexpected a meaning." [56] Farrar writes:

> To him [Augustine] are due . . . above all the bitter spirit of theological hatred and persecution. His writings became the Bible of the Inquisition. His name was adduced — and could there be a more terrible Nemesis on his errors? — to justify the murder of Servetus. [57]

There was wide acclaim from Catholics and Protestants alike for the burning of Servetus. The Inquisition in Vienne burned him in effigy. Melanchthon wrote Calvin a letter in which he called the burning "a pious and memorable example to all posterity" and gave "thanks to the Son of God" for the just "punishment of this blasphemous man." Others, however, disagreed; and Calvin became the target of criticism.

Calvin's Self-Justifications

Some critics argued that burning Servetus would only encourage the Roman Catholics of France to do the same to the Huguenots (70,000 would be slaughtered in one night in 1572). Stung by such opposition, in February 1554, Calvin published a broadside aimed at his critics: *Defensio orthodoxae fidei de sacra Trinitate contra prodigiosos errores Michaelis Serveti*. He argued that all who oppose God's truth are worse than murderers because murder merely kills the body whereas heresy damns the soul for eternity (was that worse than predestination by God to eternal damnation?) and that God had explicitly instructed Christians to kill heretics and even to smite with the sword any city that abandoned the true faith:

> Whoever shall maintain that wrong is done to heretics and blasphemers in punishing them [with death] makes himself an accomplice in their crime . . . it is God who speaks, and it is clear what law He would have kept in the Church even to the end of the world . . . so that we spare not kin nor blood of any, and forget all humanity when the matter is to combat for His glory. [58]

Historian R. Tudor Jones declares that this tract, which Calvin wrote in defense of the burning of Michael Servetus, "is Calvin at his most chilling . . . as frightening in its way as Luther's tract against the rebellious peasants." [59] Eight years later Calvin was still defending himself against criticism and still advocating the burning of heretics. In a 1561 letter to the Marquis de Poet, high chamberlain to the King of Navarre, Calvin advises sternly:

> . . . do not fail to rid the country of those zealous scoundrels who stir up the people to revolt against us. Such monsters should be exterminated, as I have exterminated Michael Servetus the Spaniard. [60]

A year later (just two years before his own death), Calvin again justifies Servetus's death, while at the same time acknowledging that he was responsible: "And what crime was it of mine if our Council *at my exhortation* . . . took vengeance upon his execrable blasphemies?" (Emphasis added.) [61] Much further documentation could be presented to expose the partisan bias of Calvinists who persist in offering one excuse after another for their hero. No wonder that even such a staunch Calvinist as William Cunningham writes:

> There can be no doubt that Calvin beforehand, at the time, and after the event, explicitly approved and defended the putting him [Servetus] to death, and assumed the responsibility of the transaction. [62]

Does The Christian Life Conform To Culture?

Today Calvin's supporters complain, "No Christian leader has ever been so often condemned by so many. And the usual grounds for condemnation are the execution of Servetus and the doctrine of predestination." [63] In fact, Servetus was only one of many such victims of Calvinism put into practice. Calvin is defended with the plea that such dealings were common practice and that he should be judged by the standard of his time. Do Calvin's defenders really mean that "new creatures in Christ Jesus" are to rise no higher than the conventions of their culture and moment in history?

God's sovereignty in controlling and causing everything that occurs is the very heart of Calvinism as conceived and taught by Calvin himself. Staunch Calvinist C. Gregg Singer declares that "the secret grandeur of Calvin's theology lies in his grasp of the biblical teaching of the sovereignty of God." [64]   Could Calvin truly have believed that he was God's instrument chosen from past eternity to coerce, torture and kill in forcing Geneva's citizens into behavior that God had predestined for them? How else could he have justified his actions?

Calvin has been acclaimed as a godly example, one who based his theology and actions upon Scripture alone. We have seen that his actions were in fact unbiblical in the extreme but were consistent with his theology. Is not that fact sufficient reason to question Calvinism itself and to examine it carefully from Scripture? That the Pope and Luther joined in unholy alliances with civil rulers to imprison, flog, torture, and kill dissenters in the name of Christ is no excuse for Calvin having done so also. Do his modern defenders really believe that Calvin's conduct conformed to Scripture? Is it not possible that some of his theology was just as unscriptural as the principles which drove his conduct? William Jones declares:

> And with respect to Calvin, it is manifest, that the leading, and to me at least, the most hateful feature in all the multiform character of popery adhered to him through life — I mean the *spirit of persecution*. [65]

Is not Christ alone the standard for His followers? And is He not always the same, unchanged by time or culture? How can the popes be condemned (and rightly so) for the evil they did under the banner of the Cross while excusing Calvin for doing much the same, though on a smaller scale? Calvin's conduct day after day and year after year was the very antithesis of what it would have been had he truly been led of the Spirit of God. We cannot escape drawing that conclusion from God's Word. The following are just two passages among many that condemn Calvin:

> But the wisdom that is from above is first pure, then peaceable, gentle, and easy to be intreated, full of mercy and good fruits, without partiality, and without hypocrisy. (James 3:17)

> He that saith he abideth in him [Christ] ought himself also so to walk, even as he [Christ] walked. (1 John 2:6)

One wonders why so many of today's Christian leaders who call themselves Calvinists are so quick to laud a man who was so far removed from the biblical exemplar reflected above.

1   W.H.C. Frend, *The Rise of Christianity* (Fortress Press, 1984), 482.
2   Philip Schaff, *History of the Christian Church* (Charles Scribner's Sons, 1910; Wm. B. Eerdmans Publishing Company, reprint 1959), II:72-73.
3   Ibid.
4   F.F. Bruce, *Light in the West*, Bk. III of *The Spreading Flame* (Wm. B. Eerdmans Publishing Co., 1956), 11-13.
5   *Codex Theodosianus*, (July 3, A.D. 321), XVI:8.1.
6   Frend, op. cit., 484.
7   Will Durant, "Caesar and Christ," Pt. III of *The Story of Civilization* (Simon and Schuster, 1950), 656.
8   Philip Hughes, *A History of the Church* (London, 1934), 1:198.
9   E.H. Broadbent, *The Pilgrim Church* (Gospel Folio Press, reprint 1999), 38-39.
10 Frend, op. cit., 492.
11 John Laurence Mosheim, *An Ecclesiastical History, Ancient and Modern*, trans. Archibald MacLaine (Applegate and Co., 1854), 101; and many other historians.
12 Laurence M. Vance, *The Other Side of Calvinism* (Vance Publications, Pensacola FL, rev. ed. 1999), 45.
13 Edward Gibbon, *The Decline and Fall of the Roman Empire* (Modern Library, n.d.), 2:233.
14 John W. Kennedy, *The Torch of the Testimony* (Christian Books Publishing House, 1963), 68.
15 John Calvin, *Institutes of the Christian Religion,* trans. Henry Beveridge (Wm. B. Eerdmans Publishing Company, 1998 ed.), III: xxv, 5
16 Loraine Boettner, *The Reformed Doctrine of Predestination* (Presbyterian and Reformed Publishing Co., 1932), 408.
17 Stefan Zweig, Eden Paul and Cedar Paul, trans.,*Erasmus: The Right to Heresy* (Cassell and Company, 1936), 207-208; cited in Henry R. Pike, *The Other Side of John Calvin* (Head to Heart, n.d.), 21-22.
18 Durant, op. cit., 474.
19 George Park Fisher, *The Reformation* (Scribner, Armstrong and Co., 1873), 224.
20 Boettner, op. cit., 410.
21 Ronald S. Wallace, *Calvin, Geneva, and the Reformation* (Baker Book House, 1990), 29.
22 Calvin, op. cit., IV:xx,2.
23 Op. cit., IV:xx,3.
24 Zweig, op. cit., 217.
25 Pike, op. cit., 26.
26 John T. McNeil, *The History and Character of Calvinism* (Oxford University Press, 1966), 189.
27 Williston Walker, *John Calvin: The Organizer of Reformed Protestantism* (Schocken Books, 1969), 259.
28 Op. cit., 107.
29 Schaff, op. cit., 8:357.
30 Durant, op. cit., VI:473.
31 Vance, op. cit., 85.
32 Durant, op. cit., 465.
33 Frend, op. cit., 669.
34 *The Register of the Company of Pastors of Geneva in the Time of Calvin*, trans. and ed. Philip E. Hughes (Wm. B. Eerdmans Publishing Co., 1966), 137-38; cited in Vance, op. cit., 84.
35 Schaff, op. cit., 8:618.
36 G.R. Potter and M. Greengrass, *John Calvin* (St. Martin's Press, 1983), 92-93.

37   *Register of Geneva*, op. cit., cited in Vance, op. cit., 201.
38   Schaff, op. cit., 502.
39   Fisher, op. cit., 222.
40   J.M. Robertson, *Short History of Freethought* (London, 1914), I:443-44.
41   Schaff, op. cit., 644.
42   Bard Thompson, *Humanists and Reformers: A History of the Renaissance and Reformation* (Wm. B. Eerdmans Publishing Co., 1996), 501.
43   Schaff, op. cit., 519.
44   C. Gregg Singer, *John Calvin: His Roots and Fruits* (A Press, 1989), 19.
45   Otto Scott, *The Great Christian Revolution* (The Reformer Library, 1994), 46.
46   Charles Beard, *The Reformation of the Sixteenth Century in Relation to Modern Thought and Knowledge* (London, 1885), 353; also see Edwin Muir, *John Knox* (London, 1920), 108.
47   Preserved Smith, *The Age of the Reformation* (New York, 1920), 174.
48   James R. White, *The Potter's Freedom* (Calvary Press Publishing, 2000), 98.
49   R.C. Sproul, *Chosen by God* (Tyndale House Publishers, Inc., 1986), 72.
50   Durant, op. cit., VI:481.
51   Roland P. Bainton, *Hunted Heretic: The Life of Michael Servetus* (Boston: The Beacon Press, 1953), 144; cited in Durant, op. cit., VI:481. See also John Calvin, *The Letters of John Calvin* (The Banner of Truth Trust, 1980), 159.
52   John Calvin, dated August 20, 1553; quoted in *Letters,* op. cit.
53   Wallace, op. cit., 77.
54   Durant, op. cit., VI:483.
55   Op. cit., 484.
56   Frend, op. cit., 672.
57   Frederic W. Farrar, *History of Interpretation* (E.P. Dutton and Co., 1886), 235-38.
58   J.W. Allen, *History of Political Thought in the Sixteenth Century* (London, 1951), 87.
59   R. Tudor Jones, *The Great Reformation* (Inter-Varsity Press, n.d.), 140.
60   John Calvin to the Marquis de Poet, in *The Works of Voltaire* (E.R. Dumont, 1901), 4:89; quoted in Vance, op. cit., 95, who gives two other sources for this quote.
61   Schaff, op. cit., 8:690-91.
62   William Cunningham, *The Reformers and the Theology of the Reformation* (The Banner of Truth Trust, 1967), 316-17.
63   Scott, op. cit., 100.
64   Singer, op. cit., 32.
65   William Jones, *The History of the Christian Church* (Church History Research and Archives, 5th ed. 1983), 2:238.

6
Arminius, Dort, Westminster and Five Points

Calvinism is often contrasted with Arminianism, so named after Jacobus Arminius (1560-1609). All those who do not fully agree with Calvinists on all five points of TULIP (see below) are often accused of being Arminians, though many against whom this charge is laid have never heard the term. Moreover, most Calvinists who malign Arminius have probably never read his works and know nothing more than hearsay about him and his beliefs. Ironically, this Dutch theologian started out as a Calvinist and even studied in Calvin's seminary in Geneva. He was a devout follower of Christ who suffered much for his faith. His entire family was murdered in his absence when Spanish Catholic troops massacred the population of his hometown of Oudewater in Holland.

Arminius was wrongfully charged with nearly every false doctrine ever invented, from Socinianism (denial of predestination, of the true nature of the Atonement and of the Trinity) to Pelagianism (the denial that Adam's sin affected his posterity, an undue emphasis upon free will, salvation by grace plus works, and the possibility of sinless perfection). Those false accusations are repeated today, often unjustly, against anyone who does not agree with Calvinism. So strong was Calvinism in certain parts of Europe in Arminius's day that to disagree with it was tantamount to a denial of the gospel and even of God's entire Word — indeed, to the endangerment of one's life.

Arminius had to bear the special onus that came upon any Protestant of his day in Holland who dared to take a second look at Calvinism from the Scriptures, a load of guilt still placed upon non-Calvinists today. He was accused of having secret leanings toward Roman Catholicism in spite of his open denunciation of Catholic sacraments and of the papacy as the kingdom of Antichrist. Indeed, upon visiting Rome to see the Vatican for himself, Arminius reported that he saw "'the mystery of iniquity' in a more foul, ugly, and destestable form than his imagination could ever have conceived." [1] While some of those who have called themselves Arminians have been guilty of all manner of heresy, having "adopted views . . . quite contrary" to what he taught, [2] it is quite a shock to discover that James Arminius was actually biblical in his beliefs and far more Christlike in his life than was Calvin. Vance writes that "Arminius was just as orthodox on the cardinal doctrines of the Christian Faith as any Calvinist, ancient or modern." [3]

In evaluating either of these two strong leaders, one must remember that just as the Five Points of Calvinism were not formulated by Calvin but by the Synod of Dort, so neither was it Arminius who articulated the five points of Arminianism but the Remonstrants after his death.

Arminius And His Teachings

There was nothing in Arminius to suggest revenge against one's enemies or the use of violence, much less the death sentence for heresy. He stood uncompromisingly for sound doctrine and believed in the infallibility and inerrancy of the Bible as inspired by God. He rejected the Mass as a denial of "the truth and excellence of the sacrifice of Christ." [4] He joined in calling the pope "the adulterer and pimp of the Church, the false prophet . . . the enemy of God . . . the Antichrist . . . [5] the man of sin, the son of perdition, that most notorious outlaw [6] . . . [who] shall be destroyed at the glorious advent of Christ," [7] and urged all true believers to "engage in . . . the destruction of Popery, as they would . . . the kingdom of Antichrist . . . ." [8]

Arminius recognized and rejected the false doctrines of Augustine for what they were. In contrast to Augustine, Arminius also rejected the Apocrypha and authority of tradition. He believed in the eternal Sonship of Christ, co-equal and co-eternal with the Father and the Holy Spirit, [9] that Christ came to this earth as a man, [10] that He was Jehovah of the Old Testament [11] who died for our sins, paying the full penalty by His one sacrifice of Himself on the cross, [12] that He was buried, rose again and ascended to heaven, [13] that man is hopelessly lost and bound by sin and that salvation is by grace alone through faith alone in Christ alone. [14]

Arminius was evangelical in the gospel he preached. Salvation was entirely through Christ as a work of grace which God alone could do in the heart. He categorically denied the false charges made against him of Pelagianism and Socinianism. [15] He also, with these words, defended himself against the false charge that he taught the doctrine of falling away: "At no period have I asserted 'that believers do finally decline or fall away from faith or salvation.'" [16]

It is astonishing with what disapproval Arminius is denounced today by Calvinists, while Augustine is praised. J.I. Packer quotes with approval "Robert Traill, the Scottish Puritan, [who] wrote in 1692, 'The principles of Arminianism are the natural dictates of a carnal mind, which is enmity both to the law of God, and to the gospel of Christ, and, next to the dead sea of Popery (into which also this stream runs), have, since Pelagius to this day, been the greatest plague of the Church of Christ, and it is like will be till his second coming.' " [17] Sheldon, however, says, "The doctrinal system of Arminius, who is confessed on all hands to have been a man of most exemplary spirit and life, was the Calvinistic system with no further modification than necessarily resulted from rejecting the tenet of absolute predestination." [18] A leading Arminian of the nineteenth century summarized his understanding of that doctrine:

> Arminianism teaches that God in Jesus Christ made provision fully for the salvation of all those who, by repentance towards God and faith in our Lord Jesus Christ, accept the terms [of the gospel], and all who do thus accept are eternally saved. All who rebel against God, and refuse to accept of Jesus on the terms of proffered mercy, sink under Divine wrath and are eternally lost. [19]

The Break With Calvinism

Arminius was as determined as Calvin to follow only the Lord and His Word. That got him into trouble because he considered himself no more "bound to adopt all the private interpretations of the Reformed" [20] than those of the Roman Catholic Church. [21] He concluded from earnest study of the scriptures that in some respects Calvinism was simply not biblical. And he suffered persecution for that careful and prayerful opinion.

Arminius was convinced that the scriptures teach that those who will be in heaven are there because they believed the gospel, not because God elected them to be saved and regenerated them without any faith on their part. He firmly believed and taught predestination as "an eternal and gracious decree of God in Christ, by which He determines to justify and adopt believers, and to endow them with life eternal, but to condemn unbelievers and impenitent persons." [22] What E.H. Broadbent in his classic *The Pilgrim Church* had to say about Arminius stands in stark contrast to the slander the latter still suffers from Calvinists:

> Brought up under the influence of Calvin's teaching, Arminius — acknowledged by all as a man of spotless character, in ability and learning unexcelled — was chosen to write in defense of Calvinism of the less extreme kind, which was felt to be endangered by the attacks made upon it. Studying the subject, however, he came to see that much that he held was indefensible;

that it made God the author of sin, set limits to His saving grace, left the majority of mankind without hope or possibility of salvation.

He saw from the Scriptures that the atoning work of Christ was for all, and that man's freedom of choice is a part of the divine decree. Coming back to the original teaching of Scripture and faith of the Church, he avoided the extremes into which both parties to the long controversy had fallen. His statement of what he had come to believe involved him personally in conflicts which so affected his spirit as to shorten his life [he died at the age of 49, Calvin at 55]. His teaching took a vivid and evangelical form later, in the Methodist revival.[23]

Fisk agrees that "Arminianism comes from the name of a man who first embraced the Calvinistic system, was called upon to defend it against the opposition, and who upon further study came around to a more moderate position." [24] McNeill, himself a Presbyterian, is honest enough to say that Arminius "does not repudiate predestination, but condemns supralapsarianism [that God from eternity past predestined the non-elect to sin and to suffer eternal damnation] as subversive of the gospel." [25] Cairns explains the major differences between the two systems:

His [Arminius's] attempt to modify Calvinism so that . . . God might not be considered the author of sin, nor man an automaton in the hands of God, brought down upon him the opposition . . . .

Both Arminius and Calvin taught that man, who inherited Adam's sin, is under the wrath of God. But Arminius believed that man was able to initiate his salvation after God had granted him the primary grace to enable his will to cooperate with God . . . . [26] Arminius accepted election but believed that the decree to save some and damn others had "its foundation in the foreknowledge of God." [27] Thus election was conditional rather than unconditional . . . .

Arminius also believed that Christ's death was sufficient for all but that it was efficient only for believers. [28] Calvin limited the atonement to those elected to salvation. Arminius also taught that men might resist the saving grace of God, [29] whereas Calvin maintained that grace was irresistible.

There are so many evangelical historians who praise Arminius as thoroughly orthodox in his doctrine that one finds it difficult to understand why he is held in such disrespect by Calvinists. There seems to be no other reason than his desire to mitigate their extremes. Of Arminius, Newman says, "He was recognized as among the ablest and most learned men of his time. His expository sermons were so lucid, eloquent, and well delivered as to attract large audiences. He was called upon from time to time to write against opponents of Calvinism, which he did in a moderate and satisfactory way. When pestilence was raging in 1602, he distinguished himself by heroic service." [30]

Arminianism And State Churches

It could only be expected that Arminius's moderate and biblical view would attract a large following. Many Protestant pastors, uncomfortable with the extremes of Calvinism and with its militancy against those who disagreed, began to see in Scripture and to preach the same modified Calvinism as Arminius. They received considerable opposition from Calvinists wherever the latter were in the majority and controlled public opinion. Furthermore, the Calvinists, following Augustine's teaching and the practice of Rome, saw church and state as partners, with the church using the state to enforce sanctions against whomever they considered to be heretics — an intolerance which Arminius and his followers opposed.

This great error of union between church and state was, as we have seen, a legacy of Constantine who had also relentlessly forbidden anyone outside the established church to meet for religious purposes and confiscated the property of those who did. Believing that baptism was "the salvation of God . . . the seal which confers immortality . . . the seal of salvation," [31] he had waited until just before his death to be baptized so as not to risk sinning thereafter and losing his salvation. Later, Emperor Theodosius issued an edict making "the religion which was taught by St. Peter to the Romans, which has been faithfully preserved by tradition" [32] the official faith of the empire; adherents were to be called "Catholic Christians," and all others were forbidden to meet in their churches. [33] One historian has explained the tragic effect for the church:

> The Scriptures were now no longer the standard of the Christian faith. What was orthodox [would] be determined by the decisions of fathers and councils; and religion propagated not by the apostolic methods of persuasion, accompanied with the meekness and gentleness of Christ, but by imperial edicts and decrees; nor were gainsayers to be brought to conviction by the simple weapons of reason and scripture, but persecuted and destroyed. [34]

Such was the official relationship between church and state which Calvin inherited from Augustine, enforced in Geneva and which the Calvinists wherever possible carried on and used to enforce their will upon those who differed with them. In league with princes, kings and emperors, the Roman Catholic Church had for centuries controlled all of Europe. The Reformation created a new state church across Europe in competition with Rome that was either Lutheran or Calvinist. The latter became known as Reformed.

The Presbyterian Church in Scotland, the Church of England, and the Dutch Reformed Church that persecuted the Arminians in Holland were all Calvinistic state churches. Tragically, they followed Constantine, Augustine and Calvin in the enormous ambition of imposing their brand of Christianity upon all in partnership with the state. As David Gay points out:

In the *Institutes* Calvin said that civil government is assigned to foster and maintain the external worship of God, to defend sound doctrine and the condition of the church. He dismissed the Anabaptists as stupid fanatics because they argued that these matters are the business of the church, not the civil authorities. Nevertheless, Calvin was wrong; they were right . . . . He was writing from the viewpoint of Constantine, not the New Testament . . . . [35]

Synods, Assemblies, Councils, And Confessions

Those who disagree with Calvinism today on the basis of their understanding of God's Word are accused of abandoning, ignoring or even defying the great confessions and established creeds of the church. We must ask, "Which church?" Roman Catholics also refer to "the Church" in a similar manner, but millions of true believers were not part of it for centuries before the Reformation, refusing to bow to the popes or to submit to Rome's heresies. Calvinists today, looking back upon the first century or so of the Reformation, refer to "the church" in much the same way, meaning state churches carrying on what Calvin began in Geneva, with those outside their membership viewed as heretics. This false view is being perpetuated by today's calculated references to "the Reformed faith," as though Calvinism deserves total credit for the Reformation.

It is amazing how diligent Calvin was to correct and persecute even to the death those who disagreed with his extreme views on sovereignty and predestination but was apparently able with no trouble to overlook the many heresies of Augustine. At least we don't find anything in his writings except praise for this man who held to so much that was unbiblical. In fact, as we have seen, Calvin not only praised Augustine, he looked to him as the authority justifying his own beliefs and policies at Geneva.

While it is dangerous to launch into an independent theology that has been unknown to believers throughout the ages, that is not necessarily what one does in ignoring or even disagreeing with the so-called established confessions. In fact, the Reformation creeds and confessions were formulated not by agreement among all Christians but by either the Lutheran or the Calvinistic segment alone. The Synod of Dort and Westminster Assembly, most often referred to by Calvinists as so clearly establishing Christian truth in opposition to Arminianism, were dominated by Calvinists and forced Calvinism as the official state religion upon everyone. So the accusation that one fails to follow these "great Reformed confessions" is merely another way of saying that one disagrees with Calvinism! It also furthers the false impression that it was the official belief held by all of the Reformers. Concerning the five points of Calvinism, Hodges writes, "None of these ideas has any right to be called normative Protestant theology. None has ever been held by a wide cross-section of Christendom. Most importantly, none of them is biblical...all of them lie outside the proper parameters of Christian orthodoxy." [36]

The Five Arminian Points

Arminius was part of the state Dutch Reformed Church, as were the leaders who carried on his beliefs after his premature death in 1609. Inevitably the differences in biblical understanding grew into open controversy over predestination and whether or not the Belgic Confession and Heidelberg Catechism should be reviewed for possible revision. To discuss the issues, forty-six Arminian ministers met privately in Gouda, Holland, on January 14, 1610. They drew up and signed a Remonstrance (protest) against Calvinism, stating that its doctrines were "not contained in the Word of God nor in the Heidelberg Catechism, and are unedifying — yea, dangerous — and should not be preached to Christian people." [37]

The Remonstrance was comprised of five brief paragraphs which became known as the five points of Arminianism. In summary they stated:

1. God from eternity past determined to save all who believe in Jesus and to "leave the incorrigible and unbelieving in sin and under wrath . . . ."

2. Christ died for and obtained redemption and forgiveness of sins for all, but these benefits are effective only for those who believe on Christ.

3. Man cannot "think, will nor do anything that is truly good," and that includes "saving faith," but must be regenerated.

4. That God's grace is absolutely essential for salvation, but that it may be resisted.

5. That those truly saved through faith in Christ are empowered by the Holy Spirit to resist sin; but whether they could fall away from the faith "must be more particularly determined out of the Holy Scripture, before we ourselves can teach it with full persuasion of our minds."

The Calvinist response came a few months later in the form of a Counter-Remonstrance which contained seven articles. The second and third points have been combined under the heading of Unconditional Election, with the sixth and seventh points combined under Perseverance of the Saints, resulting in what has become known as the Five Points of Calvinism. Vance summarizes this declaration well as follows:

1. Because the whole race has fallen in Adam and become corrupt and powerless to believe, God draws out of condemnation those whom he has chosen unto salvation, passing by the others.

2. The children of believers, as long as they do not manifest the contrary, are to be reckoned among God's elect.

3. God has decreed to bestow faith and perseverance and thus save those whom he has chosen to salvation.

4. God delivered up his Son Jesus Christ to die on the cross to save only the elect.

5. The Holy Spirit, externally through the preaching of the Gospel, works a special grace internally in the hearts of the elect, giving them power to believe.

6. Those whom God has decreed to save are supported and preserved by the Holy Spirit so that they cannot finally lose their true faith.

7. True believers do not carelessly pursue the lusts of the flesh, but work out their own salvation in the fear of the Lord. [38]

The Growing Controversy

The Counter-Remonstrance was in turn answered by The Opinion of the Remonstrants. This was a far more lengthy document which went into great detail to establish what the Remonstrants "in conscience have thus far considered and still consider to be in harmony with the Word of God . . . ." It contained lengthy objections to Calvinism under four headings, the main points of which are summarized in the following excerpts:

From Section I (10 paragraphs):

3. God . . . has not ordained the fall . . . has not deprived Adam of the necessary and sufficient grace, does also not . . . bring some [men] unto [eternal] life, but deprive others of the benefit of life . . . .

4. God has not decreed without intervening actual sins to leave by far the greater part of men, excluded from all hope of salvation, in the fall.

5. God has ordained that Christ should be the atonement for the sins of the whole world, and by virtue of this decree He has decided to justify and to save those who believe in Him, and to provide men with the means necessary and sufficient unto faith . . .

6. No one is rejected from eternal life nor from the means sufficient thereto by any antecedent absolute decree . . . .

From Section II (4 paragraphs):

1. The price of salvation, which Christ offered to God . . . paid for all and every man, according to . . . the grace of God the Father; and therefore no one is definitely excluded from . . . the benefits of the death of Christ by an absolute and antecedent decree of God.

3. Although Christ has merited reconciliation with God and the forgiveness of sins for all men . . . no one becomes an actual partaker of the benefits of the death of Christ except by faith . . . .

From Section III (12 paragraphs):

5. The efficacious grace by which anyone is converted is not irresistible, and although God through the Word and the inner operation of His Spirit so influences the will that He both bestows the power to believe . . . and indeed causes man to believe, nevertheless man is able of himself to despise this grace, not to believe, and thus to perish through his own fault.

6. Although according to the altogether free will of God the disparity of divine grace may be very great, nevertheless the Holy Spirit bestows, or is ready to bestow, as much grace upon all men and every man to whom God's Word is preached as is sufficient for the furtherance of the sufficient grace unto faith and conversion whom God is said to be willing to save according to the decree of absolute election, but also they who are not actually converted.

12. We also hold to be false and horrible that God should in a hidden manner incite men to the sin which He openly forbids; that those who sin do not act contrary to the true will of God . . . that it is according to justice a crime worthy of death to do God's will.

From Section IV (8 paragraphs):

3. True believers can fall from true faith and fall into such sins as cannot be consistent with true and justifying faith, and not only can this happen, but it also not infrequently occurs.

4. True believers can through their own fault . . . finally fall away and go lost.

5. Nevertheless we do not believe, though true believers sometimes fall into grave and conscience-devastating sins, that they immediately fall from all hope of conversion, but we acknowledge that it can happen that God according to His abundant mercy, again calls them to conversion through His grace . . . .

6. Therefore we heartily reject the following doctrines, which are daily spread abroad among the people in public writings, as being harmful to piety and good morals; namely: 1) That true believers cannot sin deliberately, but only out of ignorance and weakness. 2) That true believers through no sins can fall from the grace of God. 3) That a thousand sins, yea, all the sins of the whole world, cannot render election invalid; when it is added to this that all men are obligated to believe that they are chosen unto salvation, and therefore cannot fall from election, we present for consideration what a wide door that opens for carnal certainty. 4) That to believers and to the elect no sins, however great and grave they may be, are imputed . . . . 5) That true believers, having fallen into corrupt heresies, into grave and shameful sins, such as adultery and murder, on account of which the Church, according to the institution of Christ, is obligated to testify that she cannot tolerate them in her external fellowship, and that they shall have no part in the kingdom of Christ, unless they repent, nevertheless cannot totally and finally fall from the faith.

8. A true believer can and must be certain for the future that he, granted intervening, watching, praying, and other holy exercises, can persevere in the true faith, and that the grace of God to persevere will never be lacking to him; but we do not see how he may be assured that he will never neglect his duty in the future, but in the works of faith, piety and love, as befits a believer, persevere in this school of Christian warfare. Neither do we deem it necessary that the believer should be certain of this. [39]

These four headings were understood to contain five points, which the Calvinists at the Synod of Dort answered with what has become known as the Five Points of Calvinism. The major difference is obvious: the Arminians put the blame for man's eternal punishment upon man himself for rejecting, by his own free will, the gospel, which he could have accepted through God's gracious enabling; whereas the Calvinists laid sin itself and the damnation of man totally upon God who simply predestined everything to turn out that way. A. W. Tozer, respected by many Calvinists, declared, "So when man exercises his freedom [of choice], he is fulfilling the sovereignty of God, not canceling it out." [40]

The State of the Netherlands, in its concern for unity among its citizens, ordered both parties to meet to iron out their differences. Six leaders from each side met in the Hague on March 31, 1611, but failed to reach an agreement. While the Arminians pleaded for tolerance, the Calvinists were determined to convene a national conference to have their opponents declared heretics. Of course, the view at that time was that the state would exact the prescribed penalties upon heretics, up to and including death.

The Great Synod Of Dort (Dordrecht)

The persisting theological differences eventually involved the government in an internal battle between political rivals. The Calvinists won out, Prince Maurice siding with them, and followed up by replacing magistrates sympathetic to the Arminians. This paved the way for the national synod which, after letters sent inviting foreign representatives, was then convened at Dordrecht on November 13, 1618, and lasted into May of the following year.

Of course, the Calvinists were convinced that they were standing for truth. Each delegate took an oath to follow only the Word of God and to "aim at the glory of God, the peace of the Church, and especially the preservation of the purity of doctrine. So help me, my Savior, Jesus Christ! I beseech him to assist me by his Holy Spirit." [41]

Calvinists have ever since hailed Dort as a gathering of history's most godly leaders who sincerely followed their oath. In John Wesley's opinion, however, Dort was as impartial as the Council of Trent. [42] In fact, Dort had been called by state officials favoring the Calvinists for the sole purpose of supporting the Calvinists and condemning the Arminians, so it can hardly be considered an impartial tribunal.

Moreover, Baptists who today point to Dort as the articulation of what they believe are, as Vance points out, [43] "not only conforming to a Dutch Reformed State-Church creed, they are following Augustine, for as the Reformed theologian Herman Hanko asserts, 'Our fathers at Dordrecht knew well that these truths set forth in the Canons could not only be traced back to the Calvin Reformation;

they could be traced back to the theology of St. Augustine . . . . For it was Augustine who had originally defined these truths.' [44] Custance insists that the Five Points were 'formulated implicitly by Augustine.'" [45]

The Arminians were not allowed to plead their case as equals, but were removed from the status of delegates to that of defendants, and were summarily expelled from the synod and publicly denounced. After Dort the Remonstrants were asked to recant or be banished. More than 200 Arminian ministers were removed from their pulpits and many exiled. There was an attempt to establish a harsh Calvinistic theocracy where only Calvinism could be publicly proclaimed, but it lasted only a short time. It was not, however, until 1625 that persecution of Arminians ceased. [46]

Cairns calls the Great Synod of Dort "an international Calvinistic assembly" in which the Arminians "came before the meeting in the role of defendants." Calvinists have called Dort "a symbol of the triumph of orthodox Calvinism in the Netherlands." [47] Louis Berkhof declares, "Five thoroughly Calvinistic Canons, in which the doctrines of the Reformation, and particularly of Calvin, on the disputed points are set forth with clearness and precision." [48]

Ever since Dort, Calvinists have hailed these Canons as "a bulwark, a defense, of the truth of God's Word concerning our salvation."[49] Such a statement, made continually by Calvinists, leaves no doubt that in their minds any disagreement with Calvinism's Five Points is a rejection of the gospel. That mindset should cause great concern in the church today in view of the resurgence of Calvinism through the efforts of esteemed evangelical leaders. The concern should be even greater when the truth is known that the "Reformed faith" as expressed in these highly honored creeds is to a large extent the theology of Augustine, a father of modern Roman Catholicism.

Fruits Of The Synod Of Dort

In evaluating the Synod of Dort and the Five Points of Calvinism which it pronounced, one cannot avoid recognition of the political nature of the gathering and the fact that the Calvinistic church leaders were acting as instruments of the state in violation of the Word of God – and the state acted on their behalf to punish their opponents. That Calvinists together with the state falsely charged, persecuted, imprisoned, sought the death of and executed some of the Arminian leaders must also be a consideration in evaluating this entire procedure and its fruits.

Although both the Arminians and Calvinists at this time were in agreement as to the church-state alliance, the Arminians had no desire to use the state to enforce their views upon their opponents. Even Calvinists admit that "the divines who composed the Synod of Dort generally held that the civil magistrate was entitled to inflict pains and penalties as a punishment for heresy" and that, in contrast, the Arminians advocated "toleration and forbearance in regard to differences of opinion upon religious subjects." [50]

Consider, for example, the fate of the four main leaders of the Arminian movement. John Uytenbogaert, who had studied at Geneva under Calvin's successor, Beza, and served as chaplain to Prince Maurice (son and successor of William of Orange), was exiled after the Synod of Dort and had his goods confiscated. Simon Episcopius, a professor of theology and chief spokesman for the Arminians at Dort, was banished. John Van Oldenbarnevelt, who was advocate-general of Holland and a national hero for helping William of Orange negotiate the Union of Utrecht, because he gave support to the Arminians found himself at odds with Maurice, was falsely charged with treason and beheaded. Hugo Grotius, a famed lawyer known worldwide for his expertise in international law, was sentenced to life in prison but escaped and later became Swedish ambassador to Paris.

What biblical basis could anyone propose for exacting such penalties for a disagreement over doctrine? If the Calvinists could be so wrong in so much that is so important, might they not also be wrong in some basic theological assumptions? It seems astonishing that in spite of a complete misunderstanding of and disobedience concerning such vital and fundamental New Testament teaching as separation of church and state and nonimposition of belief by force, these men are hailed as "great divines," and the doctrine they forcefully imposed on others is embraced as the truth of God to be accepted by all today!

The Westminster Assembly

Dort was followed in 1643 by a similar prestigious gathering of "divines" in England. The Westminster Assembly was also under the auspices of the state. That Assembly formulated The Westminster Confession of Faith, which has been called "the most systematically complete statement of Calvinism ever devised." [51] Vance reminds us that "Due to the close relationship between Church and state that existed at the time, the acceptance of Calvinism in England, culminating in the Westminster Assembly, is deeply intertwined with the civil and religious history of England." [52] A brief word about that history is in order.

In the two preceding centuries, England had gone through a long struggle to escape Rome. At times she made progress, at other times she fell back into bondage. Henry VII had been proclaimed king in 1486 by a papal bull of Pope Innocent VIII. The Latin Vulgate was the official Bible. Wycliffe's Bible was suppressed, and the Provincial Council at Oxford in 1408 had forbidden the translation and printing of "any text of Holy Scripture into the English or other language . . . ." [53] Henry VIII, who had written to Erasmus from London in 1511 that "many heretics furnish a daily holocaust," [54] at the behest of Cromwell reversed himself and encouraged the Bible in English to be opened in every house and parish church — but a year before his death banned "the New Testament of Tyndale's or Coverdale's translation." [55]

During his brief reign, King Edward VI turned England away from Rome and welcomed Reformed theologians from the Continent to England, giving Calvinism a foothold there that it would never relinquish. In the late sixteenth century the University of Cambridge became a Calvinist stronghold. Edward's sister, Bloody Mary, succeeding him, brought England back under popery, forbade possession of any Protestant books and burned at the stake those who would not accept Rome's doctrines.

After Mary's death, the Geneva Bible came into use. Elizabeth I expelled the Jesuits from England. Under her, the Thirty-Nine Articles of the Church of England (mildly Calvinistic, but rejecting limited atonement) were formulated; they remain the official creed of that church to this day. John Knox held forth in Scotland, while the Puritans rose in England, only to be forced to conform by King James, who gave us the King James Bible in 1611.

Charles I succeeded James. There were debates in Parliament over Calvinism, with its proponents gaining the upper hand. The Long Parliament ordered the printing of a book by John Owen which denounced Arminianism and upheld limited atonement. It was in the context of this tumultuous background and the continued partnership of the church with the state that the Westminster Assembly was convened by Parliament. The Parliament "waged a civil war against the king . . . abolished episcopacy, ejected two thousand royalist ministers . . . summoned the Westminster Assembly, executed Archbishop Laud, and eventually executed the king himself in 1649." [56]

Once again the deck was stacked. Westminster was not a gathering of those representing all true believers, but only of the Calvinists, who had gained the upper hand in Parliament. Today's boast is that "all of the Westminster divines were Calvinists." [57] Furthermore, as Vance wisely comments, " . . . like the Synod of Dort, the presence of government officials at an ostensibly religious assembly raises some questions about its legitimacy." [58] Expenses of the members were borne by the State. Even Calvinists admit, "The Assembly was the creature of Parliament and was never able to escape from Parliamentary supervision." [59]

Logan confesses, " . . . the Assembly . . . was clearly and completely subservient to the political authority of Parliament." [60] De Witt also declares that the Assembly "was answerable, not to the King of Kings, but to the Lords and Commons of the English Parliament." [61] Schaff points out that "the Assembly . . . clung to the idea of a national state church, with a uniform system of doctrine, worship, and discipline, to which every man, woman, and child in three kingdoms should conform." [62] Bettany writes:

> In 1643 also the Westminster Assembly of divines was convened by Parliament to reform the Church of England "on the basis of the word of God, and to bring it into a nearer agreement with the Church of Scotland and the Reformed Churches on the Continent." The Scotch commissioners now required, as the price of their co-operation with the English Parliament against Charles, the adoption of the Solemn League and Covenant [drawn by a Scottish revolutionary committee requiring signers to extirpate prelacy in all its forms in Scotland, Ireland and England] . . . .

> With this weapon . . . and the test of loyalty to the king, ejections of Episcopalians from their livings . . . amounted to some thousands . . . . So many vacancies were created that they could not be filled . . . . Finally the Westminster Assembly was ordered to draw up a scheme for ordination . . . . The Westminster Assembly laboured to evolve an acceptable scheme of Presbyterianism, the Independent members, however . . . proposing toleration for all sects . . . .

> The question soon arose . . . should presbyteries have the power of including or excluding members, or should each Independent congregation wield that power? Parliament undertook to settle the whole matter by ordaining that all persons aggrieved by the action of a presbytery might appeal to Parliament . . . . Cromwell in vain tried to reconcile Independents and Presbyterians. The latter predominated in Parliament, and in 1648 showed their continued intolerance by enacting that all who denied God, or the Trinity, or the atonement, or the canonical books of Scripture, or the resurrection of the dead and a final judgment were to 'suffer the pains of death, as in case of felony, without benefit of clergy.' . . . A long catalogue of heresies of the second class was specified, to be punished by imprisonment . . . . [63]

Lessons To Be Learned

The so-called Reformation synods and councils and the confessions and decrees they generated, which all evangelicals today are supposed to honor as stating the true doctrine of Christ, were promoted by an established state church in partnership with the civil rulers — contrary to the Word of God. Always the overriding concern was for unity, and those who did not agree with the majority position were silenced, persecuted, imprisoned, banished and sometimes executed.

Just as the Roman Catholic Church had persecuted and killed those who did not agree with her down through the centuries, so the newly established Protestant churches began to do the same. Anabaptists, for example, were persecuted and killed by both Catholics and Protestants because the latter still believed in Augustine's baptism of infants with its magical powers of regeneration into the family of God.

These were the men and the motives behind the established creeds and confessions. Unquestionably, their *modus operandi* followed in the footsteps of Constantine. Not a true Christian and thus not interested in truth but in the "unity" of the empire, Constantine used "Christianity" to that end. Under him, the church, once persecuted by the world, became the persecutor. True Christians were still the ones being persecuted. The only change was that a false church had joined the world to persecute those not subscribing to its dogmas.

The new persecution was done in the name of Christ, but was the very antithesis of all Christ taught and lived and for which He died. Following in the footsteps of Rome, which in most matters they opposed, the Protestant churches continued the same practice. We cannot, and dare not, ignore these facts in evaluating the early creeds and statements of faith, coming as they did from councils and synods called by the state for the sake of unity.

Augustine had been happy to use the state in an unbiblical partnership to enforce "faith" upon heretics. Driven by the same belief, Calvin used the same system in Geneva. Nor can one deny the obvious relationship between this intolerant forcing of "faith" upon the unwilling, and the two major doctrines of both Augustine and Calvin – Total Depravity and double Predestination with their concomitant denial of any genuine choice for mankind. Freedom of conscience was the natural victim, a form of oppression which even the unsaved can tolerate only for so long.

Defining Calvinism

In spite of many differences of opinion among Calvinists today, Calvinism is generally explained by the acronym, TULIP. Philip F. Congdon writes that "a tulip is a beautiful flower, but bad theology. The fruit of the flower is appealing; the fruit of the theology is appalling . . . works, as an *inevitable result*, are necessary for salvation. To be fair, Classical Calvinists usually object to this by describing the gospel message as *not* 'faith + works = justification,' but 'faith = justification + works' . . . . This is no more than a word game. It is best seen in the old Calvinist saying: 'You are saved by faith alone, but the faith that saves you is never alone . . . . '" [64]

Some readers may have never heard of TULIP. Others, while knowing that it has something to do with Calvinism, find it difficult to remember what each letter stands for. Here, in brief, is a summary of common explanations. In each case, in order to avoid the charge that they are not properly stated, they are presented in the words of the major Calvinistic creeds or confessions:

> "T" stands for Total Depravity: that man, because he is spiritually dead to God "in trespasses and in sins" (Ephesians 2:1; Colossians 2:13), is incapable of responding to the gospel, though able to make other moral choices.

> The Westminster Confession of Faith declares: "Our first parents . . . became dead in sin, and wholly defiled in all the faculties and parts of soul and body . . . wholly inclined to all evil . . . . Man, by his fall into a state of sin, hath wholly

lost all ability of will to any spiritual good accompanying salvation . . . being altogether averse from that good, and dead to sin, is not able by his own strength, to convert himself, or to prepare himself thereunto." [65]

"U" stands for Unconditional Election: that God decides on no basis whatsoever but by the mystery of His will to save some, called the elect, and to allow all others to go to Hell even though He *could* save them *all* if He so desired.

The Canons of Dort declare: "That some receive the gift of faith from God, and others do not receive it proceeds from God's eternal decree . . . [by] which decree, he graciously softens the hearts of the elect, however obstinate, and inclines them to believe, while he leaves the non-elect in his just judgment to their own wickedness and obduracy." [66]

"L" stands for Limited Atonement: that these elect are the only ones for whom Christ died in payment of the penalty for their sins and that His death is efficacious for no others.

Dort declares: "For this was the sovereign counsel, and most gracious will and purpose of God the Father, that . . . the most precious death of his Son should extend to all the elect . . . all those, and those only, who were from eternity chosen to salvation . . . he purchased . . . by his death." [67]

"I" stands for Irresistible Grace: that God is able to cause whomever He will to respond to the gospel, that without this enabling no one could do so, and that He only provides this Irresistible Grace to the elect and damns the rest.

The Westminster Confession states: "All those whom God hath predestinated unto life, and those only, he is pleased, in his appointed and accepted time, effectually to call, by his Word and Spirit, out of that state of sin and death . . . effectually drawing them to Jesus Christ; yet so, as they come most freely, being made willing by his grace." [68]

"P" stands for Perseverance of the saints: that God will not allow any of the elect to lose the salvation which He has sovereignly given them.

The Westminster Confession states: "They, whom God hath accepted in his Beloved, effectually called, and sanctified by His Spirit, can neither totally nor finally fall away from the state of grace, but shall certainly persevere therein to the end, and be eternally saved. This perseverance of the saints depends not upon their own free will, but upon the immutability of the degree of election. [69]

William Cunningham speaks for most Calvinists when he writes that "No synod or council was ever held in the church, whose decisions, all things considered are entitled to more deference and respect [than the Synod of Dort]." [70] The Bible is our authority, not the beliefs of either John Calvin or Jacobus Arminius, or any council, synod, assembly, or creed. In the following pages, the points of TULIP are compared with the Bible, one point at a time, and in order.

1   Jacobus Arminius, *The Works of James Arminius,* trans. James and William Nichols (Baker Book House, 1986), I:26.
2   From the old *Edinburgh Encyclopedia* (Scotland: n.p.,n.d.); quoted in Arminius, op. cit., 1:306.
3   Laurence M. Vance, *The Other Side of Calvinism* (Vance Publications, Pensacola FL, rev. ed., 1999), 126.
4   Arminius, op. cit., 2:243-44.
5   Op. cit., 2:264-65.
6   Op. cit., 1:298.
7   Op. cit., 1:299.
8   Op. cit., 1:644.
9   Op. cit., 2:115-18, 138, 141-43, 145, etc.
10 Op. cit., 2:379.
11 Op. cit., 2:141.
12 Op. cit., 2:443
13 Op. cit., 2:387-88.
14 Op. cit., 2:157, 256; 1:659-60.
15 Op. cit., 1:102.
16 Op. cit., 1:741.
17 J.I. Packer, "*Sola Fide:* The Reformed Doctrine of Justification" (www.the-highway.com/ Justification_Packer.html).
18 Henry C. Sheldon, *History of Christian Doctrine* (Harper and Bros., 2nd ed. 1895), 2:34-35.
19 George L. Curtiss, *Arminianism in History* (Cranston and Curts, 1894), 10.
20 Arminius, op. cit., 1:103.
21 Op. cit., 2:81.
22 Op. cit., 2:623.
23 E.H. Broadbent, *The Pilgrim Church* (Gospel Folio Press, reprint 1999), 255.
24 Samuel Fisk, *Calvinistic Paths Retraced* (Biblical Evangelism Press, 1985), 120.
25 John T. McNeil, *Makers of the Christian Tradition* (Harper and Row, 1964), 221.
26 Arminius, op. cit., 1:329; 2:472-73.
27 Op. cit., 1:248.
28 Op. cit., 1:316-17.
29 Op. cit., 1:254; 2:497.
30 Albert H. Newman, *A Manual of Church History* (American Baptist Publication Society, 1933), 2:340.
31 Eusebius Pamphilius of Caesaria, advisor to Constantine, *The Life of Constantine* (n.p., c. A.D. 335), 3.62.
32 Philip Schaff, *History of the Christian Church* (Charles Scribner, 1910; Wm. B. Eerdmans Publishing Co., reprint 1959), 142.
33 Ibid.
34 William Jones, *The History of the Christian Church* (Church History Research and Archives, 5th ed. 1983), 1:306.
35 David Gay, *Battle for the Church: 1517-1644* (Brachus, 1997), 44.
36 Zane C. Hodges, "The New Puritanism, Pt. 2: Michael S. Horton: Holy War with Unholy Weapons" (*Journal of the Grace Evangelical Society*, Spring 1994), 6:11.
37 Curtiss, op. cit., 69.
38 Vance, 151-52.
39 From The Opinions of the Remonstrants (presented at Dordrecht, Holland), 1619.
40 A.W. Tozer, "The Sovereignty of God" (Christian Publications, 1997) Audiotape.
41 Quoted in full in Vance, op. cit., 153-54.

42 Quoted in Arminius, op. cit., I:lxiii.

43 Vance, op. cit., 158-59.

44 Herman Hanko, "Total Depravity," in Herman Hanko, Homer C. Hoeksema, and Gise J. Van Baren, *The Five Points of Calvinism* (Reformed Free Publishing Association, 1976), 10.

45 Arthur C. Custance, *The Sovereignty of Grace* (Presbyterian and Reformed Publishing Co., 1979), 71.

46 Earle E. Cairns, *Christianity Through the Centuries: A History of the Christian Church* (Zondervan Publishing, 1981), 325.

47 Cited in Vance, 148.

48 Louis Berkhof, *The History of Christian Doctrines* (Baker Book House, 1937), 152.

49 Homer Hoeksema, *The Voice of Our Fathers* (Reformed Free Publishing Association, 1980), 114.

50 William Cunningham, *The Reformers and the Theology of the Reformation* (Banner of Truth Trust, 1967), 2:381; cited in Vance, op. cit., 153.

51 M. Howard Rienstra, "The History and Development of Calvinism in Scotland and England," in Bratt, ed., *The Rise and Development of Calvinism*, 110; cited in Vance, op. cit., 159.

52 Vance, op. cit.

53 Alfred W. Pollard, ed., *Records of the English Bible*, Oxford University Press, 1911), 1.

54 H. Maynard Smith, *Pre-Reformation England* (Russell and Russell, 1963), 289.

55 Paul L. Hughes and James F. Larkin, eds., *Tudor Royal Proclamations* (Yale University Press, 1964), 1:374.

56 Vance, op. cit., 167.

57 William S. Barker, "The Men and Parties of the Assembly," in John L. Carson and David W. Hall, eds., *To Glorify and Enjoy God: A Commemoration of the 350th Anniversary of the Westminster Assembly*, 52; cited in Vance, op. cit., 171.

58 Vance, op. cit., 172.

59 John T. McNeil, *The History and Character of Calvinism* (Oxford University Press, 1966), 324.

60 Samuel T. Logan, "The Context and Work of the Assembly," in Carson and Hall, op. cit., 36.

61 John R. de Witt, "The Form of Church Government," in op. cit., 148.

62 Philip Schaff, *The Creeds of Christendom* (Baker Book House, 1990), 1:730.

63 G.T. Bettany, *A Popular History of the Reformation and Modern Protestantism* (Ward, Lock and Bowden, Ltd, 1895), 414-20.

64 Philip F. Congdon, "Soteriological Implications of Five-point Calvinism" (*Journal of the Grace Evangelical Society*, Autumn 1995), 8:15, 55-68.

65 Westminster Confession of Faith (London: n.p., 1643), VI:i,ii,iv; IX:iii.

66 Canons of Dort (Dordrecht, Holland, 1619), 1:6.

67 Op. cit., II:8.

68 Westminster, op. cit., X:I.

69 Op. cit., XVII:i,ii.

70 William Cunningham, *Historical Theology* (Still Waters Revival Books, n.d.), 2:379.

7
Total Depravity

Of the ten words making up the acronym TULIP, four (total, depravity, unconditional and irresistible) are not even found in the Bible and two (limited and perseverance) are each found only once. As for the phrases expressed by each letter (Total Depravity, Unconditional Election, Limited Atonement, Irresistible Grace and Perseverance of the Saints), *none* of them appears anywhere from the beginning of Genesis to the end of Revelation! We have, therefore, good cause to be at least cautious in approaching these key Calvinist concepts. The burden is upon their promoters to show that these ideas, in spite of their absence from Scripture, are indeed taught there.

More than the spelling of the word TULIP gives the doctrine of Total Depravity its first place. Calvinism offers a special definition of human depravity: that depravity equals inability – and this special definition necessitates both Unconditional Election and Irresistible Grace. As the Canons of Dort declare, "Therefore all men . . . without the regenerating grace of the Holy Spirit . . . are neither able nor willing to return to God . . . nor to dispose themselves to reformation." [1] That statement is an expression of human opinion without biblical support.

It is, in fact, unreasonable to say that a person is unwilling to do what he is unable to do. There is no way either to prove or to disprove the statement. How can it be said, for example, that a man is unwilling to fly like a bird? If he were able he might very well be willing. One thing is sure: his alleged unwillingness to fly like a bird cannot be blamed as the reason he doesn't do so. Nor can he be held accountable for failing to fly so long as flying is impossible for him. Yet Calvinism is guilty of both absurdity and injustice by declaring man to be incapable of repentance and faith, then condemning him for failing to repent and believe.

Calvinism's Admitted Irrationality

Such undeniable contradictions are innate within Calvinism and have caused divisions among Calvinists, who cannot agree among themselves on the fine points of TULIP. Consider the controversy over the fitness for ordination of Gordon H. Clark. "Cornelius Van Til led the seminary faculty in a *Complaint* against Clark's understanding of the Confession of Faith." [2] In essence, Clark was accused of "rationalism" for his unwillingness to pretend that salvation was sincerely offered by God to those whom God, according to Calvinism, had consigned to the blindness of total depravity. Clark considered it to be a direct contradiction that God could seek the salvation of those "He has from eternity determined not to save."

A similar controversy which originated among the faculty at Calvin Seminary "had plagued the Christian Reformed Church during the 1920's . . . [and in 1924] ended with the exodus of the Calvinists from the Christian Reformed Church under the leadership of Herman Hoeksema, and the formation of a new church, the Protestant Reformed Church." [3] Van Til, in disagreement with the Westminster Confession, argued that Clark was making "logic rule over Scripture . . ." Van Til insisted that Scripture contains irreconcilable paradoxes which "have of necessity the appearance of being contradictory." [4]

Attempting to escape the irrationality of blaming the non-elect for failing to do what they can't do, some Calvinists insist that man is able but simply not willing to turn to Christ. This is a minority view and partially correct. The problem with sinners is indeed unwillingness. For a person to be unwilling, however, he must have a will and thus by an act of that will could become willing. Furthermore, Calvin and his followers have declared in the clearest language that man is *unable* to believe the gospel, to turn to Christ or to seek God or good: "He is free to turn to Christ, but not able." [5] Inability is certainly the major view.

There is not a verse in the Bible, however, which presents Calvinism's radical idea that the sinner is incapable of believing the very gospel which offers him forgiveness and salvation and yet he is condemned by God for failing to believe. In fact, as we shall see, the Bible declares otherwise. "All men everywhere" (Acts 17:30) are repeatedly called upon to repent and to believe on Christ. One would never derive from Scripture the idea that the unregenerate are unable to believe. Dave Breese, highly respected and brilliant author and expositor of Scripture, declared that it "cannot be shown that 'total depravity' is in fact a scriptural truth." [6]

Yet Talbot and Crampton write, "The Bible stresses the total inability of fallen man to respond to the things of God . . . . This is what the Calvinist refers to as '*total depravity*.' " [7] Palmer calls this doctrine "the most central issue between the Arminian and the Calvinist, what Martin Luther even said was the hinge on which the whole Reformation turned." [8]

As a consequence of the above, the Calvinist insists that regeneration must precede salvation: "once he [the sinner] is born again, he can *for the first time* turn to Jesus . . . asking Jesus to save him" [emphasis added]. [9] R.C. Sproul declares, "A cardinal point of Reformed theology is the maxim, 'Regeneration precedes faith.' " [10] Nowhere in Scripture, however, is there a suggestion that man must be *regenerated before* he can be saved by faith in Christ. Indeed, many scriptures declare the opposite, for example: " . . . to make thee wise unto salvation through faith which is in Christ Jesus" (2 Timothy 3:15), and "ye are all the children of God by faith in Christ Jesus" (Galatians 3:26). Faith *always* precedes salvation/regeneraton. There is not one scripture which states clearly the doctrine that regeneration comes first and then faith follows – *not one*.

Nevertheless, viewing depravity as inability, which necessitates regeneration before salvation, is the very foundation of Calvinism. Engelsma acknowledges, "Deny this doctrine and the whole of Calvinism is demolished." [11] To be fair, we must, says Engelsma, "let Calvinism speak for itself." [12] That is exactly what I am trying to do.

Inasmuch as Total Depravity requires regeneration *before* faith or salvation, the Calvinist assumes it could take place – and probably does – in infancy. Thus Hoeksema reasons that "regeneration can take place in the smallest of infants . . . in the sphere of the covenant of God, He usually regenerates His elect children from infancy." [13] One would therefore expect that the children of Calvinists would behave in a sanctified way far different from other children, but that cannot be shown to be the case.

Depravity Equals Inability?

Most Christians, if asked whether man by nature is totally depraved, would likely respond in the affirmative with, perhaps, some reservation concerning the word "totally." However, the Calvinists' view of the obvious sinfulness of mankind goes far beyond the average Christian's ordinary understanding of depravity. As another leading Calvinist states, "Paul's assessment of persons apart from Christ may justly be summed up in the theological categories of 'total depravity' and 'total inability.' " [14]

The idea that depravity is inability may seem at first to be reasonable, but what does it mean? An *inability*, to be meaningful, must indicate the absence of some particular *ability*. We are told that total depravity causes an inability which prevents every man, woman, boy and girl from believing the gospel or responding to God in any way except by rejection and rebellion. What, then, is the particular ability which is lacking?

The Bible repeatedly presents man's sinfulness and warns that rejecting the salvation God has provided in Christ leaves the sinner to suffer eternal punishment under the wrath of God. Never, however, does the Bible suggest that because of Adam's original sin all of his descendants lack the ability to turn to God through faith in Christ. Indeed, the Bible is filled with invitations to all men to repent toward God and to believe on Christ to the saving of their souls. Paul went everywhere preaching to everyone he encountered throughout the Roman Empire "repentance toward God, and faith toward our Lord Jesus Christ" (Acts 20:21). Apparently he believed that anyone could respond, not just a few elect whom God had sovereignly without any faith on their part regenerated and then given them faith to believe.

In fact, *all* are *commanded* to repent and turn to Christ. As Paul declared on Mars' Hill in Athens, God "commandeth all men everywhere to repent" (Acts 17:30). To say that God commands men to do what they cannot do without His grace, then withholds the grace they need and punishes them eternally for failing to obey, is to make a mockery of God's Word, of His mercy and love, and is to libel His character. Rather than affirming any inability, the psalmist declares, "The wicked, through the pride of his countenance, will not seek after God" (Psalms 10:4).

It is neither stated in Scripture nor does it follow logically that anyone, as a result of his depravity, even if his every thought is evil, is thereby unable to believe the glad tidings of the gospel and receive Christ as his Savior. Here once again we find ourselves under the long shadow of Augustine's influence. As noted earlier, it is claimed that Augustine was "perhaps the first after Paul to realize the Total Depravity of man"; [15] indeed, that Augustine invented "the exaggerated doctrine of total human depravity . . . ." [16] In reading the *Institutes*, one feels compelled to ask whether Calvin relied more upon Augustine than upon the Bible.

This turning of depravity into a special kind of inability is never stated in the Bible but comes from human reasoning. Once arrived at, however, it leads inevitably to points 2 and 4: that God must unconditionally elect those who will be saved; and that He must effect that work through irresistible grace. Yet even the claim of inability turns out to be misleading.

What Ability Is Needed To Receive A Gift?

The Bible makes it clear that salvation is the *gift* of God through Jesus Christ, and thus no one can purchase, earn or merit his salvation. It must be received as a free gift. What ability of any kind is required to receive a gift? None, of course. Then how can any sinner suffer from an inability to receive the free gift of eternal life?

Unquestionably, to receive the gift of salvation one must believe the gospel. Never does the Bible declare this to be impossible for the natural man. The very command, "Go ye into all the world, and preach the gospel to every creature" (Mark 16:15) implies the ability of every person to believe the gospel. Indeed, that everyone knows the truth of God's existence, his moral responsibility to God and his breach of the moral laws, is stated repeatedly in Scripture:

> The heavens declare the glory of God; and the firmament sheweth his handywork . . . . There is no speech nor language, where their voice is not heard. (Psalms 19:1-3)

> For the wrath of God is revealed from heaven against all ungodliness and unrighteousness of men, who hold the truth in unrighteousness; because that which may be known of God is manifest in them; for God hath shewed it unto them. For the invisible things of him from the creation of the world are clearly seen, being understood by the things that are made, even his eternal power and Godhead; so that they are without excuse . . . .

> For when the Gentiles, which have not the law, do by nature the things contained in the law, these, having not the law (i.e., given to the Jews through Moses), . . . shew the work of the law written in their hearts, their conscience also bearing witness, and their thoughts the mean while accusing or else excusing one another . . . . (Romans 1:18-2:15)

> For the grace of God that bringeth salvation hath appeared to all men . . . . (Titus 2:11)

Yes, "the natural man receiveth not the things of the Spirit of God: for they are foolishness unto him: neither can he know them, because they are spiritually discerned" (1 Corinthians 2:14). However, this cannot be speaking of the gospel. In scores of places the gospel is plainly offered to the whole world. That Paul does not here have the gospel in mind is clear from the context. Paul is not referring to the gospel that is to be preached to all mankind, but to "the wisdom of God in a mystery, even the hidden wisdom, which God ordained before the world unto our [the believers'] glory . . . the things which God hath prepared for them that love him . . . the deep things of God . . . the things that are freely given to us of God . . . which the Holy Ghost teacheth . . . [which] are spiritually discerned" (1 Corinthians 2:7-16).

In contrast to those deeper spiritual truths which can be understood only through God's Spirit indwelling the believer, the gospel can be understood by sinners. Yes, it can only be as the Holy Spirit convicts and convinces "of sin, and of righteousness, and of judgment," but Christ said He would bring that reproving conviction upon the whole world (John 16:7-11). As Paul reminded his converts at Thessalonica, "For our gospel came not unto you in word only, but also in power, and in the Holy Ghost, and in much assurance . . . " (1 Thessalonians 1:5). Indeed, Christ says that the Holy Spirit will "reprove the world of sin . . . because they believe not on me" (John 16:7-11). Surely for unbelief to be sin the sinner must understand what he is rejecting and have the capacity to repent and to believe the gospel.

Just as no ability is required on the part of the endangered person to be rescued from drowning or from a burning building, or on the part of the imprisoned criminal who is pardoned to accept his release, so no ability is required of the person whom Christ rescues from eternal condemnation. Thus Calvinism's very foundation in its special definition of human depravity as inability is as unreasonable as it is unbiblical. In fact, Calvinists disagree among themselves as to the reason for and extent of this alleged inability.

Born Again Before Salvation?

Explaining Calvinism carefully, Palmer reiterates that no man can understand the gospel and that this "lack of understanding is also a part of man's depravity . . . all minds are blind, unless they are regenerated." [17] The thoroughly Calvinistic London Baptist Confession of 1689 stated, "As a consequence of his fall into a state of sin, man . . . is not able, by any strength of his own, to turn himself to God, or even to prepare himself to turn to God." [18] According to the Bible, however, and according to Christ himself, man's problem is not inability. Men fail to come to Christ not because they *cannot*, but because they *will not*: "And ye will not come to me, that ye might have life" (John 5:40).

James White devotes an entire chapter to "The Inabilities of Man." He recites a long list of man's sins, of his evil, of his depravity and explains that he is a "*fallen creature*, a slave to sin, spiritually dead, incapable of doing what is pleasing to God." He cites many scriptures concerning man's estrangement from God and the deceitfulness of his heart, that he can no more change his heart than the leopard can change his spots, that his mind is hostile toward God, that no man can come to Christ except the Father draw him, and so forth. White declares, "The Reformed assertion is that man cannot understand *and embrace* the gospel nor respond in *faith and repentance* toward Christ without God first freeing him from sin and giving him spiritual life (regeneration). [19] Nowhere, however, does he cite a scripture that declares man's *inability* to believe the gospel or to receive the free gift of eternal life which God offers to all.

Calvinists can, of course, find many scriptures describing man's evil heart and practices. None of these scriptures, however, states that a man cannot believe the gospel unless he is one of the elect and has been given that faith by a sovereign act of God. Pink declares that "the sinner, of himself, *cannot* repent and believe." [20] For all of their insistence upon man's inability to believe the gospel and to receive Christ, however, Calvinists cannot agree among themselves. J.I. Packer contradicts his fellow Calvinists (and what he himself says elsewhere) in declaring that regeneration *follows* faith and justification: "God elected men from eternity in order that in due time they might be justified, upon their believing. Their adoption as God's sons follows upon their justification; it is, indeed, no more than the positive outworking of God's justifying sentence." [21]

As we have seen, defining depravity as inability requires God to sovereignly *regenerate* man, and without any recognition, understanding or faith on man's part, bring him to spiritual life. Only then can He give man the faith to believe the gospel. As Dort, quoted above, says, " . . . without the regenerating grace of the Holy Spirit, they are neither able nor willing to return to God . . . ." [22] *Enabling* grace is needed for faith, but not *"regenerating* grace." Where does the Bible say one must be *regenerated* before one can believe the gospel? Not one verse can be cited where that proposition is stated clearly.

Most non-Calvinists have thought that being "born again," as Christ presented it to Nicodemus in John 3, is the same as being saved. Therefore, they are shocked and astounded to learn that Calvinism teaches that one must experience the new birth which Christ describes in John 3 *before* one can be saved. As Sproul emphasizes once again, "The Reformed view of predestination teaches that before a person can choose Christ . . . he must be born again . . . one does not first believe, then become reborn . . . ." [23] This is nothing more than human reasoning. In fact, the Bible always presents faith as the condition of salvation.

The Appalling Consequences

Acceptance of this theory, however, leads to a corollary which is even more unbiblical as well as appalling to the innate sense of compassion which God has placed within even unregenerate man: that God *could* save all mankind but deliberately withholds from multitudes the salvation He gives to the elect. Obviously, what God does for the elect He could do for all if He so desired. That He doesn't would prove that the One who *is love* lacks love for all mankind — which is contrary to *all* Scripture: "But the wisdom that is from above is . . . easy to be entreated, full of mercy . . . without partiality . . . " (James 3:17).

If lost sinners suffer from such an inability that they can be saved only by God's sovereign act of regeneration (and all men are not saved), it follows that God limits His mercy and grace to a *select few*. As one of the most fervent Calvinists, Arthur W. Pink, writes to the elect, "Then do you not see that it is due to no lack of power in God . . . that *other rebels* are not saved too? If God was able to subdue *your* will and win *your* heart, and that *without* interfering with your moral responsibility, then is He not able to do the same for others [i.e., the non-elect]? Assuredly He is." [24]   But He doesn't. Why?

Here we confront a major problem with Calvinism: its denial of God's infinite love for all. That God would choose to save only a select few and leave the rest to suffer eternal damnation would be contrary to His very nature of infinite love and mercy as the Bible presents Him, and as shall be documented in the process of examining Calvinism from Scripture. Incredibly, however, the very damnation of perhaps billions is said by the Calvinist to have been foreordained from eternity past because it pleases and glorifies God! The Westminster Confession of Faith, paraphrasing Calvin himself, declares:

> By the decree of God, for the manifestation of his glory, some men and angels are predestinated unto everlasting life; and others foreordained to everlasting death . . . . Those of mankind that are predestinated unto life, God . . . hath chosen in Christ unto everlasting glory . . . to the praise of his glorious grace . . . . The rest of mankind, God was pleased, according to the unsearchable counsel of his own will . . . for the glory of his sovereign power over his creatures . . . to ordain them to dishonor and wrath for their sin, to the praise of his glorious justice. [25]

Even Sproul admits, "If some people are not elected unto salvation then it would seem that God is not at all that loving toward them. Further. it seems that it would have been more loving of God not to have allowed them to be born. That may indeed be the case." [26] God's love, however, is infinite and perfect. It is therefore an oxymoron to suggest that God was ever toward anyone "not all that loving" and might "have been more loving." No Calvinist has ever satisfactorily explained such lack of love with which God is charged. Who could fail to be gravely concerned for this gross misrepresentation of our loving God!

The great Apostle Paul could declare unequivocally, "I am not ashamed of the gospel of Christ!" It almost sounds as though Sproul has some reservations concerning the gospel according to Calvinism. If the gospel is not good news to everyone, but only to the elect, is that cause for us to be ashamed of a God who is less than loving to all? Paul did not have the problem of believing that God was "not all that loving."

Which Comes First, Salvation Or Faith?

Nowhere from Genesis to Revelation does the Bible teach that sinful man, without first being regenerated, is incapable of repenting of his sins, turning to God and believing the gospel. On the contrary, it is all too clear that faith precedes salvation and is in fact a condition of salvation. There are scores of verses declaring that we are saved through faith, through believing on the Lord Jesus Christ as He is presented in the gospel. This sequence of events is undeniable:

. . . then cometh the devil, and taketh away the word out of their hearts, lest they should believe and be saved . . . . (Luke 8:12)

He that believeth . . . shall be saved . . . . (Mark 16:16)

Believe on the Lord Jesus Christ, and thou shalt be saved . . . . (Acts 16:31)

I am not ashamed of the gospel of Christ: for it is the power of God unto salvation to every one that believeth . . . . (Romans 1:16)

Moreover, brethren, I declare unto you the gospel which I preached unto you, which also ye have received, . . . by which also ye are saved, . . . unless ye have believed in vain. (1 Corinthians 15:1-2)

For by grace are ye saved through faith . . . . (Ephesians 2:8)

. . . for a pattern to them which should hereafter believe on him to life everlasting. (1 Timothy 1:16).

How then can one maintain that regeneration must precede faith and thus salvation? In order to support this doctrine it must be proved that the new birth is distinct from salvation, that being born again is different from and precedes being saved. For this, there is no biblical backing.

In numerous places the Bible declares that upon believing in Christ according to the gospel we receive eternal life from God as a free gift: " . . . that whosoever believeth in him should . . . have everlasting life (John 3:16); He that heareth . . . and believeth . . . hath everlasting life . . . (5:24); . . . that ye might believe that Jesus is the Christ, the Son of God; and that believing ye might have life through his name" (20:31). Believing is obviously a condition for receiving the gift of eternal life. Could one be "regenerated" and remain unsaved?

The Bible clearly teaches that the moment one believes in and receives the Lord Jesus Christ as the Savior who died for one's sins, that person has been born (regenerated of the Spirit of God) into the family of God and has thereby become a child of God. Surely there are not two kinds of life which God freely gives to sinners through regeneration. The eternal life received as a free gift through believing in Christ can only be the same life one receives upon being born again. Christ speaks to Nicodemus first of being born again. Then, in explaining the new birth, He refers to eternal or everlasting life which is received by believing in Him and His sacrifice on the cross. Was He changing the subject?

Certainly Christ gives Nicodemus no reason to believe that the life of God received from the Holy Spirit through the new birth differs in any way from the eternal life one receives by faith in Him. The fact that eternal life comes through faith and that eternal life is only by the new birth indicates quite clearly that faith precedes regeneration. Believing in Christ unto salvation is not the result of regeneration but the cause of it.

Verse after verse, in the plainest possible language, puts believing *before* regeneration. Repeatedly we are told that believing the word of truth, the gospel, is the means of regeneration. Paul tells his children in the faith, "in Christ Jesus I have begotten you through the gospel" (1 Corinthians 4:15), while Peter declares that we are "born again . . . by the word of God" (1 Peter 1:23).

Being born again by the Word of God can only refer to regeneration, but the Word of God is effectual only to those who believe. Paul declares under the inspiration of God, "faith cometh by hearing, and hearing by the word of God" (Romans 10:17) and he even calls it "the word of faith which we preach" (verse 7). Of those who are lost, we are told that "the word preached did not profit them, not being mixed with faith" (Hebrews 4:2).

On the basis of abundant testimony from Scripture, we can only conclude that faith in Christ through the gospel precedes regeneration. Therefore, the new birth does not take place by an act of God apart from a person's understanding of and faith in the gospel but as a result thereof. The doctrine that one must be born again (regenerated) before one can believe is simply not biblical.

Even Spurgeon, in spite of his claim to being a staunch Calvinist, could not accept the teaching that regeneration came before faith in Christ through the gospel. Calvinists quote him when he supports them, but they ignore statements such as the following:

> If I am to preach faith in Christ to a man who is regenerated, then the man, being regenerated, is saved already, and it is an unnecessary and ridiculous thing for me to preach Christ to him, and bid him to believe in order to be saved when he is saved already, being regenerate. Am I only to preach faith to those who have it? Absurd, indeed! Is not this waiting till the man is cured and then bringing him the medicine? This is preaching Christ to the righteous and not to sinners. [27]

Biblical Support For Total Depravity?

The words "total" and "depravity," as already noted, are not found in the Bible. Of course, neither is the word "trinity," but the Bible overwhelmingly teaches that doctrine. The Bible does not, however, teach the inability of Total Depravity as defined in Calvinism: that all men are by nature unable to believe the gospel.

To show that the Bible does indeed teach total depravity as inability, the Calvinist cites such scriptures as "And GOD saw that the wickedness of man was great in the earth, and that every imagination of the thoughts of his heart was only evil continually" (Genesis 6:5; 8:21). Other verses offered in alleged proof of this doctrine include Jeremiah 17:9, "The heart is deceitful above all things, and desperately wicked," and Romans 3:10-18, "There is none righteous

... none that seeketh after God ... none that doeth good ... no fear of God before their eyes," and so forth.

Obviously, however, that man's thoughts are only evil continually, that his heart is desperately wicked and deceitful, and that he neither seeks nor fears God, does not say that he is therefore unable, unless first of all regenerated by God, to believe the gospel even if convicted and convinced thereof by the Holy Spirit. Paul teaches otherwise: "ye were the servants of sin, but ye have obeyed from the heart that form of doctrine which was delivered you" (Romans 6:17). Clearly, servants of sin responded to the command to repent and believe in Christ — then they were saved, regenerated, changed.

Nor does the statement that "none seeks after God" deny that any man, no matter how depraved, can respond by intelligent choice without first being regenerated if God seeks and draws him. Neither does the Bible teach that God only seeks and draws an "elect" but no others. Indeed, many passages affirm that under the drawing of the Holy Spirit sinful man *can* make a moral response: "Draw me, we will run after thee" (Song of Solomon 1:4); "And ye shall seek me, and find me, when ye shall search for me with all your heart" (Jeremiah 29:13); " ... he [God] is a rewarder of them that diligently seek him" (Hebrews 11:6). Even the wicked are commanded to turn unto the Lord, with never so much as a hint that this is impossible until God first regenerates them (Isaiah 55:6-7).

Yes, God was speaking to "Israel mine elect" in Isaiah 45:4, but most of them did not heed His call. Furthermore, that this offer is not just for a select elect is clear. The "everyone that thirsteth" reminds one of Christ's cry, "If any man thirst, let him come unto me, and drink" (John 7:37). All those who thirst are offered the same "living water" which Christ offered to the woman at the well (John 4:10). And it is with this same promise to *whosoever will* that the Bible ends: "And whosoever will, let him take of the water of life freely" (Revelation 22:17).

The universality of God's offer of salvation is presented repeatedly throughout the Bible; for example: "Look unto me, and be ye saved, all the ends of the earth ... " (Isaiah 45:22). It would take considerable manipulation to maintain that the offer of salvation is extended only to the elect, or even that only the elect could respond, and even then not until they had been sovereignly regenerated. Paul confirms this desire of God for all nations when he declares to the Greek philosophers on Mars' Hill:

> God that made the world and all things therein ... hath made of one blood all nations of men for to dwell on all the face of the earth, and hath determined the times before appointed, and the bounds of their habitation;

That they should seek the Lord, if haply they might feel after him, and find him, though he be not far from every one of us:

For in him we live, and move, and have our being; as certain also of your own poets have said . . . . (Acts 17:24-28)

Is it really possible that Paul's "all nations of men" and "every one of us" and "we" referred to an elect of whom the Greeks had never heard? On the contrary, Paul is clearly including his listeners and antagonists on Mars' Hill as among those who have their physical life and being from God and who may seek and find Him. This was what the Greek poets to whom he refers had said (surely these philosophers were not referring to the elect), and Paul is affirming that general understanding and declaring the person of the true God to them, a God who is "not far from every one of us," who commands all men to seek Him, and who may be found by all.

Is There A Bias At Work?

If God intends that all mankind seek Him, and if He must be sought before He is found, then we can only conclude that those who have not yet found God and thus are not yet regenerated are capable of a genuine seeking after God as he draws *all men* unto Him (John 12:32). Calvinism's conclusion, that man must be regenerated before he can believe or even seek God, is contrary to the clear teaching of Scripture. This is dealt with in more depth in subsequent chapters.

Calvinists often cite John 1:13 as proof that man's inability as totally depraved requires that he must first be regenerated before he can believe the gospel or receive Christ as his Savior. It speaks of those "Which were born, not of blood, nor of the will of the flesh, nor of the will of man, but of God." Commenting on this verse, Calvin writes, "Hence it follows, first, that faith does not proceed from ourselves, but is the fruit of spiritual regeneration; for the Evangelist affirms that no man can believe, unless he be begotten of God; and therefore faith is a heavenly gift." [28] In fact, Calvin's conclusion doesn't follow at all from this passage. Far from deriving his belief from the text, he is reading into it something not there in order to support his peculiar doctrine.

The context makes John's meaning quite clear; "He came unto his own, and his own received him not. But as many as received him, to them gave he power [the right or privilege] to become the sons of GOD, even to them that believe on his name" (verses 11-12). His own people, the Jews, rejected Christ. In contrast, however, to those who did not receive Him, all those who did receive Him and believe on His name are, *as a result of receiving Him and believing*, given the right to become the sons of God. This new birth (verse 13) by an act of God regenerating them into His family through His Spirit is for those who have received Christ and believed "on his name" (verse 12). Calvin's conclusion could not be refuted more clearly than John does: that faith in Christ and receiving Him precede regeneration! We deal with this in more depth in Chapter 21.

Is God Sincere?

If the doctrine of Total Depravity as defined in TULIP were true, then from Genesis to Revelation we have a God who pleads for thousands of years with a seemingly endless procession of billions of individuals to repent and turn to Him, individuals who are so hopelessly depraved that they can do nothing except persist in rebellion against Him unless He regenerates them. If He really wants those with whom He pleads to repent and turn to Him, would God not give them the necessary grace to do so? He does that for the elect. Why not for all?

If man cannot respond without God's sovereign act of regeneration, then all of God's pleas are obviously useless. There is no question that if Calvinism were true, there would be no reason for God to urge men to repent — yet He does. God's sovereign act of regeneration is alleged to require no faith or participation of any kind on man's part. Thus the entire history of God's dealings with man as recorded in the Bible loses credibility.

Calvinism drives us into an irrational dead end. It is both useless and senseless for God to plead with the elect. He has already predestined them to salvation and will effect it sovereignly *before* any faith is exercised on their part. Nor does it make any better sense for God to present the gospel to and plead with the non-elect who *cannot* believe it until they have been sovereignly regenerated — but that won't happen because they are damned by God's eternal decree. Yet He continues to plead and blame them for not repenting even while He withholds from them the essential grace which He gives only to the elect! Such is the unbiblical and unreasonable misrepresentation of God by Calvinism.

Calvin's Inconsistency

In his discussions of Total Depravity, Calvin sometimes seemed confused and unable to articulate his ideas well. He theorized that totally depraved man naturally loves truth, *but not enough*; still he has great gifts from his Creator, and everyone should know that whatever truth he has comes from God — yet he cannot fully know the truth and thus be saved. One is left to wonder about the exact meaning of this terminology and where it is stated in Scripture. At other times Calvin further contradicts himself concerning this key doctrine and in some places even indicates that "total" doesn't *really* mean total. For example, Calvin engaged in the following confusing speculation which seems to teeter on the brink of Total Depravity, fall over the edge at times, then recover itself:

The human mind . . . is naturally influenced by the love of truth [but] this love of truth fails before it reaches the goal [yet] man's efforts are not always so utterly fruitless as not to lead to some result . . . and intelligence naturally implanted . . . should lead every individual for himself to recognize it as a special gift of God . . . .

Therefore . . . the human mind, however much fallen and perverted from its original integrity, is still adorned and invested with admirable gifts from its Creator. If we reflect that the Spirit of God is the only fountain of truth, we will be careful, as we would avoid offering insult to him, not to reject or contemn truth wherever it appears. In despising the gifts, we insult the Giver . . . .

He . . . by the virtue of the Spirit . . . has been pleased to assist us . . . with great talents for the investigation of truth [but] not based on a solid foundation of truth . . . . The Lord has bestowed on [philosophers] some slight perception of his Godhead, that they might not plead ignorance as an excuse for their impiety, and has, at times, instigated them to deliver some truths, the confession of which should be their own condemnation . . . . Their discernment was not such as to direct them to the truth, far less to enable them to attain it, but resembled that of the bewildered traveler . . . .

An Apostle declares, "When the Gentiles . . . do by nature the things contained in the law, these . . . shew the work of the law written in their hearts . . . " (Romans 2:14-15) [so] we certainly cannot say that they are altogether blind . . . . Nothing, indeed, is more common, than for man to be sufficiently instructed in a right course of conduct by natural law . . . . The end of the natural law, therefore, is to render man inexcusable . . . . [29]

Confusion and contradictions reign here. Is man totally depraved or isn't he? And if he is, exactly what does that mean? That the natural man doesn't understand the things of God unless they are revealed to him by God cannot be denied — the Bible says so. That is true of everything we have; it all comes from God:

... he giveth to all life, and breath, and all things . . . for in him we live, and move, and have our being . . . . (Acts 17:25, 28)

Every good gift and every perfect gift is from above, and cometh down from the Father of lights, with whom is no variableness, neither shadow of turning. (James 1:17)

But without biblical warrant, Calvin introduces the idea of degrees: All men by nature receive much truth from God, but in varying degrees. Most of them just don't receive enough — such grace is only for the elect. Unregenerate man can see, yet he is blind, but not *totally* blind. What exactly does Calvin mean? We are left to wonder.

Faced With A Choice

Calvinists object to the assertion that the natural man is "not *so* totally depraved that he can't hear God's voice and come to Christ." They respond, "Totally depraved is totally depraved. It makes no sense to say man isn't *so* totally depraved." Not only is Total Depravity not a biblical concept, but as the quote above shows, Calvin *himself* said that man is not *so* totally depraved that he cannot receive much truth from God; he just doesn't get enough truth because God withholds it. Why? Calvin says God withholds truth in order "to render man inexcusable . . . ." That is like crippling a man to render him inexcusable for failing to run fast enough and to jump high enough!

Calvin says that truth comes only from the Spirit of truth, so whatever truth man has is received from God. Then if God gives man some truth, why doesn't He give him enough to know and seek God? Is God limited, that He can only give a limited amount of truth? Surely God can give man as much truth as He desires to give. Calvin cannot show us that man naturally has a capacity for *this* much truth but not for *that* much. How was *depravity* redefined as an *incapacity* which isn't total but is just enough to damn the soul? There is nothing anywhere in Scripture to support such speculation.

When Peter confessed to Jesus, "Thou art the Christ," Jesus told him, "Flesh and blood hath not revealed it unto thee, but my Father which is in heaven (Matthew 16:15-17). Peter must have been a totally depraved natural man when the Father revealed Christ to him. Surely he hadn't yet been born of the Spirit. Though he acknowledged Jesus as the Christ, he still lacked any understanding about Christ dying for his sins. Could not the Father, therefore, reveal Christ to everyone as He did to Peter? Why not? Clearly Peter had a revelation from the Father concerning Christ before he was regenerated.

For all the importance Calvinism places upon the doctrine of Total Depravity, inasmuch as that is the condition of all mankind and the elect are delivered out of it, being totally depraved is not what keeps men in darkness after all, but God's withholding the needed light. The lost are kept out of heaven not by their sin, but by God withholding the grace they need for salvation, because He has already predestined them to eternal torment.

Given what the Bible tells us of God's dealings with man and Calvinism's doctrine of man's inability to believe, there are only two choices: either to charge the Infinite God with acting insincerely and in limited love and limited grace, or to admit that Calvinism is in error. In fact, this leads to another conclusion just as devastating to Calvinism, to be considered in the next chapter.

1   Canons of Dort (Dordrecht, Holland, 1619), III, IV:3.
2   Garrett P. Johnson, "The Myth of Common Grace," *The Trinity Review*, March/April 1987), 1.
3   Ibid.
4   Cornelius Van Til, *Common Grace and the Gospel* (Presbyterian and Reformed Publishing Company, 1973), 165-66; cited in Johnson, op. cit.
5   Frank B. Beck, *The Five Points of Calvinism* (Covenanter Press, 2nd Australian ed., 1986), 9.
6   Dave Breese, "The Five Points of Calvinism" (self-published paper, n.d.).
7   Kenneth G. Talbot and W. Gary Crampton, *Calvinism, Hyper-Calvinism and Arminianism* (Still Waters Revival Books, 1990), 20.
8   Edwin H. Palmer, *the five points of calvinism* (Baker Books, enlarged ed., 20th prtg. 1999), 19; citing Martin Luther, *The Bondage of the Will*, trans. J.I. Packer and O.R. Johnston (Fleming H. Revell, 1957), 319.
9   Palmer, op .cit., 19.
10 R.C. Sproul, *Chosen by God* (Tyndale House Publishers, Inc., 1986), 10.
11 David J. Engelsma, "The Death of Confessional Calvinism in Scottish Presbyterianism" (*Standard Bearer*, December 1, 1992), 103.
12 David J. Engelsma, *A Defense of Calvinism as the Gospel* (The Evangelism Committee, Protestant Reformed Church, n.d.), 18.
13 Homer Hoeksema, *Reformed Dogmatics* (Reformed Free Publishing Association, 1966), 464.
14 Douglas Moo, *The Epistle to the Romans* (Wm. B. Eerdmans Publishing Co., 1996), 488.
15 Arthur C. Custance, *The Sovereignty of Grace* (Presbyterian and Reformed Publishing Co., 1979), 18.
16 Frederic W. Farrar, *History of Interpretation* (E.P. Dutton and Co., 1886), 24.
17 Palmer, op. cit., 16.
18 Quoted in *A Faith to Confess: The Baptist Confession of Faith of 1689, Rewritten in Modern English* (Carey Publications, 1986); cited in James R. White, *The Potter's Freedom* (Calvary Press Publishing, 2000), 78.
19 White, op. cit., 101.
20 Arthur W. Pink, *The Sovereignty of God* (Baker Book House, 2nd prtg. 1986), 149.
21 J.I. Packer, "*Sola Fide:* The Reformed Doctrine of Justification" (www.the-highway.com/Justification_Packer.html).
22 Dort, op. cit., III,IV:3.
23 Sproul, op. cit., 72.
24 Pink, op. cit., 50.
25 Westminster Confession of Faith (London: n.p., 1643), III:iii,v,vii.
26 Sproul, op.cit., 32.
27 C.H. Spurgeon, "The Warrant of Faith" (Pilgrim Publications, 1978), 3. One-sermon booklet from 63-volume set.
28 John Calvin, *Commentary on the Gospel According to John* (Baker Book House, 1984), 43; cited in White, op. cit., 182-83.
29 John Calvin, *Institutes of the Christian Religion*, trans. Henry Beveridge (Wm. B. Eerdmans Publishing Company, 1998 ed.), II:ii,12-22.

8
The Solemn Issue: God's Character

Why does God waste His time and effort and the time and effort of His many prophets pleading with those who, allegedly, cannot hear Him and who, even if they could, being totally depraved, would never respond to His appeal by believing and obeying Him? Why create this elaborate fiction of mourning and weeping over multitudes who God knows will not only refuse to repent but who, unless He regenerates them, *cannot* repent because of their total inability to do so? Pink argues that "to affirm that he [man] is a free agent is *to deny that he is totally depraved.* [1]

Why does the Holy Spirit through Scripture give the impression that God desires all men to repent while at the same time He withholds from all but a select few the essential means of repenting? Why would God weep over and plead with those He has predestined to eternal damnation? Beck declares, "He [man] is free to turn to Christ but not able." [2] That is like saying that man is free to go to Mars any time he pleases. Is this a joke? The Calvinist seems unaware of the contradiction in what he is saying. Bryson raises a logical question:

> And since the unregenerate are reprobate [predestined to damnation by God's decree] as a result of a choice made by God alone, how could they be responsible for their lostness . . . and inevitable damnation? [3]

It would be a mocking, a taunt for God to promise man that if he would earnestly and sincerely seek Him he would find Him, if in fact it were impossible for man to do so unless God regenerated him. As inspired by the Holy Spirit, however, the entire Bible from Genesis to Revelation gives the clear impression that those with whom God pleads could of their own volition repent and turn to Him if they would. Taking Scripture at face value, H.A. Ironside put it like this:

> The gospel preacher can declare without any kind of mental reservation the blessed fact that whosoever will, may take the water of life freely (Revelation 22:17). This is not at all a question of being *allowed* to take Christ as Saviour. It is an earnest entreaty to do so. (Emphasis added) [4]

Choice And Human Responsibility

Frederic Farrar has rightly said, what God commands "must be in the power of the will, since ability is the measurement of obligation." [5] G. Campbell Morgan stated firmly, "We cannot study this Bible without being brought face to face with personal responsibility . . . when the voice of God speaks, man's will is free to obey or to disobey." [6] Kenneth Foreman said, "If there is anything the Bible shows it is that God does hold men responsible for their actions. God's 'thou shalt' is spoken to free persons, not to puppets." [7]

Yet Gerstner astonishingly says, "It is your decision to choose or reject Christ, but it is not of your own free will." [8] How it can be my decision when I am not free to choose is meaningful only to Calvinists. To all others the statement is an obvious contradiction.

Calvinism clearly requires its own peculiar understanding. Pink wrote, "Those who speak of man's 'free will,' and insist upon his inherent power to either accept or reject the Saviour, do but voice their ignorance of the real condition of Adam's fallen children." [9] Yet Jesus clearly taught that the unregenerated man can indeed decide in his will to do God's will and thereby know the truth: "If any man will do [i.e., wills to do] his [God's] will, he shall know of the doctrine, whether it be of God, or whether I speak of myself" (John 7:17). He spoke this not to the elect but to the unregenerated multitude and rabbis who would soon crucify Him. Bishop J.C. Ryle, who stood so firmly against Romanism in England in the nineteenth century, commented:

> The English language here fails to give the full force of the Greek. It is literally, "If any man is willing to do — has a mind and desire and inclination to do God's will . . . ." It should never be forgotten that God deals with us as moral beings, and not as beasts or stones. [10]

Through the centuries a non-Calvinist understanding of Scripture concerning human responsibility and ability has been ably expressed by many Christian leaders. A prominent Baptist wrote, "The individual not only must act for himself; he is the only one who can. God has made him competent." [11] A.H. Strong insisted, "Yet there is a certain remnant of freedom left to man . . . . The sinner can . . . seek God from motives of self-interest . . . the sinner can . . . give attention to divine truth." [12]   Griffith Thomas wrote, "Total depravity does not mean the absolute loss of . . . the freedom of the soul in choosing, enabling it to determine conscious action. In this sense our freedom is real and the Fall has not affected it . . . . Fallen man has the faculty of will, as he has other faculties . . . ." [13]   In the same vein, W. L. Pettingill argued from Scripture, "Whosoever will may come. He is only to come, and God does all the rest." [14]

What God Is This?

For God to act as Calvinism teaches would be inconsistent with the repeated assurance in His Word that He is merciful and loving toward *all*. The committed Calvinist W.G.T. Shedd wrote, "The charges that have been made . . . from time immemorial are, that Calvinism represents God as a tyrannical sovereign who is destitute of love and mercy for any but an elect few, that it attributes to man the depravity of devils, deprives him of moral freedom, and subjects him to the arbitrary cruelty of a Being who creates some men in order to damn them." [15] In fact, Shedd admitted that this charge had been made even by some Calvinists, against what they called hyper-Calvinism. [16]

In defending his doctrine, the Calvinist argues that for God to graciously regenerate all mankind instead of only the elect "would violate His justice, which requires just punishment for sin." [17]   However, if what God does for the elect is no violation of His character or justice, neither would it be a violation for Him to do the same for all mankind. Why must God's infinite mercy be limited to a select few?

It is also argued that imploring those who cannot respond "is a just and necessary way for God to act if man is to be held accountable as a fallen and sinful creature, regardless of his inability to respond." [18] The very suggestion is offensive to man's God-given conscience that God implores men to do what they cannot do in order to hold them accountable. Yet Calvin, though a lawyer, claimed this was God's justice in action.

After declaring that God only regenerates an elect few, Palmer exults, "What a good God!" [19] The Calvinistic elect can say that, but how is God being good to those whom, instead of regenerating, He damns to eternal suffering? In fact, the God of the Bible is not only good to a few but to all:

> For thou, Lord, art good, and ready to forgive; and plenteous in mercy unto all them that call upon thee. (Psalms 86:5)

> The hand of our God is upon all them for good that seek him . . . . (Ezra 8:22) Jesus of Nazareth . . . went about doing good, and healing all that were oppressed of the devil; for God was with him. (Acts 10:38) [Were only the elect "oppressed of the devil"?]

> The LORD is good to all: and his tender mercies are over all his works. (Psalms 145:9)

How could it increase the responsibility of those who are incapable of responding to plead with and warn them? Instead, whoever withheld the help which someone needed would be held accountable. Yet this immoral, deliberate withholding of salvation is attributed to God under the excuse that it is "God's good pleasure to do so." Would someone who stood by and watched a person drown whom he could have saved be exonerated if he explained that it had been his "good pleasure" to do so? Doesn't God have an even higher — yes, a perfect — standard of love and concern?

A Question Not Of Sovereignty But Of Character

This is not to deny that God has the right to damn us all. However, it is not true that His justice requires Him to damn the non-elect any more than the elect. Nor is it rational that God, who is infinite in love and mercy, would allow *anyone* to be damned whom He could justly deliver. Many scriptures clearly declare that God sent His Son "to be the Saviour of the world" (John 4:42; 1 John 4:14) and that Christ on the cross paid the penalty for the sins of the whole world so that God "might be just, and the justifier of him which believeth in Jesus" (Romans 3:25-26). The ultimate problem with Calvinism is the limit it places upon Christ's redemption and God's infinite mercy and love.

Amazingly, however, most Calvinists see no contradiction between the God of love presented in Scripture "who will have all men to be saved" (1 Timothy 2:4) and the God who "saves whom he wills of his mere good pleasure" [20] and leaves the rest of mankind without His mercy and grace because "it was his good pleasure to doom [them] to destruction." [21]

In attempting to escape the clear implications of this lamentable doctrine, it is argued that although totally depraved man can do nothing but reject the gospel, God is just in holding him accountable and damning him. Paul explains how God can justly forgive sinners (Romans 3:21-30) but nowhere does Scripture explain how God could justly condemn for sinning those whom He predestined to sin and to eternal destruction.

With no apparent sense of irony, a Calvinist friend who critiqued the first rough draft of the manuscript for this book wrote in a lengthy response:

> Nor do Calvinists deny that men can respond to the gospel or that God withholds the ability to respond. They do respond . . . negatively. And this response has nothing to do with God withholding anything . . . . God does not prevent man from coming to Him. They are free to come to Him if they want to. What God does withhold is His mercy, which He is under no obligation to give since it is man's desire not to know God. [22]

Not A Question Of Obligation

Such rationalization simply won't work. Of course Calvinism's God prevents the non-elect from coming to Him. He very clearly does so by withholding the grace without which they can't believe. Furthermore, He has predestined them to eternal damnation. Could there be any stronger means of preventing the non-elect from coming to Him? What this friend apparently means is that God withholds nothing that He is under obligation to bestow.

Obviously God is under no obligation to extend mercy or grace to *anyone*. By very definition, mercy and grace are completely without obligation. Thus one cannot excuse the Calvinistic God's failure to extend grace and mercy to all by simply saying He is under no obligation to do so. Obligation is not the basis for extending grace and mercy, but rather, love and the desire to meet the sinner's need.

All of God's qualities are infinite and in perfect balance. Among those qualities is mercy: "But thou, O Lord, art a God full of compassion, and gracious, longsuffering, and plenteous in mercy and truth" (Psalms 86:15). All through Scripture it is made clear that God is a God of mercy. He requires of us that we "love mercy," and He "delighteth in mercy" (Micah 7:18; 6:8). Paul tells us that God "is rich in mercy" (Ephesians 2:4). His "tender mercies are over all his works" (Psalms 145:9) and He has pronounced both Jews and Gentiles "all in unbelief, that he might have mercy upon all" (Romans 11:32).

How could any of these scriptures be interpreted to mean that God limits His grace to a select few?

Contrary to the theory of Total Depravity, the biblical accounts of God's dealings with man would lead one to conclude that, in all good faith, God lovingly, graciously and mercifully extends an offer of repentance and salvation to all mankind — and that all are therefore able to make a moral choice to believe in and accept or to reject Christ. The plain language of Scripture which repeatedly offers salvation to all seems to proclaim that God truly desires to convince and to save all who are lost and that they all have the capacity to turn to Him if they so desire. That conclusion is impressed upon the reader by hundreds of seemingly clear statements in the Bible calling upon men to repent and turn to God. Calvinism, however, robs these scriptures of their plain meaning.

Why Does God Strive?

In the very context of the first exposé of man's wicked heart, which the Calvinist offers as proof of Total Depravity, we hear God saying, "My spirit shall not always strive with man" (Genesis 6:3). How can there be a real "striving" if man is dead in sin and therefore cannot even hear, much less be persuaded? The Calvinist insists that being spiritually dead in sin means that man can no more hear the gospel or respond to God than a physically dead man could. Why would the Spirit of God *strive* with a corpse?

Furthermore, could God be sincerely striving with anyone to believe while at the same time He withholds the only means whereby one could believe?

All through the Bible we see God striving and pleading with man until, at various times and with various persons, we are told that because of man's continued rebellion He ceased to strive with him: "so [He] gave them up unto their own hearts' lust" (Psalms 81:12); "Wherefore God also gave them up to uncleanness through the lusts of their own hearts" (Romans 1:24).

To "give them up" indicates there was a time when God was genuinely striving to convince and win them and had not given them up. But a change has come in God's actions toward them, a change *not in God's heart or desire* — which are unchangeable — but a change in His *dealings* toward those who have so hardened their hearts toward Him that there is no point on His part in further striving with them.

If Calvinism is true, however, there is no genuine striving at all, no bona fide offer of repentance and faith and redemption, no sincere desire on God's part to see the non-elect saved. Indeed, the Calvinists' God strives with no one, for the salvation or doom of all is a matter not of their response to the gospel but of His having predestined them to one or the other. So it would be meaningless for such a God to say that His Spirit will no longer strive with man. If Calvinism is true, then we have God wasting His time and effort in insincere pleadings with those who not only cannot respond without His help, but whom He doesn't really want to save anyway. How can it be said that He truly wants to save those whom He has already doomed?

A Clear Contrast

Calvinism doesn't only present a feigned pleading and striving on the part of God with those who cannot possibly obey. In addition, it confronts us with the mystery of a God of infinite mercy and love who nevertheless doesn't love everyone and therefore lets multitudes perish whom He could save. In fact, Calvin himself declared that it is to God's glory that He fills hell with those whom He could save. This horrible doctrine also, Calvin admits, comes from Augustine:

> There is nothing inconsistent with this when we say, that God, according to the good pleasure of his will . . . elects those whom he chooses for sons, while he rejects and reprobates others. For fuller satisfaction . . . see Augustine Epist. 115, et ad Bonif., Lib. ii, cap. 7 . . . . The Lord therefore may show favour to whom he will, because he is merciful; not show it to all, because he is a just judge. [23]

On the contrary, not showing mercy *at all* could be explained as resulting from justice; but not showing mercy *to all* when all are equally guilty is a perversion of justice. Mercy can only be shown to the *guilty* on a righteous basis; and if not, then justice has been perverted. This fact poses a serious problem for Calvinism which John Piper in his major attempt to justify Calvinism's God fails to consider in its entire 220 pages. [24] In revealing His glory to Moses as "merciful and gracious, longsuffering and abundant in goodness and truth," God declares that He "will by no means clear the guilty" (Exodus 34:6-7).

God being both just and merciful, neither of these qualities can triumph over the other. God can only be merciful justly, not in spite of His justice. Thus God could only forgive sinners because the penalty for sin was fully paid, as Paul declares in Romans 3:19-31. And that the penalty was paid for all, making it possible for God to justly and mercifully forgive all, and not just a special class of the elect, is declared repeatedly in Scripture, as we shall see.

Taken at face value, the Bible's clear language would compel any reader to conclude that God loves all, that God is genuinely striving to convince wicked men to repent and to accept His offer of salvation, that men have the capability of responding when drawn by the Holy Spirit and convicted of their guilt and need, and that though all are drawn, some are convinced and willingly respond while others refuse.

The Bible repeatedly presents a God who so loves the whole world that He sent His Son that "the *world* through him might be saved" (John 3:16; 1 John 4:14), who "will have *all men* to be saved" (1 Timothy 2:4) and who "is not willing that *any* should perish" (2 Peter 3:9). The Bible repeatedly presents Christ as the One "who gave himself a ransom for *all*" (1 Timothy 2:6), who is "the Saviour of *all men*, specially of those that believe" (1 Timothy 4:10), and Whose death provided a propitiation "for the sins of the *whole world*" (1 John 2:2). Christ calls unto *all* who are spiritually thirsty, hungry and weary of their sin's heavy load, "come unto me and I will give you rest," living water, the bread of life, eternal life. That invitation has touched the hearts of the thirsty, hungry, weary and heavy laden for two thousand years. Yet Calvinism attempts to make all such promises apply only to a select few.

Two Conflicting Views

Calvinism presents us with the mystery of why God Who *is love* and Who is infinite in mercy toward all lets billions go to hell whom He could rescue. The Bible on the other hand, confronts us with quite another mystery: why anyone who is offered salvation as a free gift of God's grace chooses to reject it. We have no answer to that question. Pusey writes:

There is something wonderfully impressive in the respect shown by the Creator to the freedom of choice which has been bestowed upon the human race. In the Christian scheme of salvation God becomes the suitor striving by extraordinary means to win the affections of men. Christ stands at the door and knocks . . . . He respects the moral freedom of man, and does not put forth His hand to destroy that high prerogative. [25]

Viewed from the biblical perspective, no one who spends eternity in the Lake of Fire can complain that he is there because God didn't want him in heaven. All of the damned will be tormented by the knowledge that they are not there by God's predestination but by their own refusal to receive the salvation God has provided and freely offered. And God will be glorified by their eternal punishment because He did not pervert His justice by unjustly forgiving those who refused salvation on His righteous terms.

The Bible presents a God who laments over a hell filled with those for whom He provided salvation but who refused to receive it. Of the rich young ruler (Mark 10:17-22) we are clearly told that Christ "beholding him loved him," yet this one who was loved "went away grieved," unable to give up his possessions to follow Christ. From the cross Christ cried concerning those who crucified and rejected Him, "Father, forgive them . . ." (Luke 23:34).

In direct contrast, Calvinism presents a God who fills hell with those whom He could save but instead damns because He doesn't love them.

These two different views of God are the major point of separation between Calvinists and non-Calvinists.

Here is the real issue that must be confronted in consideration of TULIP: Is Calvinism not a misrepresentation of the God of the Bible who is love? Based upon his understanding of God and His Word, H.A. Ironside argued:

Turn to your Bible and read for yourself in the only two chapters in which this word "predestinate" or "predestinated" is found. The first is Romans 8:29-30. The other chapter is Ephesians 1:5,11. You will note that there is no reference in these four verses to either Heaven or Hell, but to Christlikeness eventually. Nowhere are we told in Scripture that God predestinated one man to be saved and another to be lost. Men are to be saved or lost eternally because of their attitude toward the Lord Jesus Christ. [26]

When Is Depravity Not Total?

To support their doctrine of Total Depravity, Calvinists must reconcile it with the obvious fact that the most ungodly people are capable of some morally good thoughts and deeds. Nor can that fact be explained away by always attributing the ungodly's good deeds to selfish motives. Some unsaved soldiers have selflessly thrown themselves upon hand grenades to save their buddies' lives — an act of heroic compassion from which many Christians would shrink.

Unquestionably, all human beings are capable of summoning a worldly altruism which can be widely admired. Acknowledging this natural goodness, a Calvinist author writes, "Total Depravity . . . does not mean that man is as evil as he could be." [27] How much more evil could one be than for *every thought* of his heart to be *only evil continually*? And how can the so-called totally depraved have good thoughts and do good deeds? Calvinists contradict themselves continually in this regard. For example, just before stating that "it is impossible for him [the non-Christian] to do good . . . he is not even able to understand the good," [28] Palmer has acknowledged what seems to be the opposite:

> Albert Schweitzer is an example of one who denied biblical Christianity and yet who put to shame many an orthodox Christian by his love and kindness. For other examples of relative good, consider . . . the non-Christian who risks his life by dashing before an oncoming truck to rescue a child . . . a blaspheming pagan who helps a beggar . . . the Jew who donates his large estate for public recreation   [29]

Another Calvinist writer admits that even the most ungodly persons "are able to love their children and even sacrifice their own lives for the sake of family . . . sometimes even for strangers . . . are honest . . . good people who do good deeds." [30] Even some Nazi guards who had spent the day in torturing and killing would come home in the evening and exhibit love and kindness to their wives and children. Multitudes of ungodly people at times exhibit much kindness and honesty. Of many unsaved businessmen it can be said, "His word is his bond," even that he "sweareth to his own hurt, and changeth not" (Psalms 15:4).

The Bible clearly teaches that the natural, unregenerated man can do good, and it offers many examples. We have already quoted from Romans 2 how unsaved Gentiles recognize God's moral laws in their consciences, seek to obey them, have guilt when they don't and even judge one another by that standard. Yes, it says "there is none that doeth good, no, not one" (Romans 3:12). But Jesus also said, " . . . ye do good to them which do good to you . . . sinners also do even the same" (Luke 6:33). We must take Scripture as a whole.

The fact that "totally depraved" men can obviously make moral choices for good would surely imply that without being regenerated they could under Holy Spirit conviction make a genuine choice to repent and turn to God. Where does God's Word say they cannot? Can even one verse be found in Scripture that clearly declares that man must be regenerated before he can believe the gospel? No, not one!

Both the examples given in Scripture and daily experience force us to conclude that the declaration that "every imagination of the thoughts of his heart was only evil continually" describes the general attitude of the heart, not what it must produce at every moment of every day. Similar statements that sound absolute but are not are found in *praise* of man. For example, God says of David that he walked before Him with a "perfect heart" and that he was a "man after mine own heart, which shall fulfill all my will" (1Kings 15:3; Acts 13:22, etc.). Yet David displeased God a number of times, even committing adultery and murder. In the same fashion we must understand the statements about man's wickedness and sin as describing his general attitude but not his necessity.

The Emperor's Clothes Again?

Many of the verses Calvinists use to support "T" (such as John 1:13 and Romans 9:16) have nothing to do with the concept of total depravity. In such passages we are simply told that by our own will we cannot force ourselves upon God. He is the author of salvation and it is all by His mercy and grace, not by our effort or will. None of such passages, however, declares that any man cannot believe the gospel when it is offered to him with the convincing and convicting power of the Holy Spirit.

Philippians 2:13 is also cited, but clearly this is talking about the Christian working out in his life the salvation he has been given; it has nothing to do with either total depravity or believing the gospel.

Calvinists consider the "T" in TULIP to be of paramount importance. One of their writers argues that "the doctrine of total depravity [is] one of the most important truths that needs to be re-emphasized in our day." He begins his booklet by associating those who reject the Calvinist definition of total depravity with the remarks of professional wrestler Macho Comacho who has no conviction of sin; with those who deny that we are "sinners saved by grace"; with those who try to attract sinners with excitement and avoid dealing with sin; with those who try to build up the sinner's self-esteem; with those who preach "a steady diet of positive inspiration . . . reminiscent of Norman Vincent Peale and Dale Carnegie," etc. [31] Yet these are all errors against which non-Calvinists write and preach just as much as Calvinists do (and do so from Scripture), while rejecting the unbiblical theory of Total Depravity.

The writer being quoted then credits the doctrine of Total Depravity with uniquely 1) causing us to despair of ourselves and to cast ourselves completely upon Christ alone for salvation, 2) humbling our pride, 3) helping us to witness to sinners as a fellow sinner, 4) causing us to fear trusting ourselves and driving us to trust totally in the Lord, 5) causing us to bear up under suffering without complaint, 6) giving us greater love and forgiveness toward those who wrong us, and 7) moving us to greater love and devotion to God for His amazing grace.[32]

One wonders how that author could seriously believe that those of us who reject Calvinism's peculiar definition of Total Depravity are therefore lacking in these supposed exclusive benefits thereof. Non-Calvinists, without embracing this theory, have understood and received directly from Scripture and the indwelling power of the Holy Spirit all seven of these graces which he credits to the doctrine of Total Depravity!

When You're Dead, Are You Dead?

Another major argument the Calvinist uses for Total Depravity is that by nature we are all "dead in trespasses and in sins" (Ephesians 2:1; Colossians 2:13). Sproul calls this statement "A predestination passage par excellence." [33] Continuing the fallacious equating of spiritual death to physical death, Gordon H. Clark writes, "A dead man cannot exercise faith in Jesus Christ." [34] Of course, neither can a dead man reject Christ, or even sin. The analogy simply doesn't fit. Nevertheless, James R. White, quoted above, whose book is endorsed by a host of evangelical leaders, continuing this analogy, writes:

> . . . the fallen sons of Adam are dead in sin, incapable of even the first move toward God . . . filled with the effect of depravity and alienation from God . . ..[35]

Here the Bible is being made to say what it does not in fact state. We are just as clearly told that Christians are "dead to sin" (Romans 6:2,7,11, etc.). Does that mean that they are therefore "incapable of the first move toward" sin? Certainly not. Take a human understanding of "dead," mix it together with the young John Calvin's immature understanding of God's Word, tainted by Augustinian philosophy, stir it up and out comes the theory of Total Depravity. White carries this humanistic reasoning to its logical conclusion, as do other Calvinists, and that leads to absurdities such as the following from Palmer:

> The biblical picture, however, is of a man at the bottom of the ocean . . . . He has been there for a thousand years and the sharks have eaten his heart . . . the man is dead and is totally unable to ask any lifeguard to save him. If he is to be saved, then a miracle must occur. He must be brought back to life and to the surface, and then ask the guard to rescue him . . . .

> When Christ called to Lazarus to come out of the grave, Lazarus had no life in him so that he could hear, sit up, and emerge . . . . If he was to be able to hear Jesus calling him and to go to Him, then Jesus would have to make him alive. Jesus did resurrect him and then Lazarus could respond.

> These illustrations reveal the most central issue between the Arminian and the Calvinist . . . . The Arminian has the cart before the horse. Man is dead in sins . . . unable to ask for help unless God . . . makes him alive spiritually (Eph. 2:5). Then, once he is born again, he can for the first time turn to Jesus, expressing sorrow for his sins and asking Jesus to save him. [36]

The Bible, of course, uses "dead" as an analogy in many ways, and none of them warrants such Calvinistic correlations between spiritual and physical death. Sproul himself admits that "Spiritually dead people are still biologically alive." [37] Even though Pink's brand of Calvinism is too extreme for many Calvinists, he correctly points out the fallacy of using physical death to explain what it means to be dead in trespasses and sins:

> There are some who say, the unregenerated are dead, and *that* ends the matter — they *cannot* have any responsibility . . . . A corpse in the cemetery is no suitable analogy of the natural man. A corpse in the cemetery is incapable of performing evil! A corpse cannot "despise and reject" Christ (Isaiah 53:3), cannot "resist the Holy Spirit" (Acts 7:51), cannot disobey the gospel (2 Thessalonians 1:8); but the natural man can and does do these things! [38]

When we come to the Calvinist's interpretation of what it means for man to be dead in sin and dead to God, the "T" of TULIP begins to overlap with the teaching on Irresistible Grace. Therefore, the remainder of the discussion will be deferred concerning man's spiritual death and alleged inability to respond to the gospel.

Leopard's Spots, Man's Skin Color — Like Sin?

That such natural deductions are the Calvinist's main weapon may explain why their doctrines are so appealing to intellectuals. White continues:

> Just as a person cannot change the color of their skin, or the leopard its spots, so the one who practices evil cannot break the bondage of sin and start doing good . . . . The New Testament continues the testimony of the radical depravity of man . . . Paul begins with a dreadfully long discussion of the universal sinfulness of man . . . Jew and Gentile alike. [39]

That no sinner can "break the bondage of sin" cannot be disputed. But it is a quantum leap beyond that fact to declare that the prisoner of sin cannot with great joy receive the deliverance Christ freely gives. What prisoner would not welcome freedom! Ah, but to be truly free one must be convicted of sin and believe the gospel. Granted. And where does it say in Scripture that the Holy Spirit neglects to bring that conviction and understanding to *every* sinner? He does that for the elect — why not for all? In fact, He does.

That one cannot change the color of his skin does not mean that one cannot gladly receive the cleansing of sin through Christ's blood. Such analogies sound good superficially but do not fit the actual situation any more than to equate physical and spiritual death. Instead of allegorical examples, we need clear teaching from God's Word. Scripture, however, does not support Calvinism unless its own peculiar meaning of words is adopted.

Sinfulness is indeed universal, but it is clearly not the same as Calvinism's Total Depravity. I agree with the Calvinist that man is enslaved by sin and would not of his own initiative seek after God. But *incapable* of being convicted of his sin and judgment to come or of believing the good news of the gospel? Does Scripture teach this? There is not a single verse in Scripture which clearly states that proposition.

Simple Confusion Over Inability

Calvinists are to be commended for their zeal to protect God's sovereignty and glory. They are concerned that if man could do anything toward his salvation, that fact would rob God of some of the credit for saving him. Confusion arises through failing to recognize the obvious distinction between man's inability to do anything for his salvation (which is biblical) and an alleged inability to believe the gospel (which is not biblical). To believe the gospel and to receive Christ requires no work or worth on man's part, contributes nothing to his salvation, gives no credit to man and detracts in no way from God's glory.

Failing to make this distinction, Hanko earnestly states that "the truth of total depravity [i.e., inability to believe the gospel] is the only truth which preserves intact the glory of God." [40] Under the same semantic delusion, Ross writes, "The teaching of the natural man's total inability concerning salvation is not only scriptural, but it is a doctrine that gives all the glory to God in the salvation of sinners." [41] Laboring under the same confusion, Storms argues, "By making election conditional upon something that man does, even if what he does is simply to repent and believe the gospel, God's grace is seriously compromised."[42]

It is simply not true that believing in and receiving Christ gives any credit to man or detracts at all from the fact that it is Christ alone who procured our redemption. Faith is not a work nor does it give any credit to the person who believes. Furthermore, what of the faith which the elect receive after they are allegedly regenerated? If that does not detract from God's glory, why would faith that leads to regeneration detract?

One cannot escape the countless times in the Bible when both unsaved (for their salvation) and saved (for their walk with Christ and fruitfulness) are commanded to believe in God, in His promises, in Christ and in His Word. Man has no relationship with God apart from faith. If faith, then, exercised by man detracts from God's glory, it would be impossible for man to have any relationship with God without lessening God's glory. Obviously, that is not the case.

Yes, man is totally unable to contribute one iota to his salvation. It does not then follow, however, that he therefore cannot receive the salvation freely offered in Christ. It is confusion at this point which creates the doctrine of Total Depravity and leads to the remainder of the Five Points. Spurgeon labored under no such delusion.

Calvinists gladly cite Spurgeon for support. There is no doubt that Spurgeon often declared himself to be a Calvinist, but he frequently made statements which contradicted pure Calvinism. The following from a British scholar who thoroughly knew Spurgeon's writings and sermons must be considered to understand him fully:

> Charles Haddon Spurgeon always claimed to be a Calvinist . . . . His mind was soaked in the writings of the Puritan divines; but his intense zeal for the conversion of souls led him to step outside the bounds of the creed he had inherited. His sermon on "Compel them to come in" was criticized as Arminian and unsound. To his critics he replied: "My Master set His seal on that message. I never preached a sermon by which so many souls were won to God . . . . If it be thought an evil thing to bid the sinner lay hold of eternal life, I will yet be more evil in this respect and herein imitate my Lord and His apostles."

> More than once Spurgeon prayed, "Lord, hasten to bring in all Thine elect, and then elect some more." He seems to have used that phrase often in conversation, and on his lips it was no mere badinage. With its definite rejection of a limited atonement, it would have horrified John Calvin . . . . The truth seems to be that the old Calvinistic phrases were often on Spurgeon's lips but the genuine Calvinistic meaning had gone out of them.

> J.C. Carlile admits that "illogical as it may seem, Spurgeon's Calvinism was of such a character that while he proclaimed the majesty of God he did not hesitate to ascribe freedom of will to man and to insist that any man might find in Jesus Christ deliverance from the power of sin." [43]

Scripture repeatedly states that man is dead in sin and in bondage to sin, that his heart is desperately wicked, that his thoughts are evil from his youth, and that he is a rebel against God by nature and practice. There is no statement, however, that he is depraved as defined by the "T" in TULIP. No matter how bleakly the Bible presents the evil of the human heart, never does it teach Calvinism's peculiar Total Depravity. That will be seen more clearly as we move on to the other four points of Calvinism and contrast them with Scripture.

1   Arthur W. Pink, *The Sovereignty of God* (Baker Book House, 2nd prtg. 1984), 138.
2   Frank B. Beck, *The Five Points of Calvinism* (Covenanter Press, 2nd Australian ed., 1986), 10.
3   George L. Bryson, *The Five Points of Calvinism "Weighed and Found Wanting"* (The Word for Today, 1996), 36.
4   H.A. Ironside, *What's the Answer?* (Zondervan, 1944), 43-44.
5   Frederic W. Farrar, *A Manual of Christian Doctrine* (The Alliance Press, n.d.), 76.
6   G. Campbell Morgan, *The Westminster Pulpit* (Fleming H. Revell, 1954), II:306-307.
7   Kenneth J. Foreman, *God's Will and Ours* (Outlook Publishers, 1954), 42.
8   John H. Gerstner, *A Primer on Free Will* (Presbyterian and Reformed Publishing Co., 1982), 10.
9   Pink, op. cit., foreword to first edition, unnumbered first page.
10 John C. Ryle, *Expository Thoughts on the Gospel of John* (Wm. Hunt and Co., 1883), III:16,22.
11 W.R. White, *Baptist Distinctives* (Sunday School Board, SBC, 1946), 24-25.
12 Augustus H. Strong, *Systematic Theology* (Judson Press, 1907), 640.
13 W.H. Griffith Thomas, *The Principles of Theology* (Longmans, Green and Co., 1930), 165, 180.
14 William L. Pettingill, *Bible Questions Answered* (Just A Word Inc., 3rd ed. 1935), 374.
15 William G.T. Shedd, *Calvinism: Pure and Mixed* (The Banner of Truth Trust, 1999), 15.
16 Ibid.
17 Calvinist friend to Dave Hunt, critical comment in manuscript draft margin. On file.
18 Calvinist reviewer to Dave Hunt, note in manuscript draft margin. On file.
19 Edwin H. Palmer, *the five points of calvinism* (Baker Books, enlarged ed. 20th prtg. 1980), 21.
20 John Calvin, *Institutes of the Christian Religion*, trans. Henry Beveridge (Wm. B. Eerdmans Publishing Company, 1998 ed.), III:xxi,1.
21 Op. cit., III:xxi,7.
22 Reviewer to Dave Hunt, marginal comment, n.d. On file.
23 Calvin, op. cit., III:xxiii, 10-11.
24 John Piper, *The Justification of God: An Exegetical and Theological Study of Romans 9:1-23* (Baker Books, 2000).
25 Edward B. Pusey, *What Is Of Faith As To Everlasting Punishment?* (England: James Parker and Co., 1881), 103-104.
26 H.A. Ironside, *Full Assurance* (Moody Press, 1937), 93-94.
27 James R. White, *The Potter's Freedom* (Calvary Press Publishing, 2000), 39.
28 Palmer, op. cit., 15
29 Op.cit., 11
30 Steven J. Cole, *Total Depravity* (Flagstaff AZ, 1999), 3.
31 Op. cit., 1-3
32 Op. cit., 9-13.
33 R.C. Sproul, *Chosen by God* (Tyndale House Publishers Inc., 1986), 113.
34 Gordon H. Clark, *The Biblical Doctrine of Man* (The Trinity Foundation, 1984), 102.
35 White, op.cit., 75
36 Palmer, op. cit., 18-19.
37 Sproul, op. cit., 120.
38 Arthur W. Pink, *Studies in the Scriptures* (n.p., 1927), 250-61; cited in Samuel Fisk, *Election and Predestination* (England: Penfold Book and Bible House, 1997), 155.
39 White, op. cit., 80-81.
40 Herman Hanko, in Herman Hanko, Homer C. Hoeksema, and Gise J. Van Baren, *The Five Points of Calvinism* (Reformed Free Publishing Association, 1976), 23.
41 Tom Ross, *Abandoned Truth: The Doctrines of Grace* (Providence Baptist Church, 1991), 45.
42 C. Samuel Storms, *Chosen for Life* (Baker Book House, 1987), 55.
43 A.C. Underwood, *A History of the English Baptists* (The Baptist Union of Great Britain and Ireland, 1947), 203-206; cited in Fisk, *Election and Predestination* (England: Penfold Book and Bible House, 1997), 69-70.

9
A Distorted Sovereignty

Having seen that Total Depravity is a key doctrine of Calvinism, we need to understand that behind this belief is something even more fundamental: a grave misunderstanding concerning the sovereignty of God. Singer reminds us that "The secret grandeur of Calvin's theology lies in his grasp of the biblical teaching of the sovereignty of God." [1] In fact, he did not grasp the biblical teaching but distorted it. Calvinism places such an emphasis upon sovereignty that it does away with any real choice for man: "No person since Adam has ever had a free will . . . every unsaved person is . . . free to go in only one direction . . . free to go down." [2] One can, however, argue with equal conviction, "Unless a man is free to will there is no basis for believing that truth [exists] in any field — science, theology, or philosophy . . . unless there is free will there is no meaning to praise or blame [and] there is no sin." [3]

The apparent tension between God's sovereignty and man's free will has been a point of study and discussion — and, sadly, of contention — among sincere Christians for centuries. Some have taken the approach of C.I. Scofield, that these are two truths that must both be accepted but which cannot be reconciled. "Both are wholly true, but the connecting and reconciling truth has not been revealed." [4] In apparent agreement, James M. Gray, a past president of Moody Bible Institute, suggested that "no one finite mind could hold . . . God's sovereignty and man's free agency . . . both equally at the same time. How necessary, however, that both be duly emphasized!" [5] Likewise, William L. Pettingill wrote, "God insists upon His sovereignty and also upon man's responsibility. Believe both and preach both, leaving the task of 'harmonizing' with Him." [6] In a similar vein, A.T. Pierson, although a leading Presbyterian, declared that both "the sovereign will of God and the freedom of man" are taught in Scripture and that "if we cannot reconcile these two, it is because the subject is so infinitely lifted up above us. Man is free . . . . Thus the last great invitation in God's Book is an appeal to the *will*." [7] R.A. Torrey agreed that we should not "try to explain away the clear teaching of the Word of God as to the sovereignty of God [and] the freedom of the human will . . . ." [8]

Unfortunately, neither Calvin nor many of his followers today have been willing to accept both sides of this biblical teaching. The result has been devastating in its consequences for the gospel: that man can only reject Christ, he cannot accept and believe in Him, unless he is sovereignly regenerated by God. Calvinism refuses to accept what so many great evangelists have recognized is essential. Edgar Mullins expresses very well the essential balance that is missing:

> Free will in man is as fundamental a truth as any other in the gospel and must never be canceled in our doctrinal statements. Man would not be man without it and God never robs us of our true moral manhood in saving us . . . . The decree of salvation must be looked at as a whole to understand it. Some have looked at God's choice alone and ignored the means and the necessary choice on man's part. [9]

A Commendable But Mistaken Zeal

Talbot and Crampton assure us that "The sovereignty of God is . . . the most basic principle of Calvinism . . . the foundation upon which all [including Christianity itself] is built." [10] Boettner agrees: "The basic principle of Calvinism is the sovereignty of God." [11] Such fervor for God's sovereignty is commendable. However, in order to make certain that everything is under His control to the extent that it must be in order for their doctrine to be consistent, Calvinists have made God the effective *cause* of every event that occurs: "Whatever is done in time is according to his [God's] decree in eternity." [12]

This perspective makes it impossible for man to have any real choice concerning *anything* he thinks or does. Spurgeon referred to "a class of strong-minded hard-headed men who magnify sovereignty at the expense of [human] responsibility." [13] The Calvinist believes that for man to be able to make a genuine choice even in his rebellion against God would be a denial that God is sovereign. Thus God must be the cause of all sin beginning with Adam and Eve. Boettner argues, "Even the fall of Adam, and through him the fall of the race, was not by chance or accident, but was so ordained in the secret counsels of God." [14] That unhappy conclusion is necessitated by a concept of sovereignty which is required neither by the Bible nor by logic.

We have noted the claim by some Calvinists that man is free to respond to God. At the same time, however, the doctrine of Total Depravity requires that he can respond only negatively and in opposition to God. Congdon points out, "Classical Calvinists may talk about man having a 'free will,' but it is a very limited freedom! That is, a person may choose to reject Christ — all people do — but only those who have been elected may choose to accept Him. This is no 'free will'! Are the open invitations to trust Christ in the Bible actually a cruel hoax? I don't think so. Are all people free to put their trust in the Lord Jesus Christ as personal Savior for their sin? Yes. That is why the call to missions is so urgent." [15]

How can there be any real freedom of choice if only one kind of choice is available, and one which has been decreed eternally? But would a Holy God decree evil? Obviously, this is not free choice at all. It is, however, the only "freedom" Calvinism can allow. Pink favorably quotes J. Denham Smith, whom he honors as a "deeply taught servant of God":

I believe in free will; but then it is a will only free to act according to nature . . . . The sinner in his sinful nature could never have a will according to God. For this he must be born again. [16]

Nowhere does the Bible support such a statement; and this is where it becomes sticky. Were Abraham and Moses "born again"? Isn't that a New Testament term? What does he mean, "a will according to God"? Even Christians don't always do God's will. A desire to know God? Surely all men are expected to seek the Lord while He may be found. That God promises to be found of those who seek Him surely implies that the unregenerated can seek Him.

Nor does it help the Calvinist to say that man can only will and act according to his sinful nature and against God. If sinful acts are admitted to come from genuine choice, then we have the same challenge to God's sovereignty which the Calvinist cannot allow. Either man has a free will, or his sin is all according to God's will. As we have seen, the latter is exactly what Calvin himself taught and many Calvinists still believe, making God the author of evil.

Could it be that Adam's nature was actually sinful, though God pronounced him "good" when He created him? How else, except by free will, can his sin be explained? The Calvinist escapes that problem by declaring that even the sin of Adam and Eve was foreordained and decreed by God. Pink argues, "God foreordains everything which comes to pass. His sovereign rule extends throughout the entire Universe and is over every creature . . . . God initiates all things, regulates all things . . . ." [17]

It is fallacious to imagine that for God to be in control of His universe He must therefore foreordain and initiate everything. In fact, it diminishes God to suggest that He cannot control what He doesn't foreordain and originate. Though he was a leading Presbyterian theologian, A.A. Hodge recognized the severe consequences of that extremist view of God's sovereignty: "Everything is gone if free-will is gone; the moral system is gone if free-will is gone . . . ." [18]

Confronting A Vital Distinction

For the Calvinist to uphold his extreme view of control, God must be the cause of man's total depravity and the negative response it produces. There is no way to escape this conclusion. If God were not the cause of man's sin, man would be acting independently of God, and that cannot be allowed for *anything* in the Calvinist scheme. It follows, then, that "He [God] could . . . have prevented it [the fall and entrance of sin into the world], but He did not prevent it: ergo, He willed it." [19] Thus one must conclude, "It is even biblical to say that God has foreordained sin." [20]

The only way, however, to defend God's integrity, love and compassion in a world filled with sin and suffering is to acknowledge that He has granted to man the power to choose for himself. It is thus man's fault that sin and suffering are the common experience of all mankind. God has provided full forgiveness of sins on a righteous basis and will eventually create a new universe into which sin can never enter, a universe to be inhabited by all those who have received the Lord Jesus Christ as Savior. God is exonerated and man alone is to blame for sin and suffering. Such is the teaching of the Bible, as we shall see in depth.

It is clear that Calvinism rests upon a mistaken view of what it means for God to be sovereign. Palmer tells us that God predestines untold multitudes to everlasting torment "for the glory of His sovereign power over His creatures . . . ." [21] Obviously, God could show His sovereign power over His creatures in many ways other than by decreeing their eternal damnation, a fate which surely is not required by sovereignty.

Right here we confront another vital distinction. It is one thing for God in His sovereignty, and without diminishing that sovereignty, to give man the power to rebel against Him. This would open the door for sin as being solely man's responsibility by a free choice. Is there any reason why God could not do this while retaining His absolute sovereignty? Of course not. A denial of free will in protection of God's sovereignty is well intentioned but unnecessary and misguided.

In order for God to be sovereign, it is not necessary for Him to control everything to such an extent that He must effectively *cause* man to sin. The basic problem for the Calvinist is a failure to see that God could sovereignly give to man the power of genuine choice. In his earnest zeal for God's sovereignty, he cannot see that it would not be lessened for God to allow man this responsibility. No other reason can be found for disallowing man's free choice except the fact that to allow it would destroy the very foundations of Calvinism.

Additionally, God's sovereignty as they define it becomes the Calvinists' justification for God saving only a select few and damning the rest. If one asks how a loving God could damn millions or perhaps billions whom He could have saved, the answer is that it "pleased Him so to do." If one persists and asks *why* it pleased Him, the response is that the reason is hidden "in the mystery of His will."

Giving man the power to make a genuine, independent choice need not diminish God's control over His universe. Being omnipotent and omniscient, God can so arrange circumstances as to keep man's rebellion from frustrating His purposes. In fact, God can and even does use man's free will to help fulfill His own plans and thus be even more glorified.

Hear It From Calvin And Calvinists

In his classic, *the five points of calvinism*, Edwin H. Palmer writes, "Although sin and unbelief are contrary to what God commands (His perceptive will), God has included them in His sovereign decree (ordained them, caused them to certainly come to pass) . . . . How is it that a holy God, who hates sin, not only passively permits sin but also certainly and efficaciously decrees that sin shall be? Our infinite God presents us with some astounding truths . . . ." [22]

"Astounding" is the wrong adjective. What Palmer admits astounds even him, a man who defends this doctrine diligently, is appalling to non-Calvinists, including most non-Christians. Palmer expounds further upon this staggering doctrine as follows:

> All things that happen in all the world at any time and in all history — whether with inorganic matter, vegetation, animals, man, or angels (both the good and evil ones) — come to pass because God ordained them. Even sin — the fall of the devil from heaven, the fall of Adam, and every evil thought, word, and deed in all of history, including the worst sin of all, Judas' betrayal of Christ — is included in the eternal decree of our holy God.

> [If] sin is outside the decree of God, then the vast percentage of human actions . . . are removed from God's plan. God's power is reduced to the forces of nature . . . . Sin is not only foreknown by God, it is also foreordained by God. In fact, because God foreordained it, He foreknew it. Calvin is very clear on this point: "Man wills with an evil will what God wills with a good will . . . ." [23]

It is clearly not true that unless something is decreed by God it could not be included in God's plan for the ages. Surely God in His infinite power and foreknowledge could fit into His plan even the most rebellious thoughts and deeds of mankind. He is perfectly able to frustrate, prevent or use man's plans in order to fulfill His own, and He can do so without destroying man's ability to exercise free choice. To make God the author of sin is to terribly misrepresent Him.

Why would God need to foreordain something in order to foreknow it? Yet Calvinists persist in this unbiblical doctrine which actually diminishes God's sovereignty in the act of defending it: "If God did not foreordain all things, then He could not know the future. God foreknows and knows all things because He decreed all things to be." [24] If God can only know what He himself has decreed, and would be taken by surprise if man had free choice, then His knowledge would not be infinite (i.e., God would not be omniscient).

Palmer and the other contemporary Calvinists we are quoting are expressing the very heart of Calvinism. They are being true to John Calvin, who in turn reminds us that the same was taught by Augustine. The latter has been described as the first of the early so-called Church Fathers who "taught the absolute sovereignty of God." [25] Reformed theologians (as they call themselves) trace Calvin's view of God's sovereignty back to Augustine. He acknowledged his debt to Augustine in his *Institutes* concerning God's absolute control over mankind's every thought, word and deed, good or bad, including all evil committed:

> [W]e hold that God is the disposer and ruler of all things — that from the remotest eternity, according to his own wisdom, he decreed . . . that, by his providence, not heaven and earth and inanimate creatures only, but also the counsels and wills of men are so governed as to move exactly in the course which he has destined . . . .
>
> In short, Augustine everywhere teaches . . . that there cannot be a greater absurdity than to hold that anything is done without the ordination of God; because it would happen at random. For which reason, he also excludes the contingency which depends on human will, maintaining a little further on, in clearer terms, that no cause must be sought for but the will of God . . . . I say, then, that . . . the order, method, end, and necessity of events, are, for the most part, hidden in the counsel of God, though it is certain that they are produced by the will of God . . . . [26]

An Irrational Position

Augustine did say that all wills are subject to the will of God, but he did not go as far as Calvin carries him. Moreover, Calvin leaps further into a number of fallacies that have been perpetuated to this day. Because it is so obvious, we need not argue the fact that, contrary to Calvin, actions by the free will of humans could not happen at random. If they did, our entire judicial system would break down, since rape, murder, robbery and all other crimes would then have to be viewed as random events beyond the control or moral responsibility of the perpetrators. This is, of course, absurd.

Ironically, Pink attempts to avoid the intolerable consequences of Calvin's strong statements, by also appealing to Augustine: "Let it be emphatically said that God does not *produce* the sinful dispositions of any of His creatures, though He does *restrain* and *direct* them to the accomplishing of His own purposes.

Attempting to justify this appalling doctrine, so many Calvinists have responded to me in discussions, in letters, and in comments written in the margin of manuscripts I sent to them for review, "God is under no obligation to extend His grace to those whom He predestines to eternal judgment." Of course God is under no obligation to man for anything. Grace and mercy, however, do not flow from obligation but rather from God's love. Evaluating a popular Calvinist author, Zane Hodges writes,

> The result of [Michael S.] Horton's theology is that non-elect people are hopelessly bound for hell because God declines to regenerate them. Thus they are *unable* to believe. Yet they are *condemned* for that unbelief! The picture of God that emerges from this is a hideous distortion of His loving character and nature. It is not surprising, therefore, to find Horton also writing: "He [God] cannot love us directly because of our sinfulness, but he can love us in union with Christ, because Christ is the one the Father loves." [35] What this amounts to is that God does not "directly" love *anyone* unless *first* He regenerates him or her, since "regeneration is the commencement of union." In other words, God does not love the elect until they are regenerated, and He *never* loves the non-elect at all. [36]

Sovereignty And Free Will

One often hears Christians say, "God is in control; He's still on the throne." But what does that mean? Was God not in control when Satan rebelled and when Adam and Eve disobeyed, but now He is? Does God being in control mean that all rape, murder, war, famine, suffering and evil is exactly what He planned and desires — as Palmer says, "— even the moving of a finger . . . the mistake of a typist . . . "? [37] That God is absolutely sovereign does not require that everything man thinks he chooses to do or not to do is not his choice at all but was foreordained by God from eternity past. There is neither logical nor biblical reason why a sovereign God by His own sovereign design could not allow creatures made in His image the freedom of moral choice.

In a chapter titled "the great mystery," Palmer insists that the non-Calvinist denies the sovereignty of God while insisting upon man's power of choice, while the "hyper-Calvinist denies the responsibility of man." He then suggests that the true

> Calvinist . . . accepts both sides of the antinomy. He realizes that what he advocates is ridiculous . . . impossible for man to harmonize these two sets of data. To say on the one hand that God has made certain all that ever happens, and yet to say that man is responsible for what he does? Nonsense! It must be one or the other. To say that God foreordains the sin of Judas, and yet Judas is to blame? Foolishness . . . ! This is in accord with Paul, who said, 'The word of the cross is to them that perish foolishness' (1 Cor. 1:18). The Greeks seek after wisdom and logic, and to them the Calvinist is irrational . . . . So the Calvinist has to make up his mind: what is his authority? His own human reason or the Word of God? If he answers, the human reasoning powers, then,

like the Arminian and hyper-Calvinist, he will have to exclude one of the two parallel forces. But . . . he believes the Bible is God's Word . . . infallible and inerrant . . . [T]he apparent paradox of the sovereignty of God and the responsibility of man . . . belongs to the Lord our God, and we should leave it there. We ought not to probe into the secret counsel of God." [38]

The confusion here should be obvious. There is no paradox except that which has been created by a distortion of sovereignty. Accepting this manmade contradiction, J.I. Packer says we must "refuse to regard the apparent inconsistency as real." [39] That pronouncement sounds more like Christian Science, Positive Thinking or Positive Confession than biblical exegesis!

On the contrary, as Reimensnyder has said, "The free-will of man is the most marvelous of the Creator's works." [40] It is indeed the gift that makes possible every other gift from God — for without the power to choose, man could consciously receive no moral or spiritual gift from God.

A Serious Contradiction

Unquestionably, men by their own choice can and do defy and disobey God. The knowledge that men continually break God's laws is common to every human conscience and experience. In spite of the fact that He is sovereign, and, obviously, without violating or lessening His sovereignty, God's will is continually being resisted and rejected as a result of Satan's and man's rebellion. Even Christians do not always perfectly fulfill God's will. If so, they would have no sin to confess and there would have been no need for the Epistles or Christ's letters to the seven churches of Asia, or for the judgment seat of Christ — or any other correction from God.

The Bible itself contains many examples of men defying and disobeying God. Through Isaiah the prophet, God laments, "I have nourished and brought up children, and they have rebelled against me" (Isaiah 1:2). They are offering sacrifices which He abhors, obviously not according to His will, and they are living lives which dishonor Him. We are told that "the Pharisees and lawyers [continuing the tradition of those before them] rejected the counsel of God against themselves" (Luke 7:30). Quite clearly, everything that happens in human affairs is *not* according to God's will.

In light of such scriptures, how can we understand the statement that God works "all things according to the counsel of His own will" (Ephesians 1:11)? Alvin Baker claims that this passage proves that "God works 'all things,' including sin, according to His eternal will." [41] However, the word "worketh" (KJV) is *energeo*, which doesn't convey the idea of controlled purpose but of stimulation. See Colossians 1:29 and 2 Thessalonians 2:7,9; see also "work out your own salvation...for it is God which worketh in [energizes] you" (Philippians 2:12-13).

Furthermore, the "all things" in Ephesians 1:11 are not all events in the universe but those things purposed in Christ.

Obviously, the eternal "counsel" of His will must have allowed man the freedom to defy His will, or sin would be God's will. We could never conclude from this passage (and particularly not in light of the many scriptures stating that men defy God's will) that mankind's every thought, word and deed is according to God's perfect will, exactly the way God desired and decreed it. Yet that is what ts erroneously concluded from Ephesians 1:11. To make that the case, as Calvin did, portrays God as the effective cause of every sin ever committed.

Christ asks us to pray, "Thy kingdom come, Thy will be done in earth, as it is in heaven" (Matthew 6:10). Why would Christ suggest such a prayer, if everything is already according to God's will, as He eternally decreed – and if we are already in the kingdom of God with Satan bound, as Calvin taught? The objection is raised: "How dare you suggest that the omnipotent God cannot effect His will!"

Christ's special commendation of "whosoever shall do the will of my Father" (Matthew 12:50; Mark 3:35), and such statements from His lips as "Not every one that saith unto me, Lord, Lord, shall enter into the kingdom of heaven; but he that doeth the will of my Father" (Matthew 7:21), show very clearly that everyone doesn't always fulfill God's will. The same truth is found in Isaiah 65:12, 1 Thessalonians 5:17-22, Hebrews 10:36, 1 Peter 2:15-16, 1 John 2:17 and elsewhere. Clearly there is a distinction between what God decrees and what He *allows*.

An Important Distinction

Many scriptures show that God's will can be, and is, defied by man, but nowhere does Scripture suggest that there is any will or plan of God with which man's will and actions are in perfect accord. Forster and Marston point out, however, that "Some Christian writers seem to have been unable to accept this . . . . If, as they believe, everything that happens is God's will, then the unrepentance and perishing of the wicked must also be God's will. Yet God himself says it is *not* his will . . . ." [42]

On the fact of human rebellion and disobedience in defiance of God, both Calvinists and non-Calvinists agree. The disagreement comes in the explanation. The former say that even man's rebellion has been decreed sovereignly by God and that God's will is the effective cause of it. The latter explain sin as the result of man's own selfish and evil desires and deeds in defiance of God's will. Thereby man is justly held morally accountable because it is in the power of his will either to obey or to disobey God. The Calvinist, however, denies that man, because he is totally depraved, has such a choice — yet holds him accountable in spite of his inability to act in any way except as God has decreed.

Calvinists insist that man's disobedience and sin have been ordained by God. To reject that claim, they say, would be to deny God's sovereignty. Thus any independent choice on man's part must be explained away to maintain their doctrine. This is especially true when it comes to salvation. Pink writes, "To say that the sinner's salvation turns upon the action of his own will, is another form of the God-dishonoring dogma of salvation by human efforts . . . any movement of the will is a work . . . ." [43]

On the contrary, there is, in fact, a huge difference between deciding or willing to do something and actually doing it — something which every lazy person and procrastinator continually demonstrates. Merely to will is not a work at all. Paul makes that distinction when he says, "To will is present with me; but how to perform that which is good I find not" (Romans 7:18). Indeed, Paul's will is not the problem but rather his inability to do the good he wills and to refrain from the evil which his will rejects.

It is the Calvinists' extreme view of God's sovereignty which causes them to reject the biblical teaching that salvation is offered freely to all, and instead to limit salvation to the elect. Otherwise, they argue, if man is free either to accept or to reject salvation, that leaves the final decision up to man and places God at his mercy. "So are you suggesting," they object, "that God wants to save all mankind but lacks the power to do so? It is a denial of God's omnipotence and sovereignty if there is anything He desires but can't accomplish." Let us consider this assertion.

Suggesting that God would be lacking in "power" (and thus His sovereignty would be denied) if He made a genuine offer of salvation, and some rejected it, is to frame the proposition wrongly. Power has no relationship to grace and love, which provide salvation. In fact, as we shall see, there are many things which God cannot do, and a lack of "power" is not the reason for any of them, nor is His sovereignty mitigated in the least.

What A Sovereign God *Cannot* Do

Vance points out, "The Calvinist perception of God as being absolutely sovereign is very much accurate; however, that doesn't mean that it takes precedence over his other attributes." [44] Clearly, God's ability and even His right to act in His sovereignty are only exercised in harmony with His other qualities, which must all remain in perfect balance. Calvinism destroys that balance. It puts such emphasis upon sovereignty that God's other qualities are made inconsequential by comparison and God is presented as acting out of character. That is why this book is subtitled, "Calvinism's Misrepresentation of God."

Throughout history, sovereign despots have misused their sovereignty for their own evil purposes. Obviously, however, God employs His sovereignty not as a despot but in love, grace, mercy, kindness, justice, and truth — all in perfect symmetry with His total character and all of His attributes. Indeed, He cannot act despotically or use His sovereignty for evil. Cannot? Yes, *cannot.*

"Heresy!" cries the Calvinist. "God is infinite in power; there is nothing He can't do." Really? The very fact that He is infinite in power means He *cannot* fail. There is much else which finite beings routinely do but which the infinite, absolutely sovereign God *cannot do because He is God.* He cannot lie, cheat, steal, be mistaken, etc. Nor did God will any of this in man. To will sin in others would be the same as practicing it Himself.

What God cannot do is not *in spite of who He is*, but *because of who He is.* This fact was recognized by Augustine, who wrote, "Wherefore, He cannot do some things for the very reason that He is omnipotent." [45] There are things which God cannot do because to do them would violate His very character. He cannot deny or contradict himself. He cannot change. He cannot go back on His Word.

God Can Neither Tempt Nor Be Tempted

Scripture must be taken in context and compared with Scripture; one isolated verse cannot become the rule. Jesus said, "With God all things are possible" (Matthew 19:26). Yet it is impossible for God to do evil, to cause others to do evil, or even to entice anyone into evil. This is clearly stated in Scripture: "Let no man say when he is tempted, I am tempted of God: for God cannot be tempted with evil, neither tempteth he any man . . . " (James 1:13-14).

What about instances in Scripture where the Bible says God tempted someone or was tempted? We are told, for example, that "God did tempt Abraham" (Genesis 22:1). The Hebrew word there and throughout the Old Testament is *nacah*, which means to test or prove, as in assaying the purity of a metal. It has nothing to do with tempting *to sin.* God was testing Abraham's faith and obedience.

As for God being tempted, Israel was warned, "Ye shall not tempt the Lord your God" (Deuteronomy 6:16). They had done so at Massah, in demanding water: "they tempted the LORD, saying, Is the LORD among us, or not?" (Exodus 17:7). Later they "tempted God in their heart by asking meat for their lust . . . they said, Can God furnish a table in the wilderness? Yea, . . . they tempted and provoked the most high God" (Psalms 78:18,41,56).

Clearly God was not being tempted to do *evil* — an impossibility. Instead of waiting upon Him in patient trust to meet their needs, His people were demanding that He prove His power by giving them what they wanted to satisfy their lusts. Their "temptation" of God was a provocation that put Him in the position either of giving in to their desire or of punishing them for rebellion.

When Jesus was "tempted of the devil" to cast himself from the pinnacle of the temple to prove the promise of God that angels would bear Him up in their hands, He quoted the same Scripture: "Thou shalt not tempt the Lord thy God" (Matthew 4:1-11). In other words, it is one thing to rely upon God to meet our needs as they arise, but it is something else to put ourselves deliberately in a situation where we demand that God *must* act if we are to be rescued or protected.

In the quotation above, James goes on to say, "every man is tempted, when he is drawn away of his own lust and enticed." Temptation to evil comes from within, not from without. The man who would never be "tempted" by an opportunity to be dishonest in business may succumb to the temptation to commit adultery and thus be dishonest with his wife. It is said that "every man has his price."

God was not tempting Adam and Eve to sin when He told them not to eat of a particular tree; He was testing them. Eve was tempted by her own natural lust, her selfish desire. This shows that even in innocence mankind can be selfish and disobedient. We see this in very young infants who as yet presumably do not know the difference between right and wrong.

What God Cannot Do To Save Man

When it comes to salvation, it is essential to realize that there are three additional things which God cannot do. First of all, He cannot forgive sin without the penalty being paid. In the Garden the night before the cross, Christ cried out in agony, "O my Father, if it be possible, let this cup pass from me . . . " (Matthew 26:39). Surely if it had been possible to provide salvation without Christ paying the penalty demanded by His justice, the Father would have allowed Him to escape the cross. We know, therefore, that it was not possible for God to save man any other way.

Secondly, God cannot force a gift upon anyone. Finally, He cannot force anyone to love Him or to accept His love. Force would pervert the transaction. It is at this point that we see why man must have a free will. By the very nature of giving and receiving, and of loving and receiving love, man must have the power to choose freely, as God has sovereignly ordained. The reception of God's gift of salvation and of God's love (all in and through Jesus Christ and His sacrifice for our sins) can only be by a free choice.

Christ repeatedly gave such invitations as "Come unto me, all ye that labour and are heavy laden, and I will give you rest" (Matthew 11:28), or "If any man thirst, let him come unto me, and drink" (John 7:37); and "whosoever will, let him take the water of life freely" (Revelation 22:17). Relying upon the ordinary meaning of words, does it not sound as though Christ is offering to all a gift which may be accepted or rejected?

There is no question that salvation is a free gift of God's grace: "For God so loved the world, that he gave his only begotten Son" (John 3:16); "If thou knewest the gift of God" (John 4:10); "But not as the offence, so also is the free gift" (Romans 5:15); "For the wages of sin is death, but the gift of God is eternal life through Jesus Christ our Lord" (Romans 6:23); "For by grace are ye saved . . . it is the gift of God" (Ephesians 2:8); "God hath given to us eternal life" (1 John 5:11), etc. By its very nature a gift must be received by an act of the will. If forced upon the recipient, it is not a gift.

Free Will Does Not Conflict With God's Sovereignty

Again, relying upon the ordinary meaning of words, when Scripture says, "He that believeth on the Son hath everlasting life: and he that believeth not the Son shall not see life; but the wrath of God abideth on him" (John 3:36), it sounds as though everlasting life is offered to all mankind and it is up to each one either to believe on the Son or to reject Him. So it is with literally hundreds of verses throughout the Bible.

The Calvinist objects that if man had the choice whether to say yes or no to Christ, then he would have the final say in his salvation and God would be at his mercy. By this reasoning, those places in the Bible where it seems to say that God desires all to be saved and is offering salvation to all either to be accepted or rejected cannot really mean what they say and must be interpreted to apply only to the elect — and they must have no choice. Thus Scripture's clear meaning is changed to make it conform to TULIP. We are testing that doctrine from God's Word.

Calvinists' sincere concern for God's sovereignty is not in question. The issue is whether they are being true to Scripture, to the character of God and to reason. The Calvinist argues that if God's desire is for all men to be saved — and obviously they are *not* all saved — then God's will is frustrated by rebellious, sinful men who by their wills have been able to overturn God's sovereignty. As a consequence, the plain meaning of numerous passages must be changed in order to conform to the Calvinist's mistaken view of sovereignty. As one of them has said, "The heresy of free will dethrones God and enthrones man." [46] In fact, this statement was rejected by Augustine himself.

It has been clearly shown that there are a number of things which a sovereign God *cannot* do, yet none of these limitations impinges in the least upon His sovereignty. God is not the less sovereign because He cannot lie or sin or change or deny Himself, etc. These follow *because* of His sinless, holy and perfect character.

Nor is God any the less sovereign because He cannot force anyone to love Him or to receive the gift of eternal life through Jesus Christ. Suggesting that God would be lacking in "power" (thus supposedly denying His sovereignty) if He offered salvation and some rejected it is missing the point. Power and love and love's gift do not belong in the same discussion. In fact, of the many things which we have seen that God cannot do, a lack of "power" is not the reason for any of them. Pusey points out that "It would be self-contradictory, that Almighty God should create a free agent capable of loving Him, without also being capable of rejecting His love . . . without free-will we could not freely love God. Freedom is a condition of love." [47]

To recognize that mankind has been given by God the capacity to choose to love Him or not and to receive or reject the free gift of salvation, far from denying God's sovereignty, is to admit what God's sovereignty itself has lovingly and wonderfully provided. In His sovereignty, God has so constituted the nature of a gift and of love that man must have the power of choice, or He cannot experience either one from God's gracious hand.

It is impossible that the power of choice could challenge God's sovereignty since it is God's sovereignty which has bestowed this gift upon man and set the conditions for loving, for receiving love, and for giving and receiving a gift. In contrast, however, both to Scripture and common sense, as Zane Hodges points out:

> If there is one thing five-point Calvinists hold with vigorous tenacity, it is the belief that there can be no human *free will* at all. With surprising illogic, they usually argue that God cannot be sovereign if man is granted any degree of free will. But this view of God actually *diminishes* the greatness of His sovereign power. For if God cannot control a universe in which there is genuine free will, and is reduced to the creation of "robots," then such a God is of truly limited power indeed. [48]

---

1   C. Gregg Singer, *John Calvin: His Roots and Fruits* (A Press, 1989), 32.

2   W.E. Best, *Free Grace Versus Free Will* (W.E. Best Books Missionary Trust, 1977], 20.

3   Peter A. Bertocci, *Free Will, Responsibility, and Grace* (Abingdon Press, 1957), 22, 96.

4   C.I. Scofield, *Scofield Bible Correspondence Course* (Moody Bible Institute, 1907), III:445.

5   James M. Gray, *Bible Problems Explained* (Fleming H. Revell, 3rd ed. 1913), 45.

6   William L. Pettingill, *Bible Questions Answered* (Just A Word Inc., 3rd ed. 1935), 209.

7   Arthur T. Pierson, *The Believer's Life: Its Past, Present, and Future Tenses* (Morgan and Scott, 1905), 24-30.

8   Reuben A. Torrey, *The Importance and Value of Proper Bible Study* (Moody Press, 1921), 80-81.

9 Edgar Y. Mullins, *Baptist Beliefs* (Judson, 4th ed. 1925), 27.

10 Kenneth G. Talbot and W. Gary Crampton, *Calvinism, Hyper-Calvinism and Arminianism* (Still Waters Revival Books, 1990), 14.

11 Loraine Boettner, *The Reformed Faith* (Presbyterian and Reformed Publishing Co., 1983), 2.

12 John Gill, *A Body of Doctrinal and Practical Divinity* (Baptist Standard Bearer, 1987), 173.

13 Charles Haddon Spurgeon, "God's Will and Man's Will," No. 442 (Newington, Metropolitan Tabernacle; sermon delivered Sunday morning, March 30, 1862).

14 Loraine Boettner, *The Reformed Doctrine of Predestination* (Presbyterian and Reformed Publishing Co., 1932), 234.

15 Philip F. Congdon, "Soteriological Implications of Five-point Calvinism" (*(Journal of the Grace Evangelical Society,* Autumn 1995), 8:15, 55-68.

16 Arthur W. Pink, *The Sovereignty of God* (Baker Book House, 2nd prtg. 1986), 138-39.

17 Op. cit., 240.

18 A.A. Hodge, quoted in D.A. Carson, *Divine Sovereignty and Human Responsibility* (John Knox Press, 1981), 207.

19 Jerom Zanchius, *The Doctrine of Absolute Predestination*, trans. Augustus M. Toplady (Baker Book House, 1977), 88.

20 Edwin H. Palmer, *the five points of calvinism* (Baker Books, enlarged ed., 20th prtg. 1999), 82.

21 Op .cit., 95, 124-35.

22 Op. cit., 97-100, 116.

23 Ibid.

24 David S. West (*The Baptist Examiner*, March 18, 1989), 5; cited in Laurence M. Vance, *The Other Side of Calvinism* (Vance Publications, Pensacola FL, rev. ed. 1999), 255.

25 C. Norman Sellers, *Election and Perseverance* (Schoettle Publishing Co., 1987), 3.

26 John Calvin, *Institutes of the Christian Religion*, trans. Henry Beveridge (Wm. B. Eerdmans Publishing Company, 1998 ed.), I:xvi,6,8,9.

27 Pink, op. cit., 156.

28 Jonathan Edwards, *Freedom of the Will*, ed. Paul Ramsey (Yale University Press, 1957), 137.

29 Palmer, op. cit., 87.

30 Will Durant, "The Reformation," Pt. VI of *The Story of Civilization* (Simon and Schuster, 1957), 90.

31 Palmer, op. cit., 97-100,116.

32 Op. cit., 16.

33 Quoted in Alan P.F. Sell, *The Great Debate* (Baker Book House, 1982), 7.

34 In Jacobus Arminius, *The Works of James Arminius*, trans. James and William Nichols (Baker Book House, 1986), 1:213.

35 Quoting from Michael S. Horton, ed., *Christ the Lord: The Reformation and Lordship Salvation* (Baker Book House, 1992), 111.

36 Zane C. Hodges, "The New Puritanism, Pt 3: Michael S. Horton: Holy War With Unholy Weapons" (*Journal of the Grace Evangelical Society,*" Spring 1994), 7:12, 17-29.

37 Palmer, op. cit., 25.

38 Op. cit., 85-87.

39 J.I. Packer, *Evangelism and the Sovereignty of God* (Inter-Varsity Press, 1961), 212.

40 Junius B. Reimensnyder, *Doom Eternal* (N.S. Quiney, 1880), 357; cited in Samuel Fisk, *Calvinistic Paths Retraced* (Biblical Evangelism Press, 1985), 223.

41 Alvin L. Baker, *Berkower's Doctrine of Election: Balance or Imbalance?* (Presbyterian and Reformed Publishing Co., 1981), 174.

42 Roger T. Forster and V. Paul Marston, *God's Strategy in Human History* (Bethany House Publishers, 1973), 32.

43 Pink, op.cit., 218.

44 Vance, op. cit., 256-57.

45 Augustine, *The City of God*, trans. Marcus Dods; in *Great Books of the Western World*, ed. Robert Maynard Hutchins and Mortimer J. Adler (Encyclopaedia Britannica, Inc., 1952), 18:V.10.

46 Best, op. cit., 35.

47 Edward B. Pusey, *What Is Of Faith As To Everlasting Punishment?* (James Parker and Co., 1881), 22-24; cited in Fisk, op.cit., 222.

48 Hodges, op. cit., 7:12.

10
Foreknowledge And Man's Will

A s with God's sovereignty, many theologians and philosophers seem to find a conflict also between God's foreknowledge and free will. If God knows what will happen before it happens, then it must happen as He foreknew or His foreknowledge would be wrong. That being the case, how could anyone be free to make a choice? We will consider that question in detail. First of all, however, we need to define some terms.

The biblical doctrine of foreknowledge simply states that God knows everything that will happen before it happens. The psalmist's statement, "For there is not a word in my tongue, but, lo, O LORD, thou knowest it altogether" (Psalms 139:4), tells us that God knows every thought and word before we speak it and has known it from eternity past. At the counsel of apostles and elders in Jerusalem, James stated clearly, "Known unto God are all his works from the beginning of the world" (Acts 15:18). For that to be true, God must have known everything related to what He would do. This biblical truth is clearly necessary if God is to be omnipotent, omniscient and omnipresent, the Creator and Sustainer of all.

Unquestionably, from eternity past, God must have known His creation inside and out. That includes the motions of the stars and electrons, and the exact location at any nanosecond of each atom and the earthly bodies they comprise, animate and inanimate. God knew everything that would happen to each one and how each would function. Before He created the universe or men or angels, God knew every event that would ever occur in heaven or the physical universe, and thus necessarily every thought, word and deed of every human or angel that would ever exist.

Creator And Creation

This cornerstone truth of Scripture was stated well by Augustine: "For to confess that God exists, and at the same time to deny that He has foreknowledge of future things, is the most manifest folly . . . . But . . . we [who] confess the most high and true God Himself, do confess His will, supreme power, and prescience." [1] No one, however, not even Calvin or Luther, stated God's foreknowledge more fully than the much defamed Arminius:

> [God] knows all things possible, whether they be in the capability of God or of the creature . . . imagination or enunciation . . . all things that could have an existence . . . those which are necessary and contingent, good and bad, universal and particular, future, present and past, excellent and vile; He knows things substantial and accidental of every kind; the actions and passions, the modes and circumstances . . . external words and deeds, internal thoughts, deliberations, counsels, and determinations, and the entities of reason, whether complex or simple. [2]

Calvinism, unfortunately, takes an unbiblical and illogical view of foreknowledge: "If God did not foreordain all things, then he could not know the future." [3] Without scriptural support, Calvin declared that God "foresees the things which are to happen, simply because he has decreed that they are so to happen . . . . " [4] Going even further, another author says that "The idea that God knows the future without having planned it and without controlling it is totally foreign to Scripture." [5] But he doesn't back up that assertion with Scripture. In fact, nowhere does Scripture say or even imply that God knows all beforehand *only because He has foreordained and caused it.*

How, then, can God be sure that what He foreknows will happen and that something will not intervene to change the future? He knows what will happen because He is all-knowing and therefore the future is as plain to Him as the past. If God had to plan and cause something to happen or even to control its occurrence in order to know it would take place He would be limited in His foreknowledge and therefore not the infinite, omniscient God that He is. Consequently, every detail of every crime and disease and of the destruction to property and the human suffering and loss of life and limb caused by natural disasters would also be foredained and caused by God.

We are told that "one day is with the Lord as a thousand years, and a thousand years as one day" (2 Peter 3:8); and that "a thousand years in thy sight are but as yesterday when it is past, and as a watch in the night" (Psalms 90:4). Some have attempted to find a hidden prophetic or cryptic message in these statements, but the prophecy enthusiasts can't agree upon what it is. In fact, there is no hidden message.

The phrases "with the Lord" and "in thy sight" are the key to understanding this rather simple and straightforward declaration. Time is part of the physical universe which God created. God is therefore by very definition outside of time and thus time is unrelated to Him.

As one scientist recently explained, "The actual existence of past, present, and future is required by Einstein's theory of relativity. All space and time form a four-dimensional continuum that simply exists; the theory does not permit time to be treated as a dimension in which the future is open or incomplete. The theory of relativity has measurable consequences and has been validated by rigorous experimental tests." He further explained:

> From a Christian point of view, it is reasonable to conclude that the temporal and the spatial extent of our universe were created together, and thus the entire four-dimensional structure resides before its Creator in an eternal present. Thus our modern scientific understanding of the nature of time fits quite well with the Christian tradition that God has knowledge of all time, past, present, and future: "Before Abraham was, I am." [6]

God's Continual Protection

God can know the future without His foreknowledge influencing it because time is part of this physical universe of which God knows everything as an outside observer. The universe is not an extension of God; He is not a part of it but is totally separate and distinct from space, time and matter. Therefore, just as He looks at the universe from outside, so He looks at time as part of it, seeing past, present and future from outside, knowing it all at once.

We are finite and God is infinite; therefore, we could not possibly understand *how* He knows the future. He has given us enough intelligence, however, to know that He *must* know it. As David said, speaking for all mankind, "Such knowledge is too wonderful for me; it is high, I cannot attain unto it" (Psalms 139:6).

Scripture makes it equally clear that God is no passive observer entirely disinterested in events taking their own course in the universe He has created. On the contrary, keeping a watchful eye and playing an active part, He fulfills His eternal purpose for all creation. As the psalmist declared, "Say unto God, How terrible [awesome] art thou in thy works! . . . Come and see the works of God: he is terrible in his doing toward the children of men . . . . He ruleth by his power for ever . . . " (Psalms 66:3,5,7).

God exerts His influence upon men and events (exactly as He has foreknown He would from eternity past) in order to create the future for us which He desires and has willed. Whatever influence or action He has foreknown would be needed on His part (in light of man's intentions and actions) to implement His plans would obviously also be part of God's foreknowledge, eliminating any necessity of emergency adjustment.

At times all Christians have an awareness of God's marvelous and gracious intervention in their lives. "Just in time" intervention (the way God from our perspective so often works) may seem like a last-minute thought on His part, but that is clearly not the case. No doubt His good hand is always upon His people, but in ways beyond human comprehension. As David said again:

> Thou has beset me behind and before, and laid thine hand upon me . . . . Whither shall I go from thy spirit? or whither shall I flee from thy presence? . . . into heaven . . . in hell . . . the uttermost part of the sea; even there shall thy hand lead me, and thy right hand shall hold me . . . .

> How precious also are thy thoughts unto me, O God! how great is the sum of them! If I should count them, they are more in number than the sand: when I awake, I am still with thee. (Psalms 139:5-18)

The Problem Of Evil

It is an inescapable fact that in spite of God's foreknowledge and sovereignty, evil predominates in human affairs. That God is not the author of evil is clearly stated in the Bible, as we have already seen. Therefore, we can only conclude that He has in His sovereignty given man moral responsibility to be exercised with free choice, allowing him to choose wickedness if he desires, though that is not what God desires for mankind. Total Depravity as defined by Calvinism is the culprit that eliminates man's power of choice. Man's alleged inability to choose good removed the faculty of free will:

> Inasmuch as Adam's offspring are born with sinful natures, they do not have the ability to choose spiritual good over evil. Consequently, man's will is no longer free...from the dominion of sin...as Adam's will was free before the fall.[7]

The Bible presents evil as the result of man's free will choosing for self instead of for God. The Calvinist, however, in denying human moral freedom, makes God the cause of all evil, insisting that He "creates the very thoughts and intents of the soul." [8] As Calvin declared, "The first man fell because the Lord deemed it meet that he should . . . because he saw that his own glory would thereby be displayed . . . . Man therefore falls, divine providence so ordaining, but he falls by his own fault . . . . I will not hesitate, therefore, simply to confess with Augustine . . . that the destruction consequent upon predestination is also most just." [9] This idea, however, is so contradictory to man's God-given conscience and sense of justice that Calvin spent much of his *Institutes* struggling unsuccessfully to justify it. Calvin himself states:

The decree, I admit, is dreadful; and yet it is impossible to deny that God foreknew what the end of man was to be before he made him, and foreknew, because he had so ordained by his decree. [10]

In defending God's sovereignty, another Calvinist, at the same time that he denies that man has a free will, implies that man's will must exist after all: "Free will is the invention of man, instigated by the devil." [11] How can free will be man's invention by an act of his will if his will doesn't exist? Calvin struggles with the problem of man's will and is forced to acknowledge that man is not rational without it:

I feel pleased with the well-known saying which has been borrowed from the writings of Augustine, that man's natural gifts were corrupted by sin, and his supernatural gifts withdrawn . . . . [In fact, man was never "supernatural."]

For although there is still [after Adam's fall] some residue of intelligence and judgment as well as will [because] reason, by which man discerns between good and evil . . . could not be entirely destroyed; but . . . a shapeless ruin is all that remains . . . the will, because inseparable from the nature of man, did not perish, but was so enslaved by depraved lusts as to be incapable of one righteous desire . . .

To charge the intellect with perpetual blindness so as to leave it no intelligence of any description whatever, is repugnant not only to the Word of God, but to common experience . . . the human mind [retains] a certain desire of investigating truth . . . [but it] fails before it reaches the goal . . . falling away into vanity . . . . unable, from dulness, to pursue the right path . . . and, after various wanderings, stumbling every now and then like one groping in darkness, at length gets so completely bewildered . . . .

Still, however, man's efforts are not always so utterly fruitless as not to lead to some results . . . . [12]

Calvin carries on in this fashion page after page. Man has *some* intelligence for discerning "between good and evil," but that ability is "a shapeless ruin . . . ." What does that mean? He can't tell us. The will did not *perish* but was so enslaved as to be morally useless in desiring the good which it dimly perceives. Where does the Bible say that? Calvin fails to support this assertion by careful exegesis of Scripture. Man has *some* desire after truth, but is unable due to "dulness" to pursue it fully so that he becomes "completely bewildered," yet his efforts are not "so utterly fruitless as not to lead to *some* results . . . ." This is doubletalk.

Why Doesn't God Stop Evil And Suffering?

Of course, man and Satan must be blamed and God must be exonerated, but this isn't easy to do if God has predestined everything. Many pages and even chapters of the *Institutes* are given to attempting to prove that everything man does, including all evil, is foreordained of God but that man is nevertheless guilty and is justly punished by God for doing evil. (See for example *Institutes* I:xv-xviii; III: xxi-xxiv.) Denying that man can will anything of himself, Calvin declares, "That men do nothing save at the secret instigation of God, and do not discuss and deliberate on anything, but what he has previously decreed with himself, and brings to pass by his secret direction, is proved by numberless clear passages of Scripture." [13]   In fact, there is no such Scripture – and Calvin's examples apply only to some men, not to all.

Could not the sinner blame for his sin and eternal suffering in the lake of fire a God who allows him to choose only evil and not good, and by eternal decree sovereignly originated his evil thoughts and caused his evil deeds and in punishment for that evil predestined him to eternal torment? But wait! Doesn't Romans 9:19-22 declare that no man has the right to complain against God? Paul certainly implies that by the way he phrases the questions: "Shall the thing formed say to him that formed it, Why hast thou made me thus? Hath not the potter power over the clay, of the same lump to make one vessel unto honour, and the other unto dishonour?" That important question will be dealt with in depth in its proper place.

Surely one could at least ask why God, if He is sovereign and all-powerful, doesn't intervene to the extent of stopping all evil. That is a meaningless question, however, if (as is claimed) God has decreed the rampant evil and suffering that plague mankind. Why would He undo what He has foreordained? Yet Calvinists insist that God *could* stop all evil if He so desired because He controls everything. But how could God change what He has predestined? He cannot change His mind or go back on His Word. Therefore, if He foreordained evil He cannot stop it. Here we uncover another contradiction.

The question with which we are continually confronted is this: Why would a good God who *is* love decree evil and suffering for billions not only in this life but for eternity in the lake of fire? That question is an embarrassment to at least some Calvinists, such as R.C. Sproul, because there is no rational (much less biblical) answer within that system of theology. This was admitted by Calvin himself: "I again ask how it is that the fall of Adam involves so many nations with their infant children in eternal death without remedy, unless that is so meet to God? Here the most loquacious tongues must be dumb." [14]

On the contrary, there is a biblical answer to this vital question: man has genuine moral responsibility to God because, beginning with Adam and Eve and down to the present "all have sinned" by their own free will, not by an imposed divine decree. Therefore, any sovereign intervention short of wiping out the human race would not solve the problem of evil, because evil is an act of self that comes from within the heart of man.

Jesus said it is the human heart itself from which "proceed . . . evil thoughts, murders, adulteries, fornications, thefts, false witness, blasphemies . . ." (Matthew 15:19). The only solution short of destroying mankind, as God almost did with the flood, is to create a new race through a complete change of the heart. Calvinism claims that God can do this through a sovereign "regeneration" of whomever He pleases without any faith or understanding on man's part. If that were the case, He could have done so with Adam and Eve and with all mankind, eliminating the sin and suffering in man's entire history.

The biblical answer is found in Christ alone. It is through His death in payment of our sins and His resurrection to live His life in believers that man can be forgiven and born again of the Spirit of God. This wonderful salvation cannot be forced upon anyone but is God's gracious gift for all who will receive it through believing the gospel of Jesus Christ. It is by faith that we are saved and created in Christ Jesus "unto good works, which God hath before ordained that we should walk in them" (Ephesians 2:8-10). To believe the gospel and to receive Christ requires the exercise of a genuine choice on man's part, a choice which Calvinism will not allow. As Oxford professor Andrew Fairbairn explained,

> While Freedom reigned in Heaven, Necessity governed on earth; and men were but pawns in the hands of the Almighty who moved them whithersoever He willed. This was the principle common to theologies like those of Augustine and Calvin . . . . It made illusions of our most common experience. [15]

Practical Consequences Of Denying Free Will

Sadly, as we have earlier seen in discussing the Calvinistic synods, assemblies and creeds, many of those who deny that God allows any free choice to man have been prone to act like the Deity they believed in by denying choice to those who disagreed with them and attempting to coerce everyone into conformity. In this they were following Calvin, who "demanded that the state must consent to be the servant of the church . . . . Liberty of conscience was not granted. Heretics and dissenters were executed or banished, and the people were compelled by the arms of the magistracy to perform what was considered their religious duties." [16]

Setting up a state church in the early days of the Reformation, Calvinists forced their views on others whenever possible. One historian writes, "A majority of the framers of the new creeds [in England and Scotland] believed in the divine right of Presbyterianism. They considered it a duty of the state to enforce uniformity, and were not prepared to make concessions of any importance to the Independents [i.e., the "free churches" that rejected the state church system]. In 1648, Parliament passed an act of extremely intolerant character. Eight [theological] errors [were] made punishable with death." [17]

The Westminster Assembly was called and financed by Parliament and was controlled by Presbyterians; Baptists and Independents were excluded by design. In fact, Baptists and Independents were regarded as "mortal enemies of the State Church." [18] Tolerance for any religious belief other than Calvinism "was denounced by leading members of the [Westminster] Assembly as the 'last and strongest hold of Satan....'" The Assembly was determined to enforce its brand of religion "upon the entire population." [19]

This small segment of history provides hundreds of examples of men who loved the Lord with their whole heart and were willing to suffer imprisonment and death in His service, yet because of some of their religious beliefs they treated other Christians in a most un-Christian manner. Samuel Rutherford was such a man. His letters from prison contained such deep spiritual insights and were so moving that nearly 400 editions were eventually published. Robert Murray McCheyne said that "the *Letters of Samuel Rutherford* were often in his hand." Richard Baxter held these letters in such regard that he said that apart from the Bible "such a book as *Mr. Rutherford's Letters* the world never saw the like." Spurgeon considered them "the nearest thing to inspiration which can be found in all the writings of mere men." [20] Historians described Rutherford as a "gracious and godly man." Yet because of his Calvinist beliefs he "denied absolutely the moral principles underlying religious toleration." [21] Sounding like the popes and the Vatican he despised, he even went so far as to declare that "there is but one true Church and all who are outside it are heretics who must be destroyed!" [22]

Never did Christ or His apostles or the early church attempt to force anyone to believe the gospel. The tolerance the early church had for the ungodly around them was not an acceptance of their errors. It was a recognition that no one could be forced against his will into the kingdom of God. They attempted to persuade the heathen to believe the gospel, but never did they attempt to force them to do so — nor did they believe in a God who could or would. The gospel is the good news of God's love in Christ and can only be received *willingly* from the heart. Since Calvinism denies the necessity of choice, it was only natural that its adherents would seek to force their views on all dissenters.

Roger Williams, one of the best-known advocates of religious freedom in his day, published a protest titled *The Bloudy Tenent [Bloody Tenet] of Persecution for Cause and Conscience*. He fled England for America, where he was badly treated by the Puritans. In England, the Westminster Assembly had his book publicly burned. [23] In 1648 the Presbyterians succeeded in enacting the "gag law . . . to punish the Baptists as 'blasphemers and heretics' . . . . Under this infamous law four hundred Baptists were thrown into prison." [24] In fact, dissenters had been suffering persecution and imprisonment for years — Protestants suffering at the hands of fellow Protestants for not being Calvinists.

Nearly thirty years before, the following entreaty, titled "A most Humble Supplication of many of the King's Majesty's loyal subjects . . . who are persecuted (only for differing in religion) contrary to Divine and human testimonies," had been smuggled out of a prison:

> Our miseries are long and lingering imprisonments for many years in divers counties of England, in which many have died and left behind them widows, and many small children; taking away our goods . . . not for any disloyalty to your Majesty, nor hurt to any mortal man . . . but only because we dare not assent unto, and practise in the worship of God, such things as we have not faith in, because it is sin against the Most High. [25]

Many Calvinists would deplore the persecution perpetrated by the early proponents of this doctrine. They would not approve of that side of the Westminster Assembly. Yet they praise its Calvinistic Confession, seemingly blind to the connection between the two. And they zealously promote Calvinism as "Reformation theology," as though the Calvinists had alone carried the Reformation on their shoulders. There were hundreds of thousands of others who were just as sincere in their faith (and we believe far more biblical) as were Calvin and Luther; and they suffered for Christ at the hands not only of the Roman Catholics but of Calvinists and Lutherans as well. Those who hold to the same biblical faith today may not be persecuted, but they are still dismissed by many Calvinists and Lutherans as heretics.

Love: The Missing Ingredient

God's love for the lost and the love of Christians for the lost — two major interrelated themes of Scripture — have no part in Calvinism. We know many who would take offense at that statement and who, indeed, are lovingly concerned for the lost. This is, however, *in spite* of their Calvinism, not because of it. Though a Presbyterian theological professor and one-time Moderator of the General Assembly, Herrick Johnson acknowledged:

> Across the Westminster Confession could justly be written: "The Gospel for the elect only." That Confession was written under the absolute dominion of one idea, the doctrine of predestination. It does not contain one of the three truths: God's love for a lost world; Christ's compassion for a lost world; and the gospel universal for a lost world. [26]

There is no escaping the fact that in Calvin's entire *Institutes of the Christian Religion* there is *not one mention* of God's love for the lost! Nor is that surprising in view of the fact that Calvin's God has no love for the lost but can only love the elect. [27] Does that not bother today's evangelical leaders who praise Calvin as the great exegete and call themselves Calvinists? Or haven't they noticed? How is that possible?

Furthermore, Calvin's concept of love is defective. He says that God "requires that the love which we bear to Him be diffused among all mankind, so that our fundamental principle must ever be, Let a man be what he may, he is still to be loved, because God is loved." [28] This is one of several places where Calvin says the Christian is to love "all mankind." Should not God, then, who *is love*, love all men also? Calvin never says so, but at least here he seems to imply an agreement with that principle — though his idea of God's love is strange indeed.

He tells us that God's "boundless goodness is displayed" to everyone, "but not so as to bring all to salvation." [29] How could a "goodness" that stops short of what it could do be seriously described as "boundless"? This goodness (in spite of stopping short) is said by Calvin to be "evidence of his [God's] love." Again we ask, how can failing to do all the good that God is able to do be evidence of His love? And evidence to whom?

This warped view of God's love is further revealed in Calvin's statement that this alleged display of God's "goodness" is not for the purpose of helping all mankind. Instead, God's intention is to bring "a heavier judgment . . . [upon] the reprobate for rejecting the evidence of his [God's] love." [30] This argument leaves one groping for ground beneath the fog. A goodness that doesn't do all the good it could but is akin to callously leaving victims of a collision to die in the wreckage could hardly be evidence of God's love! Would it not, instead, be evidence of a *lack* of love?

Follow Calvin's reasoning: God loves and saves only the elect; He neglects to save those whom He hasn't elected to salvation. In the process, however, somehow through "shin[ing] the light of his word on the undeserving," he reveals His goodness and love by withholding it from them! And He withholds His love, the better to damn them for "rejecting the evidence of his love"! Such twisted logic is an integral part of Calvinism in its attempt to show that God loves those whom He damns!

The very same destruction of reason has infected many of today's Calvinists as well. Consider the following from John Piper, well-known author and pastor and leading Calvinist:

> We do not deny that all men are the intended beneficiaries of the cross *in some sense* . . . . What we deny is that all men are intended as the beneficiaries of the death of Christ *in the same way*. All of God's mercy toward unbelievers — from the rising sun (Matthew 5:45) to the worldwide preaching of the gospel (John 3:16) — is made possible because of the cross . . . . Every time the gospel is preached to unbelievers it is the mercy of God that gives this opportunity for salvation. [31] (Emphasis in original)

Reading such obviously contradictory statements and trying to reason with their supporters leaves one with a sense of complete frustration. Proclaiming the gospel to those He has predestined to damnation is an act of God's mercy giving "opportunity for salvation" to those who can't be saved?! And the gospel being preached to the doomed stems from God's "mercy toward unbelievers" flowing from the Cross?

Somehow, words such as love, grace and mercy have lost what once seemed to be their meaning! It is impossible to reason with those for whom the above seems reasonable. I believe Calvinists are saved and most of them do preach the gospel. At the same time, however, there is the distinct impression that we are talking about two different "Gods" and two different "gospels." One is described in the Bible; the other is a product of Calvin's peculiar interpretation.

Differentiating Foreknowledge From Predestination

It cannot be denied that Calvinism's view of predestination, which for Calvin was seemingly empty of love, is a large part of the problem. Central to that belief is the denial that God's foreknowledge has anything to do with knowing something in advance. Instead, foreknowledge is defined as foreordaining and is equated with predestination. As we have seen, Pink says, "God foreknows what will be because He has decreed what shall be." [32] He was following Calvin, who said that "God foreknew what the end of man was to be . . . because he had so ordained by his decree." [33]

For God to foreknow something without having decreed it is not allowed by Calvin. Thus when Paul writes, "For whom he did foreknow, he also did predestinate" (Romans 8:29), Calvin insisted that it must be read, "For whom He predestinated He also did predestinate" — an obvious redundancy. This will be discussed when we come to Predestination. It is mentioned here only to show why this view was adopted by Calvin, a view which is followed loyally by his followers today.

To know something in advance is not the same as predetermining that it will happen. Foreordination and foreknowledge are not the same, but they can overlap. Whatever God has predestined He obviously knows will happen. His foreknowledge, however, is not limited to what He has predestined. He does not need to predestine something in order to know it will happen. Were that the case, as we have seen, God would not be infinite in His knowledge.

Predestination, as we shall see in more detail later, is a foundational doctrine in Calvinism. Pink claims that "God *decreed* from all eternity that Judas should betray the Lord Jesus" because through Zechariah "God declared that His Son should be sold for 'thirty pieces of silver' (Zechariah 11:12) . . . . In prophecy God makes known what *will* be, and in making known what will be, He is but revealing to us what He has ordained *shall be*." Pink goes on to argue that nevertheless Judas was "a *responsible agent* in fulfilling this decree of God."[34]

Philosophers and theologians have speculated about how God could know the future without *causing* the future. The consequences of whether or not this is true are serious. We have already given two reasons why God's foreknowledge of what will happen need have no influence upon what to man are future events. Even Calvin wrote, "I, for my part, am willing to admit, that mere prescience lays no necessity on the creatures; though some do not assent to this, but hold that it is itself the cause of things." [35] Calvin's reason, however, was the fact that he held foreknowledge and predestination to be one and the same: "but since he foresees the things which are to happen, simply because he has decreed that they are so to happen, it is vain to debate about prescience, while it is clear that all events take place by his sovereign appointment." [36]

There is obviously a vast difference between saying that God fully *foresees* everything that will happen and *allows* much that is not His perfect will (which Calvin would not permit because of his view that everything is predestined) — and in saying that God *predetermines* everything that occurs and thus is the *cause* of it (which Calvin insisted is the case). The latter view, which is the foundational doctrine of his system, makes man a mere automaton and reveals God as the effective cause behind all evil, wickedness and sin. Thus a terrible blemish is imposed upon God's holy character!

Luther likewise asserts that "God foreknows and wills all things." And he argues that if this is not true, then "how can you believe, trust and rely on His promises?" [37] The answer is, "Quite easily. We rely upon God's promises because He is God, knows all and cannot lie."

Luther is simply mistaken here as he was on much else. Scripture nowhere indicates that God must *will* all things in order to *know* them — or in order to make and keep promises. What God promises to do He will do regardless of the will or actions of man or nature, yet without violating human will. That He is able to protect us and bring us to heaven does not require that He must will every event that swirls about us — much less that He must be the direct cause of sin we commit or of which we may become the victims.

Foreknowledge As Proof

More than simply claiming that God knows the future in advance, Scripture proves this fact by revealing His infinite foreknowledge in the hundreds of accurate prophecies recorded therein. God foretells the future through His prophets for a number of reasons, the greatest being to prove that He is the one true God as opposed to false gods and to prove beyond question that, in contrast to all other sacred books of world religions, the Bible is His only and infallible written Word to mankind. Thus God declares:

Behold, the former things [which I foretold] are come to pass, and new things do I declare: before they spring forth I tell you of them. (Isaiah 42:9)

I am God, and there is none like me, declaring the end from the beginning, and from ancient times the things that are not yet done, saying, My counsel shall stand, and I will do all my pleasure . . . . (Isaiah 46:9-10)

I have even from the beginning declared it to thee; before it came to pass I shewed it thee: lest thou shouldest say, Mine idol hath done them, and my graven image, and my molten image, hath commanded them. (Isaiah 48:5)

For at least two reasons, one cannot deny God's complete foreknowledge of the future. First of all, one would be denying God as He necessarily is and as the Bible presents Him. Secondly, one would be denying the very foundation of Christianity. Old Testament prophecies comprise the major evidence God offers to man's faith that Jesus of Nazareth is the Christ, the Messiah of Israel, and that without Him there is no Christianity. So complete is this proof that no one who makes a careful investigation can honestly deny who the Lord Jesus Christ truly is.

The Apostle Paul firmly links the gospel of our salvation in Christ with God's foreknowledge expressed through His prophets: " . . . separated unto the gospel of God (which he had promised afore by his prophets in the holy scriptures), concerning his Son Jesus Christ our Lord . . . " (Romans 1:1-3). Often overlooked is the fact that in setting forth the essential elements of the gospel which must be believed if one is to be saved, Paul substantiates the message of salvation with prophecy. Twice he supports his delineation of the gospel with the phrase, "according to the scriptures," meaning, of course, Old Testament prophecies as well as the record in the New Testament:

Moreover, brethren, I declare unto you the gospel which I preached unto you, which also ye have received, and wherein ye stand; . . . how that Christ died for our sins *according to the scriptures*; and that he was buried, and that he rose again the third day *according to the scriptures* . . . (1 Corinthians 15:1-4). (Emphasis added)

Unless God's prophets, through His foreknowledge, had told us how, where and when the Messiah would be born, and of His sinless life and miracles, His betrayal for thirty pieces of silver by one of His disciples, His rejection by His people the Jews, His cruel crucifixion and His glorious resurrection, we would have had no way of identifying the Messiah when He came. Had the precise details not been foretold by prophets who had already been proved to be inspired of God, His betrayal, rejection and crucifixion would have been enough to convince us (as they convince the Jews to this day who neglect their own prophets) that

He could not have been the Messiah. The detailed identification leaves those who reject Christ without excuse.

God's foreknowledge expressed through His prophets is the very root of the gospel and of the Christian faith. None of the world's religions has such prophetic evidence for its validity. There are no prophecies for Buddha, Confucius, Muhammad or any other leader of the world's religions, whereas there are literally hundreds of prophecies establishing the truth concerning Jesus Christ.

Likewise, it is God's proven foreknowledge in prophecies already fulfilled which gives us confidence that those prophesied events which are yet future will indeed come to pass. It is right here that we confront another odd contradiction (beyond the scope of this book, but which we have dealt with in other writings): that those of the so-called Reformed position who put such emphasis upon foreknowledge and predestination have, following Augustine's lead yet further, rejected the premillennial rapture of the church, the literal thousand-year reign of Christ on David's throne, and the literal fulfillment of all of God's promises to His chosen people, Israel, along with so much else that is clearly prophesied for the future. Instead, like Augustine, they have chosen to allegorize and spiritualize away this massive and vital portion of God's revealed foreknowledge.

What About Man's Will?

As surely as we recognize that God is sovereign, we also recognize that we have at least limited freedom to act within whatever bounds He may have established for human actions. This recognition seems to be continually validated by daily experience. What L.S. Keyser says could hardly be argued: "That man has a conscience which distinguishes between right and wrong and free will by which he is able to choose between them scarcely seems to require any argument .... His whole experience tells him that he is a free moral being." [38] Alexander Maclaren, one of England's great Baptist preachers, put it in similar terms:

> If I cannot trust my sense that I can do this or not do it, as I choose, there is nothing that I can trust. Will is the power of determining which of two [or more] roads I shall go ... God, the infinite Will, has given to men, whom He made in His own image, this inexplicable and awful power of coinciding with or opposing His purpose and His voice .... [39]

It is not only Calvinists and Lutherans who deny free will, but for thousands of years atheists and skeptics have also argued against this belief. Even Arminius made pronouncements about free will which at times sounded as though they could have come from Calvin or Luther. He declared that "the Free Will of man towards the True Good is ... imprisoned, destroyed, and lost ... it has no powers whatsoever except such as are excited by Divine grace." [40] Of course, neither can man think rationally or even breathe except by God's grace — but we do think and breathe and we make choices by our own wills as well as by God's grace.

No matter how vague our understanding of free will may be or what questions and disagreements surround it, it hardly seems reasonable that our perception of making choices, some of which we agonize over for days, could simply be an illusion and that we are mere puppets of God's foreordination. In his *Confessions*, Augustine, supposed originator of "absolute sovereignty," wrote:

> I knew as well that I had a will as that I lived: when then I did will or nill anything, I was most sure that no other than myself did will and nill: and I all but saw that there was the cause of my sin." [41]

The very fact that John tells us that the redeemed are born again "not of the will of man" indicates that there must be much else for which the will of man is to be credited. Peter's statement that men "willingly are ignorant" (2 Peter 3:5) of God's truth indicates that depravity is not something beyond man's control but the product of his willing choice. That God says to Israel, "If ye be willing and obedient, . . . but if ye refuse and rebel . . . " (Isaiah 1:19-20), indicates again that man can be reasoned with and can choose by an act of his will either to obey or to disobey God. There are numerous statements in Scripture indicating that God has given man a free will to make moral and spiritual choices for which he alone bears responsibility and is to be blamed.

While God works "all things after [according to] the counsel of His own will" (Ephesians 1:11) this does not prove that God *causes* everything that happens in the universe. It is perfectly compatible with God's sovereignty for Him to allow man to disobey Him. Indeed, we have also noted that the power of choice was given to man as a decision of God's sovereignty so that man might receive God's love, love Him in return and receive the gift of salvation.

Confusion Where Clarity Is Needed

While Calvinism rejects free will, its adherents can't agree upon what this means. Some allow man freedom in the sphere of earthly matters and deny it only when it comes to believing in Christ. Palmer defines "free will" as "the kind of freedom that no man has," not only "to believe on Christ or to reject Him," but even "the ability or freedom to choose either good or evil." [42] Spencer further explains, "*Total Depravity* insists that man does not have a 'free will' in the sense that he is *free* to trust Jesus Christ as his Lord and Saviour." [43] Vance counters that "No philosopher who denies to man a free will does so on the basis of man's depravity." [44] Nor did or could Calvin produce any scripture to support his undefined assertions that man can choose *some* good but *not enough* good or that he is therefore unable to believe in Christ to the saving of his soul.

Even defining terms divides Calvinists. Charles Hodge insists that "the [Calvinist] doctrine of man's inability, therefore, does not assume that man has ceased to be a free moral agent." [45] Pink, however, declares that "'free moral agency' is an expression of human invention [46] [which denies] that he [man] is totally depraved . . . [47] the sinner's will is . . . free in only one direction, namely in the direction of evil." [48] Spurgeon said, "Free will is nonsense." [49] Pink quotes J.N. Darby in another *non sequitur*: "If Christ came to save that which is lost, free will has no place." [50]

On the other hand, equally strong Calvinists Talbot and Crampton rightfully insist that to deny that man has "free moral agency would be to allege that he could never make a choice about anything at all. That would be absurd." [51] Another Calvinist points out that "Calvin retains [to man] so little of the will . . . that he cannot explain adequately the moral character of human action [in] choices between good and evil." [52] If nothing else, the confusion among Calvinists forces each of us to come to his own conclusion based upon Scripture.

Arthur W. Pink is best known for his strong views on God's sovereignty, especially through his book *The Sovereignty of God*. Vance points out that "Pink's Calvinism upset some Calvinists so bad[ly] that an attempt was made to tone it down by The Banner of Truth Trust, by issuing, in 1961, a 'British Revised Edition' of *The Sovereignty of God* in which three chapters and the four appendices were expunged. For this they have been severely criticized (and rightly so) by other Calvinists." [53]

Do Outside Influences Destroy Free Will?

In order to support the doctrine of total depravity, the Calvinist must show that man's will is totally enslaved by sin. The argument has been used that no choice could be made without some influence. There is an element of truth in this statement. Obviously, whatever choice one makes is impacted to some extent by multiple factors: health or mental mood, the weather, financial pressures, temptations, lust, timing, opportunity and so forth. And many if not most of these influences (which could be nearly infinite in number) would seem to be beyond the control of the chooser. How then can the will ever be free?

In pressing this point, Talbot and Crampton write, "If this Arminian concept of free will is taken to its logical conclusion, then it would be sinful to preach the gospel to fallen man. Why? Because it would be an attempt to *cause* him to turn to Christ, which would be a violation of his free will." [54] In other words, it would be wrong to attempt to influence man to believe the gospel because his choice would not have been made freely. Echoing this same argument, Pink imagines he delivers a death blow to free will with this broadside: "There is something which *influences* the choice; something which *determines* the decision." [55]

First of all, it is fallacious and naive to label free will an "Arminian concept." For thousands of years many non-Christian philosophers have marshaled excellent arguments in favor of man's free will. Nor is any influence upon a decision necessarily determinative, but merely one of many factors taken into consideration *by the will* in arriving at its decision.

Further, the very fact that various influences are brought to bear in arriving at any choice is in itself evidence that man has a free will. If man had no will, there would be nothing for these "influences" to affect. Without the will, would the immaterial and impersonal "influences" fight it out among themselves as to which decision to make? Influences don't make decisions. The will takes into consideration all factors, and no matter how compelling any influences may have been, the will still makes its own choice.

That it may have been influenced to some greater or lesser extent in no way proves that the will did not take all factors into consideration and make its own decision. No matter how it reached a resolution, only the will could have decided. Although the Calvinist looks to Augustine for so much and avidly quotes him for support, here again Augustine is ignored, for he argued persuasively on this very point:

> For if that is to be called *our necessity* which is not in our power . . . it is manifest that our wills by which we live uprightly or wickedly are not under such a necessity; for we do many things which, if we were not willing, we should certainly not do. This is primarily true of the act of willing itself — for if we will, it *is*; if we will not, it *is* not — for we should not will if we were unwilling. [56]

Back to Talbot and Crampton. Their admonition has some merit and should be taken to heart by many of today's preachers who through psychological and salesmanship techniques entrap multitudes in purely intellectual or emotional false professions of faith. Nevertheless, Paul said, "Knowing therefore the terror of the Lord, we persuade men . . . " (2 Corinthians 5:11). There is obviously a godly persuasion which does not violate free will. Moreover, as we have already seen, if Calvinism were true, Paul's use of persuasion would be misguided for other reasons: the elect would need no persuasion and the non-elect, being totally depraved and predestined to eternal damnation, could not be persuaded.

Foreknowledge And Man's Will

Given the above, a central issue has engaged philosophers, skeptics and theologians in debate for thousands of years: *how* can God's foreknowledge and man's free will both be true? Surely, whatever God's foreknowledge tells

Him will happen must happen, or God's knowledge of the future would be wrong. If God knows what every person will think or do, and if nothing can prevent what God foreknows from happening, then how can man be a free moral agent? How can a man choose by his own free will a particular course of action if God knew ahead of time that he would take that action and thus it would have been impossible for him not to have taken the action God foreknew?

To phrase it another way, inasmuch as God knows everything, and thus knows what everyone will ever think or do, isn't everything therefore predetermined? And wouldn't that fact rule out any possibility that man could make a free choice concerning anything at all? Doesn't God's foreknowledge destroy the possibility of any free choice on man's part, leaving us with nothing but deterministic fatalism?

We have already seen why God's foreknowledge has no causative effect upon man's free choice. God, being timeless, lives in one eternal now. He sees what to us are future events as though they had already happened – thus His foreknowledge has no effect on man's will. There is no reason why in His omniscience God cannot know what man will freely choose to do before he chooses to do it.

There is yet another question which troubles many: If man is free to choose between options, would that not in itself deny both God's sovereignty and His foreknowledge? Luther claimed that this question was the very heart of the Reformation and of the gospel itself. In fact, Luther dogmatically insisted that it was impossible for God to foreknow the future and for man at the same time to be a free agent to act as he wills.

Believing firmly in God's foreknowledge, Luther wrote an entire book titled *The Bondage of the Will* to prove that the very idea of man's free will is a fallacy and an illusion. Several reasons have already been given why Luther was wrong on this point and that issue will be dealt with further in the next chapter.

Though Calvin took so much from Augustine, like Luther he also rejected the Augustinian belief that God could foreknow the future and that at the same time man could have a free will. Calvin states no less dogmatically than Luther that this important issue isn't even open to discussion. According to him, foreknowledge leaves no room whatsoever for free will. Period. And why? Because foreknowledge to the Calvinist, as we have seen, is the same as predestination. God knows the future because He has decreed it. Such was Calvin's argument. He put it like this:

> If God merely foresaw human events, and did not also arrange and dispose of them at his pleasure, there might be room for agitating the question [of free will] . . . but since he foresees the things which are to happen, simply because

he has decreed them, they are so to happen, it is vain to debate about prescience
. . . .

If this frigid fiction [of free will] is received, where will be the omnipotence of
God, by which, according to his secret counsel on which everything depends,
he rules over all? [57]

We are astonished that Calvin repeatedly uses such fallacious reasoning,
and doubly astounded that so many leading evangelicals continue to praise him
for being such a great exegete. These objections have been answered. While
the Bible is clear that God foreknows all, never does it declare that His
foreknowledge is based on decreeing all. Nor is it biblically or rationally sound to
suggest that free will would even challenge God's sovereignty, much less destroy
it. The Calvinist assumes a contradiction between sovereignty and free will
which doesn't exist. The fact that God is able to allow man freedom of choice
while still effecting His purposes unhindered is all the more glorifying to His
sovereign wisdom, power and foreknowledge.

Augustine On Free Will

In taking so much else from him, the Calvinist overlooks the fact that
Augustine clearly affirmed the free will of man. [58] Moreover, Augustine argued
that there *is no incompatibility* between God's absolute sovereignty and man's
free will; and that to deny that fact, as did Luther and Calvin, would be "impious"!
In his refutation of Cicero's philosophical rejection of God's foreknowledge,
Augustine writes persuasively:

Nor let us be afraid lest, after all, we do not do by will that which we do by will,
because He, Whose foreknowledge is infallible, foreknew that we would do it
. . . . Now, against the sacrilegious and impious darings of reason, we assert
both that God knows all things before they come to pass and that we do by
our free will whatsoever we know and feel to be done by us only because we
will it . . . .

[F]or our wills themselves are included in that order of causes which is certain
to God and is embraced by His foreknowledge, for human wills are also causes
of human actions; and He Who foreknew all the causes of things would
certainly among those causes not have been ignorant of our wills . . . . Wherefore
our wills also have just so much power as God willed and foreknew that they
should have. [59]

Therefore we are by no means compelled, either, retaining the prescience of
God to take away the freedom of the will, or, retaining the freedom of the will,
to deny that He is prescient of future things, which is impious. But we embrace
both. We faithfully and sincerely confess both. [60]

Augustine holds to freedom of the human will even into the eternal state:
"Neither are we to suppose that, because sin shall have no power to delight

them, free will must be withdrawn. It will, on the contrary, be all the more truly free, because set free from delight in sinning to take unfailing delight in not sinning." [61]

When it came to free will, Calvin ignored Augustine completely. On the other hand, at the end of his life Augustine seemed to develop doubts on this subject about which he had made such firm pronouncements earlier. Those very pronouncements, however, were never withdrawn.

So once again, rather than looking to men, no matter how great their reputations, we are driven to come to our own conclusions on the basis of Scripture alone. In understanding what God's Word intends, however, we are obliged to use the reasoning powers with which God has endowed us. And it seems clear that all of these great men allowed their understanding of Scripture to be colored by prejudice as well as by faulty reasoning.

Nowhere is the failure to use sound reason in exegeting Scripture more apparent than in Luther's debate with Erasmus over free will. This will be considered next.

---

1   Augustine, *The City of God*, trans. Marcus Dobs. In *Great Books of the Western World*, ed. Robert Maynard Hutchins and Mortimer J. Adler (Encyclopaedia Brittanica, Inc., 1952), V.9.

2   Jacobus Arminius, *The Works of James Arminius*, trans. James and William Nichols (Baker Book House, 1986), 2:120.

3   David S. West (*The Baptist Examiner*, March 18, 1989), 5.

4   John Calvin, *Institutes of the Christian Religion*, trans. Henry Beveridge (Wm. Eerdmans Publishing Company, 1998 ed.), III:xxiii,6.

5   Grover E. Gunn, *The Doctrine of Grace* (Footstool Publications, 1987), 13.

6   Michael J. Kane, Ph.D., "Letters" (*Christianity Today*, July 9, 2001), 9.

7   David N. Steele and Curtis C. Thomas, *The Five Points of Calvinism* (Presbyterian and Reformed Publishing Co., 1963), 25.

8   Loraine Boettner, *The Reformed Doctrine of Predestination* (Presbyterian and Reformed Publishing Co., 1932), 32.

9   Calvin, op. cit., III: xxiii, 8.

10   Op.cit., III: xxiii, 7.

11   David O. Wilmouth (*The Baptist Examiner*, September 16, 1989), 5.

12   Calvin, op. cit., II: ii, 12-13.

13   Op. cit., I: xviii, 1.

14   Op. cit., III:xxiii,7.

15   Andrew M. Fairbairn, *The Philosophy of the Christian Religion* (The MacMillan Co., 1923), 179.

16   John Horsch, *History of Christianity* (John Horsch, 1903), 270.

17   George Park Fisher, *History of the Christian Church* (Charles Scribner's Sons, 1902), 406.

18   A.C. Underwood, *A History of the English Baptists* (The Baptist Union of Great Britain and Ireland, 1970), 72.

19   Albert H. Newman, *A Manual of Church History* (American Baptist Publication Society, 1933), II:286-87.

20   *Letters of Samuel Rutherford* (The Banner of Truth Trust, 1996; 1st ed. 1664), back cover.

21   David Gay, *Battle for the Church, 1517-1644* (Brachus, 1997), 438.

22   Underwood, op. cit.

23   C. Sylvester Horne, *A Popular History of the Free Churches* (James Clarke and Co., 1903), 124-27.

24   John T. Christian, *A History of the Baptists* (Sunday School Board of the Southern Baptist Convention, 1922), I:296-97.

25   Gay, op. cit., 367.

26   Quoted in Augustus H. Strong, *Systematic Theology* (Judson Press, 1907), 779.

27   Calvin, op. cit., II:xvi,3-4; II:xvii,2-5.

28   Op. cit., II:viii,55.

29   Op. cit., III:xxiv,2.

30   Ibid.

31   John Piper and Pastoral Staff, "TULIP: What We Believe about the Five Points of Calvinism: Position Paper of the Pastoral Staff" (Desiring God Ministries, 1997), 14.

32   Arthur W. Pink, *The Doctrine of Election and Justification* (Baker Book House, 1974), 172.

33   Calvin, op. cit., III:xxiii,7.

34   Pink, op. cit., 155.

35   Calvin, op. cit., III:xxiii,6.

36   Ibid.

37   Martin Luther, *The Bondage of the Will*, trans. J.I. Packer and O.R. Johnston (Fleming H. Revell, 1957, 11th prtg. 1999), 83-84.

38   Leander S. Keyser, *Election and Conversion* (Lutheran Literary Board, 1914), 96.

39   Alexander Maclaren, *Expositions of Holy Scripture* (Hodder and Stoughton, n.d.), II:333-34

40   Jacobus Arminius, *The Works of James Arminius*, trans. James and Williams Nichols (Baker Book House, 1986), 2:192.

41   Augustine, *The Confessions*, VII:5; in *Great Books of the Western World*, ed. Robert Maynard Hutchins and Mortimer J. Adler, trans. Edward Bonverie Pusey (Encyclopaedia Britannica, Inc., 1952), vol. 18.

42   Edwin H. Palmer, *the five points of calvinism* (Baker Books, enlarged ed., 20th prtg. 1980), 36.

43   Duane Edward Spencer, *TULIP: The Five Points of Calvinism in the Light of Scripture* (Baker Book House, 1979), 27.

44   Laurence M. Vance, *The Other Side of Calvinism* (Vance Publications, Pensacola FL, rev. ed. 1999), 201.

45   Charles Hodge, *Systematic Theology* (Wm. B. Eerdmans Publishing Co., 1986), 2:260.

46   Arthur W. Pink, *The Sovereignty of God* (Baker Book House, 2nd prtg. 1986), 143.

47   Op. cit., 138.

48   Op. cit., 135.

49   Charles H. Spurgeon, *Free Will – A Slave* (Free Grace Publications, 1977), 3.

50   Pink, *Sovereignty*, 138.

51   Kenneth G. Talbot and W. Gary Crampton, *Calvinism, Hyper-Calvinism and Arminianism* (Still Waters Revival Books, 1990), 18.

52   Dewey J. Hoitenga, *John Calvin and the Will: A Critique and Corrective* (Baker Books, 1997), 70.

53   Marc D. Carpenter, Pt. 1 of "The Banner of Truth Versus Calvinism" (*The Trinity Review*, May 1997), 1-4; cited in Vance, op. cit., 24.

54   Talbot and Crampton, op. cit., 21.

55   Cited in Vance, op.cit., 202.

56   Augustine, *City of God*, V.10

57   Calvin, op. cit., III:xxiii,6-7.

58   Augustine, *Confessions*, VII:iii,5; and *City of God*, V.9-10.

59   Augustine, *City of God*, V.9.

60   Op. cit., V.10.

61   Op. cit., XXII.30.

11
Erasmus And Luther In Debate

A s we have seen, nearly any in-depth discussion with Calvinists eventually touches on the issue of free will. When that happens, the challenge is almost always issued, "Have you read Luther's *Bondage of the Will?*" John Armstrong declares enthusiastically, "This is what the Reformation is ultimately all about . . . . Roman Catholic medieval theology had a synthetic idea . . . somehow God wasn't the sole and sufficient cause of the whole thing [salvation]. This is where the Reformers in *The Bondage of the Will*, Luther and other such treatments attack as it were. And why Luther said this is *the* important book because it...takes us back where the real battle is." [1]

Calvinists are not alone in their high regard for this lengthy treatise. Many evangelicals, even without having read *Bondage,* much less having given it serious thought, hold it and Luther in high regard simply because of the key role he played in the Reformation. Not only so-called Protestants but the entire Western world owes Martin Luther a debt of gratitude. That does not mean, however, that we need accept everything that came from his pen without comparing it carefully to God's Word.

Appalled by the licentiousness he had seen in the Vatican and among the clergy in his visit to Rome, and by the sale of indulgences as tickets to heaven (financing the ongoing construction and remodeling of St. Peter's Basilica), on October 31, 1517, Luther nailed his *Disputation on the power and efficacy of Indulgences* (known as *The Ninety-five Theses* [2]) to the door of the Wittenberg Castle Chapel. (John Calvin was then eight years old.) Copies translated from the original Latin were widely distributed in many languages, inciting heated debate all across Europe and arousing hope among multitudes that the yoke of Rome could at last be loosened, if not removed.

When one studies his 95 theses, however, there is an ambivalence which makes it seem that Luther, not desiring to break with his Church, was not entirely opposed to indulgences themselves but only to their abuses. For example his twenty-fourth thesis states, "For this reason most people are necessarily deceived by that indiscriminate and high-sounding promise of release from penalty." Why "most people"? Why not *all*? Consider the following excerpts of that daring document:

21. Thus those indulgence preachers are in error who say that a man is absolved from every penalty [but he is from *some*?] and saved by papal indulgences.

37. Any true Christian, whether living or dead, participates in all the blessings of Christ and the church; and this is granted him by God, even without indulgence letters [which offer some help?].

45. Christians are to be taught that he who sees a needy man and passes him by, yet gives his money for indulgences, does not buy papal indulgences but God's wrath [but under other circumstances he could buy something of value?].

52. It is vain to trust in salvation by indulgence letters, even though the indulgence commissary, or even the pope, were to offer his soul as security [but a promise of something less than salvation, such as forgiveness to lessen suffering in purgatory is acceptable?].

62. The true treasure of the church is the most holy gospel of the glory and grace of God [Does that still allow for indulgences to dispense a lesser treasure?].

76. We say on the contrary that papal indulgences cannot remove the very least of venial sins as far as guilt is concerned [but can they lessen the purgatorial suffering for sins?].

82. Why does not the pope empty purgatory for the sake of holy love and the dire need of the souls that are there if he redeems an infinite number of souls for the sake of miserable money with which to build a church [the implication is that he could but won't do it without being paid]?

83. Why are funeral and anniversary masses for the dead continued . . . [i.e., how do we know how many are needed and thus when to stop]?

90. To repress these very sharp arguments of the laity by force alone, and not to resolve them by giving reasons, is to expose the church and the pope to the ridicule of their enemies and to make Christians unhappy [i.e., there are good reasons for indulgences?]. [3]

A Few Relevant Facts

On October 12, 1518, Luther was summoned to Rome by order of Pope Leo X. Arrested, he was held at Augsburg for trial before Cardinal Cajetan. Refused an impartial tribunal, Luther fled for his life by night. On January 3, 1521, a formal bull was issued by the Pope consigning Luther to hell if he did not recant. The Emperor, pledging Luther's safety, summoned him to appear before the Imperial Diet in Worms on April 17, 1521. The Chancellor of Treves, orator of the Diet, demanded that he retract his writings. Humbly but firmly Luther made this fearless and famous reply:

> I cannot submit my faith either to the pope or to the councils, because it is clear as day that they have frequently erred and contradicted each other. Unless therefore I am convinced by the testimony of Scripture, or by the clearest reasoning . . . I cannot and I will not retract . . . . Here I stand; I can do no other; may God help me. Amen! [4]

Now an outlaw by papal edict, Luther fled again and was "kidnaped" on his way back to Wittenberg by friends who took him for safekeeping to Wartburg Castle. From there he disseminated more "heresy" in writings which further shook all Europe. Rome's determination to eliminate Lutheran infidelity, as expressed by the Catholic authorities in March 1529 at the second Diet of Speyer, provoked a number of independent princes to assert the right to live according to the Bible. They expressed this firm resolve in the famous "Protest" of April 19, 1529, from which the term "Protestant" was coined.

The Imperial Diet was convened in Augsburg for a thorough examination of Protestant heresies. (Luther, being a wanted man, dared not appear.) On June 25, 1530, the Augsburg Confession (prepared by Melanchthon in consultation with Luther) was read before about 200 dignitaries. It delineated the clear differences between Lutheranism and Catholicism. In particular, Article IV affirmed that men "are freely justified . . . their sins are forgiven for Christ's sake, who, by His death, has made satisfaction for our sins." Article XIII declared that "the Sacraments were ordained . . . to be signs and testimonies" and condemned "those who teach that the Sacraments justify by the outward act . . . . ." Article XV admonished "that human traditions instituted to propitiate God, to merit grace, and to make satisfaction for sins, are opposed to the Gospel and the doctrine of faith. Wherefore vows and traditions concerning meats and days, etc., instituted to merit grace and to make satisfaction for sins, are useless and contrary to the Gospel." [5]

Luther still hoped that the Church could be reformed from within. Thus the Augsburg Confession, in spite of many good provisions, still viewed the Roman Catholic Church as the true Church, and those signing it claimed to be true Catholics. Several times that document refers to the steadfastness of the preparers' traditional Catholic faith, particularly in their stand for the real presence of Christ in the Eucharist and for the regenerative power of infant baptism in opposition to the "heretical Anabaptists."

Amazingly, that rather Catholic document has been the creed of most Lutherans ever since, explaining why some of Rome's errors still hang on in Lutheranism to this day. Thus it is not surprising that in Augsburg on October 31, 1999 (the date and place could hardly be a coincidence), in what can only be construed as a slap at Luther, the Lutheran World Federation and representatives of the Roman Catholic Church signed a Joint Declaration on Justification By Faith, claiming agreement on the major point that had divided Lutherans and Catholics for nearly 470 years.

Contradictions, Contradictions . . .

It would be amusing, were it not so tragic, that while this "agreement" was being reached to heal a theological schism which had begun over indulgences, Pope John Paul II was offering special indulgences for the year 2000: forgiveness of sins for giving up cigarettes for a day, for making a pilgrimage to Rome, for walking through one or more of four "Holy Doors" he would open, and so forth. In spite of this new "agreement," not one change could be noted in Roman Catholic beliefs and practices. Everything that Martin Luther had so vigorously opposed was still fully in place, including the wearing of scapulars promising that "Whosoever dies wearing this scapular shall not suffer eternal fire" (John Paul II, whom many evangelicals call a "fine Christian," has worn one since childhood), the wearing of supposedly miraculous medals for protection, the use of "Holy Water", prayers to saints, and especially to Mary, for help and even salvation, pilgrimages to shrines (some pilgrims walking on bloodied knees, the better to earn forgiveness of their sins) and too many other unbiblical and superstitious practices to enumerate.

The Pope even had the impertinence to remind the world that the practice of Holy Pilgrimages for forgiveness of sins had been initiated in 1300 by Pope Boniface VIII. Apparently John Paul II thought we had forgotten that Boniface was an anti-Christian, murderous, openly fornicating pope who had been so evil (though hardly more evil than many others) that Dante's *Inferno* had him buried upside down in the deepest crevasse of hell. Boniface had issued a Papal Bull in 1302 (still in full force and effect today) declaring that there was no salvation outside the Roman Catholic Church and that for anyone to be saved it was "altogether necessary . . . to be subject to the Roman Pontiff."

Less than a year after the Joint Declaration, John Paul II, not to be outdone by Boniface, confirmed again that there was no salvation outside his Church. Lutherans were offended, as though this were something new. In fact, the Pope had made such pronouncements before, and the same dogma has long been stated in Catholic catechisms and numerous other official documents. Yet that Romish heresy was only one of many which the new "agreement" between Lutherans and Catholics had failed to address biblically and to correct.

Credit Where Credit Is Due

Be that as it may, Martin Luther was a great reformer to whom we owe (by God's grace) much of the freedom of worship, conscience and speech that exists throughout the Western world today, in contrast, for example, to the almost total absence of such blessings in the Muslim and Communist worlds. Much took place, however, prior to Luther which made possible what he accomplished. That fact must be taken into account in evaluating his contributions.

Luther himself said, "We are not the first to declare the papacy to be the kingdom of Antichrist, since for many years before us so many and so great men . . . have undertaken to express the same thing so clearly . . . ." [6] For example, in a full council at Rheims in the tenth century the Bishop of Orléans called the Pope the Antichrist. In the eleventh century Rome was denounced as "the See of Satan" by Berenger of Tours. The Waldensians identified the Pope as Antichrist in an A.D. 1100 treatise titled "The Noble Lesson." In 1206 an Albigensian conference in Montréal, France indicted the Vatican as the woman "drunk with the blood of the martyrs," which she has continued to prove to this day in spite of shameful new "agreements" such as Evangelicals and Catholics Together and the more recent Joint Declaration.

A movement among priests and monks calling for a return to the Bible began many centuries before Luther. The reformation movement within the Roman Church can be traced as far back as Priscillian, Bishop of Avila. Falsely accused of heresy, witchcraft and immorality by a Synod in Bordeaux, France, in A.D. 384 (seven of his writings which prove these charges false were recently discovered in Germany's University of Wurzburg library), Priscillian and six others were beheaded at Trier in 385. Millions of true Christians were martyred at the hands of "Christian" Rome in the succeeding centuries.

Jumping ahead to the late 1300s, John Wycliff, called the "morning star of the Reformation," championed the authority of the Scriptures, translated and published them in English (while almost as fast, the Catholics burned them) and preached and wrote against the evils of the popes and Catholic dogmas, especially transubstantiation. Influenced by Wycliff, Jan Hus, a fervent Catholic priest and rector of Prague University, was excommunicated in 1410. He was burned as a "heretic" in 1415 — 100 years before Luther and the Protestant Reformation — for calling a corrupt church to holiness and the authority of God's Word. In 1429 Pope Martin V commanded the King of Poland to exterminate the Hussites.

Many others who lived even closer to Luther's time played an important part in preparing Europe for the Reformation. Because of the role Erasmus played, however, in provoking Luther to write what some have called his masterpiece, *The Bondage of the Will*, this fascinating man, called by some historians "the bridge to the Reformation," must occupy some of our attention. At the height of the Reformation, it was popularly said in Paris that "Luther had only opened the door, after Erasmus had picked the lock." [7]

Erasmus Of Rotterdam

Erasmus is one of the most interesting and enigmatic — and in many ways tragic — figures in history. He was born out of wedlock, a fact unknown to his father, Gerard, who, having fled in guilt from Holland to Rome, was told that his lover, Margaret, had died. Consumed with grief and remorse, Gerard entered the priesthood. Upon later returning to Holland, he discovered to his great joy that Margaret was alive, as was the son she had borne him. Gerard would not, however, break his sacerdotal vows, nor would Margaret marry any other. Together they devoted themselves to their child, Erasmus, whom they put into school at the early age of four.

Despite being orphaned in his teens and living for years in desperate poverty, Erasmus, though somewhat less brilliant than either Calvin or Luther, pursued the study of Greek, Latin and the classics and became possibly the most eloquent scholar of his day. Ordained an Augustinian priest at the age of 24, the year Columbus sailed to America, his splendid intellect and unusual clarity of expression eventually made Erasmus famous. He was courted by the powerful and rich, including kings, princes, prelates and even popes, who curried his favor. Henry VIII invited Erasmus to England, where he lectured at Cambridge University and was a friend of luminaries such as Archbishop Warham, John Colet and Sir Thomas More. All the while, Erasmus made no secret of his dislike of many of his Church's practices.

Both Erasmus's rejection of Rome's central doctrine of transubstantiation and his sense of humor (and no less his ability to remain in the good graces of important people in spite of offending them) are illustrated by a famous incident. Sir Thomas had loaned Erasmus a horse to carry him to the ship that would take him across the Channel to the continent. The ever irascible Erasmus took the horse with him aboardship and, reaching shore, rode it all the way home. When More complained, Erasmus wrote back (reflecting the many times More had attempted to convert him to transubstantiation) a brief jingle as follows:

You said of the bodily presence of Christ:
Believe that you have, and you have him.
Of the nag that I took my reply is the same:
Believe that you have, and you have him. [8]

Erasmus the renegade had already channeled his keen wit into the most cutting satire, which he used to "unveil and combat the vices of the [Roman Catholic] Church . . . [he] attacked the monks and the prevailing abuses [with] elegant and biting sarcasms against the theology and devotion of his age . . . he immolated . . . those schoolmen and those ignorant monks against whom he had declared war." Erasmus cleverly used fiction as a weapon. In *The Praise of Folly*, written largely at More's home, he personified the goddess Folly as Moria, to whom he gave such lines as

> Do we not see every country claiming its peculiar *saint*? Each trouble has its saint, and every saint his candle. This cures the toothache; that assists women in childbed, a third restores what a thief has stolen . . . especially [virtuous is] the virgin-mother of God, in whom the people place more confidence than in her Son . . . .

Moria attacks the bishops "who run more after gold than after souls." Even the highest officials in Rome cannot escape. She asks, "Can there be any greater enemies to the Church than these unholy pontiffs, who . . . allow Jesus Christ to be forgotten; who bind him by their mercenary regulations; who falsify his doctrine by forced interpretations; and crucify him a second time by their scandalous lives?" [9]

The Forerunner Of The Reformation

The Praise of Folly appeared in 27 editions and in every European language during the lifetime of Erasmus and "contributed more than any other [writing] to confirm the anti-sacredotal tendency of the age." He urged men to get back to the "Christianity of the Bible" and pointed out that the *Vulgate* "swarmed with errors." One year before Luther nailed his 95 theses to the Wittenberg Chapel Door, Erasmus published his own translation of the New Testament in Greek, which contributed immensely to Luther's later success by opening a clearer picture of God's truth to many serious students of Scripture.

D'Aubigné informs us of many ways in which Erasmus raised his voice "against that mass of church regulations about dress, fasting, feast-days, vows, marriage and confessions which oppressed the people and enriched the priests." Eloquently he pressed his attack, of which the following is representative:

> In the churches they scarcely ever think of the gospel. The greater part of their sermons must be drawn up to please the commissaries of indulgences. The most holy doctrine of Christ must be suppressed or perverted to their profit. There is no longer any hope of cure, unless Christ himself should turn the hearts of rulers and of pontiffs, and excite them to seek for real piety. [10]

From today's perspective it is almost impossible to appreciate the courage it took for Erasmus and a few others of influence to make such public declarations. There are so many unsung heroes of the Reformation, it is a pity that we cannot give them all due credit. Perhaps the meekest and least appreciated was Oecolampadius, who had declared himself in favor of Luther at Augsburg in late 1518. Later when Oecolampadius took refuge in Basel, crowds filled St. Martin's Church whenever he took the pulpit. Erasmus fled to Basel also and they became friends. Fearing that Erasmus's friendship with Oecolampadius would soften the latter's stand against Rome, Luther wrote to warn him with these guarded words: "I much fear that Erasmus, like Moses, will die in the country of Moab, and never lead us into the land of promise." [11]

In spite of their serious differences, however, "the friends of Luther, and even the reformer himself had long hoped to see Erasmus unite with them against Rome." [12] Unfortunately, in his heart Erasmus (like some of the equally tragic Jewish religious leaders in Christ's day and some evangelical leaders in our own) was willing to displease God in order to gain praise from men. In the growing controversy, he attempted to remain in the good graces of the Church hierarchy while "endeavouring to obtain concessions from [Rome] that would unite the extreme parties. The vacillations and inconsistency of Erasmus disgusted Luther. 'You desire to walk upon eggs without crushing them,'" [13] complained Rome's fearless and uncompromising enemy.

Finally The Open Antagonism

As the breach grew between him and Luther, Erasmus "was applied to from all quarters; the pope, the emperor, kings, princes, scholars, and even his most intimate friends, entreated him to write against the reformer. 'No work,' wrote the pope, 'can be more acceptable to God, and worthier of yourself and of your genius.'"

In spite of his own opposition to Rome's corruptions, so often and eloquently expressed, he had remained in good standing within the Church. She had the power to provide him with great honors. Erasmus could not bring himself to make the sacrifice of coming out fully on the side of what he felt was Luther's extremism. Yet he preferred not to oppose Luther. "It is a very easy thing to say, 'Write against Luther,' replied he to a Romish theologian; but it is a matter full of peril . . . ."

This indecision on the part of Erasmus "drew on him the attacks of the most violent men of both parties. Luther himself knew not how to reconcile the respect he felt for Erasmus's learning with the indignation he felt at his timidity." [14] Finally, Luther, desiring to free himself from any lingering hope of gaining Erasmus's half-hearted help, wrote to the latter in April 1524. The letter revealed both his impatience and continued respect for the man seventeen years his elder and seemingly offered an olive branch so uncharacteristic of Luther. In part he said:

You have not yet received from the Lord the courage necessary to walk with us against the papists. We put up with your weakness . . . . But do not . . . pass over to our camp . . . since you are wanting in courage, remain where you are. I could wish that our people would allow your old age to fall asleep peacefully in the Lord. The greatness of our cause has long since gone beyond your strength. But on the other hand, my dear Erasmus, refrain from scattering over us with such profusion that pungent salt which you know so well how to conceal under the flowers of rhetoric; for it is more dangerous to be slightly wounded by Erasmus than to be ground to powder by all the papists put together. Be satisfied to remain a spectator of our tragedy; and publish no books against me; and for my part, I will write none against you. [15]

Luther must have known the reaction which such patronizing words would arouse from Erasmus. The master rhetorician was a proud man who took Luther's condescension as an insult to his genius and integrity. Now the die was cast. D'Aubigné comments, "Thus did Luther, the man of strife, ask for peace; it was Erasmus, the man of peace, who began the conflict . . . if he had not yet determined to write against Luther, he probably did so then . . . . He had other motives besides."

Henry VIII and other nobility "earnestly pressed him to declare himself openly against the Reformation. Erasmus . . . suffered the promise to be wrung from him . . . . He was fond of glory, and already men were accusing him of fearing Luther, and of being too weak to answer him; he was accustomed to the highest seat, and the little monk of Wittenberg had dethroned the mighty philosopher of Rotterdam . . . . All Christendom that adhered to the old worship implored him . . . A capacious genius and the greatest reputation of the age were wanted to oppose the Reformation. Erasmus answered the call." [16]

Erasmus had once rejoiced in Luther's fulminations against Rome. While cautioning the reformer to be more moderate and prudent, he had defended Luther with these words: "God has given men a physician who cuts deep into the flesh, because the malady would otherwise be incurable." On another occasion he had told the Elector of Saxony, "I am not at all surprised that it [Luther's criticism] has made so much noise; for he has committed two unpardonable crimes; he has attacked the pope's tiara and the monks' bellies." [17]

Erasmus's greatest weakness was the love of praise from those in high authority, and he cherished telling friends of the latest flatteries sent his way. Coming out openly against Luther would bring more praise than remaining on the sidelines. "'The pope,' wrote he with childish vanity to a friend . . . when he declared himself the opponent of Luther, 'has sent me a diploma full of kindness and honourable testimonials. His secretary declares that this is an unprecedented honour, and that the pope dictated every word himself.'" [18] In the final analysis, vanity had won out over truth.

The epitaph which Scripture has written over the life of Erasmus applies equally to the evangelical leaders and churches who in our day are making similar compromise with Rome: "For they loved the praise of men more than the praise of God" (John 12:43).

A Hopeless Strategy

Erasmus could not in good conscience defend Rome's heresies and abuses. Neither could he call for the strong measures Luther was pressing, though he had once commended them. What should he do, what tack should he take? He chose to attack Luther, not on his opposition to Rome, which he could not honestly do, but on what Erasmus thought was an obscure point.

In the autumn of 1524, Erasmus published his now famous *Dissertation on the Freedom of the Will,* known thereafter to Luther and his supporters as the *Diatribe.* He wrote to Henry VIII, "Trust me, this is a daring act. I expect to be stoned for it." [19] Yet what did that really matter, when those with the most power and greatest rewards were fully on his side? The works of Erasmus had long before been listed on Pope Paul IV's *Index of Prohibited Books* along with those of Calvin, Luther and Zwingli. Now he received nothing but praise from every corner of the Church.

Luther's first reaction was anger that Erasmus would consider insignificant an issue of such great importance as whether man's will was free to act in response to the gospel. Nevertheless, at first he disdained to reply to a polemic which he considered so weak as to be unworthy of the battle. His silence brought exclamations of triumph from Rome's clergy: "Well, where is your Luther now ...? Ah, ah! He has met with his match at last! He has learnt now to remain in the background; he has found out how to hold his tongue." [20]

Luther's Provoked Response

With uncharacteristic reluctance, Luther finally forced himself to prepare an answer, which he began to work on toward the end of 1525 (ten years before Calvin would write his *Institutes of the Christian Religion*). Melanchthon wrote to assure Erasmus that Luther's reply would be moderate, which Erasmus knew was an impossibility. Perhaps God had to choose men with defiant and even proud personalities to stand up to the pressure which Rome brought to bear upon those who dared to oppose her vaunted authority, a pitiless authority almost unchallenged, for more than a thousand years. The language in Calvin's *Institutes* reveals a man the equal of Rome in his utter contempt of and lack of patience or sympathy for those whose opinions diverged from his dogmas. Luther's writings reveal much the same, and he was brutal in his sarcastic put-down of Erasmus. The following is just a small sample of his *ad hominem* reply:

By so doing, you merely let us see that in your heart you cherish a Lucian, or some other hog of Epicurus' herd . . . . Surely at this point you are either playing tricks with someone else's words, or practising a literary effect! [21]

You ooze Lucian from every pore; you swill Epicurius by the gallon. [22]

Here again, as usual, you muddle everything up . . . and so you fall once more to insulting and dishonouring Scripture and God . . . let them blather who will . . . . The truth is, you fetch from afar and rake together all these irrelevancies simply because you are embarrassed . . . . since you cannot overthrow . . . foreknowledge . . . by any argument, you try meantime to tire out the reader with a flow of empty verbiage . . . . [23]

See, I pray you, what abundance of by-ways and bolt-holes a slippery mind will seek out in its flight from truth! Yet it does not escape . . . . [24]

I'll be hanged if the Diatribe itself knows what it is talking about! Perhaps we have here the rhetorical trick of obscuring your meaning when danger is at hand, lest you be trapped in your words. [25]

Luther had not thought this subject through as thoroughly as he was forced now to do. He was willing to concede that man could indeed exercise his will in making choices with regard to earthly matters. But when it came to the question of man exercising any freedom of will toward his salvation, Luther laid the ground for what Calvin (who was about fifteen years old at this time) would ten years later present in his *Institutes* after his conversion to Luther's Protestantism. In his much admired *The Bondage of the Will*, Luther pompously chides and browbeats Erasmus:

In this book of mine . . . I shall harry you and all the Sophists till you tell me exactly what "free-will" can and does do; and I hope to harry you (Christ helping me) as to make you repent of ever publishing your Diatribe . . . .

God foreknows nothing contingently [i.e., no events depend upon something other than His will] . . . He foresees, purposes, and does all things according to His own immutable, eternal and infallible will. This bombshell knocks "free will" flat, and utterly shatters it; so that those who want to assert it must either deny my bombshell, or pretend not to notice it . . . .

You insist that we should learn the immutability of God's will, while forbidding us to know the immutability of His foreknowledge! Do you suppose that He does not will what He foreknows, or that He does not foreknow what He wills? If he wills what He foreknows, His will is eternal and changeless, because His nature is so. From which it follows, by resistless logic, that all we do, however it may appear to us to be done mutably and contingently, is in reality done necessarily and immutably in respect to God's will . . . the will of God, which rules over our mutable will, is changeless and sure . . . . [26]

Here, as often elsewhere in *Bondage*, Luther boasts of his conclusion without giving any valid supporting arguments. He secures his thesis by his own mere definition, not by logic or Scripture. His assertions above do not follow. Nor does he provide sufficient biblical support in this entire work to make his case for the will being in bondage. In bondage to what or whom? He often implies the answer but fails to develop it fully or to face the consequences.

Luther is arguing that God's sovereignty *ipso facto* eliminates any possibility that man could exercise a free will: "This bombshell knocks 'free will' flat, and utterly shatters it . . . . " That God foreknows the future, Luther argues, means the future is already predetermined and that in itself proves that man could not act freely. This is a mere assertion on Luther's part which he doesn't support by Scripture. Augustine considers the same problem far more carefully and comes to the opposite conclusion. As we have already seen, the fact that God *knows* something will happen does not *cause* it to happen and thus does not eliminate free will.

It is true that because God knows Mr. Jones will make a certain decision, the latter surely will make that decision, but that does not mean that Mr. Jones cannot exercise a genuine choice in coming to that decision. It simply shows that God knows in advance what Mr. Jones's free choice will be. We have already established that free will is neither logically nor biblically incompatible either with God's sovereignty or His foreknowledge. God could surely in His sovereignty provide man with the gift of genuine choice, and the Bible clearly says He has done so. Moreover, it diminishes God's foreknowledge and denies His omniscience to suggest that God could not know in advance what a free-will decision would be.

Is the will in bondage because God is sovereign and He has already determined all that will occur? Luther seems to argue as much. Ten years later Calvin would come to the same conclusion, no doubt influenced by Luther, though he would word his thesis somewhat differently and avoid giving Luther any credit. That God's sovereignty and foreknowledge eliminate man's free will, however, only creates a far worse dilemma: man's will must be in bondage to God's will!

If that is the case and therefore man cannot do anything except as God wills it, then we are driven back to the same dead end: God must be the author of evil. That unhappy conclusion is forced upon us by this extreme emphasis upon sovereignty which we have already seen is contradicted both by Scripture and reason. There is no way to assert that man can only do what God wills without admitting that God is therefore the invisible Hand effecting all the evil which man commits.

Is The Will Really In Bondage?

The defense of Calvinism traps even the best minds into contradictions. Spurgeon himself couldn't seem to make up his mind. In spite of referring to "the equally sure doctrine, that the will of man has its proper position in the work of salvation and is not to be ignored," Spurgeon also claimed that the idea of free will "left the whole economy of Grace and mercy to be the gathering together of fortuitous atoms impelled by man's own will!" [27] That, obviously, was not true. "Fortuitous atoms" have nothing to do with "Grace and mercy," nor does anyone who believes in man's power to make moral choices imagine that he can control atoms with his will! Spurgeon should have stayed with biblical exegesis.

He went on to lament, "We cannot tell on that theory whether God will be glorified or sin will triumph." Hardly. That we wouldn't know how something would turn out means nothing. The outcome was and is known to God. We have already seen that God's foreknowledge does not determine or even influence in any way man's actions, nor is His sovereignty diminished at all by man's free choice.

Sadly, great preacher that he was, in that sermon Spurgeon erected and destroyed one straw man after another: "It must either be as God wills, or as man wills . . . . If not God, then you put man there, to say, 'I will,' or 'I will not.' If I will it, I will enter Heaven. If I will it, I will . . . conquer the Holy Spirit, for I am stronger than God and stronger than Omnipotence. If I will it, I will make the blood of Christ of no effect . . . it shall be *my* purpose that shall make His purpose stand, or make it fall." [28]

With all respect to Spurgeon, this is nonsense. Even the rankest Arminian would never imagine he could "conquer the Holy Spirit" or that he was "stronger than God" or that man's will could ever "make the blood of Christ of no effect" or force an entrance into heaven!

Like so many other Calvinists in their zeal to defend God's sovereignty to the exclusion of human will, Spurgeon stooped to twisting scripture to his own ends. For example, he quotes Christ's indictment of the rabbis, "You *will not* come to Me that you might have life." He then declares, "Where is free will after such a text as that? When Christ affirms that they will not, who dares say they will . . . ? Man is so depraved, so set on mischief, the way of salvation is so obnoxious to his pride, so hateful to his lusts, that he cannot like it and will not like it, unless he who ordained the plan shall change his nature and subdue his will." [29]

Here we have more confusion and misapplication. First of all, Christ is making this statement specifically to the rabbis, not to all men. Secondly, the statement itself says that they have a will, that by their own will they are rejecting

Him: "You *will not* come to Me . . . ." Nor does Christ say that they cannot will to do otherwise. Indeed, Christ's statement would be meaningless unless they *could* of their own will repent and come to Him. Only two chapters later Christ declares, "If any man will do God's will, he shall know of the doctrine, whether it be of God . . . " (John 7:17). Spurgeon himself in this same sermon quotes this scripture as proof that man's will has a part to play in coming to Christ. [30]

Is the will really in bondage? If so, to what or to whom — and is it possible to set the captive will free from its bondage? If so, how can this be done? We must consider those questions carefully — and we will do so in the context of a further examination of Luther's treatise.

---

1   John Armstrong, "Reflections from Jonathan Edwards on the Current Debate over Justification by Faith Alone" (quoted in speech delivered at Annapolis 2000: A Passion for Truth conference). Transcript available from The Jonathan Edwards Institute, P.O. Box 2410, Princeton NJ 08542.

2   http://www.iclnet.org/pub/resources/text/wittenberg/wittenberg-luther.html.

3   Ibid.

4   J.H. Merle d'Aubigné, *History of the Reformations of the Sixteenth Century* (London: n.p., 1846; rev. ed. by Hartland Institute, Rapidan VA, n.d.), 245.

5   Ibid.

6   Ewald Plass, *What Luther Says* (Concordia Publishing House, 1987), 1:35.

7   S. Fontaine, *Histoire Catholique de Notre Temps* (Paris: Pordre de St. Francois, 1562); cited in d'Aubigné, op. cit., 411.

8   Cited in d'Aubigné, op. cit., 414.

9   Ibid.

10   Op.cit., 42.

11   Op. cit., 412.

12   Op. cit., 414.

13   Op. cit., 413.

14   Op. cit., 414.

15   Ibid.

16   Op. cit., 414-15.

17   Op. cit., 101.

18   Op. cit., 43.

19   Op. cit., 415.

20   Op. cit., 416.

21   Martin Luther, *The Bondage of the Will,* trans. J.I. Packer and O.R. Johnston (Fleming H. Revell, 1957, 11th prtg. 1999), 70.

22   Op. cit., 44.

23   Op. cit., 86-87.

24   Op. cit., 223.

25   Op. cit., 228.

26   Op. cit., 80-81.

27   Charles Haddon Spurgeon, "God's Will and Man's Will," No. 442 (Newington: Metropolitan Tabernacle; sermon delivered Sunday morning, March 30, 1862).

28   Ibid.

29   Ibid.

30   Ibid.

12
The Bondage Of The Will?

Luther was unquestionably the leading figure in the Reformation at this time and the one above all others to whom Protestants today owe the largest debt regardless of serious disagreements with much of his theology. Although many others before him had opposed Rome, some openly, most less conspicuously, Luther had been able to publish and distribute his challenge throughout Europe. Rome had always been able to silence her critics with bribery or death; now she was faced with a man who could not be bought and whose telling arguments had aroused so many powerful local rulers in his favor that he remained outside of her vengeful grasp.

The Pope had one last hope: that the arguments put forth by Erasmus and widely published by Luther's enemies would persuade the masses who had defected from the Roman Catholic tradition to return to the shelter of the one true Church. And what could be more convincing than the fact that although Erasmus had criticized the Church he had not been martyred, had not left her fold, was still on the best of terms with the Pope, and it was he who was pointing out Dr. Luther's errors. That a reformation was needed even the Church was willing to concede, but it was the kind Erasmus and others had long pleaded for — an inward transformation to correct acknowledged abuses, not a trashing of the traditions of centuries to start all over again from nothing!

Nor is there any doubt that the arguments Erasmus presented were powerfully persuasive to those who wanted to remain within the ancient fold. He was writing from a Roman Catholic perspective, defending Catholic dogma, a tactic calculated to strengthen Catholics in their beliefs but which would hardly be effective for those who had already embraced Luther's rebellion. Perhaps all Erasmus intended to accomplish was to flatter those who could reward him the most.

We do not defend Erasmus, for much that he says is even more indefensible and unbiblical, if possible, than some of Luther's irrationalities. Notwithstanding to whatever extent he has rejected the efficacy of sacraments and her other paraphernalia in his past satires, Erasmus is still bound to Rome's heresy that grace aids man in achieving salvation by works. He writes, "Though sin abounds by the law, and it is where sin abounds that grace also abounds, it does not hence follow that man cannot with God's help make himself acceptable before grace, and prepare himself by morally good works for God's favour." [1] Of course, it is because man has already morally failed to keep God's law (and cannot mend that breach by keeping it thereafter, no matter how perfectly) that he needs grace — God's *unmerited* favor for which no preparation is possible.

An Awkward Duel

Luther lunges mercilessly to attack his foe at every turn. There is no point in dueling with the Pope. Neither he nor his cardinals and bishops will listen. Power is all they understand. At least in Erasmus, Luther has an antagonist who will listen and respond, and he vents his pent-up anger against Rome upon this man who dares to defend her blasphemous sacraments.

At times neither antagonist argues to the point. Though Luther is so clearly his master when it comes to exegesis of Scripture, it is often Erasmus who is the more reasonable of the two. The latter points out, for example, what seems both rational and biblical and in favor of which we are arguing in these pages: "If it is not in the power of every man to keep what is commanded, all the exhortations in the Scriptures, and all the promises, threats, expostulations, reproofs, adjurations, blessings, curses and hosts of precepts, are of necessity useless." [2]

Luther quotes this statement, then responds for more than three pages with much ridicule but little substance. He triumphantly points out that the Old Testament passages Erasmus cites, such as Deuteronomy 30 and others, "only demand duty" but say nothing concerning free will. [3] Of course, that was all Erasmus intended to show, since the implication that follows is clear. Nor can Luther cite one verse in Scripture which refers to "the bondage of the will."

Luther then demands of Erasmus why, if man can will to keep the law, he (Luther) must "labour so hard . . . ? What need now of Christ? What need of the Spirit?" [4]

Erasmus had not even implied that there was no need of Christ or of the Holy Spirit. He had simply suggested that it would be reasonable to conclude from God's many commands and appeals to reason and obedience that man must be capable of a willing response. But Luther doesn't deal with that; he is simply bombastic in arguing beside the point, even ridiculing Erasmus for admitting that free will can only operate by God's grace. [5]

Luther pounces like a tiger on that admission, rather than agreeing with Erasmus and reasonably admitting the obvious: the fact that free will needs grace no more nullifies free will than breathing is nullified by the fact that it, too, is dependent upon God's grace. Surely man has the power and responsibility to do both in cooperation with God's grace and power!

Here and throughout *Bondage* Luther is like a bully who will not listen to reason. Yet Packer and other Calvinists praise the "dialectical strength of Luther's powerful Latin." [6]   B.B. Warfield calls *Bondage* "a dialectic and polemic masterpiece." [7] Luther's *Bondage* contains so many contradictions and so much fallacious reasoning that one wonders how it obtained the reputation of being such a logically drawn treatise.

One wonders, also, how evangelicals in their praise of Luther seemingly overlook the extent to which he was still in bondage to his Roman Catholic background. This was especially evident in his view of the efficacy of the sacraments by which in his *Small Catechism* he declares, "God *offers, gives, and seals* unto us *the forgiveness of sins* which Christ has earned for us." (Emphasis in original)[10] This Catechism is used in nearly all Lutheran churches today as their basic book of doctrine.

In answer to the question, "*What does Baptism give or profit?*" the *Catechism* declares, "It works forgiveness of sins, delivers from death and the devil, and gives eternal salvation to all who believe this, as the words and promises of God declare." [11] As for the Lord's Supper or Communion, Luther states, "It is the true body and blood of our Lord Jesus Christ under the bread and wine, for us Christians to eat and to drink . . . . In, with, and under the *bread* Christ gives us His *true body*; in, with, and under the *wine* He gives us His *true blood* . . . in the Sacrament forgiveness of sins, life, and salvation are given . . . ." (Emphasis in original)[12]

Here we have Rome's false gospel of sacramentalism which survived the Reformation and is still honored in many Protestant churches. Lutherans who trust in baptism and the Lord's Supper for their salvation are just as lost as Roman Catholics who trust in Rome's sacraments. Recognizing Luther's mistaken view of salvation may help some to realize that his view of free will and human responsibility could be equally wrong.

To What Is The Will In Bondage?

That the will — contrary to what Luther argues in his greatest treatise — is not bound is clear. We have already refuted the argument that because the will is always beset with influences proves that it is not free. There are, of course, as Paul admits in his case, things which often prevent man from doing what he would like to do. This is true at times, but not at all times. Paul doesn't say that he *never* can do what he wills. The fact that we sometimes are driven by our own lust or other pressures to act contrary to what we willed only proves that we have a will against which these pressures act. Nor does anyone lack the experience of having made decisions and carried them out in spite of, and at other times even in the absence of, prohibiting pressures.

Luther imagines he does away with freedom of human will by arguing, "For if it is not we, but God alone, who works salvation in us, it follows that, willy-nilly, nothing we do has any saving significance prior to His working in us." [13] His argument doesn't follow. Of course salvation is not our doing; but that we cannot earn salvation does not prove that we cannot freely choose to receive salvation as a gift of God's love. Throughout his entire treatise Luther continues to confuse the ability to *will* with the ability to *perform* and mistakenly imagines he has disproved the former by disproving the latter. Of course there is no relationship between the two.

Erasmus argues that for God to command man to do what he cannot do would be like asking a man whose arms are bound to use them. Luther responds that the man is "commanded to stretch forth his hand . . . to disprove his false assumption of freedom and power . . .." [14] Luther wins that small skirmish, but only because Erasmus's analogy is pitifully weak. Neither man even comes close to the Bible.

That God would not just command but earnestly plead and persuade and beseech man endlessly through His prophets, promising and giving blessing for obedience and warning of and bringing destruction for disobedience, cannot be explained away by Luther's clever but trite rejoinder. Furthermore, we have numerous examples throughout Scripture of prophets and kings and ordinary persons from Enoch to Noah to Abraham to David and onward, who, though not perfect, were indeed obedient to God and pleased Him. What happened to Luther's "bondage of the will" in those cases?

The Book of Proverbs is one huge treatise refuting Luther's thesis. Solomon is appealing to his son to "know wisdom and instruction; to perceive the words of understanding; to receive the instruction of wisdom, justice, and judgment, and equity . . . " (Proverbs 1:2-3). He declares that "A wise man will hear, and will increase learning" (verse 5) and he admonishes his son, "if sinners entice thee, consent thou not" (verse 10). He exhorts, "My son, despise not the chastening of the LORD; neither be weary of his correction: for whom the LORD loveth he correcteth; even as a father the son in whom he delighteth" (3:11-12). Are these not appeals to the will?

We could go on to quote the entire book, but that should hardly be necessary. Everything Solomon writes by way of persuasion that wisdom is to be desired in place of folly and that the reward for serving God and righteousness far exceeds serving selfish lusts and desires is surely an appeal to the will. How else could one heed the voice of wisdom? That the Lord corrects and that an earthly father corrects is not, as Luther disparagingly insists, simply to show that no correction is possible, but because the wise son will heed instruction — which is obviously only possible by an act of the will. Luther fails either to make his case for the bondage of the will or to demonstrate what it is that has the will bound.

The Will Must Be *Willing*

One searches *Bondage* in vain to find where it deals with the literally hundreds of biblical passages from Genesis 24:58 to 1 Samuel 1:11 to 2 Samuel 6:21-22 to Psalms 4:8; 5:2-3; 9:1-2; 18:1; 30:1; to John 7:17, etc., which clearly indicate that man can indeed will to do God's will. The clear passages where men express their willingness to obey and please God and prove it in their performance are conspicuous by their absence. Nor does Luther acknowledge, much less deal with, the fact that of the dozens of times the words "bondage" and "bound" occur in Scripture, not once are they used in reference to the human will.

Luther's argument that the will is bound is in itself an admission of the existence of the will. Nor does Luther, any better than Calvin, explain how the will is supposedly *unbound* so that man may believe the gospel. He argues that because even in Christians "human nature" lusts against the spirit, "how could it endeavor after good in those who are not yet born again of the Spirit . . . ?"[15] This is no proof of *bondage* of the will. Even the drunkard at times determines with his will to be sober. It is not that the will is in bondage but that the man's bodily desires overcome his will. Many have willed to be free of addiction to alcohol and have been successful even without becoming Christians.

Once it is admitted that man has a will, it is impossible to maintain either that it is in bondage or to explain how it was delivered except by its own choice. The Westminster Confession says that the elect come to Christ "most freely, being made willing by his [God's] grace." So the will which was totally depraved and set against God has been made willing through regeneration. It is not a new will but the same will the person had before, now made willing. No one, however, is made willing against his will but must have been willing to be made willing.

There is no explaining away the fact that man has a will, as Augustine and even Calvin admitted and everyone experiences countless times each day. No one can persuade man to believe or do anything without his will being involved — unless he has been drugged or hypnotized. "Regeneration" will not solve the problem of the will. If it would, then God would have made Adam and Eve and all of us that way in the beginning. The whole point is that for man to be a morally accountable being, able to love and receive love, he must have a free will. At this point we uncover the Achilles heel in Luther's argument (and we see the same problem with Calvin when we come to Unconditional Election).

Once it is acknowledged that man has a will there is no escape from it. Whatever change takes place in a man must involve his will; and for that to happen the will must be willing. If the will was in bondage and has been delivered, the will must have been willing to be delivered. We deal with this further in the next chapter.

A Prejudicial Misuse Of Scripture

It is disappointing that Luther so often forces Scripture to prove his point, instead of allowing it to speak for itself. For example, taking a statement by a psalmist concerning a temporary state of mind from which he has repented — "I was as a beast before thee" (Psalms 73:22) — he likens man's will to a beast and launches into an analogy that has nothing to do with what the psalmist says: "So man's will is like a beast standing between two riders. If God rides, it wills and goes where God wills . . . . If Satan rides, it wills and goes where Satan wills. Nor may it choose to which rider it will run, or which it will seek; but the riders themselves fight to decide who shall have and hold it." [16]

This analogy doesn't follow from this or any other scripture. The psalmist simply says that when he compared the prosperity of the wicked to his own trouble he became envious of them. He realized that in so doing he had become as foolish *as* a beast. There is nothing to suggest that his will *was* a beast — the problem was his understanding. Yet this same metaphor is offered repeatedly by Calvinists as alleged proof that the human will is in bondage. And both Luther and Calvin ignored the psalmist's repentance and the scores of other verses throughout Scripture where it is clear that man responds to God in obedience by an act of his will.

Throughout his rebuttal of Erasmus (and we are not taking the side of Erasmus in pointing out these fallacies), Luther fails to distinguish between man's freedom to will and his lack of ability to carry out what he wills. Remember, Paul says, "To will is present with me; but how to perform that which is good I find not" (Romans 7:18). Obviously, it is not the will that is in bondage but the man who wills to do good while lacking the power to do it because of indwelling sin. Thus he would surely be free to believe the gospel and to receive Christ because to do so would require no ability on his part. Sin does not prevent him from willing, but from doing. Christ, however, accomplishes all in salvation.

Forcing Scripture To Say What It Doesn't

Luther's abuse of Scripture continues throughout *Bondage*. For example, he quotes "For the wrath of God is revealed from heaven against all ungodliness, and unrighteousness of men . . . " (Romans 1:18). He then claims that Paul's statement proves that man cannot will to do any good. [17] On the contrary, that men are unrighteous and that God's wrath is aroused against their ungodliness does not even suggest, much less prove, that they *must* act in that manner. In fact, it suggests the opposite — that God is angry with them for failing to do what they could. Nor does Paul even come close to saying that all men lack the ability to make a choice to receive Christ through the gospel. This is inexcusable eisegesis.

Luther goes on to quote Paul's quotation of Psalms 14:4: "There is none that doeth good, no, not one" (Romans 3:10-12). Like Calvin ten years later, he makes this an absolute statement about man's unchangeable state rather than about his usual practice. [18] That it must be the latter is clear from the abundance of scriptures telling us of good done even by the heathen and the exhortations even to the ungodly to do good. Nowhere does the Scripture tell us that man is in such total bondage to evil that he cannot respond obediently to God. Otherwise he could not be held accountable. We have covered this earlier in the chapter concerning Total Depravity, but now offer several more examples from Scripture.

Abimelech, a pagan idol-worshiping king of the Philistines, could say to Isaac, "we have done unto thee nothing but good" (Genesis 26:10-11,29). Laban, another idol worshiper, in obedience to God, refrained from harming Jacob (Genesis 31:25-29). The Psalms are filled with exhortations to "do good" (Psalms 34:14; 37:3, etc.). Of a virtuous wife it is said that she will do her husband "good and not evil all the days of her life" (Proverbs 31:12). Jesus counsels the Jews to "do good to them that hate you" (Matthew 5:44). There are literally scores of other verses in the Bible indicating that even the ungodly can do good at times.

Luther goes on to argue, "To say: man does not seek God, is the same as saying: man cannot seek God . . . . " [19] That this is not the same we have already discussed. Luther repeatedly makes such elementary mistakes, frequently offending both Scripture and reason. To say that Mr. Brown never goes into town is obviously not the same as saying that Mr. Brown cannot go into town. Instead, one would logically conclude that for some either valid or imagined reason Mr. Brown doesn't want to or may even be afraid to go into town.

Not only does God call upon men repeatedly throughout the Bible to seek Him, as we have already seen—implying that man can and does seek God; we have many scriptures commending those who have sought and found. For example, "every one that sought the LORD went out unto the tabernacle" (Exodus 33:7). Asa could say, "we have sought the LORD our God" (2 Chronicles 14:7); and we are told that when Israel did "turn unto the LORD God of Israel, and sought him, he was found of them" (15:4). Ezra told the king, "The hand of our God is upon all them for good that seek him . . . " (Ezra 8:22). Asaph says, "In the day of my trouble I sought the Lord" (Psalms 77:2). Zephaniah refers to them "that have not sought the LORD," (Zephaniah 1:6), surely implying that there were some who did seek Him. We could offer many more references showing that men have sought and found the Lord. Therefore we must conclude that Psalms 14 and Paul's quotation thereof in Romans 3 do not mean that no man ever has or ever will or could seek the Lord, but that the general attitude of mankind is being described.

Luther goes on to argue that "the doctrine of salvation by faith in Christ disproves 'free-will.'" [20] In what way does it *disprove* free will? He offers no explanation of this alleged disproof. On the contrary, as we have seen, there is no salvation without a genuine choice. The gospel promises salvation as a gift to those who will receive it; and one must have the power of choice or one cannot receive the gift. The gospel is an invitation to come to Christ, to receive Him, to believe on Him, to accept His death in one's place in payment of the penalty for one's sins. To respond meaningfully to that offer one must also be able either to accept or reject it. Surely calling upon men to believe does not prove that they *cannot*!

Confusing The Issue

Many of the scriptures and arguments Luther marshals for support throughout the length and breadth of *Bondage* are not even apropos of the question of free will. Here is the gist of his reasoning from Romans 3:

> Here Paul utters very thunderbolts against "free-will." First: "The righteousness of God without the law," he says, "is manifested." He distinguishes the righteousness of God from the righteousness of the law; because the righteousness of faith comes by grace . . . without the works of the law . . . a man is justified by faith without the deeds of the law (v. 28) . . . .

> From all this it is very plain that the endeavour and effort of "free-will" are simply null; for if the righteousness of God exists without the law, and without the works of the law, how shall it not much more exist without "free-will"? For the supreme concern of "free-will" is to exercise itself in moral righteousness, the works of that law by which its blindness and impotence are "assisted." But this word "without" does away with morally good works, and the moral righteousness, and preparations for grace. Imagine any power you can think

of as belonging to "free-will," and Paul will still stand firm and say: "the righteousness of God exists without it . . . !"

And what will the guardians of "free-will" say to what follows: "being justified freely by His grace" . . . ? How will endeavour, and merit, accord with freely given righteousness . . . ? The Diatribe itself argued and expostulated throughout in this strain: "*If there is no freedom of will, what place is there for merit? If there is no place for merit, what place is there for reward?*" *To what will it be ascribed if man is justified without merit?*" Paul here gives the answer — there is no such thing as merit at all, but all that are justified are justified freely, and this is ascribed to nothing but the grace of God. [21]

Luther presents some excellent biblical arguments against salvation by works, but these scriptures and his reasoning therefrom have nothing to do with whether man has a will or not. Much less is there anything about the will being in bondage. No Christian who believes that man has the power of choice sovereignly bestowed by God upon him as a moral agent imagines that this power has been given to man so that he could become righteous enough to merit salvation or even to contribute to his salvation in any way. Furthermore, the very fact that Paul refers to the righteousness that comes by the law indicates that man has some power to choose to keep the law and to actually do so in at least some respects.

Paul is not primarily arguing that man cannot do any good works, but that good works will not avail to justify a sinner. One breach of the law dooms man forever because keeping the law perfectly in the future, even if that could be attained, could never make up for having broken the law, no matter on what point, in the past. Moreover, the fact that Paul says, "by the deeds of the law there shall no flesh be justified in his sight" (Romans 3:20), indicates that it is possible for man to keep some provisions of the law, such as not to commit murder, not to steal, not to commit adultery. Paul's argument is not that it is impossible to keep for one moment one provision of the law, but that even to keep the law perfectly would not be enough. In his determination to prove the alleged bondage of the will, Luther misses Paul's whole point.

J.I. Packer says, "*The Bondage of the Will* is the greatest piece of theological writing that ever came from Luther's pen. This was his [Luther's] own opinion." [22] Warfield called *Bondage* "the embodiment of Luther's reformation conceptions, the nearest thing to a systematic statement of them that he ever made . . . in a true sense the manifesto of the Reformation." [23] Packer described it as "a major treatment of what Luther saw as the very heart of the gospel." [24] If so, one wonders who could be saved, because *Bondage* encompasses some 300 pages much of which the average person would find rather difficult to follow. One wonders, too, how Paul's simple "Believe on the Lord Jesus Christ, and thou shalt be saved" (Acts 16:31) has become so complicated. And how would proving that man *cannot* believe (if that were indeed the case) encourage him to believe the gospel?

1 Martin Luther, *The Bondage of the Will*, trans. J.I. Packer and O.R. Johnston (Fleming H. Revell, 1957, 11th prtg. 1999), 246.
2 Op. cit., 171; quoting Erasmus.
3 Ibid.
4 Op. cit., 172.
5 Op. cit., 173.
6 Op. cit., "Translators' Note," 11.
7 Benjamin B. Warfield, "The Theology of the Reformation," in *Studies in Theology* (n.p., n.d), 471; quoted in "Historical and Theological Introduction" to *The Bondage of the Will* by Parker and Johnston, op. cit., 40-41.
8 Op. cit., 102.
9 Op. cit., 161.
10 Op. cit., 313.
11 *A Short Explanation of Dr. Martin Luther's Small Catechism: A Handbook of Christian Doctrine* (Concordia Publishing House, 1971 ed.), 169.
12 Op. cit., 174.
13 Luther, *Bondage*, op. cit., 102.
14 Op. cit., 161.
15 Op. cit., 313.
16 Op. cit., 103-104.
17 Op. cit., 273-275.
18 Op. cit., 279-280.
19 Op. cit., 281.
20 Op. cit., 288-95.
21 Op. cit., 289, 292.
22 Op. cit., 40.
23 Warfield, op. cit., 471; cited in Luther, op. cit., 41.
24 Luther, *Bondage*, 41.

13
Unconditional Election

Unconditional Election — another phrase that is not found in the Bible — "necessarily follows from total depravity." [1] This doctrine is really the heart of Calvinism, as many of its leading apologists testify. Herman Hanko declares, "No man can claim ever to be either Calvinistic or Reformed without a firm and abiding commitment to this precious truth." [2] Sproul, though a staunch Calvinist, fears that the term "can be misleading and grossly abused." [3] While all Calvinists don't agree on this doctrine, I am trying to be faithful to the majority view.

The Canons of Dort explained the tenet as "the unchangeable purpose of God, whereby, before the foundation of the world, he hath out of mere grace, according to the sovereign good pleasure of his own will, chosen, from the whole human race . . . a certain number of persons to redemption in Christ . . . . " [4] Unconditional Election is the outworking of the Calvinistic view of sovereignty and predestination. Once the latter two are accepted, this doctrine inexorably follows.

Why so few were chosen by the God who "is love" (1 John 4:8) and the rest damned is, as we have already seen, a major problem which Calvin himself recognized. Yet throughout his *Institutes* he offered no satisfactory explanation. "That is a question for which I have no answer," admitted one of the staunchest critics of the first draft of this book. Unable to integrate God's love into the process of Unconditional Election, Calvin simply struck back sharply at his critics while pleading Augustine's authority:

I admit that profane men lay hold of the subject of predestination to carp, or cavil, or snarl, or scoff. But if their petulance frightens us, it will be necessary to conceal all the principal articles of faith, because they and their fellows leave scarcely one of them unassailed with blasphemy . . . .

The truth of God is too powerful, both here and everywhere, to dread the slanders of the ungodly, as Augustine powerfully maintains . . . . Augustine disguises not that . . . he was often charged with preaching the doctrine of predestination too freely, but, as it was easy for him to do, he abundantly refutes the charge . . . .

The predestination by which God adopts some to the hope of life, and adjudges others to eternal death . . . is greatly cavilled at, especially by those who make prescience its cause. [5]

Calvin in typical fashion ridicules those who he claims "cavil, or snarl" against his views on predestination. He mocks what he calls "the slanders of the ungodly" as though anyone who disagrees with him is automatically ungodly. Conspicuous by their absence, however, are sound biblical reasons either to refute these critics or to substantiate irrefutably his dogmas.

While some soften their stance by calling themselves four-point or three-point Calvinists, Palmer declares, "The first word that Calvinism suggests to most people is predestination; and if they have a modicum of theological knowledge, the other four points follow . . . . The Five Points of Calvinism all tie together. He who accepts one of the points will accept the other points. Unconditional election necessarily follows from total depravity." [6] Many others agree: "If any one of the five points of Calvinism is denied, the Reformed heritage is completely lost . . . the truth of unconditional election stands at the foundation of them all [five points]. This truth is the touchstone of the Reformed faith. It is the very heart and core of the gospel." [7] So again the claim is made that Calvinism *is* the gospel. If that were true, then only Calvinists could be saved!

Unconditional Election: The Heart Of Calvinism

The term "unconditional election" was chosen because it conveys the meaning that "salvation is of the Lord and not of man." Spurgeon declared, "All true theology is summed in these two short sentences: Salvation is all of the grace of God. Damnation is all of the will of man." [8] There is a confusion, however, between salvation, which could only be effected through the sacrifice of Christ for our sins, and our acceptance thereof, which the Bible clearly states is a *condition*: "as many as *received him* . . . become the sons of God" (John 1:12). The Calvinist insists, however, that salvation cannot be conditioned upon any act or belief on man's part. Thus George L. Bryson states in summation:

Calvinistic Election says to the unregenerate elect, "Don't worry, your Depravity is no obstacle to salvation," and to the unelect, "Too bad, you have not been predestined for salvation but [to] damnation." [9]

R.C. Sproul writes, "The term *election* refers specifically to one aspect of divine predestination. God's choosing of certain individuals to be saved." [10] This choosing can only be from God's side: "By making election conditional upon something that man does, even if what he does is simply to repent and believe the gospel, God's grace is seriously compromised." [11] Sproul adds, "The Reformed view teaches that God positively or actively intervenes in the lives of the elect to insure their salvation." [12]

Why does the Calvinist insist that to be saved one cannot even believe the gospel but that God must first "intervene" sovereignly to "regenerate" the elect without their even knowing it is happening or without having any faith in Christ or understanding of the gospel? Because it is claimed that "faith" is a "work." This declaration is made repeatedly: "To reject [Calvinistic] election is to reject salvation by grace and promote salvation by works." [13]

Yet if anything is clear in Scripture it is the undisputable fact that faith is not work but its very antithesis: "By grace are ye saved, through faith; . . . not of works" (Ephesians 2:8-9); "But to him that worketh not, but believeth . . . " (Romans 4:5). Nothing could be clearer than the fact that, by believing, one is doing no work. In fact, faith and work are contrasted.

The Vital Importance Of Sovereignty

Unconditional Election demands the same distorted view of God's sovereignty that undergirds all of Calvinism,. We have already shown that this perspective is unbiblical, but to the Calvinist it is the very foundation of his belief: "The all-out emphasis on the almighty sovereignty of Jehovah God is the truth and beauty of Calvinism." [14] Another writer adds, "Only the Calvinist . . . recognizes God's absolute sovereignty." [15] On the contrary, all Christians believe that God is absolutely sovereign; but many do not accept the unbiblical definition of what that means which Calvinists attempt to force on all of us.

Without any serious effort to reconcile the theory to God's love and mercy or to man's inherent sense of what is right, Palmer declares with no apparent sense of contradiction that "God . . . has foreordained . . . even sin." [16] In fact, sin is rebellion against God, so it could hardly be willed by God. Nevertheless, like Palmer, Gordon H. Clark insists that

> . . . every event is foreordained because God is omniscient; and no detail . . . escapes his foreknowledge and deliberate counsel. Everything is part of his plan. Of everything God says, 'Thus it must be . . . .' Must not they who say that God does not foreordain evil acts now hang their heads in shame? [17]

God's omniscience does not require Him to foreordain everything. Here is another form of the discredited argument that God can only foreknow what He has foreordained. As already pointed out, if that were the case, far from supporting a belief that God is omniscient, it would limit His knowledge.

Clark, Palmer and Pink are simply echoing Calvin, who said that God "foresees the things which are to happen, simply because he has decreed that they are so to happen . . . ." Calvin goes on to reason that it is therefore "vain to debate about prescience, while it is clear that all events take place by his [God's] sovereign appointment." [18] Following their leader, many Calvinists argue, "If a single event can happen outside of God's sovereignty, then He is not totally sovereign, and we cannot be assured that His plan for the ages will be accomplished." [19]

This theory, as we have seen, had its roots in Calvin's Roman Catholicism and love of Augustine; it cannot be found in Scripture. John R. Cross, who made the great New Tribes Mission video, *Delivered from the Power of Darkness*, has said it well:

> From the third chapter of Genesis on, the scriptures shout "free will." The whole volume talks about choices, and the associated consequences. God saw fit to write an entire book on choices, the Book of Wisdom (Proverbs). Having a free will makes sense of God's free love . . . .
> Suppose you met someone who . . . showed real love for you — going out of his way to do special things for you . . . telling you they loved you. Then you found out that they had no choice — they were programmed to "be loving" . . . well, it would be a terrible disappointment. It would all seem so artificial, so meaningless, so empty. And it would be.
> Man was given a choice . . . . Having this choice defined man as a human being: to eat or not to eat, to obey or disobey, to love or not to love. Man was not a robot. Man was able to love by his own free choice [without which love is not love]. [20]

Does God Cause Man To Sin?

For the omniscient God to know all, it is clearly not necessary that He must *plan and cause* all. That very idea, as we have shown, limits the scope of God's knowledge and thus actually denies omniscience. Ironically, the major tenets of Calvinism follow directly from this misconception about sovereignty and omniscience.

It is true that God, being omniscient, knows all before it happens and therefore nothing can happen that He doesn't know. However, Calvin went much further in stating that God knows only what He has decreed. From that hypothesis it necessarily follows that God is the cause of all and therefore the cause of evil. The doctrine of Unconditional Election then follows: that just as evil is God's doing, so salvation, too, must be all of God without even faith on man's part.

Pink readily confesses the logical conclusion to which Calvinism's view of sovereignty and omniscience ultimately lead:

> . . . to deny God's foreknowledge is to deny His omniscience . . . . But we must go further: not only . . . did His omniscient eye see Adam eating of the forbidden fruit, but He *decreed* beforehand that he *should* do so. (Emphasis in original.)[21]

Here again the confused belief is offered that God's foreknowledge *causes* what He foreknows to occur, thus denying any choice to man. We have already seen that God, being separate from the time-space-matter universe He created, observes it from outside of time; thus His observation of the future leaves man free to choose. In fact, for God there *is* no time. Past, present and future are meaningful only to man as part of his temporary existence in this physical universe.

God's knowledge of what to Him is one eternal present would have no effect upon what to man is still future. Calvin himself accepted this view without realizing its devastating impact upon his denial of man's ability to make genuine choices:

> When we ascribe prescience to God, we mean that all things always were, and ever continue, under his eye; that to his knowledge there is no past or future, but all things are present, and indeed so present, that it is not merely the idea of them that is before him (as those objects are which we retain in memory), but that he truly sees and contemplates them as actually under his immediate inspection. This prescience extends to the whole circuit of the world, and to all creatures. [22]

Are "Tempting" And "Testing" Meaningless Terms?

Calvinism reasons that God, having foreordained from eternity past that Adam and Eve would eat of the Tree of Knowledge, forbids them to eat of it so He can punish them for doing what He foreordained and caused them to do! Then by Unconditional Election He saves a select few of their descendants to show His grace. That incredible scenario is unbiblical and dishonors God. It is contrary to the very character of a holy and just God who "cannot be tempted with evil, neither tempteth he any man" (James 1:13). Far from *causing* sin, God doesn't even *tempt* man to sin, as we have already seen.

We have noted that the Hebrew word translated "tempt" is *nacah*. It means to test or prove, not to entice to sin. When God asked Abraham to sacrifice Isaac, He was not enticing Abraham to commit murder but was *testing* Abraham's faith and obedience. To suggest that Abraham's every thought, word and deed had already been foreordained by God makes any "test" of Abraham's faith meaningless. The same would be true of the hundreds of times God tested the faith and obedience of individuals and nations in the Bible. What is the point if they have no free will to make a genuine choice but God's predestination has already determined what they will and must do? There would be nothing in man to test.

God was not tempting Adam and Eve to sin when He told them not to eat of a particular tree — much less had He predestined them to eat of it, though He knew they would. He gave them the easiest possible command. There must have been thousands of trees in the Garden bearing delicious fruit. They could eat of any or all of them — except one: "Of every tree of the garden thou mayest freely eat: but of the tree of the knowledge of good and evil, thou shalt not eat of it: for in the day that thou eatest thereof, thou shalt surely die" (Genesis 2:16-17). This command was a necessary test of obedience and of love for their Creator and could not have been simpler or easier to keep.

God was *testing,* not *tempting,* His creatures. But this whole concept of warning man not to tempt God and God testing man's obedience and faith which occupies so many pages of Scripture is meaningless if all has been eternally foreordained by God. This doctrine makes a mockery of all of God's pleadings through His prophets for man to repent and renders the gospel itself redundant. Why plead with or warn or preach to those whose response has been foreordained from eternity past?

Incapable And Predestined, Yet Accountable?

According to the "T" in TULIP, man is unable to respond to God in any way except rebellion. He is free to pursue sin and to reject the gospel, but because he is totally depraved (totally incapable by the Calvinist definition of that term) he cannot believe the gospel or have any degree of faith in God. He can respond to God only in unbelief and disobedience. Palmer declares that "the non-Christian is hostile to God . . . he is not even able to understand the good." [23]

Allegedly, by His eternal decree God has predestined man's every thought, word and deed, including the most heinous of atrocities committed by the world's worst criminals. Man's rebellion is only the acting out of what God has predetermined man will and must do.

Such doctrine defames the God of love and justice and turns man into a puppet with "God" pulling the strings. In defense of the character of the true God, John Wesley argued reasonably and biblically:

> He [God] will punish no man for doing anything he could not possibly avoid; neither for omitting anything which he could not possibly do. Every punishment supposes the offender might have avoided the offence for which he is punished. Otherwise, to punish him would be palpably unjust, and inconsistent with the character of God . . . . [24]

Astonishingly, Calvinists see neither injustice nor inconsistency in God foreordaining man's sin and then punishing him for what he could not avoid doing. This extreme view of sovereignty and predestination is applied to salvation by the doctrine of Unconditional Election. Although the Bible declares clearly and repeatedly that faith is the condition for salvation ("believe . . . and thou shalt be saved . . . he that believeth not shall be damned," etc.), Calvinism's Unconditional Election will not even allow faith unto salvation — God simply decides to save some, sovereignly regenerates them, and damns the rest.

Scripture and conscience impose upon *man* the duty to rescue everyone possible. But the Calvinist insists that it glorifies God for *Him* to rescue only a limited "elect" from those whom He has predisposed to evil. John MacArthur says that the elect are "those chosen by God for salvation . . . ." [25] That He chooses to damn the rest is said to show how wonderful it was that He saved at least some, thus causing the elect to be exceedingly grateful.

By this doctrine, if anyone is to be saved, God must both sovereignly *choose* to do so and He must *effect* within the sinner a saving response to the offer of salvation through Irresistible Grace (which we will come to later). With little sympathy for those who question Calvinism, Clark admitted, "The two theses most unacceptable to the Arminians are that God is the cause of sin and that God is the cause of salvation . . . ." [26] Referring to the pronouncement of this doctrine at the Synod of Dort, England's King James of King James Bible fame, though he was no Arminiam, expressed his repugnance:

> This doctrine is so horrible, that I am persuaded, if there were a council of unclean spirits assembled in hell, and their prince the devil were to [ask] their opinion about the most likely means of stirring up the hatred of men against God their Maker; nothing could be invented by them that would be more efficacious for this purpose, or that could put a greater affront upon God's love for mankind than that infamous decree of the late Synod . . . . [27]

A Strained And Unwarranted Redefinition Of Words

Who could argue with the king's concern? Nevertheless, in spite of the natural revulsion of the human conscience to this doctrine that depicts God without love or the least compassion for the billions He has been pleased to damn, it forms the foundation of Calvinism's concept of salvation. That concept rests not upon Scripture but upon a badly flawed philosophical system, although an attempt is made to support it biblically.

This is done by redefining certain words and phrases such as "world," "whosoever," "any," "all men" and even "sinners" to mean only the elect. For example, Paul's statement that "Christ Jesus came into the world to save sinners" (1 Timothy 1:15) seems on its face to mean that His desire was for all sinners to be saved. That understanding would, of course, refute Calvinism. Therefore, the word "sinners" is redefined to mean only "the elect among sinners."

There is nothing, however, in this statement, in its context or anywhere else in the Bible, to cause one to think that "sinners" really means the elect. The words "sinner" and "sinners" are found nearly seventy times in the Bible: "the wealth of the sinner is laid up for the just" (Proverbs 13:22); "we know that this man is a sinner" (John 9:24); "the men of Sodom were wicked and sinners" (Genesis 13:13); "behold, the Son of man is betrayed into the hands of sinners" (Mark 14:41); "for sinners also love those that love them" (Luke 6:32); "we know that God heareth not sinners" (John 9:31); "the law is not made for a righteous man, but for . . . the ungodly and for sinners" (1 Timothy 1:9); "but this man [Christ] . . . is holy, harmless, undefiled, separate from sinners" (Hebrews 7:24-26), etc. Surely in no case could "sinners" be construed to mean "the elect."

Throughout the New Testament the same Greek word is used for "sinners." Thus there is no license whatsoever to give it a different meaning in this *one* case which could not possibly apply anywhere else. That change in meaning is required only to salvage Calvinism, which would collapse if the Bible really meant that Christ came to save *all* sinners without discrimination, instead of only *some* sinners, i.e., the elect among them.

Who Are The Elect, And Why?

The Bible uses the term "elect" in a variety of ways. The term is used for Israel, Christ, a lady, a church and angels. Never, however, is this word used to indicate that there is a select group who alone have been predestinated to be saved. *Never.* Ironside declared, "Nowhere in the Bible are people ever predestinated to go to hell, and nowhere are people simply predestinated to go to Heaven. Look it up and see . . . predestination is always to some special place of blessing." [28]

Calvinism defines the elect as that select group whom alone God has from eternity past appointed to salvation. All others are predestined by God to inescapable damnation. The gospel can be preached with passionate appeal to the latter, both day and night — yet without effect because they are totally incapable of believing it and God has no desire whatsoever to open their blind eyes and give them the faith to believe, though He does that for the elect (through Unconditional Election) and could do so for all.

The Westminster Confession of Faith states, "By the decree of God, for the manifestation of His own glory, some men and angels are predestinated unto everlasting life, and others foreordained to everlasting death." [29] Even Calvin admitted that this idea was foreign to human conscience and reason:

To many this seems a perplexing subject, because they deem it most incongruous that of the great body of mankind some should be predestinated to salvation and others to destruction. [30]

The decree, I admit, is dreadful; and yet it is impossible to deny that God foreknew what the end of man was to be before he made him, and foreknew, because he had so ordained by his decree. [31]

Once again we are faced with the clear and repeated declaration that God decreed everything that would ever happen, from Adam's fall to the final doom of billions. But the Bible says the opposite: that "God so loved the *world,* that he gave his only begotten Son, that *whosoever* believeth in him should not perish, but have eternal life" (John 3:16). Both "world" and "whosoever" must be changed to "elect" for Calvinism to be sustained.

Perplexing Indeed!

Calvinism's "elect" are unconditionally (i.e., without any faith, understanding or choice on their part) elected to salvation simply because in the mystery of His sovereign will God decided, for no reason at all, to save them and *only* them. The Calvinist objects when we say, "for no reason at all." It is claimed that God needs no reason, that it simply pleased Him so to do, or that the reason is hidden in the mystery of His will: "We do not know what God bases His choice on . . . ." [32]

Even God, however, must have a reason for saving some and damning others. Otherwise He would be acting unreasonably, which would be contrary to His Being. In fact, He gives foreknowledge as the reason for predestination. Election/predestination is always explained in the Bible as resulting from God's foreknowledge. [33] Those whom He foreknew would believe, He predestined to special blessings, which He decided would accompany salvation from sin's penalty.

God continually explains why man is separated from Him and what the solution is, and He offers to reason with man about this matter: "Come now, and let us reason together" (Isaiah 1:18). He reasons with Israel, sends His prophets to warn her and explains repeatedly why He punishes them: "because of the wickedness of thy doings" (Deuteronomy 28:20); "they have forsaken the covenant of the LORD" (Deuteronomy 29:25); "because they have forsaken my law" (Jeremiah 9:13), etc. God explains that He gave His Son to die for our sins because of His great love for all mankind: "For God sent not his Son into the world to condemn the world; but that the world through him might be saved" (John 3:17); "And we have seen and do testify that the Father sent the Son to be the Saviour of the world" (1 John 4:14).

Yet God never declares through His prophets, through Christ or the Apostles — or anywhere in Scripture — a reason for saving a select few and damning the vast majority. Surely such an important doctrine would be clearly explained. From this lack of a reason, which is so contrary to God's character and dealings with man, it can only be concluded that Unconditional Election is but a human invention.

Scripture And Conscience Are United Against It

Nor does this doctrine find support in the conscience which God has given us. In fact, the conscience and Scripture cry out in protest against such an idea. God is entirely "without partiality" (James 3:17), is "no respecter of persons" (Acts 10:34), and all men are equally worthy of His condemnation and equally unworthy of His grace. Calvinists admit that the "elect," like all mankind, were once totally depraved, incurably set against God and incapable of believing the gospel, with no more to commend them to God's grace than the "non-elect." Then why did He select them to salvation and damn all the rest?

Even more troubling, why did Calvin's God choose to save so few when He could have saved all? Without apology, James White informs us, "Why is one man raised to eternal life and another left to eternal destruction . . . ? It is 'according to the kind intention of His will.' " [34] So it is God's *kindness* that causes Him to save so few and to damn so many! We are aghast at such a concept, and we are offended on behalf of our God.

Biblically, there is no question that God has the right to save whom He will and no one could complain. But we are repeatedly told that God *is love* and that He is merciful to *all*, exactly what we would expect of Him. We surely would not expect the "Father of mercies, and the God of all comfort" (2 Corinthians 1:3) to withhold mercy from *any* who so desperately need it — much less that He would take pleasure in doing so. Every attempt by Calvin to explain this contradiction falls short. For example:

> Why should God blame men for things the necessity of which he has imposed by his own predestination . . . ? Now . . . he arranges all things by his sovereign counsel, in such a way that individuals are born, who are doomed from the womb to certain death, and are to glorify him by their destruction . . . . If your mind is troubled, decline not to embrace the counsel of Augustine . . . . [35]

> We admit that the guilt is common, but we say, that God in mercy succours some. Let him (they say) succour all. We object, that it is right for him to show by punishing that he is a just judge . . . . Here the words of Augustine most admirably apply . . . . Since God inflicts due punishment on those whom he reprobates, and bestows unmerited favour on those whom he calls, he is free from every accusation . . . . [36]

I will not hesitate . . . to confess with Augustine that the will of God is necessity, and that everything is necessary which he has willed . . . [and] that the destruction consequent upon predestination is also most just . . . . The first man fell because the Lord deemed it meet that he should: why he deemed it meet, we know not. It is certain, however, that it was just, because he saw that his own glory would thereby be displayed . . . . [37]

What "Justice" Is This?

For God to act justly would indeed glorify Him, but Calvin has it backwards — that something which glorifies God must therefore be just. There is much that glorifies God which isn't even related to justice. Nor does God resort to judgment in order to demonstrate that He is a just judge. God *is* perfectly just, and His judgment falls upon those who deserve it and who reject His pardon through Christ — not upon a vast multitude whom He predestines to eternal torment because it pleases and glorifies Him! That is Calvin's belief which he learned from Augustine and it libels the God of the Bible.

That God would impose "the necessity of sinning" upon man, then condemn him for sinning, cannot be called just by any semantic maneuver. Yet this is exactly what Calvin taught and defended:

The reprobate would excuse their sins by alleging that they are unable to escape the necessity of sinning, especially because a necessity of this nature is laid upon them by the ordination of God. We deny that they can thus be validly excused . . . every evil which they bear is inflicted by the most just judgment of God. [38]

The heartlessness which Calvin attributes to God is appalling. Surely, as Wesley argues, to punish for failure to do what is impossible to do, or for doing what one is forced to do, is the opposite of justice. If that were not bad enough, that God would predestine man to sin so that He would have someone to judge is abhorrent even to the ungodly because it is so offensive to the conscience God has given all mankind. Calvin attributes evil to God, then calls it just because God is just: "everything which he [God] wills must be held to be righteous by the mere fact of his willing it." [39]

But Calvin hasn't shown us from Scripture that God wills and does what he ascribes to Him. Indeed, the many clear statements that God has "no pleasure in the death of the wicked; but that the wicked turn from his way and live" (Ezekiel 33:11) and that He is "not willing that any should perish, but that all should come to repentance" (2 Peter 3:9) contradict Calvin's repeated assertions that it pleases God to damn so many. [40]

Evading The Issues

Moreover, in all of his talk about God's sovereignty and justice, Calvin takes no account of God's other attributes such as His love and mercy, nor does he explain how the latter can be reconciled to his theory. Not one place in the nearly 1,300 pages of his *Institutes* does Calvin expound upon God's love for mankind or attempt to explain how God who *is* love could take pleasure in damning billions whom He could save if He so desired. Here is the great question which the very conscience God has implanted in all mankind finds so troubling − but Calvin never addresses it!

Biblically God's sovereignty is exercised only in perfect unity with His total character. He is not a despotic sovereign. His sovereignty is enforced in harmony with His love, grace, mercy, kindness, justice and truth − but Calvin has almost nothing to say about these attributes because they cannot be reconciled with his theory.

It is only reasonable to ask why God, who "is love," lacks the love and compassion to save all whom He could save and instead predestines billions to eternal torment. Calvin repeatedly hides his lack of an answer behind the word "mystery." But asserting that the reason for this predestination of some to salvation and others to damnation is hidden in the mystery of God's will offers no reason at all. Pleading "mystery" cannot cover up the horror of this doctrine. Yet that is the best Calvin can do, along with appealing to Augustine's authority. He pleads:

> Let us not be ashamed to be ignorant in a matter in which ignorance is learning. Rather let us willingly abstain from the search after knowledge, to which it is both foolish as well as perilous, and even fatal to aspire. [41]

> How sinful it is to insist on knowing the causes of the divine will, since it is itself, and justly ought to be, the cause of all that exists . . . . God, whose pleasure it is to inflict punishment on fools and transgressors . . . no other cause can be adduced . . . than the secret counsel of God . . . . Ignorance of things which we are not able, or which it is not lawful to know, is learning, while the desire to know them is a species of madness. [42]

Pleading "mystery" and exalting ignorance is contrary to God's Word, which tells us that we must "be ready always to give an answer to every man that asketh you a *reason* . . . " (1 Peter 3:15). Yet Calvin said it was wrong to seek a reason. Moreover, he called it "blessed ignorance" not to know. That won't do!

The only Greek word translated "mystery" is *musterion*. It is *never* used as Calvin used it to denote a secret not to be revealed. Rather, it *always* refers to knowledge which is being revealed − sometimes to all mankind but most often only to those who belong to Christ and are led of the Spirit. For example:

"I would not . . . that ye should be ignorant of this mystery . . . " (Romans 11:25); "I shew you a mystery . . . " (1 Corinthians 15:51); "made known unto me the mystery . . . " (Ephesians 3:3); "Even the mystery which hath been hid . . . but now is made manifest . . . " (Colossians 1:26); "I will tell thee the mystery . . . " (Revelation 17:7), etc. The word is *never* used as Calvin uses it in relation to salvation, predestination, or sovereignty, and certainly not concerning some being saved and others damned. Calvin simply invented a concept that is unknown in Scripture in order to cover up a repulsive doctrine which lies at the very heart of his teaching.

No Escape By Semantics

According to the doctrine of Unconditional Election, both the faith to believe and the salvation the elect receive are imposed upon them by God's sovereignty overriding entirely their human incapacity to choose and their depraved will's rejection of the gospel. The Calvinist objects to the phrase "imposed upon them" and insists that God simply removed from the elect their natural resistance to the gospel.

Any removal, however, of the alleged natural rejection would have to be contrary to a rebellious sinner's desire. And why would such a removal uncover within the totally depraved heart a willingness to believe the gospel? Palmer admits, "He even *makes* me, who really did not love Jesus, want to love Him and believe in Him." (Emphasis added) [43] It is axiomatic, however, that no one can be *made* either to love or to accept a gift, much less to change his mind without the willingness to do so. That willingness must come from the will that was already there; it can't be created out of thin air.

No one can be forced to change his mind. The old saying still holds: "A man convinced against his will, is of the same opinion still." No matter how he attempts to reword his explanation of Unconditional Election, the Calvinist cannot escape a basic fact recognized by all mankind: that in any meaningful change of attitude or belief, the human will must be involved. But that commonsense fact undermines God's sovereignty, according to Calvinism.

The Calvinist claims that, according to Ephesians 2:8-10, faith is bestowed as a gift (we discuss that in depth later). The Greek construction, however, demands that salvation, not faith, is the gift of God. Moreover, even if faith were the gift, it would have to be received, an act in itself requiring faith and the exercise of one's will in making the choice. Saving faith cannot come after the fact. It is an absolutely essential element in any relationship and transaction between man and God, as many scriptures declare unequivocally: "He that *cometh* to God must *believe* that he is . . . " (Hebrews 11:6). Jesus said, "According to *your* faith be it unto you" (Matthew 9:29). These are odd expressions if no one can come to God or have faith unless God sovereignly overrides that totally depraved person's unwillingness and unbelief by regenerating him without his consent or even knowing what is happening.

Calvin insists that God changes the will of the elect without either understanding or acceptance on their part. How God effects that change without conscious acquiescence on the part of the elect cannot be explained. Furthermore, such teaching is clearly not biblical. Scripture repeatedly depicts God as appealing to man's reason, conscience and will in order to persuade him to repent and believe.

1   Edwin H. Palmer, *the five points of calvinism* (Baker Books, enlarged ed., 20th prtg. 1999), 27.
2   Herman Hanko, Homer C. Hoeksema, and Gise J. Van Baren, *The Five Points of Calvinism* (Reformed Free Publishing Association, 1976), 28.
3   R.C. Sproul, *Chosen by God* (Tyndale House Publishers, Inc., 1986), 155.
4   Canons of Dort (Dordrecht, Holland, 1619), 1:7.
5   John Calvin, *Institutes of the Christian Religion*, trans. Henry Beveridge (Wm. Eerdmans Publishing Company, 1998 ed.), III:xxi,4,5.
6   Palmer, foreword to op.cit., 27.
7   Herman Hanko; cited in Laurence M. Vance, *The Other Side of Calvinism* (Vance Publications, Pensacola FL, rev. ed. 1999), 245.
8   Charles Haddon Spurgeon, *Spurgeon at His Best,* ed. Tom Carter (Baker Book House, 1988), 122.
9   George L. Bryson, *The Five Points of Calvinism "Weighed and Found Wanting"* (The Word For Today, 1996), 36.
10 R.C. Sproul, *Grace Unknown* (Baker Books, 1997), 141.
11 C. Samuel Storms, *Chosen for Life* (Baker Book House, 1987), 55.
12 Sproul, *Chosen*, 142.
13 Carl Morton, in *The Berean Baptist Banner*, January 5, 1995, 19.
14 David J. Engelsma, *Hyper-Calvinism and the Call of the Gospel* (Reformed Free Publishing Association, 1980), 133.
15 Leonard J. Coppes, *Are Five Points Enough? The Ten Points of Calvinism* (Denver CO: self-published, 1980), 15.
16 Palmer, op. cit., 25.
17 Gordon H. Clark, *Predestination* (Presbyterian and Reformed Publishing Co., 1987), 63-64; cited in Vance, op. cit., 265.
18 Calvin, op. cit., III:xxiii,6.
19 Calvinist pastor in Arizona to Dave Hunt, August 11, 2000. On file.
20 John R. Cross, *The Stranger on the Road to Emmaus* (Good Seed International, 1997), 56-57.
21 Arthur W. Pink, *The Sovereignty of God* (Baker Book House, 2nd prtg. 1986), 249.
22 Calvin, op. cit., III:xxi,5.
23 Palmer, op. cit., 15.
24 In Vance, op. cit., 236.
25 *The MacArthur Study Bible* (Word Publishing, 1997), 1939.
26 Clark, op. cit., 185.
27 King James I; in Jacobus Arminius, *The Works of James Arminius*, trans. James and William Nichols (Baker Book House, 1986), 1:213.
28 H.A. Ironside, *In the Heavenlies, Addresses on Ephesians* (Loiseaux Brothers, 1937), 34.
29 Westminster Confession of Faith (London: n.p., 1643), III:3.
30 Calvin, op. cit., III:xxi,1.
31 Op. cit., III:xxiii,7.
32 Palmer, op. cit., 26.
33 See, for example, Romans 8:29 and 1 Peter 1:2.
34 James R. White, *The Potter's Freedom* (Calvary Press Publishing, 2000), 177.
35 Calvin, op. cit., III:xxiii, 5,6.
36 Op. cit., III:xxiii,11.
37 Op. cit., III:xxiii,8,9.
38 Ibid.
39 Op. cit., III:xxiii,2.
40 Op. cit., III:xxiii,1,2,4, etc.
41 Op. cit., III:xxi,2.
42 Op. cit., III:xxiii,4,8.
43 Palmer, op. cit., 21.

14
Is Salvation Available To All?

It was God who determined of His own will to provide salvation. He devised the plan and set the rules to satisfy His justice. It is folly for anyone to imagine that man can set the requirements for salvation and impose them upon God. It is no less obvious that God, because He is God, has the prerogative of offering salvation to whomever He will.

God told Moses, "[I] will be gracious to whom I will be gracious, and will shew mercy on whom I will shew mercy" (Exodus 33:19). That statement is often misunderstood and misused. God does not say that He will be gracious and merciful to some and not to others. He is simply saying that grace and mercy are by His initiative. They cannot be demanded nor is He under any obligation to extend them to anyone.

Scripture makes it very clear that it is only by God's grace and mercy that salvation comes to man: "By grace are ye saved . . . not by works of righteousness which we have done, but according to his mercy he saved us" (Ephesians 2:8; Titus 3:5). Such scriptures are numerous throughout the Bible. This is the clear biblical message from beginning to end. Since salvation is by grace, it cannot be earned, merited or demanded on any basis whatsoever.

By their very nature, grace and mercy need not be extended to all but can be given to whomever God should decide. However, far from indicating that His grace is limited because He has decided to save only a select few and that salvation is provided for them alone, the Bible very clearly states that "God so loved the world" that He gave His Son to die "that the world through him might be saved" (John 3:16-17). In order to accomplish salvation for all, Christ the Lamb of God came to take "away the sin of the world" (John 1:29) and He became the propitiation "for the sins of the whole world" (1 John 2:2). The same thought is presented all through Scripture. Indeed, God repeatedly declares that He is gracious and merciful to all. And so it is with God's love, from which His grace and mercy flow — without partiality it reaches out to all mankind.

Furthermore, in contrast to the literally hundreds of places where God's love is clearly expressed for all of Israel (most of whom rejected Him) and for the whole world (most of whom also reject Him), *nowhere* does the Bible declare that God doesn't love and desire the salvation of all. *Nowhere* in Scripture is there any indication that God's love and salvation are limited to a select few. If this were the case, surely it would be stated clearly somewhere in order to avoid confusion in view of the many places where the opposite is so clearly declared. Unable to find *one* such scripture, the Calvinist is forced to claim that in expressions of God's desire for or offer of salvation, words such as "world" or "any" or "whosoever" or "sinners" or "all men" actually mean "the elect."

Sovereignty And Salvation

Although we could not demand that God save us from the penalty His law prescribes for sin, and although He is in no way obligated to provide salvation for *anyone*, the Bible repeatedly makes it clear that God's purpose is for all mankind to be saved: "Who will have all men to be saved, and to come unto the knowledge of the truth . . . Christ Jesus . . . gave himself a ransom for all . . . " (1 Timothy 2:4-6). "Whosoever believeth in him . . . whosoever will, let him take of the water of life freely" (John 3:16; Revelation 22:17) sounds like a genuine *offer* that can be accepted or rejected.

It is equally clear that everyone is not saved. How is that possible if the sovereign God truly wants all to be saved, as the offer of salvation seems to imply? Could a sovereign God who "worketh all things after the counsel of his own will" (Ephesians 1:11) merely express His will in an *offer* that man could by *his* will accept or reject?

Why not? Surely a command is stronger than an offer, yet the Ten Commandments which God gave from Mount Sinai to Moses and has written in every human conscience are broken continually by man's self-will. God's sovereignty would no more be undermined if some accepted the offer of salvation and others rejected it than for billions of humans continually to disobey the Ten Commandments.

The word "whosoever" is defined in *Webster's New Universal Unabridged Dictionary* as "whoever; whatever person: an emphatic form." There are no alternate meanings—it always means whoever or whatever person. The word is so universally understood that no one could possibly misinterpret it. Yet Calvinism requires that in certain places "whosoever" actually means "the elect."

In those places where "the elect" is substituted for "whosoever," there is nothing in the text or context that would even suggest such a change. The only reason that such a reinterpretation could be imposed would be to defend Calvinism, which would otherwise collapse if the normal meaning for "whosoever" were allowed.

The word "whosoever" is found 183 times in 163 verses in the Bible, beginning with "whosoever slayeth Cain" (Genesis 4:15) and ending with "whosoever will, let him take of the water of life freely" (Revelation 22:17). The meaning is just as unequivocal in the Bible as the dictionary presents it. "Whosoever" clearly means everyone without exception. It is found in warnings ("whosoever eateth leavened bread" - Exodus 12:15) and in promises of reward ("whosoever smiteth the Jebusites first shall be chief - 1 Chronicles 11:6). Among the scores of other examples are "whosoever heareth, his ears shall tingle" (Jeremiah 19:3) and "whosoever shall call on the name of the LORD shall be delivered" (Joel 2:32). Not once in its 183 appearances in the Bible is there any reason to imagine that the word "whosoever" means anything except "whosoever"! But in those places where salvation is offered to whosoever will believe and receive Christ, the Calvinist insists that the exact same Hebrew or Greek word changes its meaning to the "elect."

The best-known Bible verse, spoken by Christ to Nicodemus a sincere seeker, promises eternal life to "whosoever believeth in him" (John 3:16). Christ's last recorded words in the Bible are, "I Jesus have sent mine angel to testify unto you these things . . . the Spirit and the bride say, Come. And let him that heareth say, Come. And let him that is athirst come. And whosoever will, let him take the water of life freely" (Revelation 22:16-17). There is nothing in these passages or in any other context to suggest that Christ offers salvation to anyone less than "whosoever."

The doctrine of Unconditional Election – in contrast to Scripture – declares that this offer, which seems to be to *whosoever will*, is effective only for a select few. Although like all others the Calvinist "elect" are by nature supposedly incapable of responding to the gospel, they out of all mankind have been unconditionally elected to salvation. In the Bible, however, God repeatedly seems to offer repentance to all who will respond and salvation to all who will believe.

If salvation is not genuinely offered to all, why did Christ command His disciples to go into all the world and preach the gospel to every creature" (Mark 16:15)? Is that not giving a false impression both to His disciples and to all who would read their account of Christ's teachings in the four Gospels? Taking our Lord's words at face value, it must have seemed to those who heard Him that

He repeatedly offered salvation to all whoever would believe and receive Him: "*He* that heareth my word, and believeth on him that sent me, hath everlasting life" (John 5:24); "If *any* man thirst, let him come unto me and drink" (7:37); I am the door . . . by me if *any* man enter in, he shall be saved (John 10:7), and so forth.

How would His disciples or the common people who heard Him make these and so many other similar statements — people who had never heard of Augustine's and Calvin's theories — come to the conclusion that salvation was only for a select few who had been unconditionally elected? Furthermore, would it not be misrepresentation of the worst sort to offer salvation to *whosoever will*, when in fact it was only intended for a select few? If the latter were true, Christ could have chosen words to convey that fact rather than seeming to offer salvation to whosoever would believe on and receive Him.

Illustrating A Point

The God of the Bible declares repeatedly throughout His Word that He is not willing that anyone should perish but wills for "all men to be saved" (1 Timothy 2:4). Continually, and in the most urgent and solemn language possible, He calls upon all men to repent and to believe in His Son as the Savior of all men. Christ holds out His nail-pierced hands and pleads, "Come unto me, *all* ye that labour and are heavy laden, and I will give you rest" (Matthew 11:28). This is a promise which *all* who labor and are heavy laden have every reason to believe is extended to *them*.

Taking what the Bible says at face value, one would come to the conclusion that just as "*all* have sinned" (Romans 3:23), so *all* are offered deliverance from sin and its penalty through the gospel. To claim that "all" means only a select group called the elect does violence to the plain meaning of language and impugns the character of God; and it does this in order to force upon the Word of God a system of religion which cannot be derived from it. In our newsletter, I have likened Calvinism to the following scenario:

> If I should hold a rope 30 feet above a man at the bottom of a well and plead with him earnestly to take hold of it so that I could pull him out, wouldn't he think that I was mocking him? And if, in addition, I berate him for not grabbing the rope, would he not begin to wish he could grab me by the throat? And how could I maintain to any reasonable persons that I really wanted to bring the man up out of the well but he was the one who wasn't willing? So how can God really want to save those to whom He doesn't extend irresistible grace, that being the only means whereby they can believe the Gospel?

In a radio discussion with me,[1] James White countered that it wasn't a matter of someone getting hold of a rope: the man at the bottom of the well was dead and couldn't grab it. The point of the illustration, however, had nothing to do with grabbing a rope. No illustration is perfect. Salvation is not by any effort on our part at all, nor do we hang onto Christ to be saved. He keeps us secure in His hand.

The point of the illustration was that the rope was being held so high above the man in the well as to make it obvious that the professed rescuer wasn't sincere in his pleadings and had no intention of pulling the man from the well. The would-be rescuer, of course, is not obligated to save the man below him. But if he does not desire to save him, why does he mock him by declaring that he wants to rescue him? Why does he chide the man at the bottom of the well for failing to grab the rope while continuing to hold it far beyond his reach?

The sincerity of the offer by the supposed rescuer was the issue and the point of the imperfect illustration. And so it is with our Lord's offer of salvation in the Bible: Calvinism turns it into an offer which unquestionably, on the face of it, seems to be extended to all but really isn't, because of a disclaimer in fine print which can't be seen by the ordinary eye.

Nor does it help to picture the man at the bottom of the well as dead. In that case, the supposed rescuer is pretending to call to a corpse that he knows cannot hear him. Furthermore, if the man at the top has the power to go into the well to raise the dead man to life and take him out to safety but doesn't do so, how could he be sincere in his offer if he doesn't do what he promises?

Such is the God of Calvinism: He pleads with men to repent, He sends forth His servants to preach a gospel that seems to offer salvation to every person, and He chides and damns those who do not believe – but at the same time He does not give to them the essential faith without which they cannot respond to His pleadings. In fact, He has from eternity past irrevocably damned them eternally to the lake of fire. Such insincerity cannot be explained away by the example of the potter and clay. The fact that the potter can do with the clay what he pleases does not excuse the potter from promising perfection to each lump of clay and then discarding many, if not most, onto the rubbish heap.

Biblically, there is no question that God sovereignly has the right to save whom He will, and no one could complain. But His sovereignty is only one facet of His Being. We are repeatedly told that God *is love* (i.e., love is the very essence of His character) and that He is merciful to all – exactly what we would expect of Him. We surely would not expect the "Father of mercies, and the God of all comfort (2 Corinthians 1:3) to withhold mercy from any who so desperately need it—much less that He would take pleasure in doing so. Surely God is being misrepresented by those who limit His love and mercy and grace to a select few.

"As Many As Were *Ordained* To Eternal Life Believed"

One of the Calvinists' favorite proof texts is Acts 13:48, where we read that "as many as were ordained to eternal life believed." Vance says, "Every Calvinist, no matter what else he believes, uses this verse to prove Unconditional Election . . . ." Nettleton claims that it is "this verse that made him a Calvinist." [2] White devotes four pages to it. [3] Palmer exults, "Here is another text with stunning clarity for whoever will read the Bible without preconceived notions . . . . The stark simplicity of this text is astounding." [4]

In fact, "*ordained* to eternal life," while it is so shown in the major translations (as White is quick to point out), [5] is at best a questionable rendering, and many Greek scholars call it a wrong translation. The Greek word is *tasso* and has a variety of meanings and usages. It is found eight times in the New Testament, and none of them carries the meaning of a decree from God nor of something that is unchangeable or eternal, so there is no basis for assigning that meaning here. The Liddell and Scott Greek dictionary offers a number of alternate meanings, but "ordain" or "foreordain" is not one of them. In 1 Corinthians 16:15 in the KJV, for example, *tasso* is translated "addicted": "the house of Stephanas . . . have addicted themselves to the ministry of the saints." In Acts 15:2 it is translated "determined" (decided): "they determined that Paul and Barnabas . . . should go up to Jerusalem." Many Greek experts suggest the same idea here: that the Gentiles had disposed themselves (i.e., determined) to believe.

Several authorities trace the KJV's wrong rendering to the corrupt Latin Vulgate, which, as T.E. Page points out, "has *praeordinati*, unfairly . . . ." [6] Cook's *Commentary* reads, "The A.V. [Authorized Version, i.e., KJV] has followed the Vulgate. Rather, [it should read] were set in order for, i.e., disposed for eternal life, as in Syriac . . . and repeatedly in Josephus, as many as had . . . placed themselves in the ranks of those who welcomed the offer of eternal life." [7] Likewise, Dean Alford translated it, "as many as were *disposed* to eternal life believed." [8] Clearly there are differences of opinion concerning the technical considerations of the Greek which only the experts are competent to discuss. That being the case, we ought to come down on the side of a rendering which harmonizes with the rest of Scripture. There are dozens of passages which declare in the plainest language that the gospel is offered to whosoever will believe it and that God desires all mankind to be saved. Consequently, it would be improper to adopt here a questionable interpretation as the basis for rejecting the overwhelming weight of Scripture.

The Expositor's Greek Testament says, "There is no countenance here for the *absolutum decretum* of the Calvinists." [9] A.T. Robertson says virtually the same thing in almost the same words:

The word "ordain" is not the best translation here . . . . The Jews had voluntarily rejected the word of God. On the other side were those Gentiles who gladly accepted what the Jews had rejected . . . . Why these Gentiles here ranged themselves on God's side . . . Luke does not tell us. This verse does not solve the vexed problem of divine sovereignty and human free agency. There is no evidence that Luke had in mind an *absolutum decretum* of personal salvation . . . . [10]

So the experts disagree. Like almost every other Greek word, *tasso* has several meanings. The best way to determine which meaning applies is to consider the context. When we do that the choice becomes clear. The Jews have just rejected the gospel and that is why Paul has turned to the Greeks. In Acts 13:46, Paul says to the Jews, "but seeing that ye put it from you, and judge yourselves unworthy of everlasting life, lo, we turn to the Gentiles."

Verse 48 presents the contrast between the Jews who had set themselves against the gospel and the Gentiles who disposed themselves to receive it. Thus it is saying that "as many [Greeks] as were *disposed* to eternal life believed." That meaning is at least *allowable* from the word *tasso* and it seems to be demanded by the context. Why not accept it? Because to do so would undermine Calvinism. We can find no other reason.

Predestination To Salvation — Or Not?

What about the statements in the Bible that certain ones have been predestined, or elected? We will examine those scriptures and in the process we will see that in the Bible predestination/election is *never* unto salvation. To the Calvinist, however, predestination/election is *always* and *only* unto salvation — a view which is imposed wrongly upon Scripture. In fact, election/predestination is always unto specific blessings that *accompany* salvation, but not to salvation itself. Knowing who would believe the gospel is a valid *reason* for electing or predestinating those persons to certain blessings. But God's knowledge that He would extend Irresistible Grace to certain persons cannot be offered as the *reason* for doing so.

What else does the Calvinist have to say about election and predestination? In his book, White has an entire chapter titled "Unconditional Election a Necessity." Indeed it is a necessity if Calvinism is to be upheld, but it is not a necessity on any other basis. To define Unconditional Election, White quotes from the 1689 London Baptist Confession of Faith, the Westminster Confession of Faith, and a number of leading theologians such as James P. Boyce. Following are some excerpts from these quotations:

Before the world was made, God's eternal, immutable purpose, which originated in the secret counsel and good pleasure of His will, moved Him to choose (or to elect), in Christ, certain of mankind to everlasting glory . . . although there was nothing in them to cause Him to choose them. (Baptist Confession) [There is nothing in any of us to cause God to save us.]

This decree . . . is made "independent" of all such foreknowledge God has of what will take place in time [and] predestines certain *specific individuals* to eternal life and others it leaves to justice. This is an election *unto salvation* and . . . is *utterly unconditional* . . . not conditioned upon *anything* in the human, either foreseen faith, actions, dispositions, or desires. (Westminster) [Salvation is conditioned upon faith: "*Believe* . . . and thou shalt be saved."]

The latter theory [i.e., the Calvinistic theory] is that God . . . of his own purpose . . . has from Eternity . . . determined to save . . . a definite number of mankind (not the whole race . . . not for . . . their faith . . .) but of his own good pleasure (simply because he was pleased so to choose). (Boyce) [11]

These are assertions — fallible human opinions — which both Boyce and White admit express merely a "theory." This theory must be tested by Scripture. Further quotations of men's opinions follow in the remainder of White's chapter. The final one is from Calvin himself:

We shall never be clearly persuaded, as we ought to be, that our salvation flows from the wellspring of God's free mercy until we come to know his eternal election, which illumines God's grace by this contrast: that he does not indiscriminately adopt all into the hope of salvation but gives to some what he denies to others. [12]

This is an astonishing statement for two reasons. First of all, who ever imagined that God "indiscriminately adopt[s] into the hope of salvation"? The Bible is very clear that Christ is the door, the only way of salvation. The Gospel is the power of God unto salvation, and only those who believe the gospel are saved. Calvin is tilting at windmills in combating the idea supposedly held by non-Calvinists that God indiscriminately gives salvation.

Giving God A Bad Name

Secondly, this statement is incredible in its defamation of God. One would think that, rather than quoting this statement, Calvinists would be almost as embarrassed by it as they should be about Calvin's totalitarian imposition of "godliness" upon the citizens of Geneva under penalty of torture and death. How could God's withholding of salvation from billions to whom He *could* give it cause us to appreciate "the wellspring of God's free mercy" and "illumine God's grace"? That is like praising a man's generosity by exposing his stinginess.

The blindness on this point is frustrating. In their chapter on "Limited Atonement," after explaining that Christ died only for a select few and that all others have been damned by God for eternity, John Piper and his staff defy all logic with this statement: "Every time the gospel is preached to unbelievers it is the mercy of God that gives this opportunity for salvation." [13] *Opportunity for salvation* for those who cannot possibly be saved because Christ did not die for them and they have been predestined to eternal damnation? What taunting, cruel mockery is this!

Far from glorifying God, Calvinism gives God a bad name —and any number of atheists and other critics of the Bible have been quick to jump on this fact, using it to paint God as some kind of monster who takes pleasure in the suffering of mankind. Calvin's God chooses, for no reason at all within Himself (He is without partiality) or in those chosen (all are equally depraved and guilty), to save only a limited number of persons even though He *could save the entire human race.* It is astonishing that such abhorrent behavior is attributable to God as proof of the greatness of His grace!

Calvin vigorously defends God's sovereignty, but we don't need such arguments to prove that God is sovereign. He *is* sovereign. Period. In our dispute with Calvinism, sovereignty is not even an issue. This continual emphasis upon God's sovereignty to the exclusion of His love, mercy and grace dominates the thinking of Calvinists. For example, in the booklet John Piper and his pastoral staff at Bethlehem Baptist Church in Minneapolis published promoting Calvinism, God's love to lost sinners is missing, while sovereignty is the repetitious, dominant theme. In the preface, Piper writes, "To know him [God] in his sovereignty is to become like an oak tree in the wind of adversity and confusion." [14] But entirely missing is *anything* about knowing God's love or loving Him.

Here we confront the real issue: God's love and character. God's love for the world is conspicuous by its absence from Calvin's *Institutes.* Indeed, God's love for anyone, including the elect, is scarcely mentioned, which is rather telling considering the vital importance it is given in the Bible. That God even loves the elect is hard to find because it is not love that brings salvation to mankind but God's sovereign choice for His good pleasure.

Surely he doesn't intend to do so, but Calvin seems to mock God by linking "the wellspring of God's free mercy"with *limiting* that mercy to a select few and denying it to others to whom He could also have been merciful. God expects man to love his enemies and to do good to all. Calvin himself admits that "God enjoins us to be merciful even to the unworthy . . . ." [15] Yet He has a lesser standard for Himself? How could it glorify God for Him to be less gracious than He commands *mankind* to be? And where does God say that He limits His mercy — much less that He is thereby glorified? How could anyone say that God is showing mercy to those whom He predestines to eternal torment?

When God says, "I will be gracious to whom I will be gracious, and will shew mercy on whom I will shew mercy" (Exodus 33:19), He is simply declaring that by their very nature grace and mercy cannot be demanded. There is no basis for concluding from this statement that grace and mercy are limited to a select few. Many scriptures have already been quoted assuring us that God's mercy is unlimited and extended to all. Calvin refers to "our most merciful Father," [16] yet he limits that mercy to the elect.

Boyce offends the God-given conscience even of atheists in saying that God chose to save only a few and to let the others perish because He "was *pleased* so to choose"! Where does God ever intimate that He is pleased to let *anyone* perish? What a libelous misrepresentation of the God of the Bible!

A Strange "Mercy" And "Kindness"

The Baptist Confession declares that God's election, which is supposedly a manifestation of His mercy, "predestines certain *specific individuals* to eternal life and others it leaves to justice." How can it be a manifestation of mercy to leave the condemned to suffer the penalty which justice demands, when they could be justified and forgiven and rescued from eternal punishment? This is not a question of the guilt of sinners or of whether they deserve judgment, which we all do. The issue is mercy. We all deserve the just judgment of God. But the Bible clearly tells us that "mercy rejoiceth against judgment" (James 2:13). Surely there can be no limit to the infinite mercy of the infinite God!

God solemnly warns man, "If thou forbear to deliver them that are drawn unto death . . . [and] sayest, Behold, we knew it not; doth not he that pondereth the heart consider . . . and shall not he render to every man according to his works?" (Proverbs 24:11) Yet Calvin's God not only fails to deliver the lost but decrees their doom! This cannot be the God of the Bible, of whom Jesus said, "it is not the will of your Father which is in heaven, that one of these little ones should perish" (Matthew 18:14)!

Having disparaged God's character, Calvin says with no apparent sense of irony, "Hence the highest proof of Scripture is uniformly taken from the character of him whose word it is." [17] How can he dare to say this while impugning God's character at the same time? Calvin then goes on to extol God's mercy and grace as the pinnacle of His character:

> There are certain passages which contain more vivid descriptions of the divine character, setting it before us . . . . Moses, indeed, seems to have intended briefly to comprehend whatever may be known of God by man, when he said [actually God said], "The LORD, The LORD God, merciful and gracious, long-suffering, and abundant in goodness and truth, keeping mercy for thousands, forgiving iniquity and transgression and sin, and that will by no means clear the guilty . . . ." (Exodus 34:6-7)

> In Jeremiah, where God proclaims the character in which he would have us to acknowledge him . . . it is substantially the same . . . . "I am the LORD which exercise loving-kindness, judgment, and righteousness in the earth . . . ." (Jeremiah 9:24) [18]

Having presented from Scripture God's infinite grace, mercy and love promised to all, one can only marvel that Calvin persists in claiming that the *withholding* of His grace, mercy and love from all except the elect enhances the goodness of His character! In fact, Paul argues that God has found "all the world guilty" (Romans 3:19) and has "concluded them all [Jew and Gentile] in unbelief, that he might have mercy upon all" (Romans 11:32). Unquestionably, the *all* who are guilty and in unbelief must be the whole world of sinners, Jews and Gentiles, *all* of whom are by nature rebels and in unbelief — and these are the *all* upon whom God is determined to have mercy. It could not be stated more clearly throughout Scripture that God's mercy extends to *all.*

Denying A Clear Contradiction

As a staunch Calvinist, White informs us, "Why is one man raised to eternal life and another left to eternal destruction . . . ? It is 'according to the kind intention of His will.'" [19] So it is God's *kindness* that causes Him to damn so many! We are astounded at such a concept.

The Calvinist, however, denies that there is any contradiction in the idea that the God of infinite love is pleased to predestine billions to eternal torment. Calvin even castigates those who point out the contradiction. He praises Augustine for throwing out of the Church any who suggest that God couldn't really love those from whom He withholds the faith to believe the gospel. He writes:

> Were anyone to address the people thus: If you do not believe, the reason is, because God has already doomed you to destruction: he would not only encourage sloth, but also give countenance to wickedness. Were any one to . . . say, that those who hear will not believe because they are reprobates [i.e., damned by God's foreordination], it were imprecation rather than doctrine. [Yet as has already been shown, this is exactly what Calvin teaches.]
>
> Wherefore, Augustine not undeservedly orders such, as senseless teachers or sinister and ill-omened prophets, to retire from the Church. [20]

Calvin is trying to escape the consequences of his own dogmas, but it won't work. He repeatedly insists throughout his *Institutes* that "God saves whom he wills of his mere good pleasure" [21] and that some are "predestinated to salvation, and others to destruction." [22] Calvin says that the latter, who it was God's good "pleasure to doom to destruction . . . are excluded from access to life . . . ." [23] How those whom the omnipotent God has "excluded from access to life" could be responsible for their doom and could be the beneficiaries of His infinite love is incomprehensible.

The situation is as if the ocean were filled with billions of people whom God has so created that they are totally depraved as far as swimming is concerned (i.e., they cannot swim a stroke) and He has thrown them into the ocean. God "mercifully" rescues a small fraction of them and leaves the rest to drown in eternal death. How could anyone with any sense of fairness say to those whom God created to drown and put in that ocean, "It is your own fault!"? How can Calvin (and Calvinists today) say it is "wickedness" and "imprecation" to say that the non-elect cannot believe the gospel because God has excluded them from faith, when, in fact, that is exactly what Calvinism teaches? Calvin has left logic and Scripture behind when he tries to maintain that those whom God foreordains to eternal doom are themselves to blame for their fate. It is even more outrageous to suggest that they are the objects of His love, mercy and grace!

Biblical Mercy, Kindness And Grace

Numerous scriptures contradict the theory that God would withhold mercy from anyone — scriptures which refute the very heart of Calvinism. We are reminded that God is "ready to pardon, gracious and merciful, slow to anger and of great kindness" (Nehemiah 9:17). Of the good and righteous man, the Bible says, "he is ever [always to all] merciful" (Psalms 37:26). Surely the very "gracious and merciful God" (Nehemiah 9:31) would be no less than always merciful to all. But Calvinism limits God's grace and mercy to a select few called the elect. Such a God has a lower standard of mercy than He expects of us.

The Apostle James points out the hypocrisy of saying to someone who is "naked, and destitute of daily food . . . be ye warmed and filled" and then failing to meet his need (James 2:15-16). The God who inspired James to write those words, however, according to Calvinism, tells a lost and perishing world, "Believe on the Lord Jesus Christ, and thou shalt be saved," but neglects to elect the perishing to the salvation He seemingly offers. Such a God sees those who are worse than physically naked and destitute and, far more serious than failing to meet their temporal needs, He fails to rescue the perishing from an eternal hell even though He could in His omnipotence and sovereignty do so. Is this really the God of the Bible, or a God that Calvin borrowed from Augustine?

The psalmist rejoices that God is "plenteous in mercy unto all them that call upon him" (Psalms 86:5) and that "his tender mercies are over all his works" (Psalms 145:9). The Calvinist, however, without any warrant from Scripture, changes the "all" to mean "all of the elect." Christ exhorts us, "Be ye therefore merciful, as your Father also is merciful" (Luke 6:36). If we took Calvinism at face value, being merciful as our Father in heaven is merciful would allow us to neglect helping multitudes and to claim that so doing reveals how merciful we are!

Jesus illustrates the mercy of His Father in many ways. He tells us that after crying out, "God be merciful to me a sinner" (Luke 18:13), the publican was mercifully justified. Paul refers to "the Father of mercies and the God of all comfort" (2 Corinthians 1:3). Would the very "Father of mercies" be any less merciful *to all* than He expects mankind to be? "Blessed are the merciful; for they shall obtain mercy" (Matthew 5:7).

These scriptures and scores more in the same vein, which could be quoted and ought to be familiar to every Christian, tell us that God's mercy is infinite and over all His works, extending to all mankind without discrimination. To arrive at any other conclusion one is required to select a few Bible verses, apply to common words a special meaning that doesn't fit the rest of Scripture, and ignore scores of verses telling us of the abundance of God's mercies and grace freely offered to all.

The psalmist says, "I will sing of the mercies of the Lord for ever . . . " (Psalms 89:1). The Calvinist would rightly say that the psalmist was one of the elect, with which we would agree, and that it is His elect who praise Him for His mercies. That is true. But it is also true that God's mercies are unto all who call upon Him. Indeed, the very glory of God is in His mercy to all mankind. When Moses asked, "I beseech thee, shew me thy glory," God declared what Calvin himself quotes from Exodus 34:7 concerning His mercy, grace, longsuffering, and goodness.

It is indisputable that God has the right to limit His mercy. However, we are so clearly told in so many passages of Scripture and in so many ways that God *does not* limit His mercy but extends it to all. One is forced to reject Calvinism on this basis if on no other, for it contradicts the very character of God which is consistently displayed throughout Scripture from Genesis to Revelation.

In response to my statement that the logical outcome of Calvinism is that God does not care if billions perish, many Calvinists have objected strenuously. Yet they say God *could* save everyone if He so desired. Then the God of Calvinism doesn't care that billions perish. If He did care, then He would rescue them by causing them to believe through Irresistible Grace.

On the other hand, the non-Calvinist believes that God has given man the power to make a genuine choice. He offers salvation to all without discrimination, but He cannot make anyone believe for that would violate their free will, destroying their ability to love and to truly serve God. Thus those who will spend eternity in the lake of fire are there because of their own choice, not because of God's choice.

Whether or not God loves all, is merciful upon all, and provides salvation for all to accept or to reject, is the real issue. The answer to that question should become increasingly clear to the reader in the following pages.

---

1   "Straight Talk Live" (KPXQ, Phoenix AZ), 11 August 11, 2000). Audiotape Ato73, available through The Berean Call, P.O. Box 7019, Bend OR 97708.

2   David Nettleton, *Chosen to Salvation* (Regular Baptist Press, 1983), 16; cited in Laurence M. Vance, *The Other Side of Calvinism* (Vance Publications, Pensacola FL, rev. ed. 1999), 345.

3   James R. White, *The Potter's Freedom* (Calvary Press Publishing, 2000), 186-90.

4   Edwin H. Palmer, *the five points of calvinism* (Baker Books, enlarged ed., 20th prtg. 1980) 29.

5   White, op. cit., 187-88.

6   T.E. Page, *The Acts of the Apostles, Greek Text with Explanatory Notes* (Macmillan and Co., 1897), 169.

7   Frederic C. Cook, ed., *The Bible Commentary* (Charles Scribner Sons, 1895).

8   Henry Alford, *The New Testament for English Readers* (Baker Book House, 1983), I:745.

9   R.J. Knowling, *The Acts of the Apostles, The Expositor's Greek New Testament* (Dodd, Mead and Co., 1900), 300.

10 Archibald Thomas Robertson, *Word Pictures in the New Testament* (Harper and Bros., 1930), III: 200.

11 White, op. cit., 125-26.

12 Op. cit., 131; citing John Calvin, *Institutes of the Christian Religion,* trans. Henry Beveridge (Wm. Eerdmans Publishing Company, 1998 ed.), III:21:1.

13 John Piper and Pastoral Staff, "TULIP: What We Believe about the Five Points of Calvinism: Position Paper of the Pastoral Staff" (Desiring God Ministries, 1997), 14.

14 Ibid.

15 Calvin, op. cit., III: xx, 15.

16 Op. cit., III: xx, 3.

17 Op. cit., I: iii, 4.

18 Op. cit., I: ii, 8, 2.

19 White, op. cit., 177.

20 Calvin, op. cit., III: xxiii, 14.

21 Op. cit., III: xxi, 1.

22 Ibid.

23 Op. cit., III:xxi, 7.

15
Foreknowledge And Predestination/Election

The terms predestination and election are used interchangeably in Scripture. The basic meaning is the same: to mark out beforehand for a special purpose and blessing. On what basis? In relation to mankind, the sole reason which is always given is *foreknowledge*. Both Peter and Paul, inspired of the Holy Spirit, declare in the plainest language that God's election / predestination to special blessings is determined by His foreknowledge: "For whom he did foreknow [Greek: *proginosko*], he also did predestinate [*proorizo*] to be conformed to the image of his Son . . . " (Romans 8:29); "Elect according to [*kata*] the foreknowledge [*prognosis*] of God the Father, through sanctification of the Spirit, unto obedience . . . " (1 Peter 1:2).

What foreknowledge would cause God to mark out certain ones to be "conformed to the image of his Son" and to walk in "obedience"? We are not told directly, but the implication is that God's foreknowledge concerned those whom He knew would believe the gospel and be saved. Surely the blessings specified are the inheritance the heavenly Father has planned from eternity past for those who would become His children through faith in Christ Jesus: "That in the ages to come he might shew the exceeding riches of his grace in his kindness toward us through Christ Jesus" (Ephesians 2:7).

Before proceeding further, it is vital to realize that neither in these passages nor anywhere else does election or predestination refer to salvation but always and only to particular benefits: "What must be borne in mind is the fact that predestination is not God's predetermining from past ages who should and who should not be saved. Scripture does not teach this view." [1] Earlier we quoted Ironside to the same effect. Here is a similar statement from another of his books: "You will note that there is no reference in these four verses [the *only* four which refer to predestination] to either heaven or hell, but to Christlikeness eventually. Nowhere are we told in Scripture that God predestined one man to be saved and another to be lost." [2]

What does it mean that foreknowledge is the basis of predestination — and why should that be? To answer that question is the purpose of this chapter.

Perverting Predestination

Edward Hulme declares of Calvin, "Predestination was his pivotal dogma. His theology begins and ends with the supremacy of God . . . . 'Everything,' says Calvin, 'depends upon the mere will of God; if some are damned and others saved it is because God has created some for death and others for life.' " [3] Here it is again in Calvin's own words: "I say with Augustine, that the Lord has created those who, as he certainly foreknew, were to go to destruction, and he did so because he so willed. Why he willed, it is not ours to ask . . . ." [4]

Palmer informs us that "The first word Calvinism suggests to most people is predestination; and if they have a modicum of theological knowledge, the other four points [of TULIP] follow." [5] John H. Leith declares, "Predestination can be taken as a special mark of Reformed theology." [6] Pink writes, "Not only has God the right to do as He wills with the creatures of His own hands, but *He exercises this right,* and nowhere is that seen more plainly than in His predestinating grace." [7] What a strange grace, that it should be limited to a few.

At the very heart of this doctrine is the unbiblical belief that predestination is the "eternal decree of God, by which . . . some are preordained to eternal life, others to eternal damnation . . . ." [8] Why did God do so? Calvin is very clear: "Those, therefore, whom God passes by he reprobates, and that for no other cause but because he is pleased to exclude them from the inheritance which he predestines to his children . . . whose pleasure it is to inflict punishment . . . ." [9] It is a libel on the character of God to say that damning billions pleases Him!

Inasmuch as predestination is such a large part of his system of religion, the Calvinist manages to find this doctrine in scriptures where no one else can detect it: he "thrusts his doctrines of election and predestination into every conceivable Scripture text." [10] Vance goes on to say:

> Clark claims that "Isaiah has some two dozen verses that bear rather directly on the doctrine of predestination." [11] What he means is that there are some two dozen verses violently wrested to prove predestination, for the word neither occurs in Isaiah nor anywhere else in the Old Testament. Custance is even bolder: "Turning more specifically to the matter of Election to salvation,

consider the following." [12] Then follows a list of twelve passages from the Old Testament in which election is not mentioned and salvation is not even in view. [13]

Turning now to the New Testament, we find the same thing. Boettner audaciously declares: "There is hardly a chapter in the Gospel of John which does not either mention or imply election or reprobation. [14] But even after a statement like that he didn't give any verses. In answering the question, "I would like for you to list the scriptures which teach that God elected individuals to salvation before the world began," one Sovereign-Grace Baptist lists six scriptures where election is not even mentioned. [15]

The Role Of Predestination In Calvinism

Calvin speaks much about God's justice and mercy, but little of His love. Furthermore, he always limits God's mercy and love to the elect. Indeed, how could it be said that God is merciful and loving toward those whom He has predestined to eternal torment? One is reminded of an Islamic expert's description of that religious system: "The Divine will is irresistible, and has decreed in every detail the entire course of the universe which He governs, and the fate each moment of every creature therein . . . . Its dogma of predestination and of fate . . . leaves no room for human free-will . . . ." [16] One must say the same of Calvinism.

Horsch comments, "According to Augustine's teaching, the history of mankind would, from a religious and spiritual point of view, be little more than a puppet show . . . ." [17] R.C. Sproul writes, "God wills all things that come to pass. It is within His power to stop whatever might come to pass . . . God desired for man to fall into sin. I am not accusing God of sinning; I am suggesting that God created sin." [18] Sheldon agrees: "The Augustinian scheme . . . does represent Him [God] as foreordaining that the fall should involve, beyond every chance of rescue, the eternal ruin and damnation of the greater part of the race, who had no responsible part in the fall, except on a notion of responsibility infinitely far-fetched." [19] Palmer explains, without any apparent embarrassment or regret, that by the teaching on predestination expressed very clearly in Calvin's *Institutes* and echoed by most Calvinists to this day, God is the author of everything and therefore even of all sin:

> Foreordination means God's sovereign plan, whereby He decides all that is to happen in the entire universe. Nothing in this world happens by chance. God is in back of everything. He decides and causes all things to happen that do happen . . . . He has foreordained everything 'after the counsel of his will' (Eph. 1:11): the moving of a finger, the beating of a heart, the laughter of a girl, the mistake of a typist – even sin." [20]

No wonder John Wesley said, "The doctrine of predestination as maintained by rigid Calvinists is very shocking, and ought utterly to be abhorred, because it charges the most holy God with being the author of sin." [21] What Wesley called an abhorrent doctrine is not taught in the Bible but is a human invention. As we have already seen in Chapters 8 and 9, God can be absolutely sovereign without being the author of everything that occurs. It is Calvinism's five points which require a sovereignty allowing man no freedom of the will and thereby necessitating that God be the predestinator and effective cause of all.

While most Calvinists would repudiate the thought, this doctrine, carried to its logical conclusion, absolves mankind of moral responsibility, and Calvinists need to acknowledge that fact. For example, in a feature article as part of *Christianity Today's* "occasional series on doctrinal renewal, sponsored by a grant from Lilly Endowment Inc.," two M.Div. students at Princeton Theological Seminary recounted with great excitement the joy of their conversion to Calvinism. This was the punch line: "Blaming God for everything has been such a joy that we decided the least we could do to express our gratitude was to tell the world how we got here." [22]

And here we find again, looming over Calvin, the long shadow of Augustine. In *Election and Predestination*, Paul K. Jewett calls Augustine "the first true Predestinarian." [23] Of Calvinism's central doctrine of salvation through Irresistible Grace and Unconditional Election, Loraine Boettner declares, "This cardinal truth of Christianity was first clearly seen by Augustine." [24] It is remarkable that one of the best-known critics of Roman Catholicism would thus praise Augustine in spite of his being called "the founder of Roman Catholicism." Of that great Catholic "Saint" (another fallacy: in the Bible all believers are saints; the Epistles are addressed to the saints living in that locality), John Horsch commented:

> Augustine . . . was by theological speculation led to the belief in predestination . . . [that] the whole human family is condemned through the sin of Adam, but God in his mercy selects and predestinates a number of them for eternal life. His grace is for these alone, and it is impossible that they should be lost. From the rest of mankind who are not predestinated for salvation, God withholds his grace, and will condemn them even if they should die in infancy . . . . [25]

Where Is God's Love?

Every passage that mentions predestination/election will be searched in vain for any reference to anyone being predestined to damnation. How, then, does the Calvinist support such a doctrine? By implication only. If some are unconditionally elected to be saved, then the corollary is that those whom God did not so choose have been just as surely damned by His eternal decree. Calvin said it is "childish" to deny this "since there could be no election without its opposite reprobation." [26] Following Calvin and Augustine, Boettner uncompromisingly declares:

The doctrine of absolute Predestination of course logically holds that some are foreordained to death as truly as others are foreordained to life. The very terms "elect" and "election" imply the terms "non-elect" and "reprobation." When some are chosen . . . others are left not chosen . . . . We believe that from all eternity God has intended to leave some of Adam's posterity in their sins, and that the decisive factor in the life of each is to be found only in God's will. [27]

What a misrepresentation of God! Moreover, we search the writings of Calvinists in vain to find some hint of regret or sympathy on their part for those who are helplessly doomed by their God's eternal decree. Of course, it would be awkward for the God who damns multitudes then to profess His love for them – and how can He regret His sovereign decrees? Sovereignty and predestination are emphasized over and over – but *love and compassion*, where shall we find these?

When it comes to the obvious lack of love on God's part as they portray him, Calvinists become defensive. They propose various theories to explain how God could really love those He predestines to eternal torment. One of the most callous theories comes from Michael Horton in a book with a foreword by J.I. Packer. He argues, "But doesn't this view limit God's love? On the contrary! This view intensifies God's love, by limiting it only to those who believe. That sure beats the indiscriminate, general benevolence we seem to be hearing much about today." [28]

This is worse than double talk! "For God so loved the world" is a despicable "indiscriminate, general benevolence"? Limiting God's love to a select few doesn't limit but intensifies God's love? In fact, there is no way either to limit or to intensify God's love: it is infinite both in its scope and timelessness.

Pastor John Piper and the pastoral staff of Bethlehem Baptist Church in Minneapolis published a booklet titled "TULIP, What We Believe about the Five Points of Calvinism." Like Calvin's *Institutes*, it glorifies God's sovereignty, but nowhere in its pages is there even a mention of God's love for sinners. John Calvin is presented as "the famous theologian and pastor of Geneva," [29] with not a word about the floggings, imprisonments, tortures, banishments and burnings at the stake that he encouraged there. Piper also praises Augustine, [30] but without a hint that he was the father of modern Roman Catholicism and held to numerous doctrines which evangelicals find repugnant. Is it honest to withhold vital facts which are so relevant to the subject at hand?

Five times in the New Testament, Christ commands us, "Thou shalt love thy neighbour as thyself" (Matthew 19:19, etc.). Paul twice, and James once, reiterate this command that one must love one's neighbor as oneself (Romans 13:9; Galatians 5:14; James 2:8). Christ makes it clear that everyone who is in need is one's neighbor (Luke 10:29-37). Surely none are in greater need than the lost whose only hope is salvation and God's forgiveness. Yet Calvinism tells us that the God who "is love," and who "so loved the world" and sent His Son "that the world through him might be saved" (John 3:17), even though He could save *all*, damns billions for His "good pleasure" and to prove His justice. Aghast at such doctrine, one can only repeat in astonishment the title of this book: *What Love Is This?*

Distorting A Metaphor

The view expressed above by Boettner is supported by most of today's Calvinists, even though it negates God's love, mercy and grace for any except the elect. "All who will finally be saved, were chosen to salvation by God the Father, before the foundation of the world, and given to Jesus Christ in the covenant of grace." [31] Piper writes, "Election refers to God's choosing whom to save. It is unconditional in that there is no condition man must meet before God chooses to save him. Man is dead in trespasses and sins. So there is no condition he can meet . . . . " [32] John MacArthur, too, declares that unbelievers are "no more able to respond to God than a Cadaver" and "are incapable of any spiritual activity . . . ." [33] Vance points out the obvious error:

> And finally, if you make an exact parallel between a physically dead man and a spiritually dead man . . . then you likewise have to say . . . [if] he can't accept Christ because he is dead then he can't reject Christ either. A [physically] dead man cannot believe on Jesus Christ, but a [spiritually] dead man can." [34]

Calvinism's very amazing view of "dead in trespasses and sins" derives from the folly Vance exposes of equating spiritual death with physical death. The physically dead can do nothing, not even commit sin, so they could hardly present a proper analogy of spiritual death. The spiritually "dead," however, are able to live active lives, get an education, earn a living, defy God and continue to sin — or submit to the conviction of the Holy Spirit, repent of their sins and believe on the Lord Jesus Christ as their Savior. Yet in another book, MacArthur reiterates:

> How can a person who is dead in sin, blinded by Satan, unable to understand the things of God, and continuously filled with evil suddenly exercise saving faith? A corpse could no sooner come out of a grave and walk. [35]

It is unquestionably to the spiritually dead that Isaiah writes: "Ho, everyone that thirsteth, come ye to the waters . . . . Let the wicked forsake his way, and the unrighteous man his thoughts: and let him return unto the LORD, and he will have mercy upon him; and to our God, for he will abundantly pardon" (Isaiah 55:1,7).

Surely one must conclude that God means what He says. We agree that none would seek the Lord unless He first seeks them. It is clear from Scripture, however, that God seeks *all*. He calls upon *all who thirst* to come to Him and drink, upon *all who are wicked* to turn unto Him in reliance upon His mercy. If the wicked are not dead in trespasses and sins, then who is? It must therefore be possible for those who are spiritually dead to hear God's voice, turn to the Lord and to believe the gospel and receive pardon by His grace. Yet the insistent denial that the unregenerate can believe in Christ is a major point in Calvinism. Steele and Thomas argue that "The sinner is dead, blind, and deaf to the things of God . . . . Consequently . . . it takes regeneration by which the Spirit makes the sinner alive and gives him a new nature. Faith is not something man contributes to salvation . . . but is God's gift to the sinner . . . ." [36] When Paul and Silas said, "Believe on the Lord Jesus Christ and thou shalt be saved" (Acts 16:31), were they suggesting that by believing the Philippian jailor would contribute faith to his salvation? Hardly.

A Simple Exegesis

The fact that foreknowledge pertains to something about those whom God then elects or predestines to some favor or blessing is clear from the passages above. The Greek *kata* carries the meaning of homogeneity or harmony. Thus God's election / predestination was in agreement, or harmony, with something He foreknew about those whom He predestined to partake of the declared blessings. What could that have been? Surely the most obvious possibility would be that God foreknew who would repent and believe the gospel and on that basis He predestined them to something unique: "to be conformed to the image of his Son" and "unto obedience." Apparently departing from his oft-professed Calvinism, Spurgeon declared:

> Mark, then, with care, that OUR CONFORMITY TO CHRIST IS THE SACRED OBJECT OF PREDESTINATION . . . . The Lord in boundless grace has resolved that a company whom no man can number . . . shall be restored to His image, in the particular form in which His Eternal Son displays it . . . the likeness of the Lord from Heaven. [Emphasis in original] [37]

In order to escape this straightforward interpretation, the Calvinist must establish another meaning for foreknow/foreknowledge that fits his theory. Generally this attempt has taken two forms. Most try to maintain that foreknow/foreknowledge, instead of meaning to know in advance, means to determine in advance, or to foreordain. Piper writes, "he [God] foreknows — that is, elects — a people for himself . . . ." [38] Others suggest that it means to love beforehand. There are, however, several reasons why neither of these stratagems will work.

Various Calvinist authors argue that "foreknowledge" is "the equivalent of a determined counsel . . . God's omniscient wisdom and intention . . . God's prerogative to 'choose beforehand.' " [39] MacArthur writes:

> ...God's foreknowledge, therefore, is not a reference to His omniscient foresight but to His foreordination. God does indeed foresee who is going to be a believer, but the faith He foresees is the faith He Himself creates. It's not that He merely sees what will happen in the future; rather He ordains it. The Bible clearly teaches that God sovereignly chooses people to believe in Him. [40]

Piper quotes C.E.B. Cranfield, who refers to the foreknowledge of Romans 8:29 as "that special taking knowledge of a person which is God's electing grace." Piper then comments that "foreknowledge is virtually the same as election . . . . He foreknows – that is, elects – a people for himself . . . ." [41]

On the contrary, Peter very clearly distinguishes counsel or determination as well as election *from* foreknowledge: "him [Christ], being delivered by the determinate [*horizo*] counsel [*boule]* and foreknowledge [*proginosko*] of God . . . " (Acts 2:23). If these are the same, then Peter is saying nonsensically that Christ was "delivered by the foreknowledge *and* foreknowledge," or by "the determined counsel *and* determined counsel" of God. Paul likewise makes a clear distinction: "For whom he [God] did foreknow, he *also* [*kai*] did predestinate . . . ." The Greek *kai* denotes a differentiation, thus making it abundantly clear that foreknowledge could not be the same as predestination, or Paul, as already pointed out, would be redundantly saying, "whom he did predestinate he *also* did predestinate."

This inspired statement by Peter on the Day of Pentecost concerning Christ's betrayal and crucifixion provides important insight into God's outworking of His eternal plan. It clearly reveals that even in declaring future events through His prophets and accomplishing them in history according to His will, God takes into account what He by His foreknowledge knows will be the actions and reactions of men. He did not *cause* Judas to betray Christ, nor did He *cause* the Jews to reject Him or the Romans to crucify Him. However, He did arrange that these particular individuals who would act in that manner were on the scene at the right time to fulfill His will through their willing ignorance and/or evil.

To foreknow is simply to know in advance and can't legitimately be turned into anything else. Clearly, to know in advance is not the same as to determine or ordain. If it were, we would again have a redundancy: whom God foreordained He predestined. Foreknowledge would have been reduced to a meaningless repetition. Why even mention it unless it has special significance?

If God simply elected / predestined certain ones because He elected / predestined them, there would be no reason to mention foreknowledge at all. On the contrary, no other interpretation fits. Clearly what God foreknew would be the response of certain persons to the gospel was the *reason* for electing / predestining them to the blessings reserved for the redeemed.

The Meaning Of Foreknowledge Is Clear

In fact, that foreknowledge means nothing more nor less than to know beforehand is clear not only in the particular scriptures above, but it can be derived from other places where the same Greek words are used in the New Testament. For example, at his trial before King Agrippa, in referring to Jewish leaders of his acquaintance who he says "knew me from the beginning [i.e., before that day]" (Acts 26:4-5), Paul uses the same word, *progonisko,* translated at Romans 8:29 "for whom he did *foreknow.*" Again in his second epistle Peter uses the same word in a different context but with the identical meaning: "ye know *[progonisko]* these things before . . . " (2 Peter 3:17).

"Foreknowledge" and "foreknow" are never used in the way the Calvinist would like to persuade us they could be. We simply can't find a verse anywhere that uses "foreknowledge" in any other way than to express the fact of knowing in advance.

The second attempt to change the meaning to fit Calvinism points to the way sexual intercourse is expressed in the Old Testament: "Adam knew [*yada*] his wife" (Genesis 4:1), "Cain knew [*yada*] his wife" (verse 17), etc. From that usage of "know," the attempt is made to show some relationship between the Hebrew *yada* and the Greek *progonisko* and then to suggest that "whom God foreknew" actually means "whom God loved beforehand." Again it won't work.

Yada is used for "knowing" in a variety of ways, most often for general knowledge. Only in that generic sense would it be related to *progonisko,* which also has to do with knowledge. While *yada* is at times used to denote a special relationship — "I did know thee in the wilderness" (Hosea 13:5), "You only have I known of all the families of the earth" (Amos 3:2) — never does it mean to know in advance, whereas that is the principle meaning of *progonisko* and *prognosis.* There is, therefore, no relationship between these words which would be of any help in supporting Calvinism.

Furthermore, to "know" one's wife in a sexual way could not be before the fact, nor does God "know" man in that manner. Therefore, the attempt to link love with foreknowledge through *yada* in order to give the meaning "foreloved" won't work. That strained effort, however, reveals the lengths to which the Calvinist is both forced and willing to go to protect his theory.

Why Not Accept The Simplest Meaning?

It certainly requires no special understanding to accept that these scriptures mean (1) that God in His omniscience has foreknown from eternity past who, when convicted of sin and drawn by His Holy Spirit, would willingly respond to the gospel; and (2) that on the basis of that foreknowledge He predestined, or elected, those particular persons to special blessings: " . . . to be conformed to the image of his Son . . . unto obedience . . . ." Paul gives the same thought elsewhere and adds another blessing: "According as he hath chosen us in him before the foundation of the world, that we should be holy and without blame before him in love" (Ephesians 1:4). Dave Breese writes, "We also notice that election in Scripture is not unto salvation, but 'unto obedience . . . .' [In] Romans chapter 8 . . . predestination is based upon the foreknowledge of God and its object is not salvation but conformity to the image of Christ." [42]

Unquestionably, the lost could be saved from eternal doom without granting them sonship and perfection and the other blessings God has graciously and lovingly planned for the redeemed. Both Paul and Peter are encouraging Christians with what God has in store for those who believe the gospel. As Paul points out elsewhere, "Eye hath not seen, nor ear heard, neither have entered into the heart of man, the things which God hath prepared for them that love him. But God hath revealed them unto us by his Spirit . . . " (1 Corinthians 2:9-10).

Furthermore, not only is predestination / election never said to be unto salvation, but Paul carefully separates predestination from salvation whether in its call, justification or glorification: "whom he did predestinate, them he *also* [*kai*] called . . . them he *also* [*kai*] justified . . . them he *also* [*kai*] glorified" (Romans 8:30). The Greek *kai* shows that a distinction is being made: predestination is not the same as calling, justification or glorification. Hobbs comments, "Predestination . . . simply means that God has predetermined that those who respond affirmatively to His call . . . will be justified . . . and furthermore will be glorified. All of this is 'according to His purpose' . . . ." [43] The plain meaning of the text is clear.

There is a further problem with the Calvinist interpretation of "foreknowledge": because it rejects knowing what man would do (i.e., repent and believe the gospel), it can involve nothing more than God knowing what He would do. What is the point in saying that God foreknew what He had predestined?

Furthermore, such a statement would not only be a redundancy but nonsense. God's predestination, purposes and actions must be from everlasting just as He himself is. Therefore it would be impossible for God to "foreknow" what He purposed to do because His purposes have always existed. As James said,

"Known unto God are all his works from the beginning of the world [*aion*]. (Acts 15:18). The Greek *aion*, rather, carries the meaning of "from all eternity."

Ironically, Rob Zins accuses non-Calvinists of teaching that "there was a time when God knew not [what man would do] . . . . However, it is our contention that God knows all things because He wills all things." [44] On the contrary, we charge God with no ignorance of any kind. Rather we affirm that from eternity past God has known all that would happen in the universe and in the minds and affairs of men — but *not* because He "wills all things." Furthermore, God's foreknowledge of what He himself would do would be nonsense.

Piper insists that "God does not foreknow the free decisions of people to believe in him because there aren't any such free decisions to know." [45] We're back to man as a puppet again, with God pulling the strings, an essential part of Calvinism. But without free choice man would not be a morally responsible being nor could he love God, know God's love, receive the gift of salvation or have meaningful communion with God or worship Him. Here is Spurgeon again in another of those un-Calvinistic statements: "Shall we never be able to drive into men's minds the truth that predestination and free agency are both facts?" [46]

Although, as we have just seen, it violates the clear distinction demanded by *kai*, White writes, "In other words, the *foreknowledge* of God is based upon His decree, plan, or purpose which expresses His will, and not upon some foreseen act of *positive volition* on the part of man." Such a conclusion is not only unbiblical but assaults reason. There is no point in saying that God knows His eternal decrees. And for God to foreknow them would be impossible. Since His decrees have always been and thus were never future to Him, there is no way in which He could foreknow them, i.e., know what they would be before they were decreed.

Neither could one say that God, because He knew in advance that He had decreed to save certain persons, therefore saved them. Foreknowledge is very clearly the *reason* given for election and predestination, and God knowing in advance what He would do could never be the *reason* for His doing it.

The most straightforward interpretation of these scriptures is that knowing in advance who would believe the gospel, God made certain that those individuals heard the gospel, and He predestined them to partake of the many blessings He planned to bestow on the redeemed throughout eternity. That certainly would be the reasonable and legitimate conclusion to be derived from the clear language expressed in these passages. Why go to such great lengths to find another meaning except to support a theory?

A Closer Look At Election

The words "predestinate" and "predestinated" are used only four times in Scripture. The first three have already been considered. The fourth will be dealt with later. Election has a similar meaning, and the words "elect," "elected," "election" and "elect's" are together used twenty-seven times in the Bible.

The objects of God's election / predestination are called the elect. The word "elect" (*bachiyr* in Hebrew, *eklektos* in Greek) is used in a variety of ways. It refers to the Messiah (Isaiah 42:1; 1 Peter 2:6), to Israel or Jews (Isaiah 45:4; 65:9, 22; Matthew 24: 31; Mark 13:27), to the church (Romans 8:33; Colossians 3:12; Titus 1:1), to both Israel and the church (Matthew 24:24; Mark 13:22; Luke 18:7), to angels (1 Timothy 5:21), and to a lady (2 John 1,13).

These verses cover every mention of the word "elect" throughout the entire Bible. As can be seen, *not once* is that word used to designate a special class of persons whom God has marked out for salvation and whom alone He loves. Contradicting Scripture, a minister of the Protestant Reformed Churches in America writes, "Thus it cannot be that God loves everyone. Since God's love is sovereign and therefore always a saving love, only those who experience the salvation of the Lord can be the objects of His love." [47] Again we must ask, *what love is this*?

Calvin taught in his *Institutes* that God loves only the elect and that He has determined to save them and them alone. Such an idea flies in the face of the literally scores of verses telling us that God loves all mankind, that His mercy extends to all, and that He desires all to be saved. Let us consider in more detail those passages where election is found, in order to see whether or not they support the Calvinist's view of Unconditional Election.

The Five Pertinent Scriptures

As we have seen above, the word "elect" is found four times in the Old Testament: once referring to the Messiah (Isaiah 42:1) and three times referring to Israel (Isaiah 45:4; 65:9, 22). None of these is pertinent to our inquiry. In the New Testament, the word "elect" is found seventeen times, the word "election" six times, the word "elect's" three times, and the word "elected" once.

Eliminating the one reference to angels, the one reference to Christ himself, the three references which could be both to Israel and the church, the three to a lady, four to those Jews who have been preserved through the Great Tribulation and survived Armageddon, and the six which are simply a name for believers in Christ, we are left with five which pertain to the general subject of election.

These five verses which we shall consider are as follows:

> . . . that the purpose of God according to election might stand, not of works, but of him that calleth . . . . (Romans 9:11)

... there is a remnant according to the election of grace. (Romans 11:5)

Knowing, brethren beloved, your election of God . . . . (1 Thessalonians 1:4)

Elect according to the foreknowledge of God the Father, through sanctification of the Spirit, unto obedience and sprinkling of the blood of Jesus Christ: Grace unto you, and peace be multiplied. (1 Peter 1:2)

Wherefore the rather, brethren, give diligence to make your calling and election sure . . . . (2 Peter 1:10)

These scriptures present us with the following truths: 1) God works a definite purpose through election; 2) election involves not all mankind but a "remnant"; 3) election is according to God's grace; 4) election is "according to the foreknowledge of God the Father"; and 5) some responsibility rests upon the elect to make their "election sure." If election is to salvation by Irresistible Grace without any intelligent or moral choice on man's part, it would be impossible to be sure of one's election. But if election is to service and blessing, Peter is reinforcing in different words Paul's exhortation to "walk worthy of the vocation wherewith ye are called" (Ephesians 4:1-6).

Nowhere in Scripture is election unto salvation but always to blessing and service. Thus to make one's election sure is to fulfill the responsibility that comes with election, not to somehow be sure that one is among the elect and thus eternally saved. Marvin R. Vincent, an authority on biblical languages explains, "*Ekloge*, election [is] used of God's selection of men or agencies for special missions or attainments . . . . [Nowhere] in the New Testament is there any warrant for the revolting doctrine that God predestined a definite number of mankind to eternal life, and the rest to eternal destruction." [48]

Calvin's Fallacious Arguments

According to Scripture, as already noted, the key to election and the way it is determined by God is *foreknowledge*: "elect *according* to the foreknowledge of God the Father." In the attempt to make predestination and election pertain to salvation so that it would fit his theory, Calvin entangled himself in fallacious reasoning and even heresy.

Consider his handling of Ephesians 1:4-5: "According as he hath chosen us in him before the foundation of the world, that we should be holy and without blame before him in love: having predestinated us unto the adoption of children by Jesus Christ to himself, according to the good pleasure of his will." Under the inspiration of the Holy Spirit, Paul seems to state simply that God's choosing / predestination / election is unto blessings. There is no mention of salvation. Here are representative excerpts from Calvin's attempt to make this passage fit his theory:

By saying they were elected before the foundation of the world, he [God] takes away all reference to worth .... In the additional statement that they were elected that they might be holy, the apostle openly refutes the error of those who deduce election from prescience since he declares that whatever virtue appears in men is the result of election." [49]

First of all, Calvin erects and then destroys a straw man. That God would predestine to certain blessings those whom He foreknew would believe the gospel has nothing at all to do with their "worth." It is utterly fallacious to suggest that some worth is ascribed to sinners if by their own free choice they believe the gospel and receive the Lord Jesus Christ as Savior. Indeed, it is because of their unworthiness and desperate need of salvation that sinners turn to Him.

Who ever suggested that the blessings which are "the result of election" (as Calvin says above) are "virtues" for which those who receive them can take credit? In fact, the *why* of election is not even mentioned here. Therefore, this scripture cannot be used to dismiss what is so clearly stated in Romans 8:29 and 1 Peter 1:2 — that God's foreknowledge is the *reason* behind predestination / election / choosing certain ones to specific blessings.

The Calvinist argues that "elect according to the foreknowledge of God .. . whom he did foreknow them he also did predestinate" can't mean what it seems to mean or God's sovereignty would be undermined. On the contrary, there is nothing inherent in the concept of sovereignty which requires that those to whom God sovereignly offers a gift cannot genuinely receive or reject it. And surely God in His foreknowledge would know in advance who those persons would be and could plan to bestow special blessings upon those who He knew would believe. This understanding of salvation presents no threat whatsoever to God's sovereignty.

The view earlier presented, that God, being outside of and independent of time, could thus view past, present and future as in the present, is not a new belief. It has been held for centuries by many who could not in good conscience accept the Calvinist definition of foreknowledge and predestination. For example, around 1780 John Wesley declared in a sermon that

... when we speak of God's foreknowledge we do not speak according to the nature of things, but after the manner of men. For if we speak properly, there is no such thing as either foreknowledge or after knowledge in God. All time, or rather all eternity (for time is only that small fragment of eternity which is allotted to the children of men), being present to him at once, he does not know one thing before another, or one thing after another; but sees all things in one point of view, from everlasting to everlasting. As all time, with everything that exists therein, is present with him at once, so he sees at once, whatever was, is or will be to the end of time. But observe; we must not think they are, because he knows them. No; he knows them, because they are. [50]

Some Important Distinctions

The blessings that God has eternally purposed to bestow upon the redeemed have nothing to do with how they are saved but *follow* their salvation. And what blessings they are! We could have been given eternal life, and even a place in heaven like the angels, without being made God's children and joint heirs with Christ of all the inheritance He has in the Father. But God in His infinite love and grace predestined believers to be part of His family, His very own children who are called "unto his eternal glory by Christ Jesus" (1 Peter 5:10). As John Wesley said, "God decrees, from everlasting to everlasting, that all who believe in the Son of his love, shall be conformed to his image . . . ." [51]

Salvation is clearly distinct from the blessings which accompany it – but Calvin had to make them one and the same or his cause was lost. Opposing this error and echoing so many other biblical scholars, Andrew Telford wrote, "Nowhere in the Bible is Election connected with the salvation or the damnation of a human soul . . . . It has to do with service. It is God's elect who serve Him." [52] Sadly, in trying to make Scripture fit his theory, Calvin seems to have fallen deeply into error, once again relying upon Augustine:

> It is wisely observed by Augustine, that in the very head of the Church we have a bright mirror of free election, lest it should give any trouble to us the members – viz. that he [Christ] did not become the Son of God by living righteously, but was freely presented with this great honour, that he might afterwards make others partakers of his gifts. Should anyone here ask, why others are not what he was, or why . . . we are all corrupt while he is purity, he would not only betray his madness, but his effrontery also. But if they are bent on depriving God of the free right of electing [to salvation] and reprobating [predestining to damnation], let them at the same time take away what has been given to Christ. [53]

Calvin seems to be denying the eternal Sonship of Christ and His eternal equality and oneness with the Father! He says that Christ *became* the Son of God, being "freely presented with this great honour . . . . " When might that have been? Christ's alleged "election" to this honor apart from "living righteously" (i.e., without any merit) is then used by Calvin as an example to prove his point about the election of humans apart from their worth or works. The comparison borders on blasphemy. Christ *is* the I AM from all eternity, one with the Father; and because of *who He is* it was He alone who could redeem us. After all, throughout the Old Testament, Jahweh, the God of Israel and great I AM, repeatedly says, "I, even I, am the Lord; and beside me there is no Saviour" (Isaiah 43:11 and many others). Jesus declares, "Before Abraham was, I am" (John 8:58).

One of the sad features of Calvin's *Institutes* is the demeaning language he continually employs (much like Luther) to vilify all who disagree with him: "Hence it is, that in the present day so many dogs tear this doctrine [predestination] with envenomed teeth . . . assail it with their bark . . . . Since some feeling of shame restrains them from daring to belch forth their blasphemies against heaven, that they may give the freer vent to their rage, they pretend to pick a quarrel with us . . . this doctrine, which perverse men undeservedly assail because it is sometimes wickedly abused . . . . The profane make such a bluster with their foolish puerilities," [54] and so forth, page after page.

Beneath Calvin's own bluster there is often little substance to his arguments, which in the end can be supported only by abusing Scripture. His obvious misunderstanding of opposing views, and the weak and unbiblical reasons Calvin adduces for rejecting foreknowledge as the basis of predestination, are reinforced with much ridicule:

> We, indeed, ascribe both prescience and predestination to God; but we say that it is absurd to make the latter subordinate to the former . . . . [55]
> Others, who are neither versed in Scripture, nor entitled to any weight, assail sound doctrine with a petulance and improbity which it is impossible to tolerate . . . they ought at least to be restrained by feelings of awe from talking so confidently of this sublime mystery. [56]

That foreknowledge is the *reason* for predestination, as Scripture declares, does not make the latter subordinate to the former. Both are among the many infinite qualities and abilities unique to God alone, none of which is either independent of or subordinate to any other. As we have repeatedly noted, all of God's qualities are exercised in perfect harmony with each other. Thus Calvin's argument entirely misses the point. And here, again, he pleads "mystery" when all else fails him.

1   Herbert Lockyer, *All the Doctrines of the Bible* (Zondervan, 1964), 153.

2   H.A. Ironside, *Full Assurance* (Moody Press, 1937), 93-94.

3   Edward Maslin Hulme, *The Renaissance, the Protestant Reformation, and the Catholic Revolution* (The Century Company, 1920), 299.

4   John Calvin, *Institutes of the Christian Religion*, trans. Henry Beveridge (Wm. Eerdmans Publishing Company, 1998 ed.), III:xxiii,5.

5   Edwin H. Palmer, foreword to *the five points of calvinism* (Baker Books, enlarged ed., 20th prtg. 1980).

6   John H. Leith, *Introduction to the Reformed Tradition* (John Knox Press, rev. ed. 1981), 103.

7   Arthur W. Pink, *The Sovereignty of God* (Baker Book House, 2nd prtg. 1986), 52.

8   Calvin, op. cit., III:xxi,5.

9   Op .cit., III:xxiii,1,4

10 Laurence M. Vance, *The Other Side of Calvinism* (Vance Publications, Pensacola FL, rev. ed. 1999), 248.

11 Gordon H. Clark, *Predestination* (Presbyterian and Reformed Publishing Co., 1987), 181.

12 Arthur C. Custance, *The Sovereignty of Grace* (Presbyterian and Reformed Publishing Co., 1979), 7.

13 Numbers 16:5; 1 Kings 19:18, Psalms 65:4; 80:18-19; 110:3; Proverbs 16:1; Isaiah 26:12; Jeremiah 10:23; 31:18-19; 50:30; Lamentations 5:21.

14 Loraine Boettner, *The Reformed Doctrine of Predestination* (Presbyterian and Reformed Publishing Co., 1932), 346.

15 "Five Common Questions on the Doctrine of Election Simply and Clearly Answered" (*The Baptist Examiner*, November 20, 1993), 5; cited in Vance, op. cit., 248.

16 Alfred S. Geden, *Comparative Religion* (Society for Promoting Christian Knowledge, 1917), 102-103.

17 John Horsch, *History of Christianity* (John Horsch, 1903), 104-105.

18 R.C. Sproul, *Almighty Over All* (Baker Book House, 1999), 54.

19 Henry C. Sheldon, *History of Christian Doctrine* (Harper and Bros., 2nd ed. 1895), II:163.

20 Palmer, op. cit., 24-25.

21 A.W. Harrison, *Arminianism* (Duckworth, 1937), 189.

22 Jennifer L. Bayne and Sarah E. Hinlicky, "Free to be Creatures Again: How predestination descended like a dove on two unsuspecting seminarians, and *why* they are so grateful" (*Christianity Today*, October 23, 2000), 38-44.

23 Paul K. Jewett, *Election and Predestination* (Wm. B. Eerdmans Publishing Co., 1985 ed.), 5.

24 Boettner, op. cit., 365.

25 Horsch, op. cit.

26 Calvin, op. cit., III:xxiii,1.

27 Boettner, op. cit., 104

28 Michael Scott Horton, *Putting Amazing Back Into Grace* (Thomas Nelson Publishers, 1991), 96.

29 John Piper and Pastoral Staff, "TULIP: What We Believe about the Five Points of Calvinism: Position Paper of the Pastoral Staff " (Desiring God Ministries, 1997), 3.

30 Op. cit., 27-28.

31 John L. Dagg, *Manual of Theology and Church Order* (Sprinkle Publications, 1982), 309.

32 Piper and Staff, op.cit., 19.

33 John F. MacArthur, Jr.,. *Faith Works: The Gospel According to the Apostles* (Word Publishing, 1993), 64-67.

34   Vance, op. cit., 522.
35   John MacArthur Jr., *Saved Without A Doubt - MacArthur Study Series* (Chariot Victor Books, 1992), 58.
36   David N. Steele and Curtis C. Thomas, *The Five Points of Calvinism* (Presbyterian and Reformed Publishing Co, 1963), 16.
37   Charles Haddon Spurgeon, *The Treasury of the New Testament* (Zondervan, 1950), II:72.
38   Piper and Staff, op. cit.
39   S. Raymond Cox, "What Caused God To Choose His People?" (self-published paper, 1980), 3.
40   MacArthur, *Saved*, op. cit., 58.
41   Piper, *We Believe*, op. cit., 22.
42   Dave Breese, "The Five Points of Calvinism" (self-published paper, n.d.).
43   Herschel H. Hobbs, *Fundamentals of our Faith* (Broadman, 1960), 94-99.
44   Robert M. Zins, "A Believer's Guide to 2nd Peter 3:9" (self-published monograph, n.d.), 2-3.
45   Piper and Staff, op.cit., 22.
46   Charles Haddon Spurgeon, *The Best Bread: Sermons Preached in 1887* (Funk and Wagnalls, 1891), 109.
47   Steven R. Houck, "God's Sovereignty In Salvation" (The Evangelism Committee, Protestant Reformed Church, South Holland IL, n.d.), 10.
48   Marvin R. Vincent, *Word Studies in the New Testament* (Charles Scribner's Sons, 1924), IV:16.
49   Calvin, op. cit., III:xxii,2.
50   John Wesley, *Sermons on Several Occasions* (New York: J. Emory and B. Waugh, for the Methodist Episcopal Church at the Conference Office, 14 Crosby Street, 1831), II:39.
51   Ibid.
52   Andrew Telford, *Subjects of Sovereignty* (Harvest Time Ministries, 1980), 55-56.
53   Calvin, op. cit., III:xxii,1.
54   Op. cit., I:xvii,2,3.
55   Op. cit., III:xxi,5.
56   Op. cit., III:xxii,1.

16
Limited Atonement

The "L" in TULIP represents one more integral theory in Calvin's scheme of salvation: "the doctrine which limits the atonement to . . . the elect." [1] This concept follows directly from the limitation Calvinists place upon God's love in spite of the fact that it, like every facet of His Being, is infinite. One of their prominent apologists declares, " . . . the Bible teaches again and again that God does not love all people with the same love . . . 'loved by God' is not applied to the world but only to the saints . . . (Romans 1:7)." [2] Calvin himself declared, "All are not created on equal terms, but some are preordained to eternal life, others to eternal damnation . . . ." [3]

A.A. Hodge explains how vital this doctrine is to Calvinism: "If they [critics] could prove that the love which prompted God to give his Son to die, as a sin-offering . . . had for its objects all men . . . that Christ actually sacrificed his life with the purpose of saving all . . . on the condition of faith, then . . . the central principle of Arminianism is true [and Calvinism is false] . . . . [4] Boettner explained further:

> The Reformed Faith has held to the existence of an eternal, divine decree which, antecedently to any difference or desert in men themselves separates the human race into two portions and ordains one to everlasting life and the other to everlasting death . . . . Thus predestined and foreordained . . . their number is so certain and definite that it cannot be either increased or decreased. [5]

Carson, who is somewhat of an exception among Calvinists, tries to take a more balanced view. He draws the line at Limited Atonement, arguing that this label "is singularly unfortunate for two reasons. *First*, it is a defensive, restrictive expression: here is atonement, and then someone wants to limit it. The notion of limiting something as glorious as the Atonement is intrinsically offensive. *Second*, even when inspected more coolly, 'limited atonement' is objectively misleading. Every view of the Atonement 'limits' it in some way, save for the unqualified universalist." [6]

Honoring God's Love Is Heresy?

To the Calvinist, as Stanley Gower, a member of the Westminster Assembly, declared, there is no greater heresy than the suggestion that "God loveth all alike, Cain as well as Abel, Judas as the rest of the apostles." [7] Thus it is great heresy and dishonoring to God to take at face value that verse familiar to every Sunday-school child, "For God so loved the world, that he gave his only begotten Son, that whosoever believeth in him should not perish, but have everlasting life" (John 3:16). For Calvinism to stand, this (and many other verses expressing the same truth) cannot mean what the words seem to say: "world" and "whosoever" cannot signify all mankind but only the elect. Sproul writes, "The world for whom Christ died cannot mean the entire human family. It must refer to the universality of the elect (people from every tribe and nation)." [8] John Owen boldly states, "That the *world* here cannot signify all that ever were or should be, is as manifest as if it were written with the beams of the sun . . . ." [9]

This limitation upon the atonement of Christ, which requires changing the meaning of key words, arises sincerely from such great concern for God's sovereignty that this facet of His eternal Being becomes of disproportionate importance and overrides His equally infinite love. Owen, "after a more than seven years' serious inquiry (bottomed, I hope, upon the strength of Christ, and guided by his Spirit) into the mind of God about these things . . . ," asked earnestly, "To what purpose serves then general ransom [i.e., the "heresy" that Christ loves all and died for all], but only to assert that Almighty God would have the precious blood of his dear Son poured out for innumerable souls whom he will not have to share in any drop thereof, and so, in respect of them, to be spilt in vain, or else to be shed for them only that they might be the deeper damned?" [10] No less sincere and earnestly concerned for truth, H.A. Ironside expressed the opposing evangelical understanding in contrast to Calvinism's limited atonement which was provided for only a select few:

No matter how far they [any sinner] have drifted from God; no matter what their sins may be, they do not have to peer into the book of the divine decrees in order to find out whether or not they are of the chosen or the elect. If they come in all their sin and guilt, confessing their iniquities and trusting in Christ, then they may have the assurance from His Word that they are saved. It has been well said that the "Whosoever *wills* are the elect, and the whosoever *won'ts* are the non-elect." [11]

Calvinists, however, are firm on this issue, following in the footsteps of Calvin who said of God, "for, (as he hates sin) he can only love those whom he justifies [i.e., the elect]." [12] Criticizing those who reject limited atonement, Gerstner argues that if John 3:16 "is supposed to teach that God so loved everyone in the world that He gave His only son to provide them an opportunity to be saved by faith...such love on God's part...would be a refinement of cruelty. As we have seen, offering a gift of life to a spiritual corpse, a brilliant sunset to a blind man, and a reward to a legless cripple if only he will come and get it, are horrible mockeries." [13] We agree that it would be mockery to offer salvation to those who could not respond to the offer. Therefore, the Calvinist, because of the dogma that depravity equals inability, must claim that universal language such as "world," "any man," "whosoever," "all," etc. actually means the elect — that salvation is *not* offered to everyone. But there is no biblical justification for that interpretation!

The Doctrine Clearly Stated

To avoid having any of Christ's blood shed for those who would not benefit thereby, "The doctrine of limited atonement is simply that the cross of Christ provides a sure, secure and real salvation for everyone God intended it to save and for them alone." [14] Homer Hoeksema confesses the dire consequences of this belief, "If Christ died for the elect only, then there are no possible benefits in that death of Christ for anyone else but those for whom he died." [15] The emphasis is upon *possible*. Likewise, Steele and Thomas insist,

> Christ's redeeming work was intended to save the elect only and actually secured salvation for them. His death was a substitutionary endurance of the penalty of sin in the place of certain specified sinners . . . . The gift of faith is infallibly applied by the Spirit to all for whom Christ died, thereby guaranteeing their salvation. [16]

Here again is a doctrine which is nowhere in the entire Bible stated in plain words but which must be reasoned into existence in order to defend the rest of TULIP. Michael Horton, for example, argues, "If Jesus died for every person, but not every person is saved, His death did not actually save anybody . . . . If Christ died for people who will be in hell, His efforts cannot accurately be called a 'saving work' [and] there is no real saving power in the blood. Rather, the power would seem to be in the will of the creature . . . . These points lie at the heart of the Christian message, for they rest at the foot of the cross." [17]   This is like saying that the $1 million has no value which a father deposits in a bank in his estranged son's name and sincerely offers to him. Clearly, the faith on the sinner's part in receiving Christ no more gives the blood of Christ saving power than the willingness of the son to accept the $1 million would give it monetary value.

With no clear statement in all of Scripture to support this dogma, it must be defended by rationalizations. For example, it is argued that "if Christ died for all men and all men are not saved, the cross of Christ is of no effect. Calvary is a sham." [18]   Of course, that doesn't follow. That would be like saying that the giving of the Ten Commandments was a sham because all men do not keep them. Even Sproul acknowledges that "the value of Christ's atonement is sufficient to cover the sins of the world . . . . " [19]   It would have to be, because His perfect sacrifice must be of infinite value. Although "the cross is to them that perish foolishness" (1 Corinthians 1:18), it is not a sham but of great effect for all who believe! As one of the most respected Bible teachers of recent years said, "By contrast to the doctrine of limited atonement, the Bible teaches most strongly the doctrine of unlimited atonement . . . . The doctrine of limited atonement is specifically denied in Scripture . . . ." [20]

Another author reasons that if everyone had the option of accepting or rejecting the benefits of Calvary, man would have the upper hand: "Only Calvinism with its effective atonement limits man's power and exalts God's power and glory." [21]   Again it doesn't follow. Obviously, God is always in charge. He offers salvation on His terms. That multitudes reject His offer does not give them "the upper hand," but sends them to hell — hardly anything of which they could boast! Nor are those who reject Christ any more "in charge" than the multitudes who daily break God's commandments. Were Adam and Eve "in charge" when they rebelled? Was Satan? This is specious reasoning.

While there are some Calvinists who, like Spurgeon, reject Limited Atonement, it is irrational to do so while accepting the other four points. A leading Calvinist author put it like this: "It is in this truth of limited atonement that the doctrine of sovereign election (and, in fact, sovereign predestination with its two aspects of election and reprobation), comes into focus." [22] In other words, the whole Calvinistic system, which is built upon an extreme view of sovereignty and predestination, collapses if limited atonement is not biblical, which indeed it is not, as the plain text of Scripture indicates.

Key, Yet Controversial, Even Among Calvinists

Limited atonement is the one point which even those Calvinists who subscribe to all five points find the most difficult to accept. It is questionable whether

Calvin himself believed in limited atonement. Certainly Spurgeon rejected it as heresy. Some consider it to be "the Achilles Heel of Calvinism." [23] On the other hand, some Calvinists consider it to be their strongest point, "the hardest one of the *Five Points of Calvinism*' for Arminians to cope with." [24] Most admit that it follows necessarily from their particular view of predestination/reprobation: "If God has elected some and not others to eternal life, then plainly the primary purpose of Christ's work was to redeem the elect." [25] We must agree that it would seem unreasonable for Christ to die for those whom God had from eternity past predestined to eternal torment. "Give up this point," says another Calvinist, "and we have lost the battle on the sovereignty of God in salvation." [26]

Far from being derived from Scripture, however, Limited Atonement must be read into and forced upon it in order to make this system hang together. The Bible contains many statements which declare in the clearest language that Christ died for all mankind, that the gospel is offered and equally available to all and that God wants all to be saved. Despite that fact, most Calvinists insist upon Limited Atonement. In fact, as Hodge points out, they must in order to support the other four points.

The Calvinist recognizes that Unconditional Election and Limited Atonement "must stand or fall together. We cannot logically accept one and reject the other." [27] In fact, without Limited Atonement the entire framework collapses.

Hodges notes that the God of Limited Atonement "is hardly the God of love whom we meet in the Bible. The deity of the determinist creates human beings for whom he has no direct love, and who have no free will, and thus they are created solely for a destiny in everlasting torment. Christ's death in no way affects them, and so they stand totally outside of any redemptive provision." He goes on to say:

> Christ's atoning work is limited to the elect. The non-elect are both unloved and doomed. The cruelty implicit in such a view is obvious to any observer outside of those who have been brought up in, or have bought into, this kind of theology. Despite specious arguments addressed to every text alleged against such theology, determinists of this type are bereft of true biblical support. It is absurd, for example to claim (as they sometimes do) that when the Bible says, 'God so loved the world,' it means only 'the world of the elect.' " [28]

In considering the scriptures bearing on this subject, it becomes clear that the only way Limited Atonement can be defended is to assign, arbitrarily, a restrictive Calvinist meaning to key words. Palmer boldly declares:

> It was just because God so loved the world of elect sinners that He sent His only begotten Son that the world [i.e., the elect by Calvinist definition] might be saved through Him (John 3:16-17). In this passage, "world" does not mean

every single person, reprobate as well as elect, but the whole world in the sense of people [elected] from every tribe and nation . . . . [29]

What evidence is there either within this passage and its context or anywhere else in Scripture that "world" has this restrictive Calvinist meaning? Palmer offers none, nor can anyone else provide it. Quite simply, the only justification is in the fact that this doctrine requires it.

Why Aren't All Men Saved?

In maintaining Limited Atonement, the Calvinist reasons, "If Christ paid the debt of sin, has saved, ransomed, given His life for *all* men, then *all* men will be saved." [30] In the same vein Palmer writes, "But if the death of Jesus is what the Bible says it is — a substitutionary sacrifice for sins . . . whereby the sinner is really reconciled to God — then, obviously, it cannot be for every man . . . for then everybody would be saved, and obviously they are not." [31] In a letter to John Wesley, George Whitefield reasoned that "You cannot make good the assertion 'that Christ died for them that perish,' without holding . . . 'that all the damned souls would hereafter be brought out of hell . . . .'" [32] Clearly, most Calvinists insist that Christ's death immediately saved all of the elect without any faith, understanding or acceptance on their part. Yet Pink said, "A Saviour *provided* is not sufficient: he must be *received*. There must be *"faith* in His blood" (Romans 3:25) and faith is a *personal* thing. *I* must exercise faith." [33]

Of course, Pink was right. That Christ "taste[d] death for every man" (Hebrews 2:9) does not automatically mean that all are delivered from eternal death, the penalty for sin. Nowhere does the Bible say that. That Christ died for our sins is the message preached in the gospel. It must be believed to be of benefit to a sinner. Christ's death is only propitiatory for those who believe: He is "the Saviour of all men, specially of those that believe" (1 Timothy 4:10). Vance points out the obvious problem if the death of Christ automatically procures salvation for those for whom He died:

> But if the nature of the atonement was such that it actually in and of itself provided salvation for those for whom it was intended, then the "elect" could never have been born "dead in trespasses and sins" (Eph. 2:1). And consequently, how could men who were saved, redeemed, reconciled, and justified be "by nature children of wrath" (Eph. 2:5) . . . ? [34]

The Passover, which Pink acknowledges as "one of the most striking and blessed foreshadowments of the Cross-work of Christ to be found anywhere in the Old Testament, is a clear example of the principle that the Atonement and its application are to be distinguished. The blood of the slain passover lamb (Exodus 12:6,21) became efficacious only after it was applied to the doorpost per instructions (Exodus 12:7,22) . . . . The death of the lamb saved no one: the blood had to be applied." [35] And so it is with Christ's death.

Palmer is not troubled in putting the blame on God: "Because God has loved certain ones and not all, because He has sovereignly and immutably determined that these particular ones will be saved, He sent His Son to die for them, to save them, and not all the world." [36] Thus all men are not saved because God doesn't want them to be and has predestined multitudes to suffer eternally. According to the Bible, however, all are not saved because *they* (the lost) don't want to be saved but want to go their own way in rebellion against God and refuse to believe on Christ. Paul writes that salvation comes "unto all... that believe...for all have sinned" (Romans 3:22-23). Surely the "all have sinned" means all mankind. Thus the "all...that believe" must mean that all mankind are free and able to believe on Christ.

Salvation Is For All

Here are some of the many verses (with key words and phrases italicized) which make up the overwhelming testimony that God (exactly as we would expect of the One who *is love* and the Father of mercies) loves everyone with infinite love, desiring that all should be saved. He does not want anyone to perish and has made the death of Christ propitiatory for the sins of all mankind if they will only believe and receive the gift of eternal life in Christ:

All we like sheep have gone astray; we have turned every one to his own way; and the LORD hath laid on him the iniquity of us *all*. (Isaiah 53:6)

Behold the Lamb of God, which taketh away the sin of *the world*." (John 1:29)

. . . even so must the Son of man be lifted up: that *whosoever believeth* in him should not perish, but have eternal life . . . . For God so loved *the world*, that he gave his only begotten Son, that *whosoever believeth* in him . . . for God sent not his Son into *the world* to condemn *the world;* but that *the world* through him might be saved. *He that believeth* on him is not condemned . . . . *He that believeth* on the Son hath everlasting life: and *he that believeth not* the Son shall not see life . . . . (John 3:14,15,16,17,18,36)

If *any man* thirst, let him come unto me, and drink. (John 7:37)
For I am not ashamed of the gospel of Christ: for *it is the power of God unto salvation to every one that believeth*; to the Jew first, and also to the Greek. (Romans 1:16)

Christ died for *the ungodly*. (Romans 5:6)

But the scripture hath concluded all under sin, that the promise by faith . . . might be given to *them that believe*. (Galatians 3:22)

For the wages of sin is death; but the *gift of God* is eternal life through Jesus Christ our Lord. (Romans 6:23)

Christ Jesus came into the world *to save sinners*. (1 Timothy 1:15)

Who will have *all men* to be saved, and to come to the knowledge of the truth. (1 Timothy 2:4)

Who gave himself a ransom *for all* . . . . (1 Timothy 2:6)

We trust in the living God, who is the *Saviour of all men*, specially of those that *believe*. (1 Timothy 4:10)

That he by the grace of God should taste death *for every man*. (Hebrews 2:9)

The Lord is . . . not willing that *any* should perish, but that *all* should come to repentance. (2 Peter 3:9)

If we confess our sins, he is faithful and just to forgive us our sins, and to cleanse us from all unrighteousness . . . . And if *any man* sin, we have an advocate with the Father, Jesus Christ the righteous: And he is the propitiation for our sins: and *not for ours only; but also for the sins of the whole world*. (1 John 1:9-2:1-2)

The Father sent the Son to be the *Saviour of the world*. (1 John 4:14)

Do only the elect go astray like lost sheep? Do only the elect thirst? Are only the elect ungodly and sinners? Are only the elect "under sin"? Obviously not. As surely as all men are sinners, so surely is salvation available to all men through faith in Jesus Christ.

Taken at face value, these verses, and many more like them, seem to state in unambiguous language that Christ was sent to be "the Saviour of the world," that His death was "a ransom for all" and that He is therefore "the Saviour of all men" if they will but believe. John Owen speaks for most Calvinists when he attempts to counter such scriptures in support of limited atonement with the following commentary upon 1 Timothy 1:15, "Christ Jesus came into the world to save sinners":

> Now, if you will ask who these sinners are towards whom he hath this gracious intent and purpose, himself tells you, Matthew 20.28, that he came to "give his life a ransom for *many*;" in other places called *us* believers distinguished from the world: for he "gave himself for *our* sins, that he might deliver *us* from this present evil *world* . . ." Galatians 1:4 . . . . Ephesians v.25-27, "He loved the church, and gave himself for *it* . . . ." Titus ii.14, "He gave himself for *us*, that he might redeem *us* from all iniquity . . . " for through him "*we* have access into the grace wherein we stand," Romans v.5:2, etc. [37]

Owen was a brilliant man beyond the intellect of either Calvin or Luther, yet his argument has no substance. The necessity to defend Calvinism seemingly blinds him to the Scriptures and to simple reason. Obviously, the multitude of verses which state clearly that God loves all and is merciful to all and that Christ died for all are not nullified by other verses declaring that Christ died for the *church*, that His death was a ransom for *many*, or the assurance that He died for *us*, etc. These passages do not say that Christ died *only* for *many* sinners, *only* for the *church*, *only* for *us*, etc. If that were the case, however, statements such as, "For if through the offense of one [Adam] many be dead . . . by one man's disobedience many were made sinners" (Romans 5:15,19), etc. must indicate that death passed not upon everyone nor were all made sinners through Adam's disobedience, but only a limited few.

Of course, Paul or Peter in writing to the believers would remind them that Christ died for *them* — but that statement does not deny that He died for all. Yet this same argument is offered repeatedly by Calvinists to this day. For example, Piper futilely quotes the same inapplicable verses in which it is said that Christ was "a ransom for many," that He "bear the sins of many," and that He "loved the church and gave himself for her," etc. as "proof" that Christ's death was not propitiatory for all. [38] By that reasoning Paul wouldn't have been able to use "you," "ye," etc. in writing to the Corinthians because that would mean the benefits of Christ's death and resurrection were *only* for them. By the same argument, for David to say, "The LORD is my shepherd . . . " (Psalms 23:1) would mean that this was true only for David. Or when Israel's prophets wrote, "O God of Israel, the Saviour...their redeemer is strong, the LORD of hosts is his name . . . " (Isaiah 45:15; Jeremiah 50:34), it meant that God was only the God and redeemer of Israel.

Equally absurd, for Paul to say "the Son of God who loved *me*" would then mean that Christ loved only Paul.

Other arguments which Calvinists employ to put their own spin on the verses quoted above are astonishing. For example, John Piper and his pastoral staff become lost in the tangled wilderness of their own words in attempting to explain 1 Timothy 4:10:

> Christ's death so clearly demonstrates God's just abhorrence of sin that he is free to treat the world with mercy without compromising his righteousness. *In this sense* Christ is the savior of *all* men. But he is *especially* the Savior of those who believe. He did not die for all men in the same sense . . . . The death of Christ actually saves from *all* evil those for whom Christ died "especially." [39] [Emphasis in original]

Can anyone make sense of their use of "sense"? Christ did not die for all men in the "*same* sense," yet He is the savior of all men in "*this* sense." What is *this* sense? Because Christ's death "demonstrates God's just abhorrence of sin . . . " He is able to "treat the world with mercy without compromising his righteousness." But He doesn't treat all with mercy because Christ "did not die for all men in the same sense . . . . " We're lost in an impenetrable fog of "sense." Neither *this sense* nor *same sense* are defined, so we can't make *any sense* out of this nonsense. But it shows again the lengths to which one must go to defend Calvin's and Augustine's delusion.

Surely Isaiah is speaking to all of Israel when he says, "all we like sheep have gone astray . . . ." And surely he speaks to all of Israel when he declares that "the iniquity of us all" would be laid upon the coming Messiah. Nor can it be denied that many Israelites who were alive then and have lived since have not been saved but have remained rebels against God. Yet as surely as they went astray so surely did God lay upon Christ the iniquity of them *all*. These and many other scriptures make it clear that the benefit of Christ's death, burial and resurrection in full payment for the sins of the world is available to be received by whosoever believes the gospel.

In spite of the testimony of Scripture to the contrary, Boettner declares that "Calvinists hold that in the intention and secret plan of God, Christ died for the elect only . . . ." [40] Otherwise, adds Boettner, "If Christ's death was intended to save all men, then we must say that God was either unable or unwilling to carry out His plans." [41] He forgets, of course, that Christ's death only benefits those who *receive* Christ (John 1:12) and that salvation, being "the gift of God" (Romans 6:23), must be willingly received. As for men being able to oppose God's plans, is the evil in the world God's plan? Why, then, are we to pray, "Thy will be done, on earth as it is in heaven"?

Abusing God's Word

One can only conclude from Scripture that salvation is available to everyone in the entire world, Jew or Gentile, who will but believe in Christ "the Lamb of God, which taketh away the sin of the world" (John 1:29). How could such clear language be denied? Exactly as Palmer does it above: by changing the definition of words ("world" becomes "elect," etc.) and by certain rationalizations which at first seem to make sense but fail upon closer examination. One correspondent, objecting to what little I had written about Calvinism in our monthly newsletter, argued, "If Christ died for all men, why aren't all men saved? Is believing necessary to make the blood of Christ efficacious for redemption? On the contrary, [it is not]."

This is Calvinistic reasoning: that Christ must have died only for the elect, not for all, otherwise all would be saved. And the elect allegedly don't even need to believe or receive Christ in order to be born again for they are sovereignly regenerated by God without any desire or understanding on their part. God simply wills it so. If man has any choice in the matter at all, Calvinism is refuted. As Palmer said sarcastically of the non-Calvinist view of the cross, "Christ not only shed His blood, He also spilled it. He intended to save all, but only some will be saved. Therefore, some of His blood was wasted: it was spilled." [42]

In the Calvinist scheme, believing the gospel is not the means of one's salvation but proof that one is among the elect and was regenerated by God and thereafter given the faith to believe. The same correspondent just quoted insisted that faith is not unto salvation but "is simply the proof that the blood of Christ has saved a man." Piper and his staff argue the same: "We do not think that faith precedes and causes new birth. Faith is the evidence that God has begotten us anew." [43] Quite clearly, however, the Bible *always* puts faith *before* salvation — so Calvinism has man regenerated before he is saved, an unbiblical concept.

The Bible repeatedly says that we are "saved, *through faith*" (Ephesians 2:8). Paul told the Philippian jailor, "*Believe* on the Lord Jesus Christ, and thou *shalt be* saved . . . " (Acts 16:31). In the Greek, "believe" is always an active verb, something the one believing does, not something done to him. But the Calvinist insists that although man can believe anything else that seems reasonable and factual, he cannot believe in Christ. Therefore, God must regenerate him first and then *cause* him to believe by giving him the essential faith — something God only does for a select few, the elect.

The many verses quoted above, however, some from the lips of Christ himself, clearly make believing a *condition* of salvation. Salvation always follows and results from faith. The biblical reason all men are not saved in spite of Christ having died for all is that not all believe the gospel. "Whosoever" implies that some won't. It's that simple. Consider the following:

> To him give all the prophets witness, that . . . whosoever believeth in him shall receive remission of sins. (Acts 10:43)

> For the scripture saith, Whosoever believeth on him shall not be ashamed. (Romans 10:11)

> For whosoever shall call upon the name of the Lord shall be saved. (Romans 10:13)

The claim that "whosoever" means only the elect flies in the face of hundreds of scriptures. Nor can *one* verse be produced where this doctrine of limited atonement is clearly stated.

What About "Double Jeopardy"?

Calvinists reason that for sinners to suffer eternally after Christ had suffered for them would mean that God was demanding double payment for their sins. Boettner insists that "Christ died not for an unorderly mass, but for His people, His Bride, His Church." [44] He goes on to argue: "For God to have laid the sins of all men on Christ would mean that as regards the lost He would be punishing their sins twice, once in Christ, and then again in them." [45] Another author offers what he considers to be sound arguments against the possibility that John 3:16 and so many other verses could really mean what they say:

> [If] Jesus died, paying for the sins of all, God cannot legally or justly accuse and condemn anyone . . . regardless of whether they hear or accept the gospel, *sin cannot be justly paid for twice* . . . . For God not to pardon a sinner for whom Christ agonized would be a *travesty* of justice . . . . [then] Jesus will never . . . "see of the travail of his soul and be satisfied" (Isaiah 53). Why? Because billions for whom He agonized, travailed and died, bearing their "sins in his own body on the tree," will suffer eternal hell. Jesus paid. They pay again. God is paid twice for one debt. [46] (Emphasis in original)

However, as we shall see in the next section, it was impossible for Christ to die for some sins and not for others. Christ had to die for sin itself, the sin which "by one man . . . entered into the world," and for the death which as a result "passed upon all men" (Romans 5:12), and thus pay the penalty owed by all. Christ's payment for sin cannot be divided into pieces in order to apply it to individuals. Nor is it automatically credited to the account of anyone who does not acknowledge his guilt before God, repent and accept Christ as his Savior.

As a result of Christ's death having paid the full penalty, no one will spend eternity in the lake of fire because of his sins; they will be there for rejecting Christ and the salvation He obtained and freely offers to all. No sin could be greater than rejecting Christ, nor would punishment for that sin constitute double payment.

Furthermore, even if it were a double payment, it is the sinner, not God, who demands it by rejecting the offered pardon. God's justice has been fully satisfied in the death of His Son. The Father has proved His love by giving His Son, and Christ has proved His love by dying in the sinner's place. Therefore, even if double payment were involved, God could not be charged with injustice on that account.

Atheists carry the argument even further, saying that it is a travesty of justice for Christ, an innocent party, to be punished in the place of the guilty and for the guilty thereby to go free. In fact, that is not the gospel according to Paul but according to Barabbas. The latter could say, "Christ died for me, in my place." That was true, but Christ's death in his place had neither an eternal nor even a moral effect on Barabbas. It merely set that criminal free to live for self again — and that is not the gospel.

The truth of the gospel was expressed by Paul when he said, "I am crucified with Christ . . . [and now] Christ liveth in me" (Galatians 2:20). In fact, all those who believe in Christ have been crucified with Him. Such was not the case with Barabbas even though Christ died in his place. Those who have not believed in Christ have not accepted His death as their death and thus will suffer "the second death" eternally (Revelation 20:14-15).

God has proved himself to be both loving and just. No one can complain that God created human beings for hell. He created them all for His glorious presence. Yes, He knew that all men would sin and come short of His glory, but He had a way whereby He could be just and yet justify *all* sinners (Romans 3:22-26) so they could be forgiven and spend eternity in His presence.

Even before man had been created and had sinned, God had planned redemption for him and for all his descendants. Anyone who will spend eternity in the lake of fire (Revelation 20:14) has sent himself there by rejecting the salvation God has offered to him as a free gift of His grace. God is exonerated — He has provided salvation for all, but He will not bend His justice to accommodate those who reject Christ. He cannot deny himself.

Was "Some" Of Christ's Blood Shed In Vain?

Acceptance of Limited Atonement by many seems to be based upon the sincere misunderstanding that if Christ's blood was shed for multitudes who will not believe, some of it would have been shed in vain. Some Calvinists seem to believe that Christ's death was *potentially* redemptive of the whole world but that the limiting factor was put upon it by God himself. Thus Gunn argues, "The cross could save everyone if God had only intended it to do so." [47]

It is argued that for anyone for whom Christ died to spend eternity in the lake of fire it would not only be double payment and a violation of justice but would mean that Christ's blood was shed in vain. C.H. Spurgeon lent his support on that very point in spite of his assertion that the value of Christ's atonement was unlimited:

> Some say that all men are Christ's by purchase. But, beloved, you and I do not believe in a sham redemption which does not redeem. We do not believe in a universal redemption which extends even to those who were in hell before the Savior died, and which includes . . . unrepentant men. We believe in an effectual redemption, and can never agree with those who would teach us that Christ's blood was shed in vain. [48]

No one can truthfully say that "Christ's blood was shed in vain." No matter how many reject Him as their savior, hundreds of millions, and perhaps billions, will be with God eternally because of Christ's blood poured out on the cross. Nevertheless, that Christ died for all, that He "tasted death for every man," is the clear teaching of Scripture.

The very idea that Christ's blood could have been shed in vain if some of those for whom it was shed rejected Him and spent eternity in the lake of fire betrays a basic misunderstanding. Could such a great preacher as Spurgeon have missed the point here? A little thought reveals that he and all Calvinists have done exactly that.

Certainly Christ's blood was not shed in vain for those who believe. How much of His blood did it take to atone for those who will be in heaven? Obviously, all of it had to be shed to redeem even one person. There is no way to divide Christ's blood so that *part* of it was shed for the redeemed and *part* of it for those who are lost and thus *some* of it was shed in vain.

Even if no one believed on Him, Christ proved God's love, mercy and grace; He proved the sinfulness of sin, the justice of the penalty and glorified God in paying that penalty in full for all. Because of Christ's death on the cross, God has been fully vindicated in His creation of man and will be eternally glorified in those in hell. That seems a horrible thought. We will deal with it in more depth later.

We do not say that "all men are Christ's by purchase." Redemption, according to the Bible, becomes effectual only if and when a sinner believes the gospel. No one could escape hell apart from Christ having paid the full penalty for sin. And the rejection of Christ is one sin for which, by its very nature, Christ could not pay the penalty. This is the "sin against the Holy Ghost," unpardonable in this life or in the life to come. Indeed, that sin carries a far worse penalty of its own:

> Of how much sorer punishment . . . shall he be thought worthy, who hath trodden under foot the Son of God, and hath counted the blood of the covenant, wherewith he was sanctified; an unholy thing, and hath done despite unto the Spirit of grace? (Hebrews 10:29)

And here again we have a clear statement that the blood of Christ was not shed for the elect alone. It was shed even for those who despise it and tread under foot the Son of God. The same truth is presented by Peter that even those who go to destruction have been bought by Christ, obviously at the price of His blood shed for sin: "But there were false prophets also among the people, even as there shall be false teachers among you, who privily shall bring in damnable heresies, even denying the Lord that bought them, and bring upon themselves swift destruction" (2 Peter 2:1).

Here the Calvinist must either admit that one who was once saved lost his salvation through turning against Christ — or that the one who "was sanctified" by Christ's blood and those who deny "the Lord that bought them" are not among the elect, yet, obviously, His blood was shed for them.

Particular Atonement?

Calvinists contend that "It makes no sense for Christ to offer atonement for those the Father does not entrust to Him for salvation." [49] This is human reasoning without even one verse of Scripture to support it. Great emphasis is placed upon what is called "particular atonement," the idea that the death of Christ had to be for a particular elect. That would mean, however, that Christ died only for particular sins. Here we find a misunderstanding of the nature of the atonement. Christ did not die for individual sins only, but for *sin itself* – a penalty which had to be paid in order for *anyone* to be saved. But His paying the penalty for sin itself could not occur without His paying for all sins and providing salvation for all mankind. Such is the teaching of the Bible.

The Apostle James reminds us that to break one commandment is to be guilty of breaking all: "For whosoever shall keep the whole law, and yet offend in one point, he is guilty of all" (James 2:10). This must be the case because of the very nature of sin. It is not merely a matter of what particular commandment may have been broken, how many times one has committed a certain sin, how "bad a sinner" someone is, etc. Sin is rebellion against God. Thus in whatever way or magnitude one rebels, no matter how insignificant it seems from a human viewpoint, one is a rebel. Sin is sin, and the penalty for what we might think is only the most trivial of sins is eternal separation from God in the lake of fire.

There is no way that Christ's death could be limited to paying only for the elect's sins. To deliver even one person from eternal punishment, no matter how few or many the sins he may have committed, Christ had to pay the penalty demanded by His infinite justice for *sin*. By very definition, then, the death of Christ on the cross paid the penalty for sin itself which hangs over the heads of the entire human race. It could not be otherwise.

Christ is the "second man . . . the last Adam" (1 Corinthians 15:45-47), the representative of the entire human race. Therefore, what He did at Calvary had to be efficacious for all mankind. He paid for Adam's sin, which brought death upon all, so in paying that penalty He has freed all who will receive the salvation He offers.

Yes, we "confess our sins" (1 John 1:9) just as the Israelites were required to bring individual offerings to be sacrificed for their individual sins. But there was "the sin offering" which made possible the forgiveness of all sin. "Sin offering" in the singular is mentioned scores of times in the Book of Leviticus, far more than the offerings for sins.

That the blood of Christ was shed "for the remission of sins" is declared in Matthew 26:28; Luke 24:47; 1 Corinthians 15:3 and many other places. We are also told, however, that He died for sin. In fact, "sin" is mentioned more than twice as many times as "sins." Here are a few of those passages:

> . . . When thou shalt make his soul an offering for sin . . . he bare the sin of many . . . . (Isaiah 53:10,12)

> Behold the Lamb of God, which taketh away the sin of the world. (John 1:29)

> Wherefore, as by one man sin entered into the world . . . . (Romans 5:12)

For the wages of sin is death . . . . (Romans 6:23)

For he hath made him to be sin for us . . . that we might be made the righteousness of God in him. (2 Corinthians 5:21)

. . . burnt offerings and sacrifices for sin . . . . (Hebrews 10:6,8; 13:11)

The Gospel Is *Personal*

To be consistent with what he said above, Spurgeon, great preacher that he was, could not in good faith tell audiences that *whosoever* among them would believe in Christ would be saved. As a Calvinist, he would have to preach an oblique gospel, not a personal one, not knowing, as taught by Jay Adams, whether any or all in his audience were among the elect. And yet, in obedience to the Bible, Spurgeon preached the gospel as a call to *whosoever* would believe, as the Bible repeatedly says we must. We can and must declare to anyone and everyone, "That if *thou* shalt confess with *thy* mouth, and shalt believe in *thine* heart that God hath raised him from the dead, *thou* shalt be saved . . . . For *whosoever* shall call upon the name of the Lord shall be saved" (Romans 10:9,13).

In fact, this is the only way it could be. Salvation cannot be offered to anyone for whom Christ did not die, yet it is to be proclaimed to all: "Preach the gospel to every creature" (Mark 16:15). In contrast, the Calvinist cannot look an unsaved person in the eye and say with confidence, "Christ died for *you!*" That person may not be one of the elect, and therefore such a statement could be untrue.

Paul could not tell the Philippian jailor, "Believe on the Lord Jesus Christ and *thou* shalt be saved, and *thy house*" if Christ had not died for him and his family. Did Paul have a special revelation that this entire family was among the elect — or is the gospel for all? How could Paul declare the same to large audiences everywhere, such as at Antioch in Pisidia: " . . . to *you* is the word of this salvation sent" (Acts 13:26), if Christ only died for the elect? Surely not everyone in the vast audiences he faced was among the elect! How could Peter say to thousands of Jews gathered on Pentecost, "Repent, and be baptized *every one of you* . . . " (Acts 2:38), if Christ had not died for each and every one of them?

At times Calvin himself seemed to be ambivalent on this subject. He made statements both supporting unlimited atonement and at other times in favor of limited atonement. Referring to Isaiah 53:12 he said, "on Him was laid the guilt of the whole world." [50] Concerning Mark 14:24, "This is my blood of the new testament, which is shed for many," Calvin said, "The word *many* does not mean a part of the world, but the whole human race." [51] On 1 John 2:2, Calvin declared, "Christ suffered for the sins of the whole world, and in the goodness of God is offered unto all men without distinction, his blood being shed . . . for the whole human race." [52]

As we shall see when we come to Perseverance of the Saints, a major problem for Calvinists is how to be certain that one is among that select group for whom alone Christ allegedly died. We see this uncertainty in Calvin himself. In his will, drawn up shortly before his death, Calvin wrote, "I humbly seek from God . . . to be washed and purified by the great Redeemer's blood, shed for the sins of the human race . . . ." [53] How is it that this greatest of exegetes seemed uncertain in spite of Scripture's promise of absolute assurance: "These things have I written unto you that believe on the name of the Son of God; that ye may *know* that ye *have* eternal life . . . " (1 John 5:13)? Such assurance comes not by a special revelation that one is among the elect, but by simple faith in Christ.

Changing The Meaning Of "World"

Instead of acknowledging the statement from Calvin which we have quoted above, White selectively quotes Calvin in another mood: "In relation to John 1:29 and 1 John 2:2 the word 'world' is viewed as intending to transcend a nationalistic Jewish particularism." [54] There is nothing anywhere either in John's gospel or epistle to suggest that odd meaning. Calvinism, however, *must* change "world" into all or part of "the elect" in order to maintain itself. What did Calvin really believe, especially at the end of his life? It has been said that he began to have doubts, and the statement quoted from his will — "of the human race" — seems to confirm it. White fails to settle that issue for us.

Calvin is quoted as the authority when it suits today's Calvinists, and at other times he is ignored. Yet this confusing doctrine upon which its adherents do not agree among themselves or even with Calvin is still called "Calvinism" by everyone.

Pink stands firm on what he believes are rational reasons for Limited Atonement: "To say that God the Father has purposed the salvation of all mankind, that God the Son died with the express intention of saving the whole human race, and that God the Holy Spirit is now seeking to win the world to Christ; when . . . it is apparent that the great majority of our fellow-men are dying in sin, and passing into a hopeless eternity: is to say that God the Father is *disappointed*, that God the Son is *dissatisfied*, and that God the Holy Spirit is *defeated*." [55]

Pink is offering human reasoning that is neither biblical nor rational but, unfortunately, is required to support Calvinism. To maintain this position one would have to say that God was insincere in the hundreds of urgent and passionate pleadings and warnings for Israel to repent and obey Him which are expressed through His prophets throughout the Old Testament. The fact is that Israel as a whole rebelled against Him continually during its entire existence and continues in unbelief and rejection of her Messiah to this day. If such disobedience does not require God to be *disappointed, dissatisfied and defeated* (emotions that He cannot have), then neither would that be God's reaction when Gentiles He loves and for whom Christ died reject the salvation He freely and lovingly offers.

We do not deny that the word "world" can have a variety of meanings, but the times that it does not mean either the physical world, the ungodly world system, or all mankind are exceedingly rare. Those instances could almost be counted on one hand out of the nearly 240 times "world" is found in the New Testament. Furthermore, we challenge the Calvinist to point out *one verse* where "world" explicitly means the elect. Please, *just one!*

Of the 80 times "world" occurs in 59 verses in John's gospel, *not once* does it mean "elect." That meaning has to be read into the text — and there is nothing in the usage to differentiate between those times when the Calvinist says it means "elect" and those times when he doesn't say so. Vance lists numerous examples from John's Gospel where "world" could not possibly mean the elect:

> The world knew not Christ (1:10). The world hates Christ (7:7). The world's works are evil (7:7). Unsaved Jews were of this world (8:23). Satan is the prince of this world (12:31; 14:30; 16:11). Christ's own are distinguished from the world (13:1; 14:19, 22). The world cannot receive the Holy Spirit (14:17). The world hates the disciples (15:18; 14:14) [and many more] . . . .

> In arguing for limited atonement, Sproul inadvertently proves that the world does not refer to the "elect" . . . : "He [Jesus] explicitly excludes the non-elect from his great high priestly prayer, 'I do not pray for the world but for those whom you have given Me' (John 17:9) . . . ." [56] So not only does the world *never* denote the "elect," it is unequivocally demeaned and condemned by God. [57]

Each of us must, of course, go by the Bible no matter what John Calvin or Charles H. Spurgeon or anyone else taught. The only justification for rejecting the ordinary meaning of "world" and assigning Calvinism's peculiar connotation (which certainly is nowhere plain from any text), is that Calvinism requires it. Richard Baxter argues persuasively:

> God telleth us as plain as can be spoken that Christ died for and tasted death for every man . . . others will deny these plain truths, because they think that [God cannot justly punish those for whom Christ hath paid the penalty] . . . . But doth the Scripture speak . . . these opinions of theirs as plainly as it saith that Christ died for all and every man?

> Doth it say as plainly anywhere that He died not for all . . . ? Doth it say anywhere that he died *only* for His Sheep, or His Elect, and exclude the Non-Elect? There is no such word in the Bible . . . . [58]

Ingenious But Irrational

A favorite ploy of the Calvinist is to suggest that "world" does not mean "all people 'without exception' but...'without distinction' . . . not [only] Jews, but also . . . Gentiles." [59] This is the same tactic as changing "all people" into "all *kinds* of people" — an ingenious idea born of desperation, but irrational. Such an idea is even more strained than to brazenly change "all people" or "world" into "elect." Under what circumstances would anyone understand "all" to mean not *all* but all *kinds*?

A merchant advertises, "Giant Sale! All merchandise half price." Eager customers, however, discover that certain items are excluded from the sale. When they complain, the merchant says, "I didn't mean all 'without exception,' but all 'without distinction.' All *kinds* of products are indeed on sale, but not every item of every kind." This would be misleading advertising, and customers would have a legitimate complaint: "If that is what you meant, then that is what you should have said."

If a shepherd said, "I'm selling *all* of my sheep," would anyone think he meant *some* of all *kinds*, i.e. *some* males, *some* females, *some* newborn lambs, etc.? If headlines read, "All males between the ages of 20 and 45 are subject to military draft," who would imagine that it really meant *some* blacks, *some* whites, *some* from Illinois, *some* from Utah, etc.? Or if the announcement were made to a group of tourists stopping at an oasis near the Dead Sea in Israel that "Whoever is thirsty should get a drink now," would anyone imagine this meant *some* women, *some* men, *some* elderly among the thirsty, etc.?

There may be some context in which such a special meaning would be implied, but it is difficult to think of an example — nor can we find one in all of Scripture. Yet the Calvinist, in order to support his theory, must insist upon this peculiar meaning for *every one* of the numerous statements concerning "all" and "world" and "whosoever," etc. throughout the entire Bible! And he *really* imagines this is what God actually meant? Wouldn't the Holy Spirit be more precise in order to avoid misunderstanding? And wouldn't the Calvinist meaning be stated clearly *at least once*?

What About 1 John 2:2?

Lacking references in the Bible which plainly say that Christ died only for the elect, Calvinists somehow have to make those that say He died for all support their theory. The scripture, 1 John 2:2, is an unambiguous declaration that Christ is "the propitiation for our sins and not for ours only, but for the sins of the whole world." Surely "our" must refer to the elect. Therefore "the whole world," being in contrast to the elect, can only refer to the unsaved and would prove that Christ's death is propitiatory for all mankind.

To acknowledge what this passage is clearly saying would be the end of Calvinism. How can that conclusion be avoided? Simply by once again adopting the Calvinists' special meaning for "world." Piper writes, "The 'whole world' refers to the children of God scattered throughout the whole world." [60] White elaborates a bit further on this brazen eisegesis which Calvinists have devised in order to rescue their Limited Atonement theory:

> The Reformed understanding is that Jesus Christ is the propitiation for the sins of all the Christians to which John was writing, and not only them, but for all Christians throughout the world, Jew and Gentile, at all times and in all places. [61]

Surely the "our" in "he is the propitiation for our sins" refers to *all* Christians, not just John's contemporaries. It certainly is a true statement for all believers in Christ, and John's entire epistle, like all of the Bible of which it is a part, is addressed to all believers in all ages. If the "our" thus refers to the elect, then "the whole world," being in contrast, could only represent those who are lost.

To escape the obvious, White claims that John was only writing to the Christians of his day and therefore "our" means those who originally read the epistle; and "the whole world" means all other Christians not alive at the time when the epistle was written. [62] Nothing in the text even hints at such a conclusion. Nor would it have been invented had it not been necessary in order to rescue Limited Atonement. Undeniably, John is writing under the inspiration of the Holy Spirit to all Christians everywhere and in all ages.

Piper reasons that "Propitiated sins cannot be punished . . . . Therefore it is very unlikely that 1 John 2:2 teaches that Jesus is the propitiation of every person in the world . . . ." [63] We have already shown that this argument doesn't work for at least two reasons: 1) Christ had to pay the penalty for all sin for even one person to be saved; and 2) the benefits of Christ's death do not come automatically but only to those who believe and receive Him. Were this not the case, then the elect also for whom the Calvinist says Christ did die would be saved without believing and before they were born.

Finally, Piper, following John Owens's argument, reasons that if Christ is really the propitiation for the sins of the whole world, then unbelief would not keep anyone out of heaven because unbelief, being a sin, would have been propitiated as well. [64] In fact, rejection of Christ "the true Light, which lighteth every man that cometh into the world" (John 1:9), in spite of the conviction of all by the Holy Spirit of "sin, and of righteousness, and of judgment" (John 16:8-11), as we have already noted, is the "blasphemy against the Holy Ghost . . . [which] shall not be forgiven . . . neither in this world, neither in the world to come" (Matthew 12:31-32).

Every Christian, by very definition, has been saved through faith in Christ, and His blood is the propitiation for their sins. This fact is so elementary and essential that one could hardly be a Christian without knowing it. It is therefore absurd to suggest that John is revealing something of importance by declaring that the blood of Christ avails not only for the people alive in his day but for all Christians in all ages. If this is what the Holy Spirit through John intended, why wasn't it stated clearly? Would the Holy Spirit use "world" to convey the meaning "all Christians in all times everywhere"? Hardly.

To Whom Did John Write?

Other Calvinists reason that "John would have been writing to a Jewish audience who had long believed that God was only the God of Israel. And so they needed to be taught and reminded that Christ died not only for the lost sheep of Israel but also for his lost sheep in all the world . . . thus, the 'whole world' is his lost sheep of Israel plus his lost sheep from among the other nations." [65] Surely no one would even imagine such a far-fetched idea, had Calvinism not been invented and an explanation required for "world" that would salvage the theory.

Neither the word "Jew" nor "Gentile" appears in 1 John. There is nothing in the entire epistle to suggest that John is addressing only Jewish believers. This is another desperate effort to rescue an unbiblical theory. John tells us quite clearly to whom he is speaking: "These things have I written unto you that believe on the name of the Son of God . . . " (1 John 5:13). That includes all Christians then and now.

Furthermore, not only is John writing to all believers in Christ, he is doing so many years after the Jerusalem counsel of Acts 15, where the whole issue of salvation for Gentiles without their keeping the law of Moses had been settled. Paul's letter to the Galatian believers, which dealt with this issue in depth, had long been in circulation. John doesn't deal with this long-settled topic at all.

Who would have imagined, without the necessity to support a special theory, that John was writing only to either the Christians of his day or to a Jewish audience? Furthermore, if John were not writing to all Christians in all ages, how could we apply his epistle to ourselves today? In fact, we know that he was writing to all believers in Christ, and Christians throughout the ages have read his gospel and epistles with that understanding.

When John writes, "He that saith, I know him, and keepeth not his commandments, is a liar . . . he that saith he is in the light, and hateth his brother, is in darkness . . . ye have an unction from the Holy One . . . the anointing which ye have received of him abideth in you . . . " (1 John 2:4,9,20,27), etc. throughout his epistle, surely what he says is for all believers in Christ in every age. When he writes, "Love not the world, neither the things that are in the world . . . " (1 John 2:15) was that only for Christians in that day but not for us today? Obviously not.

What About The Meaning Of "The Whole World"?

White quotes the song of the redeemed in Revelation 5:9-10. Because it says that Christ has redeemed by His blood men "out of every kindred, and tongue, and people, and nation," White reasons, "We suggest that this passage, then, sheds significant light upon 1 John 2:2, for it is obvious that the passage in Revelation is not saying that Christ purchased every man from every tribe, tongue, people and nation. Yet, obviously, this is a parallel concept to 'the world' in 1 John 2:2." He then quotes the High Priest Caiaphas (John 11:49-52) that it is expedient "that one man die for the people, and that the whole nation perish not." [66] Surely Caiaphas really *meant* the whole nation, so what is the point?

Sadly, this is one more example of how far Calvinists have to reach: to suggest that a future song in heaven and a statement by Caiaphas about the nation of Israel prove that "world" in 1 John 2:2 really means "all *Christians* throughout the world . . . "! The song in heaven is by the redeemed, those who make up the "our" in 1 John 2:2. They are redeemed "from" or "out of" every tribe and tongue and people and nation. In fact, White is helping us to see a contrast: John does not say "from" or "out of" the whole world; he clearly says "the whole world."

Why must White go so far afield? Within this very epistle there are plenty of better comparisons that define "world" for us. In 1 John 3:1 we have the phrase, " . . . the world knoweth us not." Surely "us" refers to the redeemed and "world" is in contrast to them and cannot possibly mean some other group of Christians. In 1 John 3:13 we find, "Marvel not, my brethren, if the world hate you." Again we have the same contrast between the redeemed and the unsaved who hate them, making the meaning of "world" quite clear. In 1 John 4:5-6 we find, "They are of the world . . . we are of God." The distinction between the unsaved world and those who are saved — which is maintained consistently throughout the entire epistle — could not be clearer. Again 1 John 5:19 declares, "We are of God, and the whole world lieth in wickedness."

To be consistent with his handling of 1 John 2:2, White must believe that "all Christians throughout the world, Jew and Gentile, at all times and in all places" hate the believers to whom John was writing and lie in wickedness. In fact, nowhere in the entire epistle does "world" mean what he tries to turn it into in 1 John 2:2!

The Calvinist has a very difficult time explaining away biblical refutation of Limited Atonement. That may be why White has nothing to say about any of these verses within this epistle which we have just quoted and which leave no doubt concerning what John (and the Holy Spirit inspiring him) meant by "world." How odd!

There can be no doubt that throughout this epistle the word "world" consistently means exactly what a reasonable reader would expect: the world of mankind at large in contrast to the body of believers. One cannot claim that "world" in 1 John 2:2 is an exception and has a different meaning from everywhere else in the epistle. We can only conclude that Christ is the propitiation for the sins of the whole world and therefore His death was not propitiatory for the elect only but for the sins of all mankind. Indeed, John says exactly that in so many words: "the Father sent the Son to be the Saviour of the world" (1 John 4:14).

Clearly, without special definitions of words and much Scripture-twisting, the doctrine of Limited Atonement crumbles and with it the rest of Calvinism.

---

1 John Murray, *Redemption Accomplished and Applied* (Wm. B. Eerdmans Publishing Co., 1955), 64.
2 Edwin H. Palmer, *the five points of calvinism* (Baker Books, enlarged ed., 20th prtg. 1999), 44.
3 John Calvin, *Institutes of the Christian Religion*, trans. Henry Beveridge (Wm. Eerdmans Publishing Company, 1998 ed.), III:xxi,5.
4 A.A. Hodge, *The Atonement* (Footstool Publishers, 1987), 348.
5 Loraine Boettner, *The Reformed Doctrine of Predestination* (Presbyterian and Reformed Publishing Co., 1932), 83-84.
6 D.A. Carson, *The Difficult Doctrine of the Love of God* (Crossway Books, 2000), 73.
7 Stanley Gower, in the first of "Two Attestations" to John Owen, Bk. 1 of *The Death of Death in the Death of Christ* (n.p., 1647); in *The Works of John Owen*, ed. William H. Goold (The Banner of Truth Trust, 3rd prtg. 1978), X:147.
8 R.C. Sproul, *Chosen by God* (Tyndale House Publishers, Inc., 1986), 207.
9 Gower, op. cit., in *Owen*, op. cit., IV:338.
10 Op. cit., I:149.
11 H.A. Ironside, *Timothy, Titus and Philemon* (Loizeaux Brothers, Inc., 1990), 55.
12 Calvin, op. cit., III: xi, 11.
13 John H. Gerstner, *Wrongly Dividing the Word of Truth: A Critique of Dispensationalism* (Wolgemuth and Hyatt, Publishers, Inc., 1991), 124.
14 Grover E. Gunn, *The Doctrine of Grace* (Footstool Publications), 1987, 17.
15 Cited in Laurence M. Vance, *The Other Side of Calvinism* (Vance Publications, Pensacola FL, rev. ed. 1999), 423.
16 David N. Steele and Curtis C. Thomas, *The Five Points of Calvinism* (Presbyterian and Reformed Publishing Co., 1963), 17.
17 Michael Scott Horton, *Putting Amazing Back Into Grace* (Thomas Nelson Publishers, 1991), 89.
18 Herman Hanko, *God's Everlasting Covenant of Grace* (Reformed Free Publishing Association, 1988), 15.
19 R.C. Sproul, *Grace Unknown* (Baker Books, 1997), 165.
20 Dave Breese, "The Five Points of Calvinism" (self-published paper, n.d.).
21 Leonard J. Coppes, *Are Five Points Enough? The Ten Points of Calvinism* (Denver CO: self-published, 1980), 49.
22 Homer Hoeksema, *Limited Atonement*, 151; cited in Vance, op. cit., 406.

23   Kenneth G. Talbot and W. Gary Crampton, *Calvinism, Hyper-Calvinism and Arminianism* (Still Waters Revival Books, 1990), 11.

24   Op. cit., 37.

25   Boettner, op. cit., 151.

26   Joseph M. Wilson, "How is the Atonement Limited?" (*The Baptist Examiner*, December 9, 1989).

27   Boettner, op. cit., 151.

28   Zane C. Hodges, "The New Puritanism, Pt. 3: Michael S. Horton: Holy War With Unholy Weapons" (*Journal of the Grace Evangelical Society,* Spring 1994), 7:12, 17-29.

29   Palmer, op. cit., 44-45.

30   W.J. Seaton, *The Five Points of Calvinism* (The Banner of Truth Trust, 1970), 15.

31   Palmer, op. cit., 44.

32   Cited in Vance, op. cit., 423.

33   Arthur W. Pink, *Gleanings in Exodus* (Moody Press, 1981), 84.

34   Vance, op. cit., 427.

35   Pink, op.cit., 88.

36   Palmer, op. cit., 50.

37   Owen, op. cit., 1:157-58.

38   John Piper and Pastoral Staff, "TULIP: What We Believe about the Five Points of Calvinism: Position Paper of the Pastoral Staff" (Desiring God Ministries, 1997), 16-17.

39   Op. cit., 14-15.

40   Boettner, op. cit., 150.

41   Op. cit., 155.

42   Palmer, op. cit., 42.

43   Piper and Staff, op. cit., 11.

44   Op. cit., 157.

45   Loraine Boettner, *Reformed Faith* (Presbyterian and Reformed Publishing Co., 1983), 14.

46   Wm. Oosterman, "Take a Long Look at the Doctrine of Election" (Ottawa, Canada: The Lord's Library Publications, n.d.), 17. Available from Westboro Baptist Church, Ottawa.

47   Gunn, op. cit., 17.

48   *Sermons of C.H. Spurgeon* (available from Pilgrim Publications, Pasadena TX, n.d.), 48:303.

49   James R. White, *The Potter's Freedom* (Calvary Press Publishing, 2000), 231.

50   George Zeller, cited in "For Whom Did Christ Die?" (The Middletown Bible Church, 349 East Street, Middletown CT 06457, 1999), 23-24.

51   John Calvin, *Calvin's New Testament Commentaries* (Wm. B. Eerdmans Publishing Co., 1994), III:139.

52   Augustus H. Strong, *Systematic Theology* (Judson Press, 1907), 778. For proof that this is an authentic quotation, see Vance, op. cit., 467-68.

53   Zeller, op. cit.

54   Cited in White, op. cit, 257.

55   Arthur W. Pink, *The Sovereignty of God* (Baker Book House, 2nd prtg. 1986), 20.

56   Sproul, *Chosen*, op. cit., 206.

57   Vance, op. cit., 435.

58   Richard Baxter, *Universal Redemption of Mankind* (London: n.p., 1694), 282-83.

59   Thomas R. Schreiner, "Does Scripture Teach Prevenient Grace in the Wesleyan Sense?", ed. Thomas R. Schreiner and Bruce A. Ware, *Still Sovereign: Contemporary Perspectives on Election, Foreknowledge, and Grace* (Baker Books, 2000), 240.

60   Piper and Staff, op. cit., 16.

61   White, op. cit., 273-74.

62   Op. cit., 274-75.

63   Piper and Staff, op. cit. 16.

64   Op. cit., 18.

65   To Dave Hunt, dated September 3, 2000. On file.

66   White, op.cit., 275.

17
Understanding Pivotal Scriptures

One of the major passages to which Calvinists look for support is Romans 9. R.C. Sproul declares that Romans 9:16 alone ("So then it is not of him that willeth, nor of him that runneth, but of God that sheweth mercy") "is absolutely fatal to Arminianism." [1] Remember, however, that we are not defending Arminianism, whose adherents also do not agree among themselves. We are simply testing TULIP by God's Word.

In Romans Chapter 9, Paul declares that God loved Jacob and hated Esau before either was born, "that the purpose of God according to election might stand" (9:11-13). Calvinists consider this to be one of the strongest passages proving that before birth all men are predestined either to heaven or to damnation.

Of this passage White writes, "it speaks of the inviolability of God's purpose in election and shows that His choices are not determined by anything in man [i.e., foreknowledge of an individual's eventual response to the gospel]." [2] Piper says that Jacob and Esau "were appointed for their respected [sic] destinies [for eternity] before they were born." [3] Hoeksema agrees: "We conclude, therefore, that the predestination of Jacob and Esau is a personal election and reprobation unto salvation and eternal desolation respectively." [4] On the contrary, that this is not the case is quite clear from a careful reading of this and related passages which Paul quotes in this same chapter.

In Romans 9:13 ("As it is written, Jacob have I loved, but Esau have I hated") Paul is quoting the prophet Malachi. Such a statement is "written" nowhere else in Scripture. Clearly as the entire book of Malachi testifies, the prophet is not referring to Jacob and Esau as individuals but to the nations which descended from them: "The . . . word of the LORD to Israel by Malachi. I have loved you . . . and I hated Esau, and laid his mountains and his heritage waste . . . . Edom saith . . . we will return . . . . They shall build, but I will throw down; and they shall call them . . . the people against whom the LORD hath indignation for ever . . . . I change not; therefore ye sons of Jacob are not consumed" (Malachi 1:1-4; 3:6). Quite clearly, Esau is Edom and Jacob is Israel.

Salvation Is Not The Subject

There is no reference in Malachi to the eternal salvation of either Jacob or Esau or their descendants, much less that one together with his descendants was predestined for heaven and the other with his descendants for hell. No verse in Malachi even implies this! Yet surely Paul's quotation of Malachi must carry over its original meaning and cannot be used to prove Calvinism's predestination and reprobation.

Furthermore, we know that many Israelites descended from Jacob were lost eternally; conversely, one cannot prove that every descendant of Esau is or will be in hell. Even Calvinists would not say that every Israelite belonged to the elect. For this reason as well, the topic could not possibly be salvation or reprobation.

Commenting on the reference to Esau and Jacob in Romans, Chapter 9, Broughton accurately stated, "Election is God choosing out a people through whom He is going to manifest Himself . . . . It is not an election to salvation, but an election to service . . . ." [5] In full agreement, Professor H.H. Rowley of the University of Manchester, England, declared, "Election is for service . . . . God chose Israel . . . not alone that He might reveal Himself to her, but that He might claim her for service." [6] Fisk comments, "Rowley, indeed, goes so far as to suggest that election is something which, if not fulfilled by the elect, may be withdrawn from them — a thought at which committed Calvinists would shudder." [7] Interestingly, this comment by Rowley was part of a series of lectures he gave at Spurgeon's College in London.

Nor does Paul, in the context of his quotation in Romans, even hint any more than does Malachi at the individual salvation of Esau, Jacob or Pharaoh. Yet what Paul says about these individuals is used by Calvinists to "prove" their peculiar doctrine of election and predestination unto salvation or damnation. Vance perceptively points out that "the basic error of Calvinism is confounding election and predestination with salvation, which they never are in the Bible, but only in the philosophical speculations and theological implications of Calvinism . . . ." [8] In fact, election and predestination always have to do with a particular purpose, ministry or blessing to which one has been elected — not salvation.

"Two Nations . . . And Two Manner Of People"

Since he is quoting Malachi and Genesis, it must follow that Paul likewise is not referring to the individuals named but to the nations descended from them. In fact, that the election and prophecy referred to nations rather than individuals was clear from the very start. During her pregnancy, as the twins "struggled together within her," God told Rebekah, "Two nations are in thy womb, and two manner of people . . . the one . . . shall be stronger . . . and the elder shall serve the younger" (Genesis 25:23). God's statement to Rebekah is definitive. If the *individuals* were in view, this would be a false prophesy because Esau never served his brother Jacob nor could it be said that Jacob was stronger than Esau during their respective lifetimes.

The prophecy was, however, perfectly fulfilled in the nations descended from Esau and Jacob. "Two nations" were unquestionably the subject of God's declaration. Yet Calvinists ignore that fact because it doesn't fit their theory and they go to great lengths to make it apply to individual salvation or reprobation. For example, in all his "proof" of election to salvation from Romans 9, White, like most Calvinists, never mentions Genesis 25:23. Is it possible that he overlooked it, or does he carefully avoid it?

Piper is almost as assiduous in his neglect of this decisive prophecy. He makes four oblique references to Genesis 25:23 but never exegetes it: 1) he quotes only "the elder shall serve the younger" but not the clear statement that two nations are involved; [9] 2) he mentions in a footnote ("Luther denies Erasmus' interpretation of both Gen 25:23 and Mal 1:2"), [10] but fails to cite this denial or to show its validity; 3) he quotes Shrenk's statement in opposition to his own and in agreement with what we are saying, "The reference here is not to salvation, but to position and historical task, cf. the quotation from Gen 25:23 in Rom 9:12: 'The elder shall serve the younger'," [11] but again there is no recognition of God's statement that He had nations in view; and 4) when he finally gives the full quote, he goes off on a tangent about how Israel became stronger than Edom and fails to make the obvious application to Romans 9: "The birth to Isaac and Rebecca of . . . Jacob and Esau was announced to Rebecca in Gen 25:23, 'Two nations are in your womb, and two peoples born of you shall be divided . . . the elder shall serve the younger.' How it became possible for Jacob and his descendants to gain the ascendancy over Esau and his descendants . . . is described in Gen 25:29-34 and Gen 27:18-29." [12] Piper goes on to discuss that aspect but gives no recognition whatsoever in his entire book of the import of two nations being the subject of God's original prophecy and of Malachi's confirmation thereof. To do so would undermine his entire thesis.

Luther, too, in the several pages dealing with these three passages, manages to avoid facing the full impact of the fact that, in both Genesis and Malachi, God is ultimately referring to nations within which not every individual is either saved or lost. Therefore he ignores the obvious consequences; i.e., that in quoting these passages Paul must have had nations in mind also. [13] While he mentions that "two peoples are clearly distinguished," [14] Luther insists upon applying it all to individual salvation, and from that conclusion continues his argument against free will.

The context and God's clear statements in Genesis 25 make it abundantly clear that the subject is not the eternal destiny of Esau and Jacob to heaven or to hell, but of the "manner of people" their descendants would be and how they would fit into God's purposes. Thus, in quoting Genesis 25:23, Paul could not be speaking of individual salvation either, but rather of God's election to a preferred position of blessing and usefulness. The indisputable fact that two future nations are the subject of God's prophecy to Rebecca completely undermines Piper's complex arguments, yet he continues on page after page in a futile attempt to prove that the salvation of individuals is Paul's topic in Romans 9. Dick Sanford writes:

> Circle that word, "*Serve.*" It's not saying, "*The elder shall be saved and the younger shall not be.*" Never mix the scripture that is talking about *service* with scripture that is talking about *salvation* . . . . Service includes works that are rewarded. Salvation is grace apart from works . . . .
>
> Here the Lord says that before they were ever born, He knew which one was going to be born first and . . . I am going to switch this *service* pattern . . . [and] the inheritance is going to come through the younger instead of the older. That is a reversal also . . . .
>
> *Jacob have I loved, but Esau have I hated.* Now it does not say, "*Jacob have I saved and said he can go to heaven and Esau have I lost and said can't go to heaven.*" That is *not* what God is saying . . . [but] *I told you that I'm going to work through Jacob, and that I haven't chosen to work through Esau* . . . the blessing is not going to come through Esau . . . the children of Esau are not going to lead up to the Messiah; it's the children of Jacob that are going to lead up to the Messiah. [15] (Emphasis in original)

What About The Individuals?

Other than the two references in Malachi and Romans, we are only told once that God loved Jacob (Psalms 47:4) and no comparison is made to Esau. Nor are we ever told throughout the entire account of his birth and life that God hated Esau. That statement only comes in Malachi and in Paul's quotation in Romans and as we have seen refers not so much to Esau as an individual but to the nation descended from him. Moreover, "loved" and "hated" are comparative terms in the Hebrew (as when Christ says we must hate father and mother in comparison to our love for Him - Matthew 10:37-38; Luke 14:26) and have nothing to do with salvation. As Forster and Marston point out,

Malachi 1:2 does not mean that in a literal hatred of Esau and his descendants God has condemned every one of them to hell. It has reference simply to the higher position of the Hebrew race in the strategy of God . . . . In the original to which Paul is referring, Esau is simply a synonym for Edom [clear from the context: Malachi 1:2-5] . . . . God's choice of Israel could not be a result of her merit or works . . . . [Paul's] introduction of the quotation from Malachi 1:2 is therefore of particular relevance here, and he uses it as he develops his theme . . . . [16]

Calvinists emphasize the statement, "For the children being not yet born, neither having done any good or evil, that the purpose of God according to election might stand, not of works, but of him that calleth . . . . " However, this statement is simply further proof that election is determined by foreknowledge. No one merits God's blessing, which is all of His grace — but that grace is given to those whom He foreknows will receive it.

Before these men were born, God knew that Jacob would hear His voice and turn to Him but that Esau would despise his birthright and reject God's grace and that his descendants would be the enemies of Israel. On that basis He hated Esau / Edom. If this were not the case, we would have God hating for no reason at all, which is contrary to all that the Bible tells us of the God who "*is love*." Furthermore, if that were the case it would render meaningless Christ's prophetic statement that "They hated me without a cause" (John 15:25).

In all of the references it is consistently more than clear that the election of Jacob and rejection of Esau had nothing to do with the salvation or damnation of either individual or of their descendants. For the Calvinist to use these passages to that end is simply faulty exegesis. Yet Palmer insists, "Thus, Romans 9 is clear in asserting that both election and preterition [passing over the non-elect] are unconditional . . . 'Jacob I loved, but Esau I hated.' " [17]

What About Pharaoh?

Pharaoh's case is more involved, but likewise has nothing to do with his eternal destiny. God knew in advance the evil, self-willed heart of this tyrant. That is in fact precisely why God raised him up at this particular time: "And in very deed for this cause have I raised thee up, for to shew in thee my power; and that my name may be declared throughout all the earth" (Exodus 9:16). God used Pharaoh's stubborn rebellion and desire for self-aggrandizement to fully judge all the gods of Egypt in the process of delivering His people from that pagan land.

God did not cause Pharaoh to sin (nor has He ever done so for anyone). Rather, He arranged circumstances and events to put this particular man, whose every quirk and wicked impulse He foreknew in detail, to be in authority at that particular time, in order to use his evil to fulfill His will. Is an act of that nature the kind of Calvinistic "sovereignty" to which we object? Not at all. We affirm as biblical and reasonable both God's ability and His sovereign right to arrange circumstances and to position on the stage of life those players whom He foreknows, so that His will is effected in human affairs — and to do so without violating their will or encouraging (much less becoming accessory to) their crimes.

Nor would God, for the many reasons already given, exercise His sovereignty to cause some and not others to believe and be saved. Having Pharaoh at the right place and time to fit into His plans for Israel and Egypt has nothing to do with any of the elements in TULIP that affect personal salvation. Nor did God either cause or override Pharaoh's moral choice in the process; He simply allowed Pharaoh's evil to run its course, even strengthening Pharaoh's evil resolve to the extent to which it fulfilled God's own purpose.

There is only one biblical explanation for God taking some to heaven and sending others to hell: Scripture declares that salvation is a genuine offer, that men may *choose* either to receive or to reject Christ, and that God in His omniscient foreknowledge knows how each person will respond. The only cogent *reason* consistent with God's character for election and predestination of the redeemed to certain blessings is God's omniscient foreknowledge of who would believe. Concerning this entire passage dealing with Esau, Jacob and Pharaoh, Ironside wrote:

> There is no question here of predestination to Heaven or reprobation to hell .
> . . . We are not told here, nor anywhere else, that before children are born it is
> God's purpose to send one to Heaven and another to hell . . . . The passage
> has to do entirely with privilege here on earth. [18]

Paul concludes this section by declaring that God, "to make his power known, endured with much longsuffering the vessels of wrath [such as Pharaoh] fitted to destruction" (Romans 9:22). Though *enduring* such vessels of wrath, God does not cause them to be or do evil. Rather, He sometimes elects to use those whose hearts are evil and endures their opposition and wickedness to the extent to which it fits into His will. In that way God is able to make the wrath of man to praise Him (Psalms 76:10). This is clearly presented by Paul in the example of Pharaoh.

"Whom He Will He Hardeneth"

In relation to Pharaoh, Romans 9:18 states, "Therefore hath he mercy on whom he will have mercy, and whom he will he hardeneth." Calvinists make a great deal of the statement that God hardened Pharaoh's heart, as though that proves Unconditional Election and Limited Atonement. On the contrary, the hardening of his heart had nothing to do with whether or not Pharaoh would go to heaven, but with God's use of Pharaoh at the time of Israel's deliverance from Egypt. God says His purpose was "that I might shew these my signs before him: and that thou mayest tell in the ears of thy son, and of thy son's son, what things I have wrought in Egypt, and my signs which I have done among them; that ye may know how that I am the LORD" (Exodus 10:1).

When God hardened Pharaoh's heart to further His purposes for Israel and Egypt, to manifest His power more fully, and specifically to complete His judgment upon the gods of Egypt, He was in fact only helping Pharaoh to do what that tyrant wanted to do. At the very outset, when He sent Moses to Egypt, God declared, "I am sure that the king of Egypt will not let you go . . . " (Exodus 3:19). This was Pharaoh's disposition from the very beginning before a word was said about God hardening his heart.

Yet Calvinists are almost unanimous in their avoidance of this scripture. Passing it by, they begin their comments with Exodus 4:21, "I will harden his heart, that he shall not let the people go." Like the others, Pink ignores 3:19 and writes, "did not God harden his heart *before* the plagues were sent upon Egypt? – see Exodus 4:21!" [19] White, too, avoids 3:19 and also uses 4:21 as foundational. [20] So does Piper. In building his lengthy argument concerning the hardening of Pharaoh's heart he relies heavily upon 4:21. His many pages of erudite citations of the original Hebrew and Greek with accompanying complicated arguments lose their luster in view of Piper's disregard of 3:19, which, had he noted it, would have changed the whole picture. [21]

One wonders why Piper flooded *The Justification of God* with Greek and Hebrew words in those alphabets without the English equivalents which authors usually supply. Thus his book can be fully understood only by Greek and Hebrew scholars, while other readers must take his word for what he says. What he has to say about the hardening of Pharaoh's heart is most interesting:

> A precise analysis of the verb forms (see table on pp. 159-160) reveals that before the first active assertion of God's hardening in Ex 9:12 there are two assertions that he [Pharaoh] hardened his own heart [כבד] and after 9:12 there are two assertions that he hardened his own heart [כבד andקשׁה]. What follows from this is that Pharaoh's "self-hardening" is equally well attested before *and after* the first statement that God has hardened him. From this it cannot be inferred that Pharaoh's "self-hardening" represents his prior independent sin for which God's hardening is the punishment. In view of the subsequent "self-hardenings" (9:34; 13:15) it is *just as probable* that "the hardening of man by God appears as self-hardening." [22] (Emphasis added)

Piper acknowledges that twice Pharaoh hardened his own heart both before and after "the first active assertion of God's hardening . . . ." Yet he can't accept the obvious consequences of this fact, so he draws an unreasonable conclusion. The best he is able to say, however, is that it is only "probable" that when we are told that Pharaoh hardened his own heart it was really God who did so. To bolster this shaky conclusion he bases everything upon 4:21 while ignoring entirely 3:19.

It is important to understand that "God did not give Pharaoh the wicked desire to rebel against him. What God did was to give him the courage to carry out that desire. Thus God's action merely made the difference between a wicked act and the suppression of an evil desire through fear." [23] Furthermore, there is nothing in the story to indicate that Pharaoh was unable to submit to God by a genuine response from his heart. Contradicting what he says elsewhere, and in a very un-Calvinistic statement that suggests free will, Calvin acknowledges that the ungodly *can* be moved to genuine repentance by God's warnings:

> Who does not now see that by threatenings of this kind [Jonah's prophecy of Nineveh's destruction, etc.], God wished to arouse those to repentance whom he terrified that they might escape the judgment which their sins deserved. [24]

In this case, however, through His foreknowledge God knew that Pharaoh, like Esau, would reject His will — just as He knew that Jacob would submit and obey (Genesis 28:7, 20-21; 32:9-11, 24-32; 49:28-33, etc.). Pharaoh was an evil man who had long abused the people of God. He selfishly desired to protect his own interests by keeping these people as slaves.

Nevertheless, the time came when the plagues were so terrifying that, contrary to what he wanted to do, Pharaoh was ready to let Israel go — not from genuine repentance, but out of abject fear of further plagues. Jahweh, however, had not finished judging the gods of Egypt. Therefore, He hardened Pharaoh's heart by giving him the courage to persist in the resistance he really wanted to pursue, and the courage to do so until God had fully executed His judgment upon Egypt's gods, bringing forth "the children of Israel, out of the land of Egypt by great judgments" (Exodus 7:4).

We gain a better understanding of God's dealings with Pharaoh through the Hebrew words translated "harden" or "hardened" in the King James. In the sense of hardening one's heart *kabed* is used four times: Exodus 7:14, 8:15, 9:7 and 9:34. *Qashah*, only used once (Exodus 7:3), means to become stiffnecked or stubborn. *Chazaq* (Exodus 4:21; 7:13,22; 8:15; 9:12,35; 10:20,27; 11:10; 14:4,8,17) means to strengthen or give courage, indicating that God was not causing Pharaoh to be an evil man or to do evil actions, but was giving Pharaoh the strength and courage, even when the plagues became overwhelmingly terrifying, to stand by his intent not to let Israel go. As Forster and Marston explain after an in-depth word study,

> The Bible does not teach that God made Pharaoh unrepentant. The main word used for the hardening of Pharaoh's heart is *chazaq*, and it seems to mean that God emboldened or encouraged Pharaoh's heart so that he had the stubborn courage to stand even in the face of very frightening miracles . . . . *God never*

prevents anyone from repenting. "Have I any pleasure in the death of the wicked? Says the Lord God: and not rather that he should return from his way and live?" [25] (Emphasis added)

The example of Pharaoh does not support the Calvinist view of Total Depravity. Far from it. If Pharaoh were totally depraved, why would God have to harden his heart? Piper says that four times Pharaoh hardened his own heart. Why even say so if he was by nature totally depraved and thus completely opposed to God? How could a totally depraved heart become harder than it already was?

Nor does it say that when Pharaoh at last let Israel go God caused him to do so with Irresistible Grace. He was simply terrified, and on that basis submitted to Jahweh's will (Exodus 12:30-33), but still without true repentance.

Clay, The Potter And Vessels Of Wrath

As Paul's final commentary (White calls it a "crescendo") [26] in this important passage, he declares that no one can complain against God for what He does because the clay has no right to demand of the potter, "Why hast thou made me thus? Hath not the potter power over the clay, of the same lump to make one vessel unto honour, and another unto dishonour? What if God, willing to . . . make his power known, endured with much longsuffering the vessels of wrath fitted to destruction: And that he might make known the riches of his glory on the vessels of mercy, which he had afore prepared unto glory, even us, whom he hath called, not of the Jews only, but also of the Gentiles?" (Romans 9:20-24). Calvinists rely heavily upon this scripture passage. In fact, White declares:

> The Potter's freedom pulses through these words, flowing inexorably into the sea of sovereignty, rushing any would-be proponent of free will out of its path. God has the perfect right to do with His creation (including men) as He wishes, just as the Potter has utter sovereignty over the clay . . . "vessels of wrath . . . . ." Are these nations . . . ? No, these are *sinners* upon whom God's wrath comes. They are said to have been specifically "prepared for destruction." That is their *purpose.* [27] (Emphasis in original)

That God the Potter (1) has the right to do with men as He pleases, and (2) endures with much longsuffering the vessels of wrath we do not deny. That is all, however, that this passage tells us — it does not tell us what His desire is. Numerous other passages, however, do tell us in the clearest terms that God desires all to come to repentance and the knowledge of the truth, that He is not willing that any should perish and takes no pleasure in the death of the wicked. We have cited these passages already.

There is *nothing* in Romans 9:20-24 to indicate that God the Potter causes anyone to be or do evil. Much less does this passage prove, as Calvinists claim, that God predestines some to heaven and others to hell. Paul is referring to God's use of the innate evil of wicked men such as Esau and Pharaoh, when it suits His purpose, to fulfill His will. In so doing, He endures "the contradiction of sinners" (Hebrews 12:3). Nor does the fact that God brings these vessels of wrath to the destruction they deserve prove that this is His will for them or that they have no choice, much less that they were predestined to destruction.

The Calvinist says God *could* through Irresistible Grace *cause* all mankind to believe in Christ and obey Him. If that be true, then the fact that He does not do so runs counter to all that the Bible says of His lovingkindness, mercy and grace. There is no explanation for this glaring contradiction: the Calvinist is forced to plead "mystery." In contrast, we believe that God has given men the power of choice. Therefore, to force Irresistible Grace upon them would itself contradict that gift. God violates no one's will. Granted, He could have been gracious and suppressed the wickedness of Pharaoh and Judas had it suited His plans — but that would not have changed either their hearts or eternal destiny. As for these "vessels unto dishonor . . . fitted to destruction," however, He chose instead to strengthen their resolve to wickedness in order to effect His will. He did not cause them to choose evil, He used their wicked choice for His own purposes and in so doing "endured" their rebellion.

Herman Hoeksema claims that the example of the Potter teaches "God's absolute sovereignty to determine the final destiny of men, either to honor or dishonor, to salvation and glory or to damnation and desolation." [28] Likewise Piper says, "It is clear that Paul still has in mind the issue of unconditional election [to salvation or damnation] raised in Romans 9:6-13." [29] We have just given a different explanation which is both a reasonable exegesis and is in agreement with God's character of love and justice. Paul is not at all dealing with the eternal destiny of Esau, Jacob and Pharaoh.

John 3:16-17 Revisited

If there is one Bible verse which every child who ever attended an evangelical Sunday school is sure to know, that verse is John 3:16. What child encountering this verse for the first time without a Calvinist teacher would conclude that "world" did not mean the whole world of mankind but a limited number of individuals chosen by God? The answer is obvious.

Calvin himself, in his commentary on John 3:16, stated that "world" included "all men without exception." Luther also said it meant "the entire human race." But White, realizing that such an admission does away with Limited Atonement, manages a desperate end run around John 3:16. He suggests that sound exegesis requires "that whosoever believeth on him should not perish" actually means "in order that everyone believing in him should not perish . . . ." [30] That slight twist allows White to suggest that Calvinism's elect *alone* believe and thus Christ died only for them. Even if that were true, Calvinism would still have to explain (in view of its insistence that men must be born again before God can give them faith) how belief can precede receiving eternal life. That question will be considered under Irresistible Grace.

Like most other apologists for Calvinism, White doesn't even attempt to deal with the unequivocal statement in John 3:17 "that the world through him might be saved" (to which his explanation of John 3:16 couldn't possibly apply). Obviously, this further comment by Christ explains the meaning of the entire section (John 3:14-18) pertaining to His death on the cross, making it very clear that God gave His Son for the salvation of the entire world. Nor does White quote Calvin or anyone else concerning John 3:17. None of the thirteen contributors to *Still Sovereign* touches it.

Of course, White's interpretation of John 3:16 must agree with his argument, dealt with in our previous chapter, that 1 John 2:2 couldn't possibly mean "that Christ's death is a satisfaction for the whole world." He justifies that view by the fact that John goes on to tell us "*not to love the world!*" [31] How does the fact that we are not to love the world prove that Christ did not die for the sins of the whole world? Obviously, John is using "world" in two different ways: the *people* of the world, and the world *system*.

Recognizing that fact, White rightly declares that in 1 John 2:15 "world" means "the *present evil system,* not the universal population of mankind." (Emphasis in original) White is now caught in a web of his own making. If the fact that "world" in verse 15 means "the present evil system" refutes the belief that in verse 2 it means all the people in the world, why would it not also refute White's view that it means "all Christians throughout the world . . . at all times and in all places"? [32] There is no way to escape the straightforward meaning: in 1 John 2:2, "world" simply means all mankind.

Christ Died For All

The scriptures which declare that Christ died to save all mankind are so numerous that only a few can be presented. In scriptures such as "For the Son of man is come to seek and to save that which was lost" (Luke 19:10), "Christ died for the ungodly" (Romans 5:6), and "Christ Jesus came into the world to save sinners" (1 Timothy 1:15), there is no suggestion that only a certain *elect* group among the "lost . . . ungodly . . . [and] sinners" is intended. There is simply no qualifier.

Surely the idea that such general language actually specifies a select "elect" would never be imagined without previous indoctrination into that particular system of thought. Amazingly, however, White sees in such verses "the particularity that is so vehemently denied by the Arminian." [33]

White argues, "Is it not the message of the Bible that Christ *saves* sinners? By what warrant do we . . . change the meaning to 'wants to save' . . . ?" We, too, could ask White, "What is the justification for changing 'sinners' to '*some* sinners'?" He then quotes Paul's declaration, "I am crucified with Christ . . . the Son of God, who loved me, and gave himself for me" (Galatians 2:20), as proof that "sinners" and "ungodly, et al. mean *particular* sinners. [34] On the contrary, Paul is giving a *personal* testimony of his own faith in Christ; it cannot be used to place a limitation upon general nouns used elsewhere. Nor does he say, "I alone . . . for me alone." Every person who has the same relationship with Christ as Paul did can make the same statement: "the Son of God, who loved *me*, and gave himself for *me*," but that does not mean He doesn't love the world and didn't die for all.

It is only to be expected that at times the inspired writers of Scripture specifically applied what they said to those who were saved: "the LORD hath laid on him the iniquity of *us* all . . . Christ died for *our* sins . . . that *we* might be made the righteousness of God in him . . . who gave himself for *our* sins . . . hast redeemed *us* to God by thy blood" (Isaiah 53:6; 1 Corinthians 15:3; 2 Corinthians 5:21; Galatians 1:4; Revelation 5:9, etc.). That fact does not in any way nullify the many verses which just as clearly say that Christ died for *all.*

Paul could not declare more clearly that Christ's purpose in coming into the world was to save sinners. That all sinners are not saved is not because Christ did not pay for their sins but because all do not accept that payment. White argues that because all sinners don't get saved, this verse must therefore mean that the "sinners" Christ came to save could only be the elect among sinners.

To sustain that argument, however, one would have to change the meaning of hundreds of other Bible verses as well. Jesus himself declared, " . . . I am not come to call the righteous, but sinners to repentance" (Matthew 9:13). Again, all sinners do not repent, so the Calvinist is compelled to say that Christ only calls *some* sinners to repentance, or else His call is in vain. How could one perceive that meaning in this statement by Christ? Only Calvinists find it there – and only because Calvinism requires it. But it doesn't follow, because even the elect who do repent often fail to do so as thoroughly as they should – so to whatever extent they fail to give full honor and glory and obedience to God, are they not frustrating God's purposes just as surely as the non-elect are said to do by rejecting the gospel?

Repeatedly the Bible states that God desires to rescue and bless all Israel and that her refusal to repent prevents Him from so doing. He sends His prophets day and night to plead with Israel to repent so He won't have to punish her. It simply cannot reasonably be said that God only wants *some* of Israel to repent. Many other examples could be given of God's desire for man remaining unfulfilled because of man's rejection of His will.

"All Men" Means *Classes* Of Men?

Nothing could be clearer in refuting Limited Atonement than Paul's declaration, "who will have all men to be saved, and to come unto the knowledge of the truth" (1 Timothy 2:4). In trying to handle this passage Piper contradicts himself. He confesses that Paul is saying that "God does not delight in the perishing of the impenitent and that he has compassion on all people." Admitting that this sounds like "double talk," he sets out to show that there are " 'two wills' in God . . . that God decrees one state of affairs while also willing and teaching that a different state of affairs should come to pass." [35] This *is* double talk.

White also attempts to get around this passage. He refers to other passages wherein the expression "all men" isn't to be taken literally, such as Ananias's statement to Paul at his conversion, "For thou shalt be his witness unto all men . . . " (Acts 22:15). White insists:

> Of course, Paul would not think that these words meant that he would witness of Christ to every single individual human being on the planet. Instead, he would have surely understood this to mean all *kinds* and *races* of men . . . . Paul speaks of *kinds* of people in other places as well . . . Greek and Jew, circumcised and uncircumcised, barbarian, Scythian, slave and freeman . . . .
>
> So it is perfectly consistent with the immediate and broader context of Paul's writings to recognize this use of "all men" in a generic fashion. [36]

On the contrary, Paul would never have understood Ananias to mean *kinds* and *races* of men. Then it would mean *all* kinds and races. Japanese? Australian aborigines? Siberian or North American Indians? If that is what Ananias meant, he was a false prophet. There were surely many kinds and races of men to whom Paul never did witness.

What would any of us understand such a statement addressed to ourselves to mean? Not all men everywhere, but all those with whom we would come in contact. But what does White's strained interpretation of a statement by Ananias have to do with Paul's clear declaration that God wants "all men to be saved"?

White argues further that because Paul says prayer is to be made "for all men; for kings and for all that are in authority," he is referring to "classes of men" and that therefore the following phrase, "who will have all men to be saved," actually means "who will have *all classes of men* to be saved." [37] In fact, "kings . . . and all in authority" only refers to one class of men, that is rulers. White is only echoing Calvin here: "For the apostle's meaning here is simply that . . . God regards all men as being equally worthy to share in salvation.

But he is speaking of classes and not of individuals, and his only concern is to include princes and foreign nations in this number." [38]

The Calvinist is struggling hard to maintain his theory. Piper grasps at the same straw: "It is possible that careful exegesis of 1 Timothy 2:4 would lead us to believe that 'God's willing all persons to be saved' does not refer to every individual person in the world, but rather to all *sorts* of persons . . . ." [39] The "careful exegesis" he suggests would support this idea is never revealed.

Calvinists love to quote Spurgeon for support, but here he accuses them (as we do) of altering the plain meaning of the text. In C.H. Spurgeon, *Metropolitan Tabernacle Pulpit*, volume 26, pages 49-52, the great preacher discusses this passage of Scripture in depth:

> What then? Shall we try to put another meaning into the text than that which it fairly bears? I trow not . . . .. You must, most of you, be acquainted with the general method in which our older Calvinistic friends deal with this text. "All men" say they "that is, some men": as if the Holy Ghost could not have said "some men" if He meant some men. "All men," say they: "that is, some of all sorts of men": as if the Lord could not have said, "All sorts of men" if He had meant that. The Holy Ghost by the apostle has written, "All men," and unquestionably he means all men . . . .. My love of consistency with my own doctrinal views is not great enough to allow me knowingly to alter a single text of Scripture.

With Spurgeon we ask again, if all *classes* is what the Holy Spirit meant to convey, why was it not stated clearly? The truth is that the Holy Spirit did very clearly declare in unequivocal language that God is not willing for any person to perish — and we are tampering with God's Word by putting a Calvinist interpretation upon it!

"Kings and all that are in authority" are mentioned as special subjects of prayer and the reason is given "that we may lead a quiet and peaceable life . . .." Can anyone seriously imagine that Paul urged prayer for kings and those in authority in order to convey to Timothy (and to us today) that *all classes of men* were meant to be the recipients of the gospel: tradesmen, sheep herders, soldiers, tinkers, tailors, robbers, etc.?

Wouldn't Paul be fearful that unless he specifically mentioned them all, some despised classes such as prostitutes or slaves might be overlooked by Timothy and by us today? No, he would not, and that is why this effort falls short. Christ already told His disciples of all ages to "preach the gospel to every creature"! That Christ means *everyone* every Christian knew then and knows now.

As for 1 Timothy 2:6 ("who gave himself a ransom for all"), White quotes R.K. Wright's reference to "the meticulous demonstration by John Gill that the Arminian exegesis of key passages (such as 2 Peter 3:9 and 1 Timothy 2:4-6) is fallacious." [40] Yet he fails to give us Gill's alleged meticulous refutation.

Concerning 1 Timothy 4:10 ("who is the Saviour of all men"), here is another scripture which states beyond doubt that Christ died for all, yet White again has nothing to say about it. He then tells us that Norm Geisler, in his book *Chosen But Free*, misinterprets John 17:9 because he also misinterprets 1 Timothy 2:4-6 and 2 Peter 3:9. [41] No explanation. We are left to guess why we shouldn't understand the "all" in 1 Timothy 2:6 to mean "all," as one would reasonably expect from the context.

Christ "Tasted Death For Every Man"

Hebrews 2:9 ("that he by the grace of God should taste death for every man") is given the by now familiar Calvinist interpretation. Verse 17 is quoted: "made like His brethren . . . a merciful and faithful high priest . . . to make propitiation for the sins of the people." White then "explains":

> What "people" is here in view? It is the "many sons" of 2:10, those He "sanctifies" (2:11), "My brethren" (2:12), "the children God gave Me" (2:13). . . . In light of this we understand the statement of Hebrews 2:9, "so that by the grace of God He might taste death for everyone." Another passage often cited without context by Arminians yet defined so plainly in the text. [42]

That is it. One is left to assume that because a few verses following Hebrews 2:9 refer to Christ's brethren given to Him by God through His sacrifice, the phrase "taste death for every man" must therefore mean He tasted death only for the elect. Undoubtedly the entire epistle is addressed to believers, as are all epistles and the entire Bible — though multitudes of unbelievers have come to faith in Christ through reading the Bible. Moreover, the Bible has a great deal to say both to and about the unsaved. Obviously, the Holy Spirit can make reference to unbelievers at any time, explaining to those whom He addresses what God has done and will do to and for unbelievers. In fact, such is often the case throughout Scripture.

Without context? Let us consider the context. Within the immediate context it is clear that even when the writer uses "we" he doesn't always refer only to believers but includes all mankind: "How shall we escape, if we neglect so great salvation . . . ?" (Hebrews 2:3). Surely this is addressed to all mankind, not just to the elect, unless the Calvinist is willing to admit that it is possible for the elect to neglect their salvation and thus to be lost. That solemn admonition introduces this entire section of Hebrews 2, which continues in the same vein into Chapters 3 and 4. Readers are given numerous warnings and exhortations to hold fast to the faith and not to harden their hearts lest they perish like the children of Israel perished in the wilderness through unbelief.

All of Israel was not saved and many perished, so Israel could hardly signify the Calvinist elect. The entire context surrounding Hebrews 2:9 contains some of the strongest verses Arminians cite to prove that one's salvation can be lost, including the following:

> Today if ye will hear his voice, harden not your hearts . . . . (Hebrews 3:7-8)

> Take heed, brethren, lest there be in any of you an evil heart of unbelief, in departing from the living God. (Hebrews 3:12)

> For we are made partakers of Christ, if we hold the beginning of our confidence stedfast unto the end . . . . (Hebrews 3:14)

> Let us therefore fear, lest, a promise being left us of entering into his rest, any of you should seem to come short of it. (Hebrews 4:1)

> . . . they to whom it [the gospel] was first preached entered not in because of unbelief. (Hebrews 4:6)

Oddly enough, in his book written to refute Arminianism and to defend Calvinism, White completely avoids these verses, which make up the entire context of Hebrews 2:9. And he does so in the process of chiding Arminians for avoiding the *context*!

Another important passage among those we cite above and referred to briefly in the last chapter is 2 Peter 2:1 ("there shall be false teachers . . . denying the Lord that bought them"). It seems to say that even those who are lost have been "bought" with the blood of Christ. Those referred to here by Peter have obviously professed faith in Christ and though within the church were never saved like those to whom Jude refers who have "crept in unawares, . . . ungodly men . . . ordained to this condemnation" (Jude 4). Yet Peter says that the Lord had bought them. This passage, too, is completely neglected by White, nor is he alone in his silence.

Very few Calvinists have attempted to deal with scriptures such as Hebrews 10:29 and 2 Peter 2:1. They tell of the destruction upon those who despise the "blood of the covenant wherewith [they were] sanctified" and "despise the Lord that bought them . . . ." No arguments have been proposed upon which all Calvinists agree, and their efforts have failed. Vance cites most of those who have made such attempts:

> Charles Bronson insists that it "approaches blasphemy to say that Christ shed His precious blood for some and then, after all, they perished in Hell." [43] Dabney dismisses both verses because: "The language of Peter, and that of Hebrews . . . may receive an entirely adequate solution, without teaching that Christ actually "bought" or "sanctified" any apostate, by saying that the Apostles speak there "*ad hominem*." [44] But because of the diversity of interpretations put on these verses by Calvinists in their attempt to evade the clear teaching of Scripture, they cannot be disregarded so easily.

Concerning those who were sanctified in Hebrews 10:29, Calvinists try to get around the obvious implications in a variety of ways. Beck claims they were "sanctified, but not saved." [45] Gill maintains that Christ Himself "is said here to be *sanctified*." [46] Owen makes them [mere] "professors . . . of the gospel," and adds the phrase "in the profession of the gospel" after "sanctified." [47] Other than a few isolated comments, Calvinists are strangely silent (Pink does not comment on this verse [Hebrews 10:29] in his books, *The Sovereignty of God, Sanctification* or his Hebrews commentary) on this passage. The context of the verse, however, is *"if we sin wilfully after that we have received the knowledge of the truth"*(Hebrews 10:26) and *"the Lord shall judge his people"* Hebrews 10:30). [48]

Understanding 2 Peter 3:9

With regard to 2 Peter 3:9, however, White has several references. The first repeats the statement about John Gill's amazing but unrevealed refutation. [49] The next two suggest that the "Reformed view" of this passage may be "a more consistent interpretation" than the one Geisler offers, but he fails to give us this "more consistent interpretation." [50] The next promises that "an exegetical interpretation of the passage" is coming. [51] Next we are told that Geisler fails to give "as meaningful and thorough a discussion" of the passage as "the Reformed exegesis" — yet neither Geisler's nor the "Reformed exegesis" is explained. [52]

Finally, we are given the Calvinistic interpretation of "The Lord is not slack . . . but is longsuffering to us-ward, not willing that any should perish, but that all should come to repentance." White declares that "the passage is not speaking about salvation as its topic." On that basis he summarily rules out the possibility that Peter means what the words he uses so clearly declare.

In fact, the passage speaks of a number of things: the last days; scoffers who would arise ridiculing the idea that Christ would return in judgment; a reminder of the flood that destroyed the world of that day and that the present world will be destroyed by fire; the fact that the Day of the Lord will come like a thief; that the entire universe will be dissolved; that we therefore ought to live godly lives; that unstable and unlearned persons twist the meaning of Paul's epistles; and finally there is an exhortation to keep from error and to "grow in grace and in the knowledge of our Lord and Saviour Jesus Christ."

Since Peter deals with so much in this final chapter of his epistle, there is no reason salvation could not be included. Nor can anyone insist that Peter cannot address both saved and unsaved in the same verse. If he does not, we have a serious contradiction. The phrase "longsuffering to us-ward" is surely directed to the elect. But it could as well be an editorial expression including all mankind. If not, the phrase which follows ("not willing that any should perish") must also apply only to the elect. But the latter can *only* mean all of mankind, since it refers to a perishing which surely does not imperil the elect.

There are only two possibilities: the reference is to 1) perishing under the penalty of sin or escaping that penalty by repenting; or 2) perishing in the fire that will destroy the world or escaping it. Certainly, perishing in the world-destroying fire of God's judgment is no more applicable to the elect than perishing under the penalty of sin. John Owen argued, "See, then, of whom the apostle is here speaking . . . . Such as had received 'great and precious promises' . . . whom he calls 'beloved' . . . . The text is clear, that it is all and only the elect whom he would not have to perish." [53] Likewise, John Gill writes, "It is not true that God is not willing that any one individual of the human race should perish, since he has made and appointed the wicked for the day of evil . . . . Nor is it his will that all men...should come to repentance, since he withholds from many both the means and grace of repentance . . . ." [54]

On the other hand, John Murray, former Westminster Seminary professor, whom Cornelius Van Til called "a great exegete of the Word of God," [55] declared, "God does not wish that any men should perish. His wish is rather that all should enter upon life eternal by coming to repentance. The language in this part of the verse is so absolute that it is highly unnatural to envisage Peter as meaning merely that God does not wish that any believers should perish...." [56] Writing in the second century, Justin Martyr suggests that God is delaying the Last Judgment because "in His foreknowledge He sees that some will be saved by repentance, some who are, perhaps not yet in existence." [57]

Are The Elect In Danger Of Perishing?

Let us assume that White is right and the subject is not salvation. "Perish," therefore, must refer to perishing in the fire of God's judgment that will, in the Day of the Lord, destroy the universe. That certainly is a valid possibility for unbelievers, but White claims the "any" and "all" refer to the elect. Now we have a new problem: how could there be any danger that the elect might perish in the final fire of God's judgment — and how would His longsuffering toward them prevent such an end?

White argues that since the epistle is addressed to believers (we agree) it can only have reference to believers throughout. One of the many letters received on this subject makes the same point: "As in all of the epistles, 2 Peter is addressed to the *elect* . . . Peter is not speaking to mankind in general here . . . ." [58] We have shown, logically and biblically, that this argument, used frequently by Calvinists in other instances as well, is unfounded. The fact that believers are being addressed is no reason that Peter cannot make a statement to believers about God's desire for the whole world, including the fate of unbelievers.

While Peter is not speaking *to* mankind in general, but only *to* the elect, he is certainly not speaking only *about* the elect. Is it the elect who will be the last-days scoffers? Was it the elect who perished in the flood? Is it the elect who will perish in the coming fire which will destroy the world and the entire universe? Surely not. Nor could those to whom God is longsuffering lest they perish in coming judgment be the elect.

Moreover, salvation is undoubtedly the topic of at least this verse, since it refers to the repentance which God desires for all; and surely a repentance unto salvation is the only means of deliverance from the wrath to come. But the elect, being already saved, don't need to repent unto salvation, so how could "*any* should perish . . . *all* should come to repentance" refer to them?

Furthermore, the doctrine of Irresistible Grace claims that God can cause anyone to repent and believe the gospel at any time — so why would longsuffering be mentioned if reference is to the elect? Whether the subject is salvation or not, Calvinism is in trouble. In spite of the contradictions we have just pointed out, the only escape is to insist that this does not refer to all mankind but only to the elect. Now we are faced with one more redundancy: God is not willing that any of those He has sovereignly elected not to perish should perish! And He is longsuffering to accomplish that goal? Such arguments are not sustainable.

The only consistent understanding of this verse is that the "us-ward" in the phrase "longsuffering to us-ward" is like an editorial "we" that includes everyone. It is true that in the only other place this expression is found in the New Testament, it clearly refers to those who are the saved. That fact, however, does not restrict the way it could be used in this particular instance. One use doesn't make a rule. "Us-ward" introduces the statements about "longsuffering" and "perish," which could only apply to the world at large.

Peter is referring to the destruction of the universe from which the elect have been delivered. The ungodly are the ones who will perish, and the only consistent understanding of the verse is that God does not want *anyone* to perish, and, as He has done with Israel, is longsuffering in pleading with them and waiting upon them to repent and be saved. This understanding is also consistent with the whole tenor of Scripture, as we are repeatedly reminded.

What About 1 Timothy 4:10?

Though all key passages cannot be covered, some further attention must be given to Paul's declaration that Christ "is the Saviour of all men, specially of those that believe." Surely "those that believe" must be the elect for whom Christ is the Saviour in a *special* way not true of "all men" in general. Thus "all men" can't possibly mean the elect. White omits reference to this passage, as do other Calvinists.

There are, of course, similar contrasts made elsewhere in Scripture. Paul exhorts prayer "for all men . . . that we may lead a quiet and peaceable life . . .

" (1 Timothy 2:1-2). Surely the "we" who are to pray must be the elect, and the "all men" must be someone else. Again Paul writes, "Let us do good unto all men, especially unto . . . the household of faith" (Galatians 6:10). The elect must be the household of faith, again set in contrast to "all men."

Here also the Calvinist adopts astonishing reasoning in order to escape the plain teaching of Scripture. Gary North explains that "Christ is indeed the Savior of all people prior to the day of judgment." [59] "Savior" in what way? Calvin is no less audacious in his claim that Savior simply means that Christ shows "kindness" to all men. [60] Where is "Savior" ever used to signify "kindness"? And what kindness would bless in this life and damn for eternity?

Calvin adds that by "Savior" the passage only means, for the non-elect, that Christ "guards and preserves." [61] Pink and Beck declare, somewhat like Calvin, that "Savior of all men" simply means that Christ is the "Preserver" of all men.

Really? In what way does God "preserve" those whom He has predestined to eternal damnation? And how is Christ "the Savior of all people prior to the day of judgment"? North doesn't explain, nor can he. And what could be meant by God's "kindness" to those He predestined before their birth to suffer eternally and from whom He withholds the salvation He could give to all? "Kindness" for the fleeting moments of time, then eternal damnation, could hardly be kindness at all! We are offended for our God at such boldness in rewriting His Word!

Grasping At Straws

The final verse listed above, among those disproving Limited Atonement, is 1 John 4:14: "the Father sent the Son to be the Saviour of the world." This is just one more scripture which White avoids, just as he avoids John 3:17 and so many others. Instead, in further attempt to prove Limited Atonement, attention is focused upon those passages which clearly refer to the blessings God has planned for His elect.

It is only to be expected that Paul and other inspired writers of Scripture would remind the redeemed that Christ died for them and that the Father delivered Christ to the cross for the sake of the elect. Such passages, however, as we have seen, do not in any way imply, much less declare, that Christ's death was *only* for them and not also for the sins of the whole world. If so, these passages would contradict the many others which declare in the plainest language that Christ did indeed die for all. But these are the only places to which the Calvinist can turn in positive support of his argument. Thus White tells us:

The Father did not spare, or hold back, His very own Son, but delivered Him over *for us all* [Romans 8:32]. The word "delivered over" refers to the giving of the Son in sacrifice. The [same] Greek word is used in this context by Paul, as in Ephesians 5:2 (where Christ gives Himself up *for us*), and 5:25 (where

Christ gives Himself *for the Church*). It is also used in Matthew 27:26 of the delivering up of Jesus to be crucified. The Father delivered over the Son to die upon the cross *for us* . . . . The Father gave the Son *in our place*, in the place of His *elect people*.

In light of the tremendous price paid for our redemption in Christ, Paul then asks, "how will He (the Father) not also with Him (Christ) freely give us all things?" To whom is Paul speaking? God's elect. Surely these words could not be spoken of every single human for two reasons: Christ is not "given" to the person who endures God's wrath in eternity, and, God obviously does not give "all things" to those who spend eternity in hell . . . this is an empty passage [if it] says God *offers* all things, but very few actually *obtain* them. No, it is clear: God gives "all things" to those for whom He gave His Son as a sacrifice. That sacrifice was *for them;* it was made in their place. (Emphasis in original) [62]

Clearly such passages as these have nothing to do with offering salvation to the world and therefore do not contradict the clear biblical teaching in many other places that Christ indeed died for all and that salvation is offered to all. That the elect should praise God for giving Christ to die for them (and that the Bible specifically reminds the elect of what Christ has done for them) does not in any way mean that Christ died *only* for them.

That some grasp at such straws only exposes the bankruptcy of their theory. If the fact that the redeemed are grateful to Christ for dying for their sins proves that He died *only* for them, then the same argument would establish that Christ loved *only* Paul and died *only* for him. After all, Paul gratefully declares, "*I* am crucified with Christ . . . the Son of God, who loved *me*, and gave himself for *me*" (Galatians 2:20).

God's Infinite Love

Limited Atonement simply cannot be supported from the Bible without avoiding many passages and adopting special interpretations for many others. Calvinists' arguments about the blood of Christ being wasted if shed for many who would not believe are specious. Then God wasted His time and the time and effort of His prophets who called, without success, upon millions of Jews for centuries to repent. From the cross Christ cried, "Father, forgive them" concerning those who were crucifying and mocking Him. Was He wasting His breath, since many if not most of those taunting and crucifying Him would never repent and thus not be forgiven? And how could He ask His Father to forgive them except on the basis of His blood, shed for sin?

Paul says concerning those who have rejected and crucified Christ, "My heart's desire and prayer to God for Israel, is that they might be saved" (Romans 10:1). In evident agony of soul he writes, "I say the truth in Christ, . . . I have great heaviness and continual sorrow in my heart . . . for my brethren, my kinsmen according to the flesh" (Romans 9:1-3). He even wishes himself accursed of God if that would save the Jews. Surely it is God's love for the lost which moves Paul to this extent. Yet Calvinism insists that God, who *is love,* willingly lets billions go to hell, while Paul, who surely is in touch with God, agonizes for their salvation! On the contrary, we are told that God desires "all men to be saved . . . "! Rob Zins writes to this author:

> Finally, you raise some philosophical problems with the *demand* of God that all men everywhere should repent and believe and the corresponding *will* of God which has determined that only some will be given the ability to do so. This is a difficult issue to face. But it is no more difficult to face than all men being condemned by the sin of one man, Adam. It is no more difficult to face than the fact of sin, corruption, evil and all other forms of sin *allowed* to continue when God could end them all. [63]

As already noted, God could end all evil only by destroying all men because all continue to sin. Even "saved sinners" continue to sin (1 John 1:9). But He is longsuffering, calling upon men to repent, turn to Him and receive the salvation He offers. There is no lack of love on God's part. Even though all have become sinners through Adam and are thus condemned, God has provided salvation and made it available to all who will believe. He cannot force it upon anyone without destroying man as a moral agent capable of loving and being loved. The problem is with Calvinism's claim that God *could save* everyone but refuses to do so because it is His "good pleasure" to damn multitudes.

Continually in Scripture, Christ and men of God from Moses to Paul expressed a fervent desire for the salvation of sinners. Obviously, not all are going to believe, yet the desire is sincerely expressed that they would do so. Calvinists change the straightforward language of such scriptures, even denying that God loves *all* in spite of the numerous clear statements that He does.

Yes, Christ in His prayer to the Father for His own says, "I pray not for the world" (John 17:9). That does not, however, nullify the Father's and Christ's love for the world, nor does it nullify the fact that He died for the sins of the whole world. He is merely setting forth the parameters and purpose of His prayer. He is declaring that the unity and blessing and separation from the world for which He prays and to which the elect have been predestined do not apply to those who will reject Him but only to those who will believe. Christ does not say that He doesn't want all to believe. *Never* does the Bible say that! Rather, He knows who will believe and who won't because He knows all and is praying for the former.

Unquestionably, there are difficult verses dealing with the whole subject of our salvation. They must be interpreted in the context of all of Scripture. And a major part of the context is the person of God himself. In the final analysis what we believe about God will determine our understanding of God's Holy Word.

The God of the Bible *is love*, His tender mercies are over all His works, He doesn't want anyone to be lost, and He so loved the world that He gave Christ to pay the penalty of sin for every man. Therefore, grace could not be irresistible or all would be saved — the subject to which we now come.

1   Cited in James White, *The Potter's Freedom* (Calvary Press Publishing, 2000), 222.
2   Op. cit., 215.
3   John Piper, *The Justification of God: An Exegetical and Theological Study of Romans 9:1-23* (Baker Books, 2000), 203-204.
4   Herman Hoeksema, *God's Eternal Good Pleasure*, ed. and rev., Homer C. Hoeksema (Reformed Free Publishing Association, 1979), 24.
5   Len G. Broughton, *Salvation and the Old Theology* (Hodder and Stoughton, n.d.), 152.
6   H.H. Rowley, *The Biblical Doctrine of Election* (Lutterworth Press, 1952), 45.
7   Samuel Fisk, *Calvinistic Paths Retraced* (Biblical Evangelism Press, 1985), 81.
8   Laurence M. Vance, *The Other Side of Calvinism* (Vance Publications, Pensacola FL, rev. ed. 1999), 35.
9   Piper, op. cit., 51.
10   Op. cit., 56.
11   Op. cit., 57.
12   Op. cit., 61-62.
13   Martin Luther, *The Bondage of the Will*, trans. J.I. Packer and O.R. Johnston (Fleming H. Revell, 1957, 11th prtg. 1999), 222-29.
14   Op. cit., 225.
15   Dick Sanford, *Predestination and Election*, ed. John R. Cross (self-published monograph, n.d.), 11-12.
16   Roger T. Forster and V. Paul Marston, *God's Strategy in Human History* (Bethany House Publishers, 1973), 75.
17   Edwin H. Palmer, *the five points of calvinism* (Baker Books, enlarged ed., 20th prtg. 1999), 32-34, 105.
18   H.A. Ironside, *Lectures on the Epistle to the Romans* (Loizeaux Brothers, 1926), 110, 116.
19   Arthur W. Pink, *The Sovereignty of God* (Baker Book House, 2nd prtg. 1986), 96.
20   White, op. cit., 211, 221.
21   Piper, op. cit., 155-81.
22   Op. cit., 163.
23   Forster and Marston, op. cit., 75.
24   John Calvin, *Institutes of the Christian Religion*, trans. Henry Beveridge (Wm. Eerdmans Publishing Company, 1998 ed.), V:xvii,14.
25   Forster and Marston, op. cit., 169-70.
26   White, op. cit., 213.
27   Op. cit., 213-14.
28   Hoeksema, op. cit., 60.
29   Piper, op. cit., 204.
30   White, op. cit., 194.
31   Op. cit., 277.
32   Op. cit., 274.
33   Op. cit., 147.
34   Op. cit., 247-49.

35   John Piper, "Are There Two Wills In God?" in *Still Sovereign*, ed. Thomas R. Schreiner and Bruce A. Ware (Baker Books, 2000), 108-109.
36   White, op. cit., 139-43.
37   Ibid.
38   John Calvin, *Calvin's New Testament Commentaries* (Wm. B. Eerdmans Publishing Co., 1994), 10:209.
39   Piper, "Two Wills," op. cit., 108.
40   Op. cit., 25.
41   Op. cit., 265.
42   White, op. cit., 246-47.
43   Charles W. Bronson, *The Extent of the Atonement* (Pilgrim Publications, 1992), 45.
44   Robert L. Dabney, *Systematic Theology* (The Banner of Truth Trust, 2nd ed. 1985), 525.
45   Frank B. Beck, *The Five Points of Calvinism* (Covenanter Press, 2nd Australian ed. 1986), 53.
46   John A. Gill, *The Cause of God and Truth* (The Baptist Standard Bearer, 1992), 58.
47   John Owen, *The Works of John Owen*, ed. William H. Goold (The Banner of Truth Trust, 3rd prtg. 1978), X:365-66.
48   Vance, op. cit., 455-56.
49   White, op. cit., 25.
50   Op. cit., 135-36.
51   Op. cit., 137
52   Op. cit., 143
53   Owen, op. cit., X: 348-49.
54   Gill, op. cit., (The Baptist Standard Bearer, 1980), 62-63.
55   Quoted in Iain H. Murray, *The Life of John Murray* (The Banner of Truth Trust, 1984), 93.
56   John Murray, *The Free Offer of the Gospel* (n.p., n.d.), 24.
57   St. Justin Martyr, Ch. 28 of *The First and Second Apologies, Ancient Christian Writers, No. 56* (Paulist Press, 1997).
58   From England to Dave Hunt, dated September 8, 2000. On file.
59   Gary North, *Dominion and Common Grace* (Institute for Christian Economics, 1987), 44.
60   Calvin, *Commentaries*, op.cit., 3:245.
61   Ibid.
62   White, op. cit., 236-38.
63   Robert M. Zins to Dave Hunt, August 24, 2000. On file.

18
Irresistible Grace

In the doctrine of Irresistible Grace we find once again the pervasive influence of Augustine. Boettner informs us, "This cardinal truth of Christianity [Irresistible Grace] was first clearly seen by Augustine" [1] – a cardinal truth which Warfield says Augustine "recovered for the Church." [2] Likewise some Baptist followers agree that "Augustine may be regarded as the father of the soteriological system which now goes by the name of 'Calvinism.'" [3] Sproul even says, "Augustinianism is presently called Calvinism or Reformed Theology." [4] Shedd declares:

> Augustine accounts for the fact that some men are renewed and some are not, by the unconditional decree (*decretum absolutum*), according to which God determines to select from the fallen mass of mankind (*massa perditionis*), the whole of whom are alike guilty and under condemnation, a portion upon whom he bestows renewing grace, and to leave the remainder to their own self-will and the operation of law and justice. [5]

Having once taught free will and that God desired to save all mankind, [6] Augustine later changed his view. Faith became something which God irresistibly bestowed upon the elect without their having believed anything or having made any decision or even having been aware that they were being regenerated. [7] By such reasoning man, being by nature dead in sin, can't even hear the gospel, much less respond to the pleadings of Christ. Irresistible Grace is necessitated by this unbiblical premise to which Calvinists cling in spite of the fact that our Lord calls to *all*, "Come unto me, *all* ye that labour and are heavy laden, and I will give you rest . . . . If *any* man thirst, let him come unto me, and drink" (Matthew 11:28; John 7:37), etc. Apparently *all*, even the spiritually dead, can hear and come and drink as other passages make very clear. Dave Breese writes, "If grace were irresistible, one fails to understand even the reason for preaching the gospel . . . ." [8]

The Serious Consequences Of Sovereignty Misapplied

To recap Calvinism up to this point, because of Total Depravity, those whom God has unconditionally elected and predestined to eternal life and for whom alone Christ died are first sovereignly regenerated without faith, understanding or even knowing it is happening to them. Thereafter (some would say simultaneously) the grace to believe on Christ as Savior and Lord is irresistibly imposed upon the newly regenerated elect whom God from eternity past has predetermined to save. Piper says that man must first

> . . . be born of God. Then, with the new nature of God, he immediately receives Christ. The two acts (regeneration and faith) are so closely connected that in experience we cannot distinguish them . . . new birth is the effect of irresistible grace . . . an act of sovereign creation . . . . [9]

No one can resist God's saving grace, irresistibly imposed by His sovereign will upon those whom He has predestined to eternal life. This Irresistible Grace is one more essential in the Calvinist theory of salvation. As Piper says, " . . . there can be no salvation without the reality of irresistible grace. If we are dead in our sins, totally unable to submit to God, then we will never believe in Christ unless God overcomes our rebellion." [10]

Here we face the deplorable consequences of this doctrine in its libel of the character of God and its denigration of God's love. Piper declares, "God is sovereign and can overcome all resistance when he wills . . . irresistible grace refers to the sovereign work of God to overcome the rebellion of our hearts and bring us to faith in Christ so that we can be saved." [11] If that is true, God could have irresistibly imposed grace upon Adam and Eve and spared mankind the suffering and evil that resulted from their rebellion. Why didn't He do so? What love is this?

We are asked to believe that God actually loves and has compassion not for the world (as the Bible says) but for a limited few only. Piper says God chose to save them alone by irresistibly imposing His grace upon them, and predestined the remainder of mankind to eternal torment. Such a scenario is abhorrent to every person who has any sense of ethics and compassion, and it maligns the God of the Bible whose "tender mercies are over all his works" (Psalms 145:9).

If, as the Bible declares, God truly loves all and has given them the power of choice in order to respond to that love, then those who are lost are responsible for their own doom through wilfully rejecting the salvation God lovingly and freely offers in Christ. Incredibly, Hodge writes, "According to the Augustinian scheme, the non-elect have all the advantages and opportunities of securing their salvation . . . ." [12] What advantages and opportunities for salvation do those have from whom God withholds the regeneration and irresistible grace without which Calvinists say no one can believe unto salvation? Can Hodge be serious?

Furthermore, how can anyone whom God created totally depraved, caused to sin, then withheld the grace he needs for salvation – how can such a person be justly held accountable? Should a paraplegic be held accountable for failing to become a world-class gymnast, or a man for failing to bear children or to breast feed the children his wife bears? Certainly that would not be the case in any court of law on earth, yet we are urged to believe that God's perfect justice operates in this fashion. Tragically, Calvinism's misrepresentation of God has caused many to turn away from the God of the Bible as from a monster.

The God of Calvinism has created all men incapable of choosing to seek Him and of believing the gospel. The only hope is in God himself, in His love and mercy and grace; but this God was pleased to limit His love to a relative few and to damn the rest in order to prove His sovereignty and justice. Such has been the underlying theme in Total Depravity, Unconditional Election and Limited Atonement. In Irresistible Grace, the next logical progression in TULIP, the God who delights to damn is presented once again. Considering himself one of the elect, Piper finds great joy in TULIP and expresses no regrets for the predestined fate of those for whom this doctrine could only cause eternal anguish:

> We need to rethink our Reformed doctrine of salvation so that every limb and every branch in the tree is coursing with the sap of Augustinian delight. We need to make plain that *total depravity* is not just badness, but blindness . . . and *unconditional election* means that the completeness of our joy in Jesus was planned for us before we ever existed [never mind that eternal doom was also planned for others]; and that *limited atonement* is the assurance that indestructible joy in God is infallibly secured for us [the elect for whom alone Christ died] by the blood of the covenant; and *irresistible grace* is the commitment and power of God's love . . . the *perseverance of the saints* is the almighty work of God to keep us . . . . [13] (Emphasis in original)

What Love, Compassion And Grace Is This?

Why doesn't the God who *is love* and infinite in grace extend Irresistible Grace to all? That question is inescapable in view of the Bible's repeated assurance that God's love and grace are boundless. Consider a few examples: " . . . for the LORD your God is gracious and merciful, and will not turn away his face from you, if ye return unto him" (2 Chronicles 30:9); " . . . thou art a God ready to pardon, gracious and merciful, slow to anger, and of great kindness . .

. for thou art a gracious and merciful God" (Nehemiah 9:17,31); "But thou, O Lord, art a God full of compassion, and gracious, longsuffering, and plenteous in mercy and truth" (Psalms 86:15); " . . . the LORD is gracious and full of compassion" (Psalms 111:4; 112:4; 145:8, etc.); "And rend your heart, and not your garments, and turn unto the LORD your God: for he is gracious and merciful . . . " (Joel 2:13); " . . . for I knew that thou art a gracious God, and merciful, . . . of great kindness" (Jonah 4:2).

Like hundreds of others, each of these scriptures is addressed to all of Israel, most of whom rejected God's grace. Never is there any hint that God's merciful compassion extends to an elect alone. Nor can we find a suggestion anywhere declaring that God's boundless love and grace is limited to a select few. "We love him because he first loved us" (1 John 4:19) declares that our love is in response to God's love. Nowhere does Scripture indicate that we love God because He made the elect love Him, and others He left without this sentiment.

Sadly, in reading scores of books by Calvinists one finds much which extols God's sovereignty but almost nothing of His love. Packer admits, "In Reformation days as since, treatments of God's love in election were often given shape, overshadowed, and indeed preempted by wrangles of an abstract sort about God's sovereignty in reprobation." [14]

Surely the Ten Commandments are not for the elect alone, but for all mankind, as they were for all Israel. The first commandment is, "And thou shalt love the LORD thy God with all thine heart, and with all thy soul, and with all thy might" (Deuteronomy 6:5). This is proof enough that all men have the power of choice necessary to love God and to receive His love, though all fail to keep this commandment just as they fail to keep the others. The Christian is to love others with God's love as his strength and example, for "love is of God" (1 John 4:7), " . . . the love of God is shed abroad in our hearts by the Holy Ghost, which is given unto us" (Romans 5:5): and "Ye yourselves are taught of God to love one another" (1 Thessalonians 4:9).

God's love flowing through the believer has a practical effect: "But whoso hath this world's good, and seeth his brother have need, and shutteth up his bowels of compassion from him, how dwelleth the love of God in him?" (1 John 3:17). Does "brother" mean fellow Christians only? Hardly, considering that we are commanded to love our enemies and to do good to all, even to those who hate us (Matthew 5:44; Luke 6:35, etc.). How odd that God's love dwelling in us would unfailingly meet through us the needs of others — yet God himself sees billions in the direst of need and refuses to help them — indeed, damns those He could save. Surely this is not the God portrayed in the Bible!

Never do we find in Scripture any support for the idea that God takes pleasure in damning His creatures. We have already seen that we are assured otherwise: "As I live, saith the Lord GOD, I have no pleasure in the death of the wicked; but that the wicked turn from his way and live: turn ye, turn ye from your evil ways; for why will ye die, O house of Israel?" (Ezekiel 33:11). Certainly "house" includes all of Israel, not merely the few who did repent and turn to God.

A Longsuffering God

Yet if Calvinism be true, these pleadings are a sham. The elect don't need them, and the non-elect can't heed them. The elect must be regenerated and infused with irresistible grace, while the rest of mankind are damned without remedy. Supposedly, to save only a select elect and to damn the rest was necessary to prove God's sovereignty and will eternally be to His greater glory. Obviously, however, God need not damn anyone in order to prove His sovereignty. If it is not a threat to God's sovereignty to save the elect, neither would it be for Him to save a million more, 100 million more – or more loving yet, to save all mankind.

Sovereignty in Calvinism, as we have seen, is such that God is behind every emotion and act of every individual, causing each sin and causing each impulse of "love." Supposedly the heart of man is "made willing" in order to love God. But as we have seen, "made willing" is an oxymoron. One can be persuaded or convinced but not *made* willing because the will, being still involved, must have been willing to reach that point.

Again we are compelled to ask, "What love is this?" If Calvin's God can be said to love at all, it is with a love which allegedly can be imposed upon *anyone* and only comes to man by that imposition. But such is not the nature of love. This "love" which allows no rejection can hardly be true love at all.

In contrast, in the Bible we see God's infinite love, grace and mercy demonstrated powerfully in His dealings with Israel. Moreover, it is the rejection and hatred against Him by disobedient Israel which causes God's true love to shine all the brighter. Though a Calvinist, D.A. Carson expresses the contradiction of Calvinism clearly:

> . . . the entire prophecy of Hosea is an astonishing portrayal of the love of God. Almighty God is likened to a betrayed and cuckolded husband. But the intensity of God's passion for the covenant nation comes to a climax in Hosea 11. "When Israel was a child," God declares, "I loved him, and out of Egypt I called my son: (11:1) . . . ." But the more God loved Israel, the more they drifted away. God was the one who cared for them . . . the one who "led them with cords of love and human kindness" (11:4). Yet they . . . sacrificed to Baals and loved idolatry. So God promises judgment. They will return to "Egypt" and Assyria, i.e., to captivity and slavery, "because they refuse to repent" (11:5). Their cities will be destroyed (11:6) . . . . Thus it sounds as if implacable judgment has been pronounced.

But then it is almost as if God cannot endure the thought. In an agony of emotional intensity, God cries,

> "How can I give you up, Ephraim?
> How can I hand you over, Israel? . . .
> My heart is changed within me;
> all my compassion is aroused.
> I will not carry out my fierce anger . . . .
> For I am God, and not man . . .
> I will not come in wrath . . . .
> I will settle them in their homes,"
> declares the LORD. [16]

There are scores of such passages which leave no doubt that God loves and desires to bless not just an elect who will be redeemed out of Israel, but all of Israel (and all mankind as well) including those who refuse His love and gracious offer of blessing. God's very character is reflected in the commandments He gave to His chosen people. They were to restore even to an enemy his ox or ass that had wandered off (Exodus 23:4). Yet God himself won't give wandering mankind the kindness He commands that man give to beasts? Such teaching doesn't ring true to Scripture.

A Foundational Misunderstanding

How does this grievous libel upon God's character arise among those who we believe truly love the Lord? As we have already seen, the problem is an overemphasis upon the sovereignty of God to the exclusion of all else. It is imagined that if man can make a choice, if even with the wooing and winning of the Holy Spirit he can willingly respond to the love of God in the gospel, God's sovereignty has been overruled. Pink insists that if man could of his own volition believe on and receive Christ, "then the Christian would have ground for boasting and self-glorying over *his* cooperation with the Spirit . . . ." [17]   Even Carson, in a book in which at times he seems to deny Limited Atonement and which has so much balanced truth to offer, falls into this error:

> If Christ died for all people with exactly the same intent . . . then surely it is impossible to avoid the conclusion that the *ultimate* distinguishing mark between those who are saved and those who are not is their own decision, their own will. That is surely ground for boasting. [18]

Although we appreciate the sincerity of those who reason thus, we have already shown the fallacy of this argument. Salvation is the gift of God's love offered to whosoever will believe. How could a gift be received and love returned without the ability to choose? The ability to say no — which is all Calvinism grants to the totally depraved — is meaningless without the accompanying ability to say yes.

Furthermore, how could accepting a gift provide a basis for boasting? If the gift is offered to all freely for the taking, those who receive the gift have no basis whatsoever for giving any credit to themselves. All has been provided in Christ, it is His work, to Him is all the glory, and it is absurd to suggest that the hopeless sinner who has been rescued without merit or effort on his part could thereby boast of anything.

The Calvinist is so fearful that any response on man's part would challenge God's sovereignty that he invents ever more untenable arguments. Charles Hodge insists that "if efficacious grace is the exercise of almighty power it is irresistible." [19] Following the same reasoning, C.D. Cole writes, "The power of grace is the power of God. This makes it fitting to speak of irresistible grace. Surely we can speak of an irresistible God!" [20]

The flaw in such reasoning is elementary. Omnipotent power has nothing to do with grace or love or bestowing a gift. Indeed, just as God himself cannot force anyone to love Him (a coerced response is the opposite of love), so it would be the very opposite of grace to force any gift or benefit of "grace" upon anyone who did not want to receive it.

Beck, like so many Calvinists, echoes the same unsound argument: "I repeat, the Gospel of Christ *is* the power of God unto salvation! *Nothing* can stop it . . . . If God's grace can be *successfully* resisted, then *God* can be overcome . . . ." [21] Such arguments are an embarassment to sound reason. God's power in salvation refers to His ability to pay the penalty so that He can be just and yet justify sinners; it does not refer to His forcing salvation upon those who would otherwise reject it. Nowhere in Scripture is there such a concept. Always it is "whosoever *will* may come," never the imposition of God's grace upon any unwilling person. Here we must agree with Arminius, who said, "Grace is not an omnipotent act of God, which cannot be resisted by the free-will of men." [22] It cannot be, or it would not be grace by very definition.

Christ's lament over Jerusalem, "How often would I have gathered thy children together, even as a hen gathereth her chickens under her wings, and ye would not!" (Matthew 23:37), is nothing less than the heart cry of Jahweh who sent His prophets generation after generation to plead for repentance from a people who steadfastly refused the offer of His grace. Why was that grace not "irresistible"?

The Bible is filled with passages in which God mourns over Israel and sinners in general, expressing His desire to forgive and save and bless, and His sorrow over their rejection of His grace. For example, "Oh that my people had hearkened unto me . . . ! I should soon have subdued their enemies, [and] have fed them also with the finest of the wheat" (Psalms 81:8-16). Instead, God's judgment fell upon Israel. Was judgment what He intended all along and His pleadings insincere? One is driven to such a conclusion by Calvinism — but the Bible teaches otherwise.

More Contradictions

No one expresses this elementary misunderstanding of omnipotence more clearly than Tom Ross: "If every man possesses a free will that is powerful enough to resist the will of God in salvation, what would prevent that same man from choosing to resist the will of God in damnation at the great white throne of judgment?" [23] Can Ross see no difference between salvation offered in God's grace, and judgment imposed by His justice? Can he be serious in suggesting that because the former could be rejected so could the latter? Not all Calvinists agree. Thus Carson writes that "God's unconditioned sovereignty and the responsibility of human beings are mutually compatible." [24]

There can be no minimizing of God's sovereignty — but that must be balanced with all of His other qualities: "I do not think that what the Bible says about the love of God can long survive at the forefront of our thinking if it is abstracted from the sovereignty of God, the holiness of God, the wrath of God, the providence of God, or the personhood of God — to mention only a few nonnegotiable elements of basic Christianity." [25] Only an unbiblical and irrational view of sovereignty requires that even in man's rebellion against God in the Garden of Eden, his continual disobedience of God's Ten Commandments and his straying like a lost sheep in rejection of God's will, the Creator is behind it all, sovereignly *causing* every sin! This error gave rise to the belief that grace must be irresistible. On the contrary, every conscience bears witness to Carson's statement that "The Scriptures do not mock us when they say, 'Like as a father pitieth his children, so the Lord pitieth them that fear him.' " [26] Yet Carson remains a Calvinist while contradicting what most of his fellows believe.

Some Calvinists attempt to escape the horrifying consequences of their doctrine by suggesting that predestination unto damnation and God's invitation to all to believe are both true even though they contradict each other. One hears it said repeatedly that finite man simply cannot understand; that we just don't know how to reconcile these apparent conflicts and are not supposed to discuss them, for all will be revealed in eternity.

The truth is that Calvinism itself has created this particular "mystery." While there is much that finite beings cannot understand, we have been given a conscience with a keen sense of right and wrong and of justice and injustice. God calls us to reason with Him about these things. He goes to great lengths to explain His justice and love and has given even to unregenerate man the capacity to understand the gospel and to believe in Christ or to reject Him.

Irresistible Grace And The Gospel

As for the gospel, how can Calvinists deal with it without contradicting their own system? On the one hand, they must honor Christ's command to "preach the gospel to every creature." On the other hand, it is difficult to uphold the importance of the gospel when the unregenerate can neither understand nor believe it, and the elect are regenerated without it, then sovereignly and supernaturally given the faith both to understand and believe it. Seemingly unaware that he is contradicting the very "Reformed Theology" of which he is a major defender, Sproul earnestly exhorts readers, "If we believe in the power of the gospel to effect our salvation, we must believe in the power of the Gospel preached to bring in His elect." [27] But Calvinism's elect have been predestined from a past eternity and it is God's soverignty, *not the gospel,* which alone can "bring in His elect."

Given TULIP, how can the gospel effect the salvation of anyone? The unregenerate, elect or non-elect, cannot understand or believe it. And even if the non-elect somehow could, it would be of no avail because they have been predestined to eternal damnation from the beginning. The elect are regenerated without the gospel and only then can they believe. But once regenerated they have already been saved unless one can be sovereignly regenerated (i.e., born again by the Spirit) and still not be saved. Having been regenerated without the gospel, subsequently hearing and believing it cannot save them, since they have surely already been saved in their regeneration.

Sproul is being faithful to God's Word, which clearly teaches that the gospel "is the power of God unto salvation to everyone who believes" it. In being true to the Bible, however, he must ignore Calvinism's teaching that one cannot believe the gospel until one has been regenerated. So he talks as though the gospel, as the Bible says, must be believed for salvation — but deep down somewhere in the subterranean caverns of his mind he holds that this can't be true because if it were then Calvinism would be false.

Elsewhere Sproul spends an entire book rebuking the signers of "Evangelicals and Catholics Together: The Christian Mission in the Third Millennium" and arguing quite rightly that "Justification by faith alone is essential to the gospel. The gospel is essential to Christianity and to salvation." [28] He ends the book with this un-Calvinistic quote from John Calvin: "Let it therefore remain settled . . . that we are justified by faith alone." [29] But Sproul believes there is no faith until regeneration, so the new birth into God's family as a child of God comes before one has believed the gospel. But if faith in Christ through the gospel is essential to justification and salvation, we have the elect born again as children of God before they are justified or saved.

When it deals with the gospel, Calvinism becomes very confusing. How can the gospel preached "bring in His elect" as Sproul declares? Even the elect can't understand or believe it until they have been regenerated – and Calvinism is firm that regeneration is the way for God to "bring in His elect." Was it not the sovereign act of regeneration that brought the elect into the fold? Then the gospel was not involved at all and Sproul is offering false motivation for preaching it.

Yes, it is difficult to make sense out of Calvinism when it comes to the preaching of the gospel. But then, the Calvinist apparently has two compartments in his mind: in one he holds to Calvinism's dogmas faithfully, and in the other he holds to the teaching of Scripture. It can't be easy or comfortable for the conscience. That faith in Christ through the gospel precedes the new birth/ salvation seems to be so clear in scores of passages such as the following:

In whom [Christ] also ye trusted, *after* that ye heard the word of truth, the *gospel* of your *salvation*: in whom also *after that ye believed*, ye were sealed with that holy Spirit of promise . . . . (Ephesians 1:13; emphasis added)

A Classic Oxymoron

On its very face, the phrase "irresistible grace" presents another irreconcilable contradiction. As far as grace is concerned, there are two possible meanings for the word "irresistible": irresistible in its appeal to all mankind; or irresistible in its imposition upon the elect alone. The former is, of course, vigorously denied by Calvinism. That system is founded upon the belief that grace has no appeal at all to the totally depraved, spiritually dead sons and daughters of Adam. Nor does grace have any appeal even to the elect until they have been sovereignly regenerated.

Only one possibility remains: that grace is irresistibly imposed upon a chosen few – and this is the teaching of Calvinism. But to impose anything upon anyone is the very antithesis of grace. Forcing even a most valuable and desirable gift upon someone who does not wish to receive it would be ungracious in the extreme. Thus the phrase "irresistible grace" is another oxymoron. Yet this is an integral element without which the other four essentials of TULIP collapse.

Moreover, this fourth point of TULIP, like the first three, confronts us with one more phrase unknown to Scripture – so how can it possibly be biblical? The word "irresistible" does not appear in the Bible. The wonderful grace of God, however, is one of the most precious truths presented in His Word. Found throughout both the Old and New Testaments, the word "grace" occurs 170 times in 159 verses. Furthermore, while grace clearly must be given by God if we are to receive it, *never* in all of those instances is there a suggestion that grace is irresistibly imposed. Always the inference is that God's grace is given freely and willingly received. Consider a few examples:

But Noah found grace in the eyes of the LORD. (Genesis 6:8)

... the LORD will give grace and glory ... (Psalms 84:11)

By whom we have received grace and apostleship ... (Romans 1:5)

Having then gifts differing according to the grace that is given to us ... (Romans 12:6)

I thank my God ... for the grace of God which is given you by Jesus Christ .. . (1 Corinthians 1:4)

Unto me, who am less than the least of all saints, is this grace given ... (Ephesians 3:8)

But unto every one of us is given grace according to the measure of the gift of Christ. (Ephesians 4:7)

Likewise, ye husbands, ... giving honour unto the wife, ... as being heirs together of the grace of life ... (1 Peter 3:7)

Yes, there are some scriptures which Calvinists look to for support of the belief that grace is irresistibly imposed, such as "And I will pour upon the house of David, and upon the inhabitants of Jerusalem, the spirit of grace and supplications ... " (Zechariah 12:10); "And with great power gave the apostles witness, ... and great grace was upon them" (Acts 4:33); "And God is able to make all grace abound toward you ... " (2 Corinthians 9:8), etc.

Even in these instances, however, although the indication is much stronger that God is sovereignly granting grace, still there is no indication that God's grace is irresistibly extended to anyone who does not choose to receive it.

Are There "Two Conflicting Wills" With God?

Many Calvinists, in upholding that system, make extreme statements such as the following: "Because God's will is always done, the will of every creature must conform to the sovereign will of God." [30] Vance comments, "That fornication and unthankfulness are actually part of God's 'secret will' should come as no surprise in light of ... the Calvinistic concept of God's all-encompassing decree." [31] We are back to the repulsive doctrine that everything that happens – including all evil – is according to God's will. Pink even rejects the distinction sometimes made between God's "perfect will" and His "permissive will" because "God only permits that which is according to His will." [32]

Calvinists struggle to reconcile a sovereignty which causes every sinful thought, word and deed and damns billions, with the repeated biblical assurances of God's goodness, compassion, and love for all. Piper devised an ingenious but unbiblical and irrational solution — the idea that God has *two wills* which contradict one another, yet are not in conflict:

> Therefore I affirm with John 3:16 and 1 Timothy 2:4 that God loves the world with a deep compassion that desires the salvation of all men. Yet I also affirm that God has chosen from before the foundation of the world whom he will save from sin. Since not all people are saved we must choose whether we believe (with the Arminians) that God's will to save all people is restrained by his commitment to human self-determination or whether we believe (with the Calvinists) that God's will to save all people is restrained by his commitment to the glorification of his sovereign grace (Eph 1:6, 12, 14; Rom 9:22-23) . . . . This book aims to show that the sovereignty of God's grace in salvation is taught in Scripture. My contribution has simply been to show that God's will for all people to be saved is not at odds with the sovereignty of God's grace in election. That is, my answer to the question about what restrains God's will to save all people is his supreme commitment to uphold and display the full range of his glory through the sovereign demonstration of his wrath and mercy for the enjoyment of his elect and believing people from every tribe and tongue and nation. [33]

Once again we have an unblushing contradiction from Piper. In His great love and compassion God "desires the salvation of all men." Yet for reasons known only to Himself, he doesn't save them all — and this in spite of the insistence that He could save all if he so desired. Let us get this straight: Piper's God desires the salvation of all men; in His sovereign imposition of Irresistible Grace he *could* save all, but doesn't because it is His "secret will" not to do so. Here we have the clearest contradiction possible. How can the Calvinist escape? Ah, Piper has found an ingenious way to affirm that God loves and really desires to save even those whom He has predestined to damnation from eternity past: God has *two wills* which, though they contradict each other, are really in secret agreement. Are we going mad?

We are asked to believe that it is no contradiction for God to contradict himself if it furthers the "sovereign demonstration of his wrath and mercy"! Reason fails Piper once again. Damning billions would certainly demonstrate God's wrath — but how would that glorify Him in his mercy? And even if that somehow were the case, there is no way to reconcile reprobation with the clear expressions of God's love and desire for the salvation of all — expressions which Piper uncalvinistically claims to accept at face value.

Piper has yet another problem. God does not contradict himself. Therefore, Piper must reconcile what he calls "two wills" of God to show that they are in agreement even though they directly disagree with and invalidate each other. And this he fails to do because it is impossible. A contradiction is a contradiction, and there is no honest way that two contradictory propositions can be massaged into agreement.

Piper is following Calvin, who fell into the same misconception. He said, "This is His wondrous love towards the human race, that He desires all men to be saved, and is prepared to bring even the perishing to safety . . . . God is prepared to receive all men into repentance, so that none may perish." [34] Could this be the same John Calvin who declared so often and so clearly that from a past eternity God had predestined billions to damnation? Is Calvin's God a schizophrenic?

Very much like Piper's "two wills," Calvin fell back upon a "secret will": "No mention is made here of the secret decree of God by which the wicked are doomed to their own ruin." [35] Sproul attempts to play the same broken string. Bryson responds reasonably and succinctly: "But certainly one so erudite as Sproul knows that: 1. If Grace is irresistible, and if: 2. Grace is essential to salvation, then it follows: 3. No saving grace is extended to the unelect." Bryson continues:

> Thus, Calvinists are in the rather awkward position of claiming to make a valid offer of salvation (to the unelect) . . . while denying [that] the only provision (i.e., Christ's death) of salvation is for the unelect . . . [and saying] that the unelect cannot possibly believe [the gospel] . . . . To add insult to injury, they are claiming this is just the way God (from all eternity) wanted it to be. [36]

Can God's Grace Be Rejected Or Resisted?

Even Christians don't always live up to our Lord's will. Consider the following: "For this is the will of God, even your sanctification . . . " (1 Thessalonians 4:3); "In every thing give thanks: for this is the will of God in Christ Jesus concerning you" (1 Thessalonians 5:18). Surely not every Christian fulfills God's will by living a perfectly sanctified life at all times and always giving thanks to God "in everything." God's will is being violated continually by unbelievers disobeying the Law and by believers failing to live as they should. Surely when John says, "These things write I unto you that ye sin not" (1 John 2:1), he expresses the will of God for every Christian. Yet he also declares that no Christian fully lives up to this desire of God: "If we say that we have no sin, we deceive ourselves . . . . If we say that we have not sinned, we make him a liar, and his truth is not in us" (1 John 1:8,10).

Furthermore, many other scriptures make it clear that while grace is unmerited, we must accept and respond to it. For example, Paul declares, "But by the grace of God I am what I am: and his grace which was bestowed upon me was not in vain; but I laboured more abundantly than they all: yet not I, but the grace of God which was with me" (1 Corinthians 15:10); "We . . . beseech you also that ye receive not the grace of God in vain" (2 Corinthians 6:1); "Thou therefore, my son, be strong in the grace that is in Christ Jesus" (2 Timothy 2:1);

"Let us therefore come boldly unto the throne of grace, that we may obtain mercy . . . " (Hebrews 4:16).

Numerous scriptures make it very clear that the reception of God's grace is not by imposition of an overwhelming omnipotent sovereignty without willingness on man's part. One could even fail to accept and properly cooperate with God's grace. There is no question that God sincerely desired to bless Israel. Nevertheless, she refused His grace and placed herself instead under His judgment by her rebellion and idolatry.

God's desire for Israel, as for all men, was good: "For I know the thoughts that I think toward you, saith the LORD, thoughts of peace, and not of evil . . . " (Jeremiah 29:11). However, because the blessings of His grace were contingent upon Israel's faith and faithfulness, she reaped instead the judgment of God. We are even told that by their rebellion they "limited the Holy One of Israel" (Psalms 78:41). Think of that — limiting the omnipotent, sovereign God, which Calvinists say is impossible! Indeed, we are told that the rabbis "rejected the counsel of God against themselves" (Luke 7:30) — but there is no hint that they thereby annulled God's sovereignty or gained control over God.

Paul intimates that Christians can also limit the work of the Holy Spirit in their lives and His empowerment for ministry. The Christian life and victory is not alone by sovereign power, but the believers' faith and obedience as "labourers together with God" (1 Corinthians 3:9) is essential: "Whereunto I also labour, striving according to his working, which worketh in me mightily" (Colossians 1:29); "work out your own salvation with fear and trembling. For it is God which worketh in you both to will and to do of his good pleasure" (Philippians 2:12-13).

God truly and powerfully works within the believer and we can do nothing but by the leading and empowering of the Holy Spirit. At the same time, however, we must give ourselves willingly to the work of God through us. Most Calvinists admit this cooperative effort when it comes to living the Christian life, but insist that there can be no such willingness in believing the gospel and accepting Christ.

Again we point out how unreasonable it is — that, if He so desires, God can sovereignly cause the totally depraved sinner to turn to him, yet His sovereignty seems to lose its Calvinistic power when it comes to causing Christians to live in victory and holiness and fruitfulness. It is certainly clear that once God has regenerated the elect they do not all live to His glory as fully as they might and as His perfect will for them clearly desires.

There is no escaping the fact that God's desire for Christians goes far beyond their experience. If that were not the case, we would be forced to admit that the shallow and unfruitful lives of so many genuine believers are exactly what God desires for them. We ask again, what is the meaning of rewards and the point of the Judgment Seat of Christ if each Christian's every thought, word and deed is exactly as God wills? And if that is the case, why aren't Christians perfect? Surely the continual disobedience both of unbelievers and believers proves that God's grace is not "irresistible." Nor does man's disobedience diminish God's sovereignty in the least. Obviously, freedom of choice itself is part of God's plan!

Yet the idea of Irresistible Grace is predicated upon the unbiblical belief that a human ability to accept or to reject the gospel would deny God's sovereignty. We have shown that reasoning to be fallacious and that the very concept is unbiblical.

The Calvinist's Unresolvable Problem

Although combining the word "irresistible" with grace is the Calvinist's own invention, he denies it to mean that grace is "imposed" by God upon the elect. Here some Calvinists begin further to contradict themselves. Sproul, for example, concedes that irresistible grace can be resisted but at the same time declares that "it is invincible." [37] We are left to wonder how something invincible can be resisted. Most Calvinists agree that Irresistible Grace produces an "effectual call" which is "ultimately irresistible." Vance quotes a number of Calvinists to this effect and explains that this concept is "derived from Chapter X in the Westminster Confession of Faith." [38]

Sproul says that for the elect God takes away all that caused them in their total depravity to resist him. Supposedly the result is akin to a dam being removed so that the water flows uninhibited. The removal, of course, is without understanding or cooperation on man's part, the understanding and faith only coming *after* and *as a result of* the breaking of the "dam," not before.

An obvious question immediately arises: What is the "dam," and whence this flow that the dam had held back? It sounds as though there were something which resides within man that could indeed respond to God. That, of course, is not acceptable and leaves the Calvinist with further contradictions.

The great problem is how to get a totally depraved man saved – a man who cannot even hear the gospel, much less understand and believe it. Remember, the Synod of Dort describes this process as not taking away man's "will and its properties" but "sweetly and powerfully bend[ing] it . . . . " [39] But to "bend" the totally depraved will (rather than to destroy and create a new one) is to admit that it is finally the original will which yields to God. Moreover, what does it mean to "bend" the will, and how is that done "sweetly" and at the same time "powerfully"? And if the human will is not destroyed and something else not put in its place, then it cannot be denied that the human will does after all decide and choose to be bent.

This is a knotty problem! After declaring that totally depraved man's will and its properties of self-determination are not taken away, Dort laid out its complaint against Arminians: "The true doctrine having been explained, the Synod *rejects* the errors of those: 1. Who teach . . . 2. Who teach . . . " and so forth, through nine numbered paragraphs. Much of what is listed as being rejected was not believed by the Arminians, nor is it believed by most non-Calvinists today.

Paragraph 8 wrestled with the difficult problem which is created by Calvinism itself: How can man's will be allowed any part in receiving Christ when it is totally depraved, man is spiritually dead, and God's sovereignty must cause all, including sin and salvation through faith in Christ? Here is the error denounced by that paragraph:

> 8. Who teach: That God in the regeneration of man does not use such powers of his omnipotence as potently and infallibly bend man's will to faith and conversion; but that all the works of grace having been accomplished, which God employs to convert man, man may yet so resist God and the Holy Spirit, when God intends man's regeneration and wills to regenerate him, and indeed that man often does so resist that he prevents entirely his regeneration, and that it therefore remains in man's power to be regenerated or not. [40]

Of course it is not in man's power to be regenerated, nor would the rankest Arminian suggest that it was. That power comes only from God and there would be nothing man could do without God's gracious provision in Christ. That man can accept or reject the offered salvation is not the same as saying that it is in his power to be regenerated.

While Ben Rose insists that "God does not bring anyone into the kingdom against his or her will," [41] yet that statement is clearly contradicted by the phrase "irresistible grace." If under the conviction of the Holy Spirit man could make a genuine choice to believe and to receive, there would be no need for grace to be "irresistible." The Westminster Confession of Faith continues the double talk:

> All those whom God hath predestinated unto life, and those alone, he is pleased . . . effectually to call . . . to grace and salvation by Jesus Christ; enlightening their minds spiritually and savingly to understand the things of God . . . renewing their wills, and, by his almighty power . . . effectually drawing them to Jesus Christ: yet so as they come most freely, being made willing by his grace. [42]

What Does The Bible Teach?

Responding to the criticism of the Pharisees that He received and ate with sinners, Christ gave the illustrations of the lost sheep, lost coin and prodigal son to show that humans seek and have great joy in finding the lost, whether sheep, coin or wayward son (Luke 15:1-32). It seems equally clear that these illustrations are intended also to tell us of God's love and joy in seeking and finding the lost. The vignettes Christ gives do not seem to represent true children of God who have simply wandered away and are being brought back by God, but examples of lost mankind.

In telling the prodigal's story, Christ uses language that seems to contradict Calvinism. The prodigal realizes his situation, comes to a decision, makes a choice and acts upon it by his will: "And when he came to himself, he said, How many hired servants of my father have bread enough and to spare, and I perish with hunger! I will arise and go to my father, and I will say unto him, Father, I have sinned against heaven, and before thee . . . ." Why doesn't Christ tell us that the prodigal, being totally incapable of understanding his situation, or of repenting and returning to the father, was irresistibly drawn by the father?

It is clearly said that the prodigal "was dead," and was "lost" (Luke 15:24), but that did not prevent him from being moved in his conscience and choosing to return to the father. If the prodigal does not represent the unregenerate lost sinner dead in sin whom God welcomes in love, then the Calvinist must abandon Perseverance of the Saints (the "P" in TULIP, to be discussed in Chapters 22 and 23) and admit that salvation can be lost — which neither side believes.

Christ declared that all men are to act like the good Samaritan toward everyone in need (Luke 10:30-37); we are even to love our enemies and to do good to those who hate us (Matthew 5:44). If this is the standard God sets for mankind, would He not behave even more benevolently toward all? If Paul did not want a single Jew to go to hell and was in continual agony of soul for their salvation, willing even to be accursed of God if that would save his "kinsmen according to the flesh" (Romans 9:1-3), would God, who surely put this selfless love in Paul's heart, be any *less* loving and concerned for lost humanity on its way to hell? Surely not the God of the Bible!

What About God's Love?

It is simply impossible to maintain that a God who damns those He could save (much less who takes pleasure in so doing!) is merciful and full of love. How then can the Calvinist escape the charge that he misrepresents the God of the Bible? Sovereignty can't excuse or justify callous neglect on God's part to rescue those He could save. That God has the right to damn everyone would not make Him loving and merciful if He did so.

As I have repeatedly emphasized, my firm disagreement with Calvinism is not over God's sovereignty, which I fully embrace and to which I submit. The issue is whether God loves all without partiality and desires all to be saved. Unquestionably, Calvinism denies such love; but the Bible, in the clearest language, repeatedly declares God's love to all and His desire that all should be saved and none should be lost.

Based upon the behavior God expects of Christians in whom the love of God dwells (1 John 3:17), it would seem that the God of the Bible would make salvation available to all in the sincere desire that all receive Christ and be saved. Surely this is exactly what so much of Scripture declares: that it is not God's will for any to perish. To take the general wording of such scriptures and say that they apply only to the elect does violence to the entire tenor of Scripture and to God's character.

If grace is irresistible, why doesn't God, who is love and full of compassion, impose it upon everyone? We have just seen that grace *cannot* be irresistible. God cannot *force* anyone to believe in Christ, much less to love Him. All who would be in God's presence for eternity must love Him sincerely, and love requires a genuine choice.

According to both the many passages in the Bible already quoted and the conscience God has given us, it is not because He did not desire to save all mankind and predestined some to eternal doom that those who reject God's offer of salvation are lost. They are eternally doomed because they rejected the salvation Christ obtained through His sacrifice on the cross and which God genuinely and lovingly offered to them through Jesus Christ. There are only two possibilities: either God causes men to go to hell or they make their own choice. Nor can it be both, or God's will would coincide with that of totally depraved sinners!

Was Paul Wrong In His Passionate Concern?

It seems reasonable that Paul, who was inspired of the Holy Spirit to provide the definitive teaching concerning foreknowledge, election / predestination, sovereignty and salvation by grace through faith, would know these subjects at least as well as Calvin knew them. Could Paul have been wrong in his continual agony over the lost sheep of the house of Israel (and indeed all men), and Calvin right in his lack of concern for the lost? Yet if God himself, as Calvin sincerely believed, is not concerned over the lost (and why should He be, having predestined their eternal torment), then we must conclude that Paul was badly out of touch with the Holy Spirit for being in continual prayerful distress for the salvation of his unsaved fleshly kinsmen.

Paul confesses, "Brethren, my heart's desire and prayer to God for Israel is, that they might be saved" (Romans 10:1). Surely he cannot be praying for Calvin's elect, for their salvation has been predestined from eternity past. Irresistible Grace will make certain they are saved, so there is no need to pray for them. And is it not an affront to God to pray for the salvation of those whom in His sovereignty He has willed to be damned? How could Paul dare to express deep concern for those whom God has placed outside of His love and grace and for whom He has no concern?

It is troubling that in all of our dealings with Calvinists we have never heard any of them express great concern for the lost, or sorrow that so many will spend eternity in hell. That attitude, however, is perfectly consistent with their beliefs. Why should one be disappointed at that which is God's sovereign good pleasure? Might it not even be rebellion for one to be concerned for the salvation of those whom God has determined not to save?

Yet even the God-given conscience of a non-Christian is troubled by such disregard for the welfare of fellow humans. How is it possible that the God who put such standards in man's conscience could Himself have no such concern? It is beyond belief that the God whose Word repeatedly exhorts us to rescue all those in need would Himself neglect multitudes of those in the greatest need of all!

What God Is This?

We have seen Calvinism's teaching that God does not desire to save all mankind and that Christ had no intention of dying for the sins of all on the cross. It is just at this point that we reach our ultimate objection to this system of religion which young Calvin learned from Augustine and further developed and passed along to millions who follow it today. This doctrine is repugnant even to unbelievers because it contradicts the conscience and sense of obligation and fairness God has implanted in every one of us. Yet a Calvinist pastor insists, "To suggest that Christ came *actually* to save all men is 'universalism' . . . a heresy openly promoted by the ecumenical churches." [43] On the contrary, universalism teaches that all men will ultimately *be saved*, not that salvation is *offered* to all.

A Calvinist editor in England writes earnestly, "The plain truth is that God does *not* wish to save all men. If He did, then He would save them . . . . If God wanted to save all men, why did He prevent Paul from preaching the gospel in certain areas?" [44] Such an argument makes sense only to a Calvinist, for whom salvation is not something man receives by faith in his heart but is imposed upon him contrary to his will and cannot be resisted. Hence the necessity for Irresistible Grace.

But what does this have to do with God preventing Paul from preaching in certain places? There could have been many reasons for redirecting Paul. Certainly he could not preach everywhere. Again Calvinists are grasping at straws.

Peter asked Christ, "Lord, how oft shall my brother sin against me, and I forgive him? till seven times?" The Lord responded that he ought to forgive "seventy times seven." Christ then told the story of the servant who because he would not forgive a fellow servant was "delivered...to the tormentors." In application, He said, "So likewise shall my heavenly Father do also unto you, if ye from your hearts forgive not every one his brother their trespasses" (Matthew 18:21-35).

Does God impose a higher standard of grace and mercy upon man than His own character produces? Surely if our heavenly Father expects us to forgive those who sin against us, how much more can we be confident that He is ready to forgive all who sin against Him. This is God as the Bible portrays Him, infinite in love, grace and mercy, ready to forgive all who call upon Him. Calvinism misrepresents Him as only loving and forgiving a select few.

The Darkest Side Of Calvinism

We consider TULIP to be a libel against our loving and merciful God as He reveals himself both in His Word and in human conscience. Because of the Lord's mercy to the rebellious house of Israel, Nehemiah praises Him: " . . . thou art a gracious and merciful God" (Nehemiah 9:31). In seeking to call His wayward people to himself, God says to disobedient Israel through the prophet Jeremiah, "I am merciful" (Jeremiah 3:12). In the spirit of all of the prophets, Joel begs Israel to repent: "[T]urn unto the LORD your God; for he is gracious and merciful, slow to anger, and of great kindness . . ." (Joel 2:13).

How could God be merciful to sinners, as Christ declared Him to be in the case of the repentant publican, and let *any* of them go to hell whom He could save? There is no way to justify the lack of concern on the part of Calvinism's God for *all* of the lost. R.C. Sproul wrote, "How we understand the person and character of God the Father affects every aspect of our lives." [45] He is right, and what effect must it have to believe in a God who limits His love, grace and mercy to a select few, takes pleasure in damning the rest of mankind, and tells us to be merciful as He is merciful!

David, who surely knew God at least as well as Calvin did, declared, "With the merciful thou wilt shew thyself merciful . . . " (2 Samuel 22:26). Not a word about being merciful to a select few only. The God of the Bible is merciful to those who have shown mercy to others. Is this not what Jesus also said in the Sermon on the Mount, "Blessed are the merciful: for they shall obtain mercy" (Matthew 5:7)? But we are to believe that those who show mercy would receive no mercy from God unless they were among the elect. Yet both Christ and David make it sound as though, even without the benefit of Irresistible Grace, some of the "totally depraved" show mercy to their fellows, and because of that God's mercy will be given to them. Apparently, showing mercy reveals a heart willing to receive (and to be grateful for) God's mercies.

This Is Election?

We have already seen — and will come to understand it even better in Chapters 22 and 23 — that a major problem for any Calvinist is knowing for certain that he or she is one of the elect. And that solemn question raises further serious problems with this unbiblical system of religion devised by an immature believer and then dogmatically upheld not only by him but by his followers today. Calvin seemed to believe that nearly everyone in Geneva was one of the elect and treated them accordingly. Why? First of all, Calvin held infant baptism to be of such value that it transformed an infant into one of the elect. In fact, to be baptized at any age, even by the most wicked and unbelieving Roman Catholic priest, was to have entered into the kingdom of God if one thereafter believed in the efficacy of that sacrament:

> God in baptism promises the remission of sins, and will undoubtedly perform what he has promised to all believers. That promise was offered to us in baptism, let us therefore embrace it in faith. [46]

This is a remarkable statement. According to Calvin, the gospel is no certain way to bring people to Christ — but baptism is. In baptism one receives a promise of remission of sins which, if thereafter believed, gives certain entrance into the kingdom of God! Furthermore, Calvin taught that the children of believers, even though not baptized, are automatically among the elect:

> Children who happen to depart this life before an opportunity of immersing them in water are not excluded from the kingdom of heaven . . . . Hence it follows, that the children of believers are not baptised in order that though formerly aliens from the Church, they may then, for the first time, become children of God, but rather are received into the Church by a formal sign, because, in virtue of the promise, they *previously belonged* to the body of Christ. [47] (Emphasis added)

Apparently from Calvin's belief that everyone in Geneva, having been baptized, was one of the elect (though he might have to burn, behead or banish them for heresy), attendance at church services was required of all. It was perhaps this rule that caused Servetus to risk drawing attention to himself by attending the service where he was recognized. Moreover, also mandatory for everyone (with few exceptions) was the partaking of the bread and wine at the celebration of the Lord's supper.

Considering Paul's clear warning that "he that eateth and drinketh unworthily, eateth and drinketh damnation to himself" (1 Corinthians 11:29), what can be said in defense of Calvin's forcing of the Eucharist upon the unwilling? Could he have sincerely believed that every citizen in his holy "City of God" belonged to Christ? Wasn't this a worse sort of "universalism" than that which Calvinists attribute now to those of us who believe Christ died for all?

There was at least one exception to this universalism which nevertheless hardly changes the picture. A notorious libertine named Berthelier had been forbidden by the Church Consistory to partake of the Lord's Supper. In 1553, together with others of his persuasion, he attempted to do so and was repulsed by Calvin. [48]

Left With Unanswered Questions

Calvinism's elect, chosen by God for salvation, must somehow be *made* to believe the gospel in spite of both their natural unwillingness and alleged inability. The gospel of God's grace, which seemingly is offered to whosoever will believe, must be imposed — and that, only upon those whom God has elected. As White explains, this is why Irresistible Grace is an absolute necessity:

> Unregenerate man is fully capable of understanding the facts of the gospel: he is simply incapable, due to his corruption and enmity, to submit himself to that gospel . . . . [49]

This is a terrible attack upon the gospel, rendering powerless what Paul declares is "the power of God unto salvation" (Romans 1:16)! And this is what White calls "the Reformed position." Yet Scripture never states this belief but rather contradicts it. With no clear support from the Bible, the "Reformed position" must be deduced from the fact that man is "dead in sin." [50] The fallacy has been already exposed of ascribing the symptoms of physical death to the spiritually dead.

Once sovereignly regenerated, the person is presumably able, under the influence of irresistible grace, to believe the gospel and thereafter to make moral choices and thus to serve Christ from the heart. Oddly enough, however, from then on, grace is evidently no longer imposed irresistibly upon the elect, as it was before they were regenerated. That fact is obvious, since the elect do not always behave as they should, much less to perfection. Yet the language Scripture uses in describing the Christlike life which believers are to live *sounds* far more irresistibly imposed than anything Calvinists can cite from the Bible concerning salvation:

> Therefore if any man be in Christ, he is a new creature: old things have passed away; behold, all things are become new. Christ liveth in me . . . . For we are his workmanship, created in Christ Jesus unto good works, which God hath before ordained that we should walk in them. For it is God which worketh in you both to will and to do of his good pleasure . . . . every one that doeth righteousness is born of him . . . whosoever abideth in him sinneth not . . . greater is he that is in you than he that is in the world . . . . " (2 Corinthians 5:17; Galatians 2:20; Ephesians 2:10; Philippians 2:13: 1 John 2:29; 3:6; 4:4.)

These passages leave us with further questions. The Calvinist cannot point to any passage in the Bible which states clearly that grace is irresistible, or that God imposes it upon the elect who otherwise could not believe the gospel. On the other hand, there are many passages such as those just quoted which state quite clearly that God intends righteousness for those who believe in Christ. In spite of that fact, however, Christians do not live up to the perfection God has ordained.

If God can irresistibly impose His grace unto salvation upon the totally depraved, why can't He impose it upon the regenerated unto perfection in Christian living? There is certainly no biblical answer to this dilemma in which we find ourselves if we accept the theory of Irresistible Grace.

Paul even gives the example of a true Christian, surely one of the elect, who does not have even *one good work* as evidence that he belongs to Christ. *None* of his works survive the fire of evaluation at the judgment seat of Christ, yet "he himself shall be saved"(1 Corinthians 3:12-15). How could God's sovereignty completely override human moral responsibility and choice, as the Calvinist insists, to the extent that man has no choice when it comes to salvation – and yet the elect are able to resist God's grace and His will and thus often fail to do the good works which God has ordained for them to fulfill to His glory?

If the elect, having been made spiritually alive by sovereign regeneration, nevertheless do not perfectly obey God, why is unbelief and rebellion equated by Calvinism with total depravity and spiritual death?

If God's sovereignty does not nullify for the elect the moral accountability to make choices, why would His sovereignty disallow a genuine choice on the part of the unsaved to accept or reject the gospel? If disobedience to God's will by the elect poses no threat to God's sovereignty, why would a rejection of the gospel by some of the unsaved pose a threat?

And would not an irresistible imposition of grace turn it into no grace at all? Some of these questions are considered in the next chapter.

1   Loraine Boettner, *The Reformed Doctrine of Predestination* (Presbyterian and Reformed Publishing Co., 1932), 365.

2   Benjamin B. Warfield, *Calvin and Augustine*, ed. Samuel G. Craig (Presbyterian and Reformed Publishing Co., 1956), 321.

3   Kenneth H. Good, *Are Baptists Calvinists?* (Backus Book Publishers, 1988), 49.

4   R.C. Sproul, *The Holiness of God* (Tyndale House Publishers, Inc., 1993 ed.), 273.

5   William G.T. Shedd, *A History of Christian Doctrine* (Charles Scribner and Co., 3rd ed. 1865), 70.

6   Augustine, *On the Spirit and the Letter*. In Laurence M. Vance, *The Other Side of Calvinism* (Vance Publications, Pensacola FL, rev. ed. 1999), 57.

7   Augustine, *On the Predestination of the Saints*, op. cit., 7,8,16.

8   Dave Breese, "The Five Points of Calvinism" (self-published paper, n.d.), 3.

9   John Piper and Pastoral Staff, "TULIP: What We Believe about the Five Points of Calvinism: Position Paper of the Pastoral Staff" (Desiring God Ministries, 1997), 12.

10   Op. cit., 9.

11   Ibid.

12   Charles Hodge, *Systematic Theology* (Wm. B. Eerdmans Publishing Co., 1986), 2:643.

13   John Piper, *The Legacy of Sovereign Joy: God's Triumphant Grace in the Lives of Augustine, Luther, and Calvin* (Crossway Books, 2000), 73.

14   J. I. Packer, "The Love of God: Universal and Particular," in *Still Sovereign,* ed. Thomas R. Schreiner and Bruce A. Ware (Baker Books, 2000) 281.

15   Piper and Staff, "TULIP," 2.

16   D.A. Carson, *The Difficult Doctrine of the Love of God* (Crossway Books, 2000), 46-47.

17   Arthur W. Pink, *The Sovereignty of God* (Baker Book House, 2nd prtg. 1986), 128.

18   Carson, op. cit., 78-79.

19   Hodge, op. cit., II:687

20   C.D. Cole, *Definitions of Doctrines* (Bible Truth Depot, n.d.), 84.

21   Frank B. Beck, *The Five Points of Calvinism* (Covenanter Press, 2nd Australian ed. 1986), 40.

22   Jacobus Arminius, *The Works of James Arminius*, trans. James and William Nichols (Baker Book House, 1986), I:525.

23   Tom Ross, *Abandoned Truth: The Doctrines of Grace* (Providence Baptist Church, 1991), 56.

24   Carson, op. cit., 52.

25   Op. cit., 11.

26   Op. cit., 29.

27   R.C. Sproul, Jr., "The Authentic Message" *(Tabletalk*, Ligonier Ministries, Inc., June 2001), 7.

28   R.C. Sproul, *Faith Alone: The Evangelical Doctrine of Justification* (Baker Books, 1995), 19, and throughout the book.

29   Op.cit., 192; citing Calvin, *The Epistles of Paul the Apostle* (a comment on Galatians 2:16), 39.

30   Steven R. Houck, *The Bondage of the Will* (Peace Protestant Reformed Church, n.d.), 3.

31   Laurence M. Vance, *The Other Side of Calvinism* (Vance Publications, Pensacola FL, rev. ed. 1999), 481.

32   Pink, op.cit., 243.

33   John Piper, "Are There Two Wills In God?" In *Still Sovereign*, ed. Thomas R. Schreiner and Bruce A. Ware (Baker Books, 2000), 130-31.

34   John Calvin, *Calvin's New Testament Commentaries* (Wm. B. Eerdmans Publishing Co., 1994), 12, 364.

35   Ibid.

36   George L. Bryson, *The Five Points of Calvinism "Weighed and Found Wanting"* (The Word For Today, 1996), 56.

37   R.C. Sproul, *Grace Unknown* (Baker Books, 1997), 189.

38   Vance, op. cit., 478.

39   Canons of Dort (Dordrecht, Holland, 1619); reproduced in Vance, op. cit., 607-26.

40   Op. cit., III, IV, "Of the Corruptions of Man, His Conversion to God, and the Manner Thereof,", 17/8.

41   Ben Lacy Rose, *T.U.L.I.P.: The Five Disputed Points of Calvinism* (Providence House Publishers, 1996), 37.

42   Westminster Confession of Faith (London: n.p., 1643), X,1.

43   Pastor in Australia to Dave Hunt, September 8, 2000. On file.

44   Editor of British Christian publication, England, to Dave Hunt, September 8, 2000. On file.

45   R.C. Sproul, *The Holiness of God* (Tyndale House Publishers, Inc. 1993 ed.), 20.

46   John Calvin, *Institutes of the Christian Religion*, trans. Henry Beveridge (Wm. B. Eerdmans Publishing Company, 1998 ed.), IV:xxv,17.

47   Op.cit., IV:xxv.22.

48   Piper, *Legacy*, 135-47; citing Henry F. Henderson, *Calvin in His Letters* (J.M. Dent and Co., 1909), 77-79.

49   James R. White, *The Potter's Freedom* (Calvary Press Publishing, 2000), 101.

50   Ibid.

19
When Grace Isn't Grace

What Calvin practiced in imposing of his *Institutes of Religion* upon those who disagreed with his new faith was in many instances far from Christianity, and was certainly neither grace nor gracious. It was, however, eminently consistent with his view of *Irresistible* Grace and a God who sovereignly imposes it upon the elect. How else could God make certain that the blood of Christ shed on the cross for sin would actually bring salvation to at least some? And how else could a sinner who could not believe be made to believe except irresistibly? In his dispute with Rome, Calvin insisted that "divine grace [acts] irresistibly . . . ." [1]

White argues that because the Bible says *Christ saves* sinners we can't change it to say that he "saves synergistically with the assistance of the sinner himself." [2] Simply *believing* the gospel and *receiving* its free gift of salvation, however, could hardly qualify as "assistance" to God. Yet Pink likewise sounds so reasonable when he argues:

> Who is regulating affairs on this earth today — God, or the Devil? What impression is made upon the minds of those men of the world who, occasionally, attend a Gospel service . . . ? Is it not that a *disappointed* God is the One whom Christians believe in? From what is heard from the average evangelist today, is not any serious hearer *obliged* to conclude that he professes to represent a God who is filled with benevolent intentions, yet unable to carry them out; that He is earnestly desirous of blessing men, but that they will not let Him? [3]

Has Pink forgotten that much of the Old Testament was written by weeping prophets who expressed God's disappointment and grief over Israel's rejection of His love and grace and proffered mercy? Nevertheless, to the Calvinist, if salvation is merely an offer that man can refuse, that puts man in charge rather than God. This argument is patently fallacious. The Calvinist's only alternative would have to be for a gift and love to be sovereignly imposed, which would destroy them both. Thus man is programmed to respond rather than turning to God willingly with his whole heart.

Calvin's sincere desire to protect God's sovereignty from any incursion by man necessitated a God who from eternity past decided to save a select few from among totally depraved mankind and to banish the rest to eternal hell. Neither the elect nor the non-elect had any choice in the matter in spite of God apparently pretending that they did have a choice by calling upon all men to repent and believe and to choose whom to serve. In Calvinisn, repentance and faith come totally from God to the extent that man has no responsible part to play:

> It is sad indeed to find one like the late Dr.[A.T.] Pierson — whose writings are generally so scriptural and helpful — saying, "It is a tremendous thought that even God Himself cannot . . . prevent me from defying and denying Him, and would not exercise His power in such a direction if He could, and could not if He would." (*A Spiritual Clinique*) It is sadder still to discover that many other respected and loved brethren are giving expression to the same sentiments. Sad, because directly at variance with the Holy Scriptures." [4]

In fact, it is Calvinism that puts its special interpretation upon Scripture to make it fit its scheme.

God The Puppet Master

The insistence upon a sovereignty which necessarily disallows any choice to man became the foundation of that system of theology known as Calvinism today. God's sovereignty and man's inability to say, think or do anything that God had not predestined has been the continuing emphasis, as any survey of the writings of Calvinists reveals. Man is thus reduced to a puppet with God pulling the strings.

Engelsma asserts, "The Apostle Paul was an avowed, ardent predestinarian, holding double predestination, election, and reprobation." [5] What Engelsma attributes to Paul, Jewett claims was the common belief of every theologian in history worth mentioning: "Every theologian of the first rank from Augustine to Barth has affirmed . . . that God's election is a righteous and holy decision that he makes according to his own good pleasure to redeem the objects of his electing love." [6] Man cannot even believe the gospel without God *causing* him to do so.

Piper writes an entire book "to defend the claim that God is not unrighteous in unconditionally predestining some Israelites [and some of all mankind] to salvation and some to condemnation." [7] There is no disagreement with Calvinism concerning God's righteousness or His justice — the issue is His love. Does He love the whole world and does He, because of His infinite love, desire all men to be saved, or doesn't He? The Calvinist limits God's love to a select few, whereas the Bible declares His love for all — and allows man the choice which love requires.

Packer makes the Calvinist position clear: "God loves all in some ways (everyone whom he creates . . . receives many undeserved good gifts . . . .) He loves some in all ways (that is . . . he brings them to faith, to new life and to glory according to his predesinating purpose)." [8] Again, the question must be faced: "What love is this that provides some *temporal* earthly benefits for those it predestines to *eternal doom*?" Christ said it was a bad bargain for a man to "gain the whole world, and lose his own soul" (Matthew 16:26). How is it that the very exchange of time for eternity, which Christ warns against, Packer calls a gift of God's love? But this is Calvinism. In his highly recommended and defining book, Palmer declares:

> Reprobation is God's eternal, sovereign, unconditional, immutable, wise, holy, and mysterious decree whereby, in electing some to eternal life, He passes others by, and then justly condemns them for their own sin — all to His own glory . . . .

> By the decree of God, for the manifestation of His glory, some men and angels are predestinated to everlasting life; and others foreordained to everlasting death . . . . God has appointed the elect to glory . . . . The rest of mankind God was pleased, according to the unsearchable counsel of His own will . . . for the glory of His sovereign power over His creatures . . . to ordain them to dishonor and wrath for their sin, to the praise of His glorious justice. [9]

A One-Sided Emphasis

In never-ending litany, Calvinism's continual emphasis is upon God's sovereignty, glory, justice and wrath. One searches its literature diligently and finds very little, if anything, of God's mercy, grace, compassion and love for the creatures He has made. So many of the attributes of God as revealed in Scripture simply don't square with reprobation and must be ignored. Yes, there is "grace," but it is "irresistible" and for the elect alone with an unapologetic emphasis upon God's withholding it from the non-elect, as though damning those whom He could save gives Him greater glory!

Irresistible Grace is a human invention with rules developed by human reasoning and then imposed upon the Bible. White writes, "We first note that 'irresistible grace' is a reference to God's sovereign regeneration of His elect:

any other use of this phrase is in error." [10] It is amazing how precisely he insists this phrase must be used — a phrase not even found in the Bible. He even describes definite rules for its operation about which Paul and the other apostles, who never used the phrase, obviously knew nothing.

When Moses asked for a revelation of God's glory, the response was, "I will make all my goodness pass before thee . . . [and] the LORD passed by before him, and proclaimed, The LORD, The LORD God, merciful and gracious, longsuffering, and abundant in goodness and truth, Keeping mercy for thousands, forgiving iniquity and transgressions and sin and that will by no means clear [i.e., forgive without the penalty being paid] the guilty . . . (Exodus 33:19; 34:6-7).

Great emphasis is placed upon God's statement, "[I] will be gracious to whom I will be gracious, and will shew mercy on whom I will shew mercy" (Exodus 33:19) — but always from the negative point of view, as though God were limiting His grace and mercy to the elect. It is true, as Piper says, that "there are no stipulations outside his own counsel or will which determine the disposal of his mercy and grace . . . in dispensing mercy and grace God is dependent on nothing but his own free and sovereign choice." [11]

That is true, but God declares repeatedly that His grace and mercy are for all. The Calvinist, however, sees in God's declaration to Moses a limiting of grace and mercy to the elect; whereas the whole tenor of Scripture tells us that His mercy and grace are boundless. The entire context requires the understanding that God is revealing the infinite expanse of His mercy and grace, not its limitations. These limitless benefits are from His "goodness" as God, and flow to all His creatures in infinite love.

A Continuing Cover-Up

We are examining closely whether the theory of Irresistible Grace is really biblical and truly represents the God of the Bible. As we have already seen, solely on the basis of Calvin's *irresistible* imposition of his brand of godliness at Geneva we have good cause for suspecting the contrary. How could a man who so outrageously violated the basic teachings of Christ, and who by his treatment of his fellows dishonored his Lord, be looked to as a theological giant by so many evangelicals today? Surely doctrine and conduct influence and reflect one another.

It is staggering, in view of his tyrannical and often brutal rule of Geneva, that anyone could defend Calvin as an outstanding Christian. Could there be any question that his dictatorial conduct which was so un-Christlike was a direct result of his view of God as a harsh Sovereign more ready to condemn than to save? Tragically, that view of God persists among this man's followers today.

Furthermore, there has been a shameful cover-up of John Calvin which continues to the present. The booklet put out by John Piper and his pastoral staff at Bethlehem Baptist Church in Minneapolis opens with "Historical Information." It begins, "John Calvin, the famous theologian and pastor of Geneva . . . . " [12] — and that is it from "history." There is not one word of the tyrannical rule of this "Protestant Pope" which we have documented in Chapter 5. Is it really fair to readers to praise Calvin without telling the truth? Doesn't that give a false impression? Isn't Calvin's conduct as important as his theology? Is there not an intimate connection between the two and shouldn't one be judged by the other?

In a new book, Piper purports to faithfully tell the truth about Augustine, Luther and Calvin, whom he calls "three famous and flawed fathers in the Christian church . . . " and thereby to show how "the faithfulness of God triumphs over the flaws of men." [13] We shake our heads in astonishment to read Piper's declaration that his aim in this book "is that the glorious Gospel of God's all-satisfying, omnipotent grace will be savored, studied and spread for the joy of all peoples — in a never-ending legacy of Sovereign Joy." [14] *All peoples*? Can he be serious?

Are Calvinists so used to changing "world" and "whosoever" and "all men" and other universal terms in God's Holy Word into "elect" that they now use broad terms to mean elect in their own books? Calvinism's gospel of "omnipotent grace will be savored, studied and spread for the joy" of the non-elect? These are supposed to savor, study and take great joy that they have been predestined to eternal doom and there is no hope whatsoever to change their fate? What mockery! Yet the Calvinist seems blind to what his theory has done to the God who *is love* and how it mitigates against any sense of urgency and responsibility to preach the gospel.

Piper reminds us that "The standard text on theology that Calvin and Luther drank from was *Sentences* by Peter Lombard. Nine-tenths of this book consists of quotations from Augustine . . . . Luther was an Augustinian monk, and Calvin immersed himself in the writings of Augustine, as we can see from the increased use of Augustine's writings in each new edition of the *Institutes* . . . paradoxically, one of the most esteemed fathers of the Roman Catholic Church 'gave us the Reformation.' " [15] Piper considers this paradox to be good; we do not, and for the many reasons we are giving, among them Rome's heresies that were carried over into the Reformation by Luther and Calvin.

His supposed exposé of Calvin's "flaws" is almost a whitewash. Piper admits that "fifteen women were burned at the stake" and that there were some cruelties. The full truth, as we have seen, is far worse. All is largely excused, however, as "Calvin's accommodation to brutal times" and as having been done "in tribute and defense of Protestant martyrs in France." [16] Piper writes:

> . . . the worst was his joining in the condemnation of the heretic, Michael Servetus, to burning at the stake in Geneva . . . . Calvin argued the case against him. He was sentenced to death. Calvin called for a swift execution, instead of burning, but he was burned at the stake on October 27, 1553.
>
> This has tarnished Calvin's name so severely that many cannot give his teaching a hearing. But it is not clear that most of us, given that milieu, would not have acted similarly under the circumstances . . . the times were harsh, immoral, and barbarous and had a contaminating effect on everyone . . . . There was in the life and ministry of John Calvin a grand God-centeredness, Bible-allegiance, and iron constancy.
>
> Under the banner of God's mercy to miserable sinners, we would do well to listen and learn . . . . The conviction behind this book is that the glory of God, however dimly, is mirrored in the flawed lives of his faithful servants. [17]

With those sweet words Piper really means that "under the banner of God's mercy to *some* miserable sinners" the favored elect may "listen and learn." But the non-elect can't listen and learn because they are totally depraved and without understanding or hope because Piper's "God" keeps them in blindness. And even if they could understand the message and wanted to believe, it would not be possible because they have been damned from eternity past by an immutable decree of the Almighty. Is it really fair to readers to give such a false impression of joy to "all peoples"?

And was it really "a grand God-centeredness, Bible-allegiance, and iron constancy" which produced the ungodly and unbiblical tyranny under Calvin at Geneva? Review Chapter 5 to see how Calvin is being protected by Piper. There were many Christians who did not practice torture and burning at the stake in Calvin's day and thus proved that no one needed to make "accommodation to brutal times." Would Paul have, or John, or Christ? Why Calvin?

And why doesn't Piper explain that the reason Calvin pushed for beheading was because that was the execution for civil crimes and the onus would not be on himself? But the charges brought against Servitus by Calvin and pressed by him in court were theological and required the flames. Calvin was simply trying to circumvent the law. Do we praise him for that? Eight years later Calvin was still advising other rulers to exterminate heretics "like I exterminated Michael Servetus. . . "! But he was a victim of his times? No, a victim rather of his theology!

Unbiblical And Unreasonable

As we have already seen, the theory of Irresistible Grace (as with the rest of Calvinism) confronts us with many serious conflicts with Scripture and with reason. One of the most astonishing in both categories is the insistence that man must be regenerated (i.e., born again) before he can believe in Christ to salvation. Sproul explains: "Reformed theology views regeneration as the immediate supernatural work of the Holy Spirit that effects the change of the soul's disposition . . . . Faith is a fruit of regeneration." [18]

We have earlier given some attention to this theory but need to examine it in more depth. That this dogma is not produced by biblical exegesis but is necessitated by the other points in TULIP is clear. Nowhere does the Bible plainly state that regeneration (i.e., the new birth, being born again, given eternal life, salvation) *precedes* faith, but there are scores of scriptures which tell us that *faith* comes first:

He that believeth and is baptized shall be saved . . . ." (Mark 16:16)

. . . to them gave he power to become [through the new birth] the sons of GOD, even to them that believe on his name (John 1:12)

He that believeth on me hath everlasting life. (John 6:47)

. . . he that believeth in me, though he were dead, yet shall he live . . . . (John 11:25)

. . . that believing ye might have life through his name. (John 20:31)

Believe on the Lord Jesus Christ, and thou shalt be saved . . . . (Acts 16:31)

. . . and many of the Corinthians hearing believed, and were baptized. (Acts 18:8)

. . . the gospel of Christ . . . is the power of God unto salvation to everyone that believeth . . . . (Romans 1:16)

That if thou shalt . . . believe in thine heart . . . , thou shalt be saved.(Romans 10:9)

. . . it pleased God . . . to save them that believe. (1 Corinthians 1:21)

. . . them that believe to the saving of the soul. (Hebrews 10:39)

Whosoever believeth that Jesus is the Christ is [as a result of believing] born of God . . . . (1 John 5:1)

It seems indisputably clear from the above scriptures and many others that only upon believing in Christ, and as a result of that faith, is one regenerated. Sproul acknowledges that if one is a Christian, one is regenerate; and if one is regenerate, one is a Christian. [19] But if faith only follows regeneration, one has become a Christian *before* believing unto salvation — a concept directly contrary to Scripture.

Robert Morey claims there is one verse in the Bible that teaches regeneration before faith: John 3:3. He declares, "Christ places regeneration by the Spirit as a requirement before one can 'see,' i.e., believe or have faith in the Kingdom of God." He states quite emphatically that "a sinner who is born of the flesh can not believe the good news of the Kingdom until he is born by the Spirit." [20]

Such loose thinking is not typical of Morey, but it is very typical of the eisegesis so many otherwise rational Calvinists are forced into in order to defend an unbiblical theory. "*See*" the kingdom means to "*believe* or have faith in the Kingdom . . . "? There is no such concept anywhere in Scripture: faith is in God and in Christ. And Christ leaves no doubt as to the meaning of "see" when He reiterates, "Except a man be born of water and of the Spirit, he cannot *enter into* the kingdom of God" (John 3:5). One must be in the kingdom of God to see it in the way Christ means. Realizing that it is absurd to speak of "faith in the Kingdom," Morey rephrases it to "believe the good news of the Kingdom," which is equally far from what Christ says.

Christ told His disciples (and us today as His disciples also) to go into all the world and preach the gospel to every person whom we encounter and who will listen. In obedience to his Lord, the Apostle Paul had a passion to get the gospel to everyone he could reach. He spent his life in trying to persuade Jews and Gentiles to believe in Christ, disputing in the synagogues and public places. But if Calvinism is true, this is a futile task. Man is totally depraved, even "dead," so that he cannot believe unto salvation, no matter how persuasively we preach the gospel.

Demeaning The Great Commission

How can God's grace reach, with regeneration, the "totally depraved" sinner who is incapable of believing the gospel? What could be more logical than something called Irresistible Grace to impose salvation upon those whom God has elected to be saved? And since man is powerless to believe unto salvation, wouldn't it follow of necessity that salvation must be imposed upon him without his first believing the gospel? If Total Depravity means that no man can believe the gospel unto salvation, then not only the theory of Irresistible Grace follows but also its corollary: man must be regenerated and made alive before he can believe and be saved.

Yet a biblical view keeps slipping in, betrayed by un-Calvinistic admissions. For example, the following from Sproul: "Once Luther grasped the teaching of Paul in Romans, he was reborn." [21] This slip of the pen contradicts the claim that one must first be regenerated and only then can the gospel be understood and believed. Which is it? We are reborn/regenerated before we can believe the gospel, or through believing the gospel? Or are we reborn twice, once by

God's sovereign act before we believe, and then again after first being regenerated and given the faith to believe?

In contrast, the Bible repeatedly declares in the plainest language (not only in the passages quoted above but elsewhere as well) that no man can be changed from unrepentant sinner to child of God without from the heart believing the gospel and, as a result of believing, being born of the Spirit of God. But if no one can believe the gospel without first being regenerated by the Spirit of God, as Calvinism declares, then not only the damnation of billions but the continuance of evil must be God's will inasmuch as He chooses to regenerate so few and to move upon so few hearts with Irresistible Grace. The Bible, reason and conscience are all contradicted. Dick Sanford has put it like this:

> The teaching that [because of God's sovereignty] a man who's saved couldn't have done anything but be saved, and a man who's lost couldn't have done anything but be lost destroys the concept of grace. It changes grace to simple programming. Love is not required . . . . Man isn't responding to a loving God's grace, he is simply doing what he was programmed to do. [22]

Building Upon A "Dead" Foundation

It was specious reasoning about "dead in sins" (which superficially seems logical, but certainly is not biblical) that gave birth to Calvin's theory of Irresistible Grace. While this issue was dealt with in Chapter 9, further discussion was promised under this heading. Care is being taken to be certain that Calvinism is fairly presented and clearly understood in order not to charge Calvinists falsely.

Inasmuch as White is recognized as an authority on Calvinism, let him elaborate further upon its assertions with regard to the "I" in TULIP:

> Reformed authors frequently point to the biblical teaching that man is "dead in sin" as substantiation of their belief that God *must* be absolutely sovereign and salvation *must* be completely of free grace and *not* a synergistic cooperation between God and man since man is not *capable* of cooperating any more than a corpse. [23]

> If men are dead in sin at all [i.e., by Calvinism's own peculiar definition], it follows that they must have spiritual life restored to them before they can do spiritually good things . . . . Spiritually dead men believe all sorts of things: just not those things that are pleasing to God. [24]

If one overlooks the continual misrepresentation of Calvinism as *the* theology of the Reformation, White's reasoning at first sounds almost persuasive. When one considers it further, however, something isn't right. Where does the Bible make this distinction that the spiritually dead can "believe all sorts of things" but not "those things that are pleasing to God"? And what does this have to do with salvation, since salvation does not depend upon being "pleasing to God"? And if spiritual death is likened to physical death, an analogy which the Calvinist uses to support his theory, then the spiritually dead shouldn't be able even to think or to believe anything. But if the analogy fails completely in that respect, how can it be valid with regard to the gospel?

To support this analogy, White offers no direct teaching from the Bible. In fact, there is none. The doctrine of Irresistible Grace was largely formulated by deduction from the biblical statement that men are spiritually dead. The only way to make it fit TULIP was to equate "spiritual death" with "physical death." That error became a major pillar of the foundation upon which Calvinism was constructed.

In the process of likening the spiritually dead person to a corpse, there arose a subtle form of materialism. The practical effect (which the Calvinist would deny) was to disregard the capabilities of the soul and spirit which continue very much alive even when the body is a corpse — and certainly ought not to be forgotten while man, though spiritually dead, is physically alive. From that basic fallacy followed a host of unwarranted conclusions in the attempt to build a coherent theory.

A Subtle Surrender To Materialism

Taken in by this error, Dabney argued, "The corpse does not restore life to itself; after life is restored it becomes a living agent." [25] What does that have to do with salvation? Who imagines that the sinner restores himself to life as though he were responsible for saving himself? All the sinner must do is to believe the gospel; it is God who, in response to faith, creates spiritual life through the new birth.

Furthermore, Dabney has forgotten the soul and spirit. The body is only the temporary earthly house for the person living within. The physical body and brain of a biologically alive person doesn't even know it's alive. The soul and spirit living within the body constitute the real person who thinks and wills. Thus, likening spiritual death to a corpse misses the point and leads to confusion. The error in this analogy becomes even clearer when one remembers that regeneration unto spiritual life has no effect on the body at the time. The person remains physically unchanged.

Clearly, in spite of the physical death of the body it once inhabited, the spirit of man continues to think and will. Christ tells of the rich man who after his death could think and speak and express desires "in hell" (Luke 16:22-31). The tissues of a living body, including even the brain, know nothing of the "issues of life" (Proverbs 4:23), yet the Calvinist founds his theory upon the fact that a corpse can't do anything. Piper also embraces the error that the spiritually dead cannot believe the gospel: "God is the one who sovereignly decides who will be shown such mercy [as to be made spiritually alive] . . . ." [26]

Likewise, Westblade calls spiritual death "a moral one that does not hinder us physically but clouds the eyes of the heart . . . . Moral corpses that we are, the only hope we have for a will that turns its passion toward God lies in the call of God [that] makes 'us alive together with Christ . . . .'" [27] Here the error goes a bit deeper. Now morals are connected with the physical body and because a corpse can't make moral choices (of course neither could the physical body when it was alive) — the natural man, being spiritually dead, is therefore imagined to be morally dead.

Where does the Bible teach this? Aren't the Ten Commandments given to spiritually dead mankind and don't the spiritually dead understand the moral issues and often keep some of the commandments? Paul says that even the spiritually dead ungodly "shew the work of the law written in their hearts, their conscience also bearing witness, and their thoughts the mean while accusing or else excusing one another) . . . (Romans 2:14-15)." Doesn't God appeal to every man's conscience continually?

Abraham reminds the rich man in hell of his past moral failure as the reason he is there. Though his body is a corpse in the grave, the rich man knows the truth of his sin, that it is too late for him, and expresses the earnest moral concern that his brothers still alive be warned so that they will not join him in hell. The Calvinist has created an analogy which has run off on its own, far away from both the Bible and common sense.

The Bible offers no justification whatsoever from Genesis to Revelation for concluding that man is morally a corpse. Prone to evil, yes; but unable to understand that he is a sinner and that Christ died for his sins, unable to recognize when he does wrong, and incapable of believing the gospel? No. Never does the Bible teach that. Nor does it teach that the spiritually dead cannot understand the gospel and believe on the Lord Jesus Christ unto salvation.

Adding To The Confusion

Nevertheless, joining the parade of evangelical leaders who support this grave error, J.I. Packer echoes the party line: "'Dead' evidently signifies total unresponsiveness to God, total unawareness of his love, and total lack of the life he gives: no metaphor for spiritual inability and destitution could be stronger." [28] *Evidently?* What does that mean? "Total unresponsiveness to God" and "total unawareness" of God's love even in the God-given conscience? Why doesn't Scripture state the Calvinist position plainly if that is what it means?

Packer offers no direct statement from the Bible supporting his assertion. There is none. He simply follows the standard Calvinist equating of *spiritual* death with *physical* death, an analogy which unwittingly embraces materialism, ignoring as it does the difference between the spirit and the physical body. Here

Calvinists become confused and contradict themselves and one another. Consider this admission from Schreiner, similar to statements already quoted from other Calvinists:

> We are not saying that they [the totally depraved and spiritually dead] are as evil as they can possibly be. Jesus says, " . . . you then, though you are evil, know how to give good gifts to your children" (Luke 11:13). If people were as evil as they possibly could be, they would not desire to give good things to their children [but] Jesus still says that they are evil. Evil people still give good gifts . . . and do kind things . . . ." [29]

If the totally depraved and spiritually dead are "moral corpses," how can they make any moral choices and do any good? That they can is undeniable. Yet the spiritually "dead" person, even though able to do *some* good, is unable to seek God or believe the gospel? That distinction is never made in Scripture.

White's elaboration has already been quoted: "Unregenerate man is fully capable of understanding the facts of the gospel: he is simply incapable, due to his corruption and enmity, to submit himself to that gospel . . . . " [30] Now White is walking a very slender tightrope: while he can believe any number of other things, the spiritually dead man cannot believe the right things and certainly not the gospel although he can understand and reject it. This unbiblical theory is a bold invention of man. Calvinism thus hinges upon a peculiar definition of the word "dead," for which there is no justification other than the necessity to prop up a system of religion. Those who are "dead in sin" can do *this*, but they can't do *that* — but these rules and definitions cannot be found anywhere in Scripture.

The gospel is to be preached to "every creature" (Mark 16:15). It would be irrational for God to send His servants out to suffer and die in preaching the gospel to those who were incapable of understanding and believing it. Yet Palmer reasons, "Only when the Holy Spirit regenerates man and makes him alive spiritually can man have faith in Christ and be saved." [31] In all the Calvinist writing we have studied, not one verse from Scripture is cited which clearly states this doctrine.

Irresistible Grace And Spiritual Death

The word "dead" is used several ways in Scripture. We have already noted that even the saved who are not just physically but now spiritually alive are said to be dead: for example, "dead to sin" (Romans 6:2,7,11). Yet every Christian must honestly confess that, so far as his own desires and conduct are concerned, "dead to sin" is not an absolute statement but must be experienced by faith. Christians are said to be dead in other ways as well: "dead with Christ" (Romans 6:8; Colossians 2:20); "dead to the law" (Galatians 2:19); "for ye are dead, and your life is hid with Christ in God" (Colossians 3:3); "For if we be dead with him

. . . " (2 Timothy 2:11), etc. Yet none of these biblical analogies fits perfectly with being physically dead.

As for sinners, the Bible unquestionably teaches that they are spiritually dead to God. But what does that mean? Adam was spiritually dead, but he heard when God spoke to him and told him the consequences of his sin. He understood why God made a covering of animal skin and told him to offer a lamb from the flock in anticipation of the Lamb of God who would one day pay the penalty for sin. Was Adam regenerated? Obviously not. Such a concept is only introduced in the New Testament. Surely the new birth was unknown before the day of Pentecost, yet many prior to that time knew God and looked forward to the Messiah.

Why should spiritual death to God be taken in an absolute sense any more than the Christian's being dead to sin? There is no biblical reason for doing so. For example, Ephesians 5:14 commands, "Awake thou that sleepest, and arise from the dead, and Christ shall give thee light." Those who are dead are being told to arise. Are they *physically* dead or *spiritually* dead? Obviously not the former; but if the latter, this presents problems to the Calvinist. How can the spiritually dead even be addressed, much less respond and arise from the dead?

Are Christians dead and yet exhorted to raise themselves from the dead — or are they just acting like those who are dead? Paul seems to be paraphrasing Isaiah 60:1-2, which was addressed to unbelieving and rebellious Israel at that time. Can those who are dead in sins raise themselves to life in order to hear Christ's voice and be given light? Or is this metaphorical language, and "dead" doesn't really mean *dead*, but asleep? After all, Paul says, "Awake, thou that sleepest . . . ."

One would think that Calvinists would want to face Ephesians 5:14 and provide an answer, but among the many whom I have read, not one has done so. White gives it a wide berth, as does Piper. None of the thirteen Calvinist authors of the essays which comprise *Still Sovereign* even mentions it. Not every author can cover every scripture — but for none of them to touch it? Isn't that odd? Even in his huge and detailed exposition of the issues on both sides, Vance is unable to quote any Calvinist concerning this scripture.

The Bible contains many difficult passages. Human logic isn't going to solve them. The Bible is one book and every passage must be interpreted in the context of the whole. For example, Jehovah's Witnesses cite "My Father is greater than I" to "prove" that Christ is not God. It sounds so logical from that one verse. But when we take all of Scripture we realize that Christ, who said, "I and my Father are one . . . before Abraham was, I AM, etc.," *is* God from eternity past, co-equal and co-existent with the Father and the Holy Spirit.

Likewise, we must compare scripture with scripture (the Bible is its own best interpreter) as we are doing in order to understand passages about Election, enduring vessels of wrath such as Pharaoh, hating Esau but loving Jacob, dead in sins, and so forth. And to liken spiritual death to physical death does not fit the Bible as a whole.

Seeking An Understanding

Difficult passages are made plain in the light of those which are very clear. And there can be no doubt that Jesus plainly taught more than once that hearing His voice and, as a result, believing the gospel and receiving the gift of eternal life, is possible for those spiritually dead. For example, Jesus said, "The hour is coming, and now is, when the dead shall hear the voice of the Son of God: and they that hear shall live" (John 5:25). A key phrase is, "now is."

Unquestionably, He could have been speaking only of multitudes of the spiritually dead, one after another, individually being made alive through hearing and believing the gospel in His day and throughout time. That He was not referring to men being *physically* raised from the dead, but to their receiving spiritual life, is clear from the fact that He also makes separate and specific reference to a later physical resurrection.

Immediately after declaring that now the dead could hear His voice and live, Christ refers to a future day of resurrection and the phrase "now is" is not included: "The hour is coming, in the which all that are in the graves shall hear his voice, and shall come forth . . . . " Graves were not mentioned in His first statement concerning the dead hearing His voice and living. Here, in contrast to the spiritually dead receiving eternal life through hearing His voice, Christ refers to a future resurrection of the physically dead coming out of their graves, some "unto the resurrection of life" and some "unto the resurrection of damnation" (John 5:28-29).

The process to which Christ first refers, whereby the spiritually dead are given life, can only be ongoing through the preaching of and believing the gospel. Surely this receiving of life by the dead comes as a result of faith in Christ exactly as He said:

> Verily, verily, I say unto you, He that heareth my word, and believeth on him that sent me, hath everlasting life, and shall not come into condemnation; but is passed from death unto life. (John 5:24)

All of Scripture bears witness to what Christ, the Living Word, is saying here: "faith cometh by hearing . . . the word of God" (Romans 10:17) and through that faith the spiritually "dead in trespasses and sins" (Ephesians 2:1) are given spiritual life, eternal life. Repeatedly we are told that he who "believeth" is given "everlasting life" through his faith and as a result passes "from death unto life." He is not regenerated by means of God sovereignly making him spiritually alive without his believing the gospel and thereafter given faith to believe in Christ, as Calvinism asserts. No, he is regenerated as a result of believing the gospel, i.e., through putting his faith in Christ.

A Calvinist friend to whom a preliminary copy of the manuscript of this book had been given for review wrote in the margin, "Regeneration and salvation are distinctly different, as are justification and sanctification." He cited no scriptures, for nowhere in Scripture is that distinction made. To be regenerated by the Spirit of God and thus to become a child of God and yet still need to be saved? Surely sovereign regeneration by the Spirit of God makes one a child of God — and yet one can believe the gospel only after this Calvinist "regneration." On the contrary, all the saved have been born again and all who are born again are saved. These are not two events, but synonyms for the same work of God.

Yet the Calvinist insists that without faith in Christ, without any understanding of the gospel or exercise of choice, the "elect" are "born again" (regeneration must be the same as the new birth) by the Spirit of God into the family of God so that God can then give them faith to believe. Since we are saved by faith — "by grace are ye saved through faith...believe and thou shalt be saved" (Ephesians 2:5, Acts 16:31) — and Calvinism says that we can't have faith until we have been regenerated, we must (according to this strange doctrine) be born again before we are saved! Though a staunch Calvinist, Dillow realizes the folly and writes, "Furthermore, the state of salvation occurs simultaneously with the exercise of this faith and does not occur before it." [32]

The "Spiritually Dead" Hear And Believe

That the unsaved, dead in trespasses and in sins, can be reasoned with and can understand and believe the gospel unto salvation is clear from many passages such as the following: "Knowing the terror of the Lord, we persuade [unsaved] men" (2 Corinthians 5:11); "And he reasoned in the synagogue [with unregenerate men] . . . and persuaded the [unbelieving] Jews and Greeks [to believe]" (Acts 18:4); "he mightily convinced the [unbelieving] Jews . . . shewing by the scriptures that Jesus was Christ" (Matthew 18:28); and so forth.

These verses (and many more like them) surely make it sound as though we are to use reason and Scripture in order to convince the lost that they need a Savior, and that the Holy Spirit will use the persuasion of God's Word, which is "quick, and powerful, and sharper than any twoedged sword" (Hebrews 4:12), to convict them and bring them to Christ. To be reasoned with, persuaded and convinced, a person must understand the arguments and believe the truth which they convey. Clearly, then, the unregenerate *can* understand the gospel and respond prior to their regeneration – or persuading them would be a fruitless effort.

God said to the unbelieving and rebellious children of Israel, most of whom refused to respond, "Come now, and let us reason together . . . though your sins be as scarlet, they shall be as white as snow . . . " (Isaiah 1:18). If Calvinism were true, God would be wasting His time and effort reasoning with spiritually dead people who could no more respond to the truth than a corpse could give itself a blood transfusion. And if the only way they could repent and believe unto eternal life was for God to impose Irresistible Grace upon them, we are faced again with the question of why He pleads and berates while at the same time He withholds the only means whereby those He addresses could respond.

According to Calvinism, God should have first regenerated Israel (or at least the elect among them) and then and only then could He have reasoned with them to any spiritual benefit. But the Bible tells us otherwise. From these few scriptures we have considered, as well as from many similar passages in the Bible, one would certainly *not* conclude that God overwhelms elect sinners with Irresistible Grace to regenerate them first and then gives them faith to believe. On the contrary, He calls upon them to repent and sends His prophets to warn and persuade them. Paul's major ministry was disputing and persuading in the synagogue, the marketplace and public gatherings such as Mars' Hill, where men met to discuss issues of the day.

The very fact that Paul, Apollos and the other early evangelists expended so much time and energy in persuading men to believe the gospel is completely contrary to the concept of both Total Depravity and Irresistible Grace. Obviously, Paul was not aware of the principles Calvin would extract from his epistles 1,500 years later. Nor apparently was Jesus, for He kept urging the unregenerate to come to Him and from the cross asked His Father to forgive the very rebels who crucified and mocked Him.

"Limited" Irresistible Grace?

Even if we assume, for sake of argument, that grace *could* be irresistible, the Calvinist's grace could hardly be called grace for another reason: it is limited. Yes, as sovereign, God can do as He pleases. He could damn everyone and no one could complain, for that is what we deserve. Sovereignly, He is under no obligation to save anyone.

But sovereignty is not a total description of God. Numerous passages have already been cited in which God is described as infinite in love, mercy and grace toward all and not willing that any perish. The Calvinist God, however, limits His grace and mercy. Christ was asked whether few would be saved and He stated that indeed there would be few (Matthew 7:13-14; Luke 13:23-28) – not because

God limits His grace, however, but because so few are willing to repent and believe the gospel by which alone they can be saved.

One would think that these passages where Christ says few will be saved would be favorites for Calvinists, especially Matthew 7:14 and Luke 13:23. Yet in searching many books by Calvinists, this author has been unable to find even one such reference. Why? Could it be because Christ so clearly puts upon the unregenerate the responsibility of entering the kingdom? Hear His words: "Enter ye in at the strait gate . . . strait is the gate, and narrow is the way, which leadeth unto life, and few there be that find it" (Matthew 7:14). Why would He even give such a warning if one could come into the kingdom solely through having been predestined to salvation and sovereignly regenerated without any understanding, repentance or faith? A.T. Pierson said it well:

> Insofar as any human being sins for himself, he must believe for himself . . . . Boasting is excluded. I have only to believe . . . to take Jesus as Saviour . . . to accept the white robe of His perfect righteousness, which is "unto all and upon all . . . that believe" [Romans 3:22]. [33]

Why aren't more saved? Why aren't *all* people saved? The Bible says it is because so few are willing to come as repentant sinners and enter in at the narrow gate of faith in Christ alone. Refusing to allow man that option of a free will, Calvinism insists that so few are saved because God only loves, cares for and saves a few, though He could save all. This God is defended by saying that He is being gracious and merciful to whomever He rescues from the hell they deserve. Indeed, Calvinism makes it appear that saving so few is to God's greater glory. Calvin has earlier been quoted to that effect:

> We shall never be clearly persuaded, as we ought to be, that our salvation flows from the wellspring of God's free mercy until we come to know his eternal election, which illumines God's grace by this contrast: that he . . . gives to some what he denies to others. [34]

Here we gain further insight into Calvin's strange thinking: God illumines His grace by not extending it to multitudes! Somehow by *limiting* His grace God enlarges our appreciation of the wellspring from which His mercy flows! And we are to praise Him all the more because He gives only to a few what He could extend to all? Well, that is Calvinism. Boettner reminds us that "if any are saved God must choose out those who shall be the objects of His grace." [35]

Imagine a man in a barge surrounded by a thousand desperate people who have no life jackets and can keep themselves afloat in the icy water only for a few more minutes. He has the means of saving every one of them from a watery grave, and more than enough room and complete provisions on the barge for them all. He plucks only 150 from certain death, leaving the rest to drown because it pleases him to do so.

The next day, would the newspapers have banner headlines praising this man for being so kind, gracious and merciful that he rescued 150 and left 850 to die – or even if he rescued 850 and left to their fate only 150 whom he could have saved? Hardly. By the conscience God has given even the "totally depraved" and spiritually dead children of Adam, everyone would condemn such despicable behavior. No one with any sense of the morals God has imprinted upon every conscience could praise such a man for leaving *anyone* to drown whom he could have saved.

Yet we are supposed to believe that God refrains from rescuing millions and perhaps billions, and we are to praise Him all the more for having limited His love, mercy and grace! W.J. Seaton says without any apparent sense of irony or shame, because this is what all Calvinists believe, " . . . if God alone can save, and if *all* are not saved, then the conclusion must be that God has not chosen to save all." [36] Pink argues that to claim that the purpose of Christ's death was to provide salvation for all "is to undermine the very foundations of our faith." [37]

What "faith" is that! How did Augustine and Calvin do away with the heavenly Father who the Bible assures us is infinitely more loving, merciful, kind and gracious than any human could ever be? What have they made of Him?

Piper ends one of his most important books, in which he attempts to justify the reprobating God of Calvinism, with this exhortation to the elect readers: " . . . we will entrust ourselves to mercy alone. In the hope of glory we will extend this mercy to others that they may see our good deeds and give glory to our Father in heaven.' [38] Why should the elect's good deeds cause those who have been predestined to eternal doom to give glory to the elect's Father in heaven who closed the door of salvation to them? The God-given conscience is offended at the Calvinists' rejoicing in their election with scarcely a word of sympathy for those who will spend eternity in utter anguish and for whom from the beginning there was never any hope.

As for mercy, only if one is absolutely certain that he is among the elect (and how can any Calvinist be one-hundred-percent certain?) dare he trust himself to the "mercy" of this otherwise unmerciful God. For the non-elect there is no real mercy. Nor need the Calvinist be merciful to all but (like his God) only toward those to whom it "pleases" him to be merciful.

Yes, the Calvinist insists that God is merciful in giving sunshine and rain and life to the lost – but only the Calvinist thinks in such terms. Would a murderer be considered merciful who gives a nice, hearty meal to his victims just before he tortures and kills them? Ah, but God is sovereign and the clay can't complain about what the potter has made of it. We are not mere lumps of clay, but creatures made in the image of God and to whom He has lovingly promised salvation. Calvinism's God offends the conscience which the God of the Bible has put within all mankind, tramples upon the very compassion with which the One who *is love* has imbued even the ungodly, and manifests a lower standard of behavior toward multitudes than He requires of us toward our enemies. Something isn't right!

Remember again that the issue before us is not only God's sovereignty. The issue is also mercy and grace motivated by love. Calvinism's "grace," for the very reason that it is *limited* and *irresistible*, is no grace at all.

1 John Calvin, *Acts of the Council of Trent: With the Antidote*, ed. and trans. Henry Beveridge (1851); in *Selected Works of John Calvin: Tracts and Letters*, 7 vols., ed. Henry Beveridge and Jules Bonnet (Baker Books, 1983), 3:111.
2 James R. White, *The Potter's Freedom* (Calvary Press Publishing, 2000), 247.
3 Arthur W. Pink, *The Sovereignty of God* (Baker Book House, 2nd prtg. 1986), 12.
4 Pink, op. cit., 144.
5 David J. Engelsma, *Hyper-Calvinism and the Call of the Gospel* (Reformed Free Publishing Association, 1980), 53.
6 Paul K. Jewett, *Election and Predestination* (Wm. B. Eerdmans Publishing Co., 1985 ed.), 3-4.
7 John Piper, *The Justification of God: An Exegetical and Theological Study of Romans 9:1-23* (Baker Books, 2000), 179.
8 J.I. Packer, "The Love of God: Universal and Particular," in *Still Sovereign,* ed. Thomas R. Schreiner and Bruce A. Ware (Baker Books, 2000), 283-84.
9 Edwin H. Palmer, *the five points of calvinism* (Baker Books, enlarged ed., 20th prtg. 1999), 95, 124-25.
10 White, op. cit., 137.
11 Piper, op. cit., 82-83.
12 John Piper and Pastoral Staff, "TULIP: What We Believe about the Five Points of Calvinism: Position Paper of the Pastoral Staff" (Desiring God Ministries, 1997), 3.
13 John Piper, *The Legacy of Sovereign Joy: God's Triumphant Grace in the Lives of Augustine, Luther, and Calvin* (Crossway Books, 2000), 18.
14 Op. cit., 38.
15 Op. cit., 24-25.
16 Op. cit., 32-35.
17 Op. cit., 34-38.
18 R.C. Sproul, *Faith Alone: The Evangelical Doctrine of Justification* (Baker Books, 1995), 26.
19 Op. cit., 23.
20 Robert A. Morey, *Studies in the Atonement* (Crowne Publications, 1989), 82.
21 R.C. Sproul, *The Holiness of God* (Tyndale House Publishers, Inc., 1993 ed.), 144.
22 Dick Sanford, *Predestination and Election*, ed. John R. Cross (self-published monograph, n.d.), 3.
23 Op. cit., 100.
24 Op. cit., 105.
25 Robert L. Dabney, *The Five Points of Calvinism* (Sprinkle Publications, 1992), 35.
26 Piper, *Justification*, 178, note 31.
27 Donald J. Westblade, "Divine Election in the Pauline Literature." In *Still Sovereign*, ed. Thomas R. Schreiner and Bruce A. Ware (Baker Books, 2000), 72-73.
28 Packer, op. cit., 283.
29 Thomas R. Schreiner, "Does Scripture Teach Prevenient Grace in the Wesleyan Sense?" in Schreiner and Ware, op. cit., 231.

30 White, op. cit., 101.
31 Palmer, op. cit., 27.
32 Joseph C. Dillow, *The Reign of the Servant Kings: A Study of Eternal Security and the Final Significance of Man* (Schoettle Publishing Co., 2nd ed. 1993), 287.
33 Arthur T. Pierson, *The Believer's Life: Its Past, Present, and Future Tenses* (Morgan and Scott, 1905), 20,33.
34 John Calvin, *Institutes of the Christian Religion*, trans. Henry Beveridge (Wm. Eerdmans Publishing Company, 1998 ed.), III:xxi,1.
35 Loraine Boettner, *The Reformed Doctrine of Predestination* (Presbyterian and Reformed Publishing Co., 1932, 95.
36 W.J. Seaton, *The Five Points of Calvinism* (The Banner of Truth Trust, 1970), 12.
37 Pink, op. cit., 260.
38 Piper, op. cit., 220.

20
Grace And Human Responsibility

In addition to the many scriptures already discussed, Calvinists have a number of other favorites which they cite in support of TULIP, and especially of Irresistible Grace. A sufficient number of these will be presented herein to allow Calvinist leaders to put forth their best arguments.

A passage used most frequently and with the greatest confidence is John 6:37,44: "All that the Father giveth me shall come to me . . . . No man can come to me, except the Father . . . draw him . . . ." Note the enthusiasm with which White "proves" his thesis from this portion of God's Word:

> If believing that man is "so dead" in sin that he is incapable of coming to Christ on his own is "extreme Calvinism," then the Lord Jesus beat Calvin to the punch by 1500 years with His preaching in the synagogue recorded in John 6. Here we have the Lord teaching almost everything Norman Geisler identifies as "extreme Calvinism." Jesus teaches that God is sovereign and acts independently of the "free choices" of men. He likewise teaches that man is incapable of saving faith outside of the enablement of the Father. He then limits this drawing to the same individuals given by the Father to the Son. He then teaches irresistible grace *on the elect* (not on the "willing") when He affirms that *all* those who are given to Him *will* come to Him. John 6:37-45 is the clearest exposition of what [Geisler] calls "extreme Calvinism" in the Bible.

> There is good reason why [Geisler] stumbles at this point: there is no meaningful non-Reformed exegesis of the passage available . . . .

> Let us listen to Jesus teach "extreme Calvinism" almost 1500 years before Calvin was born . . . . "All that the Father gives me will come to me . . . ." The action of giving by the Father *comes before* the action of coming to Christ by

the individual. And since *all* those so given *infallibly come*, we have here both unconditional election and irresistible grace . . . in the space of nine words . . . !

Since the action of *coming* is dependent upon the action of *giving*, we can see that it is simply not exegetically possible [to deny that] God's giving results in man's coming. Salvation is of the Lord . . . . [1]

"Unconditional election and irresistible grace" are found in this passage? Yarbrough, [2] Piper, [3] D.A. Carson [4] and J.I. Packer [5] (among others) also think so. Yet the words "unconditional" and "irresistible" aren't even there, nor can they be found elsewhere in the Bible. And God "limits this drawing to the same individuals given by the Father to the Son"? Read the entire passage carefully; that is not what Christ says, as we shall see. Whatever Christ means, it must be in agreement with the message of God's entire Word — and neither Unconditional Election nor Irresistible Grace qualifies.

Careless Extrapolation

Every Christian would surely agree that the "enablement" of God is essential not only for coming to Christ but for *anything* a saved or even unsaved man does. Without it no one can even draw a breath. Enablement, however, is a far cry from irresistible enforcement *causing* man's action. Yet Yarbrough makes it even stronger with his assertion that "whoever comes to the Son does so as the result of the Father's forceful attraction." [6] Where does one find such teaching in this passage?

Sproul asserts that a "crucial point of dispute between Rome and the Reformation [by this he means Calvinism] . . . was the efficacy of divine grace. Is grace irresistible and efficacious on its own, or is it resistible and dependent on human cooperation?" Of course, he believes it is irresistible and quotes Thomas Aquinas in support. However, the language Aquinas uses is ambivalent: "divine help . . . the help of God . . . the help of grace, etc." [7] To help someone is obviously not the same as causing or forcing them to do something — but the Calvinist is not timid when it comes to unwarranted extrapolations.

More than adequate biblical proof has been offered that the first four theories making up Calvinism (thus far considered) contradict the overall message of Scripture concerning God's love and grace and the response He requires of man as He has created him. We are therefore confident that nothing of TULIP can be found in this particular passage.

A Troubling Tendency

Attention has already been called to a sad tendency among Calvinists which comes as a direct result of this system of thought. It is a troubling apparent lack of sympathy for the lost. And how could it be otherwise? According to Calvinism, God himself has no sympathy for the lost but has been pleased to predestine their doom.

Such a theory logically leads to apathy toward evangelism, though many Calvinists do not succumb to the practical consequences of their belief. Custance reasons, "If Election guarantees the salvation of all that are predestined to be saved, why should we be bothered with evangelism . . . ? What possible difference can it make whether we speak to men or not?" [8] He is right. If God irresistibly draws to Christ a limited elect and predestines the rest to damnation, that fact presumably should be reflected in the attitude and actions of the elect toward the rest of humanity.

It would be only reasonable for a Calvinist to adopt the attitude that "I'm one of the elect. Let the non-elect be damned; there's nothing I can do for them. To be concerned would be to complain against God for predestining them to their just fate." Would that attitude be unloving? Not if God had the same attitude, which Calvinism affirms.

God, according to Calvinism, as we have repeatedly shown in quotations from its leading proponents, does not love the lost enough to save them all; he lacks mercy for the lost sufficient to give them the faith to believe unto salvation — and is even glorified in sovereignly damning so many and saving so few. Morey writes approvingly, "Calvin taught that God loved the elect and planned their holiness and salvation while . . . He hated the reprobate and planned their sin and damnation." [9] "Planned" even "*their sin*"? Yes, even "the mistake of a typist" — that's Calvinism! Yet the Bible reveals God to be infinite in love and mercy without partiality to *all* mankind.

The Overwhelming Testimony Of Scripture

Many scriptures have been quoted in which God expresses genuine concern for rebellious Israel, sending His prophets to plead with His people to repent so He will not have to punish them — and there are hundreds more. We have noted Paul's passion for the lost, his willingness even to be accursed if that might rescue his brethren the Jews from hell, a passion also for the salvation of Gentiles which could only have come from the indwelling Holy Spirit. We have seen the Lord Jesus Christ weeping over Jerusalem, identifying himself as Jahweh, the One who has wept over His rebellious children (Isaiah 1:1-9) for centuries.

We have heard Jesus call out to *whosoever* was weary, burdened or thirsty, "Come unto me." We have heard our Lord repeatedly declare that *whosoever* would believe on Him would be saved. And we have seen the many scriptures which, if the ordinary meaning of words can be accepted, offer salvation to the whole world and declare that God wants the whole world to be saved, that He gave His Son for the salvation of the whole world, that He is not willing that any should perish and that Christ died for the sins of all.

To annul this plain teaching of Scripture, the Calvinist has boldly changed "world" to mean "elect" in no fewer than twenty scriptures. He has changed "whosoever" and "all" into "elect" at least sixteen times each. In addition, the phrase "every man" has been turned into "elect" six times and "everyone" into "elect" three times. In every instance where these changes have been made there is nothing in the text to justify "elect" as the meaning of the word for which it must be substituted. The change has been made for one reason only: to accommodate Calvinism! For example, when Christ says He would draw "all men" to himself (John 12:32), the Calvinist must say, "The 'all' plainly refers to all of God's *elect*." [10] *Plainly*? Only if one is a Calvinist.

One would think that the overwhelming testimony of Scripture that God *is love*, that He is ever merciful to all and wants all to come to the knowledge of the truth, would be accepted gratefully and joyfully by all of Christ's true followers, and that this good news would be proclaimed to the world as Christ commanded. Instead, we have seen that in those places where God's desire for the salvation of all mankind is clearly stated, Calvinists still insist that God has chosen to save only a select few. Great effort is made, even calling upon distant verses unrelated to the context of these loving statements, in order to deny what is so clearly affirmed of God's undeserved and unlimited love for all.

A Simple, Straightforward Declaration

Were these hundreds of scriptures to be taken at face value, one could then in all good faith, biblically and rationally, approach statements such as "All that the Father giveth me shall come to me" (John 6:37) and "no man can come to me, except the Father draw him" (John 6:44) with complete confidence that they could not possibly contradict the Bible's consistent overall message of God's love for everyone. In that spirit, one would then look carefully at the context to seek an understanding in agreement with what Scripture elsewhere so often and consistently declares of God's love and desire for all to be saved.

Piper goes to great lengths in an unsuccessful attempt to "show from Scripture that the simultaneous existence of God's will for 'all persons to be saved' (1 Timothy 2:4) and his will to elect unconditionally those who will actually be saved [John 6:37 is among verses referenced] is not a sign of divine schizophrenia or exegetical confusion." [11] In his zeal to defend Calvinism he must not only change the meaning of words, but maintain that the contradiction thereby created isn't really a contradiction after all.

Christ's words are so simple and straightforward. "All that the Father giveth me shall come to me" does not say that "all that the Father draws shall come to me." Nor does "No man can come to me, except the Father . . . draw him" say that all that the Father draws come to Christ. And surely "I will raise him up at the last day" (John 6:40,44,54) refers to those who actually come to Christ, not all who are drawn. It certainly would not include those who are drawn and then "draw back unto perdition" (Hebrews 10:39). The Calvinist is reading into Christ's words more than He actually says.

The Calvinist's Best Foot Forward

This book is not intended to win a purely intellectual debate. We are defending our God's honor and character. In the process, great care has been taken not to misunderstand Calvinism or to misjudge its proponents. So let us carefully consider White's arguments as he develops them from the context of John 6:37-45, a scripture which he calls "the clearest exposition of what [critics] call 'extreme Calvinism.'" In examining White's and other Calvinists' methods of interpretation, one often finds eisegesis forcing the text to say what it doesn't say in order to fit their theories. White writes:

> Literally Jesus says, "No man is able to come to me." These are words of *incapacity* and they are placed in a universal context. All men . . . lack the ability to come to Christ in and of themselves . . . . That is Paul's "dead in sin" (Ephesians 2:1) and "unable to please God" (Romans 8:8). It is the Reformed doctrine of total depravity: man's inability [here being] taught by the Lord who knows the hearts of all men . . . . .

> All men would be left in the hopeless position of "unable to come" *unless* God acts, and He does by drawing [some but not all] men unto Christ . . . . No man can "will" to come to Christ outside of this divine drawing . . . . Reformed scholars assert that the ones who are drawn are the ones who are given by the Father to the Son: i.e., the elect . . . .

> Obviously, then, it cannot be asserted that . . . the Father is drawing *every single individual human being* [or] universalism [everyone is saved] would be the result, for *all* who are drawn are likewise *raised up* at the last day. [12]

Where in this passage does Jesus mention "total depravity" or "dead in sin" or *"incapacity"* or "unable to please God" or anything about an "elect"? None of these Calvinist theories is there — nor is any part of TULIP even implied. Jesus does not say that the drawing must be limited to the elect or universalism would be the result, or that the drawing is either *irresistible* or *unconditional*. Yet Sproul says "draw" means to "compel," [13] and Pink insists it means "impel." [14] Yarbrough writes, "It is hard to imagine a more explicit description of the Lord's selective and effectual drawing activity. [15] Those ideas are imposed upon the text because a system of religion requires them, not because anything Christ says gives such an indication.

It is quite clear that Christ does *not* say that everyone who is drawn will actually come to Him and be saved. That simply is not in the text. Nevertheless, White is joined by a host of others who consider this to be one of the premier "predestination passages" [16] and a prooftext for Irresistible Grace. Vance cites no less than thirteen authors of that persuasion. [17] Schreiner and Ware assert with White that "the one who is drawn is also raised up on the last day." [18] Yet Christ clearly says it is those who actually come to Him whom He will raise up at the last day.

Calvinists go far beyond what Christ says, reading into His words what isn't there. Let us quote Christ's own words (John 6:37,39, 40,44) to see exactly what He said:

1. All that the Father giveth me [not all He draws] shall come to me;

2. and him that cometh to me [not everyone the Father draws] I will in no wise cast out.

3. And this is the Father's will, . . . that of all which he giveth me [not all whom He draws] I should lose nothing, but should raise it up again at the last day.

4. And . . . that every one which seeth the Son, and believeth on him [not all who are drawn], may have everlasting life: and I will raise him up . . . .

5. No man can come to me, except the Father which hath sent me draw him: and I will raise him up at the last day [all who will be raised up have been drawn, but not all who have been drawn will be raised up].

Read the entire text again carefully. Christ does not say that all whom the Father *draws,* but all whom He *gives* to the Son, will come to Him, and He will lose none of them whom the Father gives Him; they will all be raised at the last day. Of whom is Christ speaking? We have seen that the Bible teaches that in God's foreknowledge He knew who would believe and who would reject the gospel. The former are those whom the Father has given to the Son. There is nothing here about causing a select few to believe unto salvation and choosing not to save the rest of mankind.

Christ says that no one can come to Him unless the Father draws him. But He doesn't say (as White and the others quoted above claim) that everyone whom the Father draws actually comes to the Son and is saved. There is a genuine desire on God's part for all to be saved and a bona fide *offer* of salvation is made to whosoever will believe — but not everyone believes. God's genuine desire for all to be saved is elsewhere stated so often and clearly by prophets, Christ and His apostles that we dare not impose any interpretation upon this passage to the contrary.

The element of the Father "drawing" is mentioned by Christ only in this one passage. On the other hand, the promise is encountered repeatedly throughout

throughout John's gospel "that whosoever believeth in him should not perish . . . he that believeth on the Son hath everlasting life: . . . he that believeth not the Son shall not see life . . . if any man thirst, let him come unto me, and drink," etc. (John 3:16-17, 36; 7:37). Furthermore, Christ's statement is clear that not everyone who is *drawn*, but "everyone which *seeth* the Son, and *believeth* on Him may have everlasting life . . . (John 6:40)."

The Burden Of Proof

There is no question that Scripture repeatedly presents God's love, compassion and concern for all Israel and the whole world, and His desire for all to repent. Nor is there any doubt that He offers salvation to all in the clearest language possible. In contrast, not one scripture can be produced where any of the tenets of Calvinism is clearly stated. The burden of proof is upon the Calvinist to show where the Bible clearly states his doctrine; yet even in this passage which White calls "the clearest exposition of Calvinism," the theory is not plainly stated but must be read into it or it could not be found there at all.

Indisputably, the phrases themselves which are represented by the first four letters in the acronym TULIP never appear in the entire Bible. That fact should speak volumes. Where is it stated in plain words that men are by nature incapable of believing the gospel or of seeking God? Where does it say in clear language that men are chosen unconditionally to salvation, or that grace is irresistible, or that Christ died only for a select few? Where does it say explicitly that one must be sovereignly regenerated without any understanding or faith before one can understand and believe the gospel? *The Calvinist cannot produce for any part of TULIP a clear, unambiguous statement from any part of Scripture!* Calvinism must therefore be imposed upon certain texts because it cannot be derived from any.

Where does the Scripture clearly say that God desires billions to perish and that it is His good pleasure and even to His glory to withhold from them the requisite irresistible grace? Where does it say in clear language that God's love is limited to a select few who alone He desires to save? In contrast to the very few verses that may (and only with considerable difficulty) be interpreted in the above manner, there are literally hundreds proclaiming in unmistakable terms His love and desire of salvation for all.

Far from being taught directly in Scripture, Calvinism is arrived at by a number of faulty analogies: what it means that the human heart is exceedingly sinful, rebellious and selfish; what it means that God is sovereign, that man is dead in trespasses and in sins, that no one can come to Christ except the Father draw him, that the thought of the heart is evil continually, etc. In each case the Calvinist has had to devise a false analogy in order to make his system work.

Those Who "Draw Back Unto Perdition"

Even in this passage about the Father drawing there is nothing to indicate either that only certain ones are drawn or that the drawing is irresistible. That conclusion must be arrived at by assumptions neither essential to nor compatible with the context. Moreover, to "draw" someone in the ordinary sense of that word doesn't mean they will necessarily come all the way, nor is there anything in either the Greek or the context to suggest, much less to demand, that conclusion.

Contrary to the eisegesis forced upon this text to produce an irresistible drawing unto Christ (which He never taught), there are many souls who are drawn partway to Christ by the Father and who then turn back. The Bible offers many such examples: " . . . if any man draw back, my soul shall have no pleasure in him. But we are not of them who draw back unto perdition [Greek, apoleia]; but of them that believe to the saving of the soul" (Hebrews 10:38-39).

The same Greek word, apoleia, is found eight times in the New Testament. It is often translated "perdition," and in each case means eternal damnation. Piper acknowledges that "Most commentators agree that . . . [apoleia] indicates clearly the eternal perdition . . . ." [19] Consider the following: "judgment and perdition of ungodly men" (2 Peter 3:7); "And the beast . . . goeth into perdition" (Revelation 17:11).

Clearly, those who "draw back unto perdition" cannot be among the elect since the elect cannot lose their salvation and be damned. Yet those who "draw back" must have been drawn to some extent. Otherwise, to "draw back" would be meaningless.

White avoids Hebrews 10:38-39. So do Pink, Sproul, Piper, and a host of other Calvinists, at least in their books which we have been able to peruse. In his exhaustive treatment, Vance is unable to quote a single Calvinist commenting on this passage.

One of many similar letters I have received declared, "You make God out to be a heavenly wimp who would sure like to save folks, but He just can't do it unless they cooperate. But the God of the Bible is mighty to save, and He does it in spite of the proud, stubborn, self-righteous will of fallen sinners!"

On the contrary, salvation is a gift of God's love. Neither a gift nor love, as God has designed them and as the Bible presents them, can be forced upon the unwilling, not even by God. This does not indicate any weakness in God but simply reflects the nature of love and a gift. That man may rebel against God, disobey His laws and refuse God's offer of the gift of His grace does not in the least demean God's sovereignty. In fact, in His sovereignty He has ordained that love and a gift would require a choice, and makes that clear in His Word. Another letter argued similarly:

> You say God loves every person in the world and it is His will that each one be saved . . . . To even think that God sovereignly allows man to thwart His divine will is heretical, demeaning to God's greatness and a fabulous invention of the mind to accommodate your bias. God controls every animal, every person and all events . . . . Your views, dear brother, make God's will subordinate to man's will, and represent God's plan of salvation as a failure since all men are not saved . . . . [20]

This is fatalism, and those who maintain this position could hardly have thought it through very carefully without recognizing the horrible consequences. We've noted the obvious: If God controls every person and event, then rape, murder and all crime and wars and suffering must be His doing according to His will — but just as obviously, that is not the case. In the *counsel* of His will He *allows* that which is not His perfect will in order to further His purpose in salvation. Evil is surely the opposite of God's will. Therefore, we can be certain that it is not God's will for evil to reign on earth. Satan is the god of this world and "the whole world lieth in wickedness [i.e., in the wicked one, Satan]" (1 John 5:18). God allows this state of affairs for now, but not for ever.

We all recognize that not everything done on this earth is the will of God. Surely God does not always impose His will upon man so that He "controls . . . all events," as most Calvinists insist. If He did, then He would be the author of evil — and He surely is not. John writes, "whosoever doeth not righteousness is not of God" (1 John 3:10). Sadly, much if not most of what occurs in the affairs of men is *not* righteousness and is therefore *not of God* and would never be willed by Him.

Without the power of choice we could not love God or one another. Man has been given the awesome responsibility to choose for himself. Sadly, most choose evil over good, self instead of God. He does not force salvation upon man any more than He forces anyone to obey the Ten Commandments. If salvation were forced it would not be a gift of love.

Is It All A Charade?

The Calvinist claims that God, in His sovereignty (if He so desired), *could* stop all sin and cause everyone always to keep the Ten Commandments perfectly. This would be possible if man had no free will. In that case, instead of causing him to do evil, God could cause him always to do only good. If that were true, however, what would be the point of giving the Law? God could have controlled human thoughts, words and deeds so that without even knowing the Law everyone would do exactly what the Law required.

Incredibly, most Calvinists teach that in His sovereignty God gave the Ten Commandments, caused man to break them, then damned him for doing what God caused him to do. The Bible is thereby turned into a charade, man into a puppet and God into a monster whom the atheist has good cause to reject.

That man himself, however, not God, is the cause of evil on earth, having selfishly and foolishly chosen to oppose God's will, there can be no doubt. Nor can it be doubted that God's Spirit has not only written His laws in every conscience but seeks to draw all men unto Christ. Yet, sadly, even those to whom God has unmistakably manifested Himself in great power, including obvious miracles, have nevertheless rejected Him and gone their own way to hell.

God said of Israel, "The LORD thy God hath chosen thee to be a special people unto himself . . . because the LORD loved you . . . " (Deuteronomy 7:6-8). Similar statements are made throughout the Old Testament, God even calling Israel His wife. Again, "[I] have taken [them] from the ends of the earth . . . " (Isaiah 41:9); "When Israel was a child, then I loved him . . . I drew them with . . . bands of love . . . my people are bent to backsliding from me . . . " (Hosea 11:1-8).

Israel is called God's elect in both Old and New Testaments (Isaiah 45:4; 65:9,22; Matthew 24:31, etc.). There is no question that God chose Israel, called her and drew her with "bands of love" unto Himself. Yet most Israelites went into idolatry, refused to repent and were surely not among the redeemed. God had to say repeatedly, "My people hath forgotten me, they have burned incense to vanity" (Jeremiah 18:15); "my people have forgotten me days without number" (Jeremiah 2:32).

Many are drawn to the Lord who refuse to believe on Him unto salvation. Christ himself said on at least two occasions, "for many are called, but few are chosen" (Matthew 20:16; 22:14). And even some who are chosen are not willing to fulfill their calling but betray the One whom they claimed was their Lord. Jesus said, "Have not I chosen you twelve, and one of you is a devil? He spake of Judas Iscariot . . . " (John 6:70-71).

Jesus had called Judas, drawn him and chosen him to be a disciple. Judas had followed Jesus with the other disciples for several years, had called Jesus "Lord," and, commissioned by Christ, went forth with the other disciples "to preach the kingdom of God, and to heal the sick" (Luke 9:2). But the heart of Judas had never been won to Christ. He was like those who will say, "Lord, Lord, have we not prophesied in thy name? . . . cast out devils? . . . done many wonderful works?" and yet Jesus will say to them, "I never knew you: depart from me" (Matthew 7:22-23). These have not *lost* their salvation, since they were never saved: "I *never* knew you: depart from me!" was Christ's pronouncement upon those who were drawn to Him but never came all the way to know Him as Savior and Lord.

Except The Father Draw Him: What Does That Mean?

No one naturally seeks the Lord; we all seek our own selfish desires, and no one can come to Christ except the Father draw him. But the Holy Spirit is in the world to convict all of their sin and need (John 16:8-11), the gospel is being preached, the Father is drawing everyone (even through the witness of creation and conscience). Sadly, many like Judas come partway, even seem to be a disciple, then draw back unto perdition.

Not only did Jesus not teach the idea of an irresistible drawing in this passage or elsewhere, He could not have taught it because it would not have been in harmony with the rest of His Word.

Yes, Christ clearly said, "No man can come to me, except the Father . . . draw him." What does that mean? White claims that "draw" indicates a total incapacity on man's part. He insists that Christ is not saying that His Father draws men so they may come to Him while still requiring their willing participation. Instead, he asserts that "draw" means man can't cooperate in any way, but is irresistibly drawn beyond his power either to agree or disagree. That's not being drawn, but propelled against one's will.

And while White's might be one possible interpretation of this statement, it is certainly not the only one possible. Nor is it obvious from the text. Of course, it is the only one which fits Calvinism, but that is not a valid reason for embracing it. Could it be that the desire to justify that theory makes it difficult for Calvinists to see legitimate alternatives which otherwise are quite obvious?

Eisegetical Illusion

To support his assertions, White quotes Calvin, to whom he refers with great admiration. Apparently, as far as White is concerned, Calvin's tyrannical rule of Geneva where he exhibited much pride, impatience and lack of love and sympathy toward those who dared to disagree with him, even resorting to torture in order to persuade, gives no cause for suspecting Calvin's understanding of and fidelity to Scripture.

Surely, that behavior so completely contrary to the Spirit of Christ and God's Word is in fact a compelling indication that Calvin's understanding of the biblical teaching concerning God's sovereignty, mercy and love could very well be flawed. As the Apostle John writes, "He that saith he abideth in him ought himself also so to walk [conduct himself], even as he [Christ] walked" (1 John 2:6). That standard applies to every Christian everywhere at every time in history — and at times Calvin acted so far from it that no excuse can justify his behavior. His actions were, in fact, consistent with what he believed about God, but not consistent with the God of the Bible or with the standard of behavior He requires of those who know and represent Him.

Nevertheless, as though oblivious to the founder of Calvinism's shortcomings, White writes:

> John Calvin is admitted, even by his foes, to have been a tremendous exegete of Scripture. Fair and insightful, Calvin's commentaries continue to this day to have great usefulness and benefit to the student of Scripture. Here are his comments on John 6:44:

> "To come to Christ being here used metaphorically for believing, the Evangelist, in order to carry out the metaphor in the apposite clause, says that those persons are drawn whose understandings God enlightens, and whose hearts he bends and forms to the obedience of Christ . . . hence it follows that all are not drawn, but that God bestows this grace on those whom he has elected.

> True, indeed, as to the kind of drawing, it is not violent, so as to compel men by external force [such as Calvin himself used!]; but still it is a powerful impulse of the Holy Spirit, which makes men willing who formerly were unwilling and reluctant. It is a false and profane assertion, therefore, that none are drawn but those who are willing to be drawn, as if man made himself obedient to God by his own efforts; the willingness with which men follow God is what they already have from himself, who has formed their hearts to obey him." [21]

It is true that Christ uses coming to Him as a metaphor of believing on Him. Schreiner and Ware write, "The 'coming' of John 6:37 is synonymous with 'believing.' That the words *coming* and *believing* are different ways of describing the same reality is confirmed by what Jesus says in John 6:35, 'I am the bread of life: he that cometh to me shall never hunger, and he that believeth on me shall never thirst.' " [22]

That fact indicates once again that faith comes first and is the condition of the new birth and salvation. Believing is synonymous with coming to Christ, not something that is bestowed after one has been regenerated. Surely coming to Christ would result in regeneration through the gospel. The fact that coming is the same as believing also contradicts Unconditional Election and Irresistible Grace for which "coming" must be without faith and is like a dead man being carried. Yes, the Father draws men to Christ, but unless they truly believe in Him they have not "come" all the way but have drawn back unto perdition.

The reader is challenged to examine this passage carefully to see for himself whether any Calvinist doctrines are actually found there. Where is there even a hint (much less a clear statement) in Christ's words of a limited and predestined group "whose hearts [God] bends and forms to the obedience of Christ," or that "God bestows this grace on those whom He has elected," or that it would be "a false and profane assertion, therefore, that none are drawn but those who are willing to be drawn," etc.? Upon examination of the text, these dogmas cannot be found plainly stated therein.

Was Calvin Really The Great Exegete?

John Calvin believed and practiced a number of things which many of those who call themselves Calvinists today would consider seriously wrong, if not heresy. For example, Calvin was a staunch believer in the efficacy of infant baptism to effect forgiveness of sins and to bring the infant into the Kingdom. Worse yet, in spite of his quarrel with the papacy and the Roman system, he taught that being baptized as a baby (or as an adult) by a Roman Catholic priest (which had happened to Calvin as an infant) was efficacious for eternity. The priest could even have been a rank unbeliever and great sinner.

Had he not maintained this Romish false doctrine, Calvin himself would have had to submit to rebaptism, and that was repugnant to him. He derided the Anabaptists for opposing infant baptism. Their valid, biblical reason — that an infant has no understanding of the gospel and has not believed in Christ — was scorned by Calvin and his wrath and that of the other Reformers came upon them. These true evangelicals were martyred by both Catholics and Protestants for being baptized by immersion after they were saved by grace alone through faith alone in Christ alone.

Rather than any natural brilliance, Calvin's arguments reflect a bias toward the sacramentalism he learned as a Roman Catholic from Augustine, which he elaborated upon and thereafter was compelled to defend. His logic often betrays a spiritual immaturity. Incredibly, Calvin argued:

> Such in the present day are our Catabaptists, who deny that we are duly baptised, because we were baptised in the Papacy by wicked men and idolaters . . . . Against these absurdities we shall be sufficiently fortified if we reflect that by baptism we were initiated . . . into the name of the Father, and the Son, and the Holy Spirit; and, therefore, that baptism is not of man, but of God, by whomsoever it may have been administered [but only so long as they were clergy].

> Be it that those who baptised us were most ignorant of God and all piety, or were despisers, still they did not baptise us into a fellowship with their ignorance or sacrilege, but into the faith of Jesus Christ, because the name they invoked was not their own but God's . . . . But if baptism was of God, it certainly included in it the promise of forgiveness of sin, mortification of the flesh, quickening of the Spirit, and communion with Christ. [23]

These astonishing statements reflect a sacramentalism which maintains that the physical act of baptism has spiritual power and imparts regeneration. To be baptized by Roman Catholic priests who were not even Christians but held to and promoted a false gospel, was perfectly acceptable to Calvin because they used the name of God when they administered it! Even to be baptized by *despisers* of Christ and God would bring the "promise of forgiveness of sin . . . "! Why would merely pronouncing the name of God and Christ by unbelievers minister spiritual power? Because they were "part of the ministerial office."

Thus, for all his legitimate complaints against the papacy, and in spite of being recognized as one of the main figures in the Protestant Reformation, nevertheless Calvin honored Rome's corrupt and unsaved priests as God's ministers! And at the same time he condemned those who came out of that Antichrist system through faith in Christ for being subsequently baptized as believers according to God's holy Word.

In this, Calvin betrays his unbiblical view of clerical dominance over the laity. So high was his regard for a clergy class, whether Roman Catholic or Protestant, that he taught that only the clergy could baptize or administer the Lord's Supper. He justified that unbiblical belief in this manner:

> It is here also pertinent to observe, that it is improper for private individuals to take upon themselves the administration of baptism; for it, as well as the dispensation of the Supper, is part of the ministerial office. For Christ did not give command to any man or woman whatever to baptise, but to those whom he had appointed apostles. [24]

Thus Calvin also accepted Rome's claim that her bishops were the successors of the twelve Apostles and from them her priests received divine authority. And he was a leader of the Reformation? Contrary to what Calvin taught about an exclusive "ministerial office," our Lord Jesus Christ clearly commanded the original disciples to make disciples and to teach every disciple they won to Him through the gospel to "observe all things whatsoever I have commanded you" (Matthew 28:20).

Tolerating Calvin's Errors

Obviously, "all things" meant that each new disciple made by the original disciples was likewise to make disciples, baptize them and teach them also to do likewise. Every true Christian today is a disciple of a disciple of a disciple all the way back to the original disciples — each one having taught the new disciples that they, too, must observe *all things* Christ commanded the original twelve. Were the twelve commanded to baptize and to minister the Lord's Supper? Then so is every other disciple. All true Christians always have been and still are today the only successors of the Apostles!

Here we have proof enough that all believers in Christ are qualified to do whatever the original disciples did, including ministering baptism and the Lord's Supper. Christ's own words effectively destroy the fiction of a special clergy class lording it over a laity. One would think that this "greatest of exegetes" could see that fact clearly from the Great Commission, but he didn't. Indeed, this elementary error was the basis of the popish power Calvin wielded in oppressing the citizens of Geneva.

Worse yet, how could the priests and bishops of the Roman Catholic Church, who were not even saved but believed and taught a false salvation through works and ritual, qualify as the successors to the Apostles? And how could Calvinist ministers who disagreed so markedly with Rome on the gospel nevertheless be co-successors, sharing with Roman Catholic clergy this exclusive right to baptize and administer the Eucharist? Calvin's "brilliant exegesis" led him not only into grave error but into contradictions so blatant that one wonders how today's Calvinists can overlook or tolerate them.

Furthermore, Calvin also taught that there was no difference between the baptism practiced by John the Baptist and the baptism Christ commanded His disciples to perform: "I grant that John's was a true baptism, and one and the same with the baptism of Christ . . . the ministry of John was the very same as that which was afterwards delegated to the apostles." [25] That is so clearly wrong that we won't take time to refute it. John's baptism "unto repentance" (Matthew 3:11) had nothing to do with the believer's identification with Christ in His death, burial and resurrection, as is the case with the baptism Christ told His disciples to practice.

The fact that Paul considered John's baptism different and inappropriate for believers in Christ (Acts 19:1-6) is explained away by Calvin with the fantastic idea that these who said they knew nothing but the baptism of John hadn't really received John's baptism [26] — and this in spite of the fact that in response to Paul's question "Unto what then were you baptized?" they replied, "Unto John's baptism."

It seems that Calvinists are willing to tolerate a great deal of error taught by John Calvin and still consider him to be one of the greatest exegetes in history. From a careful study of what Calvin taught in his *Institutes*, however, we have a far different opinion. It is a mystery how, in spite of so much false teaching and his un-Christian behavior at Geneva, he can be held in such high regard by evangelicals today.

That Calvin was wrong on so many other points ought to ease the pain of having to admit that perhaps he was also wrong on TULIP. Yet the high regard in which Calvin is held seems to create an impassable barrier preventing this simple admission of error on his part.

Finding The "Unavailable" Exegesis

There is no question that the Calvinist interpretation of John 6:37-45 is contrary to the entire tenor of Scripture. Let us examine it, too, in this specific context. In John 6:65, Jesus uses slightly different language in saying the same thing: "no man can come unto me, except it were *given* [Greek, *didomi*] unto him of my Father." Note this is not a giving of the sinner to the Son, but a giving to the sinner (given *him*), making it possible for him to come to Christ.

Surely it is justifiable to take what He says in verse 65 as at least a *possible* indication of what Christ meant by the Father drawing: i.e., that the Father *gives* the opportunity to come — and we have an abundance of scriptures indicating that this opportunity is given to the whole world through the gospel. We need no more than this simple understanding to refute White's claim that "there is no meaningful non-Reformed exegesis of the passage available." Certainly this is at least a *possible* one.

In fact, we find that the very same Greek word (*didomi*) is used for "given" multiple times in the New Testament in a way that allows a distinctly non-Calvinist interpretation of Christ's words here and which is also consistent with the overall biblical emphasis upon God's love and mercy. For example, Paul uses *didomi* when he says that God "giveth to all life, and breath, and all things" (Acts 17:25). Some of the many other places where *didomi* is used to indicate something given by God and which men can either receive or reject, obey or disobey, and which involves their cooperation are as follows:

> . . . the law was given by Moses . . . (John 1:17). (No one is forced to obey, although there are serious consequences for disobedience.)

> . . . [I] would have given thee living water (John 4:10). (The water would not be forced upon her against her will. She would have to want it and willingly receive it.)

> I have given them thy word . . . (John 17:14). (The disciples had to willingly receive the Word and obedience thereto was by their choice, it wasn't forced upon them.)

> . . . the cup which my Father hath given me, shall I not drink it? (John 18:11). (Jesus pleaded with the Father that if salvation could come to mankind any other way to spare Him this cup. However, He drank it out of obedience to the Father and love for us.)

> . . . through the grace given unto me . . . (Romans 12:3; 15:15; Galatians 2:9, etc.). (Paul uses this expression with this same Greek word a number of times. This is not Calvinism's mythical Irresistible Grace. God's grace was not imposed upon him so that he could not disobey or fail to fulfill all God's will or did not need to cooperate in the fulfillment thereof.)

Surely all of these usages (and others like them) give us ample reason for the very non-Reformed exegesis which White says is not "available." The Father draws the lost to Christ by giving (*didomi*) to them the opportunity to believe. The giving of those who believe to the Son is of another nature. And those who are drawn by the Father must, in response to the Father's drawing, "see" Him with the eyes of faith and believe on Him to be saved. The giving of the Father to the Son is something else — a special blessing for those who believe.

Christ is saying that we cannot demand salvation but it must be given to us from God. Salvation involves a new birth and no man can regenerate himself into God's family; that privilege can only be given of God and only God has the power to effect it by His Holy Spirit. In all of this, however, there is no rationale for believing that God only grants this for a select few and withholds it from the rest of mankind or that He irresistibly forces it upon anyone.

Christ does not say that the Father forcefully pulls or drags or irresistibly compels anyone to come to Him. In fact, Christ gives every indication that there is definite responsibility on the part of those who are being drawn to believe in Him: "he that believeth on me shall never thirst...ye also have seen me, and believe not" (John 6:35-36); "ye will not come to me, that ye might have life" (John 5:40). Not ye *cannot* because my Father will not allow it, but ye *will not*.

Instead, the Calvinist view of "draw him" renders "come to me" meaningless, absolving the sinner of any responsibility to come, repent or believe. One cannot be held responsible for what one cannot do, and as we have more than amply documented, Calvinism teaches that the sinner is dead and *cannot* respond unless God first of all regenerates him through Irresistible Grace and then causes him to believe. That idea is clearly an invention to make a theory work.

Jesus said, "My Father giveth you the true bread from heaven" (John 6:32). There is no indication of force-feeding. In fact, Christ says, "I am the bread of life: he that cometh to me shall never hunger; and he that believeth on me shall never thirst...this is the will of him that sent me, that every one which seeth the Son, and believeth on him, may have everlasting life . . . he that believeth on me hath everlasting life" (John 6:35,40,47). He goes on to say, "I am the living bread which came down from heaven: if any man eat of this bread, he shall live for ever . . ." (verse 51).

The metaphor Christ chose of eating and drinking contradicts Calvinism. It is clear from this entire passage that eating and drinking Christ's body and blood is a metaphor for believing on Him, as Schreiner and Ware admit: "To come to Jesus is to satisfy one's hunger and to believe in him is to quench one's thirst." [27] While the Calvinist tries to say that the faith to believe is given by God in order to *cause* the elect to believe, that idea hardly fits the metaphor of eating and drinking. Surely it is the responsibility of the one to whom the Father gives the "bread of life" to eat it. There is no hint that the bread of life is force-fed to the elect through Irresistible Grace without their willingly receiving and eating it.

Human Responsibility

Christ's words, "No man can come to me except the Father draw him," are not the same as White's interpretive "No man is *able* to come to me." Christ is not denying either the necessity or capability on man's part of active acquiescence and faith. He is actually saying, "Men *can* come to me *if* the Father draws them — i.e., if *given* to them of the Father." And hundreds of passages tell us that this giving (*didomi*) is a gift of God's love, and like the giving of the Son to die for our sins, is for the whole world. Such an understanding is consistent with Scripture's repeated invitations to come, invitations which would be meaningless without a definite responsibility on man's part *and ability* to "come" when he is "drawn." Man has a choice to make: to come or not to come, to eat and drink of Christ or of the things of this world and Satan.

Yes, the Bible says that "there is none that seeketh after God" (Romans 3:11). But that is only one side and the Bible makes it clear that this statement does *not* mean, as Calvinism insists, that no man is *able* to seek. It is not that man lacks the ability to seek God or that God holds back the essential grace for coming. The problem is that man, in and of himself, lacks the desire to seek God. Blinded by sin and obsessed with self, man seeks everything except God (including false gods he finds more appealing) until, by the Holy Spirit, convicted of sin and convinced of his need of a Savior, he is drawn to Christ.

In infinite love and boundless grace, God continually encourages man to seek Him. Though many, perhaps the vast majority (broad is the road to destruction), reject the wooing of the Holy Spirit and Christ's call to come to Him, many respond to this call in repentance toward God and faith in our Lord Jesus Christ, the message that Paul preached (Acts 20:21). That is why Paul expended himself — preaching the gospel in the attempt to *persuade* men (2 Corinthians 5:11) to come to Christ — and we should also.

Men are responsible to respond to conscience and to the gospel and to the striving of the Holy Spirit in their lives (Genesis 6:3). Nor can we as believers avoid our responsibility to obey Christ's command to preach the gospel and to do so in the power of the Holy Spirit and with sincere conviction and persuasion. Paul and Barnabas "so spake, that a great multitude both of the Jews and also of the Greeks believed" (Acts 14:1). So must we, "as the oracles of God" (1 Peter 4:11).

The Universal Thirst That Only God Can Quench

David said, "When thou saidst, Seek ye my face, my heart said unto thee, Thy face, LORD, will I seek" (Psalms 27:8). The sons of Korah sang, "As the hart panteth after the water brooks, so panteth my soul after thee, O God" (Psalms 42:1). Others could be quoted in the same vein. Not just an elect, but all men in all times and places (and that includes even the wicked and unrighteous, which we all are by nature) are exhorted thus:

> Seek ye the LORD while he may be found, call ye upon him while he is near: let the wicked forsake his way, and the unrighteous man his thoughts: and let him return unto the LORD, and he will have mercy upon him; and to our God, for he will abundantly pardon. (Isaiah 55:6-7)

> God that made the world . . . hath made of one blood all nations of men for to dwell on all the face of the earth . . . that they should seek the Lord, if haply they might . . . find him, though he be not far from every one of us . . . . (Acts 17:24-27)

There is no way that "wicked . . . unrighteous . . . all nations of men" can be turned into the "elect"! Unquestionably, the Bible teaches human responsibility to believe in and seek the Lord. It does not teach that only an elect few are irresistibly made to come to God and to Christ without any willingness or desire on their part. Christ's invitation, "Come unto me," surely means that though man would not come of his own accord without the Father drawing him, yet when the Father through the Holy Spirit draws men to Christ they are able as moral agents to yield and to come by a genuine act of faith and volition — or to resist and not come.

Why would God urge to seek Him, and Christ invite to come to Him, men who, if Calvinism is true, are totally depraved and dead in sin to the extent that they can't even hear His voice or make a move toward Him? Indeed, if Calvinism were true, why would Christ even say "come unto me and drink" to *anyone*? That invitation wouldn't be appropriate for the elect, since their coming is only by the Father irresistibly drawing them. Nor would it be appropriate for the non-elect, because there is no way they can come even if they had the desire.

The extreme view which interprets human depravity and being dead in sin to mean that the natural man cannot seek after and find God is repudiated by literally hundreds of Bible verses. The few places where it says man doesn't seek God are far outweighed by the scores of passages which encourage seekers after God. Here are just a few:

> Seek the LORD . . . seek his face continually. (1 Chronicles 16:11)

> . . . if ye seek him, he will be found of you . . . . (2 Chronicles 15:2)

> . . . thou, LORD, hast not forsaken them that seek thee. (Psalms 9:10)

> . . . they shall praise the LORD that seek him . . . . (Psalms 22:26)

> . . . they that seek the LORD shall not want any good thing. (Psalms 34:10)

> Let all those that seek thee rejoice and be glad . . . . (Psalms 40:16)

... let not those that seek thee be confounded .... (Psalms 69:6)

... they that seek the LORD understand all .... (Proverbs 28:5)

... for it is time to seek the LORD .... (Hosea 10:12)

Seek ye the LORD, all ye meek of the earth .... (Zephaniah 2:3), etc.

If men not only do not but *cannot* seek God unless He causes them to do so with Irresistible Grace, what do all these passages mean? That unregenerate man can be motivated to seek after and even to find God is clear from many scriptures. Thus God encourages unbelieving and rebellious Israel, "And ye shall seek me, and find me, when ye shall search for me with all your heart" (Jeremiah 29:13). As for being drawn irresistibly without any understanding, we are told, "he that cometh to God must believe that he is, and that he is a rewarder of them that diligently seek him" (Hebrews 11:6). Again, the coming is "seeing" with the eyes of faith and truly believing.

More Contradictions

Calvin himself at times contradicted his own theories. He taught that all men "are born and live for the express purpose of learning to know God" and therefore "it is clear that all those who do not [on their own initiative] direct the whole thoughts and actions of their lives to this end fail to fulfill the law of their being." [28] Indeed, this is what the Bible says — but it contradicts Calvinism. How could the very "law of their being" compel all mankind to seek God when they are unable to do so? It would make sense for men to be *unwilling* to fulfill the "law" of their being, but to be *unable* to do so must be blamed on the Creator and turns much of the Bible into fiction.

Having acknowledged the fact that God made man to seek, to find, and to know Him, how could Calvin then develop the theory of Total Depravity? Would God have made all men for the very purpose of seeking after and knowing Him, as Paul plainly said on Mars' Hill (Acts 17:26-28), and at the same time neglect to provide the very grace which they need for that seeking and knowing?

Calvin further contradicted himself and Scripture with the added argument that when men "do think of God it is against their will; never approaching him without being dragged into his presence, and when there, instead of the voluntary fear flowing from reverence of the divine majesty, feeling only that forced and servile fear which divine judgment extorts ... which, while they dread, they at the same time also hate." [29] Calvin paints this horrible picture without any biblical warrant. No wonder he embraced the idea of Irresistible Grace.

What about the elect? Aren't they all formerly totally depraved men who have been drawn to God? And what of the many scriptures (some of which we have quoted) testifying to the many who took pleasure in seeking God? Where does it ever say that Enoch (who walked with God) or Abraham (the friend of God) or Moses (who spoke with God face to face) or David (whose psalms testify to a perpetual seeking after and thirst for God) or Daniel (for whom time with God in prayer was so precious that the threat of being thrown into the lions' den could not cause him to give it up), et al., were irresistibly drawn by God, who changed their wills without willing cooperation on their part? Where does it say that the men and women of God in the Old Testament were regenerated and then given the faith and desire to seek God? Isn't the New Birth something which only New Testament saints experience? How then without sovereign regeneration could the believers before Pentecost know God?

The Bible contains abundant testimony to the fact that men can be drawn to God and do indeed eagerly come and fall down and worship Him. But even if the picture of totally depraved mankind Calvin paints were true, wouldn't that be all the more reason for a God who *is* love to extend His grace to all mankind in order to fulfill the purpose for which even Calvin admits He created them?

Calvinists seem far too eager to take hold of every verse that says man *doesn't* seek the Lord and too reluctant to compare them with the much greater number of verses which say God desires man to seek and find Him and that it is possible for man so to do. That attitude is only the logical reflection of the "God" they believe in and follow, a God who takes pleasure in damning billions. In defense of God's true character, it must be insisted again that such is *not* the God of the Bible.

1   James R. White, *The Potter's Freedom* (Calvary Press Publishing, 2000), 155-56.
2   Robert W. Yarbrough, "Divine Election in the Gospel of John." In *Still Sovereign: Contemporary Perspectives on Election, Foreknowledge, and Grace*, ed. Thomas R. Schreiner and Bruce A. Ware (Baker Books, 2000), 50-51.
3   John Piper, "Are There Two Wills In God?" In Schreiner and Ware, op. cit., 107.
4   D.A. Carson, "Reflections on Assurance." In op. cit., 263.
5   J.I. Packer, "The Love of God: Universal and Particular." In op. cit., 283.
6   Yarbrough, op. cit., 50.
7   R.C. Sproul, *Faith Alone: The Evangelical Doctrine of Justification* (Baker Books, 1995), 137-38.
8   Arthur C. Custance, *The Sovereignty of Grace* (Presbyterian and Reformed Publishing Co., 1979), 277.
9   Robert A. Morey, *Studies in the Atonement* (Crowne Publications, 1989), 296.
10 Arthur W. Pink, *Exposition of the Gospel of John* (Zondervan Publishing House, 1975), 682.
11 Piper, ibid.
12 White, op. cit., 158-60.
13 R.C. Sproul, *Chosen by God* (Tyndale House Publishers, Inc., 1986), 69.
14 Pink, op. cit., 338.
15 Yarbrough, op. cit., 51.
16 D.A. Carson, *Divine Sovereignty and Human Responsibility* (John Knox Press, 1981), 174.
17 Laurence M. Vance, *The Other Side of Calvinism* (Vance Publications, Pensacola FL, rev. ed. 1999), 508.
18 Schreiner and Ware, Introduction to *Still Sovereign*, op. cit., 15.
19 John Piper, *The Justification of God: An Exegetical and Theological Study of Romans 9:1-23* (Baker Books, 2000), 201.
20 To Dave Hunt, n.d., received September 10, 2000. On file.
21 John Calvin, *Commentary on the Gospel of John, The Comprehensive John Calvin Collection* (Ages Digital Library, 1998); cited in White, op. cit., 161.
22 Schreiner and Ware, op.cit., 14.
23 John Calvin, *Institutes of the Christian Religion*, trans. Henry Beveridge (Wm. B. Eerdmans Publishing Company, 1998 ed.), IV:xv,16-17.
24 Op. cit., IV:xv,20.
25 Op. cit., IV:xv,7,18.
26 Ibid.
27 Schreiner and Ware, op. cit., 14.
28 Calvin, op. cit., I:iii,3.
29 Op. cit., I:iv,4.

21
Persuasion, The Gospel And God

A thorough examination of the passage in John 6, which is extolled as the clearest presentation of Calvinism in Scripture, has failed to reveal therein any support for TULIP. But if Calvinism were actually true, then as Luther said approvingly, Jesus would indeed have been "taunting and mocking" the Jews something like this:

> You must believe on Me as the bread of God come down from heaven to give life unto the world. But you lack the ability to believe unto salvation, and My Father is only going to give that ability to a few of you.

> By "world," of course, I really mean "elect." Though no one recognizes that yet, one day it will be revealed through a system called Calvinism.

> You must by faith eat My flesh and drink My blood [i.e., believe that I as God became a real flesh-and-blood man to die for your sins, fulfilling the Levitical sacrifices which the priests ate]. If you don't believe on Me, you will perish in your sins.

> You naively think this is a real offer of salvation, but in fact it is intended the better to damn you. You couldn't believe on Me if you tried.

> You wretches are all so totally depraved that you can't come to Me except My Father regenerates you and gives you the faith to believe. And He has already decided in a past eternity (for reasons hidden in His will and to His glory) that He will only do that for some but not all of you.

> Yes, He could cause *all* of you to believe on Me, but it is His good pleasure only to rescue *some* from hell. And don't think I'm going to die needlessly for

those of you whom My Father has predestined to eternal destruction — that would be a waste of My blood. I will die only for the sins of the elect.

What love is this? Some Calvinists willingly admit that the real issue is "whether it can properly be said that God *desires* the salvation of all men." [1] Calvinists insist that God has no such desire. In zealously defending God's sovereignty, Calvinism brings a reproach upon His character.

If God *could* by His power bend anyone and everyone's heart "to the obedience of Christ" without any desire on their part, why doesn't He do it for all? And why didn't He do this for Adam and Eve at the very beginning, and thereafter for all their descendants? Why needlessly allow sin to bring the horror of evil and suffering that would plague billions — and then only save a relatively few when *all* could be rescued? Worse yet, why would God *cause* Adam and Eve and all mankind to sin and then punish them for doing what He caused them to do?

In support of this abhorrent doctrine, Calvin quotes Augustine: "Wherefore, it cannot be doubted that the will of God (who hath done whatever he pleased in heaven and in earth . . .) cannot be resisted by the human will . . . ." [2] This unbiblical belief created the appalling dogma that everything happening on earth, including all wickedness of the grossest nature, is caused by God. How could it be otherwise if man can do nothing contrary to God's will? Thus Calvinism, taken to its logical conclusion, leads to fatalism, from which come both predestination to damnation and irresistible grace.

Calvinism And Evangelism

If grace truly is irresistible, if only those elected by God to salvation can be saved, if no one can believe the gospel until regenerated by God and thereafter given the faith to believe, would it not be vain to attempt to persuade anyone through the gospel — or for those who hear to attempt to believe in Christ? Since there is nothing one can do to change one's eternal destiny (if one of the elect, nothing can stand between the soul and heaven; and if not among the elect, nothing can be done to escape hell) shouldn't one just go on with life and let the inevitable take its course? While many Calvinists would object to this view, it cannot be denied that this is the practical conclusion to which that dogma leads.

Yet Calvinists often contradict themselves because they slip into an evangelism mode. At times, D. James Kennedy, founder of Evangelism Explosion, makes it sound not only as though salvation is available to all but even that faith precedes regeneration: "Place your trust in [Christ]. Ask Him to come in and be born in you today." [3] Contrary to his professed Calvinism, Spurgeon taught that "soul-winning is the chief business of the Christian . . . ." [4] Kennedy trains others to evangelize and in the process contradicts Calvinism: "For if it is true that we must be born again, then it is also true that we *may* be born again . . . . That, my friends, is the *good news.*" [5] Does he seriously mean that salvation for the elect alone is *good news* for *everyone?*

In attempting to show that evangelism has some place in Calvinism, Boettner declared that every preacher should "pray for them [to whom he presents the gospel] that they may each be among the elect." [6] But what is the point of either praying or preaching the gospel if it is not the gospel but sovereign regeneration which brings men to Christ and the fate of each has been predestined from a past eternity?

As for Kennedy's "*good*" news, are those who have been predestined to eternal torment expected to rejoice that their doom is sealed and there is nothing that can be done to change it? Can he and other evangelistically inclined Calvinists seriously think their practice matches their belief? In disagreeing with Hoeksema, another Calvinist rightly points out that "for them [the elect] alone the gospel is good news." [7]

Many Calvinists are convinced, and logically so, "that the doctrines of grace are contrary to soul winning." [8] Engelsma callously declares that the call of the gospel "does not express God's love for them [the non-elect]" nor is it "a saving purpose. On the contrary, it is his purpose to render them inexcusable and to harden them." [9] No wonder that by their own admission so many Calvinists lack the Apostle Paul's zeal for winning the lost. Vance quotes a Sovereign Grace Baptist leader who admits that

> We do not win many souls. A few of our kind of churches win a soul now and then, but most of us do very, very little of this . . . . Our preachers are not soul winning men. We do not have soul winning members . . . we almost never give any instructions on why and how to win souls. We do not really work at soul winning in our churches. [10]

But this is consistent with Calvinism. Why "work at soul winning"? Persuasion is meaningless for those whose eternal destiny has already been decided without regard to any response they could possibly make to the gospel. Fatalistically, Sproul insists, "Those whom [the Father] regenerates come to Christ. Without regeneration no one will ever come to Christ. With regeneration no one will ever reject him." [11] Jay Adams adds his agreement: "Repentance and faith are the acts of *regenerated* men, not of men *dead in sins.*" [12] And in spite of the quote above, Boettner declares, "Only those who are quickened (made spiritually alive) by the Holy Spirit ever have that will [to come to Christ]." [13]

Calvinism presents a further contradiction: If God is able to bend the hearts of the elect to the obedience of Christ while they are totally depraved sinners,

354 What Love Is This?

why couldn't He be at least as effective in transforming the elect after He has regenerated them? Why doesn't God's irresistible grace that is so powerful toward sinners create perfectly obedient lives after sinners are saved? Why is grace irresistible for lost sinners, bending their wills to His, but not for saved sinners who so often fail to do His will? Something isn't right!

Another Favorite Verse

John 1:13 is cited by Calvinists as absolute proof that man can have no part whatsoever in his salvation, not even in believing the gospel (hence the necessity of Irresistible Grace): "Which were born, not of blood, nor of the will of the flesh, nor of the will of man, but of God." Van Baren writes, "It is only by the irresistible grace of God that one is born again." [14] In spite of saying that the will plays an important part in salvation, Spurgeon declared, "It is utterly impossible that human language could have put a stronger negative on the vainglorious claims of the human will than this passage does . . . ." [15]

Since a baby has nothing to do with its birth, then supposedly neither can the sinner have anything to do with being born of the Spirit of God through believing in and receiving Christ. That spiritual birth is nothing at all like physical birth, however, is a major point of this very passage: "not of blood . . . flesh . . . will of man." Yet Palmer reasons that because an unborn baby doesn't exist, neither does an unsaved person: "a nonbeing does not exist and therefore can have no desires to go to Christ." [16] Neither can it sin or reject Christ or have the least need of being regenerated if it "does not exist."

That spiritually mature believers today continue to approve such specious reasoning and to promote it as biblical is astonishing. Calvin even said that "infants . . . are saved . . . regenerated by the Lord," [17] even though he admits that an infant is too young to understand the gospel. [18] Garrett declares, "John the Baptist was born again while in his mother's womb." [19] In fact, the new birth was not experienced by Old Testament saints. Furthermore, it comes only by believing "the word of God . . . which by the gospel is preached" (1 Peter 1:23-25) — hardly possible for infants, much less for a fetus.

Palmer continues his unbiblical reasoning: "A baby never desires or decides . . . [or] contributes one iota toward his own birth . . . . In a similar fashion, the unbeliever cannot take one step toward his rebirth." [20] Even Pink points out the fallacy: "Regeneration is not the creating of a person which hitherto had no existence, but the renewing and restoring of a person whom sin had unfitted for communion with God . . . ." [21] Vance explains the obvious contradictions:

. . . is a baby responsible for any of its actions before it is born? If not, then neither would an unsaved man be responsible for any of his [so he could hardly be a sinner]. [22]

The Simplicity Of What John Says

The declaration in John 1:11-13 is simple and to the point: flesh and blood have no relationship to the new birth, which is spiritual and completely unrelated to physical birth. Thus those who treat the two as analogous fall into error. That was in fact the very mistake Nicodemus made: "How can a man be born when he is old? Can he enter the second time into his mother's womb, and be born" (John 3:4)? Christ makes a clear distinction: "That which is born of the flesh is flesh; and that which is born of the Spirit is spirit" (John 3:6). These are two different births, and any seeming similarities are only superficial and cannot become the basis of sound conclusions.

John also explains that the new birth — which Christ tells Nicodemus is essential for entering the kingdom of God (John 3:3,5) — does not come by man's will but by the will of God. Man did not conceive of the new birth nor can he effect it by his efforts. Nor does the non-Calvinist believe that he can. Yet we are accused of that. Bishop imagines that he is refuting the non-Calvinist when he declares that the sinner "cannot renew his own will, change his own heart, nor regenerate his bad nature." [23] But who claimed he could?

How does maintaining that we must believe the gospel to be saved suggest that we can regenerate ourselves? The Calvinist is attacking a straw man created by a serious misunderstanding of the non-Calvinist position.

Then what brings about the new birth? John does not explain that in verse 13 but in the previous one: by receiving Christ and believing in His name. Yet verse 12 is commonly overlooked or even avoided by most Calvinists, who reason from verse 13 alone. The basis of the new birth is answered specifically and repeatedly in numerous other passages as well. All John tells us in verse 13 is that the new birth comes to man by the initiation and power of God alone.

Is the new birth imposed upon man in spite of his contrary will by a sovereign God's irresistible grace? If so, this verse gives no such suggestion. Moreover, dozens of passages declare that eternal life is a gift from God to be received by "whosoever believeth." Even Calvin said, "Now it may be asked how men receive the salvation offered to them by the hand of God? I reply, by faith." [24] Yet we are criticized for saying that salvation is offered by God to man and must be and can be accepted by faith.

Staggering Deductions

Commenting on John 1:12-13, Calvin links it quite biblically and logically with James 1:18 ("Of his own will begat he us with the word of truth . . . ."). Clearly James, like John, is saying that regeneration was God's idea, it originated with Him "of his own will," and that He effects it ("begat he us"). James likewise confirms Peter's declaration that we are born again by "the word of truth," i.e., through believing the gospel of Jesus Christ — impossible for infants, and something which baptism cannot effect even in adults. Calvin himself acknowledges that faith in the "word of truth" is essential to salvation — but in the next breath he contradicts himself again:

> We confess, indeed, that the word of the Lord is the only seed of spiritual regeneration; but we deny the inference that, therefore, the power of God cannot regenerate infants . . . . But *faith*, they say, *cometh by hearing*, the use of which infants have not yet obtained . . . . But they observe not that where the apostle makes hearing the beginning of faith, he is . . . not laying down an invariable rule . . . . [25]

There is nothing about "hearing" being the *beginning* of faith; nor would that concept help Calvin at all. If hearing the "word of the Lord" is the beginning of faith, then an infant, baptized or not, hasn't even begun to possess what Calvin admits is "the only seed of spiritual regeneration." Calvin retained throughout his life the unbiblical view of baptism which, as a devout Roman Catholic, he learned from Augustine, the greatest saint of that apostate Church. Baptism became a substitute for the faith in Christ through the gospel which Christ and His apostles declare so plainly is essential to salvation or the new birth.

This is a deadly error related to the denial of man's responsibility and ability to believe the gospel. These unbiblical ideas then led to another astonishing heresy: children of believers are automatically among the elect and thus already regenerated from the womb. That false assurance has probably led millions astray! Here it is again from Calvin's pen:

> Hence it follows, that the children of believers are not baptised, in order that . . . they may then, for the first time, become children of God, but rather are received into the Church by a formal sign, because in virtue of the promise, they previously belonged to the body of Christ. [26]

Following Calvin, the Counter-Remonstrance declared that "the children of believers, as long as they do not manifest the contrary, are to be reckoned among God's elect." [27] So a well-behaved baby, toddler or young child of believing parents is considered to be automatically a regenerated child of God without understanding or believing the gospel! Even for adults, as we shall see when we come to Perseverance of the Saints, behavior rather than faith becomes the Calvinist's assurance of salvation — another deadly error, considering the undeniable capacity of the unsaved to live seemingly good lives.

While the belief that children of the elect are themselves elect might be compared to the belief that young children who die prior to reaching an understanding of the gospel are covered by the blood of Christ and taken to heaven, there is a grave difference between the two concepts because the former ultimately involves those who, rather than having been taken to heaven in infancy, continue to live into adulthood. Why should the Calvinist youth, when he comes of age, be challenged to believe the gospel, inasmuch as both by birth and baptism he has been declared to be one of the elect?

Confirmation merely confirms what infant baptism — or being born into a Calvinist family — already accomplished. Indeed, what need is there to preach the gospel to *anyone,* since the elect are regenerated without it and the non-elect cannot understand or believe it? To defend his dogmas, Calvin managed to rationalize an interpretation of John 1:13 and James 1:18 which actually contradicts both:

> Hence it follows, first, that faith . . . is the fruit of spiritual regeneration; for the Evangelist affirms that no man can believe, unless he be begotten of God; and therefore faith is a heavenly gift. It follows, secondly, that faith is not bare or cold knowledge, since no man can believe who has not been renewed [reborn] by the Spirit of God. [28]

Neither of these verses even mentions faith, and certainly there is no intimation that faith is either a gift or the fruit of regeneration. Search these verses, pray about them, and you will never find anything to suggest that the faith to believe in and receive Christ comes after and as a result of the new birth. Far from deriving this teaching from either text, Calvin imposed his own ideas upon them to create his own unique doctrine of faith.

Look At The Context

Yes, faith must be involved. The "word of truth" mentioned by James obviously must be believed to be of any effect — which Calvin acknowledged was both essential and impossible for the very young. Unquestionably, faith must be in operation to believe the word of truth of the gospel and thereby bring about the new birth — it would be too late for faith to result from regeneration. John also teaches that the new birth is given by God to those who believe in and receive Christ. Far from teaching that "no man can believe, unless he be begotten of God," both passages teach the opposite: that faith in Christ qualifies one (gives the "power [Greek, *exousia*, meaning authority or right] to become the children of God") and that it is through believing "the word of truth" that one is regenerated.

In John 1:12 we have the simple and straightforward statement that "as many as received him . . . that believe on his name" are given authority "to become the sons of God." It is only those who have believed on and received Christ who then become the sons of God. It couldn't be said more clearly that receiving Christ and believing on His name *precede* regeneration, or being born again. Faith in Christ is the condition God requires for effecting the new birth.

Calvin, the great exegete, contradicted himself on this subject as on others. For example, " . . . it is said that believers, in embracing Christ, are 'born, not of blood, nor of the will of the flesh, nor of the will of man, but of God' (John 1:13)..." [29] Here he clearly admits the biblical order: one embraces (i.e., believes in) Christ and as a result of this faith is born of God, i.e., regenerated. In this same section of his *Institutes*, however, he refers to regeneration as preceding faith.

How can Calvinists claim that these verses teach that one must be born again *before* one can believe on and receive Christ? They reverse the clear biblical order, acknowledged at times even by Calvin. From this unbiblical twisting of Scripture flows the doctrine of Irresistible Grace: God must irresistibly regenerate the elect before they can even believe in Christ.

Calvinists make some surprising deductions from John 1:13, such as that "man does not have a free will when it comes to the matter of salvation." [30] Pink insists, "In and of himself the natural man has power to reject Christ; but . . . not the power to receive Christ." [31] Palmer asserts, "Only when the Holy Spirit regenerates man and makes him alive spiritually can man have faith in Christ and be saved." [32] Custance declares, "What could possibly be a plainer statement than this of the fact that salvation is conferred upon a select number who are conceived by the Holy Spirit and born again by the will of God alone?" [33] Yet that is not what this passage says at all. Vance provides an astounding list of quotes from Calvinists related to sovereign regeneration occurring apart from any understanding or faith on man's part:

A person is regenerated before he believes. [34]

A man is not saved because he believes in Christ; he believes in Christ because he is saved. [35]

A man is not regenerated because he has first believed in Christ, but he believes in Christ because he has been regenerated. [36]

We do not believe in order to be born again; we are born again in order that we may believe. [37]

. . . being quickened and renewed by the Holy Spirit, [man] is thereby enabled . . . to embrace the grace offered and conveyed in it. [38]

Read John 1:11-13 and James 1:18 and meditate upon these passages and pray about them. You will find that there is nothing in either to substantiate such statements: in fact they teach the opposite! Calvinism cannot be derived from but is being imposed upon them. Nor can the doctrine of regeneration before faith be derived from any other passage in God's holy Word. Bob Thompson challenges any Calvinist "to point to one instance in the Bible where God implanted

His Holy Spirit in . . . an individual *before* he or she took God at His Word and was saved . . . ." [39]

Another Verse Most Calvinists Avoid

The major problem when it comes to John 1:13 is the failure to take into account that it follows verse 12 — and verse 12 follows verse 11: "He came unto his own, and his own received him not." It is to this fact that John refers when he begins verse 12 with the word "but." In contrast to those who did not receive Christ, John writes, "*But* as many as received him . . . even to them that believe on his name" is given to become the sons of God. Verse 13 then explains that those who believe and receive Christ cannot give the new birth into God's family to themselves but are born "of God." And is it not repeatedly made clear in Scripture that "the gospel of God" (Romans 1:1) offers the new birth to those who will repent and believe?

This passage offers an insight of great importance in relation to the doctrine of predestination / election: that becoming a child of God through the new birth is a special blessing that would not automatically follow believing the gospel. Men could be saved from eternal hell and be given eternal life without being adopted as children into the family of God. Clearly, being predestined / elected / chosen to be the children of God is not predestination unto salvation but to a special blessing which God has graciously and lovingly made to accompany salvation.

It is no coincidence that most Calvinists avoid John 1:12. No reference is made to it in the 600 pages of the *Selected Writings of John Knox*, [40] and Pink avoids it in *The Sovereignty of God*. Piper makes two oblique references to it in *The Justification of God*, but without substantive comment. [41] Not one of the thirteen authors in *Still Sovereign: Contemporary Perspectives on Election, Foreknowledge and Grace* confronts it. To his credit, White gives it four and one-half pages [42] because Norm Geisler mentions it in his book, *Chosen But Free* (Bethany House, 1999), and White's book was written specifically as a rebuttal to Geisler.

White attempts a response to Geisler's statement that "verse 12 [John 1:12] makes it plain that the means by which this new birth is obtained is by [sic] 'all who receive him [Christ]'." [43] Geisler means that verse 12 gives the qualification ("as many as received him . . . who believe on his name") for receiving the new birth mentioned in verse 13, and that the new birth is totally "of God." This is obviously correct.

Confusing Man's Faith With God's Work

The problem in White's response is simple and twofold: 1) He introduces (without any biblical support) the favorite argument about faith being impossible without the new birth. That assertion is contrary to the numerous passages calling upon the unregenerate to believe and offering salvation through faith; and 2) he fails to distinguish between man's believing and God's regenerating. Neither Geisler nor anyone else critical of the Calvinist interpretation of John 1:13 imagines that man's faith *causes* regeneration. Thus the Calvinist is arguing against something his critics don't even espouse.

Jesus tells Nicodemus that he must be born of the Spirit of God. He makes it equally clear that man must believe in order to be saved: "that whosoever believeth in him should not perish, but have everlasting life .... He that believeth . . . is not condemned: but he that believeth not is condemned already . . . " (John 3:16,18). And surely salvation and the new birth are one and the same: no one who is saved is not also and at the same time born again, and no one who is born again has not been saved. Yet White proceeds to demolish the same old straw man:

> Nothing is said in the text that the new birth is "received" by an "act of free will." In fact, *the exact opposite is stated clearly*, "the ones born *not* of the will of man . . . . " It is an amazing example of how preconceived notions can be read into a text that CBF [*Chosen But Free*] can say the text makes the new birth dependent upon an act of the "free will" when the text says the opposite.

> [Furthermore], if a person can have saving faith without the new birth, then *what does the new birth accomplish?* Evidently one does not need the new birth to obey God's commands or have saving faith. [44]

White confuses man's side with God's side. That the new birth is "not of the will of man, but of God" does not deny that man must believe for God to effect this work in him. Man's faith in Christ no more causes the new birth than faith causes forgiveness of sins and reconciliation to God. Forgiveness of sins, the new birth into God's family, and the many other blessings we have in Christ are all the work of God bestowed on those who believe. Believing did not *create* these blessings, it merely fulfilled God's condition for bestowing them. Yes, regeneration is not by man's fleshly will but all of God; however, God regenerates only those who have received and believed on Christ.

Unquestionably, not only James 1:18 ("begat he us with the word of truth") but numerous other passages teach that believing "the word of truth" is essential for and must precede the new birth. The gospel is the specific "word of truth" which must be believed for the new birth to occur: "Believe on the Lord Jesus Christ, and thou shalt be saved" (Acts 16:31). Peter puts it succinctly: "Being born again . . . by the word of God" (1 Peter 1:23).

In response to Nicodemus's question about how a man can be born again into God's kingdom, Christ explains that He is going to be "lifted up" for sin upon the cross like the brazen serpent in the wilderness, "that whosoever believeth in him should not perish, but have everlasting life" (John 3:15-16). Salvation is not of works, but by faith: "But to him that worketh not, but believeth on him that justifieth the ungodly, his faith is counted for righteousness" (Romans 4:5). As Paul repeatedly says, the sinner is "justified by faith" (Romans 5:1). Clearly, the sinner must hear and believe the gospel *before* regeneration, not after it. Calvin reversed the biblical order, as do his followers today.

Is Faith, Or Salvation, The Gift Of God?

More than one of the critical letters I received charged me with ignorance on this count: "You don't seem to understand that *faith itself* is a God-given gift." That faith is a gift is a major foundational principal of Calvinism. The favorite passage offered as proof is Ephesians 2:8-10. Mathison says, "Saving faith is a gift of God, a result of the regenerating work of the Holy Spirit." [45] Storms claims, "Numerous texts assert that such [saving] faith is God's own gracious gift (see especially Ephesians 2:8-9 . . .)." [46] Clark declares:

> A dead man cannot . . . exercise faith in Jesus Christ. Faith is an activity of spiritual life, and without the life there can be no activity. Furthermore, faith . . . does not come by any independent decision. The Scripture is explicit, plain, and unmistakable: "For by grace are ye saved through faith, and that not of yourselves, it is the gift of God" (Ephesians 2:8). Look at the words again, "It is the gift of God." If God does not give a man faith, no amount of will power and decision can manufacture it for him. [47]

On the contrary, the subject of the preceding seven verses is *salvation*, not faith. Verse 8 then declares concerning salvation, "by grace are ye saved . . . it [obviously salvation] is the gift of God." It is not saving faith, but *being saved* that is God's gift. We are repeatedly told that eternal life is "the gift of God" (Romans 6:23; see also John 4:10; Romans 5:18; Hebrews 6:4, etc.). No less definitive, as Calvin admitted, then tried to deny, is the statement that "faith comes by hearing and hearing by the Word of God." There is no biblical basis for suggesting that God gives saving faith to a select few and withholds it from others.

Furthermore, the construction of the Greek in Ephesians 2:8-10 makes it impossible for faith to be the gift. Such is the verdict of many Greek authorities including Alford, [48] F.F. Bruce, A.T. Robertson, [49] W.E. Vine, Scofield and others. [50] Vance notes that "A witness to the truth of Scripture against the Calvinist 'faith-gift' interpretation can be found in the Greek grammarians." He lists W. Robertson Nicoll, [51] Kenneth S. Wuest, [52] Marvin R. Vincent [53] and others. [54]

Among the reasons the experts cite is the fact that the word *faith* is a feminine noun, while the demonstrative pronoun *that* ("and that not of yourselves, *it is* the gift") is neuter and thus could not refer to faith. Nor will the grammar, as W.G. MacDonald says, "permit 'faith' to be the antecedent of 'it.' " [55] Of course, "it is" is not in the Greek but was added for clarity by the KJV translators, thus is italicized. Nor does it require a knowledge of Greek, but simply paying attention to the entire context of Ephesians 2:8-10, to realize that salvation, not faith, is "the gift of God" – as all of Scripture testifies.

A number of other Greek authorities could be cited to that effect. Though a Calvinist, F.F. Bruce explains, "The fact that the demonstrative pronoun 'that' is neuter in Greek (*tauto*), whereas 'faith' is a feminine noun (*pistis*), combines with other considerations to suggest that it is the whole concept of salvation by grace through faith that is described as the gift of God. This, incidentally, was Calvin's interpretation." [56] Calvin himself acknowledged, "But they commonly misinterpret this text, and restrict the word 'gift' to faith alone. But Paul . . . does not mean that faith is the gift of God, but that salvation is given to us by God . . . ." [57] Thus White and other zealous Calvinists who today insist that faith is the gift are contradicting John Calvin himself.

Furthermore, even if saving faith were the gift (which it could not be), there is nothing in Ephesians 2 (or anywhere else) to indicate that it is irresistibly given by God only after He has sovereignly regenerated the totally depraved sinner and not before. Indeed, that very passage says we are "saved, through faith"; i.e., faith is the means of our salvation/regeneration, not something which follows it.

The Biblical Order: Faith Brings Salvation

In fact, John 1:12 is only one of many verses which make it clear that God effects the new birth / regeneration only in those who have placed their faith in Christ. We need not repeat the many verses already quoted proving that salvation is by faith in Christ ("believe on the Lord Jesus Christ, and thou shalt be saved," etc.). There are many others.

For example, Galatians 3:14 declares that we "receive the promise of the Spirit *through faith*"; and verse 26 says, "ye are all the children of God *by faith* in Christ Jesus." Likewise Paul tells the Ephesian believers, "In whom ye also trusted, after that ye heard the word of truth, the gospel of your salvation: in whom also after that ye believed, ye were sealed with that holy Spirit of promise, which is the earnest of our inheritance . . . " (Ephesians 1:13-14). It could not be stated more clearly that a permanent relationship with the Holy Spirit begins only *after believing the gospel*. No wonder, then, that White and other Calvinists avoid this scripture as well.

Consider Christ's own words, "that every one which seeth the Son, and believeth on him, may have everlasting life" (John 6:40). Clearly, seeing the Son and believing on Him precede receiving eternal life. Calvin turned it around to say that everyone who is elected and sovereignly given everlasting life by Irresistible Grace will then see the Son and believe on Him. We should not need any more verses to disprove Calvin's amazing reversal of the biblical order, but there are many more.

Jesus said, "He that heareth my word and believeth on him that sent me, hath everlasting life" (John 5:24). Again, hearing and believing precede receiving eternal life, which comes through the new birth. Surely no one could be regenerated by the Holy Spirit without receiving simultaneously the gift of eternal life. Galatians 3:22 presents the same truth: "But the scripture hath concluded all under sin, that the promise by faith of Jesus Christ might be given to them that believe." The promised new birth and eternal life are given "by faith . . . to them that believe."

John says of Jesus, "In him was life; and the life was the light of men . . . the true Light, which lighteth every man that cometh into the world" (John 1:4,9). Once again the words "every man" tell us clearly that the unregenerated can be given the light of the gospel. "I am the light of the *world*:" said Jesus. "He that followeth me shall not walk in darkness, but shall have the light of life" (John 8:12). White has no comment on these verses in his book nor upon other similar passages such as John 16:8, where Jesus said that when the Holy Spirit came He would "reprove the *world* of sin, righteousness and judgment." Many other verses could be cited in the same vein.

Did Christ Really Weep Over Jerusalem?

In a radio discussion with James White, I referred to Christ's weeping over Jerusalem. I pointed to His expression of desire ("how often would I") and His lament over Jerusalem's hard-hearted response ("ye would not") as proof of His sincere offer of grace, and man's right and ability to receive or reject salvation:

> O Jerusalem, Jerusalem, thou that killest the prophets, and stonest them which are sent unto thee, how often would I have gathered thy children together, even as a hen gathereth her chickens under her wings, and ye would not! (Matthew 23:37)

White countered that Christ was not weeping over Jerusalem and that the ones He wanted to gather were Jerusalem's children, not the religious leaders who rejected Him. "Ye would not," he insisted, expressed the attitude of the rabbis, not of Jerusalem's "children" whom He wanted to gather under His care. Nor does White's argument help him, considering the fact that very few if any of Jerusalem's "children," any more than her leaders, ever believed on Christ, whereas Christ is expressing His desire for all.

We need to set the scene. From comparing the gospel accounts it is clear that Jesus had just made His triumphal entry into Jerusalem and was in the temple when He made the statement in Matthew 23. Luke specifically declares that as He rode into the city on the colt of an ass He wept as He beheld Jerusalem from a vantage point:

> And when he was come near, he beheld the city, and wept over it, saying, If thou hadst known, even thou, at least in this thy day, the things which belong unto thy peace! but now they are hid from thine eyes. For . . . thine enemies shall . . . lay thee even with the ground, and thy children within thee; . . . because thou knewest not the time of thy visitation. (Luke 19:41-44)

There is no doubt that Christ wept over the city of Jerusalem as He looked upon it. Nor can there be any doubt that when in the temple He lamented, "O Jerusalem, Jerusalem," He was referring to the city and all of its inhabitants down through history, not to any certain segment of the population. "Thy children" could only mean the inhabitants of Jerusalem, not the babes and youth. To suggest, as White stated in a letter, that "those who were 'unwilling' were not those Jesus sought to gather" does violence to what Jesus says: "How often would I . . . but ye would not." He is specifically saying that He wanted to gather them but they were unwilling. He is addressing the inhabitants of Jerusalem as that city's children: "Return, ye backsliding children . . ." (Jeremiah 3:22).

Furthermore, Christ's very words, "how often would I," were a direct claim to deity, a claim which White, in his zeal to defend Calvinism, misses completely. Christ is claiming multiple past pleadings over Jerusalem, yet no such instances are recorded in the gospel accounts during His incarnation. Unquestionably, Christ is presenting Himself as the God of Israel who had sent His prophets generation after generation to warn the inhabitants of Jerusalem, often called "the children of Israel . . . the children of Judah," that if they did not repent, His wrath would be poured out upon them.

Many passages could be quoted which alone could explain Christ's statement. Here are but a few of such lamentations and warnings from God at the mouth of only one of His prophets, Jeremiah. Only in this context is there justification for Christ to use the words "how *often* would I":

> Go and cry in the ears of Jerusalem, . . . Thus saith the LORD; I remember thee, the kindness of thy youth, the love of thine espousals, when thou wentest after me in the wilderness . . . . Israel was holiness unto the LORD . . . [but] my people have . . . forsaken me . . . .

> My bowels, my bowels! I am pained at my very heart . . . O my soul, the sound . . . of war. Destruction upon destruction . . . . For my people is foolish, they

have not known me, they are sottish children . . . . Woe unto thee, O Jerusalem! wilt thou not be made clean?

I spake unto you, rising up early and speaking, but ye heard not; and I called you, but ye answered not . . . I have even sent unto you all my servants the prophets, daily rising up early and sending them: yet they hearkened not unto me . . . .

Thus saith the LORD of hosts, the God of Israel; Behold, I will bring evil upon this place . . . because they have forsaken me . . . and have burned incense . . . unto other gods . . . and have filled this place with the blood of innocents; they have built also the high places of Baal, to burn their sons with fire for burnt offerings unto Baal . . . . I will make this city desolate . . . because of all the houses upon whose roofs they have burned incense unto all the host of heaven, and have poured out drink offerings unto other gods.

For this city hath been to me as a provocation of mine anger and of my fury from the day that they built it even unto this day . . . because of all the evil of the children of Israel and of the children of Judah . . . they, their kings, their princes, their priests, and their prophets, and the men of Judah, and the inhabitants of Jerusalem . . . though I taught them, rising up early and teaching them, yet they have not hearkened to receive instruction. (Jeremiah 2:2-3,13; 4:19-22; 7:13, 25-26; 13:27; 19:3-13; 32:31-33; etc.)

If these and hundreds of similar declarations from the prophets, echoed by Christ, do not express a genuine concern on God's part for Israel to repent so that His wrath need not be poured out upon her, then words have no meaning. Such sincere concern in the face of Israel's refusal to repent completely refutes the theories of Total Depravity, Unconditional Election, Limited Atonement and Irresistible Grace. Otherwise, God's pleadings and warnings are a sham.

If men are totally depraved (as by the Calvinist definition), then there is no point in God pleading with them. If only a few are among the elect and God is not making a bona fide offer of grace, but withholds the Irresistible Grace without which they cannot repent, then hundreds of pages in the Bible are a farce, the insincere pleadings from a Calvinist God who has no real intention of helping those over whom He supposedly weeps. To support TULIP from the Bible the Calvinist must do violence to Scripture with interpretations which are so strained as to make the Bible say what only a Calvinist would derive from it, and then only because Calvinism requires it.

Is There A Real Battle For Souls?

Paul tells us that Satan, "the god of this world, hath blinded the minds of them which believe not, lest the light of the glorious gospel of Christ . . . should shine unto them" (2 Corinthians 4:4). Why would it be necessary for Satan to blind men's eyes if all are totally depraved as Calvinism defines it and are thus already as spiritually blind as one could ever be? Indeed, they are *dead*, and dead men can't see. Calvinism is again refuted because it makes this passage meaningless, as it does so many others.

As for the elect, if, as Calvinism declares, they are sovereignly regenerated and by Irresistible Grace given the faith to believe, and nothing can prevent them from hearing and believing the gospel, it would be impossible for Satan to blind them and therefore there would be no point in his even trying. There would be no real battle between God and Satan for souls, no real conflict within the human heart, the whole thing having already been decided by God with nothing Satan or man could do to change that fact. Paul would have simply been wasting his time disputing and persuading — and the same would be true of our seeking to win to Christ those whom God has predestined to hell.

Calvinism, if it were true, would be great news to Satan. He wouldn't need to deceive the lost to prevent them from believing the gospel because God himself would already have consigned them to hell. As for the elect, because of irresistible Grace, Satan would be wasting his time trying to blind or harden them. There would be no point in trying to blind *anyone*.

If by withholding irresistible grace God were already doing a better job of damning souls than Satan ever could, and man had no choice in the matter, that enemy of souls could go on a long vacation. Yet the Bible declares, "the great dragon . . . that old serpent, called the Devil, and Satan, . . . deceiveth the whole world" (Revelation 12:9). We wonder what is the need for deception, and why "whole world" doesn't mean the elect here, as it supposedly does in other places.

"As many as received him . . . " sounds as though the volitional act of receiving is required on the part of the convicted sinner. Eternal life is a free gift. A gift cannot be merited, earned or paid for in any way, but it *must* be received. Surely to "receive" requires some acquiescence on the part of the recipient. Anything imposed upon someone by a grace that is "irresistible" is not a gift received.

Indeed, how can grace be irresistible? The very term "irresistible grace" is self-contradictory. How can it be an act of "grace" to force upon someone something he hasn't believed and doesn't desire? "God doesn't force anyone," says the Calvinist. Then what does "irresistible" mean? "God is just removing their resistance," is the reply. *Irresistibly* removing it? If it is not against their will, why must it be irresistible?

Would that not fill heaven with those who were unwilling to believe in Christ, to love God or even to be there, but who had been irresistibly *made* willing? "Not so," counters the Calvinist in defense of his theory. "God through Irresistible Grace has wrought a regenerative transformation so that those thus blessed truly love God from their hearts."

But if this could be done for the elect, it could be done for all mankind. How could the infinite love of God leave anyone out? That brings us back to the compelling question: What love is this that loves so few? And why would the God of truth plead with a world of totally depraved individuals to repent and believe the gospel when He had already predestined them to doom?

Luther's Astonishing "Answer"

In his debate with Luther, Erasmus pointed out this apparent insincerity by arguing that God's pleadings with a man to repent and to obey who could not do so would be like asking someone whose hands were tied to use them. Luther countered that God, by calling us to do what we can't do, is "trying us, that by His law He may bring us to a knowledge of our impotence, if we are His friends . . . [and] deservedly taunting and mocking us, if we are His proud enemies." [58] He went on to argue that Erasmus might just as well conclude from " 'if thou wilt keep the commandments, they shall preserve thee' . . . therefore, man is able to keep the commandments." [59]

Luther seemed to have forgotten that even unsaved men keep at least much of the Law most of the time. Even Calvin himself admitted that "total depravity" doesn't mean man is necessarily as wicked as he could be. We've seen that both Scripture and experience prove that all men are capable of doing some good; and some "totally depraved" men at times exceed in kindness and thoughtfulness the behavior of some genuine Christians.

Furthermore, that I am shown my impotence to keep the Law is of no value unless there is a remedy that I can know of and receive. That remedy is the gospel which requires that I come to Christ in faith, believing in Him as the One who paid the penalty for my sins. Nor does the fact that I cannot perfectly keep the Law prove in the least that I cannot come to Christ and believe on Him and receive by faith the benefit of His payment for my breach of the Law.

Paul declares that "the law was our schoolmaster to bring us unto Christ" (Galatians 3:24). While the Calvinist would say that "us" refers to the elect, even the elect were unregenerate like the rest of mankind before they came to Christ. If being "dead in trespasses and in sins" means that man is morally a corpse, how could the Law bring *anyone* to Christ? This is not the Father irresistibly dragging the elect to Christ and sovereignly regenerating and then giving them faith to believe. This is the Law working upon the conscience like a "schoolmaster." How could the Law affect the conscience of "moral corpses"?

If man were totally incapable of keeping even one commandment for one moment, then the giving of the Law would not only be a mockery but to no purpose. But if unregenerate man (as is the case) does understand the Law, keeps it in part at least some of the time, and has a guilty conscience for breaking it, then how can he morally be a corpse? And if unregenerate man can choose to obey or disobey the Law, why cannot he choose to believe the gospel which Paul says brings us to Christ — and where does the Bible say that he can't?

That Inescapable Will Again!

It is interesting to see how *The Canons of Dort* handle this problem. That man has a will with which he could make moral choices is admitted, but it became depraved by the fall. As a consequence, man is supposedly impotent to respond to the gospel. The Holy Spirit must therefore sovereignly regenerate him in order to "heal" that deficiency:

> But as man by the fall did not cease to be a creature, endowed with understanding and will, nor did sin which pervaded the whole race of mankind, deprive him of the human nature, but brought upon him depravity and spiritual death; so also the grace of regeneration does not treat man as senseless stocks and blocks, nor takes away their will and its properties, neither does violence thereto; but spiritually quickens, heals, corrects, and at the same time sweetly and powerfully ends it; that where carnal rebellion and resistance formerly prevailed, a ready and sincere spiritual obedience begins to reign; in which the true and spiritual restoration and freedom of our will consist. [60]

The will is a knotty problem for Calvinists, which they massage around but don't solve. Dort offers a strange solution: "the grace of regeneration . . . spiritually quickens, heals, corrects, and at the same time sweetly and powerfully ends [the will] . . . ." What an odd "healing" that puts an *end* to what it "heals"! Why wasn't this "ready and sincere spiritual obedience" implanted in Adam and Eve? And now that the elect have this new will through regeneration, why don't they always obey God perfectly?

The reason can only be that a "will" is *no will* unless the person whose will it is wills with it. The will can be used for good or evil. The will cannot be denied or dismissed. Calvin and Luther tried to explain it away, but that is not possible. The will is mentioned several thousand times in the Bible. Unregenerate men are frequently called upon to exercise the will in choosing to obey God.

Even the regenerated have a fleshly will that, despite Dort, apparently wasn't *ended* at the new birth: "For the flesh lusteth against the Spirit, and the Spirit against the flesh: and these are contrary the one to the other . . . " (Galatians 5:17).

"Where Is Boasting Then?"

The Calvinist counters that if salvation must be received by an act of faith, then man could exercise his will in deciding whether to believe and therefore could boast that he had contributed to his salvation. Furthermore, it is asserted that man's will is not free to act in that manner. When presenting his belief that "of the great body of mankind some should be predestined to salvation, and others to destruction," [61] Calvin argues that there is "no other means of humbling us as we ought, or making us feel how much we are bound to him [Christ] . . . . It is plain how greatly ignorance of this principle detracts from the glory of God, and impairs true humility." [62]

On the contrary, Paul tells us that although the choice is ours, because all we can do is to *believe*, there is nothing to boast about at all. "Where is boasting then?" asks Paul. "It is excluded," he declares definitively, "by . . . faith" (Romans 3:27). So rather than faith giving cause for boasting, it is the very reason why there can be no boasting. Once again, Calvin is seen to be in direct opposition to Scripture. Nevertheless, Palmer insists that "Calvin simply expounded the Bible . . . [he] uncovered truths that had been in the Bible all the time." [63]

A Calvinist author declares, "If God only saves people who of their own supposed free will accept Jesus, then they merit salvation. They *deserve* to be saved . . . . The notion of free will exalts man because man elects God and God only ratifies man's choice." [64] There is great confusion on this matter of the will because there is no escaping the fact that, as Spurgeon admitted, "Man's will has its proper place in the matter of salvation . . . . When a man receives the Divine Grace of Christ, he does not receive it against his will . . . . Nor again, mark you, is the will taken away. For God does not come and convert the intelligent free agent into a machine." [65] In the same sermon, however, Spurgeon denounces the idea that man can choose whether to believe in Christ or not as making "the purpose of God in the great plan of salvation entirely contingent [upon man's will]." His objection is to man's "coming to God [being] the result of his unassisted nature." [66]

Who would say that man can come to God "unassisted" by the Holy Spirit? Not even the rankest Arminian! But Calvinism makes that false charge against those who disagree with its extremism. Indeed, it goes beyond man being assisted [i.e., drawn by God through the conviction and power of the Holy Spirit and the Word] to insist that man must be forced, caused, made to come completely against his will. It is that word "irresistible" associated with grace that causes the problem because it allows no willingness on man's part. And that raises the same libel against God that we have referred to repeatedly: if man is totally incapable of believing and must be irresistibly dragged to Christ, then Calvin's reprobation results. If it detracts from God's glory for man to be able to respond willingly to the gospel, then surely it also detracts from God's love for Him not to cause *all mankind* to respond.

There is no escaping the fact that the will is essential in any meaningful relationship between man and man, and between man and God. After denouncing "free will," Spurgeon ends that sermon by quoting, "Whosoever will, let him come, and take the water of life freely." [66] Unless one can say yes or no to the offer of salvation it could not be a gift of God's love. Nor does God ratify man's choice; man simply repents and believes the gospel, accepting the free gift of salvation offered in Christ.

Moreover, it is foolish to suggest that receiving a gift means we *deserve* it. Again Calvinism denies the very distinction the Bible makes: "For the wages of sin is death; but the gift of God is eternal life through Jesus Christ our Lord" (Romans 6:23). The distinction could not be clearer between wages, which are deserved, and a gift, which cannot be earned or merited but is simply received and thus provides no cause for boasting.

We are commanded to come to the Lord Jesus Christ, believing in Him as our Savior, but that does not mean that we are forced to do so. And, yes, the Father draws us. But without a willing choice on our part, for Him to irresistibly cause us to believe in and receive Him would not be a gift received, nor would it establish a love relationship between us and God, either on His side or ours.

A drowning man who yields himself into the hands of his rescuer has nothing to boast about, nor has he done any work to assist in his rescue. So it is with the lost sinner. He is simply allowing Christ to rescue him: he has nothing to boast of for he has played no part at all in his salvation.

Solomon said, "he that winneth souls is wise" (Proverbs 11:30). To win someone over to believe in Christ requires persuasion. This is the job of the Holy Spirit through the gospel and He graciously uses human instruments. Our hearts are won as the Father draws us and as Christ's love arouses a response of love within us: "We love him, because he first loved us" (1 John 4:19).

Commissisoned By God To Persuade Men

Calvinism denies that there is any winning or any persuading – salvation comes by sovereign regeneration and Irresistible Grace imposed. If one must be regenerated and then is made to believe, the gospel would have no part in the new birth, preaching it would be pointless, there would be no convincing the unregenerate sinner and it would be a waste of time attempting to do so. Yet Paul expended himself for Christ doing exactly that, disputing and persuading in the attempt to win people to Christ

As soon as he was converted, Paul "confounded the Jews . . . at Damascus, proving that this is very Christ . . . " (Acts 9:22). Everywhere he went Paul "disputed . . . in the synagogue . . . and in the market daily . . . " (Acts 17:17). The last chapter of Acts tells us that even under house arrest in Rome, Paul was still at it: " . . . there came many to him, . . . to whom he expounded, . . . persuading them concerning Jesus . . . " (Acts 28:23).

Paul said, "I am made all things to all men, that I might by all means save some" (1 Corinthians 9:22). Through his powerful preaching of the gospel he won many to Christ wherever he went. There is not a word about Irresistible Grace regenerating the sinners to whom Paul preached and God then giving them faith.

Paul wrote to the Thessalonian believers: "For our gospel came not unto you in word only, but also in power, and in the Holy Ghost, and in much assurance; as ye know what manner of men we were among you for your sake" (1 Thessalonians 1:5). The Holy Spirit brought conviction and assurance, and the lives Paul and his companions lived before them were part of that conviction. Why all of this explanation if for everyone it is the same sovereign regeneration and then irresistibly imposed "faith"? Calvinism just doesn't fit the diligent and fruitful preaching of the gospel by the Apostles to sinners from city to city.

Through the Word of God preached by Paul and Barnabas, Jews and Greeks were *persuaded* to believe and as a result they were regenerated. Paul said to those at Corinth whom he had won to Christ, "for in Christ Jesus I have begotten you through the gospel" (1 Corinthians 4:15). Clearly their acceptance of the gospel Paul preached brought about their regeneration. Yet Palmer reasons, "Only when the Holy Spirit regenerates man and makes him alive spiritually can man have faith in Christ and be saved." [68]

Empowered by the Holy Spirit, Paul diligently persuaded multitudes by the preaching of the gospel. To this he devoted his life: "Knowing, therefore the terror of the Lord, we persuade men" (2 Corinthians 5:11). Where did Paul get this notion, so contrary to Calvinism, that men had to be *persuaded* to believe the gospel? He received this clear understanding from Christ himself. When Christ appeared to Paul on the road to Damascus, He sent him to Jews and Gentiles

> . . . to open their eyes, and to turn them from darkness to light, and from the power of Satan unto God, that they may receive forgiveness of sins, and inheritance among them which are sanctified by faith . . . (Acts 26:18)

What would be the need of Paul opening men's eyes and turning them from darkness to light through the Spirit-empowered preaching of the gospel if it all happens through sovereign regeneration with irresistible grace imposed upon the lost without any understanding or faith? Yet this is precisely what Christ commissioned Paul to do as He had the other Apostles. In relating this encounter with Christ to King Agrippa, Paul declared:

> I was not disobedient . . . but shewed first unto them of Damascus, and at Jerusalem, and throughout all the coasts of Judaea, and then to the Gentiles, that they should repent and turn to God . . . . I continue unto this day,

witnessing both to small and great, saying none other things than those which the prophets and Moses did say . . . . (Acts 26:19-23)

In spite of his staunch support for Calvinism at times, what Spurgeon said at other times undermined it. As though he had forgotten about irresistible grace, he argued:

We are not saved against our will. Nor . . . is the will taken away. For God does not come and convert the intelligent free agent into a machine . . . . But we do hold and teach that though the will of man is not ignored . . . the work of the Spirit . . . is to change the human will, and so make men willing . . . .

Now, Brethren, how is your heart and my heart changed in any matter? Why, the instrument generally is *persuasion*. A friend sets before us a truth we did not know before. He pleads with us. Puts it in a new light and then we say, "Now, I see that," and our hearts are changed towards the thing . . . . The Spirit makes a revelation of the Truth of God to the soul, whereby it sees things in a different light from what it ever did before. And then the will cheerfully bows that neck which once was stiff as iron and wears the yoke which once it despised . . . .

Yet, mark, the will is not gone . . . . If you are *willing*, depend upon it that God is willing. Soul, if you are anxious after Christ, He is more anxious after you . . . . Let your willingness to come to Christ be a hopeful sign and symptom.

He ended the sermon with, "It is not of him that wills, nor of him that runs, but of God that shows mercy. Yet — 'whosoever will, let him come, and take the water of life freely.' " [69]

The Bottom Line

In a personal letter accompanied by some of his writings, author and apologist Rob Zins states, "The Word of God teaches that all men are responsible before God and *accountable*. That all men are equally 'unable' to please God is also undeniable. But, inability does not diminish responsibility." He goes on to argue:

To say that God "allows it" but does not "will it" but *lets* it take place, puts you in no better position than the Calvinist who says that God *could* give irresistible grace to all but does not want to do so. How is it that one can feel better about God *allowing* corruption, abortion, murder and lust, when He *could* stop it . . . ? [70]

We've covered this already. Yes, God *could* stop all evil immediately, but because man has the genuine power of choice, the cessation of sin could only come by destroying the human race as He once did by the flood. However, in His grace he allowed Noah and his family to survive, and through them sin survived and grew into the horror reported daily in the media. The God of the

Bible, however, has a full solution for sin for all who will believe the gospel and receive the Lord Jesus Christ as Savior.

Calvinism, on the other hand, claims that God *could* rescue everyone from hell by imposing His will upon them. He could deliver everyone from all suffering and disease and death. He could have left this world a paradise without sin ever invading it, because man has no real choice under Calvinism and therefore God himself is even the author of evil. That "God," being the cause of even the typist's error, could have a world without any sin or suffering or death — but for His own good pleasure chose the world of rampant evil and suffering as it is today.

The issue we have been dealing with is very simple: Which God is the biblical One — the God of Calvinism, or the God of love who is not willing that any perish, but has given them the right to choose? There is no question which God rings true to the conscience given even to the unsaved.

Man is a created being. As such he is necessarily less than his Creator. That being the case, man can only make less than perfect choices. The amount and degree of evil on this earth will be limited only by man's imagination and the extent to which constituted authority controls human behavior. As Paul foretold, so it has happened: "But evil men and seducers shall wax worse and worse, deceiving, and being deceived" (2 Timothy 3:13).

God Contrasted With False Gods

Suffering and rampant evil are the fault of man's willful choices which have corrupted everything he touches. Sin, suffering and death are not God's fault nor anything God could stop without destroying the world — which He will do one day: "the heavens shall pass away with a great noise, and the elements shall melt with fervent heat, the earth also and the works that are therein shall be burned up . . . . Nevertheless we, according to his promise, look for a new heavens and a new earth, wherein dwelleth righteousness" (2 Peter 3:10-13).

Until then, God "is longsuffering to us-ward, not willing that any should perish" (2 Peter 3:9). God himself has come as a man to pay the infinite penalty demanded by His infinite justice for the sin of the whole world (1 John 2:2). He offers pardon to all and sends forth the gospel of salvation to "whosoever will believe."

Men are responsible for their sin and for their eternal destiny because salvation is offered to all as a free gift and all have the ability either to receive it or to reject it. Calvinism insists that man has no such capability, yet he is responsible anyway. To hold someone responsible for failing to do what he cannot do would be like saying that a paraplegic is responsible to run the 100-meter high hurdles in world-record time.

How can a just God hold sinners responsible to repent and believe in Christ when He withholds from them the essential ability to do so? The very sense of justice which God himself has instilled in human conscience cries out against such a travesty! And here we confront once again the real issue: God's merciful and loving character.

Zins quotes R.L. Dabny "to the effect that the absence of volition in God to save all does not imply a lack of love. God has true love which is constrained by consistent and holy reasons known only to Himself." [71] Such reasoning fails. There is no whitewashing Calvinism's God from His failure to rescue those whom He could rescue. Nor can this evident lack of love and compassion be excused due to "reasons known only to Himself."

The Bible contrasts the truth, purity, love and mercy of the true God with the capricious destructiveness of pagan gods. In the process, the prophets appeal to our reason and to the conscience God has given us. Baal is exposed as a false god not worthy of worship because of its demand that children be sacrificed in the sacred fires on its altars. Would the true God cause billions to burn whom He could deliver?

If it is legitimate to appeal to conscience and reason in exposing false gods, surely no lesser standard should be applied to determine which is the true God. And if He is presented as being less gracious, less loving, less kind and merciful than He expects mankind to be, then surely there is a legitimate reason for declaring that the one depicted cannot be the true God. To attribute to Him *any* lack of love and mercy is surely to misrepresent the true God.

---

1   John Murray and Ned B. Stonehouse, *The Free Offer of the Gospel* (n.p., n.d.), 3.
2   John Calvin, *Institutes of the Christian Religion*, trans. Henry Beveridge (Wm. B. Eerdmans Publishing Co., 1998 ed.), III:xxiii,14.
3   D. James Kennedy, *Why I Believe* (Word Publishing, 1980), 140.
4   Charles Haddon Spurgeon, *The Soul Winner* (Wm. B. Eerdmans Publishing Co., 1963), 15.
5   Kennedy, op. cit., 138.
6   Loraine Boettner, *The Reformed Doctrine of Predestination* (Presbyterian and Reformed Publishing Co., 1932), 285.
7   James Daane, *The Freedom of God* (Wm. B. Eerdmans Publishing Co., 1973), 24.
8   Joseph M. Wilson, "Soul Winning" *(The Baptist Examiner*, February 15, 1992), 1.
9   David J. Engelsma, *Hyper-Calvinism and the Call of the Gospel* (Reformed Free Publishing Association, 1980), 17-18.
10   Wilson, op.cit., 1-2; cited in Laurence M. Vance, *The Other Side of Calvinism* (Vance Publications, Pensacola FL, rev. ed. 1999), 542.
11   R.C. Sproul, *Chosen by God* (Tyndale House Publishers, Inc., 1986), 125.
12   Jay E. Adams, *Decisional Regeneration* (Free Grace Publications, 1972), 12.
13   Boettner, op. cit., 11.
14   Gise J. Van Baren, "Irresistible Grace," in Herman Hanko, Homer C. Hoeksema, and Gise J. Van Baren, *The Five Points of Calvinism* (Reformed Free Publishing Association, 1976), 77.

15 Charles Haddon Spurgeon, "God's Will and Man's Will," No. 442 (Newington: Metropolitan Tabernacle; sermon delivered Sunday morning, March 30, 1862).

16 Edwin H. Palmer, *the five points of calvinism* (Baker Books, enlarged ed., 20th prtg. 1999), 17.

16 Op. cit., 17.

17 Calvin, op. cit., IV:xvi, 16-19.

18 Ibid.

19 Eddie K. Garrett, "The Purpose of the Gospel" *(The Hardshell Baptist*, December 1990, 4); cited in Vance, op. cit., 525.

20 Palmer, op. cit., 17.

21 Arthur W. Pink, *The Doctrine of Salvation* (Baker Book House, 1975), 26-27.

22 Vance, op. cit., 522.

23 George S. Bishop, *The Doctrines of Grace* (Baker Book House, 1977), 146.

24 John Calvin, *Calvin's New Testament Commentaries* (Wm. B. Eerdmans Publishing Co., 1994), 11:144.

25 Op. cit., IV:xvi, 18.

26 Calvin, *Institutes*, IV:xvi,18-21; IV:xv,22.

27 Vance, op. cit., 151-52.

28 John Calvin, *Commentary on the Gospel According to John* (Baker Book House, 1984), 43; cited in James R. White, *The Potter's Freedom* (Calvary Press Publishing, 2000), 183.

29 Calvin, *Institutes*, II: ii,19.

30 Manford E. Kober, *Divine Election or Human Effort?* (n.p., n.d.), 31; cited in Vance, op. cit., 216.

31 Arthur W. Pink, *The Sovereignty of God* (Baker Book House, 2nd prtg. 1986 ed.), 128.

32 Palmer, op. cit., 27.

33 Arthur C. Custance, *The Sovereignty of Grace* (Presbyterian and Reformed Publishing Co., 1979), 188.

34 W.E. Best, *Simple Faith (A Misnomer)* (W.E. Best Book Missionary Trust, 1993), 34.

35 Boettner, op. cit., 101.

36 Arthur W. Pink, *The Holy Spirit* (Baker Book House, 1978), 55.

37 Grover E. Gunn, *The Doctrines of Grace* (Footstool Publications, 1987), 8.

38 Westminster Confession of Faith (London: n.p., 1643), Chapter X.

39 Bob Thompson, "The 5 Points of Calvin's Doctrine of Predestination" (self-published monograph, 4056 Skyline Rd., Carlsbad CA 92008, n.d.), 6.

40 John Knox, *Selected Writings of John Knox* (Presbyterian Heritage Publications, 1995).

41 John Piper, *The Justification of God: An Exegetical and Theological Study of Romans 9:1-23* (Baker Books, 2000), 31, note 154.

42 James R. White, *The Potter's Freedom: A Defense of the Reformation and a Rebuttal of Norman Geisler's Chosen But Free* (Calvary Press Publishing, 2000), 182-86.

43 Cited in White, op. cit., without footnote reference.

44 Op. cit., 185.

45 Keith A. Mathison, *Dispensationalism: Rightly Dividing the People of God?* (Presbyterian and Reformed Publishing Co., 1995), 99.

46 C. Samuel Storms, "Prayer and Evangelism under God's Sovereignty;" in Thomas R. Schreiner and Bruce A. Ware, eds., *The Grace of God, The Bondage of the Will* (Baker Books, 1995), 221.

47 Gordon H. Clark, *Predestination* (Presbyterian and Reformed Publishing Co., 1987), 102; cited in Vance, op.cit., 515-16.

48 Henry Alford, *The New Testament for English Readers* (Baker Book House, 1983), 3:216.

49 Archibald Thomas Robertson, *Word Pictures in the New Testament* (Harper and Bros., 1930), 4:525.

50 Cited in Samuel Fisk, *Divine Sovereignty and Human Freedom* (Loizeaux Brothers, 1973), 32-36.

51 W. Robertson Nicoll, ed., *The Expositor's Greek Testament* (Wm. B. Eerdmans Publishing Co., n.d.), 3:289.

52 Kenneth S. Wuest, *Ephesians and Colossians in the Greek New Testament* (Wm. B. Eerdmans Publishing Co., 1953), 69.

53 Marvin R. Vincent, *Word Studies in the New Testament* (Charles Scribner's Sons, 1924), 3:376.

54 Vance, op. cit., 517.

55 MacDonald, W.G., *Grace Unlimited,* ed. Clark H. Pinnock (Bethany Fellowship, Inc., 1976), 87; quoted in Samuel Fisk, *Calvinistic Paths Retraced* (Biblical Evangelism Press, 1985), 22.

56 F.F. Bruce, *The Epistles to the Colossians, to Philemon, and to the Ephesians* (Wm. B. Eerdmans Publishing Co., 1984), 220-21.

57 John Calvin, *Calvin's New Testament Commentaries* (Wm. B. Eerdmans Publishing Co., 1994), 11:145.

58 Martin Luther, *The Bondage of the Will*, trans. J.I. Packer and O.R. Johnston (Fleming H. Revell, 1957, 11th prtg. 1999), 153.

59 Op. cit., 154.

60 Canons of Dort (Dordrecht, Holland, 1619), sec. III/IV, para.16; cited in Vance, op.cit., 619.

61 Calvin, *Institutes*, III:xxi,1.

62 Ibid.

63 Palmer, foreword to *five points*, 2.

64 Wm. Oosterman, "Take a Long Look at the Doctrine of Election" (Ottawa, Canada: The Lord's Library Publications, n.d.), 3. Available from Westboro Baptist Church, Ottawa.

65 Palmer, op. cit., 27.

66 Charles Haddon Spurgeon, "God's Will and Man's Will," No. 442 (Newington: Metropolitan Tabernacle; sermon delivered Sunday morning, March 30, 1862).

67 Ibid.

68 Ibid.

69 Spurgeon, "God's Will," op. cit.

70 Robert M. Zins to Dave Hunt, August 23, 2000. On file.

71 Zins, ibid.

22
Perseverance Of The Saints

Before beginning what turned into an urgent and in-depth study of Calvinism, I had thought that I was at least a one-point Calvinist. Surely my belief in eternal security, the assurance of salvation eternally in God's presence, must be the same as Calvinism's Perseverance of the Saints. That turned out, however, not to be the case. Why?

Biblical assurance of salvation does not depend upon one's performance but upon the gospel's declaration that Christ died for the sins of the world and upon His promise that whosoever believes in Him receives the gift of eternal life. In contrast, the Calvinist's assurance is in God having predestined him to eternal life as one of the elect — and his performance plays a large part in helping him to know whether or not he is among that select group. Coppes insists that "God's answer to doubt . . . the only proper fount of assurance of salvation . . . of getting to heaven (glorification) is the doctrine of predestination." [1] That view has serious problems, as we shall see.

I believe in my Savior the Lord Jesus Christ and therefore, according to His promise, my sins are forgiven, I have been born again into God's family as His dear child and heaven is my eternal home. Christ calls, "Come unto me, all ye that labour and are heavy laden, and I will give you rest" (Matthew 11:28). Laden with sin, I came to Him and as He promised found rest in Him alone. Christ guaranteed, "him that cometh to me I will in no wise cast out" (John 6:37). I came to Him by faith in His Word and He will never cast me out — i.e., I can never be lost. My assurance is in His promise and keeping power, not in my efforts or performance. He said, "I give unto them [my sheep] eternal life; and they shall never perish" (John 10:28). It would be strange "eternal life" indeed if it were here today and gone tomorrow.

Yet many professing Christians (including many Five-Point Calvinists who believe in Perseverance of the Saints) are troubled with doubts concerning their salvation. Doubts even assail leading Calvinists. Zane C. Hodges points out that "The result of this theology is disastrous. Since, according to Puritan belief, the genuineness of a man's faith can only be determined by the life that follows it, assurance of salvation becomes impossible at the moment of conversion." [2] And, one might add, at any time thereafter as well, for reasons we will show.

Piper and his staff write, " . . . we must also own up to the fact that our final salvation is made contingent upon the subsequent obedience which comes from faith." [3] No wonder, then, as R.T. Kendall has commented, that "nearly all of the Puritan 'divines' went through great doubt and despair on their deathbeds as they realized their lives did not give perfect evidence that they were elect." [4] Arminius, on the other hand, contrary to the false label attached to him by his enemies, had perfect assurance and said that the believer can "depart out of this life . . . to appear before the throne of grace, without any anxious fear . . . " [5]

An Endemic Uncertainty Of Salvation

Why such uncertainty among Calvinists? Why such doubts? And in what can the Calvinist find assurance? Oddly enough, certainty of salvation and confidence of one's eternal destiny is not to be found in the fifth point of Calvinism where one would expect it — nor can it be found in the other four points. While many Calvinists would deny it, uncertainty as to one's ultimate salvation is, in fact, built into the very fabric of their system.

Congdon writes, "*Absolute assurance of salvation is impossible in Classical Calvinism* . . . . [emphasis his]. Understand why: Since works are an *inevitable* outcome of 'true' salvation, one can only know he or she is saved by the presence of good works. But since no one is perfect . . . any assurance is at best imperfect as well. Therefore, you may *think* you believed in Jesus Christ, may *think* you had saving faith, but be sadly mistaken . . . and because unsaved, be totally blind to the fact you are unsaved . . . ! R.C. Sproul . . . in an article entitled 'Assurance of Salvation,' writes: 'There are people in this world who are not saved, but who are convinced that they are . . . .'

"When our assurance of salvation is based *at all* on our works, we can never have absolute assurance . . . ! But does Scripture discourage giving objective assurance of salvation? Hardly! On the contrary, the Lord Jesus (John 5:24), Paul (Romans 8:38-39), and John (1 John 5:11-13) have no qualms about offering absolute, objective assurance of salvation. Furthermore, works are *never* included as a requirement for assurance." [6]

Bob Wilkin of Grace Evangelical Society reports what he heard at Sproul's Ligonier National Conference (with about 5,000 present), June 15-17, 2000 in Orlando, Florida:

> John Piper . . . described himself as "a seven point Calvinist" . . . [and said] that no Christian can be sure he is a true believer; hence there is an ongoing need to be dedicated to the Lord and deny ourselves so that we might make it. [We must endure to the end in faith if we are to be saved.] [7]

> This struck me as odd, since there was so much emphasis on the sovereignty of God in this conference. Yet when it comes right down to it, within a Reformed perspective God uses fear of hell to motivate Christians to live for Him.
> My heart is heavy as I write this from Orlando. I feel such a burden for the people here. Why? Because their theology makes assurance impossible. It [lack of assurance] permeated the whole conference. [8]

What a commentary, that lack of assurance of salvation permeated the Ligonier National Conference featuring major Calvinist leaders! Why should that be? Because the Calvinist cannot rely upon Christ's promise of eternal life or upon the gospel, which are only for the elect. Instead, his security lies in knowing that he is one of the elect. Piper writes, " . . . we believe in eternal security . . . the eternal security of the elect." [9] And there one confronts a serious problem: How can one be certain that one is among that select predestined company?

Though Christ commanded that the gospel be preached to every person living in the entire world, the Calvinist says it is effective only for the elect. Others can *imagine* they believe the gospel, but not having been sovereignly regenerated, their faith is not from God and will not save. As Sproul and his fellow editors declare, "The fruit of regeneration is faith. Regeneration precedes faith." [10] Indeed, the gospel offers false hope to the non-elect and in fact condemns them. Thus, believing the gospel is of no value unless one has been predestined to salvation. Yet predestination was determined by God in eternity past and, as Packer writes, "decreed by his counsel secret to us" [11] – so how can that doctrine give assurance to anyone today? Who can know that he is among the secretly predestined elect?

No wonder, then, that Calvinists are plagued by doubts concerning their salvation. When facing such doubts, VanOverloop gives the cheering advice to "wait prayerfully for a season of richer grace." [12] Otis, on the other hand, suggests that "One of the proofs that we are genuinely saved is that our faith will persevere to the end of our lives." [13] But what if doubts come, such as confronted "nearly all of the Puritan 'divines' "?

Disagreement On A Vital Point

Admittedly, there is no general agreement on this point. Many Calvinists do affirm that believing the gospel brings assurance. In a Calvinist symposium, the essay on assurance by D.A. Carson, which attempts to give a balanced biblical view, does not offer any typical Calvinist arguments for perseverance of the saints at all and comes to no definitive conclusion.[14] As we have seen, Calvin taught that being born into a Calvinist family automatically made the child one of the elect, as did infant baptism, so long as one believed in its efficacy. Thus, while believing the gospel is no sure way to be saved, believing in one's infant baptism is. Sproul even says, "Infants can be born again, although the faith they exercise cannot be as visible as that of adults." [15] For the Calvinist, however, seeking assurance that one's faith is genuine raises further difficulties. For him, faith is a gift from God and has nothing to do with man's volition.

But how can one know whether one's faith is from God or not? Dillow quotes Dabney that each one must examine his faith because it is possible to have a false faith. This only raises further questions. Would God give false faith? Calvin said He would and does. So if God gives true faith to some and false faith to others, how could one know whether the faith he thinks he has is genuine?

Yet Boettner carries on at length about faith being the assurance that one is among the elect, and he argues that since faith "is not given to any but the elect only, the person who knows that he has this faith can be assured that he is among the elect." [16] But what about the false faith and assurance that Calvin says God gives to the non-elect, the better to damn them? The New Geneva Study Bible makes no mention of that problem and even suggests that John wrote his first epistle "to assure those who have believed that they actually possess the priceless gift [of eternal life]." [17]

Attempting to fortify his argument from a different angle, Boettner writes, "Every person who loves God and has a true desire for salvation in Christ is among the elect, for the non-elect never have this love or this desire." [18] By that standard, however, the Christians in the church at Ephesus would have doubted their salvation because they no longer had that fervent love (Revelation 2:4-5) — yet there is no suggestion that they were not true Christians. And what about a false love and desire given by Satan to deceive?

The Puritans struggled with this very question. Dillow accuses Dabney of vainly trying to defend an "issue which dominated three hundred years of English Puritan debate" [19] — considerable dissension indeed, and on a very key point. Arminius, however, declared, " . . . my opinion is, that it is possible for him who believes in Jesus Christ to be certain . . . that he is a son of God, and stands in the grace of Jesus Christ." [20]

Dillow, though a staunch Calvinist, disagrees that faith must be examined. He argues, "The Bible never raises this issue . . . . Does a man struggle to know if he loves his child . . . ? We know we have believed aright if we have believed according to biblical truth . . . . The issue is not a rational examination of our faith . . . [but] a rational examination of the object of faith, Jesus Christ, and the gospel offer." [21] He goes on to accuse fellow Calvinists of being taken up with preserving a dogma:

> Finally, the Bible explicitly and implicitly affirms that assurance is part of saving faith . . . . "Faith is the assurance of things hoped for" (Hebrews 11:1). But in addition, the scores of passages which tell us that "whosoever believes has eternal life" surely imply that a person who has believed has eternal life . . . . Belief and assurance are so obviously inseparable that only the interest of preserving the Experimental Predestinarian doctrine of perseverance can justify their division. [22]

Uncomfortable With Jesus?

Following Calvin's teaching, however, like the Jehovah's Witnesses and Mormons, many Calvinists believe that the only way to make one's "calling and election sure" (2 Peter 1:10) is not through faith but through good works. Oddly, although the first four points of Calvinism insist that man can do nothing, the fifth depends, in the view of many, upon human effort. Boettner quotes Warfield: "It is idle to seek assurance of election outside of holiness of life." [23] Likewise, Charles Hodge declares, "The only evidence of our election . . . [and] perseverance, is a patient continuance in well-doing." [24]

But finding assurance in one's works always leaves questions unanswered in view of the undeniable fact, which we have commented upon earlier, that the apparent good works of the unsaved sometimes put Christians to shame. Furthermore, one's performance could be excellent most of one's life, but if failure comes at some point, one has lost the performance-based assurance. R.C. Sproul expressed the same concern:

> A while back I had one of those moments of acute self-awareness . . . and suddenly the question hit me: "R.C., what if you are not one of the redeemed? What if your destiny is not heaven after all, but hell?" Let me tell you that I was flooded in my body with a chill that went from my head to the bottom of my spine. I was terrified.
>
> I tried to grab hold of myself. I thought, "Well, it's a good sign that I'm worried about this. Only true Christians really care about salvation." But then I began to take stock of my life, and I looked at my performance. My sins came pouring into my mind, and the more I looked at myself, the worse I felt. I thought, "Maybe it's really true. Maybe I'm not saved after all."
>
> I went to my room and began to read the Bible. On my knees I said, "Well, here I am. I can't point to my obedience. There's nothing I can offer I

knew that some people only flee to the Cross to escape hell . . . . I could not be
sure about my own heart and motivation. Then I remembered John 6:68 . . . .
Peter was also uncomfortable, but he realized that being uncomfortable with
Jesus was better than any other option! [25]

Uncomfortable with Jesus?! Where is the comfort and assurance in that?
Couldn't a Muslim obtain similar assurance through being *uncomfortable* with
Muhammad and the Qur'an, or a Mormon through being uncomfortable with
Joseph Smith? Why is it better to be uncomfortable with Jesus than with Buddha?
Where does the Bible suggest, much less commend, being *uncomfortable* with
Jesus? Nor is that taught in this passage. This idea seems all the more pitiful,
coming from a Christian leader and theologian!

There is no escaping the necessity of evidence, and solid faith based upon it,
which the Bible and the Holy Spirit provide in abundance to the believer. Peter
could not understand what Christ meant about eating His body and drinking His
blood. But that did not change the fact that he knew that Jesus was the Messiah.
The important statement from Peter was, " . . . thou hast the words of eternal
life. And we believe and are sure that thou art that Christ, the Son of the living
God" (John 6:68-69). But such faith is not sufficient to give the Calvinist assurance
and would still leave him uncomfortable because the non-elect often think they
believe in Christ. According to Calvin, God even helps them with this delusion.

We have every reason to be very comfortable with Jesus – and this is one
of the great blessings and part of the joy of our salvation. We have absolute
proof that the Bible is God's Word, that Jesus is the Christ, that the gospel is
true, and we have the witness of the Holy Spirit within. The Bible promises
absolute assurance: "These things have I written unto you that believe in the
name of the Son of God; that ye may know that he have eternal life . . . " (1
John 5:13). That assurance, according to this scripture and many others, is for
all those who simply believe in Christ. There is no other basis for assurance of
sins forgiven and eternal life.

Why doesn't Sproul rely upon such promises? Because for a Calvinist the
question is not whether one has believed the gospel but whether or not one was
from eternity past predestined by God to be among the elect, and that is an
elusive question, as many a Calvinist has discovered to his dismay.

The Gospel: God's Power Unto Salvation

In the following pages, the question of assurance will be illustrated
(compositely as we have heard it related by a number of people) through a
fictitious couple whom we shall call Al and Jan. They've been married almost
ten years and have two children. A devout Roman Catholic all of his life with
two brothers who are priests and a sister who is a nun, Al became a Christian a

few months after his marriage. After six weeks of struggling to resolve the obvious contradictions between the Catholicism he had known all of his life and his growing understanding of what the Bible teaches, Al left that Church and has been ostracized by his devoutly Catholic family ever since.

Jan, on the other hand, was a typical New Ager who had absolutely rejected absolutes and was open to anything — except, of course, biblical Christianity, which she disliked for being "too narrow." It seemed like a glorious miracle to both of them when Al was able to lead Jan to Christ about six months after his own conversion.

For nearly eight years Al was happy in the faith, witnessing to friends and family and seeing some come to Christ. He was crystal clear on the gospel and the basis of his salvation. There was no doubt in his mind that he had been convicted of sin, of righteousness and of judgment to come by the Holy Spirit (as all the world is, according to John 16:7-11). Having believed the gospel that Christ died for his sins and that "whosoever believeth on him should not perish, but have everlasting life," Al had placed his faith in the Lord Jesus Christ as his Savior.

At least he was sure at the time he had believed on the Lord Jesus Christ exactly as Paul exhorted the Philippian jailor, "Believe on the Lord Jesus Christ, and thou shalt be saved" (Acts 16:30-31). As a result (or so it had seemed to him), his life was changed and this was the testimony he had enthusiastically shared publicly in church, in street meetings and to individuals. From the beginning of his new life in Christ, Al had had a hunger for God's Word as his spiritual food. He had read his Bible regularly with great interest and enjoyment, and he and Jan had become part of a seemingly vibrant fellowship of Bible-believing Christians and rejoiced together in their new life in Christ.

Enter A Troubling Uncertainty

Then Calvinism was introduced into a small men's Bible study group that Al attended. Lively discussions followed which he found intriguing. At about the same time, Calvinistic doctrines entered the pastor's sermons with increasing frequency and fervency. Although the pastor didn't insist (as some Calvinist pastors do) that every church member be a Calvinist, a number of families left the church in protest over the new emphasis. They felt they were no longer receiving the well-rounded teaching which had attracted them in the first place. Instead, the pastor seemed to bring an unbalanced emphasis upon God's sovereignty into everything he taught — though of course he didn't think so. After all, he was only presenting an exegesis of Scripture, though with a different understanding than his sermons had reflected in previous years. It proved to be

true once again, as William MacDonald, author of more than 80 books, has
stated:

> It is the practice of many Calvinists to press their views relentlessly upon
> others, even if it leads to church division . . . . This "theological grid" or
> system becomes the main emphasis of their conversation, preaching, public
> prayers and ministry. Other issues seem to pale in comparison. The *system*
> itself is only a deduction they make from certain verses and is not directly
> taught in Scripture. [26]

Al was intrigued and swept along with the pastor's new emphasis. This
was the man who had led him to Christ and discipled him and now Al was eager
to follow into what seemed to be a deeper understanding of biblical truth. Jan,
however, was not happy with the implication that God didn't love everyone and
had predestined multitudes to eternal suffering, and that Christ had not died for
the sins of the world as she thought the Bible clearly declared. She knew, however,
that Al was happy and seemed to be studying his Bible more diligently than ever,
so she kept her misgivings to herself.

Seeing his interest, the pastor lent Al some books and tapes by Piper, Sproul
and others. Al began listening to Sproul's daily Calvinist teaching on radio and
bought a copy of the New Geneva Study Bible. Its notes convinced him that
Calvinism was the faith of the Reformation and the true gospel. Gradually the
new "truth" began to make more sense and Al became convinced that what he
was learning followed logically from God's sovereignty.

Al became obsessed with sovereignty and was greatly influenced by a book
by Bruce Milne in which its author said that God's will "is the final cause of all
things . . . and even the smallest details of life. God reigns in his
universe . . . ." [27] Only later would he learn that these words were an echo from
John Calvin in his *Institutes*. Of course, the premier writer on sovereignty was
A.W. Pink and it wasn't long before Al was immersed in Pink's *The Sovereignty
of God*, at the recommendation of friends.

It bothered Al at first to think that God had sovereignly ordained everything,
even having "decreed from all eternity that Judas should betray the Lord
Jesus." [28] Pink explained that "God does not *produce* the sinful dispositions of
any of His creatures . . . He is neither the Author nor the Approver of sin." [29] Al
pondered how God's sovereignty meant that He controlled and literally *caused*
everything and yet that man was to blame for the sin God caused him to commit.
The pastor explained that some things "couldn't be reconciled."

The more Al read, the more the whole matter of man's will became an
enigma. He was especially puzzled by seemingly contradictory statements on
that subject by a number of Calvinist authors. Pink, for example, rejected the
very idea of free will, [30] a concept which he denounced repeatedly. Yet in order

to encourage the study of "the deeper things of God [i.e., Calvinism]," he declared, "it is still true that 'Where there's a will, there's a way' . . . . ." [31] If God had to make the elect willing to be saved because they had no will, why did their will have any role to play? Such questions only bothered Al briefly and were soon forgotten.

Growing Confusion

In order to share his new "faith" with Jan and to bring her along this exciting path of learning with him, Al immersed himself in a detailed study of each of the five points of TULIP. And that turned out to be the start of a downward slide in his faith. Beginning with a deepening understanding of the doctrine of Total Depravity, doubts began to disturb the security Al had once known in Christ. How could he be sure he was truly saved? After all, as a totally depraved person he couldn't possibly have believed in Christ with saving faith unless God had first sovereignly regenerated him. Looking back on his conversion, Al tried to assure himself that that was what had actually happened, even though he didn't remember it that way.

Well, of course, he must have been sovereignly regenerated. That was the only way he could have believed the gospel. All the Calvinists were very firm on that point. But how could he know for sure? After all, regeneration had to happen without his knowledge and before he understood the gospel. How could he possibly be sure that something he wasn't even aware of when it happened had actually occurred?

If Christ's promise in John 3:16 "that whosoever believeth in him should not perish, but have everlasting life" was a genuine offer to the entire world (as he had once thought but no longer believed), then he could have assurance by simply believing. But if "whosoever" really meant "the elect" and salvation was restricted to them, his only assurance would be in knowing he was among the elect, and that question began to trouble him.

First John 5:10-13 ("These things have I written unto you that believe on the name of the Son of God; that ye may know that ye have eternal life . . . ") had once given him great comfort. Now, however, with his new understanding, Al was convinced that John was writing to the elect; and if he wasn't really one of the elect, then his believing would be in vain.

Yet all through this epistle, over and over again it was "believe and have eternal life" — and nothing about being one of the elect. Al took that problem to the pastor, who explained that John was writing *to* the elect, so he didn't need to define who they were. Of course.

Al could not, however, escape a host of questions that kept coming back to haunt him. The Bible clearly said that faith came by hearing the Word of God, and certainly one couldn't hear the Word without faith to believe. But the totally depraved couldn't have faith until they were regenerated and given that faith from God . . . but one had to have faith to believe the gospel in order to be regenerated . . . so how could one be regenerated before believing? It was an impossible conundrum.

There was a brief and heated dispute among his Calvinist friends at the discussion group when Al raised this troubling question. Various Calvinist authors were consulted along with the New Geneva Study Bible, which they all read daily, devouring the notes. There was no question: it was not just a consensus among Calvinist authorities, but unanimous that regeneration had to precede faith. Before the evening was over, they accused Al of having Arminian tendencies, which he denied, of course, but remained uncertain.

Al became convinced that his doubts had to be an attack from Satan. Could this be what Paul wrote about in Ephesians 6? Al turned there and only became more bewildered when he came to these words: "Above all, taking the shield of faith, wherewith ye shall be able to quench all the fiery darts of the wicked" (Ephesians 6:16). *Taking* the shield of faith? Why would that be necessary if faith was a gift from God, sovereignly bestowed?

There was no unanimity in the discussion group when this question came up a few days later. Al thought that *taking* the shield of faith indicated that faith must involve volition on man's part. Some argued that this was written to believers and that of course we had responsibility to believe after we were regenerated.

"But isn't it only *after* we've been sovereignly regenerated that God gives us the faith to believe?" asked Al. "Why is that initial faith *without* volition but afterwards it's different? Wouldn't a faith given sovereignly by God be better than a faith for which we are responsible?"

The lengthy discussion that evening ended without a consensus or further accusations about "an Arminian tendency." Now Al was not the only one having doubts.

A Victim Of Subtle Deception?

Al went back over some of the Calvinist authors he had earlier found so helpful. Now their words only added to his confusion and doubts about his own salvation. Some emphasized total depravity to such an extent that the unsaved were incapable of even understanding the gospel. Others, however, said that the non-elect could understand it but not believe it unto salvation without the faith God gives. Most agreed that the unregenerate could not believe unto salvation. White made that as clear as anyone:

... it is *not* the Reformed position that spiritual death means "the elimination of all human ability to understand or respond to God." Unregenerate man is . . . simply incapable [of] submit[ting] himself to that gospel. [31]

Reading those words really bothered Al. If while remaining a spiritually dead lost soul he *could* have understood the gospel, then what he'd thought was faith could have been purely humanistic consent without salvation! How would he know the difference? He had been sure he had understood the gospel and had believed it. But if he had only understood it as a spiritually dead and totally depraved sinner, and not as one who had been regenerated and given faith by God, he would still be lost!

Once happy in the Lord, now Al could no longer be certain that his repentance and what he had thought was faith in Christ for salvation had not been purely human emotions. Indeed, that had to be the case unless God had first regenerated him without any act of faith on his part. But that wasn't how he remembered it as happening, and he couldn't talk himself into pretending that he had been regenerated prior to what he had always referred to as his conversion.

The Impact Of "Unconditional Election"

Al realized that if he had been elected unto salvation, it could only have been unconditionally and thus completely apart from any "faith" he could have placed in Christ. That faith had to be given to him *after* he was saved and could not have involved any volitional belief on his part.

Looking back on what he had once thought was a clear memory of responding to the gospel by simply believing in Christ, his confusion only grew. He remembered the night he was saved (or thought he got saved). It was as if a light had gone on when the pastor who had led him to Christ quoted Romans 1:16: "For I am not ashamed of the gospel of Christ: for it is the power of God unto salvation to every one that believeth." A lifetime of sacraments, confession, penance, prayers to Mary, and wearing of medals and scapulars suddenly was revealed as useless. The *gospel* was God's means of saving souls and all he had to do was believe. He had believed the gospel, knew he was saved and never had a doubt about his salvation for eight happy years.

Al had even presented that same gospel to others, believing it was God's power unto salvation for them as well if they would but believe. Now he knew that he had been spreading an Arminian lie which had deceived him into imagining he was saved! And to think that he had deceived others as well!

How mistaken he had been to imagine that the gospel was an offer that included him! What *presumption* on his part at the time! That was the unfortunate result of having heard the gospel from a non-Calvinist — and now he was *paying the price*. So were those to whom he had passed this misunderstanding in the days when he had been under the delusion that *"whosoever* believeth in him should not perish" meant salvation was an offer to be accepted by anyone who was willing under the conviction of the Holy Spirit.

His pastor tried to encourage Al to believe that his doubts were good, that they helped him obey Peter's admonition, "Wherefore the rather, brethren, give diligence to make your calling and election sure: for if ye do these things, ye shall never fall . . . " (2 Peter 1:10).

"But how can I make sure an election I don't have if I'm not one of the elect?" Al asked in desperation.

"I've seen your works, Al," came the reassuring response. "There are several in our church that you led to Christ."

"Led to Christ? Isn't that an Arminian idea?" Al blurted out in despair. "What do you mean, *led* to Christ! The elect don't need to be led to Christ but are sovereignly regenerated without any understanding or faith on their part — and the non-elect *can't* be led to Christ. How could you have offered me the gift of salvation through the gospel without knowing I was one of the elect?"

"I wasn't a Calvinist then," replied the pastor awkwardly. "Anyway, since we don't know who the elect are, we preach the gospel to all and leave it to the Lord."

"If we don't know who the elect are," demanded Al earnestly, "then how does anyone know he's one of the elect? That's what's bothering me! Peter says to make our election sure, but how can I do that when I can't be sure I'm elected?"

"You've got the fruits" — the pastor began, but Al looked at his watch, muttered an excuse and headed for the door.

"Limited Atonement" Adds To His Despair

The theory of Limited Atonement further undermined the simple faith Al once had in Christ. At the moment when he had thought he got saved, he had believed that Christ died "for all . . . for the ungodly . . . for sinners . . . for every man," and thus for *him*. He had thought that Christ's sacrifice on the cross was the propitiation "for the sins of the whole world" and thus it had paid the penalty for his sins. How easily he had been deceived by an Arminian lie!

It had finally become the "truth" to Al that Christ's blood was shed only for the elect; otherwise some of it would have been wasted.

How could he have dared to imagine that Christ had paid the full penalty for all sin and thus had died for *him*! The very idea must have come from his own pride. Honesty forced Al to admit that he'd never had any proof that he was one of the elect for whom Christ had died. Nor could he imagine how he could ever hope to find such proof.

Al had offered what he had thought was the good news of the gospel to friends and relatives and acquaintances. He had told many of them with great zeal and confidence, "Christ died for *you*! How can you reject Him when you realize that He loves *you* so much that He came all the way from heaven to pay the full penalty for *your sins* so that He could rescue *you* from hell? If you were the only person on earth, Christ would have died for *you*!"

Leading others to Christ with the gospel had once given him great joy and satisfaction, knowing he would meet them in heaven. Now he knows that the gospel he preached was a lie that had led many astray into imagining that Christ had died for them. How many he has deceived, he can't know, since he doesn't know who, if any, among them were predestined to salvation.

Al is now in great despair, not only for himself but for those whom he surely led astray. Formerly it had brought him great joy that he had become fruitful for Christ in winning a number of people to his Lord. Now he knows there is no such thing as "winning people to Christ." It is a delusion of human pride to think that anyone may say "yes" or "no" to God! Whether one will be saved or lost has all been decided by God an eternity ago and nothing can change that fact.

"Irresistible Grace" — The Final Blow

The theory of Irresistible Grace had once brought great comfort. Learning that even the faith to believe was all of God had at first seemed so humbling, but now it troubled him deeply. Looking back on his "conversion" as he remembered it, Al could find nothing "irresistible" about his salvation.

Leading up to his "conversion," he had agonizingly weighed the choice between a few years of sinful enjoyment or eternal bliss with Christ. In fact, he had procrastinated. Then an auto "accident" which the doctors said he shouldn't have survived became what he had often referred to thereafter as his "wake-up call." In the hospital, as the man who was now his pastor had presented the gospel, Al had "given his heart to the Lord," as he had heard it so often expressed. He had believed in Christ and knew he had passed from death to life because of Christ's promise.

That was then — but this was now. Now he knew it all had been a fleshly or even satanic delusion. Yes, he had been absolutely convinced that the gospel was true and he knew he needed a Savior. He had believed with all his heart that only through Christ having paid the penalty for his sins could he be saved from God's just judgment. But now he knew that even those who were doomed for eternity could come to such rational conclusions and think they had believed in Christ.

No, he had no proof that Christ had died for him, that he was one of the elect. Even less did he have any indication that he had been drawn to Christ by the Father's Irresistible Grace. Even now he wanted to believe, wanted to be saved. He felt that he loved Christ for having died in his place. But it had to be wishful thinking of a totally depraved mind.

Turning To Calvin For Help

The fact that he had read at least some, though not all, of that imposing and intellectually challenging volume, Calvin's *Institutes of the Christian Religion,* had once given Al considerable pride. One of the things that had first attracted him to Calvinism was the fact that so many of its adherents seemed to be more intelligent than ordinary Christians, and especially gave that impression when they talked about election. He enjoyed the company of the elect and there was an exhilarating sense of camaraderie in knowing that outsiders simply didn't understand the truth discovered by Augustine and passed on to Calvin.

Now he turned to the *Institutes* for comfort, hoping that Calvin would offer something to quell his rising doubts. Instead, he was horrified. The answer Calvin gave to his questions seemed to credit God with working an almost fiendish deception upon the reprobate, "enlightening some with a present sense of grace, which afterwards proves evanescent." [33] Al was shocked that God would intentionally deceive sincere seekers and wondered why he hadn't noticed such statements before. The deception Calvin attributed to God sounded almost diabolical, leaving Al severely shaken: "There is nothing to prevent his [God's] giving some a slight knowledge of his gospel, and imbuing others thoroughly . . . the light which glimmers in the reprobate is afterward quenched . . . ." [34]

So the totally depraved, dead-in-trespasses-and-sins moral corpses are nevertheless not *completely* "dead" but able to have "a slight knowledge" of the gospel, a light God gives them that glimmers and then is quenched, while unable to understand enough to be saved! Seemingly diabolical, yes. Yet it rang so true to his own experience. How else could he explain the fact that he had once been so sure of his salvation but was now in despair?

Al desperately searched the Bible but could not find any statement about such a difference between the elect and non-elect, especially that a false light was given to those whom God had predestined to damnation in order to deceive them. Wasn't Satan the one who deceived those who didn't believe, in order to prevent the light of the gospel from penetrating their hearts? He thought of John 1:9 and read it again. It seemed to say that Jesus Christ was "the true Light, which lighteth every man that cometh into the world." He searched Pink's *The Sovereignty of God* and White's *The Potter's Freedom,* Piper's *The Justification of God,* and the works of other Calvinist authors, looking for help, but could find none of them who addressed this important verse. Why was it avoided? At last he found where Schreiner dealt with it in detail. Al was excited to read, "This illumination . . . makes it possible for men and women to choose salvation." [35] Reading on, however, his enthusiasm vanished when he saw that Schreiner was explaining Wesley's view and went on to debunk it. The light of Christ shines upon all men only to reveal "the moral and spiritual state" of each heart, not to reveal Christ to them. [36] That certainly agreed with Calvin.

It seemed that Calvin was saying that God not only predestined multitudes to eternal doom and there was nothing they could do about it, but He deliberately deceived some of them into imagining that they were truly saved, when they weren't! Al could not remember anything in the Bible that would support such doctrine and noticed that Calvin didn't give any biblical references to back up what he said. With horror Al read what now seemed to be sadistic reasoning:

> . . . experience shows that the reprobate are sometimes affected in a way similar to the elect, that even in their own judgment there is no difference between them . . . . Not that they truly perceive the power of spiritual grace and the sure light of faith; but the Lord the better to convict them, and leave them without excuse, instills into their minds such a sense of his goodness as can be felt without the Spirit of adoption.

> Still it is correctly said, that the reprobate believe God to be propitious to them, inasmuch as they accept the gift of reconciliation, though confusedly and without due discernment . . . . Nor do I even deny that God illumines their minds to this extent, that they recognize his grace; but that conviction he distinguishes from the peculiar testimony which he gives to his elect in this respect, that the reprobate never obtain to the full result or to fruition. When he shows himself propitious to them, it is not as if he had truly rescued them from death, and taken them under his protection. He only gives them a manifestation of his present mercy. In the elect alone he implants the living root of faith, so that they persevere even to the end.

> There is nothing to prevent His giving some a slight knowledge of his Gospel, and imbuing others thoroughly. [37]

What "God" Is This!

What could Calvin possibly have meant by "present mercy"? No matter how "merciful" God was to these poor souls in this life, could it be called "mercy" at all if its ultimate end was destruction? Was it not cynical to call temporary favor "mercy" upon those whom this God had predestined for eternal damnation? Who could believe in such a God! Now Al found himself wrestling with thoughts of atheism and only with great effort suppressed such rebellion.

Luther, too, in *The Bondage of the Will*, seemed to present a "God" who was just as sadistic, "deservedly taunting and mocking" [38] the lost by calling upon them to come to Christ when they couldn't without the help He refused to give them! It is one thing to mock those who, having been given a genuine choice, have wilfully rejected salvation and have persisted in their attempt to dethrone God. It is something else for Calvin's and Luther's God, having created man without the possibility of repenting and believing the gospel, then to mock him in the doom to which he has been predestined.

Al could not equate such deceit with the loving, gracious, merciful God of the Bible! But this was the God of Augustine, the premier "saint" of Roman Catholicism to whom not only Calvin and Luther looked as their mentor but whom so many leading evangelicals praised highly. He was further shaken when he came across this statement in a book he was reading: "The Reformation was essentially a revival of Augustinianism and through it evangelical Christianity again came into its own." [39] As a former Catholic, the acknowledgment that Augustine was the founder of Calvinism and, indeed, of "evangelical Christianity" shook him to the core.

What was the truth after all?

Searching for assurance, Al found where Calvin explained that his teaching that some are predestined to salvation and others to destruction was "the only sure ground of confidence [that one was truly saved]," a confidence that only the elect possess. [40] Al thought about that and prayed about it but could not see how the belief that God had predestined some to heaven and others to hell could give anyone confidence that he was chosen for heaven. Was he blind, totally reprobate and unable to see the truth?

His inability to make sense of Calvin seemed to be the final confirmation that he was eternally lost without any hope. The only encouragement he received during those dark days came from the Westminster Confession: "True believers may have the assurance of their salvation divers ways shaken, diminished, and intermitted . . . by God's withdrawing the light of his countenance, and suffering even such as fear him to walk in darkness and to have no light . . . ." [41] That seemed to bring a ray of light, but he couldn't find the biblical basis for true believers lacking the assurance which the Bible promises to simple faith.

Then a friend gave him a book which he said had resolved all of his questions. It was *The Reformed Doctrine of Predestination* by Loraine Boettner. The back cover declared it to be "One of the most thorough and convincing statements on predestination to have appeared in any language . . . the authoritative work in this field." [42] Al began to read it with high hopes. Instead of helping him, however, the book shook him further. The recommendation by *Christianity Today* that "The chapter on Calvinism in history will prove illuminating to many" [43] caused him to read that part first.

Al was immediately troubled by Boettner's admission that early Christian leaders would have rejected Calvinism's view of predestination and that "This cardinal truth of Christianity was first clearly seen by Augustine . . . . " [44] He knew very well that Augustine was responsible for most of Catholicism's doctrines and practices. There had even been a recent newspaper article telling that the

Pope and the Roman Catholic Church had just held some kind of commemorative observance in which this "Saint" had been hailed as the "Doctor of the Church." How could Calvinism be a "cardinal truth of Christianity" if centuries had passed with Christian leaders believing the opposite until Augustine, the greatest of Roman Catholics, "discovered" it?

Is There No Way Of Escape?

Throughout the nearly twenty-five years of his life during which he had been a Catholic, Al had trusted the Church and its sacraments for his eternal destiny. Of course, under that system of salvation by works, rituals, medals, scapulars and intervention of the "saints," he never could be sure he was saved. The longing for assurance had been a key factor in causing him even to consider listening to what he had been taught from childhood were Protestant heresies.

And now in his despair he considered turning back to Rome, even though he knew he'd find even less assurance there than in Calvinism. His former Church had taught him that one never could be sure of getting to heaven; in fact, it was a sin to claim such confidence. He vaguely remembered the anathema pronounced by the Council of Trent upon those who commit the sin of presumption by saying they *know* they are saved and will never be lost.

In a new flash of sudden insight, Al understood at last that ancient anathema, and why Cardinal O'Connor, before his death, declared:

> Church teaching is that I don't know, at any given moment, what my eternal future will be. I can hope, pray, do my very best — but I still don't *know*. Pope John Paul II doesn't *know* absolutely that he will go to heaven, nor does Mother Teresa of Calcutta, unless either has had a special divine revelation. [45]

That must be it — a special revelation from God was what he needed! How else could one be certain, either as a Catholic or a Calvinist, of being among the elect and destined to persevere to the end? Paul had exhorted the Corinthians, "Examine yourselves, whether ye be in the faith; prove your own selves" (2 Corinthians 13:5). Al had thought that was a call to examine his heart to make certain that his faith in Christ was sincere and being lived out in his life through the guidance and empowering of God: " . . . work out your own salvation with fear and trembling. For it is God which worketh in you both to will and to do of his good pleasure" (Philippians 2:12-13).

But a Calvinist author he had read argued from that Scripture, " 'It is God who works in you both to will and do.' If this is true after conversion, when I am made free in Christ, it must be even more so before conversion when I am a slave to sin." [46] No further proof was needed of sovereign election. It is God who does all. Then what good would self-examination do? It would never reveal whether one was among the elect. One could be lost because of not being among the elect and yet be totally deceived by the fleshly delusion of having sincerely believed in Christ and even imagining that one was seeking to live for Him. If God had not done a work in him, all the believing Al could work up would be to no avail. There could be no more subtle delusion — and none more frightening!

After his conversion Al had become a strong believer in the necessity of apologetics. Reared in Roman Catholic schools, he had been taught that evolution was true. In university, it had been a debate about evolution between a Christian geneticist and a professor in the same field which had first started him on an investigation which ultimately led to his conversion to Christ. He had carefully weighed a great deal of evidence and found that it all pointed to the validity of the Bible and Christianity.

As a Calvinist, however, he had lost his interest in apologetics. Some of his Calvinist friends from the study group were heavily into apologetics — but what was the point? The elect needed no evidence or persuasion and it would do the non-elect no good. For a time he felt somewhat confused and even guilty over his change of mind, but that dissipated when a fellow Calvinist (who had been in it longer than he) pointed out from Calvin's *Institutes* where such an attitude was justified.

Calvin's Weakness As An Apologist

It would of course be consistent with Calvinism to look upon evidence and reason as of little if any value in establishing faith. After all, faith is a gift of God bestowed only upon the elect after their regeneration as a result of a secret predestination. Indeed, why should a Calvinist be concerned (though Al noted that many, inconsistently, were) to offer to the ungodly evidence for the existence of God and that the Bible is true in every word? The totally depraved cannot be swayed by truth, while the elect don't need such persuasion since they are regenerated in order to cause them to believe and evidence has nothing to do with it. No wonder Calvin had so little use for evidence and proof:

> The prophets and apostles . . . dwell [not] on reasons; but they appeal to the sacred name of God, in order that the whole world may be compelled to submission . . . . If, then, we would . . . save [ourselves] from . . . uncertainty, from wavering, and even stumbling . . . our conviction of the truth of Scripture must be derived from a higher source than human conjectures, judgments, or reasons; namely, the secret testimony of the Spirit . . . it is preposterous to attempt, by discussion, to rear up a full faith in Scripture . . . .

> Profane men . . . insist to have it proved by reason that Moses and the prophets were divinely inspired. But I answer, that the testimony of the Spirit is superior to reason. For as God alone can properly bear witness to his own words, so these words will not obtain full credit in the hearts of men, until they

are sealed by the inward testimony of the Spirit . . . . Let it therefore be held as fixed, that . . . Scripture, carrying its own evidence along with it, deigns not to submit to proofs and arguments, but owes the full conviction with which we ought to receive it to the testimony of the Spirit . . . . We ask not for proofs or probabilities on which to rest our judgment, but we subject our intellect and judgment to it as too transcendent for us to estimate . . . .

Such, then, is a conviction which asks not for reasons; such, a knowledge which accords with the highest reason, namely, knowledge in which the mind rests more firmly and securely than in any reasons . . . the conviction which revelation from heaven alone can produce . . . the only true faith is that which the Spirit of God seals on our hearts . . . .

This singular privilege God bestows on his elect only, whom he separates from the rest of mankind . . . . If at any time, then, we are troubled at the small number of those who believe, let us . . . call to mind that none comprehend the mysteries of God save those to whom it is given. [47]

It seemed only reasonable to Al that the witness of the Holy Spirit, being subjective, would need to be supported by external proof. The Bible is filled with evidence and the examples of prophets, the Apostles and Christ himself applying such proof to persuade unbelievers to come to faith in God, and to strengthen the faith of believers. Surely that verification ought to be called upon in presenting the gospel and in reinforcing the assurance of believers.

Al realized that from their perspective Muslims could give their own testimony to most of what Calvin said about the inner witness of the Spirit. They think they don't need proof, because they have an inner conviction that Allah spoke through his prophet Muhammad and Allah's name is great. Internal and external evidence, however, would reveal to them that the Qur'an was not true and that Muhammad was a false prophet. Mormons, too, are able to hold fast to their "faith" in spite of the total lack of evidence to support in any way the Book of Mormon (indeed, much evidence refutes it) because its validity was supposedly verified to them by God through a "burning in the bosom." Such is the secret "faith" of every convinced cult member.

Having belittled proofs, Calvin did go on to offer some, but they were generally weak and hardly sufficient to convince an intelligent skeptic. They involved the majesty of language and sublime truths set forth in Scripture more than evidences for its inspiration. He did touch briefly on a few prophecies, but they were of the kind which were fulfilled in short order, such as the restoration of the children of Israel under Cyrus. The most powerful prophecies fulfilled in Israel throughout history and in the coming of her Messiah were almost completely neglected — the former, no doubt, because of the rejection of Israel as God's people which Luther and Calvin carried over from their Catholicism.

Calvin did spend several chapters speaking of the evidences that God exists and that the Bible is the Word of God, and that God is the only true God in contrast to the false gods of the heathen. But why do this if it isn't important? The elect surely don't need any proof. Moreover, the proofs he offered were weak and superficial and would carry little weight with any intelligent skeptic. So many others have written apologetics which are far superior to Calvin's that he wasted his time.

We do not minimize the witness of the Holy Spirit within the believer. However, the Bible offers proof upon proof, as did the Apostles and prophets. We have the prophecies fulfilled, the historical evidence, and the scientific and logical evidence. These are important in establishing the Word of God and the gospel it contains as the truth of God. Paul told Titus that an elder should "be able by sound doctrine both to exhort and to convince the gainsayers" (Titus 1:9).

Al had not entirely lost his interest in apologetics, but it seemed of little value in light of his new understanding. Furthermore, he found no hope in apologetics of ever being able to prove that he was one of the elect. In fact, there was no way that apologetics could establish the truth of election — much less determine the identity of the elect. That realization began to trouble him, though he wasn't sure why . . . .

---

1   Leonard J. Coppes, *Are Five Points Enough? The Ten Points of Calvinism* (Denver CO: self-published, 1980), 25, 27.

2   Zane C. Hodges, author's preface to *The Gospel Under Siege* (Kerugma, Inc., 2nd ed. 1992), vi.

3   John Piper and Pastoral Staff, "TULIP: What We Believe about the Five Points of Calvinism: Position Paper of the Pastoral Staff" (Desiring God Ministries, 1997) 25.

4   R.T. Kendall, *Calvin and English Calvinism to 1649* (Oxford University Press, 1979), 2; cited without page number by Bob Wilkin, "Ligonier National Conference" (*The Grace Report*, July 2000).

5   Jacobus Arminius, *The Works of James Arminius*, trans. James and William Nichols (Baker Book House, 1986), 1:667; cited in Laurence M. Vance, *The Other Side of Calvinism* (Vance Publications, Pensacola FL, rev. ed. 1999), 591.

6   Philip F. Congdon, "Soteriological Implications of Five-point Calvinism" (*Journal of the Grace Evangelical Society*, Autumn 1995), 8:15, 55-68.

7   Piper and Staff, op. cit., 23.

8   Wilkin, op.cit., 1-2.

9   Piper and Staff, op. cit., 24.

10 New Geneva Study Bible, "Regeneration: The New Birth" (Thomas Nelson Publishers, 1995), 1664.

11 J.I. Packer, "The Love of God: Universal and Particular." In *Still Sovereign: Contemporary Perspectives on Election, Foreknowledge and Grace*, ed. Thomas R. Schreiner and Bruce A. Ware (Baker Books, 2000), 281.

12 Ronald VanOverloop, "Calvinism and Missions: Pt. 2, Unconditional Election" (*Standard Bearer*, January 15, 1993), 185; cited in Vance, op. cit., 403.

13 John M. Otis, *Who is the Genuine Christian?* (n.p., n.d.), 39; cited in Vance, op. cit., 595.

14 D.A. Carson, "Reflections on Assurance." In Schreiner and Ware, op. cit., 247-48.
15 New Geneva Study Bible, ibid.
16 Loraine Boettner, *The Reformed Doctrine of Predestination* (Presbyterian and Reformed Publishing Co., 1932), 308.
17 New Geneva Study Bible (marginal note commenting upon 1 John 5:13), op. cit., 1993.
18 Boettner, op. cit., 309.
19 Joseph C. Dillow, *The Reign of the Servant Kings: A Study of Eternal Security and the Final Significance of Man* (Schoettle Publishing Co., 2nd ed. 1993), 192-93.
20 Arminius, op. cit., 1:667.
21 Dillow, op. cit., 193.
22 Op. cit., 291.
23 Boettner, op. cit., 309.
24 Charles Hodge, *A Commentary on Romans* (The Banner of Truth Trust, 1972), 292.
25 R.C. Sproul, "Assurance of Salvation" (*Tabletalk,* Ligonier Ministries, Inc., November 1989), 20.
26 William MacDonald to Dave Hunt (marginal note in review copy). On file.
27 Bruce Milne, *Know the Truth* (InterVarsity, n.d.), 66.
28 Arthur W. Pink, *The Sovereignty of God* (Baker Book House, 4th ed., 2nd prtg. 1986), 155.
29 Op. cit., 156.
30 Op. cit., 1.
31 Pink, foreword to 1st ed. 1918, op. cit.
32 James R. White, *The Potter's Freedom* (Calvary Press Publishing, 2000), 100-101.
33 John Calvin, *Institutes of the Christian Religion*, trans. Henry Beveridge (Wm. Eerdmans Publishing Company, 1998 ed.), III:ii,11.
34 Op. cit., III:ii,12.
35 Thomas R. Schreiner, "Does Scripture Teach Prevenient Grace in the Wesleyan Sense," in *Still Sovereign*, op. cit., 237.
36 Op. cit., 240.
37 Calvin, op. cit., III:ii,11-12.
38 Martin Luther, *The Bondage of the Will*, trans. J.I. Packer and O.R. Johnston (Fleming H. Revell, 1957, 11th prtg. 1999), 153.
39 Boettner, op. cit., 367.
40 Calvin, op. cit., III:xxi,1.
41 Westminster Confession of Faith (London: n.p., 1643), XVIII:iv.
42 Boettner, op. cit., back cover.
43 Ibid.
44 Op. cit., 365.
45 Sam Howe Verhovek, "Cardinal Defends a Jailed Bishop Who Warned Cuomo on Abortion" (*The New York Times*, February 1, 1990), A1, B4.
46 Wm. Oosterman, "Take a Long Look at the Doctrine of Election" (Ottawa, Canada: The Lord's Library Publications, n.d.), 7. Available from Westboro Baptist Church, Ottawa.
47 Calvin, op. cit., 71-73.

23
Resting In God's Love

The more deeply Al studied the subject of assurance, the more confused he became at the frequent contradictions among Calvinists. He read where John MacArthur said that "those whose faith is genuine will prove their salvation is secure by persevering to the end in the way of righteousness." [1] But Joseph Dillow, in a book which had been highly recommended to him by his pastor as giving the clearest word on assurance of salvation, criticized MacArthur and (with many quotations from Calvin to support him) declared that "Saving faith in Calvin and in the New Testament is a passive thing located in the mind." [2] In that case it would be independent of any works.

Calvin argued that " . . . if we are in communion with Christ, we have proof sufficiently clear and strong that we are written in the Book of Life." [3] But considering the deceitfulness of every human heart, how could we possibly be sure that we were in communion with Christ — and what about all the other things Calvin said in contradiction to this statement? Al was now exactly where Calvin had said he would be: " . . . all who do not know that they are the peculiar people of God must be wretched from perpetual trepidation.[4] So his wretchedness was, after all, to be endless.

Al's confusion only grew (but with it a glimmer of hope) when he read the admission from Gerstner that those who think they have full assurance that they are saved "ground themselves in the faulty definitions of saving faith which we received from the first Reformers. They . . . defined saving faith as a belief that 'Christ has saved me,' making the assurance of hope its necessary essence.

Now, the later Reformers . . . have subjected this view to searching examination, and rejected it (as does the Westminster Assembly) on scriptural grounds." [5] That could only mean that Al's former assurance of salvation had actually been in agreement with the early Reformers and it was the later ones who retreated from that position! Whom should he believe – and why such disagreement among Calvinists?

Al wondered how he had missed the fact that so many Calvinists seemed to insist that assurance was *impossible*. Kenneth Gentry wrote, "Assurance is subjective . . . . Dabney rightfully notes that [absolute assurance] requires a revelation beyond the Scripture because the Bible does not specifically speak to the individual in question. Nowhere in the Bible do we learn . . . that Ken Gentry is among the elect." [6] Al was badly shaken. From Gentry's article and similar statements from other leading Calvinists, was he to conclude that Calvinism actually opposed the assurance he was seeking? That seemed to be what Walter Chantry was saying:

> Few seem to appreciate the doubts of professing Christians who question whether they have been born again. They have no doubt that God will keep His promises but they wonder whether they have properly fulfilled the conditions for being heirs to those promises . . . . They are asking a legitimate question, "Have we believed and repented? Are we the recipients of God's grace . . . ?" Since we read of self-deceived hypocrites like Judas, it is an imperative question. "What must I do to be saved?" is an altogether different question from, "How do I know I've done that?" You can answer the first confidently. Only the Spirit may answer the last with certainty. [7]

Al was not only confused but deeply troubled by the very selectiveness of leading Calvinist apologists which he began to notice and we have documented in earlier chapters. In his zeal to deny that volition had anything to do with faith, and to show that it was entirely a mental attitude produced by the Holy Spirit without man's will, Dillow cited Ephesians 6:23 ("Peace be to the brethren, and love with faith, from God the Father and the Lord Jesus Christ.") [8] but neglected to mention 6:16 ("Above all, taking the shield of faith . . . "). Since "taking" surely was something we must do, so believing must be our responsibility as well. But that contradicted the very sovereignty Dillow was declaring. No wonder he hadn't mentioned this verse!

Al found little comfort from his Calvinist friends. They had their own doubts, which they generally denied, only admitting them in rare moments of candor. It was all sovereignty with no part for man to play at all – except that one had to persevere to the end and demonstrate it in one's life. And Al knew he was failing that test.

A friend had given Al an article by R.C. Sproul titled "Assurance of Salvation." Al had read it eagerly, hoping for help, only to come across this troubling statement: "There are people in this world who are not saved, but who are convinced that they are . . . ." [9]

That seemed to describe the very false assurance he once had. Now he knew better. The more he researched, the more convinced he became that assurance of heaven was beyond his reach. And to his surprise, Al was discovering that uncertainty of salvation was rather common among Calvinists. A statement by I. Howard Marshall seemed to go right through his heart because it was so true of his own situation: "Whoever said, 'The Calvinist knows that he cannot fall from salvation but does not know whether he has got it,' had it summed up nicely." [10] Was Calvinism itself, then, the root of his doubts?

The more Al read, the more confused he became. Dillow went on and on about the faith that brings assurance [11] until it became far too complex theologically for the Philippian jailor to have known what Paul meant when he said, "Believe on the Lord Jesus Christ and thou shalt be saved" (Acts 16:31). But could it really be that simple?

The Central Issue: God's Love

Al's troubled countenance and frequent moodiness finally provoked Jan to break her silence. "Let me get this straight," she began. "The God you now believe in — "

"What do you mean, 'the God I now believe in'?" Al interjected testily. "He's the same God I always believed in and the One you believe in too!"

"Really? I listen carefully to Pastor Jim . . . and a lot of people besides me aren't happy. The God of the Bible that I believe in (and you used to) loves the whole world and wants everyone saved. He gives us all the right to choose — so it's not His doing if anyone goes to hell . . . ."

"That's *your* interpretation," interrupted Al.

"Let me finish, please . . . ? Your *new* God gives no one a choice. He regenerates certain elect ones against their will, and — "

"That's not true!" Al shot back quickly. "He makes us willing by changing our hearts."

"Were *you* willing to be regenerated?"

"I didn't know I was being regenerated. That has to come first before anyone can understand or believe the gospel. We're regenerated and then given faith — "

"Exactly what I said. Your will was set against God. Out of the blue He regenerated you. If that isn't against your will . . . ."

"Well . . . I'll have to think about that."

"You didn't have a choice. He just elected you."

"Grace has to be *irresistible* because no one wants it. You think a sovereign God is going to let man have the last word! Then He's not sovereign! The God I believe in isn't going to let puny man frustrate His purposes! You don't understand sovereignty . . . God doesn't share His throne!"

"Sovereignty, foreknowledge, free will . . . Calvinists make it all so complicated," cautioned Jan. "But the Bible is simple enough for a child to understand. The real issue is love — and that simplifies everything. You actually believe that God who *is* love only loves certain ones and predestines the rest to eternal damnation? What love is this?"

"Well . . . the Bible does teach election. You admit that . . . ."

"Forget election for the moment — "

"It's in the Bible, for heaven's sake! How can you forget it?"

"I mean that's too complicated. There's something simpler — God's love. I can't believe that the God I know sends anyone to hell that He could rescue!"

"It doesn't make *me* comfortable, either. But the Bible teaches this is God's good pleasure."

"*Where* does the Bible say that! My Bible says that God has no pleasure in the destruction of the wicked but wants all to be saved. Al, I love you, but I can't go along with this. That's not the God of love I know and read of in the Bible. I think the Calvinism you and pastor are into misrepresents God! But I don't want to discuss it — we just argue."

"We're not arguing, Jan. This is important. I've been studying this for months . . . ."

"Al, I admire you for the effort you've put into it. But it takes no study to see that God loves the whole world so much that He sent His Son to die for everyone's sins so that 'the world through him might be saved.' And that's just one verse."

"*World* there means the elect," Al countered. "You just don't understand. But a little more study—"

"Don't you think I've been studying too? I know enough verses to tell me that Calvinism libels the God who Paul said wants 'all men to be saved' (1 Timothy 2:4) and Peter said 'is not willing that any should perish' (2 Peter 3:9)."

"*All men* and *any* means the elect. If you'd let me explain—"

"Please, Al, don't complicate the Bible. When it says God loves the whole world and doesn't want any to perish, why work so hard to make it say *elect*?" Jan shrugged her shoulders helplessly. "You go ahead and study Calvinism. I'll stick with my simple faith, and let's not argue about it."

"We're not arguing — just discussing."

But Jan had turned to the kitchen sink and was busying herself cleaning up the dinner dishes.

Hell: Whose Choice?

It was deeply troubling to Al (though he wasn't ready to admit it to Jan) that in spite of the biblical presentation from Genesis to Revelation of God's love, grace, and mercy to all, Calvinism portrayed God as pleased to damn billions. At one time this view had seemed the only way to uphold God's sovereignty, but now he wondered whether an overemphasis upon sovereignty had diminished God's love. He read where White said:

> We know, naturally, that we are to have God's glory as our highest goal, our highest priority. So it should not be at all surprising that the most profound answer Scripture gives to the question of "what's it all about" is that it is about God's glory. *All* of salvation results in the praise of the glory of *His* grace. [12]

Those were nice words to which a few months earlier Al would have assented without much thought. Now he wondered how predestining multitudes to eternal torment could be to the glory of God's grace — and how even the salvation of the elect could glorify God if He could have done the same for all, but didn't.

Jan's words from months earlier came back to haunt him: "The Bible teaches that those in hell will be there because, although God didn't want them to go there and lovingly provided and freely offered full salvation, they rejected it."

To say God's sovereignty would be denied if man had a choice no longer seemed quite as foolproof as it once had. Couldn't God make a sovereign decision to allow man free will? He began cautiously to read some critics of Calvinism and came across the following, which seemed to make a lot of sense:

> What takes the greater power (omnipotence): to create beings who have no ability to choose — who are mere pawns on God's cosmic chessboard — or to create beings who have the freedom to accept or reject God's salvation? I submit, the latter . . . . Would a God who ordained the existence of immortal beings without making any provision for them to escape eternal torment be a cruel being? What kind of God would call on mankind to "believe and be saved" when He knows they cannot [and] what kind of relationship is there between God and people who could never choose Him — but are "irresistibly" called . . . ? For these and other reasons I question the idea that individual unconditional election and five-point Calvinism best reflect the attributes of God. A God who sovereignly offers salvation to all through His elect Savior reflects both power and love. [13]

Perseverance Of The Saints?

Al continued wrestling with the matter of assurance. Even aside from the question of whether he was one of the elect, he was still confused about whether his experience of trusting Christ was biblical. Reading again James White's *The Potter's Freedom*, he came across the statement once more that "something must happen *before* a person can 'hear' or believe in Christ: and that is the work of God in regenerating the natural man and bringing him to spiritual life." [14] That certainly hadn't been the sequence of events in his coming to Christ, as he remembered it. He had thought that he had been regenerated (born again) *following* his faith in Christ and as a *result* of believing the gospel.

But much like White, Jonathan Edwards also taught that there had to be "the principle of holiness that precedes faith . . . the alteration made in the heart of the sinner before there can be action [i.e., faith in Christ]." [15] Going back in his memory to that decisive night, Al could not see how that could have been the case.

Al was listening to a tape by John Armstrong, a man he greatly admired as a leading Calvinist, and was shocked to hear him say, "I was asked the question about a year ago by a group of pastors in Pennsylvania . . . 'What do you think is the one doctrine that is the most destructive in the life of the church . . . today?' And I said, the doctrine of Eternal Security." [16]

Al couldn't believe his ears. He had to rewind the tape and listen to it again. Sure enough, he'd heard it right the first time. So the worst thing possible was to have assurance of salvation? Armstrong seemed to explain why any apparent assurance could only be false: "God justifies, but man must have faith and he must obey . . . . Romans 2:13-14, when it says the one who obeys the law is justified, it means exactly that. That is not a hypothetical verse, ladies and gentlemen, the way many Protestants have read it. And when James 2:13-14 says, 'The doers of the law shall be justified,' it means the doers of the law shall be justified. That's why Paul and James are not in conflict . . . . Let me suggest . . . [also] Ephesians 2:8-10 . . . . We are saved unto good works. They're necessary consequential works. Without them there is no salvation. Right?" [17]

No wonder there could be no assurance of salvation: it depended upon our keeping the law! The Bible says no one has kept the law, so who could be saved? Al was devastated. Was Armstrong right or was Dillow? Yet both of them not only contradicted one another but themselves as well. On the same tape, Armstrong said that man had no will, Luther's *Bondage of the Will* was what the Reformation was all about and that even the faith to believe was a gift of God. So how could it be man's responsibility to believe and keep the law? Al was bewildered. Nor did it help when Armstrong gave his antidote: " . . . perseverance, and here's the point, is the necessary attribute of justification." [18] What did that mean? Who could make any sense of this?

Perseverance was everything for some Calvinists, but not for others. Who should Al believe? And how could a failure to persevere after the fact prove that one had not been saved in the first place? Why, that would mean that one could *never* be sure he had ever been saved until he died and thus knew whether he had truly persevered to the end! Al had once been so happy with the fifth point of Calvinism because he thought it meant that God would do the persevering: "for it is God which worketh in you both to will and to do of his good pleasure" (Philippians 2:13). Now he discovered that the persevering in good works and keeping the law was up to him — and he knew that he couldn't do it.

Why hadn't he noticed earlier this emphasis upon *one's own* perseverance? Al knew that his "performance" had deteriorated lately, and that meant that his perseverance in the faith was far from what it ought to be. The very fact that he was plagued by doubts was further proof that he was not persevering. And the doubts only grew, the more he studied the writings of leading Calvinists, ancient or modern. Could it be Calvinism itself that fostered the doubts? Perhaps Calvin was admitting this when he wrote:

> For there is scarcely a mind in which the thought does not sometimes rise, Whence your salvation but from the election of God? But what proof have you of your election? When once this thought has taken possession of any individual, it keeps him perpetually miserable, subjects him to dire torment, or throws him into a state of complete stupor . . . . Therefore, as we dread shipwreck, we must avoid this rock, which is fatal to every one who strikes upon it . . . . [19]

Al was devastated. To try to be sure you're one of the elect would be *fatal*? Wait a minute! Wasn't it Calvinism's doctrine of election that had caused his uncertainty? Non-Calvinists had no such doubts. If he abandoned this doctrine would he find peace?

More And More Unanswered Questions

Al began to ask Christian friends how they knew they were saved. The Calvinists said they were among the elect and had the works to prove it, though at times they weren't especially comfortable. The non-Calvinists simply replied that they had believed the gospel. Christ had promised eternal life to all who would come to Him in faith, and that was good enough for them.

The more Al studied, the more the troubling questions mounted. If man is totally depraved by nature, how can he aspire to and even do good deeds? But he does. If Total Depravity isn't total in that regard, then why is it total when it comes to believing the gospel? Why would God repeatedly appeal to men to repent if they couldn't? Why send His prophets day after day, year after year, to unregenerate Israel if their pleadings were of no avail? If it was all Irresistible Grace, why not just zap everyone with it?

Everyone? It always came back to Jan's main complaint — how could God who *is* love allow *anyone* to perish whom He could save? Even worse, how could the God of all grace (1 Peter 5:10) and mercy will anyone's destruction? He had never admitted it to Jan, but the importance of that question was beginning to push everything else into the background. Jan's earnest query haunted him: "*What love is this?*"

Somehow a little booklet by Spurgeon fell into Al's hands and he was excited to read that even that great preacher and staunch Calvinist admitted that he'd had no perception at the time of his conversion that God had sovereignly regenerated him nor could he imagine at what point that could have happened. Spurgeon confessed, "When I was coming to Christ, I thought I was doing it all myself – I sought the Lord earnestly . . . ." It was not until some time later that he realized that "God was at the bottom of it all . . . . He was the Author of my faith, and so the whole doctrine of grace opened up to me . . . ." [20] He closed his sermon declaring that those Christians who are most pious, reverent and devoted to the Lord "believe that they are saved by Grace, without works, through faith, and that not of themselves, it is the gift of God." [21] That sounded like his non-Calvinist friends, and the way he had believed before becoming a Calvinist!

To God Be The Glory!

Al remembered that before he'd become a Calvinist he had praised God for being the Author of salvation and the Savior of sinners, had given all credit and glory to Him, and had understood very clearly that he would never have sought Him had God not moved upon him by His Spirit to do so. But he had also believed that it was his responsibility to respond in faith from his heart. Surely, for man to respond to God by gratefully receiving the gift of salvation would not nullify anything Spurgeon said. And how could it challenge God's sovereignty for man to receive gratefully what God offered while giving God all the glory?

Jan, in fact, had some time previously suggested, "It seems to me that my praise and gratitude to the Lord is more genuine and more glorifying to God than any Calvinist's."

"How can you say that?" Al had protested.

"Because my gratitude and praise comes from my heart. I wasn't programmed to accept Christ – "

"*Programmed*? No Calvinist teaches that!"

"You don't call it that, but you were totally opposed to God and instead of your heart being won to Christ by His love and grace and mercy, you were *made* to believe – "

"Not *made* to believe," Al interrupted impatiently. *When would she ever understand?* "Our wills are changed graciously!"

"Okay, you were *caused* to believe. Al, you can't get around the fact that God did something to your will so that you believed what you formerly didn't believe. And it didn't come about by any conviction on your part, any understanding, any faith on your part . . . . I've been reading some of those Calvinist books you've got."

Like every other argument – yes, that's what they had become – this one, too, ended with neither of them giving any ground. But Al was increasingly shaken in his confidence that Calvinism was the truth of God. Most troubling had been the realization that his uncertainty seemed to arise out of Calvinism itself. No wonder Calvin had voiced so many warnings about doubts:

> Among the temptations with which Satan assaults believers, none is greater or more perilous, than when disquieting them with doubts as to their election, he at the same time stimulates them with a depraved desire of inquiring after it out of the proper way . . . I mean when puny man endeavors to penetrate to the hidden recesses of the divine wisdom . . . in order that he may understand what final determination God has made with regard to him. [22]

So it wasn't proper to want to know God's "final determination . . . with regard to him"? But there was nothing so important! It seemed that Calvin kept contradicting himself. Sometimes he even seemed to say that we should just trust God for our election: "Our confidence ought to go no farther than the word . . . ." [23] Al realized that if he did that, he would turn from Calvinism back to simple faith in the gospel. Perhaps, thought Al in despair, he ought to go back even before what he had thought was his conversion and return to the Church of his upbringing.

Desperation — And Enlightenment

Al began to think more seriously of returning to Catholicism. Embarrassed and uncertain, he went back to his old parish and found that a new priest who didn't know him was in charge. That made it easier. In the process of telling the new man that he wanted to explore possibly returning to Roman Catholicism, somehow the name of Calvin, came up. In the next fifteen minutes, to his utter amazement Al discovered that this priest knew even more about Calvinism than did Pastor Jim.

A well-worn copy of Calvin's *Institutes of the Christian Religion* was pulled from a shelf and the priest began to read a section which he was sure would settle any question in Al's mind of returning to the true Church. Al almost jumped up and shouted, "Hallelujah!" when what Calvin had said about baptism was read to him. He could hardly believe his ears that, according to Calvin, his baptism as a baby into the Roman Catholic Church had made him one of the elect! All he had to do was to believe the promise inherent in his Catholic baptism!

Al was ecstatic. The Catholic Church had done more for him than he had known. So he was one of the elect after all: Calvin himself had said it! All Al needed to do was to trust his baptism!

But this new assurance lasted for only a few days. Was his faith to be in his baptism as an infant too young to understand anything, and at the hands of a Catholic priest who himself believed and taught a false gospel? Was that really the biblical foundation of eternal salvation? Well, Calvin had thought so.

What about the true gospel he had believed, "the power of God unto salvation," and as a result had been born again? If being baptized as a baby when he didn't even know what was happening had made him a child of God, as Calvin had insisted, even to the persecution of those who disagreed, then what was the point of his believing the gospel? No, he couldn't accept that, even if Calvin had declared it. Al had finally come to a fish in the Calvinism pond too large to swallow.

Now he faced new doubts: If Calvin had been so wrong about infant baptism — and there was no doubt that like Luther he had been — maybe the rest of his teaching was equally false. Why should he believe TULIP at all? It seemed impossible that Calvin could have ever written such heresy as he had about baptism — there was no other name for it — but the priest had shown it to him right there in the *Institutes* and Al had looked it up for himself when he got home.

A Forgotten Challenge

Al turned again to his collection of Calvinist writers and began going through their books and listening to their tapes once more, hoping to find the elusive answer he'd been seeking. Tucked inside one of the books, he found a letter received from a friend a few months after he'd become a Calvinist. Now the forgotten and important role it had played in beginning his doubts flooded his memory. He read it again carefully and thoughtfully:

> As for the doctrine of election humbling you, have you ever considered how you know you are one of the elect? Calvin literally said that God causes some of the non-elect to imagine they have believed and are among the elect, the better to judge them. Is that the God you now believe in? Are you sure you aren't just imagining you are one of the elect?

> What qualifies you to be one of the elect? Calvin said there was no reason for God to choose you except that it pleased Him to do so. He also says that it pleased and glorified Him to predestine billions to burn in an eternal hell. Doesn't that bother you? Do you want to accept grace from *that* "God"? I think that's a libel on God's character!

There was more to it, a host of verses (which Al knew very well by now) declaring that God was not willing that any perish, that He wanted all to know the truth and to be set free, that Christ came to seek and to save sinners, not *some* sinners, etc. Al folded the letter thoughtfully and carefully put it back in the book. Originally it had made him so angry that he hadn't answered it. He must reply at last — and much differently from the way he would have responded before. But he didn't want Jan to see the letter or his reply — at least not yet.

The Turning Point

One day the fact struck Al with compelling force that his wife, whom he had "led to the Lord," had the very assurance of salvation that he was seeking. From the very first when he had been intrigued by Calvinism's intellectual appeal, she had tried to avoid discussing the subject whenever he had brought it up. All she would say was that she was resting in Christ's love and promise and that the gospel couldn't be as complicated as having to change the obvious meaning of words into something else to make God less loving than the Bible said He was.

What the Bible said! Those words suddenly took on a new meaning and became his deliverance. Getting back to the Bible was the turning point. Al stopped listening to and reading Calvinist experts and began to seriously study the Bible itself. It felt as if a burden had rolled off his shoulders just to be able to take the words of Scripture for what they said rather than having to change them to fit Calvinism.

Among the last issues he wrestled with was Christ's statement, "Ye have not chosen me, but I have chosen you" (John 15:16). In pondering those words, Al realized he was complicating something that was rather simple. Christ was saying nothing more than any employer could say to each employee — that the employer's choosing was decisive. The employee could not force the employer to hire him; but neither could the employer force someone to work for him. The employee had to consent to being hired.

Likewise, we can't force Christ to choose us. He is under no obligation to us; salvation is alone by His grace and mercy and love. But our faith is essential. Salvation is only for those who believe in and receive Christ.

Al took up his remaining doubts with his pastor. They had some long discussions and in spite of the pastor's efforts to keep him in the fold, Al's faith in Calvinism had been too badly eroded; while his confidence in the simple gospel was slowly being restored. Finally, only one problem remained which he had to wrestle with on his knees: there was no question that the Bible stated quite clearly that God blinded people's eyes to the gospel. How could that be reconciled with the infinite love which Al now believed God had for all without discrimination?

Calvinism's Last Stand

A favorite scripture of Calvinists and one to which White gives considerable attention [24] is John's comment: "Therefore they could not believe, because that

Esaias said again, He hath blinded their eyes, and hardened their heart" (John 12:39-40). White also quotes John 8:34-48, "Why do you not understand what I am saying? It is because you cannot hear My word . . . ." He then declares:

> Again the Reformed and biblical view of man is presented with force: Jesus teaches that the Jews *cannot* (there's that word of *inability* again) hear His word and do *not* understand what He is saying . . . they lack the spiritual ability to appraise spiritual truths. [25]

Far from proving Total Depravity, however, and thus the necessity of Irresistible Grace, Al could now see that these passages proved the opposite. If the unregenerate Jews were totally depraved and dead in sins as Calvinism defines it, unable in that condition to see or believe, surely God would not have needed to blind their eyes and harden their hearts. The fact that God finds it necessary to blind and harden anyone would seem to be proof that unregenerate men are *not* unable to understand or believe the gospel.

But why would a loving God deliberately blind the eyes of the lost to prevent them from believing the gospel? This seemed especially puzzling to Al in view of God's continual lamentations over Israel for her refusal to obey and His repeated expressions of desire to forgive and to bless her.

Since Israel was already in rebellion against God, why would He further harden hearts? There would have to be a good reason for doing this, a reason which would not diminish God's love and mercy; a reason which must apply equally to the Jews in Isaiah's day and speak prophetically of those in Christ's day. What could that be?

Inspired of God, Israel's prophets laid out her sin, rebellion and stubbornness. For example, God through Isaiah laments, "Hear, O heavens, and give ear, O earth: . . . I have nourished and brought up children, and they have rebelled against me" (Isaiah 1:2). God knew their hard hearts and that there was no point in pleading with them further. But He was going to use them to fulfill His purposes declared by His prophets, just as He used Pharaoh.

God would send His Son to reveal His great love, to open the eyes of the blind, heal the sick, raise the dead, feed the hungry, offer Himself to Israel as their Messiah, weep over Jerusalem here on earth as He had done repeatedly from heaven through His prophets in ages past, and die for their sins and for the sins of the world. He would not allow that purpose to be frustrated by a momentary sentimentality on the part of the Jews which might cause them, while still rejecting Him, not to insist upon the cross.

They were going to cry, "Away with Him, crucify Him!" This was what their hard hearts really wanted. And to make certain that they did not relent at the last minute out of humanistic pity, God hardened their hearts and blinded their eyes. So Peter could say, "Him, being delivered by the determinate counsel and foreknowledge of God, ye have taken, and by wicked hands have crucified and slain" (Acts 2:23).

Al could see a similar example in the blindness that will be given to those left behind at the Rapture who have heard and rejected the gospel. Paul states specifically, "And *for this cause* God shall send them strong delusion, that they should believe a lie: that they all might be damned . . . " (2 Thessalonians 2:10-12). For *what* cause? Because "they received not the love of the truth, that they might be saved . . . who believed not the truth, but had pleasure in unrighteousness." God would help them to believe the lie their already hardened hearts wanted to believe.

Here we see not a God who arbitrarily blinds people so they can't be saved, but a loving God who is also perfectly just in giving unrepentant rebels the desire of their hearts, which leads to their damnation. They rejected the truth, so God helps them to persist in that rejection. Nor would He need to blind them if they were totally depraved as Calvinism defines it.

Yes, "the natural man receiveth not the things of the Spirit of God: . . . neither can he know them, because they are spiritually discerned [i.e., revealed alone by the Holy Spirit]" (1 Corinthians 2:14). But there Paul is not referring to the gospel which is to be preached "to every creature" (Mark 16:15). He is addressing believers and referring to "the hidden wisdom . . . the deep things of God," which are only revealed by the Spirit of God to those who are indwelt by and walking in obedience to the Holy Spirit.

The Final Question

Pastor Jim, learning of Al's weakening confidence in Calvinism, had challenged him: "If you are going to return to the belief that you had the ability to say yes to God in believing the gospel, how can you be sure that some time you may not decide to say no to God — even in eternity in heaven?" Zins expresses that problem as well as anyone:

> It is ironic that many . . . who adamantly argue that God forces no one to come to Him have no problem believing that God forces those who have come to Him *to stay with Him.* For most evangelicals, free will mysteriously disappears after one chooses salvation . . . . "God will not make you come, but He will make you stay," might be their theological sentiment. [26]

Al asked Jan about this, and her reply was as simple as the Bible itself: "Why would I ever want to give up heaven? There would be nothing to tempt me away from our Lord, who is so wonderful that nothing could!" She smiled at him and went back to ironing his shirts.

One's eternal security as saved by grace depends entirely upon God and not upon oneself. Neither salvation nor the assurance thereof is by works, nor can works be a sign of the reality of one's salvation or the means of providing assurance. Even the apparent working of miracles, casting out of demons and prophesying in Christ's name are no proof that one belongs to Him, as Christ himself solemnly declared:

> Not every one that saith unto me, Lord, Lord, shall enter into the kingdom of heaven; but he that doeth the will of my Father which is in heaven. Many will say to me in that day, Lord, Lord, have we not prophesied in thy name? and in thy name have cast out devils? and in thy name done many wonderful works? And then will I profess unto them, I never knew you: depart from me, ye that work iniquity. (Matthew 7:21-23)

On the other hand, there could be in the life of a particular person not one good work to indicate the reality of salvation, yet that person could be truly saved and thus elected of God to the blessings He has planned for the redeemed of all ages. All of one's works could be consumed in the fire of God's testing of motives and deeds; yet that person not be lost, according to Paul, in spite of no outward evidence of salvation:

> Every man's work shall be . . . revealed by fire; and the fire shall try every man's work of what sort it is. If any man's work abide . . . he shall receive a reward. If any man's work shall be burned, he shall suffer loss: but he himself shall be saved; yet so as by fire. (1 Corinthians 3:11-15)

Paul, of course, was speaking of those who are truly saved through faith in Christ. Al could now see his problem clearly: not one verse in the Bible tells how to know one has been elected. If being one of the elect is the basis for assurance of salvation, then there can be no assurance.

But one had to be *certain* about eternity! Yet Calvinists couldn't agree among themselves on the answer to what was obviously the most crucial question. Al decided at last that he was through with that theory for good.

Assurance For Eternity

Biblical assurance of eternal life in heaven with Christ rests alone upon His promises, the promises of the Bible and upon the foreknowledge, predestination/election and keeping power of God. Christ said, "Come unto me," and we came. The gospel says, "Believe on the Lord Jesus Christ and thou shalt be saved," and we believed. Christ and His Word promise:

> Elect according to the foreknowledge of God the Father, through sanctification of the Spirit, unto obedience and sprinkling of the blood of Jesus Christ . . . . (1 Peter 1:2)

> According as he hath chosen us in him before the foundation of the world, . . . having predestinated us unto the adoption of children by Jesus Christ to himself, according to the good pleasure of his will, . . . in whom we have

redemption through his blood, the forgiveness of sins, according to the riches of his grace . . . . (Ephesians 1:4-7)

For whom he did foreknow, he also did predestinate to be conformed to the image of his Son, . . . whom he did predestinate, them he also called: and whom he called, them he also justified: and whom he justified, them he also glorified. (Romans 8:29-30)

But as many as received him, to them gave he power to become the sons of GOD, even to them that believe on his name: which were born [again], not of blood, nor of the will of the flesh, nor of the will of man, but of God. (John 1:12-13)

For God sent not his Son into the world to condemn the world; but that the world through him might be saved. He that believeth on him is not condemned: but he that believeth not is condemned already, . . . he that believeth on the Son hath everlasting life . . . . (John 3:17-18,36)

And this is the record, that God hath given to us eternal life, and this life is in his Son. He that hath the Son hath life; and he that hath not the Son of God hath not life. These things have I written unto you that believe on the name of the Son of God; that ye may know that ye have eternal life . . . . (1 John 5:11-13)

Verily, verily, I say unto you, He that heareth my word, and believeth on him that sent me, hath everlasting life, and shall not come into condemnation; . . . but is passed from death unto life. (John 5:24)

We believed, were saved "according to the promise of life which is in Christ Jesus" (2 Timothy 1:1), and are simply resting in His abundant promises that "whosoever believeth in him should not perish, but have everlasting life" (John 3:16). By simple faith in God's promise, the God who cannot lie, the believer knows that he has passed from death to life and will never perish — and he has been given the witness of the Holy Spirit within. "He that believeth on the Son of God hath the witness in himself . . . " (1 John 5:10). And "the Spirit itself beareth witness with our spirit, that we are the children of God: . . . heirs of God, and joint-heirs with Christ . . . (Romans 8:16-17).

Having "heard the word of truth, the gospel of [our] salvation: in whom also after that [we] believed, [we] were sealed with that holy Spirit of promise, which is the earnest of our inheritance until the redemption of the purchased possession . . . " (Ephesians 1:13-14). Those who believe on Christ know they are saved and will never perish because God cannot lie. Our trust is in Him for now and eternity.

Paul said, "I know whom I have believed, and am persuaded that he is able to keep that which I have committed unto him against that day" (2 Timothy 1:12). We, too, have believed and know the One in whom we are eternally secure. We, too, are fully persuaded that "the God and Father of our Lord Jesus Christ, . . . according to his abundant mercy hath begotten us again unto a lively hope by the resurrection of Jesus Christ from the dead, to an inheritance incorruptible, and undefiled, and that fadeth not away, reserved in heaven for [us], who are kept by the power of God through faith unto salvation ready to be revealed in the last time" (1 Peter 1:3-5).

We have the many infallible proofs of prophecy fulfilled in Israel (and still being fulfilled before our eyes) and those which promised in detail the coming of the Messiah — prophesies which have without question been fulfilled in the life, death and resurrection of our Lord and Savior Jesus Christ. We have the historical proofs, the archaeological proofs, the scientific proofs and the internal proofs that the Bible is God's Word. The Bible offers a true and infallible testimony of the creation of this earth, the fall of Adam and Eve, the redemption through Christ's blood poured out in death upon the cross, of His soon return for His bride, and of His Second Coming to rescue Israel and to establish His millennial kingdom, when He will rule with a rod of iron over the nations from His father David's throne in Jerusalem — and of the coming new heavens and new earth.

We simply believe God's Word in all things and therefore we are certain that we are saved and that He is coming back to take us to His Father's house of many mansions to fulfill His promise "that where I am, there ye may be also" (John 14:1-3). As Paul said, " . . . and so shall we ever be with the Lord. Wherefore comfort one another with these words" (1 Thessalonians 4:17-18).

A Final Word

My heart has been broken by Calvinism's misrepresentation of the God of the Bible whom I love, and for the excuse this has given atheists not to believe in Him. My sincere and earnest desire in writing this book has been to defend God's character against the libel that denies His love for all and insists that He does not make salvation available to all because He does not want all to be saved. It is my prayer that readers will recognize that Christian authors and leaders, ancient or modern and no matter how well respected, are all fallible and that God's Word is our only authority.

God's Word declares that the gospel, which is "the power of God unto salvation to *every one that believeth*" (Romans 1: 1 6), is "good tidings of great joy," not just to certain elect, but "to *all* people" (Luke 2:10). Sadly, the insistence that only a select few have been elected to salvation is *not* "good tidings of great joy to all people"! How can such a doctrine be biblical?

It is my prayer that Calvinist readers who may have gotten this far have been fully persuaded to misrepresent no longer the God of love as having predestinated multitudes to eternal doom while withholding from them any opportunity to understand and believe the gospel. How many unbelievers have rejected God because of this deplorable distortion we do not know — but may that excuse be denied everyone from this time forth! And may believers, in confidence that the gospel is indeed glad tidings for *all* people, take God's good news to the whole world!

1   John F. MacArthur, Jr., *The Gospel According to Jesus* (Academie Books, Zondervan Publishing House, 1988), 98.
2   Joseph C. Dillow, *The Reign of the Servant Kings: A Study of Eternal Security and the Final Significance of Man* (Schoettle Publishing Co., 2nd ed. 1993), 253.
3   John Calvin, *Institutes of the Christian Religion*, trans. Henry Beveridge (Wm. Eerdmans Publishing Company, 1998 ed.), III:xxiv,5.
4   Op. cit., III:xxi,1.
5   *Discussions by Robert L. Dabney*, ed. C.R. Vaughn (Presbyterian Committee of Publication, 1890), 1:183.
6   Kenneth Gentry, "Assurance and Lordship Salvation: The Dispensational Concern" (*Dispensationalism in Transition*, September 1993); quoted by Robert N. Wilkin, "When Assurance Is Not Assurance" (*Journal of the Grace Evangelical Society*, Autumn 1997), 10:19, 27-34.
7   Walter D. Chantry, *Today's Gospel: Authentic or Synthetic?* (The Banner of Truth Trust, 1970), 75-76.
8   Dillow, op. cit., 280.
9   Cited in Philip F. Congdon, "Soteriological Implications of Five-point Calvinism" (*Journal of the Grace Evangelical Society*, Autumn 1995), 8:15, 55-68.
10 I. Howard Marshall; cited in D.A. Carson, "Reflections on Christian Assurance" (*Westminster Theological Journal*), 54:1,24.
11 Dillow, op.cit., 272-91.
12 James R. White, *The Potter's Freedom* (Calvary Press Publishing, 2000), 178.
13 Congdon, op. cit., 8:15, 56-57.
14 White, op. cit., 112-13.
15 John Armstrong, "Reflections from Jonathan Edwards on the Current Debate over Justification by Faith Alone" (quoted in speech given at Annapolis 2000: A Passion for Truth conference, sponsored by Jonathan Edwards Institute, PO Box 2410, Princeton NJ 08543). For more information on Jonathan Edwards's view on justification, contact Grace Evangelical Society, (972) 257-1160.
16 Ibid.
17 Ibid.
18 Ibid.
19 Calvin, op. cit.., III:xxiv,4..
20 Charles Haddon Spurgeon, "A Defense of Calvinism," single-sermon booklet (Still Waters Revival Books, n.d.), 3-4.
21 Op. cit., 22.
22 Calvin, op. cit.
23 Op. cit., III:xxiv,3.
24 White, op. cit., 105-109.
25 Op. cit., 112-14.
26 Robert M. Zins, "A Believer's Guide to 2nd Peter 3:9" (self-published monograph, n.d.), 3.

BIBLIOGRAPHY

Adams, Jay E. *Competent to Counsel*. Baker Book House, 1970.

———. *Decisional Regeneration*. Free Grace Publications, 1972.

A Faith to Confess: The Baptist Confession of Faith of 1689, Rewritten in Modern English. Carey Publications, 1986.

A Short Explanation of Dr. Martin Luther's Small Catechism: A Handbook of Christian Doctrine. Concordia Publishing House, 1971 ed.

Alford, Henry. *The New Testament for English Readers.* Baker Book House, 1983.

Allen, J.W. *History of Political Thought in the Sixteenth Century.* London, 1951.

Anderson, Sir Robert. *The Bible or the Church?* Pickering and Inglis, 2nd ed., n.d.

"Arminian / Calvinist Response." *SBC Life*, August 1995.

Arminius, Jacobus. *The Works of James Arminius.* Trans. James and William Nichols. Baker Book House, 1986.

Armstrong, John. "Reflections from Jonathan Edwards on the Current Debate over Justification by Faith Alone." Quoted in speech given at Annapolis 2000: A Passion for Truth conference. Sponsored by Jonathan Edwards Institute, PO Box 2410, Princeton NJ 08543. For more information on John Edwards's view on justification, contact Grace Evangelical Society, (972) 257-1160.

Augustine, *Gift of Perseverance*.

———. *On the Soul and its Origins.*

———. *The City of God.* Trans. Marcus Dods. In *Great Books of the Western World.* Ed. Robert Maynard Hutchins and Mortimer J. Adler. Encyclopaedia Brittanica, Inc., 1952.

———. *The Confessions.* In *Great Books of the Western World.* Ed. Robert Maynard Hutchins and Mortimer J. Adler. Trans. Edward Bouverie Pusey. Encyclopaedia Brittanica, Inc., 1952.

Baine, Jennifer L., and Sarah E. Hinlicky. "Free to be Creatures Again: How predestination descended like a dove on two unsuspecting seminarians, and *why* they are so grateful." *Christianity Today*, October 23, 2000.

Bainton, Roland P. *Hunted Heretic: The Life of Michael Servetus*. Boston: The Beacon Press, 1953.

Baker, Alvin L. *Berkouwer's Doctrine of Election: Balance or Imbalance?* Presbyterian and Reformed Publishing Co., 1981.

Baxter, Richard. *Universal Redemption of Mankind*. London: n.p., 1694.

Beard, Charles. *The Reformation of the Sixteenth Century in Relation to Modern Thought and Knowledge.* London, 1885.

Beck, Frank B. *The Five Points of Calvinism.* Covenanter Press, 2nd Australian ed. 1986.

Berkhof, Louis. The History of Christian Doctrines. Baker Book House, 1937.

Bertocci, Peter A. *Free Will, Responsibility, and Grace.* Abingdon Press, 1957.

Best, W.E. *Free Grace Versus Free Will.* W.E. Best Books Missionary Trust, 1977.

————. *Simple Faith (A Misnomer).* W.E. Best Books Missionary Trust, 1993.

Bettany, G.T. *A Popular History of the Reformation and Modern Protestantism.* Ward, Lock and Bowden, Ltd, 1895.

Billion, James F. *True Wisdom Has Two Sides: Calvinism — is it Biblical?* Edinburgh: Grace Mount Publishers, n.d.

Bishop, George S. *The Doctrines of Grace.* Baker Book House, 1977.

Boettner, Loraine. *The Reformed Doctrine of Predestination.* Presbyterian and Reformed Publishing Co., 1932.

————. *The Reformed Faith.* Presbyterian and Reformed Publishing Co., 1983.

Bouwsma, William J. *John Calvin: A Sixteenth Century Portrait.* Oxford University Press, 1988.

Breese, Dave. "The Five Points of Calvinism." Self-published paper, n.d.

Broadbent, E.H. *The Pilgrim Church.* Gospel Folio Press, reprint 1999.

Bronson, Charles W. *The Extent of the Atonement.* Pilgrim Publications, 1992.

Broughton, Len G. *Salvation and the Old Theology.* Hodder and Stroughton, n.d.

Bruce, F.F. *The Books and the Parchments.* Pickering and Inglis, Ltd., 1950.

————. *The Epistles to the Colossans, to Philemon, and to the Ephesians.* Wm. B. Eerdmans Publishing Co., 1984.

————. *Light in the West*, Bk. III of *The Spreading Flame.* Wm. B. Eerdmans Publishing Co., 1956.

Bryson, George L. *The Five Points of Calvinism "Weighed and Found Wanting."* The Word For Today, 1996.

Butterworth, Charles C. *The Literary Lineage of the King James Bible.* University of Pennsylvania Press, 1941.

Cairns, Earle E. *Christianity Through the Centuries: A History of the Christian Church.* Zondervan Publishing, 1981.

Calvin, John. *Calvin's New Testament Commentaries*. Wm. B. Eerdmans Publishing Co., 1994.

———. *Institutes of the Christian Religion*. Trans. Henry Beveridge. Wm. B. Eerdmans Publishing Company, 1998 ed. First published in Latin (Basel, Switzerland, 1586); later in French.

———. *John Calvin, Calvin's Calvinism*. Trans. Henry Cole. Reformed Free Publishing Association, 1987.

———. *Letters of John Calvin.* The Banner of Truth Trust, 1980.

———. *Selected Works of John Calvin: Tracts and Letters.* Ed. Henry Beveridge and Jules Bonnet. Baker Books, 1983.

Canons of Dort. Dordrecht, Holland, 1619.

Carson, D.A. *Divine Sovereignty and Human Responsibility*. John Knox Press, 1981.

———. "Reflections on Christian Assurance." *Westminster Theological Journal,* Vol. 54.

———. *The Difficult Doctrine of the Love of God,* Crossway Books, 2000.

Carson, John L. and David W. Hall, eds. *To Glorify and Enjoy God: A Commemoration of the 350th Anniversary of the Westminster Assembly.* The Banner of Truth Trust, 1994.

Chafer, Lewis Sperry. *Systematic Theology*. Dallas Seminary Press, 1948.
Chantry, Walter D. *Today's Gospel: Authentic or Synthetic?* The Banner of Truth Trust, 1970.

———. *Predestination.* Presbyterian and Reformed Publishing Co., 1987.

Christian, John T. *A History of the Baptists*. Sunday School Board of the Southern Baptist Convention, 1922.

Clark, Gordon H. *The Biblical Doctrine of Man*. The Trinity Foundation, 1984.

Codex Theodosianus. N.p., July 3, A.D. 321.

Cole, C.D. *Definition of Doctrines*. Bible Truth Depot, n.d.

Cole, Steven J. *Total Depravity*. Flagstaff AZ, 1999.

Congdon, Philip F. "Soteriological Implications of Five-point Calvinism." *Journal of the Grace Evangelical Society,* Autumn 1995.

Cook, Frederic C., ed. *The Bible Commentary.* Charles Scribner Sons, 1895.

Coppes, Leonard J. *Are Five Points Enough? The Ten Points of Calvinism*. Denver CO: self-published, 1980.

Cox, S. Raymond. "What Caused God To Choose His People?" Self-published paper, 1980.

Cross, John R. *The Stranger on the Road to Emmaus*. Good Seed International, 1997.

Cunningham, William. *Historical Theology*. Still Waters Revival Books, n.d.

Curtiss, George L. *Arminianism in History*. Cranston and Curts, 1894.

Custance, Arthur C. *The Sovereignty of Grace*. Presbyterian and Reformed Publishing Co., 1979.

Daane, James. *The Freedom of God*. Wm. B. Eerdmans Publishing Co., 1973.

Dabney, Robert L. *Discussions by Robert L. Dabney*. Ed. C. R. Vaughn. Presbyterian Committee of Publication, 1980.

————. *Systematic Theology*. The Banner of Truth Trust, 2nd ed. 1985.

————. *The Five Points of Calvinism*. Sprinkle Publications, 1992.
Dagg, John L. *Manual of Theology and Church Order*. Sprinkle Publications, 1982.

d'Aubigné, J.H. Merle. *History of the Reformations of the Sixteenth Century*. London: n.p., 1846; rev. ed. by Hartland Institute, Rapidan VA, n.d.

Davis, Jimmie B. In "The Berean Baptist Banner," February 5, 1995.

Dillow, Joseph C. *The Reign of the Servant Kings: A Study of Eternal Security and the Final Significance of Man*. Schoettle Publishing Co., 2nd ed. 1993.

Douty, Norman F. *The Death of Christ*. Williams and Watrous Publishing Company, n.d.

Duncan, Mark. *The Five Points of Christian Reconstruction from the Lips of Our Lord*. Still Waters Revival Books, 1990.

Durant, Will. *The Story of Civilization*. Simon and Schuster, 1950.

Edinburgh Encyclopedia. Scotland: n.p., n.d.

Edwards, Jonathan. *Freedom of the Will*. Ed. Paul Ramsey. Yale University Press, 1957.

Engelsma, David J. *A Defense of Calvinism as the Gospel*. The Evangelism Committee, Protestant Reformed Church, n.d.

————. *Hyper-Calvinism and the Call of the Gospel*. Reformed Free Publishing Association, 1980.

————. "The Death of Confessional Calvinism in Scottish Presbyterianism." *Standard Bearer*, December 1, 1992.

Eusebius Pamphilius of Caesaria, advisor to Constantine. *The Life of Constantine*. N.p., c. A.D. 335.

Fairbairn, Andrew M. *The Philosophy of the Christian Religion*. The MacMillan Co., 1923.

Farrar, Frederic W. *A Manual of Christian Doctrine*. The Alliance Press, n.d.

———. *History of Interpretation*. E.P. Dutton and Co., 1886.

Fisher, George Park. *History of the Christian Church*. Charles Scribner's Sons, 1902.
———. *The Reformation*. Scribner, Armstrong and Co., 1873.

Fisk, Samuel. *Calvinistic Paths Retraced*. Biblical Evangelism Press, 1985.

———. *Divine Sovereignty and Human Freedom*. Loizeaux Brothers, 1973.

———. *Election and Predestination*. England: Penfold Book and Bible House, 1997.

Foreman, Kenneth J. *God's Will and Ours*. Outlook Publishers, 1954.

Forster, Roger T. and V. Paul Marston. *God's Strategy in Human History*. Bethany House Publishers, 1973.

Frend, W.H.C. *The Rise of Christianity*. Fortress Press, 1984.

Gay, David. *Battle for the Church: 1517-1644*. Brachus, 1997.

Geden, Alfred S. *Comparative Religion*. Society for Promoting Christian Knowledge, 1917.

Geisler, Norman L. *What Augustine Says*. Baker Book House, 1982.

———. *Chosen but Free*. Bethany House, 1999.

George, Timothy. *Theology of the Reformers*. Broadman Press, 1988.

Gerstner, John H. *A Primer on Free Will*. Presbyterian and Reformed Publishing Co., 1982.

———. *Wrongly Dividing the Word of Truth: A Critique of Dispensationalism*. Wolgemuth and Hyatt, Publishers, Inc., 1991.

Gibbon, Edward. *The Decline and Fall of the Roman Empire*. Modern Library, n.d.

Gill, John A. *A Body of Doctrinal and Practical Divinity*. Baptist Standard Bearer, 1987.

———. *The Cause of God and Truth*. The Baptist Standard Bearer, 1992.

Good, Kenneth H. *Are Baptists Calvinists?* Backus Book Publishers, 1988.

Goold, William H., ed. *The Works of John Owen*. The Banner of Truth Trust, reprint 1978.

Grady, William P. *Final Authority: A Christian's Guide to the King James Bible*. Grady Publications, 1993.

Gunn, Grover E. *The Doctrine of Grace*. Footstool Publications, 1987.

Hanko, Herman. *God's Everlasting Covenant of Grace*. Reformed Free Publishing Assocation, 1988.

Hanko, Herman, Homer C. Hoeksema, and Gise J. Van Baren. *The Five Points of Calvinism*. Reformed Free Publishing Assocation, 1976.

Harkness, Georgia. *John Calvin: The Man and His Ethics*. Abingdon Press, 1958.

Harrison, A.W. *Arminianism*. Duckworth, 1937.

Henderson, Henry F. *Calvin in His Letters*. J.M. Dent and Co., 1909.

Hobbs, Herschel H. *Fundamentals of our Faith*. Broadman, 1960.

Hodge, A.A. *The Atonement*. Footstool Publishers, 1987.

Hodge, Charles. *A Commentary on Romans*. The Banner of Truth Trust, 1972.

———. *Systematic Theology*. Wm. B. Eerdmans Publishing Co., 1986.

Hodges, Zane C. *The Gospel Under Siege*. Kerugma, Inc., 2nd ed. 1992.

———. "The New Puritanism, Pt. 3: Michael S. Horton: Holy Wars With Unholy Weapons." *Journal of the Grace Evangelical Society,* Spring 1994.

Hoeksema, Herman. *God's Eternal Good Pleasure*. Ed. and rev. Homer C. Hoeksema, Reformed Free Publishing Association, 1979.

Hoeksema, Homer. *Reformed Dogmatics*. Reformed Free Publishing Association, 1966.

———. *The Voice of Our Fathers*. Reformed Free Publishing Association, 1980.

Hoitenga, Dewey J. *John Calvin and the Will: A Critique and Corrective*. Baker Books, 1997.

Horne, C. Sylvester. *A Popular History of the Free Churches*. James Clarke and Co., 1903.

Horsch, John. *History of Christianity*. John Horsch, 1903.

Horton, Michael Scott. *Putting Amazing Back Into Grace*. Thomas Nelson Publishers, 1991.

———., ed. *Christ the Lord: The Reformation and Lordship Salvation*. Baker Book House, 1992.

Houck, Steven R. "God's Sovereignty In Salvation." The Evangelism Committee, Presbyterian Reformed Church, South Holland IL, n.d.

———. *The Bondage of the Will.* Peace Protestant Reformed Church, n.d.

http://www.iclnet.org/pub/resources/text/wittenberg/wittenberg-luther.html.

Hughes, Philip. *A History of the Church.* London, 1934.

Hughes, Paul L. and James F. Larkin, ed. *Tudor Royal Proclamations.* Yale University Press, 1964.

Hulme, Edward Maslin. *The Renaissance, the Protestant Reformation, and the Catholic Revolution.* The Century Company, 1920.

Hutchins, Robert Maynard and Mortimer J. Adler, ed. *Great Books of the Western World.* Encyclopaedia Brittanica, Inc., 1952.

IFCA International. *What We Believe*: www.ifca.org

Ironside, H.A. *Full Assurance.* Moody Press, 1937.

———. *In the Heavenlies, Addresses on Ephesians.* Loizeaux Brothers, 1937.

———. *Lectures on the Epistle to the Romans.* Loizeaux Brothers, 1926.

———. *Timothy, Titus and Philemon.* Loizeaux Brothers, Inc., 1990.

———. *What's the Answer?* Zondervan, 1944.

Jewett, Paul K. *Election and Predestination.* Wm. B. Eerdmans Publishing Co., 1985 ed.

John Paul II, Sovereign Pontiff. *Augustineum Hyponensem.* Apostolic Letter, August 28, 1986. Available at www. cin.org/jp2.ency/augustin.html.

Jones, R. Tudor. *The Great Reformation.* Inter-Varsity Press, n.d.

Jones, William. *The History of the Christian Church.* Church History Research and Archives, 5th ed. 1983.

Kane, Michael J., Ph.D., "Letters." *Christianity Today,* July 9, 2001.

Kennedy, D. James. *Why I Believe.* Word Publishing, 1980.

———. *Why I Am a Presbyterian.* Coral Ridge Ministries, n.d.

Kennedy, John W. *The Torch of the Testimony.* Christian Books Publishing House, 1963.

Keyser, Leander S. *Election and Conversion.* Lutheran Literary Board, 1914.

Knowling, R.J. *The Acts of the Apostles, The Expositor's Greek New Testament.* Dodd, Meade and Co., 1900.

Knox, John. *Selected Writings of John Knox.* Presbyterian Heritage Publications, 1995.

Leith, John H. *Introduction to the Reformed Tradition.* John Knox Press, rev. ed. 1981.

Lockyer, Herbert. *All the Doctrines of the Bible.* Zondervan, 1964.

424 **What Love Is This?**

Luther, Martin. *The Bondage of the Will*. Trans. J.I. Packer and O.R. Johnston. Fleming H. Revell, 1957, 11th prtg. 1999.

———. *A Short Explanation of Dr. Martin Luther's Small Catechism: A Handbook of Christian Doctrine*. Concordia Publishing House, 1971 ed.

MacArthur, John F., Jr. *Faith Works: The Gospel According to the Apostles*. Word Publishing, 1993.

———. *Saved Without A Doubt–MacArthur Study Series*. Christ Victor Books, 1992.

———. *The Gospel According to Jesus*. Academie Books, Zondervan Publishing House, 1988.

Maclaren, Alexander. *Expositions of Holy Scripture*. Hodder and Stoughton, n.d.

St. Justin Martyr. *The First and Second Apologies*. Ancient Christian Writers, No. 56. Paulist Press, 1997.

Mathison, Keith A. *Dispensationalism: Rightly Dividing the People of God?* Presbyterian and Reformed Publishing Co., 1995.

McGrath, Alister E. *A Life of John Calvin*. Blackwell Publishers, 1990.

McNeil, John T. *Makers of the Christian Tradition*. Harper and Row, 1964.

———. *The History and Character of Calvinism*. Oxford University Press, 1966.

Milman, Henry H. *History of Christianity*. A.C. Armstrong and Son, 1886.

Milne, Bruce. *Know the Truth*. InterVarsity, 1982.

Moo, Douglas. *The Epistle to the Romans*. Wm. B. Eerdmans Publishing Co., 1996.

Morey, Robert A. *Studies in the Atonement*. Crowne Publications, 1989.

Morgan, G. Campbell. *The Westminster Pulpit*. Fleming H. Revell, 1954.

Morrison, James. *The Extent of the Atonement*. Hamilton, Adams and Co., 1882.

Mosheim, John Laurence. *An Ecclesiastical History, Ancient and Modern*. Trans. Archibald MacLaine. Applegate and Co., 1854.

Morton, Carl. In *The Berean Baptist Banner*, January 5, 1995.

Muir, Edwin. *John Knox*. London, 1920.

Muller, Richard A. *Christ and the Decree*. Baker Book House, 1988.

Mullins, Edgar Y. *Baptist Beliefs*. Judson, 4th ed. 1925.

Murray, Iain H. *The Life of John Murray*. The Banner of Truth Trust. 1984.

Murray, John. *Redemption Accomplished and Applied*. Wm. B. Eerdmans Publishing Co. 1955.

————. *The Free Offer of the Gospel.* N.p., n.d.

Murray, John and Ned B. Stonehouse. *The Free Offer of the Gospel.* N.p., n.d.

New Geneva Study Bible. Thomas Nelson Publishers, 1995.

Newman , Albert H. *A Manual of Church History.* American Baptist Publication Society, 1933.

Nicoll, W. Robertson, ed. *The Expositor's Greek Testament.* Wm. B. Eerdmans Publishing Co., n.d.

Noll, Mark A., ed. *The Princeton Theology*. Presbyterian and Reformed Publishing Co., 1983.

North, Gary. *Dominion and Common Grace.* Institute for Christian Economics, 1987.

Oosterman, Wm. "Take a Long Look at the Doctrine of Election." Ottawa, Canada: The Lord's Library Publications, n.d. Available from Westboro Baptist Church, Ottawa.

Ostling, Richard N. "The Second Founder of the Faith." *Time*, September 29, 1986.

Owen, John. *The Works of John Owen.* Ed. William H. Goold. The Banner of Truth Trust, 3rd prtg. 1978.

Packer, J.I. *Evangelism and the Sovereignty of God.* Inter-Varsity Press, 1961.

————. "The Love of God: Universal and Particular," in *Still Sovereign,* eds. Thomas R. Schreiver & Bruce A. Ware. Baker Books, 2000.

Page, T.E. *The Acts of the Apostles, Greek Text with Explanatory Notes.* Macmillan and Co., 1897.

Palmer, Edwin H. *the five points of calvinism*. Baker Books, enlarged ed., 20th prtg. 1999.

Pettingill, William L. *Bible Questions Answered.* Just A Word Inc., 3rd ed. 1935.

Phelps, Fred. "The Five Points of Calvinism." *The Berean Baptist Banner,* February 5, 1990.

Pierson, Arthur T. *The Believer's Life: Its Past, Present, and Future Tenses*. Morgan and Scott, 1905.

Pike, Henry R. *The Other Side of John Calvin.* Head to Heart, n.d.

Pink, Arthur W. *Exposition of the Gospel of John.* Zondervan Publishing House, 1975.

————. *Gleanings in Exodus.* Moody Press, 1981.

————. *The Doctrine of Election and Justification.* Baker Book House, 1974.

————. *The Doctrine of Salvation*. Baker Book House, 1975.

————. *The Holy Spirit*. Baker Book House, 1978.

————. *The Sovereignty of God.* Baker Book House, 2nd prtg. 1986 ed.

Pinnock, Clark H, ed. *Grace Unlimited*. Bethany Fellowship, Inc., 1976.

Piper, John. *The Justification of God: An Exegetical and Theological Study of Romans 9:1-23*. Baker Books, 2000.

————. "Are There Two Wills in God?," in *Still Sovereign,* eds. Thomas R. Schreiver & Bruce A. Ware. Baker Books, 2000.

————. *The Legacy of Sovereign Joy: God's Triumphant Grace in the Lives of Augustine, Luther and Calvin*. Crossway Books, 2000.

Piper, John and Pastoral Staff. "TULIP: What We Believe about the Five Points of Calvinism: Position Paper of the Pastoral Staff." Desiring God Ministries, 1997.

Plass, Ewald. *What Luther Says*. Concordia Publishing House, 1987.

Pollard, Alfred W., ed. *Records of the English Bible*. Oxford University Press, 1911.

Potter, G.R. and M. Greengrass. *John Calvin*. St. Martin's Press, 1983.

Rice, N.L. *God Sovereign and Man Free*. Sprinkle Publications, 1985.

Robertson, Archibald Thomas. *Word Pictures in the New Testament,* Harper and Bros., 1930.

Robertson. J.M. *Short History of Freethought*. London, 1914.

Robinson, H. Wheeler. *The Bible In Its Ancient and English Versions*. Clarendon Press, 1940.

Rose, Ben Lacy. *T.U.L.I.P.: The Five Disputed Points of Calviniam.* Providence House Publishing, 1996.

Ross, Tom. *Abandoned Truth: The Doctrines of Grace*. Providence Baptist Church, 1991.

Rowley, H.H. *The Biblical Doctrine of Election*. Lutterworth Press, 1952.

Ruckman, Peter S. *The History of the New Testament*. Pensacola Bible Baptist Bookstore, 1982.

Rutherford, Samuel. *Letters of Samuel Rutherford*. The Banner of Truth Trust, 1996; 1st ed. 1664.

Ryle, John C. *Expository Thoughts on the Gospel of John*. Wm. Hunt and Co., 1883.

Sanford, Dick. *Predestination and Election.* Ed. John R. Cross. Self-published monograph, n.d.

Schaff, Philip. *History of the Christian Church.* Charles Scribner, 1910; Wm. B. Eerdmans Publishing Co., reprint 1959.

———. *The Creeds of Christendom.* Baker Book House, 1990.

Schreiner, Thomas R. and Bruce A. Ware, eds. *Still Sovereign: Contemporary Perspectives on Election, Foreknowledge and Grace.* Baker Books, 2000.

———. *The Grace of God, The Bondage of the Will.* Baker Books, 1995.

Scofield, C.I. *Scofield Bible Correspondence Course.* Moody Bible Institute, 1907.

Scott, Otto. *The Great Christian Revolution.* The Reformer Library, 1994.

Seaton, W.J. *The Five Points of Calvinism.* The Banner of Truth Trust, 1970.

Sell, Alan P.F. *The Great Debate.* Baker Book House, 1982.

Sellers, C. Norman. *Election and Perseverance.* Schoettle Publishing Co., 1987.

Shedd, William G.T. *Calvinism: Pure and Mixed.* The Banner of Truth Trust, 1999.

———. *A History of Christian Doctrine.* Charles Scribner and Co., 3rd ed. 1865.

Sheldon, Henry C. *History of Christian Doctrine.* Harper and Bros., 2nd ed. 1895.

Singer, C. Gregg. *John Calvin: His Roots and Fruits.* A Press, 1989.

Smith, H. Maynard. *Pre-Reformation England.* Russell and Russell, 1963.

Smith, Preserved. *The Age of the Reformation.* New York, 1920.

Souter, Alexander. *The Earliest Latin Commentaries on the Epistles of St. Paul.* N.p., 1927.

Spencer, Duane Edward. *TULIP: The Five Points of Calvinism in the Light of Scripture.* Baker Book House, 1979.

Sproul, R.C. *Almighty Over All.* Baker Book House, 1999.

———. "Assurance of Salvation." *Tabletalk.* Ligonier Ministries, Inc., November 1989.

———. *Chosen by God.* Tyndale House Publishers, Inc., 1986.

———. *Faith Alone: The Evangelical Doctrine of Justification.* Baker Books, 1995.

———. *Grace Unknown.* Baker Books, 1997.

———. *The Holiness of God.* Tyndale House Publishers, Inc., 1993 ed.

Sproul, R.C., Jr. "The Authentic Message." *Tabletalk*. Ligonier Ministries, Inc., June 2001.

Spurgeon, Charles Haddon. "A Defense of Calvinism." Still Waters Revival Books, n.d. Single-sermon booklet.

————. *Autobiography of Charles H. Spurgeon*. American Baptist Society, n.d.

————. *Free Will–A Slave*. Free Grace Publications, 1977.

————. "God's Will and Man's Will," No. 442. Newington: Metropolitan Tabernacle; sermon delivered Sunday morning, March 30, 1862.

————. *Spurgeon at His Best*. Ed. Tom Carter. Baker Book House, 1988.

————. *Sermons of C.H. Spurgeon.* Available from Pilgrim Publications, Pasadena TX, n.d.

————. *The Best Bread: Sermons Preached in 1887.* Funk and Wagnalls, 1891.

————. *The Soul Winner*. Wm. B. Eerdmans Publishing Co., 1963.

————. *The Treasury of the New Testament.* Zondervan, 1950.

————, ed. *Exposition of the Doctrine of Grace.* Pilgrim Publications, n.d.

Steele, David N. and Curtis C. Thomas. *The Five Points of Calvinism.* Presbyterian and Reformed Publishing Co., 1963.

"Straight Talk Live." KPXQ, Phoenix AZ, August 11, 2000. Audiotape Ato73, available through The Berean Call, PO Box 7019, Bend OR 97708.

Strong, Augustus H. *Systematic Theology*. Judson Press, 1907.

Storms, C. Samuel. *Chosen for Life*. Baker Book House, 1987.

Talbot, Kenneth G. and W. Gary Crampton. *Calvinism, Hyper-Calvinism and Arminianism*. Still Waters Revival Books, 1990.

Telford, Andrew. *Subjects of Sovereignty*. Harvest Time Ministries, 1980.

The Opinions of the Remonstrants. Presented at Synod of Dort, Dordrecht, Holland, 1619.

The Register of the Company of Pastors of Geneva in the Time of Calvin. Trans and ed. Philip E. Hughes. Wm. B. Eerdmans Publishing Co., 1966.

Thomas, W.H. Griffith. *The Principles of Theology*. Longmans, Green and Co., 1930.

Thompson, Bard. *Humanists and Reformers: A History of the Renaissance and Reformation*. Wm. B. Eerdmans Publishing Co., 1996.

Thompson, Bob. "The 5 Points of Calvin's Doctrine of Predestination." Self-published monograph, 4056 Skyline Rd., Carlsbad CA 92008, n.d.

Torrey, Reuben A. *The Importance and Value of Proper Bible Study.* Moody Press, 1921.

Tozer, A.W. "The Sovereignty of God." Christian Publications, 1997. Audiotape.

Underwood, A.C. *A History of the English Baptists.* The Baptist Union of Great Britian and Ireland, 1970.

Unger, Merrill F. *Unger's Bible Dictionary*. Moody Press, 1969.

Vance, Laurence M. *The Other Side of Calvinism*. Vance Publications, Pensacola FL, rev. ed. 1999.

Verduin, Leonard. *The Reformers and Their Stepchildren.* Christian Hymnary Publishers, 1991.

Verhovek, Sam Howe. "Cardinal Defends a Jailed Bishop Who Warned Cuomo on Abortion." *The New York Times,* February 1, 1990.

Vincent, Marvin R. *Word Studies in the New Testament.* Charles Scribner's Sons, 1924.

Voltaire. *The Works of Voltaire.* E.R. Dumont, 1901.

Wallace, Ronald S. *Calvin, Geneva, and the Reformation.* Baker Book House, 1990.

Walker, Williston. *John Calvin: The Organizer of Reformed Protestantism*. Schocken Books, 1969.

Ware, Bruce A. "Effective Calling and Grace," in *Still Sovereign,* eds. Thomas R. Schreiver & Bruce A. Ware. Baker Books, 2000.

Warfield, Benjamin B. *Calvin and Augustine*. Ed. Samuel G. Craig. Presbyterian and Reformed Publishing Co., 1956.

————. "Five Common Questions on the Doctrine of Election Simply and Clearly Answered." *The Baptist Examiner*. November 20, 1993.

Wendell, Francois. *Calvin: Origins and Development of His Religious Thought.* Baker Books, 1997.

Wesley, John. *Sermons on Several Occasions*. New York: J. Emory and B. Waugh, for the Methodist Episcopal Church at the Conference Office, 14 Crosby St., 1831.

West, David S. *The Baptist Examiner,* March 18, 1989.

Westblade, Donald J. "Divine Election in the Pauline Structure," in *Still Sovereign,* eds. Thomas R. Schreiver & Bruce A. Ware. Baker Books, 2000.

Westminster Confession of Faith. London: n.p., 1643.

White, James R. *The Potter's Freedom: A Defense of the Reformation and a Rebuttal of Norman Geisler's Chosen But Free.* Calvary Press Publishing, 2000.

White, W.R. *Baptist Distinctives.* Sunday School Board, SBC, 1946.

Wilkin, Robert N. "Ligonier National Conference." *The Grace Report,* July 2000.

————. "When Assurance Is Not Assurance." *Journal of the Grace Evangelical Society,* Autumn 1997.

Wilmouth, David O. *The Baptist Examiner*, September 16, 1989.

Wilson, Joseph M. "How is the Atonement Limited?" *The Baptist Examiner,* December 9, 1989.

————. "Soul Winning." *The Baptism Examiner,* February 15, 1992.

Wuest, Kenneth S. *Ephesians and Colossians in the Greek New Testament.* Wm. B. Eerdmans Publishing Co., 1953.

Yarbrough, Robert W. "Divine Election in the Gospel of John," in *Still Sovereign,* eds. Thomas R. Schreiver & Bruce A. Ware. Baker Books, 2000.

Zanchius, Jerom. *The Doctrine of Absolute Predestination.* Trans. Augustus M. Toplady. Baker Book House, 1977.

Zeller, George. In "For Whom Did Christ Die?" The Middleton Bible Church, 349 East St., Middletown CT 06457, 1999.

Zins, Robert M. "A Believer's Guide to 2nd Peter 3:9." Self-published monograph, n.d.

Scripture Reference Index